Genealogical & Local History Books In Print

Fourth Edition

Volume 3

Compiled by Netti Schreiner-Yantis

GENEALOGICAL BOOKS IN PRINT
Springfield, Virginia
1985

Printed in the United States of America

Library of Congress Catalog Number 75-4225
ISBN 0-89157-034-9 (Paper)
ISSN 0146-616X

The Library of Congress cataloged this serial as follows:

Genealogical & local history books in print. 4th ed.
   [Springfield, Va., s.n.] 1976-
      v. 22 cm.
      Continues: Genealogical books in print, ISSN 0147-426X
      Key title: Genealogical & local history books in print,
         ISSN 0146-616X

      1. United States——Genealogy——Bibliography——Periodicals
      2. United States—History, Local—Bibliography——Periodicals
      3. Genealogy—Bibliography—Periodicals

   Z5313.U5G45   016.929'1'0973   77-648320
   [CS47]   77[7708]   MARC-S

ORDER FROM GENEALOGICAL & LOCAL HISTORY BOOKS IN PRINT

Title: _____

_____

Author: _____ Vendor # _____ Price: $ _____
Last name sufficient

Tax, if you live in same state as the vendor: _____

Postage, if vendor specified as extra : _____

TOTAL: _____

_____ _Mailing Label – Please print or type clearly the portion that says "SHIP TO"_

From:

SHIP TO: _____

_____

_____

BOOK – SPECIAL 4TH CLASS RATE

✂

ORDER FROM GENEALOGICAL & LOCAL HISTORY BOOKS IN PRINT

Title: _____

_____

Author: _____ Vendor # _____ Price: $ _____

Tax, if you live in same state as the vendor: _____

Postage, if vendor specified as extra: _____

TOTAL: _____

_____ _Mailing Label – Please print or type clearly the portion that says "SHIP TO"_

From:

SHIP TO: _____

_____

_____

BOOK – SPECIAL 4th CLASS RATE

ORDER FROM GENEALOGICAL & LOCAL HISTORY BOOKS IN PRINT

Title: _____

_____

Author: _____ Vendor # _____ Price: $ _____
Last name sufficient

Tax, if you live in same state as the vendor: _____

Postage, if vendor specified as extra : _____

TOTAL: _____

_____ *Mailing Label – Please print or type clearly the portion that says "SHIP TO"*

From:

SHIP TO: _____

_____

_____

BOOK – SPECIAL 4TH CLASS RATE

✂

ORDER FROM GENEALOGICAL & LOCAL HISTORY BOOKS IN PRINT

Title: _____

_____

Author: _____ Vendor # _____ Price: $ _____

Tax, if you live in same state as the vendor : _____

Postage, if vendor specified as extra: _____

TOTAL: _____

_____ *Mailing Label – Please print or type clearly the portion that says "SHIP TO"*

From:

SHIP TO: _____

_____

_____

BOOK – SPECIAL 4th CLASS RATE

Family Genealogy Section

[Included in this section- besides Family Genealogies- are Family Newsletters and Biographies. Other works, such as early diaries and publications about Indian captivity, have also been listed here since this makes it possible to include the author's or Indian prisoner's name in the index.]

Surname Index #

1 - THE COURTRIGHT (KORTRIGHT) FAMILY by John Howard Abbott. Tobias A. Wright, pub. 1922.
168pp—GE4-OP47569--Vendor #D1555

2 - GENEALOGICAL HISTORY OF ROBERT ADAMS OF NEWBURY, MASSA-CHUSETTS...1635-1900. Andrew Napoleon Adams, comp. 1900. Rutland, VT: Tuttle Co.
675pp—GE4-OP70845--Vendor #D1555

3 - A GENEALOGY OF THE LAKE FAMILY OF GREAT EGG HARBOUR...IN NEW JERSEY by Arthur Adams. 1915. Hartford: Priv. Pr.
473pp—GE4-OP72025--Vendor #D1555

4 - THE FAMILY OF JAMES THORNTON, FATHER OF HON. MATTHEW THORNTON by Charles Thornton Adams. 1905. New York City.
54pp—GE4-BH21427--- Vendor #D1555

5 - HISTORY OF THOMAS ADAMS AND THOMAS HASTINGS FAMILIES... AMHERST, MASSACHUSETTS by Herbert Baxter Adams. 1880. Amherst, MA.
68pp—GE4-OP13253--Vendor #D1555

6 - GENEALOGY AND HISTORY OF...NEWBURY ADAMS FAMILY...OF DEV-ONSHIRE, ENGLAND....by Smith Adams. 1895. Calais, ME.
62pp—GE4-BH11672--- Vendor #D1555

7 - CHARLES KILGORE OF KING'S MOUNTAIN...HISTORY OF THE KILGORE FAMILY by Hugh Milburn Addington. 1935. Nickelsville, VA: Service Pr.
176pp—GE4-OP62616--Vendor #D1555

8 - THE SUTTON-DUDLEYS OF ENGLAND AND THE DUDLEYS OF MASSA-CHUSETTS....by George Adlard. 1862. New York.
212pp—GE4-OP62590--Vendor #D1555

9 - WHITTEN AND ALLIED FAMILIES by Virginia Wood Alexander. ca. 1966. Columbia, TN.
312pp—GE4-OP66178--Vendor #D1555

10 - FAMILY BIOGRAPHIES OF FAMILIES OF ALEXANDER, WILKINSON, SPARR AND GUTHRIE....by William G. Alexander. 1892. Cripple Creek: XL Job Pr. Ofc.
194pp—GE4-BH21131   --Vendor #D1555

11 - GENEALOGICAL HISTORY OF BRANCH OF ALGER FAMILY...FROM THOMAS ALGER....by Arthur Martineau Alger. 1876. Boston: D. Clapp & Son.
72pp—GE4-OP62885--Vendor #D1555

12 - GENEALOGY OF THE ALLEN AND WITTER FAMILIES: AMONG THE EARLY SETTLERS....by Asa W. Allen. 1872. Salem, OH: L. W. Smith.
270pp—GE4-BH21006--- Vendor #D1555

13 - RECORD...FAMILY OF ISAAC VAN NUYS (OR VANNICE) OF HARRODS-BURG, KENTUCKY....by Carrie E. Allen. New Jersey: n.p.
321pp—GE4-OP62864--Vendor #D1555

14 - THE GENEALOGY AND HISTORY OF THE SHREVE FAMILY FROM 1641 by Luther Prentice Allen. 1901. Greenfield, IL: Priv. Pr.
744pp—GE4-OP46430--Vendor #D1555

15 - DESCENDANTS OF JOHN FAIRMAN, OF ENFIELD, CONNECTICUT, 1683-1898 by Orrin Peer Allen. 1898. Palmer, MA: C. B. Fiske & Co.
56pp—GE4-BH21203--Vendor #D1555

16 - DESCENDANTS OF NICHOLAS CADY OF WATERTOWN, MASSACHUSETTS 1645-1910 by Orrin Peer Allen. 1910. Palmer, MA: C. B. Fiske & Co. text 633pp—supp. 40pp—GE4-OP52743--------------------------Vendor #D1555

17 - GENEALOGY OF SAMUEL ALLEN OF WINDSOR, CONNECTICUT AND SOME...DESCENDANTS by Willard Spencer Allen. 1876. Boston: Priv. Pr. 94pp—GE4-BH21161--Vendor #D1555

18 - A GENEALOGY OF THE ALLEN FAMILY FROM 1568 TO 1882 by William Allen. Rev. by Joshua Allen. Farmington, MO: Chronicle Book. 54pp—GE4-BH21007-- Vendor #D1555

19 - ALSPACH FAMILY, 1738-1967. HENRY ALSPACH, 1773-1825...THEIR DESCENDANTS by Clifford F. Alspach. 1968. Akron, OH. 232pp—GE4-OP65069--Vendor #D1555

20 - A BARONIAL FAMILY IN MEDIEVAL ENGLAND: THE CALRES, 1217-1314 by Michael Altschul. 1965. Baltimore: Johns Hopkins Pr. 352pp—GE4=2004926-- Vendor #D1555

21 - THE AMBLER FAMILY OF PENNSYLVANIA, 1688-1968 by Frank Rhoades Ambler. Mary Grace Ambler, ed. 1968. Jenkintown, PA: Old York Road Pub. Co. 168pp—GE4-OP65483--Vendor #D1555

22 - HANNA, BLAIR AND ALLIED FAMILIES, GENEALOGICAL AND BIO-GRAPHICAL by American Historical Company, Inc., New York. Prep. for Eliza Hanna Hayden. 1927. Hayden, NY. 66pp—GE4-OP16807---Vendor #D1555

23 - MUSSER AND ALLIED FAMILIES, A GENEALOGICAL STUDY WITH BIO-GRAPHICAL NOTES by American Historical Company, Inc., New York. 1941. comp. and priv. pr. for Dorothy Musser. 399pp—GE4-OP67695--Vendor #D1555

24 - HISTORICAL ACCOUNT...FAMILY OF FRISEL OR FRASER...FRASER OF LOVATT....by John Anderson. 1825. Edinburg: Wm. Blackwood. 221pp—GE4-OP64537---Vendor #D1555

25 - DONALD ROBERTSON...WIFE, RACHEL ROGERS, OF KING AND QUEEN COUNTY, VIRGINIA...POSTERITY by William Kyle Anderson. 1900. Detroit: Winn & Hammond, pr. 318pp—GE4-OP13114---Vendor #D1555

26 - GENEALOGICAL HISTORY OF JOHN AND MARY ANDREWS...FARMING-TON, CONNECTICUT, 1640....by Alfred Andrews. 1872. Chicago: A. H. Andrews & Co. 675pp—GE4-OP13705---Vendor #D1555

27 - GENEALOGY OF ANDREWS OF TAUNTON AND STOUGHTON, MASSA-CHUSETTS...BOSTON, MASSACHUSETTS....by George Andrews. 1887. Rochester, NY: E. R. Andrews, pr. 100pp—GE4-BH21175---Vendor #D1555

28 - HISTORY OF HAMLIN FAMILY WITH GENEALOGIES EARLY SETTLERS ...IN AMERICA....by Henry Franklin Andrews. 1894. Exira, LA: G. W. Guernsey. 150pp—GE4-BH21151-- --------------------------------Vendor #D1555

29 - DESCENDANTS OF JOHN PORTER OF WINDSOR, CONNECTICUT by Henry Porter Andrews. 1882. Saratoga Springs, NY: George W. Ball. 137pp--GE4-OP66525 ---Vendor #D1555

30 - GENEALOGY OF DESCENDANTS OF THOMAS ANGELL...SETTLED IN PROVIDENCE, 1636 by Avery F. Angell. 1872. Providence: A. C. Greene, pr. 322pp—GE4 BH19198---Vendor #D1555

31 - VAUX OF HARROWDEN, A RECUSANT FAMILY by Godfrey Anstruther. ca. 1953. Newport, RH: Johns Ltd. 561pp—GE4-OP52980---Vendor #D1555

32 - GENEALOGY OF ANTHONY FAMILY FROM 1495 TO 1904...GERMANY TO
ENGLAND...TO AMERICA by Charles Lawton Anthony. 1904. Sterling, IL.
381pp-GE4-OP50668--Vendor #D1555

33 - RECORDS OF THE ANTRIM FAMILY OF AMERICA by Harriet Stockton
Antrim. 1899. Burlington, NJ.
248pp-GE4-OP33109---Vendor #D1555

34 - GENEALOGICAL HISTORY OF THE ARCHER FAMILY...JAMES ARCHER
...1803-1919 by Martin B. Archer. 1919. Columbus, OH: F. J. Heer
Pr. Co.
100pp-GE4-OP57081---Vendor #D1555

35 - INDEX OF PERSONAL NAMES, "GENEALOGICAL HISTORY OF THE
ARCHER FAMILY....by M. B. Archer. 1919. George W. Archer, comp.
1976. Arlington, VA: Archer.
76pp-GE4-AU00169---Vendor #D1555

36 - CHRONICLES OF THE ARMSTRONGS by James Lewis Armstrong. 1902.
Jamaica: Marion Pr.
426pp-GE4-OP62742---Vendor #D1555

37 - THE ARNOLD FAMILY by William Hendrick Arnold. 1935. Texarkana,
AR: West Pub. Co.
218pp-GE4-OP46433---Vendor #D1555

38 - THE ASPINWALL GENEALOGY compiled by Algernon Aikin Aspinall.
1901. Rutland, VT: Tuttle Co.
262pp-GE4-OP13751---Vendor #D1555

39 - AUSTEN PAPERS, 1704-1856 edited by Richard Arthur Austen-Leigh.
1942. Spottiswoode: Ballantyne.
380pp-GE4-OP30973---Vendor #D1555

40 - ONE LINE OF THE HICKS FAMILY by John Osborne Austin. 1894.
Providence: E. L. Freeman & Son, pr.
34pp-GE4-BH21202---Vendor #D1555

41 - THE GROTON AVERY CLAN, 2 vols. by Elroy McKendree Avery and
Catharine Hitchcock (Tilden) Avery. 1912. Cleveland.
Vol. 1 814pp-Vol. 2 758pp-GE4-CD00133----------------------Vendor #D1555

42 - THE AXTELL FAMILY IN AMERICA. FIRST FIVE GENERATIONS by
Seth Jones Axtell. 1899. Boston.
24pp-GE4-BH21168---Vendor #D1555

43 - THE BRASHEAR STORY; A FAMILY HISTORY by Troy L. Back and
Leon Brashear. ca. 1963 n.p.
434pp-GE4-OP57034---Vendor #D1555

44 - GENEALOGY OF THE LINTHICUM AND ALLIED FAMILIES by Matilda
Phillips (Jones) Badger. 1936. Baltimore, MD.
262pp-GE4-OP71093---Vendor #D1555

45 - BAILEY GENEALOGY. JAMES, JOHN AND THOMAS, AND THEIR
DESCENDANTS edited by Hollis Russell Bailey. 1899. Somerville, MA:
Citizen Co.
490pp-GE4-BH02113---Vendor #D1555

46 - GENEALOGY AND HISTORY OF BAKER, ANDRUS, CLARK AND ADAMS
FAMILIES....by Albert Clark Baker. 1920. Decorah, IA.
428pp-GE4-OP34895---Vendor #D1555

47 - GENEALOGY OF RICHARD BAKER, BORN IN ENGLAND: DIED IN
DORCHESTER, MASSACHUSETTS, OCTOBER 25, 1689 by Edmund James
Baker. 1889. Boston: D. Clapp & Son, pr.
40pp-GE4-BH21130---Vendor #D1555

48 - GENEALOGY OF BENJAMIN FAMILY IN THE UNITED STATES OF AMER-
ICA FROM 1632 TO 1898...MOUNT WASHINGTON, MASSACHUSETTS by
Ellis Benjamin Baker. 1898. New Haven, CT: Press of Tuttle, Morehouse & Taylor.
162pp-GE4-BH19033---Vendor #D1555

49 - BALDWIN FAMILY PAPERS 1734-1832...PERTAINING TO DAVID BALD-
WIN...ST. JOHN'S, NEWFOUNDLAND by David Baldwin. n.p. n.d.
140pp—GE4-OP64435---Vendor #D1555

50 -THE BALFOURS OF PILRIG, A HISTORY FOR THE FAMILY by Barbara
Gordon Balfour-Melville. 1907. Edinburg: T. A. Constable.
546pp—GE4-OP40290---Vendor #D1555

51 - EDWARD BALL AND SOME OF HIS DESCENDANTS...THE SIXTH GEN-
ERATION compiled by Nicholas Ball. 1891. Newport, RI: Mercury Pr.
26pp—GE4-BH19034---Vendor #D1555

52 - BALL FAMILY OF SOUTHWEST VIRGINIA:...DESCENDANTS OF MOSES
BALL OF FAIRFAX COUNTY, VIRGINIA.... by Palmer Ray Ball. 1933.
45pp—GE4-OP71090---Vendor #D1555

53 - FRANCIS BALL'S DESCENDANTS...WEST SPRINGFIELD BALL FAMILY
FROM 1640 TO 1902 by Timothy Horton Ball. 1902. Crown Point, IN:
J. J. Wheeler Pr.
101pp—GE4-BH16063---Vendor #D1555

54 - GENEALOGICAL RECORDS OF THE DINWIDDIE CLAN OF NORTHWEST-
ERN INDIANA by Timothy Horton Ball. 1902. Crown Point, IN: J. J.
Wheeler, pr.
180pp—GE4-BH17348---Vendor #D1555

55 - A FRISIAN FAMILY: THE BANTA GENEALOGY by Theodore Melvin
Banta. 1893. NY.
426pp—GE4-OP00470---Vendor #D1555

56 - SAYRE FAMILY, LINEAGE OF THOMAS SAYRE by Theodore Melvin
Banta. 1901. NY: De Vinne.
954pp—GE4-OP24217---Vendor #D1555

57 - GENEALOGY OF BARBER FAMILY; DESCENDANTS OF ROBERT BARBER,
LANCASTER COUNTY, PENNSYLVANIA by Edwin Atlee Barber. 1890.
Philadelphia: W. F. Fell & Co.
200pp—GE4-BH21176---Vendor #D1555

58 - GENEALOGY PREPARED AND PUBLISHED IN 1864...APPENDIX TO HIS
BOOK ENTITLED MY WIFE AND MY MOTHER by Heman H. Barbour. 1885.
Hartford: Pr. of Wiley, Waterman & Eaton.
110pp—GE4-BH21238---Vendor #D1555

59 - FRYE GENEALOGY; ADRIAN OF KITTERY, MAINE, JOHN OF ANDOVER,
MASSACHUSETTS, JOSHUA OF VIRGINIA, THOMAS OF RHODE ISLAND
by Elizabeth Frye Barker. rev. ed. 1920. NY: Tobias A. Wright, pr.
203pp—GE4-OP47981---Vendor #D1555

60 - EARLY MALTBY WITH SOME ROADES HISTORY...MAULBSY FAMILY IN
AMERICA...EMIGRANTS FROM NOTTINGHAMSHIRE, ENGLAND TO PENN-
SYLVANIA by Ella Kent Barnard. 1909. Carlisle, PA: Cornman Pr.
432pp—GE4-OP42084---Vendor #D1555

61 - JOSEPH WEST AND JANE OWEN by Celeste Jane (Terrell) Barnhill.
1930. Greenfield, IN: Wm. Mitchell.
118pp—GE4-OP16823---Vendor #D1555

62 - RICHMOND, WILLIAM AND TIMOTHY TERRELL, COLONIAL VIRGINIANS
by Celeste Jane (Terrell) Barnhill. 1934. Greenfield, IN: Mitchell Co.
364pp—GE4-OP36919---Vendor #D1555

63 - RECORD OF THE BARTHOLOMEW FAMILY, HISTORICAL, GENEALOGI-
CAL AND BIOGRAPHICAL by George Wells Bartholomew. 1885. Austin,
TX.
775pp—GE4-OP61425---Vendor #D1555

64 - GENEALOGY...RUSSELL FAMILY...DESCENDANTS OF JOHN RUSSELL,
OF WOBURN, MASSACHUSETTS, 1640-1878 by John Russell Bartlett. 1879.
Providence: Priv. pr. [by Providence Pr. Co.].
256pp—GE4-BH21248---Vendor #D1555

65 - GREGORY STONE GENEALOGY...GREGORY STONE OF CAMBRIDGE,
MASSACHUSETTS, 1320-1917 by Joseph Gardner Bartlett. 1918. Boston:
Stone Family Assoc.
966pp—GE4-OP41948---Vendor #D1555

66 - HENRY ADAMS OF SOMERSETSHIRE, ENGLAND AND BRAINTREE, MASSACHUSETTS...HIS DESCENDANTS by Joseph Gardner Bartlett. 1927. New York: n.p.
198pp—GE4-OP62672--Vendor #D1555

67 - ROBERT COE, PURITAN: HIS ANCESTORS AND DESCENDANTS, 1340-1910 by Joseph Gardner Bartlett. 1911. Boston.
682pp—GE4-OP31027--Vendor #D1555

68 - THE BARTLETTS: ANCESTRAL, GENEALOGICAL, BIOGRAPHICAL, HISTORICAL...JOHN BARTLETT, OF WEYMOUTH, AND CUMBERLAND by Thomas Edward Bartlett. 1892. New Haven, CT: Pr. of Stafford Pr. Co.
96pp—GE4-BH21152--Vendor #D1555

69 - BARTOW GENEALOGY. PART 1. CONTAINING EVERY ONE OF NAME BARTOW DESCENDED FROM DOCTOR THOMAS BARTOW....by Evelyn Pierrepont Bartow. 1878-79. Baltimore: Innes & Co., prs.
348pp—GE4-BH21231--Vendor #D1555

70 - ADDITIONAL BASKERVILLE GENEALOGY:SUPPLEMENT TO AUTHOR'S GENEALOGY OF BASKERVILLE FAMILY OF 1912 by Patrick Hamilton Baskervill. 1917. Richmond: W. E. Jones Sons,Inc.
240pp—GE4-OP41309--Vendor #D1555

71 ANDREW MEADE OF IRELAND AND VIRGINIA...ANCESTORS...DESCENDANTS...THEIR CONNECTIONS by Patrick Hamilton Baskervill. 1921. Richmond, VA: Old Dominion Pr.
226pp—GE4-OP34904--Vendor #D1555

72 - GENEALOGY OF BASKERVILLE FAMILY AND SOME ALLIED FAMILIES ...FROM 1266A.D. by Patrick Hamilton Baskervill. 1912. Richmond: W. E. Jones Sons, Inc.
198pp—GE4-OP41310--Vendor #D1555

73 - GENEALOGY BASS-JONES. IN MEMORY OF FRANK N. BASS by Frank Nelson Bass. Freeport, IL: C. T. Bass, n.d.
71pp—GE4-OP53212--Vendor #D1555

74 - BATES, ET AL. OF VIRGINIA AND MISSOURI compiled by Onward Bates. 1914. Chicago: pr. for priv. dist.
164pp—GE4-OP4676--Vendor #D1555

75 - GENEALOGY OF THE DESCENDANTS OF EDWARD BATES OF WEYMOUTH, MASSACHUSETTS by Samuel Austin Bates. 1900. S. Braintree, MA: F. A. Bates.
158pp—GE4-BH21223--Vendor #D1555

76 - SKETCH OF WILLIAM BEARDSLEY;...ORIGINAL SETTLERS OF STRATFORD, CONNECTICUT...DESCENDANTS....by Eben Edwards Beardsley. 1867. New Haven: Bassett & Barnett.
46pp—GE4-BH19169--Vendor #D1555

77 - RECORD OF FAMILY OF CHARLES BEATTY...IRELAND TO AMERICA ...1729 by Charles C. Beatty. 1873? Steubenville, OH: Pr. of W. R. Allison.
128pp—GE4-BH21265--Vendor #D1555

78 - HISTORY AND GENEALOGY OF THE BIEBER, BEAVER, BIEVER, BEEBER FAMILY by Irvin Milton Beaver. 1939. Reading, PA: I. M. Beaver.
988pp—GE4-OP64280--Vendor #D1555

79 - MONOGRAPH OF DESCENT OF FAMILY OF BEEBE...BROUGHTON, ENGLAND, 1650 compiled and edited by Clarence Beebe. 1904? New York.
168pp—GE4-OP41322--Vendor #D1555

80 - BEESON GENEALOGY by Japser Luther Beeson. Macon, GA: Burke Co. n.d.
150pp—GE4-OP50130--Vendor #D1555

81 - CONCERNING...ANCESTORS...DESCENDANTS...ROYAL DENISON BELDEN AND OLIVE CADWELL BELDEN by Mrs. Jessie Perry (Van Zile) Belden. 1898. Philadelphia: J. B. Lippincott Co.
358pp—GE4-OP72618--Vendor #D1555

82 - THE BENNETT, BENTLY AND BEERS FAMILIES by Stephen Beers
Bennett. 1899. Pittston?, PA.
66pp—GE4-BH21149---Vendor #D1555

83 - GENEALOGY OF FAMILY OF BENSON OF BANGER HOUSE AND NORTH-
WOODS...PATELEY BRIDGE by Arthur Christopher Benson. 1895. Eton:
G. New.
44pp—GE4-OP70994--Vendor #D1555

84 - BENSON FAMILY RECORDS...DESCENDANTS OF JOHN BENSON OF
OXFORDSHIRE, ENGLAND....by Fred Harvey Benson. 1920. New York:
Craftsman Pr.
208pp—GE4-OP72642--------------------------------------Vendor #D1555

85 - WALTER ALLEN OF NEWBURY, MASSACHUSETTS, 1640...NOTES ON
ALLEN FAMILY....by Allen Herbert Bent. 1896. Boston: D. Clapp &
Son, prs.
72pp—GE4-BH21157--Vendor #D1555

86 - BERGEN FAMILY;...DESCENDANTS OF HANS HANSEN BERGEN...
NEW YORK AND BROOKLYN....by Teunis G. Bergen. 1876. Albany:
Joel Munsell.
700pp—GE4-OP65482--Vendor #D1555

87 - REPRINT OF BETHAM'S HISTORY, GENEALOGY AND BARONETS OF
BOYNTON FAMILY IN ENGLAND....TO WHICH IS ADDED BURKE'S
PEERAGE by William Betham. John Farnham Boynton, ed. 1884. Syracuse, NY: Smith & Bruce, Prs.
44pp—GE4-OP41566--Vendor #D1555

88 - MATTHEW THORNTON'S FAMILY AND DESCENDANTS by George E.
Betton. n.p., n.d.
9pp—GE4-BH19084---Vendor #D1555

89 - VAWTER FAMILY IN AMERICA WITH ALLIED FAMILIES OF BRANHAM,
WISE, STRIBLING, CRAWFORD, LEWIS, GLOVER, MONCRIEF by Grace
Vawter Bicknell. 1905. Indianapolis: Hollenbeck Pr.
448pp—GE4-OP44241---Vendor #D1555

90 - NOTES ON THE GENEALOGY OF THE BIDDLE FAMILY by Henry D.
Biddle. 1895. Philadelphia: W. S. Portescue & Co.
94pp—GE4-OP57651--Vendor #D1555

91 - HOUSE OF BIERBAUER. TWO HUNDRED YEARS OF FAMILY HISTORY,
1742-1942 compiled by Charles William Bierbower and James Culver Bierbower. 1942. New Wilmington: Globe Pr. Co.
192pp—GE4-OP57619--Vendor #D1555

92 - HISTORY OF THE BILL FAMILY edited by Ledyard Bill. 1867.
368pp—GE4-OP47912---------------------------------------Vendor #D1555

93 - HISTORY OF THE WALDENSES, Vol. 2 by Rev. Adam Blair. 1832.
642pp—GE4-OP67606---------------------------------------Vendor #D1555

94 - THE MICHAEL SHOEMAKER BOOK (SCHUMACHER) by Williams T. Blair.
1924. Pr. for J. L. Shoemaker, Wyoming, PA. Scranton, PA: Intl. Text
Book Pr.
1088pp—GE4-BH09833-------------------------------------Vendor #D1555

95 - THE BLAKENEYS IN AMERICA AND SOME COLLATERALS by John Oscar
Blakeney. 1928. Little Rock, AR.
54pp—GE4-OP34915---Vendor #D1555

96 - THE BLEDSOE FAMILY by John T. Bledsoe (Pine Bluff, Ark.). 1973.
Perdue.
298pp—GE4-2050419---------------------------------------Vendor #D1555

97 - THE BLEDSOE FAMILY: SUPPLEMENT by John T. Bledsoe. ca. 1976.
Ann Arbor: Xerox Univ. Microfilms.
385pp—GE4·AU00051--------------------------------------Vendor #D1555

98 - A FAMILY STORY by John T. Bledsoe. 1980. Ann Arbor: Univ. Microfilms Intl.
200pp—GE4-AU00102--------------------------------------Vendor #D1555

99 - GENEALOGY OF THE BOLLES FAMILY IN AMERICA by John Augustus
Bolles. 1865. Boston: H. W. Dutton & Son.
86pp—GE4-BH19107--Vendor #D1555

100 - MEMOIR OF PORTION OF BOLLING FAMILY IN ENGLAND AND VIR-
GINIA by Robert Bolling. 1868. Pr. for priv. dist. Richmond, VA:
W. H. Wade & Co.
82pp—GE4-BH17414--Vendor #D1555

101 - MEMOIR OF PORTION OF BOLLING FAMILY IN ENGLAND AND VIRGINIA
by Robert Bolling. 1868. Richmond, VA: W. H. Wade & Co.
138pp—GE4-OP67666--Vendor #D1555

102 - THE FAMILY OF BOLTON IN ENGLAND AND AMERICA, 1100-1894 by
Henry Carrington Bolton and Reginald Pelham Bolton. 1895. NY.
584pp—GE4-OP30875--Vendor #D1555

103 - GENEALOGICAL AND BIOGRAPHICAL ACCOUNT OF FAMILY BOLTON:
IN ENGLAND AND AMERICA....by Rev. Robert Bolton. 1862. NY:Gray.
284pp—GE4-BH21481--Vendor #D1555

104 - HIGH WATER OVER THE ROAD: SEVEN GENERATIONS OF AMERICAN
FAMILY by Ted Booth. ca. 1968. Grand Rapids, MI: Eerdmans.
236pp—GE4-2012910--Vendor #D1555

105 - GENEALOGY OF ONE BRANCH OF SHERMAN FAMILY FROM SAMUEL
SHERMAN OF STRATFORD, CONNECTICUT....by Walter Sherman Booth,
Juliette Fairchild Northrup and Mrs. H. B. Northrup. 1900. Milwaukee,
WI: Pr. of the Evening Wisconsin Co.
24pp—GE4-BH19091--Vendor #D1555

106 - HISTORY OF THE BORNEMAN FAMILY IN AMERICA...1721 to 1878 by
John H. Borneman. 1881. Govertown, PA: J. H. Borneman.
116pp—GE4-OP45900--Vendor #D1555

107 - A BRIEF GENEALOGY OF THE WHIPPLE FAMILY by John H. Boutell.
1857. Lowell: E. D. Green & Co.
36pp—GE4-BH21297--Vendor #D1555

108 - BOWIES AND THEIR KINDRED. A GENEALOGICAL AND BIOGRAPHICAL
HISTORY by Walter Worthington Bowie. 1899. Washington: Pr. of Corm-
well Bros.
528pp—GE4-OP42027--Vendor #D1555

109 - BOWLES FAMILY OF ENGLAND [A GENEALOGY] by John Bowles. n.p.n.d.
2pp—GE4-BH19262--Vendor #D1555

110 - GEORGE BOWMAN AND HIS DESCENDANTS compiled by Anna Harman
Bowman. 1962. n.p.
240pp—GE4-OP65032--Vendor #D1555

111 - SOME KENTUCKIANS MOVE WEST, CREEKMORES, BLAKEYS AND RE-
LATED FAMILIES compiled by Anna Harman Bowman. 1970. n.p.
112pp—GE4-OP65029--Vendor #D1555

112 - THE BOWSER FAMILY HISTORY by Addison Bartholomew Bowser. 1922.
Excelsior.
310pp—GE4-OP14800--Vendor #D1555

113 - THE TERRELL JACKSON ANCESTRY by Margaret Jackson Boyette.
1926. Pinebluff, AR.
3pp—GE4-OP66952--Vendor #D1555

114 - BOYNTON FAMILY. GENEALOGY OF DESCENDANTS OF WILLIAM AND
JOHN BOYNTON...YORKSHIRE, ENGLAND...SETTLED AT ROWLEY,
ESSEX COUNTY, MASSACHUSETTS compiled by John Farnham Boynton
and Caroline (Harriman) Boynton. 1897. Groveland?, MA.
434pp—GE4-OP41818--Vendor #D1555

115 - DESCENDANTS OF ISAAC BRADLEY OF BRANFORD AND EAST HAVEN,
NEW YORK by Leonard Abram Bradley. 1917. NY: Priv. Pr.
187pp—GE4-OP70192--Vendor #D1555

116 - SURVEY OF THE ISHAMS IN ENGLAND AND AMERICA; EIGHT HUN-
DRED AND FIFTY YEARS OF HISTORY AND GENEALOGY by Homer
Worthington Brainard. 1938. Rutland, VT: Tuttle Pub. Co., Inc.
682pp—GE4-OP44264---Vendor #D1555

117 - GARY GENEALOGY; THE DESCENDANTS OF ARTHUR GARY OF ROX-
BURY, MASSACHUSETTS by Lawrence Brainerd. 1918. Boston.
239pp—GE4-OP23255---Vendor #D1555

118 - THE BRASHEAR-BRASHEARS FAMILY, 1449-1929 by Henry Sinclair
Brashear. 1929. Texarkana, TX.
178pp—GE4-OP47237---Vendor #D1555

119 - LONGSWORTH FAMILY HISTORY; DESCENDANTS OF SOLOMON LONGS-
WORTH, SR., OF MARYLAND compiled by Mary Esther Longsworth Breese.
1951. Lima, OH.
281pp—GE4-2051676---Vendor #D1555

120 - BRERETON, A FAMILY HISTORY by John Brereton. 1919. San
Francisco.
72pp—GE4-OP63584---Vendor #D1555

121 - BRIEF NOTICE OF THE LATE THOMAS KEYES OF WEST BOYLSTON...
HIS DESCENDANTS...ANCESTRY by John Brereton. 1857. Worcester:
H. J. Howland
15pp—GE4-OP47240---Vendor #D1555

122 - GENEALOGIES OF...FAMILIES BEARING NAME OF KENT IN THE
UNITED STATES....by Lloyd Vernon Briggs. 1898. Boston: Rockwell
& Churchill Pr.
402pp—GE4-OP69085---Vendor #D1555

123 - WE AND OUR KINSFOLK. EPHRAIM AND REBEKAH WATERMAN BRIGGS,
...ANCESTORS.... by Mary Balch Briggs. 1887. Boston: Beacon Pr.
174pp—GE4-BH19170---Vendor #D1555

124 - BOOK OF THE VARIAN FAMILY...SPECULATIONS AS TO THEIR
ORIGIN....by Samuel Briggs. 1881. Cleveland, OH: Theo. C. Schenck
121pp—GE4-OP61542---Vendor #D1555

125 - PARTIAL RECORD OF DESCENDANTS OF WALTER BRIGGS OF WEST-
CHESTER, NEW YORK by Samuel Briggs. 1878. Cleveland, OH: pr. for
priv. circulation only, Fairbanks, Briggs & Co.
64pp—GE4-BH21027---Vendor #D1555

126 - THE FAMILY OF JORIS DIRCKSEN BRINCKERHOFF, 1638 by Roeliff
Brinckerhoff. 1887. New York: R. Brinkerhoff.
213pp—GE4-2000499---Vendor #D1555

127 - HISTORY OF THE BROADDUS FAMILY...IN THE UNITED STATES...
TO YEAR 1888 by Andrew Broaddus. St. Louis: Central Baptist Pr., n.d.
208pp—GE4-OP64586---Vendor #D1555

128 - THE BROCKWAY FAMILY. SOME RECORDS OF WOLSTON BROCKWAY,
AND HIS DESCENDANTS compiled by D. Williams Patterson for Francis
E. Brockway. 1890. Owego, NY: Brockway's Power Pr.
190pp—GE4-BH19106---Vendor #D1555

129 - FAMILY RECORD OF SILAS BROWN, JR. by Augustus Cleveland Brown.
1879. NY: G. Macnamara, pr.
188pp—GE4-BH21031---Vendor #D1555

130 - THE MACLAUGHLINS OF CLAN OWEN. A STUDY IN IRISH HISTORY
by John Patrick Brown. 1879. Boston: W. J. Schofield.
96pp—GE4-OP42387---Vendor #D1555

131 - MY ANCESTORS AND THEIR DESCENDANTS by William Luther Brown.
ca. 1937. Atlanta: Artcraft Pr. Co.
222pp—GE4-OP66527---Vendor #D1555

132 - THE BABBITT FAMILY HISTORY by William Bradford Browne. 1912.
Taunton, MA: C. A. Hack & Son.
900pp—GE4-OP72646---Vendor #D1555

133 - GENEALOGICAL RECORD OF DESCENDANTS OF THOMAS BROWNELL,
1619 TO 1910 by George Grant Brownell. 1910. Jamestown, NY.
366pp—GE4-OP71411--Vendor #D1555

134 - GENEALOGICAL RECORD OF DESCENDANTS OF THOMAS BROWNELL,
1619 TO 1910 by George Grant Brownell. 1910. Jamestown.
368pp—GE4-OP22091--Vendor #D1555

135 - MAGNA CHARTA BARONS AND THEIR DESCENDANTS by Charles Henry Browning. 1915. Philadelphia: Baronial Order of Runnemede.
395pp—GE4-OP13602--Vendor #D1555

136 - THE BRUBACHER GENEALOGY IN AMERICA by Jacob N. Brubacher.
1884. Elkhart, IN: Mennonite.
244pp—GE4-OP27953--Vendor #D1555

137 - FATHER JULIUS AND MOTHER EMILIE: PERSONAL BIOGRAPHY OF
MIDWESTERN PIONEERS by George C. Bubolz. ca. 1975. Hicksville,
NY: Exposition Pr. (An Exposition-Lochinvar bk.)
196pp—GE4-2010735--Vendor #D1555

138 - HISTORY OF ANCIENT SURNAME OF BUCHANAN AND ANCIENT SCOTTISH SURNAMES....by William Buchanan. 1793. Glasgow: Buchanan.
366pp—GE4-BH15522--Vendor #D1555

139 - GENEALOGY OF SAMUEL BUCK FAMILY OF PORTLAND, CONNECTICUT,
...YEAR 1894 by Horace Blake Buck. 1894. Worcester, MA: O. B. Wood.
72pp—GE4-BH21171--Vendor #D1555

140 - LE JOUVENCEL. INTO., BIOGRAPHIQUE ET LITTERAIRE, PAR CAMILLE FAVRE, 2 vols. by Jean de Bueil, comte de Sancerre. 1887-1889. Paris.
Vol. 1 569pp—Vol. 2 515pp—GE4-OP51787--------------------Vendor #D1555

141 RITTERZEIT UND RITTERWESEN, 2 vols. by Johann Gustav Gottlieb
Bueschig. 1823. Leipzeig: F. A. Brockhaus.
Vol. 1 455pp—Vol. 2 308pp—GE4-OP65176--------------------Vendor #D1555

142 - HISTORY AND GENEALOGY OF FAMILIES OF BELLINGER AND DE
VEUX...FAMILIES by Joseph Gaston Baillie Bulloch. 1895. Savannah,
GA: Morning News Print.
109pp—GE4-BH19201--Vendor #D1555

143 - HISTORY AND GENEALOGY OF FAMILY OF BAILLIE OF DUNAIN,
DOCHFOUR....by Joseph Gaston Baillie Bulloch. 1898. Green Bay,
WI: Gazette Pr.
118pp—GE4-BH19051--Vendor #D1555

144 - HISTORY AND GENEALOGY OF THE HABERSHAM FAMILY by Joseph
Gaston Baillie Bulloch. 1901. Columbia, SC: R. L. Bryan Co.
245pp—GE4-OP66869--Vendor #D1555

145 - INCIDENTS IN THE LIFE AND TIMES OF STUKELEY WESTCOTE...
DESCENDANTS by Jonathan Russell Bullock. 1886. n.p.
244pp—GE4-BH19062--Vendor #D1555

146 - THE BURGESS GENEALOGY by Ebenezer Burgess. 1865. Boston:
Pr. of T. R. Marvin & Son.
226pp—GE4-OP69027--Vendor #D1555

147 - HISTORY AND GENEALOGY OF BURGNER FAMILY...SWISS EMIGRANT
OF 1734 by Jacob Burgner. 1890. Oberlin, OH: Oberlin News Pr.
216pp—GE4-OP52602--Vendor #D1555

148 - GENEALOGY AND HISTORY OF INGALLS FAMILY IN AMERICA...
LYNN, MASSACHUSETTS....by Charles Burleigh. 1903. Malden, MA:
G. E. Dunbar.
354pp—GE4-OP46478--Vendor #D1555

149 - BURNHAM FAMILY; GENEALOGICAL RECORDS OF DESCENDANTS...
EARLY SETTLERS IN AMERICA by Roderick Henry Burnham. 1869.
Hartford: Pr. of Case, Lockwood & Brainard.
592pp—GE4-BH14014--Vendor #D1555

150 - GENEALOGICAL RECORDS OF HENRY AND ULALIA BURT...FROM
1640-1891 by Roderick Henry Burnham. 1892. Warwick, NY: Miss
Elizabeth Burt.
371pp—GE4-CD00090--—Vendor #D1555

151 - HANSARD MILITARY RECORDS OF CIVIL WAR;...CHEROKEE RECORDS
...HANSARD NAME by Annie Walker Burns. 1964? [ca. 1978] Washington, DC.
64pp—GE4-AU00050--Vendor #D1555

152 - HANSARD-CHRISTIAN FAMILY HISTORY RECORDS by Annie Walker
Burns. 1951? Washington, D.C. [Repr. 1978, Knoxville, TN for Hansard Family Register]
141pp—GE4-AU00048--Vendor #D1555

153 - GENEALOGY OF THE BURROUGHS FAMILY by Lewis Amos Burroughs.
1894. Carretteville, OH: Peirce Pr. Co.
26pp—GE4-OP14099---Vendor #D1555

154 - EARLY DAYS IN NEW ENGLAND LIFE...HENRY BURT OF SPRING-
FIELD....by Henry Martyn Burt. 1893. Springfield, MA: C. W. Bryan
Co., prs.
683pp—GE4-CD00013---Vendor #D1555

155 - BRANCHIANA; BEING PARTIAL ACCOUNT OF BRANCH FAMILY OF
VIRGINIA by james Branch Cabell. n.d. Richmond, VA: Whittet &
Shepperson.
207pp—GE4-OP57095---Vendor #D1555

156 - THE CALKINS MEMORIAL MILITARY ROSTER by William Wirt Calkins.
ca. 1903. Chicago: M. A. Donahue & Co.
222pp—GE4-OP61986---Vendor #D1555

157 - GENEALOGY OF DESCENDANTS OF LAWRENCE AND CASSANDRA
SOUTHWICK...SAME, MASSACHUSETTS by James Moore Caller and
Maria A. Ober. 1881. Salem: J. H. Choate.
674pp—GE4-OP17634---Vendor #D1555

158 - GENEALOGY OF THE SPOTSWOOD FAMILY IN SCOTLAND AND
VIRGINIA by Charles Campbell. 1868. Albany, J. Munsell.
44pp—GE4-BH19092---—Vendor #D1555

159 - SOME BRYSONS AND SWEARINGENS by Sarah Ellen (Smith) Campbell.
1965. Kalamazoo, MI: H. C. Nycum.
308pp—GE4-OP40189---Vendor #D1555

160 - CANTRELL FAMILY; BIOGRAPHICAL ALBUM AND HISTORY OF DE-
SCENDANTS OF ZEBULON CANTRELL....compiled by Carmi G. Cantrell.
1898. Springfield, IL: Illinois State Register Pr. House.
179pp—GE4-OP64225---Vendor #D1555

161 - HISTORY OF CARLOCK FAMILY AND ADVENTURES OF PIONEER
AMERICANS by Marion Pomeroy Carlock. 1929. Los Angeles, CA:
Wm. B. Straube Pr. Co.,Inc.
654pp—GE4-OP70099---Vendor #D1555

162 - HISTORY AND GENEALOGY OF CARPENTER FAMILY IN AMERICA...
1637-1901 by Daniel Hoogland Carpenter. 1901. Jamaica, NY: Marion Pr.
406pp—GE4-OP42018---Vendor #D1555

163 - HISTORY AND GENEALOGY OF HOOGLAND FAMILY IN AMERICA...
1638-1891 by Daniel Hoogland Carpenter. 1891. NY: J. Polhemus.
286pp—GE4-OP15571---Vendor #D1555

164 - GENEALOGICAL NOTES OF CARPENTER FAMILY, INCLUDING...DR.
SEYMOUR D. CARPENTER....by Seymour David Carpenter. 1907.
Springfield, IL: Illinois State Journal Co., Prs.
289pp—GE4-OP63542---Vendor #D1555

165 - CARR FAMILY RECORDS: EMBRACING RECORD OF FIRST FAMILIES
...IN AMERICA....by Edson Irving Carr. 1894. Rockton,IL: Herald
Pr. House.
540pp—GE4-OP57259---Vendor #D1555

166 - SAWYERS IN AMERICA;...HISTORY...IMMIGRANT SAWYERS, WHO
SETTLED IN NEW ENGLAND....by Amory Carter. 1883. Worcester:
Pr. of E. R. Fiske.
120pp—GE4-BH19063--Vendor #D1555

167 - HOLLISTER FAMILY OF AMERICA; LIEUTENANT JOHN HOLLISTER OF
WETHERSFIELD, CONNECTICUT....compiled by Lafayette Wallace Case.
1886. Chicago: Fergus Pr. Co.
805pp—GE4-OP63999--Vendor #D1555

168 - BAIRD AND BEARD FAMILIES; GENEALOGICAL, BIOGRAPHICAL...
HISTORICAL COLLECTION OF DATA by Fermine (Baird)Catchings.
ca. 1918. Nashville: Baird-Ward Pubs.
150pp—GE4-BH06546--Vendor #D1555

169 - THE HOUSE OF CESSNA, 2nd series by Howard Cessna. 1935. Berlin:
Berlin Pub. Co.
198pp—GE4-OP50181--Vendor #D1555

170 - THE HOUSE OF CESSNA by Howard Cessna. n.d. Bedford, PA: Pr.
of Pennsylvania Hawkeye.
194pp—GE4-OP54836--Vendor #D1555

171 - CHANDLER FAMILY. DESCENDANTS OF WILLIAM AND ANNIS
CHANDLER...ROXBURY, MASSACHUSETTS, 1637 by George Chandler.
1883. Worcester, MA: Pr. of Charles Hamilton.
1340pp—GE4-OP62648--Vendor #D1555

172 - GENEALOGY OF FOLSOM FAMILY: JOHN FOLSOM AND DESCENDANTS,
1615-1882 by Jacob Chapman. 1882. Concord, NH: Pr. by Republican
Pr. Assn.
316pp—GE4-BH21172--Vendor #D1555

173 - GENEALOGY OF PHILBRICK AND PHILBROOK FAMILIES...THOMAS
PHILBRICK, 1583-1667 by Jacob Chapman. 1886. Exeter, NH: Exeter
Gazette Steam Pr. House.
230pp—GE4-BH21173--Vendor #D1555

174 - GENEALOGICAL HISTORY OF CHAPPELL, DICKIE, AND KINDRED
FAMILIES OF VIRGINIA...., rev. ed., compiled by Phil Edward Chappell. 1900. Kansas City, MO: Hudson-Kimberly.
434pp—GE4-OP30894--Vendor #D1555

175 - THE HIERONYMUS STORY by Lou's Ryan Chenault, et al. 1959.
Salt Lake City: The Salt Lake Times.
161pp—GE4-OP66513--Vendor #D1555

176 - CHISOLM GENEALOGY...A.D. 1254, WITH SHORT SKETCHES OF
ALLIED FAMILIES by William Grnett Chisolm. 1914. NY: Knickerbocker
Pr.
102pp—GE4-OP04484--Vendor #D1555

177 - DESCENDANTS OF RICHARD CHURCH OF PLYMOUTH, MASSACHU-
SETTS by John Adams Church. 1913. Rutland, VT: Tuttle Co.
354pp—GE4-OP44265--Vendor #D1555

178 - THE CHURCHILL FAMILY IN AMERICA compiled by Gardner Asaph
Churchill and Nathaniel Wiley Churchill. George M. Bodge, ed. [n.p.]
rev. ed. 1904.
779pp—GE4-OP14120--Vendor #D1555

179 - CHUTE FAMILY IN AMERICA IN THE TWENTIETH CENTURY by George
M. Chute. n.p., n.d.
116pp—GE4-PB01779--Vendor #D1555

180 - CLAIBORNE PEDIGREE, GENEALOGICAL TABLE OF DESCENDANTS OF
SECRETARY WILLIAM CLAIBORNE....by George Mason Claiborne. 1900.
Lynchburg, VA: J. P. Bell Co.
58pp—GE4-BH11554--Vendor #D1555

181 - JOHN WOOD OF RHODE ISLAND, AND EARLY DESCENDANTS ON THE
MAINLAND by Bertha W. Clark. 1966. n.p.
162pp—GE4-OP69166--Vendor #D1555

182 - GILL, ABSTRACTS FROM RECORDS IN SOUTHERN STATES AND
GENEALOGICAL NOTES compiled by Eva Turner Clark. 1939. NY:
Richard R. Smith.
204pp—GE4-OP54630--Vendor #D1555

183 - GENEALOGIES OF CLARK, PARKS, BROCKMAN, AND DEAN, DAVIS
AND GOSS FAMILIES IN FIVE PARTS by Henry William Clark. 1905.
Montgomery, AL.
Vol. 1, pt. 1 Clark Family 186pp—Vol. 1, pt. 2 Parks Family 150pp—
Vol. 1, pt. 3 Brockman and Dean Families 184pp—Vol. 2, pt. 1
Davis Family 136pp—Vol. 2, pt. 2 Goss Family 222pp-GE4-OP61847-Vendor #D1555

184 - CLARKE'S KINDRED GENEALOGIES by Augustus Peck Clarke. 1896.
Cambridge, MA: Harvard Pr. Co.
406pp—GE4-OP15142---Vendor #D1555

185 - GENEALOGY OF THE DESCENDANTS OF NATHANIEL CLARKE OF
NEWBURY, MASSACHUSETTS by George Kuhn Clarke. 1883. Boston:
Pr. of T. R. Marvin & Son.
134pp—GE4-BH19190---Vendor #D1555

186 - HISTORY AND GENEALOGY OF...CLARKE FAMILY...CONNECTION
WITH SHATTUCKS by George Washington Clarke. 1898. Detroit: Pr.
of Morrison Pr. Co.
78pp—GE4-BH21280--Vendor #D1555

187 - RECORDS OF SOME DESCENDANTS OF JOHN FULLER, NEWTON,
1644-98 by Samuel Clarke Clarke. 1869. Boston: Pr. by D. Clapp & Son.
30pp—GE4-BH21235---Vendor #D1555

188 - RECORDS OF SOME DESCENDANTS OF RICHARD HULL, NEW HAVEN,
1639-1662 by Samuel Clarke Clarke. 1869. Boston: Pr. by D. Clapp
& Son.
60pp—GE4-BH21236--Vendor #D1555

189 - RECORDS OF SOME DESCENDANTS OF WILLIAM CURTIS, ROXBURY,
1632 by Samuel Clarke Clarke. 1869. Boston: David Clapp & Sons.
29pp—GE4-OP64243---Vendor #D1555

190 - GENEALOGY AND HISTORY OF THE CLAY FAMILY by Hiland Henry
Clay. 1916. n.p.
159pp—GE4-OP46502---Vendor #D1555

191 - THE CLAY FAMILY...THE MOTHER OF HENRY CLAY...GENEALOGY
OF THE CLAYS by Mrs. Mary Rogers Clay and the Clay Family. 1899.
Louisville, KY: John P. Morton & Co.
295pp—GE4-OP64527--Vendor #D1555

192 - DEWITT FAMILY WITH CHART SHOWING ANCESTRY OF MRS.
LOUISA B. DEWITT by Edward A. Claypool. n.p., n.d.
63pp—GE4-BH21286--Vendor #D1555

193 - GENEALOGY OF WILLIAM KELSEY by Edward A. Claypool. 1928.
New Haven, CT: tuttle, Morehouse & Taylor.
296pp Vol. 1—GE4-OP16995---------------------------------Vendor #D1555

194 - GENEALOGY OF THE CLEVELAND AND CLEAVELAND FAMILIES, 3 vols.
compiled by Edmund Janes Cleveland. Hartford, CT: Pr. for subscribers
by Case, Lockwood & Brainard Co. 1899.
Vol. 1 1070pp—Vol. 2 1137pp—Vol. 3 974pp—GE4-OP63567------Vendor #D1555

195 - COGGESHALLES IN AMERICA; GENEOLOGY DESCENDANTS OF JOHN
COGGESHALL OF NEWPORT....by Charles Pierce Coggeshall and Thell-
well Russell Coggeshall. 1930. Boston: C. E. Godspeed.
396pp—GE4-OP35268---------------------------------------Vendor #D1555

196 - ISAAC KOOL (COOL OR COLE) AND CATHERINE SERVEN...NEW YORK
CITY by David Cole. 1876. NY: John F. Trow & Son Prs.
307pp—GE4-OP62732---------------------------------------Vendor #D1555

197 - DESCENDANTS OF JAMES COLE OF PLYMOUTH, 1633 by Ernest Byron
Cole. 1908. NY: Grafton Pr.
451pp—GE4-OP27378--------------------------------------Vendor #D1555

198 - EARLY GENEALOGIES OF THE COLE FAMILIES IN AMERICA. (IN-
CLUDING...COWLES)....by Frank Theodore Cole. 1887. Columbus,
OH: Pr. by Hann & Adair.
400pp—GE4-BH19271--Vendor #D1555

199 - HISTORY AND GENEALOGY OF COLEGROVE FAMILY IN AMERICA...
SKETCHES, PORTRAITS, ETC. by William Colegrove. 1894. Chicago, IL.
840pp—GE4-OP22314---------------------------------------Vendor #D1555

200 - PEDIGREE AND GENEALOGICAL NOTES...FAMILY OF PENN, OF ENG-
LAND AND AMERICA....by James Coleman. 1871. London: J. Coleman.
40pp—GE4-BH11673--Vendor #D1555

201 - GENEALOGY OF LYMAN FAMILY, IN GREAT BRITAIN AND AMERICA
...RICHARD LYMAN....by Lyman Coleman. 1872. Albany, NY: J.
Munsell.
572pp—GE4-BH21162---------------------------------------Vendor #D1555

202 - GENEALOGICAL RECORD OF DAVISON, DAVIDSON, DAVISSON FAM-
LY OF NEW ENGLAND by Henry Rugers Remsen Coles. 1899. NY.
143pp—GE4-OP4762---Vendor #D1555

203 - GENEALOGICAL RECORD OF DESCENDANTS OF QUARTERMASTER
GEORGE COLTON:...PRIVATE SOURCES by George Woolworth Colton.
1912. Lancaster, PA: Wickersham Pr. Co.
636pp—GE4-PB01510---------------------------------------Vendor #D1555

204 - COLVER-CULVER GENEALOGY; DESCENDANTS OF EDWARD COLVER
OF BOSTON,...CONNECTICUT by Frederick Lathrop Colver. ca. 1910.
NY: Frank Allaben Gen. Co.
271pp—GE4-OP65487---------------------------------------Vendor #D1555

205 - GENEALOGY OF DESCENDANTS OF REVEREND RICHARD DENTON OF
HEMPSTEAD, LONG ISLAND....by George Dawson Aylesworth Combes.
1936. Rockville Center, NY.
109pp—GE4-OP66724---------------------------------------Vendor #D1555

206 - HISTORY AND GENEALOGY OF CONANT FAMILY IN ENGLAND AND
AMERICA....by Frederick Odell Conant. 1887. Portland: Priv. Pr. Pr.
of Harris & Williams.
698pp—GE4-OP43991---------------------------------------Vendor #D1555

207 - THE CONKLINGS IN AMERICA by Ira Broadwell Conkling. 1913.
Washington, D.C.: Charles H. Potter & Co., Inc.
132pp—GE4-OP66926---------------------------------------Vendor #D1555

208 - THE WHITTINGHILL FAMILY IN AMERICA, 1770-1970 by Michael Lewis
Cook. 1971. Evansville, IN: Unigraphic, Inc.
139pp—GE4-OP62465---------------------------------------Vendor #D1555

209 - RATHBONE GENEALOGY, COMPLETE HISTORY OF RATHBONE FAM-
ILY, DATING FROM 1574....by John Clark Cooley. 1898. Syracuse,
NY: Pr. of the Courier Job Pr.
866pp—GE4-OP57857---------------------------------------Vendor #D1555

210 - GENEALOGICAL RECORD OF LeVAN FAMILY...DANIEL LeVAN AND
MARIE BEAU (HUGUENOTS)....by Warren Patten Coon. 1927. Newark, NJ.
358pp—GE4-OP60471---------------------------------------Vendor #D1555

211 - THE JACKSON FAMILY GENEALOGY AND HISTORY by William Ross
Cooper and Eleanor (Jackson) Baldwin. n.p., n.d.
39pp—GE4-OP72685--Vendor #D1555

212 - THE JACKSON FAMILY HISTORY AND GENEALOGY by William Ross
Cooper and Eleanor (Jackson) Baldwin. 190? n.p.
39pp—GE4-OP66914--Vendor #D1555

213 - GENEALOGY OF BAILY FAMILY OF BROMHAM, WILTSHIRE, ENGLAND,
...CHESTER COUNTY, PENNSYLVANIA by Gilbert Cope. 1912. Lancaster, PA: Wickersham Pr. Co.
761pp—GE4-OP70980---------------------------------------Vendor #D1555

214 - GENEALOGY OF THE DUTTON FAMILY OF PENNSYLVANIA by Gilbert Cope. 1871. West Chester, PA: Hickman.
112pp—GE4-OP31470--Vendor #D1555

215 - THE WAITE FAMILY OF MALDEN by Deloraine Pendre Corey. 1878. Malden, MA: Pr. for priv. dist. by D. Clapp & Sons.
24pp—GE4-BH21239--Vendor #D1555

216 - GENEALOGY OF CORLEYS BEGINNING WITH DANIEL CORLEY... JONATHAN CHEATHEM CORLEY by Dewitt Clinton Corley. 1927. Decatur, IL.
242pp—GE4-OP31771--Vendor #D1555

216 - CORLISS-SHELDON FAMILIES, GENEALOGICAL, BIOGRAPHICAL by Mary Corliss. 1934. Hartford, CT: States Hist. Soc., Inc.
127pp—GE4-OP66947--Vendor #D1555

217 - GENEALOGY OF CORNELL FAMILY...DESCENDANTS OF THOMAS CORNELL OF PORTSMOUTH, RHODE ISLAND by John Cornell. 1902. NY: Pr. of T. A. Wright.
552pp—GE4-OP56094--Vendor #D1555

218 - GENEALOGY OF CORSER FAMILY IN AMERICA...APPENDIX BY E. B. CORSER by Samuel Bartlett Gerrish Corser. 1903. Concord, NH: I. C. Evans Co.
471pp—GE4-OP66844--Vendor #D1555

219 - CORTELYOU GENEALOGY, A RECORD OF JACQUES CORTELJOU AND ...HIS DESCENDANTS by John Van Zandt Cortelyou. 1941. Lincoln, NE: Pr. of Brown Pr. Serv.
625pp—GE4-OP41800--Vendor #D1555

220 - THE CORWIN GENEALOGY (CURWIN, CURWEN, CORWINE) IN THE UNITED STATES by Edward Tanjorie Corwin. 1872. NY: S. W. Green.
325pp—GE4-OP70833--Vendor #D1555

221 - COUNTRYMAN GENEALOGY by Alvin Countryman and John E. Countryman. 1925. Lux-Brothers & Heath.
360pp—GE4-OP51931--Vendor #D1555

222 - THE COVINGTONS, BEING A COLLECTION OF FAMILY INFORMATION by William Slaughter Covington. 1941. Omaha, NE: Citizen Pr. Co.
203pp—GE4-OP72657--Vendor #D1555

223 - DeMOTT AND ALLIED FAMILIES by Estella DeMotte Craig and Phoebe DeMotte Norman. 1953. n.p.
110pp—GE4-OP16411--Vendor #D1555

224 - GENEALOGY OF FELLOWS-CRAIG, AND ALLIED FAMILIES, FROM 1619 TO 1919 compiled by Frank H. Craig. 1919. Kewanee, IL: Kewanee Pr. & Pub. Co.
160pp—GE4-OP64372--Vendor #D1555

225 - DESCENDANTS OF JANE TALIAFERRO CRAIG, EMIGRANT ANCESTRESS, WITH...ALLIED FAMILIES....by Harry LaVird Craig. 1960. Twin Falls?, ID.
177pp—GE4-OP72055--Vendor #D1555

226 - GENEALOGY OF THE CRANE FAMILY, 2 vols., by Ellery Bicknell Crane. 1895-1900. Worcester, MA: Pr. of C. Hamilton.
Vol. 1 220pp—Vol. 2 686pp—GE4-OP16773---------------------Vendor #D1555

227 - RAWSON FAMILY, REVISED MEMOIR OF EDWARD RAWSON...INCLUDING NINE GENERATIONS by Ellery Bicknell Crane. 1875. Worcester: Pub. by the family.
422pp—GE4-OP44904--Vendor #D1555

228 - CRAUN FAMILY IN AMERICA compiled by Victor S. Craun. 1950. Harrisonburg, VA: Craun Reunion Assn.
354pp—GE4-AU00005--Vendor #D1555

229 - "PERVERSE WIDOW":...CATHARINA, WIFE OF WILLIAM BOEVEY, ESQ. OF FLAXLEY ABBEY....by Arthur William Crawley-Boevey. 1898. London, NY: Longmans, Green & Co.
498pp—GE4-BH19109--Vendor #D1555

230 - ANCESTRY OF...JAMES WILLIAM WHITE, M.D. WITH...FAMILIES OF
WHITE, NEWBY....by William Francis Cregar. 1888. Philadelphia: Pr.
of Patterson & White.
236pp—GE4-BH21227--- --- Vendor #D1555

231 - THE BLUNTS OF ISLE OF WIGHT COUNTY, VIRGINIA AND THEIR
DESCENDANTS by James Francis Crocker. 1914. Portsmouth, VA:
Whitson & Shepherd.
10pp—GE4-OP35023---Vendor #D1555

232 - THE VANDERBILTS AND THE STORY OF THEIR FORTUNE by William
Augustus Croffut. 1886. Chicago: Belford, Clarke.
376pp—GE4-OP30182---Vendor #D1555

233 - SIMON CROSBY THE EMIGRANT: HIS ENGLISH ANCESTRY...HIS
AMERICAN DESCENDANTS by Eleanor Francis Davis Crosby. 1914.
Boston: G. H. Ellis Co.
193pp—GE4-OP57156---Vendor #D1555

234 - PARTIAL GENEALOGY OF THE FERRIS FAMILY compiled by Charles
Edward Crowell. 1899. New Jersey, Atlantic Highlands: C. E. Crowell
& A. Rasines.
64pp—GE4-OP63502---Vendor #D1555

235 - THE BUCKNERS OF VIRGINIA...ALLIED FAMILIES OF STROTHER
AND ASHBY edited by William Armstrong Crozier. 1907. NY: The
Genealogical Assn.
437pp—GE4-OP46108---Vendor #D1555

236 - GENEALOGY OF THE CULBERTSON AND CULBERSON FAMILIES, rev.
ed., by Lewis Rogers Culbertson. 1923. Zanesville: The-Couier Co.
Prs. & Binders.
487pp—GE4-OP47899--Vendor #D1555

237 - HISTORICAL RECORD OF THE HOLMSLEY FAMILY by Carrie Holmsley
Cunningham. 1958? n.p.
94pp—GE4-OP46194---Vendor #D1555

238 - SOME SCRAPS OF HISTORY REGARDING THOMAS KUNDERS AND HIS
CHILDREN....by Henry Cunreds. 1891. Wilmington: Pr. of W. Costa.
136pp—GE4-BH17349---Vendor #D1555

239 - THE CURFMAN-KURFMAN-CORFMAN-KORFFMANN GENEALOGY by
Robert Joseph Curfman. 1971. Denver: [s.n.]
143pp—GE4-AU00178---Vendor #D1555

240 - PADDOCK GENEALOGY: DESCENDANTS OF ROBERT PADDOCK OF
PLYMOUTH COLONY, BLACKSMITH...1646 by Robert Joseph Curfman.
1977. Fort Collins, CO: Curfman.
267pp—GE4-AU00218---Vendor #D1555

241 - PETTY-PETTIS GENEALOGY: DESCENDENTS OF JOHN PETTY OF
SPRINGFIELD, MASSACHUSETTS, 1668 compiled by Robert Joseph Curfman. 1974. Kansas City, MO: Robert Joseph Curfman.
88pp—GE4-AU00179---Vendor #D1555

242 - GENEALOGY OF THE CURRENT AND HOBSON FAMILIES by Annie E.
Current. 1906. New Castle, IN: M. O. Watters.
434pp—GE4-OP37963---Vendor #D1555

243 - DESCENDANTS OF THOMAS (5) BUELL, PIONEER IN MADISON COUN-
TY, NEW YORK....compiled by Harlow Dunham Curtis. 1956. Portland,
OR: Nathan Deloss Buell.
349pp—GE4-OP64546---Vendor #D1555

244 - THE CUSTER FAMILIES by Milo Custer. 1912. Bloomington, IL.
55pp—GE4-OP62744---Vendor #D1555

245 - CUTLER MEMORIAL AND GENEALOGICAL HISTORY...FAMILIES ALLIED
TO CUTLERS BY MARRIAGE compiled by Nahum Sawin Cutler. 1889.
Greenfield, MA: Pr. of E. A. Hall & Co.
713pp—GE4-OP63956---Vendor #D1555

246 - DANN AND MONTGOMERY CHRONICLES; OUR FARM AND OUR FAMILY by Harvey Montgomery Dann. 1943. NY: Tripps Color Pr. Corp.
186pp—GE4-OP55739--Vendor #D1555

247 - STAMMTAFEL UND REGISTER DER NACHKOMMENSCHAFT DES SAMUEL ALEXANDER LEVI (DANN) AUS FRANKFURT...by Wilhelm Dann. 1870. Frankfurt A.M.
98pp—GE4-BH14089---Vendor #D1555

248 - HISTORY AND GENEALOGY OF DAVENPORT FAMILY IN ENGLAND AND AMERICA....by Amzi Benedict Davenport. 1851. NY: S.W. Benedict
398pp—GE4-OP33489---Vendor #D1555

249 - SUPPLEMENT TO HISTORY...DAVENPORT FAMILY, IN ENGLAND AND AMERICA...1850 by Amzi Benedict Davenport. 1876. Stanford, CT.
469pp—GE4-OP33548--Vendor #D1555

250 - WARREN, JACKSON, AND ALLIED FAMILIES...JESSE WARREN AND BETSEY JACKSON by Betsey (Warren) DAvis. 1903. Philadelphia: Pr. for priv. circulation by J. B. Lippincott Co.
275pp—GE4-OP70827---Vendor #D1555

251 - CHARLES AND HANNAH (MATSON) DAVIS...DESCENDANTS, REVISED TO OCTOBER 1962 compiled by Earl Harris Davis. 1956. n.p.
388pp—GE4-OP13416---Vendor #D1555

252 - SKETCHES OF THE LIFE AND CHARACTER OF BERRYMAN KENCHIN DAVIS by Frederick Parker Davis. 1929? Sioux City, IA: priv. pr. by author.
217pp—GE4-OP12567---Vendor #D1555

253 - SAMUEL DAVIS, OXFORD, MASSACHUSETTS AND JOSEPH DAVIS, DUDLEY, MASSACHUSETTS...DESCENDANTS by George Lucien Davis. 1884. North Andover, MA: G. L. Davis.
638pp—GE4-BH21163--Vendor #D1555

254 - BILLINGSLEY FAMILY (BILLINGSLY-BILLINGSLEA) IN AMERICA by Harry Alexander Davis. 1936. Washington, D.C. [Rutland, VT: Tuttle Pub. Co., Inc.]
988pp—GE4-OP72668--Vendor #D1555

255 - NORRIS FAMILY OF MARYLAND AND VIRGINIA; GENEALOGY OF THOMAS NORRIS...., 4 vols. by Harry Alexander Davis. 1941. Washington, D.C.
1453pp—GE4-OP66923---Vendor #D1555

256 - DOLAR DAVIS; SKETCH OF HIS LIFE WITH RECORD...EARLIER DE-SCENDANTS by Horace Davis. 1881. Dambridge: Riverside Pr.
76pp—GE4-BH21150--Vendor #D1555

257 - DAVIS FAMILY: HISTORY OF DESCENDANTS OF WILLIAM DAVIS,... MARY MEANS by Thomas Kirby. 1912. Norwood, MA: Impr. for family by Plimpton Pr.
342pp—GE4-OP45949--Vendor #D1555

258 - ANCESTRY OF ANNIS SPEAR, 1775-1858 OF LITCHFIELD, MAINE by Walter Goodwin Davis. 1945. Portland, ME: Southworth-Anthoensen Pr.
185pp—GE4-OP47145--Vendor #D1555

259 - HISTORY OF THE HART FAMILY OF WARMINSTER, BUCKS COUNTY, PENNSYLVANIA by William Watts Hart Davis. 1867. Doylestown, PA: Pr. priv. W. W. H. Davis, Pr. (Best copy available pp10-11 App.faded)
162pp—GE4-OP67663--Vendor #D1555

260 - COLLECTION OF FAMILY RECORDS...BEARING NAME DAWSON, OR ALLIED...FAMILIES....by Charles Carroll Dawson. 1874. Albany, NY: J. Munsell.
606pp—GE4-BH13677---Vendor #D1555

261 - GENEALOGICAL REGISTER OF DESCENDANTS IN MALE LINE OF ROBERT DAY, 2nd ed., by George Edward Day. 1848. Northhampton: J. & L. Metcalf. 130pp—GE4-OP54406-----------------------Vendor #D1555

262 - DESCENT OF FAMILY OF DEACON OF ELSTOWE AND LONDON...KIR-
ton by Edward Deacon. 1898. Bridgeport, CT.
498pp—GE4-BH21423--Vendor #D1555

263 - GENEALOGY OF DESCENDANTS OF JAMES DEAN,ONE...FIRST SETT-
LERS OF OAKHAM, MASSACHUSETTS by Gardner Milton Dean. 1889.
Boston: Pr. of T. W. Ripley.
38pp—GE4-BH21178--Vendor #D1555

264 - GENEALOGY OF FAMILY OF ARNOLD IN EUROPE AND AMERICA....
by John Ward Dean, et al. 1879. Boston: Pr. of D. Clapp & Son.
32pp—GE4-BH19175--Vendor #D1555

265 - BIOGRAPHICAL SKETCH OF ELKANAH WATSON...EARLY SETTLED IN
PLYMOUTH COLONY by William Reed Deane. 1864. Albany, NY: J. Munsell.
28pp—GE4-BH21160--Vendor #D1555

266 - GENEALOGY OF DECOUR FAMILY...FAMILY IN AMERICA FROM
LEUREN DES COU compiled by Sarah Ella Decou and John Allen Decou.
1926. n.p.
289pp—GE4-OP63446--Vendor #D1555

267 - THE DE FORESTS OF AVESNES (AND OF NEW NETHERLAND)...1494
TO PRESENT TIME....by John William De Forest. 1900. New Haven,
CT: Tuttle, Morehouse & Taylor.
312pp—GE4-AC81102--Vendor #D1555

268 - ROLL OF THE HOUSE OF LACY, PEDIGREES, MILITARY MEMORIES...
HISTORY by Edward De Lacy-Bellingari. 1928. Baltimore: Waverly Pr.
459pp—GE4-OP55728--Vendor #D1555

269 - HASLER FAMILIES AND WHERE THEY CAME FROM by Helen Hassler
Dempsey. 1946. Rutland, VT: Tuttle Pub. Co.
408pp—GE4-OP46387--Vendor #D1555

270 - SCHELL; OR, RESEARCHES AFTER DESCENDANTS OF JOHN CHRIS-
TIAN SCHELL AND JOHN SCHELL by Christian Denissen. ca. 1896.
Detroit: J. F. Eby & Co.
105pp—GE4-CD00251--Vendor #D1555

271 - HAND-BOOK OF HARTWELL GENEALOGY, 1636-1887...WILLIAM HART-
WELL OF CONCORD, MASSACHUSETTS....by Lyman Willard Densmore.
1887. Boston: Pr. of G. E. Crosby & Co.
202pp—GE4-BH13665--Vendor #D1555

272 - ST. PAUL'S CHURCH, RED HOOK, DUCHESS COUNTY, NEW YORK...
ROSE HILL...DE PEYSTER FAMILY..."Anchor" by John Watts DePeyster.
1881. NY: C. H. Ludwig, Pr.
92pp—GE4-BH21164--Vendor #D1555

273 - COUNTING KINDRED OF CHRISTIAN DEPPEN AND HISTORY OF
CHRISTIAN RUCHTY....by Elmer Ellsworth Deppen and M. L. Ellsworth.
ca. 1940. Sinking Spring, PA.
626pp—GE4-OP62796--Vendor #D1555

274 - DESCENDANTS OF THOMAS WHITE, OF MARBLEHEAD AND MARK
HASKELL OF BEVERLY, MASSACHUSETTS....by Perley Derby. 1872.
Boston: Pr. of D. Clapp & Son.
124pp—GE4-BH19049--Vendor #D1555

275 - JOHN WOODBURY AND SOME OF HIS DESCENDANTS...LATE PERLEY
DERBY by Perley Derby. 1900? Salem?, MA.
40pp—GE4-BH21224--Vendor #D1555

276 - DESCENT OF SAMUEL WHITAKER PENNYPACKER FROM ANCIENT
COUNTS OF HOLLAND. 1898.
36pp—GE4-BH11676--Vendor #D1555

277 - LIFE OF GEORGE DEWEY, REAR ADMIRAL, U.S.N.: AND DEWEY
FAMILY HISTORY compiled by Louis Marinus Dewey; edited by Adelbert
Milton Dewey. ca. 1898. Westfield, MA: Dewey Publ Co.
1007pp—GE4-OP60559--Vendor #D1555

278 - TERRELL GENEALOGY by Emma Dicken. 1952. San Antonio,TX.
320pp—GE4-OP22922--Vendor #D1555

279 - GENEALOGY OF THE DICKEY FAMILY by John Dickey. 1898. Worcester, MA: F. S. Blanchard & Co.
345pp—GE4-OP57132--Vendor #D1555

280 - RECORD OF THE LAMBERT-DICKINSON FAMILY by Wharton Dickinson. 1901. NY.
315pp—GE4-OP71150--Vendor #D1555

281 - DICKINSON FAMILY HISTORY 1830. 1830. n.p.
3pp—GE4-BH21285--Vendor #D1555

282 - DENNY GENEALOGY, 3 vols., by Margaret Collins (Denny) Dixon and Elizabeth Chapman Denny Vann. 1944. NY: National Historical Soc.
Vol. 1 641pp—Vol. 2 460pp—Vol. 3 568pp—GE4-CD00097--------Vendor #D1555

283 - THE MOBLEYS AND THEIR CONNECTIONS by William Woodward Dixon. 1915. SC.
164pp—GE4-OP41677--Vendor #D1555

284 - DANIEL DOBYNS OF COLONIAL VIRGINIA: HIS ENGLISH ANCESTRY AND AMERICAN DESCENDANTS by Kenneth W. Dobyns and Margaret Stum Thorpe. 1969. Arlington, VA.
188pp—GE4-2005247--Vendor #D1555

285 - EARLY RECORDS OF THE DODGE FAMILY IN AMERICA by Reuben Rawson Dodge. 1879. Sutton, MA: R. R. Dodge.
30pp—GE4-BH9171--Vendor #D1555

286 - TRISTRAM DODGE AND HIS DESCENDANTS IN AMERICA...BLOCK ISLAND AND COW NECK, LONG ISLAND....by Robert Dodge. 1886. NY: Pr. of J. J. Little & Co.
252pp—GE4-BH17343--Vendor #D1555

287 - GENEALOGICAL HISTORY OF ONE BRANCH OF THE DODGE FAMILY by Thomas Hutchins Dodge. 1880. Worcester: Pr. of C. Hamilton.
52pp—GE4-BH21125--Vendor #D1555

288 - THE DONNELL FAMILY....DESCENDANTS OF THOMAS DONNELL, OF SCOTLAND by Camille Donnell and Emma A. Donnell. 1912. Greenfield, IN: William Mitchell Pr. Co.
84pp—GE4-OP42342--Vendor #D1555

289 - A GENEALOGY OF DONNELL, LANGFORD AND OTHER FAMILIES by Charles E. Donnell. 1949. Plainview, TX.
142pp—GE4-AU00221--Vendor #D1555

290 - THE DOOLITTLE FAMILY IN AMERICA compiled by William Frederick Doolittle. 1901-1908. pt. 1-7.
832pp—GE4-OP62797--Vendor #D1555

291 - DOTY-DOTEN FAMILY IN AMERICA; DESCENDANTS OF EDWARD DOTY ...MAYFLOWER by Ethan Allen Doty. 1897. Brooklyn, NY.
1036pp—GE4-OP16810--Vendor #D1555

292 - GENEALOGY OF THE DOWNING FAMILY...by William Colwell Downing and R. Wilberforce. 1901. Philadelphia, Pr. of Dando Pr. & Pub. Co.
272pp—GE4-OP70844--Vendor #D1555

293 - GENEALOGICAL AND BIOGRAPHICAL ACCOUNT OF FAMILY OF DRAKE IN AMERICA by Samuel Gardner Drake. 1845. n.p.
51pp—GE4-OP66912--Vendor #D1555

294 - BEMIS HISTORY AND GENEALOGY;...DESCENDANTS OF JOSEPH BEMIS OF WATERTOWN, MASSACHUSETTS by Thomas Waln-Morgan Draper. 1900. San Francisco, CA.
298pp—GE4-OP52752--Vendor #D1555

295 - THE DRAPERS IN AMERICA, BEING A HISTORY AND GENEALOGY... NAME AND CONNECTION by Thomas Waln-Morgan Draper. 1892. NY.
346pp—GE4-OP51016--Vendor #D1555

296 - GENEALOGY OF SAMUEL WILLIAMS, OF GRAFTON, NEW HAMPSHIRE,
...RICHARD WILLIAMS, OF TAUNTON by Josiah Hayden Drummond.
1899. Portland: Smith & Sale, Prs.
22pp—GE4-BH21140--—--Vendor #D1555

297 - THE JOHN ROGERS FAMILIES IN PLYMOUTH [MASSACHUSETTS] AND
VICINITY by Josiah Hayden Drummond. 1895. Portland, ME.
42pp—GE4-BH21194---Vendor #D1555

298 - JOHN ROGERS OF MARSHFIELD AND SOME OF HIS DESCENDANTS
by Josiah Hayden Drummond. 1898. West Hanover, MA: R. R. Ellis.
240pp—GE4-BH21240--Vendor #D1555

299 - THE ROGERS FAMILY OF GEORGETOWN [MAINE] by Josiah Hayden
Drummond. 1897? n.p.
58pp—GE4-BH21241---Vendor #D1555

300 - BI-CENTENARY REUNION OF DESCENDANTS OF LOUIS AND JACQUES
DUBOIS...NEW YORK, 1875 by William Ewing Dubois. 1876. Philadelphia: Pr. of Rue and Jones.
194pp—GE4-OP46569--Vendor #D1555

301 - PEDIGREE OF DUDLEY by Dean Dudley. n.p., n.d.
2pp—GE4-BH21200---Vendor #D1555

302 - SCRUGGS GENEALOGY; WITH...FAMILIES BRISCOE, DIAL, DUNKLIN,
LEAKE AND PRICE by Ethel Hastings Scruggs Dunklin. 1912. NY: La-
plante & Dunklin Pr. Co.
245pp—GE4-OP50160---Vendor #D1555

303 - RECORDS OF THE GUTHRIE FAMILY OF PENNSYLVANIA, CONNECTI-
CUT AND VIRGINIA....by Harriet Nancy Dunn and Eveline Guthrie
Dunn. 1898. Chicago: H. N. & S. L. Dunn.
314pp—GE4-BH21216--Vendor #D1555

304 - HENRY DUNSTER AND HIS DESCENDANTS by Samuel Dunster. 1876.
Central Falls, RI: E. L. Freeman & Co.
356pp—GE4-BH21165---Vendor #D1555

305 - THE HUGUENOT BARTHOLOMEW DUPUY AND HIS DESCENDANTS by
Benjamin Hunter Dupuy. 1908. Louisville: Courier-Journal Job. Pr. Co.
460pp—GE4-OP66945---Vendor #D1555

306 - GENEALOGICAL HISTORY OF DUPUY FAMILY...WITH ADDITIONS BY
...HERBERT DUPUY by Charles Meredith DuPuy. 1910. Philadelphia:
J. B. Lippincott Co.
293pp—GE4-OP66713---Vendor #D1555

307 - STEELE FAMILY. A GENEALOGICAL HISTORY OF JOHN AND GEORGE
STEELE....by Daniel Steel Durrie. 1859. Albany, NY: Munsell & Roland.
157pp—GE4-OP72122---Vendor #D1555

308 - GENEALOGICAL RECORDS OF DESCENDANTS OF THOMAS CARHART,
OF CORNWALL, ENGLAND by Mary Elizabeth Carhart Dusenbury. 1880.
NY: A. S. Barnes & Co.
142pp—GE4-OP57055---Vendor #D1555

309 - HISTORY OF THE DESCENDANTS OF ELDER JOHN STRONG, OF
NORTH HAMPTON, MASSACHUSETTS, 2 vols. by Benjamin Woodbridge
Dwight. 1871. Albany, NY: J. Munsell.
Vol. 1 878pp—Vol. 2 834pp—GE4-BH02119-------------------Vendor #D1555

310 - SOME RECORDS OF THE DYER FAMILY by Catherine Cornelia Joy
Dyer. 1884. NY: Thomas Whittaker.
130pp—GE4-OP12209---Vendor #D1555

311 - FAMILIES OF EATON—SUTHERLAND, LAYTON—HILL by Arthur Wentworth Hamilton Eaton. 1899. NY: Priv. pr.
36pp—GE4-BH21198--Vendor #D1555

312 - THE OLIVESTOB HAMILTONS by Arthur Wentworth Hamilton Eaton.
1893. NY: Priv. pr.
48pp—GE4-BH21199--Vendor #D1555

313 - EBERSOL FAMILIES IN AMERICA, 1727-1937, INCLUDING...EBERSOLE, EBERSOL, EVERSOLE, EVERSULL compiled and published by Rev. Charles E. Ebersol. 1937. Lansing, MI: Pr. by Franklin Deklein Co.
289pp—GE4-OP54008--Vendor #D1555

314 - JOHN BROWNE, GENTLEMAN OF WANNAMOISETT by Aimee May Huston Eck. 1951. Minneapolis.
194pp—GE4-OP50624--Vendor #D1555

315 - WILLIAM HUSTON OF VOLUNTOWN, CONNECTICUT AND SOME OF HIS DESCENDANTS by Aimee May Huston Eck. 1950. Minneapolis, MN.
130pp—GE4-OP47573--Vendor #D1555

316 - THE RANDOLPHS by Hamilton James Eckenrode. 1946. Indianapolis: Bobbs-Merrill.
332pp—GE4-OP14357- --Vendor #D1555

317 - SOME HISTORICAL NOTES ON THE EDEN FAMILY by Robert Allan Eden. 1907. Baldes East & Blades.
128pp—GE4-OP66978--Vendor #D1555

318 - GENEALOGICAL COLLECTIONS CONCERNING THE SCOTTISH HOUSE OF EDGAR by Andrew Edgar. Edited by comm. of the Grampian Club. London: Pr. for Grampian Club.
108pp—GE4-OP72625--Vendor #D1555

319 - HISTORY OF CLAN EGAN: THE BIRDS OF THE FOREST OF WISDOM by Joseph J. Egan and Mary Joan Egan. ca. 1979. Pub. for the Irish American Cultural Inst. by Univ. Microfilms Intl.
322pp—GE4-2019862--Vendor #D1555

320 - GENEALOGICAL RECORD OF FAMILIES OF BEATTY, EGLE, MUELLER, MURRAY, ORTH AND THOMAS by William Henry Egle. 1886. Harrisburg: L. S. Hart, pr. & binder.
144pp—GE4-BH19039--Vendor #D1555

321 - GENEALOGICAL RECORD: THE BRADFORDS, FULLERS, AND ELLISES, A.D., 1550-1900 by Caleb Holt Ellis. 1900. Fort Fairfield, ME: Leader Pr.
64pp—GE4-BH11671--Vendor #D1555

322 - BIOGRAPHICAL SKETCHES OF RICHARD ELLIS, FIRST SETTLER OF ASHFIELD, MASSACHUSETTS....compiled by E. R. Ellis. 1888. Detroit, MI: Graham Pr. Co.
502pp—GE4-OP65074--Vendor #D1555

323 - THE HOUSE OF MANSUR by Mary Rebecca Ellis. 1926. Jefferson City, MO: Hugh Stevens Pr.
307pp—GE4-OP47704--Vendor #D1555

324 - NOTICES OF THE ELLISES OF ENGLAND, SCOTLAND, AND IRELAND by William Smith Ellis. 1857-1866. n.p.
700pp—GE4-OP62525--Vendor #D1555

325 - ELWELL FAMILY IN AMERICA; GENEALOGY OF ROBERT ELWELL OF DORCHESTER.... by Jacob Thomas Elwell. Rev. by Rev. Charles Henry Pope. 1899. Boston, MA: C. H. Pope.
44pp—GE4-BH21132--Vendor #D1555

326 - GENEALOGICAL RECORDS OF DESCENDANTS OF JOHN AND ANTHONY EMERY...1590-1890 by Rufus Emery. 1890. Salem, MA: E. Cleaves.
636pp—GE4-BH21024--Vendor #D1555

327 - HOWLAND HEIRS:...STORY OF A FAMILY...MRS. HETTY H. R. GREEN by William Morrell Emery. 1919. New Bedford, MA: E. Anthony & Sons, Inc.
498pp—GE4-OP42033--Vendor #D1555

328 - GENEALOGY OF ESTABROOK FAMILY; INCLUDING ESTERBROOK AND ESTERBROOKS IN THE UNITED STATES by William Booth Estabrook. 1891. Ithaca, NY: Andrus & Church.
375pp—GEr-OP47839--Vendor #D1555

329 - ESTES GENEALOGIES, 1097-1893 by Charles Estes. 1894. Salem, MA: E. Putnam. Pr. for the family.
440pp—GE4-BH19038--Vendor #D1555

330 - BEN OLIEL AND SEELEY by Dorothy Wood Ewers. 1966. Crete?, IL.
204pp—GE4-PB01481--Vendor #D1555

331 - BOGGS ANCESTRY OF RUBIE RAY BOGGS...AND OTHER BOGGS
RECORDS by Dorothy Wood Ewers. 1965. Crete, IL.
95pp—GE4-OP70900---Vendor #D1555

332 - DAN FOGLE'S FAMILY: "LEST WE FORGET" by Dorothy Wood Ewers.
1974. Colorado Springs: Ewers.
394pp—GE4-PB1480--Vendor #D1555

333 - DESCENDANTS OF JOHN WOOD,...DIED IN PORTSMOUTH, RHODE
ISLAND IN 1655, 6 vols. and 2 suppls. by Dorothy Wood Ewers. 1978.
Colorado Springs.
Vol. 1 133pp—Vol. 2 448pp—Vol. 3 374pp—Vol. 4 189pp—Vol. 5 194pp—
Vol. 6 100pp—1st suppl. 132pp—2nd suppl.—114pp—GE4-AU00057--Vendor #D1555

334 - GENEALOGICAL WORKBOOK RE PURDUM by Dorothy Wood Ewers.
1965. Crete, IL.
26pp—GE4-OP70905--Vendor #D1555

335 - LITTLE COMPTON WOODS;...FIFTH GENERATIONS OF WOOD DE-
SCENDANTS IN LITTLE COMPTON, RHODE ISLAND by Dorothy Wood
Ewers. 1978. Colorado Springs, CO.
95pp—GE4-AU00056---Vendor #D1555

336 - ONE HUNDRED NINETY-SIX GRANDPARENTS;...DESCENDANTS OF
JOHN WOOD OF RHODE ISLAND....by Dorothy Wood Ewers. 1961?
Crete, IL.
187pp—GE4-OP70089---Vendor #D1555

337 - PROOFS FOR EWERS-JANNEY RELATIONSHIP...WILLIAM EWERS AND
AMY GREGG by Dorothy Wood Ewers. 1963. Crete, IL.
26pp—GE4-OP70902--Vendor #D1555

338 - RUMMEL (RUMMELL) by Dorothy Wood Ewers. 1965. n.p.
13pp—GE4-OP70904--Vendor #D1555

339 - THIS ALSO IS EWERS by Dorothy Wood Ewers. 1975. (Typescript)
157pp—GE4-PB01482--Vendor #D1555

340 - THIS IS EWERS (YOURS) by Dorothy Wood Ewers. 1962. Crete, IL.
993pp—GE4-OP69618--Vendor #D1555

341 - VALENTIN RUMMEL'S ANCESTRY AND SOME OTHER RELATIONSHIPS
by Dorothy Wood Ewers. 1977. Colorado Springs, CO.
22pp—GE4-AU00055---Vendor #D1555

342 - WORKBOOK OF FAMILIES ALLIED TO WOOD by Dorothy Wood Ewers.
1963. Crete, IL.
336pp—GE4-OP70091---Vendor #D1555

343 - WORKBOOK OF LINES ALLIED TO EWERS AND BOGGS by Dorothy
Wood Ewers. 1977. n.p.
102pp—GE4-PB01743--Vendor #D1555

344 - CLAN EWING OF SCOTLAND by Elbert William Robinson Ewing. ca. 1922.
VA: Cobden Pub. Co.
388pp—GE4-OP56559--Vendor #D1555

345 - THE EYRE FAMILY OF PHILADELPHIA. n.p., n.d.
24pp—GE4-BH21290--Vendor #D1555

346 - FAC-SIMILIES OF MEMORIAL STONES...LAST ENGLISH ANCESTORS
OF GEORGE WASHINGTON.... 1862. Boston: W. White, Pr. to the state.
28pp—GE4-BH21211---Vendor #D1555

347 - FAMILY REGISTER OF GERRET VAN SWERINGEN AND DESCENDANTS
compiled by a member of the family, 2d ed. 1894. Washington.
86pp—GE4-BH02410---Vendor #D1555

348 - EIGHT CENTURIES OF SPANGLERS, 22 GENERATIONS FROM 1150 A.D.
TO 1939 A.D. compiled by Belmont Mercer Farley. 1939. Washington,DC.
68pp—GE4-OP60905---Vendor #D1555

349 - THE HISTORY OF THE BOWLES FAMILY compiled by Thomas M. Farquhar. 1907. Philadelphia.
255pp—GE4-OP66520--Vendor #D1555

350 - FAY GENEALOGY by Orlin Prentice Fay. 1898. Cleveland, OH.
419pp—GE4-OP4180--Vendor #D1555

351 - GENEALOGY OF THE FELL FAMILY IN AMERICA compiled by Sarah M.
Fell. 1891. Philadelphia: A. H. Sickler.
532pp—GE4-OP30202---Vendor #D1555

352 - GENEALOGY OF DESCENDANTS OF JOHN FERGUSON, A NATIVE OF
SCOTLAND....by Arthur Bixby Ferguson. 1911. Salem, MA: Newcomb
& Gauss.
172pp—GE4-OP72105---Vendor #D1555

353 - THE FERGUSON FAMILY IN SCOTLAND AND AMERICA by Martin
Luther Ferguson. 1905. Canadaigua, NY: Times Presses.
278pp—GE4-OP71166--Vendor #D1555

354 - FERNER, FARNER, FURNER FAMILIES by O. A. Ferner. 1941?
Alliance, OH: Roy Y. Ferner.
31pp—GE4-AU00168--Vendor #D1555

355 - HOSLER FAMILIES by Vernon D. Ferrell. ca. 1977. n.p.
139pp—GE4-AU00034--Vendor #D1555

356 - RECORD OF THE LIFE OF DAVID DUDLEY FIELD. HIS ANCESTORS
....by Emilia A. Rausch Field. 1931. Denver, n.p.
269pp—GE4-OP57158---Vendor #D1555

357 - RUNKLE FAMILY; BEING AN ACCOUNT OF THE RUNKELS IN EUROPE,
....by Benjamin Van Doren Fisher. 1899. NY: T. A. Wright.
378pp—GE4-BH09842--Vendor #D1555

358 - RUNKLE FAMILY; BEING AN ACCOUNT OF THE RUNKELS IN EUROPE,
....by Benjamin Van Doren Fisher. 1899. NY: T. A. Wright.
436pp—GE4-BH21167--Vendor #D1555

359 - HISTORY OF THE FITCH FAMILY, A.D. 1400 TO 1930...., 2 vols. by
Roscoe Conkling Fitch. 1930. Haverfield, MA: Record Pub. Co.
Vol. 1 430pp—Vol. 2 486pp—GE4-OP45755--------------------Vendor #D1555

360 - FAMILY RECORDS OF DESCENDANTS OF GERSHOM FLAGG...OF LAN-
CASTER, MASSACHUETTS....by Norman Gershom Flagg. 1907.
Quincy, IL.
172pp—GE4-OP17926---Vendor #D1555

361 - FLETCHER FAMILY HISTORY; DESCENDANTS OF ROBERT FLETCHER
OF CONCORD, MASSACHUSETTS by Edward Hatch Fletcher. 1881.
Boston: Rand, Avery.
648pp—GE4-OP17009--Vendor #D1555

362 - FLICKINGER FAMILY HISTORY, INCLUDING FLICKINGER FAMILIES
IN THE UNITED STATES OF AMERICA....by Robert Elliott Flickinger.
1927. Des Moines, IA: Success Comp. & Pr. Co.
829pp—GE4-OP72133--Vendor #D1555

363 - GIBSON FLOURNOY AND RELATED FAMILIES by Emma Madgelaine
Flournoy. 1972?
128pp—GE4-AU00183--Vendor #D1555

364 - FOGG FAMILY OF AMERICA, THE REUNION OF FOGG FAMILIES
1902-3-4-5-6 edited by Adna James Fogg and John Lemuel Murray Willis.
1907. Eliot, ME.
143pp—GE4-OP06977---Vendor #D1555

365 - MEMOIRS OF A HUGUENOT FAMILY...THE REVEREND JACQUES JAMES
FONTAINE by Jacques James Fontaine, translated and compiled by Ann
Maury. 1853. NY: George P. Putnam & Co.
512pp—GE4-OP63439---Vendor #D1555

366 - ...GENEALOGY OF BENNERS, CLAPPERS, ETTLEMANS, FORNEYS
AND STUDYS by Charles William Forney. ca. 1931. Boone, IA: Standard Pr. Co.
389pp—GE4-OP62761---Vendor #D1555

367 - SKETCHES AND GENEALOGY OF THE FORNEY FAMILY; FROM LAN-
CASTER, PENNSYLVANIA....by John Keller Forney. 1926. KS: Re-
flector Pr. Co.
118pp—GE4-OP54010--Vendor #D1555

368 - A GENEALOGY OF THE FOR(R)ESTER FAMILY. DESCENDANTS OF
REGINALD FOSTER....by Edward Jacob Forster. 1876. Boston: Pr.
by D. Clapp & Son.
38pp—GE4-BH21177--Vendor #D1555

369 - WORKS OF SIR JOHN FORTESCUE, KNIGHT, CHIEF JUSTICE OF
ENGLAND...., 2 vols. by Sir John Fortescue. 1869. London.
Vol. 1 1223pp—Vol. 2 484pp—GE4-OP65511---------------------Vendor #D1555

370 - PEDIGREE OF JESSE W. FOSTER. IN LINES OF FOSTER, COGIN....
by George Everett Foster. 1897. Ithaca, NY: West Hill Pr.
630pp—GE4-BH19186--Vendor #D1555

371 - HISTORY OF THE WELD FAMILY FROM 1632-1878 by Charlotte Weld
Fowler. Middletown: Pelton & King.
66pp—GE4-OP25483---Vendor #D1555

372 - OUR PREDECESSORS AND THEIR DESCENDANTS, rev. ed. by Robert
Ludlow Fowler. 1905. NY: Priv. Pr. for circulation among family.
98pp—GE4-BH21225---Vendor #D1555

373 - FOX GENEALOGY INCLUDING THE METHERD, BENNER AND LEITER
DESCENDANTS...COMPILED IN 1914 by Daniel G. Fox. 1924. n.p.
172pp—GE4-OP61558--Vendor #D1555

374 - DANIEL FOX OF EAST HADDAM, CONNECTICUT, AND SOME OF HIS
DESCENDANTS by William Freeman Fox. 1890. Albany: Brandow Pr. Co.
44pp—GE4-BH19172---Vendor #D1555

375 - WOLFENSBERGER IN AMERICA compiled by Frances C. B. Francis.
1967. n.p.
34pp—GE4-OP65485---Vendor #D1555

376 - FREESE FAMILIES by John Wesley Freese. 1906. Cambridge, MA:
Caustic-Claffin Co., Prs.
108pp—GE4-OP30372--Vendor #D1555

377 - CROCKETT FAMILY AND CONNECTICING LINES by Janie Preston
Collup French and Zella Armstrong. ca. 1928. Bristol, TN: King Pr. Co.
625pp—GE4-OP63432--Vendor #D1555

378 - ANCESTORS AND DESCENDANTS OF SAMUEL FRENCH, THE JOINER
OF STRATFORD CONNECTICUT by Joseph Mansfield French. 1940.
Ann Arbor: Edwards Bros. Inc.
470pp—GE4-OP66867--Vendor #D1555

379 - BRIEF HISTORY OF BISHOP HENRY FUNK AND OTHER FUNK PION-
EERS,....by Abraham James Fretz. 1899. Elkhart, IN: Mennonite Pub.
874pp—GE4-OP69107--Vendor #D1555

380 - GENEALOGICAL RECORD OF DESCENDANTS OF WILLIAM NASH...
BRUSH COUNTY, PENNSYLVANIA by Abraham James Fretz. 1903.
Butler, NJ: Pr. of Pequannock Valley Argus.
132pp—GE4-OP62111--Vendor #D1555

381 - GENEALOGICAL RECORD OF DESCENDANTS OF LEONARD HEADLEY
OF ELIZABETHTOWN, NEW JERSEY by Abraham James Fretz. 1905.
Milton, NJ: J. W. Headley.
110pp—GE4-OP17675--Vendor #D1555

382 - GENEALOGICAL RECORD OF DESCENDANTS OF MARTIN OBERHOLT-
ZER by Abraham James Fretz. 1903. Milton, NJ: Pr. of Evergreen News.
346pp—GE4-OP61988--Vendor #D1555

383 - ANCESTRY AND POSTERITY (IN PART) OF GOTTFRIED FREY, 1605-
1913, 2nd ed., by Samuel Clarence Frey. 1914. York, PA: Dispatch-
Daily Print.
403pp—GE4-OP47861--Vendor #D1555

384 - DE JARNETTE AND ALLIED FAMILIES IN AMERICA (1699-1954) compiled by Earl C. & Mary (Miller) Frost. 1954. San Bernardio, CA.
249pp—GE4-OP70031--Vendor #D1555

385 - FROST GENEALOGY: DESCENDANTS OF WILLIAM FROST OF OYSTER BAY,...WITH WINTHROP,....by Josephine C. Frost. 1912. NY: Frederick H. Hitchcock.
462pp—GE4-OP66901--Vendor #D1555

386 - THE HAVILAND GENEALOGY by Josephine C. Frost. 1914. NY: Lyons Gen. So. (pt. 1-2)
564pp—GE4-OP00527--Vendor #D1555

387 - STRANG GENEALOGY, DESCENDANTS OF DANIEL STREING...WHITNEY AND THORNE FAMILIES by Josephine C. Frost. 1915. NY: Bowles-pr.
206pp—GE4-BH11322--—Vendor #D1555

388 - UNDERHILL GENEALOGY, 4 vols., by Josephine C. Frost. 1932. n.p. Pub. priv. by M. C. Taylor. Vol. 1 140pp—Vol. 2 729pp—Vol. 3 580pp—Vol. 4 323pp—GE4-OP66060---------------------Vendor #D1555

389 - PEFFLEY—PEFFLY—PEFLEY FAMILIES IN AMERICA AND ALLIED FAMILIES, 1729-1938 by May Miller Frost and Earl C. Frost. 1938. Los Angeles.
275pp—GE4-OP71037--Vendor #D1555

390 - FAMILY HISTORY OF LIEUTENANT COLONEL FREDERICK FUEGER, ...AND HIS DESCENDANTS by Frederick Fueger. 1904. Detroit: Winn & Hammond.
69pp—GE4-OP12729--Vendor #D1555

391 - CURD FAMILY IN AMERICA, GENEALOGY OF...EDWARD CURD... VIRGINIA, 1704 by Frand K. Fuller, Thomas Henry Shelton Curd. 1938. Rutland, VT: Tuttle Pub. Co., Inc.
163pp—GE4-OP62735--Vendor #D1555

392 - GENEALOGY OF FULLER FAMILIES DESCENDING FROM ROBERT FULLER OF SALEM....by Newton Fuller. 1898. New London, CT.
51pp—GE4-2051850--Vendor #D1555

393 - GENEALOGY OF FULTON FAMILY, BEING DESCENDANTS OF JOHN FULTON, LANCASTER....by Hugh Ramsey Fulton. 1900.
318pp—GE4-OP24754--Vendor #D1555

394 - HISTORY AND PEDIGREE OF HOUSE OF GAILLARD OR GAYLORD... AND UNITED STATES by William Gaillard. 1872. Cincinnati: Wm. Gaillard.
75pp—GE4-OP60988--Vendor #D1555

395 - A PENNSYLVANIA PIONEER;...THE EXECUTIVE COMMITTE OF BALL ESTATE ASSOCIATION by Emmett Williams Gans. 1900. Mansfield,OH: R. J. Kuhl.
712pp—GE4-OP35062--Vendor #D1555

396 - THE ARMISTEAD FAMILY, 1635-1910 by Virginia Armistead Garber. 1910. Richmond, VA: Whittet & Shepperson.
328pp—GE4-OP57214--Vendor #D1555

397 - LION GARDINER, AND HIS DESCENDANTS 1599-1890 edited by Curtiss Crane Gardiner. 1890. St. Louis: A. Whipple.
206pp—GE4-OP66539--Vendor #D1555

398 - CHRONICLES OF GARNIERS OF HAMPSHIRE DURING FOUR CENTURIES, 1530-1900....by Arthur Edmund Garnier. 1900. Norwich & London: Jarrold & Sons, Empire Pr.
262pp—GE4-BH21197--Vendor #D1555

399 - BENSON FAMILY OF NEWPORT, RHODE ISLAND...BENSON FAMILIES IN AMERICA...DESCENT by Wendell Phillips Garrison. 1872. NY: Nation Pr. (Priv. pr.)
72pp—GEr-OP70997--Vendor #D1555

400 - WILLIAM GAULT FAMILY HISTORY, 1735-1948, ...PART 2 IN 1948 by
Pressley Brown Gault and Elizabeth Pinkerton Leighty. 1948. Sparta, IL.
171pp—GE4-OP40313--Vendor #D1555

401 - ROOTS AND SOME OF THE BRANCHES OF THE PUCKETT FAMILY...
by Christine South Gee. 1958. Greenwood, SC.
140pp—GE4-OP36396--Vendor #D1555

402 - GENTRY FAMILY IN AMERICA, 1676 TO 1909, INCLUDING...HAGGARD
AND TINDALL by Richard Gentry. 1909. NY: Grafton Pr.
492pp—GE4-OP44915--Vendor #D1555

403 - HEINRICH GERNARDT AND HIS DESCENDANTS. HISTORICAL FACTS.
by Jeremiah Meitzler Mohr Gernerd. 1904. Williamsport, PA: Pr. of the
Gazette & Bulletin.
394pp—GE4-OP61566--Vendor #D1555

404 - THE GIBBS FAMILY OF RHODE ISLAND by George Biggs. 1933. NY:
Privately printed.
276pp—GE4-OP70096--Vendor #D1555

405 - BIOGRAPHICAL SKETCHES OF THE BORDLEY FAMILY, OF MARYLAND,
FOR THEIR DESCENDANTS by Elizabeth Bordley Gibson. 1865. Philadelphia: H. B. Ashmead.
159pp—GE4-AC81592--Vendor #D1555

406 - GIDDINGS FAMILY; OR, DESCENDANTS OF GEORGE GIDDINGS,...
FROM ST. ALBANS, ENGLAND....by Minot Samuel Giddings. 1882.
Hartford, CT: Pr. of Case, Lockwood & Brainard Co.
248pp—GE4-BH03412--Vendor #D1555

407 - GENEALOGICAL AND BIOGRAPHICAL RECORD OF THAT BRANCH OF
FAMILY OF GILMAN....by Arthur Gilman. 1863. J. Munsell.
64pp—GE4-BH21234--Vendor #D1555

408 - TO THE DESCENDANTS OF TIMOTHY INGRAHAM, INFORMATION...
GREAT INGRAHAM ESTATE....by Gilbert R. Gladding. 1859. Providence: H. L. Tillinghast.
82pp—GE4-OP42325--Vendor #D1555

409 - RECORD OF CASPER GLATTFELDER, CANTON ZURICH, SWITZER-
LAND, IMMIGRANT, 1743...FAMILIES by Noah Miller Glatfelter. 1901.
St. Louis: Nixon-Jones Pr. Co.
136pp—GE4-BH11381--Vendor #D1555

410 - BOARDMAN GENEALOGY, 1525-1895. ENGLISH HOME AND ANCESTRY
OF SAMUEL BOREMAN....by Charlotte Goldthwaite. 1895. Hartford,
CT: Pr. of the Case, Lockwood & Brainard Co.
848pp—GE4-BH21153--Vendor #D1555

411 - GOODRICH FAMILY IN AMERICA by Goodrich Family Memorial Assn.
1889. Chicago: Fergus Pr. Co.
462pp—GE4-OP16966--Vendor #D1555

412 - GOODRIDGE GENEALOGY; HISTORY OF DESCENDANTS OF WILLIAM
GOODRIDGE...WATERTOWN, MASSACHUSETTS by Edwin Alonzo Goodridge. 1918. NY: Privately pr.
320pp—GE4-OP50838--Vendor #D1555

413 - GORSUCH GENEALOGY AND PEN PICTURES by Charles W. Gorsuch.
1905. Lebanon, OH.
124pp—GE4-OP24992--Vendor #D1555

414 - JOHN GRADY (1710-1787) OF DOBBS AND DUPLIN by Benjamin Grady.
1930. Wilson, NC: P. D. Gold.
104pp—GE4-OP37538--Vendor #D1555

415 - EARLY HISTORY OF THE TRUBY-GRAFF AND AFFILIATED FAMILIES
by Mary Lavinia Truby Graff. ca. 1941. Kittanning, PA.
390pp—GE4-OP61985--Vendor #D1555

416 - GENEALOGY OF CLAYPOOLE FAMILY OF PHILADELPHIA, 1588-1893 by
Rebecca Irwin Vanuxen Trimble Graff. 1893. Philadelphia: J. B. Lippincott Co.
232pp—GE4-OP40728--Vendor #D1555

417 - LAUNCELOT GRANGER OF NEWBERRY, MASSACHUSETTES, AND
SUFFIELD, CONNECTICUT. GENEALOGICAL HISTORY by James Nathaniel Granger. 1893. Hartford, CT: Case, Lockwood & Brainard Co. Pr.
756pp—GE4-OP45952---Vendor #D1555

418 - UNTANGLING SOME OF THE WRIGHTS OF BEDFORD COUNTY, VIRGINIA by Robert N. Grant. 1977. n.p.
985pp—GE4-AU00037--—Vendor #D1555

419 - GENEALOGY OF GRAVES FAMILY IN AMERICA by John Card Graves.
1896. Buffalo, NY: Baker, Jones & Co.
616pp—GE4-BH21418--Vendor #D1555

420 - WOODCOCK, OF CURDEN, OF NEWBURGH AND OF WIGAN COUNTY,
LANCASTER by Andrew Edward Paillimore Gray. 1882. Canterbury:
Ginder.
28pp—GE4-OP01289---Vendor #D1555

421 - DESCENDANTS OF GEORGE HOLMES OF ROXBURY, 1594-1908 by
George Arthur Gray. 1908. Boston: David Clapp & Son Pr.
445pp—GE4-OP62487--Vendor #D1555

422 - GREENES OF RHODE ISLAND, WITH HISTORICAL RECORDS OF ENGLISH ANCESTRY, 1534-1902....by George Sears Greene. 1903. NY:
Knickerbocker Pr.
964pp—GE4-OP62475--Vendor #D1555

423 - GENEALOGY OF GREENLEE FAMILIES IN AMERICA, SCOTLAND, IRELAND, AND ENGLAND by Ralph Stebbins Greenlee and Robert Lemuel
Greenlee. 1908. Chicago.
961pp—GE4-OP66658--Vendor #D1555

424 - WEAVER FAMILY OF NEW YORK CITY by Isaac John Greenwood. 1893.
Boston: D. Clapp & Sons Prs.
30pp—GE4-BH21237---Vendor #D1555

425 - PARTIAL HISTORY OF GRIFFIN FAMILY IN MASSACHUSETTS...OF
METHUEN by Charles Griffin. 1888. Lowell, MA: Campbell & Hanscom.
34pp—GE4-BH19174---Vendor #D1555

426 - THE HARRINGTON FAMILY by Ian Grimble. 1957. London: J. Cape.
270pp—GE4-OP24441--Vendor #D1555

427 - THE GRIMES FAMILY...BY MARY A. GRIMES AND ELLA A. EUSTIS
by Emma Elizabeth Grimes. ca. 1946. Minneapolis?
108pp—GE4-OP71578--Vendor #D1555

428 - THE GROOME FAMILY AND CONNECTIONS: A PEDIGREE by Harry
Connelly Groome. 1907. Philadelphia: J. B. Lippincott Co. Pr.
113pp—GE4-OP46261--Vendor #D1555

429 - HISTORY AND GENEALOGY OF GROVES FAMILY IN AMERICA...
OF BEVERLY, MASSACHUSETTS by William Taylor Groves. 1915. Ann
Arbor, MI: the author.
59pp—GE4-OP53542---Vendor #D1555

430 - STILES FAMILY IN AMERICA; GENEALOGIES OF MASSACHUSETTS
...ROBERT STILES...1659-1891....by Mary Stiles (Paul) Guild. 1892.
Albany: J. Munsells.
72ppp—GE4-OP35124--Vendor #D1555

431 - PARK OF KENTUCKY, 1749-1929;...EBENEZER PARK...MADISON
COUNTY, KENTUCKY....by Nell Marshall Park Gum. 1929. Frankfort, KY.
176pp—GE4-OP69020--Vendor #D1555

432 - COMPLETE FAMILY RECORD: DESCENDANTS OF REUBEN GUNN,
...REV. JAMES DUNN by Benjamin Jesse Gunn. 1891. Ft. Scott, KS:
Monitor Pub. House & Book Bindery.
114pp—GE4-BH21272--Vendor #D1555

433 - GENEALOGY OF DESCENDANTS OF HUGH GUNNISON, OF BOSTON...
1610-1876....by George W. Gunnison. 1880. Boston: George A. Foxcroft.
223pp—GE4-OP42475--Vendor #D1555

434 - ADDRESS...EDWARD HAWES THE EMIGRANT AND SOME OF HIS DE-
SCENDANTS by Gilbert Ray Haines. 1895. n.p.
27pp—GE4-BH21283---Vendor #D1555

435 - ANCESTRY OF HAINES, SHARP, COLLINS, WILLS, GARDINER, PRICK-
ITT, EVES, EVANS, MOORE, TROTH, BORTON AND ENGLE FAMILIES
by Richard Haines. 1902. Camden, NJ: Sinnickson Chew & Sons Co.
506pp—GE4-OP62889--Vendor #D1555

436 - GENEALOGY OF STOKES FAMILY, DESCENDED FROM THOMAS AND
MARY STOKES....by Richard Haines. 1903. Camden, NJ: Sinnickson
Chew & Sons Co. Prs.
443pp—GE4-OP64230--Vendor #D1555

437 - SIX CENTURIES OF MOORES OF FAWLEY, BERKSHIRE, ENGLAND...
GREAT BRITIAN AND AMERICA by David Moore Hall. 1904. Richmond,
VA: O. E. Flanhart Pr. Co.
112pp—GE4-OP41669--Vendor #D1555

438 - THOMAS NEWELL, WHO SETTLED IN FARMINGTON, CONNECTICUT,
A.D. 1632....by Mary A. Newell Hall. 1878. Southington, CT: Cochrane Bros. Book & Job Prs.
278pp—GE4-CD00093--Vendor #D1555

439 - DESCENDANTS OF NICHOLASS PERKINS OF VIRGINIA by William
Kearney Hall. 1957. Ann Arbor, MI: Edwards Brothers, Inc.
703pp—GE4-OP66531--Vendor #D1555

440 - OUR VAN HORNE KINDRED by Elsie Overbaugh Hallenbeck. 1959.
Amsterdam?, NY.
274pp—GE4-CD00045--Vendor #D1555

441 - HALLOCK GENEALGY:...PETER HALLOCK, WHO LANDED AT SOUTH-
OLD, LONG ISLAND, NEW YORK....by Lucius Henry Hallock. 1928.
Riverhead, NY: Harry Lee Pub. Co.
771pp—GE4-CD00113--Vendor #D1555

442 - BRIEF SKETCH OF HALLOCK ANCESTRY IN THE UNITED STATES...
JEREMIAH AND MOSES HALLOCK....by William Allen Hallock. 1866.
NY: American Tract Soc.
30pp—GE4-BH21205---Vendor #D1555

443 - STORY OF THE HALSTEDS OF THE UNITED STATES by William Leon
Halstead. Ann Arbor. n.d.
120pp—GE4-OP12731--Vendor #D1555

444 - FAMILY OF HAMLEY, HAMBLY, HAMLYN AND HAMBLING by Edmund
H. Hambly. 1946? Royal Coll. of Surgeons, Gloucester. Pr. by J. Bellows.
163pp—GE4-CD00134--Vendor #D1555

445 - GENEALOGY OF THE HAMILTON FAMILY by Salome Hamilton. 1894.
Minneapolis: A. C. Bausman, Pr.
145pp—GE4-OP10830--Vendor #D1555

446 - GENEALOGY OF THE HAMILTON FAMILY FROM 1716 TO 1894 by
Salome Hamilton. 1894. Minneapolis: A. C. Bausman, Pr.
160pp—GE4-BH21179--Vendor #D1555

447 - HISTORY AND GENEALOGIES OF HAMMOND FAMILIES IN AMERICA...
1000-1902, 2 vols. by Frederick Stam Hammond. 1902-04. NY: Ryan &
Burkhart, Prs.
Vol. 1 748pp—Vol. 2 967pp—GE4-OP63481--------------------Vendor #D1555

448 - SWANZEY HAMMOND GENEALOGY compiled by Joseph Hammond. 1890.
Marlboro, NH: W. L. Metcalf.
18pp—GE4-OP66059---Vendor #D1555

449 - HISTORY AND GENEALOGY OF DESCENDANTS OF WILLIAM HAMMOND
...ELIZABETH PENN....by Roland Hammond. 1894. Boston: David
Clapp & Son.
376pp—GE4-OP63578--Vendor #D1555

450 - HAMRICK AND OTHER FAMILIES; INDIAN LORE by Mayme Herbert
Hamrick. ca. 1939. Scottdale, PA: Mennonite Pub. House.
144pp—GE4-OP72820--Vendor #D1555

451 - A CONTRIBUTION TO THE GENEALOGY OF THE HANDERSON FAMILY
by Henry Ebenezer Handerson. 1885. NY: the author.
82pp—GE4-BH10990- -Vendor #D1555

452 - THE HANNA FAMILY OF ENOREE RIVER by Frank Allan Hanna. 1969.
Durham, NC.
126pp—GE4-OP52903- -Vendor #D1555

453 - THE HOUSE OF HANNA by Sarah Ann Hanna. 1906. Brookville, IN.
142pp—GE4-OP44354- -Vendor #D1555

454 - HUCKINS FAMILY by Henry Winthrop Hardon. 1916. Boston: D.
Clapp & sons, Pr.
213pp—GE4-OP66507- -Vendor #D1555

455 - HISTORY AND GENEALOGY OF THE HARLAN FAMILY...CHESTER
COUNTY, PENNSYLVANIA by Alpheus Hibben Harlan. 1687. Baltimore: Lord Baltimore Pr., n.d.
1132pp—GE4-OP51185- -Vendor #D1555

456 - HARMAN GENEALOGY (SOUTHERN BRANCH) WITH BIOGRAPHICAL
SKETCHES, 1700-1924 by John Newton Harman. 1925. Richmond, VA:
W. C. Hill Pr. Co.
376pp—GE4-OP61444- -Vendor #D1555

457 - HARMAN-HARMON GENEALOGY AND BIOGRAPHY, WITH HISTORICAL
NOTES compiled and edited by John William Harman. 1928. Parsons,WV.
570pp—GE4-OP60932- -Vendor #D1555

458 - THE HARMON GENEALOGY, COMPRISING ALL BRANCHES IN NEW
ENGLAND by Artemas Canfield Harmon. 1920. Washington, DC: Gibson
Bros., Inc.
320pp—GE4-OP63857- -Vendor #D1555

459 - COLONIAL MEN AND TIMES...JOURNAL OF COLONEL DANIEL TRABUE,
...ANCESTRY....by Lillie Du Puy Van Culin Harper. 1916. Philadelphia,
PA: Innes & Sons.
715pp—GE4-OP61413- -Vendor #D1555

460 - GENEALOGICAL RECORD OF THOMAS BASCOM, AND HIS DESCEND-
ANTS by Edward Doubleday Harris. 1870. Boston, MA: W. P. Lunt.
100pp—GE4-BH19054- -Vendor #D1555

461 - NEW ENGLAND ANCESTORS OF KATHERINE-BRATTLE AND WILLIAM-
CARY HARRIS...WHEELOCK by Edward Doubleday Harris. 1887. NY:
C. H. Ludwig.
46pp—GE4-BH21190- -Vendor #D1555

462 - NEW-ENGLAND ROYALLS. REPRINT FROM THE NEW ENGLAND HIS-
TORICAL AND GENEALOGICAL REGISTER....by Edward Doubleday
Harris. 1885. Boston: D. Clapp & Son, pr.
54pp—GE4-BH21193- -Vendor #D1555

463 - WILLIAM AND ANNE ROBINSON OF DORCHESTER, MASSACHUSETTS
...THEIR DESCENDANTS by Edward Doubleday Harris. 1890. Boston:
D. Clapp & Son.
82pp—GE4-BH21189- -Vendor #D1555

464 - RECORD OF HARRIS FAMILY DESCENDED FROM JOHN HARRIS...
WILTSHIRE, ENGLAND by Joseph Smith Harris. 1903. Philadelphia:
G. F. Lasher Pr.
156pp—GE4-BH21204- -Vendor #D1555

465 - HARRIS FAMILY OF VIRGINIA FROM 1611 TO 1914...FREDERICKS-
BURG, VIRGINIA by Thomas Henry Harris. 1914. n.p.
36pp—GE4-OP63495- -Vendor #D1555

466 - A CENTURY AND A HALF OF THE ISAAC HARRISON FAMILY, 1744-
1899 by Ella Warren Harrison. 1902? n.p.
162pp—GE4-BH21220- -Vendor #D1555

467 - THE DEVON CARYS, 2 vols. by Fairfax Harrison. 1920. NY: De Vinne.
Vol. 1 488pp—Vol. 2 378pp—GE4-OP22842- - - - - - - - - - - - - - - - - -Vendor #D1555

468 - THE VIRGINIA CARYS by Fairfax Harrison. 1919. NY: De Vinne.
306pp—GE4-OP23177--Vendor #D1555

469 - GENEALOGY OF THE NESBIT, ROSS, PORTER,TAGGART FAMILIES
OF PENNSYLVANIA by Blanche Taggart Hartman. 1929. Pittsburgh,
PA: Priv. pr.
362pp—GE4-OP72667--Vendor #D1555

470 - ORIGIN, HISTORY AND GENEALOGY OF BUCK FAMILY...JAMES BUCK
AND ELIZABETH SHERMAN...by Cornelius Burnham Harvey. 1889.
Jersey City, NJ: J. J. Griffiths.
286pp—GE4-BH19176--Vendor #D1555

471 - FAMILY TREE OF FIVE HARVEY BROTHERS...THOMAS, JAMES,
PETER, PHILIP AND ANDREW....by Lester Malcom Harvey. 1955.
Skaneateles, NY: Priv. pr.
173pp—GE4-OP65129--Vendor #D1555

472 - HARVEY BOOK...AMERICAN FAMILIES OF HARVEY, NESBITT, DIXON
AND JAMESON...by Oscar Jewell Harvey. 1899. Wilkesbarre, PA.
1207pp—GE4-OP62685--Vendor #D1555

473 - GENEALOGICAL HISTORY OF CONCORD HARWOODS...JOHN HARWOOD
OF LONDON, ENGLAND by Watson Herbert Harwood. 1912. Chasm
Falls, NY.
163pp—GE4-OP47149--Vendor #D1555

474 - NARRATIVE OF THOMAS HATHAWAY...INCIDENTS IN LIFE OF JEMIMA
WILKINSON....by Mrs. William Hathaway, Jr. 1869. New Bedford: E.
Anthony & Sons.
56pp—GE4-BH21191--Vendor #D1555

475 - CHRONICLES OF THE COCHRANS by Ida Clara Cochran Haughton.
1915. Columbus: Stoneman Pr. Co.
159pp—GE4-OP12855--Vendor #D1555

476 - BARLOW AND ALLIED FAMILIES, ARRANGED AND MULTIGRAPHED BY
THE LATTER....by Laura Campbell Hawkins and Emma Campbell
De Vries. 1930. n.p.
260pp—GE4-OP43705--Vendor #D1555

477 - PLYMOUTH ARMADA HEROES, THE HAWKINS FAMILY. WITH ORIG-
INAL PORTRAITS...ILLUSTRATIONS by Mary Wise Savery Hawkins.
1888. Plymouth: William & Son.
211pp—GE4-OP57983--Vendor #D1555

478 - GENEALOGICAL AND BIOGRAPHICAL RECORD OF PIONEER THOMAS
SKIDMORE...SKIDMORE FAMILY by Emily Carrie Hawley. 1911. CT:
E. C. Hawley.
382pp—GE4-OP10761--Vendor #D1555

479 - POLLOCK GENEALOGY; BIOGRAPHICAL SKETCH OF OLIVER POLLOCK,
ESQUIRE OF CARLISLE....by Horace Edwin Hayden. 1883. Harrisburg, PA.
64pp—GE4-OP61850--Vendor #D1555

480 - GEORGE HAYES OF WINDSOR AND HIS DESCENDANTS by Charles
Wells Hayes. 1884. Buffalo, NY: Baker, Jones & Co., prs.
336pp—GE4-BH00187--Vendor #D1555

481 - THE HAYES FAMILY, ORIGIN, HISTORY AND GENEALOGY compiled by
Royal Scott Hayes. 1928. Cincinnati, OH.
462pp—GE4-OP70196--Vendor #D1555

482 - HAYMOND FAMILY, WITH BRIEF SKETCHES, OFFICIAL PAPERS AND
LETTERS by Henry Haymond. 1903. Morganstown, WV: Acme Pub.Co.
96pp—GE4-OP46532--Vendor #D1555

483 - RECORD OF THE HAYMOND FAMILY by William C. Haymond. n.d.
Winnamac, IN: Gorrell & Son.
138pp—GE4-OP56579--Vendor #D1555

484 - THE HAYWARD FAMILY by Charles Hayward. 1896. Chicago.
83pp—GE4-OP35344--Vendor #D1555

485 - BRIEF HISTORY AND GENEALOGY OF HEARNE FAMILY FROM A.D.
1066,....by William Thomas Hearne. 1907. Independe, MO: Examiner
Pr. Co. Press.
759pp—GE4-OP63513--Vendor #D1555

486 - RECORDS OF THE CARRICK MOORE FAMILY by George Heath. 1912.
380pp—GE4-OP30266--Vendor #D1555

487 - HISTORY OF HEATWOLE FAMILY FROM BEGINNING OF SEVENTEENTH
...PRESENT TIME by Cornelius Jacob Heatwole. 1907. n.p.
292pp—GE4-OP50412--Vendor #D1555

488 - FAMILY RECORDS OF DESCENDANTS OF HENRY HAEFFNER, 1754-
1886...NOTES by George Henry Heffner. 1886. Kutztown, PA: Journal Steam Job Pr.
56pp—GE4-BH13664--Vendor #D1555

489 - GENEALOGY OF THE HENRY FAMILY by David Ford Henry. 1919. n.p.
79pp—GE4-OP71186--Vendor #D1555

490 - GENEALOGICAL RECORD OF REVEREND HANS HERR...BIRTH A.D.
1639...13,223 PERSONS by Theodore Witner Herr. 1908. Lancaster, PA.
806pp—GE4-OP65071--Vendor #D1555

491 - SPRUNGER FAMILY: DESCENDANTS OF PETER SPRUNGER, BORN
1757...1565-1575 compiled by William E. Herr. 1975. Los Angeles:
W. E. Herr.
298pp—GE4-AU00116--Vendor #D1555

492 - HERRICK GENEALOGY...REVISED, AUGMENTED AND BROUGHT TO
A.D.1885....by Jedediah Herrick. 1885. Columbus, OH.
568pp—GE4-OP66998--Vendor #D1555

493 - HERSHEY FAMILY HISTORY compiled by Henry Hershey. 1929. Scottdale, PA: Mennonite Pub. House.
291pp—GE4-OP12590--Vendor #D1555

494 - HISTORY AND RECORDS OF HERSHEY FAMILY FROM YEAR 1600 by
Scott Funk Hershey. 1913. New Castle, PA: Petite Book Co.
108pp—GE4-OP30192--Vendor #D1555

495 - BRIEF BIOGRAPHIC MEMORIAL OF JACOB HERTZLER...COMPLETE
GENEALOGICAL FAMILY REGISTER by John Hertzler. 1885. Elkhart:
Mennonite Pub. Co.
388pp—GE4-OP24737--Vendor #D1555

496 - JUDGE JOHN SPEED AND HIS FAMILY....PREPARED FOR FILSON
CLUB....by John Healy Heywood. 1894. Louisville: J. P. Morton & Co.
50pp—GE4-BH19089--Vendor #D1555

497 - HISTORY OF CHENOWETH FAMILY, BEGINNING 449 A.D. by Cora
Viola Chenoweth Hiatt. ca. 1925. Winchester Pub. Co.
252pp—GE4-BH13773--Vendor #D1555

498 - GENEALOGY OF HIBBARD FAMILY WHO ARE DESCENDANTS OF
ROBERT HIBBARD....by Augustine George Hibbard. 1901. Woodstock.
464pp—GE4-OP30225--Vendor #D1555

499 - EDWARD HIGBY AND HIS DESCENDANTS by Clinton David Higby.
1927. Boston, PA: T. R. Marvin.
496pp—GE4-OP17312--Vendor #D1555

500 - EARLY HILDRETHS OF NEW ENGLAND. READ...AT CHELMSFORD,
JUNE 16TH, 1894 by Arthur Hildreth. 1894? Boston: T. W. Ripley Pr.
74pp—GE4-BH21244--Vendor #D1555

501 - HILL AND HILL-MOBERLY CONNECTIONS OF FAIRFIELD COUNTY,
SOUTH CAROLINA by George Anderson Hill. 1961. Ponca City, OK.
336pp—GE4-AU00074--Vendor #D1555

502 - GENEALOGICAL NOTES OF WHIPPLE-HILL FAMILIES...RECORDS OF
OTHER FAMILIES by John Whipple Hill. 1897. Chicago: Fergus Pr. Co.
122pp—GE4-BH19059--Vendor #D1555

503 - DESCENDANTS OF HENRY HINES, SR. EDITED BY J. ADGER STEW-
ART by James Davis Hines. 1925. Louisville, KY: J. P. Morton.
42pp—GE4-OP17364--Vendor #D1555

504 - GENEALOGY OF HITCHCOCK FAMILY...DESCENDED FROM MATTHIAS
HITCHCOCK OF EAST HAVEN, CONNECTICUT....by Mary Lewis Judson.
1894. Amherst, MA.
595pp—GE4-OP64483---Vendor #D1555

505 - SHANNON GENEALOGY; GENEALOGICAL RECORD AND MEMORIALS
...SHANNON FAMILY IN AMERICA by George Enos Hodgdon. 1905.
Rochester, NY: Genesee Pr.
626pp—GE4-OP70947---Vendor #D1555

506 - SIZER GENEALOGY. HISTORY OF ANTONIO DE ZOCIEUR WHO
CHANGED NAME TO ANTHONY SIZER by Lillian Josephine Hubbard
Holch. 1941. Brooklyn, NY: Bowles-Pr.
498pp—GE4-OP62764---Vendor #D1555

507 - GENEALOGY OF DESCENDANTS OF BANFIELD CAPRON FROM A.D.
1660TO 1859 by Frederic Augustus Holden. 1859. Boston: G. C. Rand
& Avery.
288pp—GE4-OP27117---Vendor #D1555

508 - HOLDERS OF HOLDERNESS, HISTORY AND GENEALOGY OF HOLDER
FAMILY...CHRISTOPHER HOLDER by Charles Frederick Holder. 1902.
Pasadena.
419pp—GE4-OP63910---Vendor #D1555

509 - WILLIAM DAWES AND HIS RIDE WITH PAUL REVERE....GENEALOGY
OF DAWES FAMILY by Henry Ware Holland. 1878. Boston: J. Wilson.
206pp—GE4-OP37816---Vendor #D1555

510 - GENEALOGY OF HOLLON AND RELATED FAMILIES by Clay Hollon.
1958. Chicago.
110pp—GE4-OP22458---Vendor #D1555

511 - LETTER OF DIRECTIONS TO HIS FATHER'S BIRTH-PLACE...GEN-
EALOGY BY B. WILLIAMS PATTERSON by John Holmes. 1865. NY:
U. Q. Club [J. M. Bradstreet & Son Pr.]
90pp—GE4-BH21218---Vendor #D1555

512 - SWEDISH HOLSTEINS IN AMERICA, FROM 1644 TO 1892...JOHN
HUGHES....by Anna Morris Ellis Holstein. 1892. Norristown, PA:
M. R. Wills, Pr. & Bdr.
468pp—GE4-BH13681---Vendor #D1555

513 - BEARDSLEY GENEALOGY: FAMILY OF WILLIAM BEARDSLEY,...
SETTLERS OF STRATFORD, CONNECTICUT by Nellie Judson Beardsley
Holt. 1951. West Hartford.
687pp—GE4-OP70779---Vendor #D1555

514 - GEORGE MICHAEL ELLER AND DESCENDANTS...WELKER, GRAYBILL,
COLYARD, WHITTINGTON, HOOK....by James William Hook. 1975.
New Haven?
504pp—GE4-OP71178---Vendor #D1555

515 - THE HUBER-HOOVER FAMILY HISTORY by Harry M. Hoover. 1928.
Scottdale, PA: Mennonite Pub. House.
353pp—GE4-OP69277---Vendor #D1555

516 - GENEALOGY OF PARK BENJAMIN by Merle Montgomery Hoover. 1948.
NY: Columbia Univ. Pr.
94pp—GE4-OP71654---Vendor #D1555

517 - FREEMAN FORBEARS...ORIGINAL HIRES OF JAMES CITY AND CHAR-
LES RIVER IN VIRGINIA by Garland Evans Hopkins. 1942. n.p.
85pp—GE4-OP62767---Vendor #D1555

518 - LOGUES IN AMERICA, AND RELATED FAMILIES, TWO PARTS by
Mabel Logue Hopkins and Leona Logue Schneiter. Edited by Albert
Marion Logue. 1955. San Leandro?, CA.
156pp—GE4-PB02252- -Vendor #D1555

519 - HOPKINS OF VIRGINIA AND RELATED FAMILIES b·· Walter Lee Hopkins. 1931. Richmond, VA: J. W. Ferguson & Sons.
460pp—GE4-OP60920- -Vendor #D1555

520 - LEFTWICH-TURNER FAMILIES OF VIRGINIA by Walter L Hopkins.
1931. Richmond, VA: J. W. Fergusson & Sons Prs.
410pp—GE4-OP66985- -Vendor #D1555

521 - BLISS BOOK, ROMANTIC HISTORY OF THE BLISS FAMILY FROM...
ENGLAND....by Charles Arthur Hoppin. 1913. Hartford, CT: Priv. pr.
221pp—GE4-OP46439- -Vendor #D1555

522 - HOSMER GENEALOGY, DESCENDANTS OF JAMES HOSMER...1635 AND
SETTLED IN CONCORD, MASSACHUSETTS by George Leonard Hosmer.
1928. Cambridge: Technical Composition Co.
301pp—GE4-OP14148- -Vendor #D1555

523 - HOUGHTON GENEALOGY; DESCENDANTS OF RALPH AND JOHN
HOUGHTON OF LANCASTER, MASSACHUSETTS by John Wesley Houghton. ca. 1912. NY: F. H. Hitchcock.
695pp—GE4-OP50081- -Vendor #D1555

524 - GENEALOGY OF HOUSER, RHERER, DILLMAN, HOOVER FAMILIES by
W. W. Houser. 1910. n.p.
245pp—GE4-OP66442- -Vendor #D1555

525 - LIFE AND LETTERS OF CHRISTOPHER HOUSTON...COMPILED BY
GERTRUDE D. ENFIELD by Christopher Houston. 1957. n.p.
205pp—GE4-OP67688- -Vendor #D1555

526 - BRIEF BIOGRAPHICAL ACCOUNTS OF MANY MEMBERS OF HOUSTON
FAMILY...TABLE by Samuel Rutherford Houston. 1882. Cincinnati:
Elm St. Pr. Co.
420pp—GE4-BH17824- -Vendor #D1555

527 - MATERIALS FOR A GENEALOGY OF THE SPARHAWK FAMILY IN NEW
ENGLAND compiled by Cecil Hampden Cutts Howard. 1892. Salem.
115pp—GE4-OP63498- -Vendor #D1555

528 - HOWARD GENEALOGY: GENEALOGICAL RECORD EMBRACING...DE-
SCENDANTS...THOMAS AND SUSANNA HOWARD....by Jarvis Cutler
Howard. 1884. Hartford, CT: Case, Lockwood & Brainard Co. for comp.
256pp—GE4-BH19162- -Vendor #D1555

529 - ABRAHAM HOWARD OF MARBLEHEAD, MASSACHUSETTS AND HIS
DESCENDANTS compiled by Joseph Platt Howard. 1897. NY: Priv. pr.
71pp—GE4-BH21154- -Vendor #D1555

530 - GENEALOGY OF BIGELOW FAMILY OF AMERICA, INCLUDING...HAR-
OLD SEARS BIGELOW by Gilman Bigelow Howe. 1890. Worcester, MA.
584pp—GE4-OP55612- -Vendor #D1555

531 - BRIEF GENEALOGICAL AND BIOGRAPHICAL HISTORY OF ARTHUR,
HENRY, AND JOHN HOWLAND....by Franklyn Howland. 1885. New Bedford, MA.
596pp—GE4-OP46806- -Vendor #D1555

532 - HISTORY OF HUBBELL FAMILY, CONTAINING...DESCENDANTS OF
RICHARD HUBBELL...., 2nd ed. by Walter Hubbell. 1915. NY.
430pp—GE4-OP55765- -Vendor #D1555

533 - HUGHES AND ALLIED FAMILIES compiled by David Darwin Hughes.
1879. Grand Rapids, MI.
256pp—GE4-BH13628- -Vendor #D1555

534 - HUGHES AND ALLIED FAMILIES compiled by David Darwin Hughes.
n.p., n.d.
266pp—GE4-BH21148- -Vendor #D1555

535 - BOOK OF THE HULLS:...HULLS OF ENGLAND, MASSACHUSETTS, CONNECTICUT, AND RHODE ISLAND by Oliver Hull. 1863. NY: pr. by P. Eckler.
50pp—GE4-BH21425--Vendor #D1555

536 - HISTORY OF THE HUME FAMILY by John Robert Hume. 1903. St. Louis, MO: Hume Gen. Assn.
326pp—GE4-OP34740--Vendor #D1555

537 - SOME MARYLAND BAXTERS AND THEIR DESCENDANTS by Allan Sparrow Humphreys. 1948. Fayetteville, AR.
143pp—GE4-OP66408--Vendor #D1555

538 - GENEALOGICAL HISTORY OF ROBERT AND ABIGAIL PANCOAST HUNT FAMILY...SUB-FAMILIES by Charles Cummins Hunt. 1906. Dixon, IL.
210pp—GE4-BH21217--Vendor #D1555

539 - THE POUND AND KESTER FAMILIES by John Eddy Hunt. 1904. Chicago: Regan Pr.
630pp—GE4-OP52089--Vendor #D1555

540 - THE THACKERAYS IN INDIA AND SOME CALCUTTA GRAVES by Sir. William Wilson Hunter. 1897. London: H. Frowde.
210pp—GE4-BH19090--Vendor #D1555

541 - GENEALOGICAL MEMOIR OF LO-LATHROP FAMILY...MARK LOTHROP OF SALEM AND BRIDGEWATER....by Elijah Baldwin Huntington. 1884. Ridgefield, CT: Mrs. Julia M. Huntington.
506pp—GE4-BH21025--Vendor #D1555

542 - PHILIP HUNTON AND HIS DESCENDANTS by Daniel Thomas Vose Huntoon. 1881. Canton, MA: Cambridge Univ. Pr.,J. Wilson & Son.
140pp—GE4-BH21184--Vendor #D1555

543 - HURLBUT GENEALOGY; OR, RECORD OF DESCENDANTS OF THOMAS HURLBUT, OF SAYBROOK....by Henry Higgins Hurlbut. 1888. Albany, NY: J. Munsell's Sons.
545pp—GE4-OP46323--Vendor #D1555

544 - HISTORY OF HUSTON FAMILIES AND THEIR DESCENDANTS 1450-1912; ...RECORD by E. Rankin Huston. 1912. Mechanicsburg, PA: Carlisle Pr. Co.
277pp—GE4-CD00405--Vendor #D1555

545 - HUTCHINS GENEALOGY by Charles Hutchins. 1885. Boston.
18pp—GE4-OP60424--Vendor #D1555

546 - ISTORIIA DVORIANSKAGO SOSLOVIIA V ROSSII by Mikhail Tikhonovich Iablochkov. 1876. S. Peterbug, Kotomin.
721pp—GE4-OP28844--Vendor #D1555

547 - LANIER FAMILY by Louise Ingersoll. n.p., n.d.
706pp—GE4-OP65555--Vendor #D1555

548 - ROOTS OF WILLIAM POWELL LEAR by Institute of Family Research. 1977?
87pp—GE4-2051627--Vendor #D1555

549 - SOME ACCOUNT OF FAMILY OF SMOLLETT OF BONHILL...DR. TOBIAS SMOLLETT by Joseph Irving. 1859. Dumbarton.
48pp—GE4-OP36680--Vendor #D1555

550 - GENEALOGY OF IVES FAMILY...MOVEMENT FROM QUINNIPIAC TO THE BLACK RIVER COUNTRY by Arthur Coon Ives. 1932. Watertown, NY: Hungerford-Holbrook Co.
330pp-=GE4-OP42020--Vendor #D1555

551 - JACOBY FAMILY GENEALOGY: RECORD OF DESCENDANTS OF PIONEER PETER JACOBY....by Henry Sylvester Jacoby. 1930. Lancaster, PA: Pr. & bound for Comm. on pub. by Lancaster Pr., Inc.
681pp—GE4-OP70065--Vendor #D1555

552 - COGSWELLS IN AMERICA by Ephraim Orcutt Jameson. ca. 1884. Boston: Alfred Mudge & Son.
770pp—GE4-OP67656--Vendor #D1555

553 - JARVIS FAMILY; OR, DESCENDANTS OF FIRST SETTLERS OF THE NAME IN MASSACHUSETTS....by George Atwater Jarvis. 1879. Hartford: Case, Lockwood & Brainard Co. Pr.
398pp—GE4-OP72157--Vendor #D1555

554 - GENEALOGICAL SKETCH OF DESCENDANTS OF SAMUEL SPENCER OF PENNSYLVANIA by Howard Malcom Jenkins. 1904. Philadelphia: Ferris & Leach.
259pp—GE4-OP70968--Vendor #D1555

555 - EDWARD JESSUP OF WEST FARMS, WESTCHESTER COUNTY, NEW YORK, AND HIS DESCENDANTS....by Henry Griswold Jessup. 1887. Cambridge: Priv. pr. for author, by J. Wilson & Son.
500pp—GE4-BH21117--Vendor #D1555

556 - JEWELL REGISTER, CONTAINING LIST OF DESCENDANTS OF THOMAS JEWELL,...MASSACHUSETTS by Pliny Jewell. 1860. Hartford: Case, Lockwood & Co. Pr.
105pp—GE4-OP71568--Vendor #D1555

557 - JOHN ADAM'S BOOK...THREE GENERATIONS OF ADAMS FAMILY, 1734-1807 compiled by Henry Adams. 1934. n.p.
12pp—GE4-OP52115--Vendor #D1555

558 - WEISER FAMILY; GENEALOGY OF FAMILY OF JOHN CONRAD WEISER, ...1710-1960 edited by Frederick S. Weiser. Prepared by John Conrad Weiser Family Assn. 1960. Manheim, PA.
906pp—GE4-OP65189--Vendor #D1555

559 - JOHNES FAMILY OF SOUTHAMPTON LONG ISLAND, 1629-1886 by Edward Rodolph Johnes. 1886. NY: Wm. Lowey.
48pp—GE4-OP50410--Vendor #D1555

560 - JOHNSON MEMORIAL. JEREMIAH JOHNSON AND THOMAZIN BLANCHARD JOHNSON...AND JAMES GIBSON by James Bowen Johnson. 1895. Washington, DC: Howard Univ. Pr.
240pp—GE4-BH21133--Vendor #D1555

561 - WINDERS OF AMERICA by Robert Winder Johnson. 1902. Philadelphia: J. B. Lippincott Co.
150pp—GE4-OP62710--Vendor #D1555

562 - AN INCOMPLETE DIRECTORY OF DESCENDANTS OF MY GREATGRANDPARENTS by A. R. Johnston. n.d. Harrisburg, PA: Pub. House of United Evangelical Church.
80pp—GE4-OP41007--Vendor #D1555

563 - THE HOUSTOUNS OF GEORGIA by Edith Duncan Johnston. ca. 1950. Athens: Univ. of Georgia Pr.
484pp—GE4-PB00108--Vendor #D1555

564 - BREWSTER GENEALOGY, 1566-1907...RECORD OF DESCENDANTS OF WILLIAM BREWSTER...., 2 vols. by Emma C. Brewster Jones. 1908. NY: Grafton Pr.
Vol. 1 710pp—Vol. 2 838pp—GE4-OP57905--------------------Vendor #D1555

565 - STILLMAN FAMILY IN THE UNITED STATES OF AMERICA, collected, compiled and published by Henry L. Jones. 1896. Wellsville, NY.
300pp—GE4-OP46048--Vendor #D1555

566 - LEVERING FAMILY;...GENEALOGICAL ACCOUNT OF WIGARD LEVERING AND GERHARD LEVERING....by Horatio Gates Jones. 1858. Philadelphia: Pr. for author, by King & Baird.
224pp—GE4-BH17347--Vendor #D1555

567 - CAPTAIN ROGER JONES, OF LONDON AND VIRGINIA...OTHER FAMILIES, VIZ: BATHURST, BELFIELD, BROWNING, CARTER, CATESBY, COCKE, GRAHAM, FAUNTLEROY, HICKMAN, HOSKINS, LATANE, LEWIS, MERIWETHER, SKELTON, WALKER, WARING, WOODFORD.... by Lewis Hampton Joanes. 1891. Albany, NY: J. Munsell's Sons.
676pp—GE4-BH21118--Vendor #D1555

568 - THROCKMORTON, BARBOUR, JONES; GENEALOGY OF THESE THREE
FAMILIES...DASHIEL FAMILIES by Otey Sherman Jones. 1939.
St. Louis, MO.
87pp—GE4-OP62684--Vendor #D1555

569 - JORDAN MEMORIAL: FAMILY RECORD OF REVEREND ROBERT JOR-
DAN...IN AMERICA by Tristram Frost Jordan. 1882. Boston: David
Clapp & Son.
514pp—GE4-OP64245--Vendor #D1555

570 - ANCESTRY OF JEREMY CLARKE OF RHODE ISLAND AND DUNGAN
GENEALOGY compiled by Alfred Rudulph Justice. 1923. Philadelphia:
Franklin Pr. Co.
584pp—GE4-OP66657--Vendor #D1555

571 - HISTORY OF KERR FAMILY, FROM 1708:...DAVID AND CORNELIA
KERR....by Samuel P. Kaler. 1898. Columbia City, IN.
134pp—GE4-BH14432--Vendor #D1555

572 - DZIWOLAGI HERALDYCZNE by Franciszek Damocki. 1916. Warsaw.
51pp—GE4-OP58041--Vendor #D1555

573 - GENEALOGY OF PART OF KASSON FAMILY IN UNITED STATES AND
IRELAND by George M. Kasson. 1882. Woodbury, CT: Arthur E. Knox.
51pp—GE4-OP67693--Vendor #D1555

574 - HISTORY OF KEAGY RELATIONSHIP IN AMERICA, FROM 1715 TO
1900 by Franklin Keagy. 1899. PA: Harrisburg Pub. Co.
675pp—GE4-OP63899--Vendor #D1555

575 - KEIM AND ALLIED FAMILIES IN AMERICA AND EUROPE...., VOLUME
I edited by De B. Randolph Keim. 1899 [1900] Harrisburg, PA.
Vol. I 420pp—GE4-BH15541--Vendor #D1555

576 - ANCESTRY OF BENJAMIN HARRISON, PRESIDENT OF UNITED STATES
OF AMERICA, 1889-1893,....by Charles Penrose Keith. 1893. Philadelphia: Pr. by J. B. Lippincott Co.
144pp—GE4-BH21138--Vendor #D1555

577 - BROOKS AND KINDRED FAMILIES by Ida Brooks Kellam. 1950. n.p.
392pp—GE4-OP62917--Vendor #D1555

578 - DESCENDANTS OF CONRAD KELLER; WITH...GWINN, NEWSOME, RIP-
LEY SLAGLE, SPEECE, VANDEN, WISEMAN AND WRIGHT....by Bennie
De Forest Keller. 1951. n.p.
242pp—GE4-OP46534--Vendor #D1555

579 - GENEALOGICAL HISTORY OF KELLEY FAMILY DESCENDED FROM
JOSEPH KELLEY OF NORWICH, CONNECTICUT....by Hermon Alfred
Kelley. 1897. Cleveland, OH: Priv. pr.
200pp—GE4-BH21119--Vendor #D1555

580 - TWO CENTURIES OF KEMMERER FAMILY HISTORY, 1730-1929 by
Kemmerer Fammily Association. 1929. Allentown, PA; Searle & Bachman.
176pp—GE4-OP46523--Vendor #D1555

581 - GENERAL HISTORY OF KEMP AND KEMPE FAMILIES OF GREAT
BRITAIN...COLONIES by Frederick Hitchin Kemp, et al. 1902. London:
Leadenhall Press Ltd.
372pp—GE4-OP04517--Vendor #D1555

582 - GENEALOGY OF FISHBACK FAMILY IN AMERICA...GERMANTOWN,
VIRGINIA 1714-1914 by Willis Miller Kemper. 1914. NY: Thomas Madison
Taylor.
383pp—GE4-OP51720--Vendor #D1555

583 - MEMORIAL OF JOSIAH KENDALL, ONE OF FIRST SETTLERS OF
STERLING, MASSACHUSETTS....by Oliver Kendall. 1884. Providence,
RI: pr. by author.
162pp—GE4-BH00067--Vendor #D1555

584 - HISTORY OF DESCENDANTS OF WILLIAM KENNEDY...MARION HEN-
DERSON 1730-1880 compiled by Elias Davidson Kennedy. 1881. Philadelphia: Pr. of Henry B. Ashmead.
87pp—GE4-OP63912--Vendor #D1555

585 - GENEALOGY: ROBERT KEYES OF WATERTOWN, MASSACHUSETTS,
1633, SOLOMON KEYES...DESCENDANTS by Asa Keyes. 1880. Battle-
boro: G. E. Selleck.
334pp−GE4-OP17549--Vendor #D1555

586 - KEYSER FAMILY, DESCENDANTS OF DIRCK KEYSER OF AMSTERDAM
by Charles Shearer Keyser. 1889. Philadelphia, n.p.
193pp−GE4-OP62351--Vendor #D1555

587 - PARTIAL HISTORY OF KYLE, KILE, COYLE FAMILY IN AMERICA...
BACKGROUND by Orville Merton Kile. 1958. Baltimore: Waverly Pr.
200pp−GE4-OP24229--Vendor #D1555

588 - KIMBALL FAMILY NEWS, BEING SUPPLEMENTARY TO HISTORY OF
KIMBALL FAMILY IN AMERICA.... 1900. Topeka, KS: G. R. Kimball.
478pp−GE4-BH21134--Vendor #D1555

589 - KING FAMILY OF SUFFIELD, CONNECTICUT...AND AMERICAN DE-
SCENDANTS A.D. 1662-1908 compiled by Cameron Haight King. 1908.
San Francisco, CA, n.p.
723pp−GE4-OP52404--Vendor #D1555

590 - KITE FAMILY: FRAGMENTARY SKETCH OF THE FAMILY FROM ITS
ORIGINS....by Virginia Ann Kite. 1908. n.p.
132pp−GE4-OP27625--Vendor #D1555

591 - SEVEN CENTURIES IN THE KNEELAND FAMILY by Stillman Foster
Kneeland. 1897. NY: the author.
670pp−GE4-BH21135--Vendor #D1555

592 - GENEALOGIES OF HALLADAY, HOWELL, ICKRINGILL, KRAFT-NICH-
OLSON AND WHITE FAMILIES by Vernon Andre Kraft-Nicholson. n.p.,n.d.
362pp−GE4-OP70684--Vendor #D1555

593 - THE HALLADAY FAMILY, 1650-1933 by Vernon Andre Kraft-Nicholson.
n.p., n.d.
108pp−GE4-OP71854--Vendor #D1555

594 - HISTORY OF KUYKENDALL FAMILY SINCE ITS SETTLEMENT IN DUTCH
NEW YORK....by George Benson Kuykendall. 1919. Portland, OR:
Kilham Stationery & Pr. Co.
693pp−GE4-OP65445--Vendor #D1555

595 - GENEALOGY OF WARNE FAMILY IN AMERICA...DESCENDANTS OF
THOMAS WARNE....by George Warne Labaw. 1911. NY: F. Allaben
Gen. Co.
732pp−GE4-OP41307--Vendor #D1555

596 - DESCENDANTS OF WILLIAM AND RACHEL KEENER compiled by Lawson
Keener Lacy. 1964. Longview, TX.
231pp−GE4-OP71180--Vendor #D1555

597 - LADD FAMILY, A GENEALOGICAL AND BIOGRAPHICAL MEMOIR compiled by Warren Ladd. 1890. New Bedford, MA: Edmund Anthony & Sons.
430pp−GE4-OP64513--Vendor #D1555

598 - GREENE FAMILY AND ITS BRANCHES, FROM A.D. 861 TO A.D. 1904
by Lora Sarah La Mance. 1904. Floral Park, NY: Mayflower.
354pp−GE4-OP33004--Vendor #D1555

599 - FAMILY RECORDS. LAMB, SAVORY by Fred William Lamb. 1900.
Harriman. n.p. A. Caldwell.
38pp−GE4-BH21182--Vendor #D1555

600 - GENEALOGICAL SKETCH OF SOME DESCENDANTS OF ROBERT SAVORY
OF NEWBURY, 1656, 2d ed., rev. & enl. by Fred William Lamb. 1904.
Manchester, NH: J. B. Clarke Co. Pr.
32pp−GE4-BH19104--Vendor #D1555

601 - DEWEES FAMILY, GENEALOGICAL DATA, BIOGRAPHICAL FACTS AND
HISTORICAL INFORMATION....by Harriet Belle Parker La Munyan. Ed.
by Ellwood Roberts. 1905. Norristown, PA; Wm. H. Roberts.
342pp−GE4-OP62110--Vendor #D1555

602 - LANTZ FAMILY RECORD: BEING A BRIEF ACCOUNT OF LANTZ
FAMILY IN UNITED STATES OF AMERICA by Jacob Wissler Lantz. 1931.
Cedar Springs, VA.
290pp—GE4-OP55965---Vendor #D1555

603 - GENEALOGY OF THE DESCENDANTS OF ISAAC AND BARBARA
STOLTZFUS LAPP compiled by C. L. Lapp. 1941. n.p.
119pp—GE4-OP15642---Vendor #D1555

604 - LARISUN FAMILY: BIOGRAFIC SCETCH OV DESCENDANTS OV JON
LARISUN...RINGOS by Cornelius Wilson Larison. 1888. NJ: Fonic Pub.
498pp—GE4-OP63254---Vendor #D1555

605 - LAUFFER HISTORY: GENEALOGICAL CHART OF DESCENDANTS OF
CHRISTIAN LAUFFER by Charles Alpheus Lauffer. 1906. Jeannete,
PA: Pr. of the Westmoreland Journal.
349pp—GE4-OP57278---Vendor #D1555

606 - THE ANCESTRY OF ABRAHAM LINCOLN by James Henry Lea and J.
R. Hutchinson. 1909. Boston: Houghton Mifflin.
212pp—GE4-OP25213---Vendor #D1555

607 - GENEALOGICAL...MEMORIALS OF READING, HOWELL, YERKES, WATTS,
LATHAM AND ELKINS FAMILIES by Josiah Granville Leach. 1898.
Philadelphia: J. B. Lippincott.
428pp—GE4-OP24697---Vendor #D1555

608 - HISTORY OF PENROSE FAMILY OF PHILADELPHIA by Josiah Granville Leach. 1903. Philadelphia: pub. for priv. circulation by D. Biddle.
294pp—GE4-BH11680---Vendor #D1555

609 - ABRAHAM LINCOLN, AN AMIERCAN MIGRATION by Marion Dexter
Learned. 1909. Philadelphia: W. J. Campbell.
163pp—GE4-OP30384---Vendor #D1555

610 - LEE CHRONICLE, STUDIES OF EARLY GENERATIONS OF LEES OF
VIRGINIA by Cazenove Gardner Lee. Comp. & ed. by Dorothy Mills
Parker. 1957. NY: N. Y. Univ. Pr.
468pp—GE4-2050258---Vendor #D1555

611 - LEE OF VIRGINIA, 1642-1892...DESCENDANTS OF COLONEL RICHARD
LEE by Edmund Jennings Lee. 1895. Philadelphia.
618pp—GE4-OP52704---Vendor #D1555

612 - HISTORY OF THE SCOTT FAMILY by Henry James Lee. ca. 1919.
NY: R. L. Polk & Co., Inc.
119pp—GE4-OP53086---Vendor #D1555

613 - MEMORANDA OF LEES AND COGNATE FAMILIES. FOR THREE HUN-
DRED YEARS....by John Newton Lee. 1898. Waukegan, IL: De Kay Bros.
64pp—GE4-BH21420---Vendor #D1555

614 - GENEALOGY OF VALE AND GARRETSON DESCENDANTS:...WITH
BIOGRAPHICAL AND HISTORICAL RECORDS by Lydia Anne Vale Leffler.
1913. Ames, IA.
194pp—GE4-OP57345---Vendor #D1555

615 - HISTORY OF LAMAR OR LEMAR FAMILY IN AMERICA by Harold Dihel
LeMar. 1941. Omaha, NE: Cockle Pr. Co.
454pp—GE4-OP66193---Vendor #D1555

616 - HISTORY OF THE LENT (VAN LENT) FAMILY by Nelson Burton Lent.
1903. Newburgh, NY.
230pp—GE4-OP30154---Vendor #D1555

617 - NEWTON GENEALOGY...DESCENDANTS OF RICHARD NEWTON OF
SUDBURY AND MARLBOROUGH, MASSACHUSETTS 1638 by Ermina Elizabeth Newton Leonard. 1915. DePere, WI: Bernard Ammidown Leonard.
879pp—GE4-OP65570---Vendor #D1555

618 - MEMORIAL: GENEALOGICAL, HISTORICAL...OF SOLOMON LEONARD,
1637, of DUXBURY AND BRIDGEWATER....by Manning Leonard. 1896.
Auburn, NY.
491pp—GE4-OP64428---Vendor #D1555

619 - GENEALOGICAL RECORD OF THE VEEDER FAMILY by Vreeland Youngman Leonard. 1937. n.p.
346pp—GE4-OP66877--Vendor #D1555

620 - RANDALL LEWIS OF HOPKINTOWN, RHODE ISLAND AND DELAWARE
COUNTY, NEW YORK...DESCENDANTS by Frank Pardee Lewis and Edward Chester Lewis. 1929. Seattle: Argus Pr.
200pp—GE4-OP61114--Vendor #D1555

621 - GENEALOGY OF LEWIS FAMILY IN AMERICA, FROM MIDDLE OF THE
SEVENTEENTH CENTURY...by William Terrell Lewis. 1893. Louisville,
KY: Courier-Journal Job Pr.
406pp—GE4-OP55320--Vendor #D1555

622 - LEWISIANA, OR, THE LEWIS LETTER: INDEX [FOR] VOL. 1-17.
1939. Syracuse.
712pp—GE4-OP56644--Vendor #D1555

623 - LEWISIANA; OR, THE LEWIS LETTER. A MONTHLY INTER-FAMILY
PAPER, 15 vols. 1907. Lisle, NY.
Vol. 1-8 1542pp—Vol. 16-17 472pp—Vol. 9-15 1188pp—
GE4-OP40351--Vendor #D1555

624 - GENEALOGY OF WALDO FAMILY; RECORD OF DESCENDANTS OF
CORNELIUS WALDO...., 2 vols. by Waldo Lincoln. 1902. Worcester,
MA: Pr. of C. Hamilton.
Vol. 1 612pp—Vol. 2 606pp—GE4-BH19041--------------------Vendor #D1555

625 - HISTORY OF LINCOLN FAMILY,...SAMUEL LINCOLN OF HINGHAM,
MASSACHUSETTS....by Waldo Lincoln. 1923. Worcester, MA: Common-
wealth Pr.
774pp—GE4-OP27217--Vendor #D1555

626 - HISTORY OF LINDLEY-LINDSLEY-LINSLEY FAMILIES IN AMERICA,
1639-1930, 2 vols. by John Milton Lindly. 1924. Winfield, LA.
Vol. 1 600pp—Vol. 2 600pp—GE4-OP41392--------------------Vendor #D1555

627 - LINDSAYS OF AMERICA by Margaret Isabella Lindsay. 1889. Albany,
NY: J. Munsell's Sons.
304pp—GE4-OP62847--Vendor #D1555

628 - HISTORY OF A FRAGMENT OF CLAN LINN AND GENEALOGY OF LINN
....by George Wilds Linn. 1905. Lebanon, PA: Report Pr.
226pp—GE4-BH13690--Vendor #D1555

629 - GENEALOGY OF JOSEPH LINNELL, SOLDIER OF THE AMERICAN REV-
OLUTION by Mary Belle Linnell. n.p., n.d.
110pp—GE4-OP56727--Vendor #D1555

630 - LIVINGSTONS OF LIVINGSTON MANOR....by Edwin Brockholst Livingston. 1910. NY: Knickerbocker Pr.
742pp—GE4-OP66680--Vendor #D1555

631 - GENEALOGY. FAMILY OF AARON AND SARAH BRADLEY, OF GUIL-
FORD, CONNECTICUT by Abigail Parkman Llloyd. 1879. Hartford, CT:
Case, Lockwood & Brainard Co. Pr.
124pp—GE4-BH21129--Vendor #D1555

632 - DESCENDANTS OF JOSEPH LOOMIS IN AMERICA, AND ANTECEDENTS
IN OLD WORLD by Elias Loomis. 1875. rev. by Elisah S. Loomis, Ph.D.,
1908. 1909. Berea, OH.
1109pp—GE4-OP66976--Vendor #D1555

633 - MEMORIAL OF FAMILY OF MORSE. COMPILED...HON. ASA PORTER
MORSE....by Henry Dutch Lord. 1896. Cambridgeport, MA: Harvard
Pr. Co.
624pp—GE4-BH21174--Vendor #D1555

634 - LOVEJOY GENEALOGY WITH BIOGRAPHIES AND HISTORY, 1460-1930
by Clarence Earle Lovejoy. 1930. NY.
520pp—GE4-OP15133------------------------------ ---Vendor #D1555

635 - GENEALOGY OF LOVELAND FAMILY IN THE UNITED STATES OF
AMERICA, FROM 1635 TO 1892, Vol. 2 by John Bigelow Loveland and
George Loveland. 1894. Fremont, OH: I. M. Keller.
288pp—GE4-OP23766--Vendor #D1555

636 - HISTORY AND GENEALOGY OF LUCY FAMILY IN AMERICA by Gregory
Ramsey Lucy. 1959. Mountain Home, AR: W. K. Lucy, Pub.
229pp—GE4-OP53660--Vendor #D1555

637 - GENEALOGY OF COLONEL ANDREW LYNN, JR. AND MARY ASHER-
CRAFT JOHNSON....by Eliza Belle Lynn. 1912. Uniontown, PA:
Uniontown Pr. Co.
90pp—GE4-OP55124--Vendor #D1555

638 - DESCENDANTS OF JACOB MOAK OF NEW SCOTLAND by Elizabeth
Janet MacCormick. 1942. NY?
126pp—GE4-OP44388--Vendor #D1555

639 - HISTORY OF CLAN MACKENZIE; WITH GENEALOGIES OF THE PRIN-
CIPAL FAMILIES by Alexander Mackenzie. 1879. Inverness: A. & W.
Mackenzie.
482pp—GE4-BH21419--Vendor #D1555

640 - MACLAYS OF LURGAN...DESCENDANTS OF CHARLES AND JOHN
MACLAY...1734 by Edgar Stanton Maclay. 1889. Brooklyn, NY:
Ogilvie pr.
120pp—GE4-BH13872--Vendor #D1555

641 - GENEALOGY OF THE MACY FAMILY FROM 1635–1868 by Silvanus
Jenkins Macy. 1868. Albany: Joel Munsell.
524pp—GE4-OP56229--Vendor #D1555

642 - MANLY FAMILY: AN ACCOUNT OF DESCENDANTS OF CAPTAIN BASIL
MANLY....by Louise Manly. 1930. Greenville, SC.
388pp—GE4-OP47087--Vendor #D1555

643 - DESCENDANTS OF ELISHA WARE, OF WRENTHAM, MASSACHUSETTS,
TO JANUARY 1ST, 1896 by Franklin Weston Mann. 1896. Milford, MA.
28pp—GE4-BH21214--Vendor #D1555

644 - MANN MEMORIAL...GENEALOGY OF DESCENDANTS OF RICHARD
MANN, OF SCITUATE, MASSACHUSETTS by George Sumner Mann. 1884.
Boston: D. Clapp & Son Pr.
271pp—GE4-OP70626--Vendor #D1555

645 - GENEALOGICAL AND BIOGRAPHICAL HISTORY OF MANNING FAMIL-
IES OF NEW ENGLAND....by William Henry Manning. 1902. Salem:
Salem Press Co.
932pp—GE4-BH13772--Vendor #D1555

646 - DESCENDANTS OF MANNSPERGS, GENEALOGY OF MANNSPERGER
FAMILY IN GERMANY AND AMERICA, Vol. 1 by Martin Matheny Mans-
perger. 1939. n.p.
209pp—GE4-OP63741--Vendor #D1555

647 - MARIS FAMILY IN THE UNITED STATES: RECORD OF DESCENDANTS
OF GEORGE AND ALICE MARIS....by George Lewis Maris and Annie M.
Pinkerton Maris. 1885. West Chester, PA.
483pp—GE4-OP23712--Vendor #D1555

648 - GENEALOGY OF THE MARK FAMILY by Gordon St. George Mark. 1953.
32pp—GE4-OP65851--Vendor #D1555

649 - ANCESTRY OF GENERAL GRANT, AND THEIR CONTEMPORARIES by
Edward Chauncey Marshall. 1869. NY: Sheldon & Co.
200pp—GE4-BH03459--Vendor #D1555

650 - MACK GENEALOGY. DESCENDANTS OF JOHN MACK OF LYME,
CONNECTICUT....,Vol. 1 by Sophia Smith Martin. 1903-04. Rutland,
VT: Tuttle Co., prs.
980pp—GE4-BH21155--Vendor #D1555

651 - THE VAN HORN FAMILY HISTORY by Francis Merton Marvin. 1929.
East Stroudsburg, PA: Press Pub. Co.
466pp—GE4-OP65850--Vendor #D1555

652 - ENGLISH ANCESTRY OF REINOLD AND MATTHEW MARVIN OF HART-
FORD, CONNECTICUT....by William Theophilus Rogers Marvin. 1900.
Boston.
291pp—GE4-OP69202--Vendor #D1555

653 - GENEALOGY OF SAMPSON MASON FAMILY by Alverdo Hayward Mason.
1902. East Braintree, MA: Pr. by A. H. Mason.
302pp—GE4-OP45196--Vendor #D1555

654 - DESCENDANTS OF ROBERT ISBELL IN AMERICA by Edna Warren
Mason. 1944. New Haven, CT: Tuttle, Morehouse & Taylor Co.
303pp—GE4-OP71438--Vendor #D1555

655 - HISTORY OF BORTON AND MASON FAMILIES IN EUROPE AND AMER-
ICA by Freeman Clark Mason. ca. 1908. Dowagiac, MI: H. E. Agnew.
424pp—GE4-OP62918--Vendor #D1555

656 - RECORD OF DESCENDANTS OF ROBERT MASON, OF ROXBURY,
MASSACHUSETTS edited by William Lyman Mason. 1891. Milwaukee:
Burdick, Armitage & Allen, prs.
80pp—GE4-BH21180--Vendor #D1555

657 - BRIEF HISTORY OF BISHOP JACOB MAST AND OTHER MAST PION-
EERS....by Christian Z. Mast. 1911. Scotdale, PA: Mennonite Pub. Hse.
522pp—GE4-OP34830--Vendor #D1555

658 - RECORD OF ANCESTRY AND DESCENDENTS OF EDWARD BARBER
...PHEBE TILLINGHAST....by Dorcas Waite Matteson. 1892. Wickford, RI.
82pp—GE4-OP50425--Vendor #D1555

659 - WRIGHT FAMILY MEMORIALS...DESCENDANTS...GRANDFATHER
JUSTUS WRIGHT, OF SOUTH HADLEY, MASSACHUSETTS by Anna
Elvira Wright Matthews. 1886. Boston: J. A. Crosby.
58pp—GE4-BH19050--Vendor #D1555

660 - OLIPHANTS OF GASK; RECORDS OF A JACOBITE FAMILY by Margaret Ethel (Blair Oliphant) Maxtone-Graham. 1910. London: J. Nisbet.
532pp—GE4-OP33110--Vendor #D1555

661 - DANFORTH GENEALOGY compiled by John Joseph May. 1902. Boston:
C. H. Pope.
535pp—GE4-OP17995--Vendor #D1555

662 - GARDNER HISTORY AND GENEALOGY by Lillian May and Charles
Morris Gardner. ca. 1907. Cleveland: Erie Pr. Co.
407pp—GE4-OP64982--Vendor #D1555

663 - DESCENDANTS OF RICHARD SARES (SEARS) OF YARMOUTH, MASSA-
CHUSETTS, 1638-1888....by Samuel Pearce May. 1890. Albany, NY:
J. Munsell's Sons.
678pp—GE4-CD00573--Vendor #D1555

664 - GENEALOGY OF THE MAYS FAMILY AND RELATED FAMILIES TO 1929
by Samuel Edward Mays. Plant City, FL. n.d.
349pp—GE4-OP62846--Vendor #D1555

665 - GENEALOGICAL RECORD OF DESCENDANTS OF COLONEL ALEXANDER
McALLISTER...NORTH CAROLINA by David Smith McAllister. 1900.
Richmond, VA: Whittet & Shepperson, Prs.
248pp—GE4-OP62806--Vendor #D1555

666 - FAMILY RECORDS...ABRAHAM ADDAMS McALLISTER AND...
JULIA ELLEN (STRATTON) McALLISTER....by James Gray McAllister.
1912. Covington, VA. n.p.
94pp—GE4-OP62979--Vendor #D1555

667 - GENEALOGIES OF THE LEWIS AND KINDRED FAMILIES edited by John
Meriwether McAllister and Lura Boulton Tandy. 1906. Columbia, MO:
E. W. Stephens Pub. Co.
424pp—GE4-OP61091--Vendor #D1555

668 - GENEALOGY OF LOUCKS FAMILY, BEGINNING WITH JOHANN DIET-
RICH LOUCKS,...TO DATE by Edwin Merton McBrier. 1940. NY: John
S. Swift Co., Inc.
332pp—GE4-CD00361--Vendor #D1555

669 - THE McCLURE FAMILY, limited ed., by James Alexander McClure.
1914. Petersburg, VA: Presses of Frank A. Owen.
232pp—GE4-OP69394--Vendor #D1555

670 - HENDRICKSONS OF NEW YORK, NEW JERSEY AND PENNSYLVANIA...
WILLIAM HENDRICKSON ("WILM HENDRICKS")....by Marie Florence
McConnell. 19? Lakeland, FL.
238pp—GE4-BH21268--Vendor #D1555

671 - WILLIAM McCOY AND HIS DESCENDANTS by Lycurgus McCoy. 1904.
Battle Creek, MI.
218pp—GE4-OP65259--Vendor #D1555

672 - THE McCUES OF THE OLD DOMINION by John Nolley McCue. 1912.
Mexico: Missouri Pr. & Pub. Co.
236pp—GE4-OP52884--Vendor #D1555

673 - SUPPLEMENT NUMBER 1 TO EDITION B OF MacDONALD GENEALOGY
....1880 by Frank Virgil McDonald. 1880. Cambridge: Univ. Pr.,J.
Wilson & Son.
184pp—GE4-BH21213--Vendor #D1555

674 - HISTORY OF McDOWELLS AND CONNECTIONS by John Hugh McDowell.
1918. Memphis: C. B. Johnston & Co., Pub.
683pp—GE4-OP50558--Vendor #D1555

675 - THE SCOTCH-IRISH McELROYS IN AMERICA A.D. 1717-A.D. 1900 by
John McConnell McElroy. 1901. Albany: Ft. Orange Pr.
241pp—GE4-OP10940--Vendor #D1555

676 - McGINNESS AND SCOTT FAMILIES AND THEIR BRANCHES; GENEA-
LOGICAL NOTES by Samuel Wilson McGinness and Mary R. Ford. 1892.
Pittsburgh: Murdoch, Kerr & Co.
304pp—GE4-OP70686--Vendor #D1555

677 - JAMES CLARK MANSFIELD, CHRISTOPHER CLARK AND ALLIED
FAMILIES by Virginia Eliza Hodge McNaught. 1934. n.p.
251pp—GE4-OP66768--Vendor #D1555

678 - KINCHELOE, McPHERSON AND RELATED FAMILIES; THEIR GENEAL-
OGIES AND BIOGRAPHIES by Lewin Dwinell McPherson. 1951. Washington, DC.
514pp—GE4-OP61004--Vendor #D1555

679 - GENEALOGICAL HISTORY OF LEE FAMILY OF VIRGINIA AND MARY-
LAND...1866....by Edward Campbell Mead. 1868. NY: Richardson & Co.
86pp—GE4-BH21413--Vendor #D1555

680 - HISTORY AND GENEALOGY OF MEAD FAMILY OF FAIRFIELD COUNTY,
CONNECTICUT....by Spencer Percival Mead. 1901. NY: Knicker-
bocker Pr.
Text 598pp—index 78pp—GE4-OP41582----------------------------Vendor #D1555

681 - THE MEADORS AND THE MEADOWS by Edward Kirby Meador. 1941.
Boston: Meador Pub. Co.
60pp—GE4-OP66741--Vendor #D1555

682 - ORIGIN AND HISTORY OF MAGENNIS FAMILY...KEYLOR, SWISHER,
MARCHBANK, AND BRYON FAMILIES by John Franklin Magianness.
1891. Williamsport, PA: Heller Bros. Pr. Hse.
279pp—GE4-OP70687--Vendor #D1555

683 -ANCESTRY OF JOHN WHITNEY by Henry Melville. 1896. NY: DeVinne Pr.
322pp—GE4-OP65930--Vendor #D1555

684 - HISTORY CORRESPONDENCE AND PEDIGREEES OF THE MENDENHALLS
by William Mendenhall. 1912. Greenville, OH: Chas. R. Kemble Pr.
299pp—GE4-OP69395--Vendor #D1555

685 - GENEALOGY OF MERRICK-MIRICK-MYRICK FAMILY OF MASSACHU-
SETTS, 1636-1902 by George Byron Merrick. 1902. Madison, WI: Tracy
Gibbs. (p. 207 missing)
534pp—GE4-OP26229--Vendor #D1555

686 - AMERICAN ANCESTORS OF GEORGE W. MERRILL OF SAGINAW,
MICHIGAN...RECORDS by William Merrill. 1903. Saginaw, MI.
40pp—GE4-BH21422--Vendor #D1555

687 - REVISED MERRITT RECORDS by Douglas Merritt. 1916. NY: T. A.
Wright.
198pp—GE4-OP15700--Vendor #D1555

688 - GENEALOGY OF A BRANCH OF METCALF FAMILY, WHO ORIGINATED
IN WEST WRENTHAM, MASSACHUSETTS....by Eliab Wight Metcalf.
1867? n.p.
28pp—GE4-BH21183--Vendor #D1555

689 - GENEALOGY OF THE MEYER FAMILY by Henry Meyer. 1890. Cleveland, OH: Pr. by Lauer & Mattill.
134pp—GE4-BH15523--Vendor #D1555

690 - MIDDLETON-DOWNING FAMILY HISTORY; BEING A PUBLICATION TO
COMMEMORATE SILVER JUBILEE.... 1932. Anderson, IN: Hazel May
Middleton Kendall.
109pp—GE4-AU00132--Vendor #D1555

691 - HISTORIC FAMILIES OF AMERICA; WILLIAM ALMY...JORIS JANSSEN
de RAPALJE....by Charles Kingsbury Miller. 1897. Chicago.
136pp—GE4-OP22669--Vendor #D1555

692 - MERRIWETHERS AND THEIR CONNECTIONS...GENEALOGY OF MERI-
WETHERS IN AMERICA....by Louisa H. A. Minor. 1892. Albany, NY:
J. Munsell's Sons.
196pp—GE4-BH06881--Vendor #D1555

693 - THE GOULDS OF RHODE ISLAND by Rebecca Gould Mitchell. 1875.
Providence: A. C. Greene.
112pp—GE4-OP36378--Vendor #D1555

694 - HISTORY AND GENEALOGY OF PETER MONTAGUE...HIS DESCEND-
ANTS, 1621-1894 by George William Montague. 1894. Amherst, MA:
Pr. of Carpenter & Morehouse.
579pp—GE4-OP67221--Vendor #D1555

695 - HISTORY AND GENEALOGY OF MONTAGUE FAMILY OF AMERICA...
LANCASTER COUNTY, VIRGINIA by George William Montague. 1886.
Amherst, MA: Pr. of J. E. Williams.
857pp—GE4-OP63443--Vendor #D1555

696 - GENEALOGICAL HISTORY OF MONTGOMERYS AND THEIR DESCEND-
ANTS by David B. Montgomery. 1903. Owensville: J. P. Cox.
466pp—GE4-OP27434--Vendor #D1555

697 - HISTORY OF DESCENDANTS AND CONNECTIONS OF WILLIAM MONT-
GOMERY AND JAMES SOMERVILLE....by Frank Montgomery. 1897.
Albany: J. Munsell.
116pp—GE4-OP34855--Vendor #D1555

698 - GENEALOGICAL HISTORY OF FAMILY OF MONTGOMERY, INCLUDING
MONTGOMERY PEDIGREE by Thomas Harrison Montgomery. 1863.
Philadelphia: pr. for priv. circulation.
158pp—GE4-OP34571--Vendor #D1555

699 - THE DARE FAMILY HISTORY by William Harry Montgomery and Nellie
Grosscup (Leddon) Montgomery. 1939-47. Poughkeepsie, NY.
358pp—GE4-OP50391--Vendor #D1555

700 - THE MOONS AND KINDRED FAMILIES by John William Moon. 1930.
Atlanta, GA: Stein Pr. Co.
138pp—GE4-OP16385--Vendor #D1555

701 -PATTEN FAMILIES; GENEALOGIES OF PATTENS FROM THE NORTH OF
IRELAND....by Howard Parker Moore. 1939. Ann Arbor: Edwards Bros.
205pp—GE4-OP66804--Vendor #D1555

702 - HISTORY OF FAMILY OF MORGAN, FROM YEAR 1089 TO PRESENT....
by James Appleton Morgan. n.d. NY.
311pp—GE4-OP57524--Vendor #D1555

703 - HARRIS GENEALOGY. HISTORY OF JAMES HARRIS, OF NEW LONDON,
CONNECTICUT...DESCENDANTS....by Nathaniel Harris Morgan. 1878.
Hartford: Case, Lockwood & Brainard Co.
260pp—GE4-BH19064--Vendor #D1555

704 - MORGAN GENEALOGY. HISTORY OF JAMES MORGAN, OF NEW LON-
DON, CONNECTICUT...DESCENDANTS by Nathaniel Harris Morgan.
1869. Hartford: Pr. of Case, Lockwood & Brainard.
320pp—GE4-BH11682--Vendor #D1555

705 - RESSIGUIE FAMILY. HISTORICAL AND GENEALOGICAL RECORD OF
ALEXANDER RESSEGUIE OF NORWALK....by John Emery Morris. 1888.
Hartford, CT: Pr. of Case, Lockwood & Brainard Co.
114pp—GE4-BH21159--Vendor #D1555

706 - GENEALOGICAL AND HISTORICAL REGISTER OF DESCENDANTS OF
EDWARD MORRIS OF ROXBURY....by Jonathan Flynt Morris. 1887.
Hartford, CT.
456pp—GE4-OP62951--Vendor #D1555

707 - LETTER FROM MRS. THOMAS MORRIS...REGARDING KANE AND
KENT FAMILIES by Sarah Kane Morris. ca. 1889. NY.
40pp—GE4-BH19165--Vendor #D1555

708 - KING GENEALOGY. CLEMENT KING OF MARSHFIELD, MASSACHU-
SETTS, 1668,...DESCENDANTS compiled by George Austin Morrison.
1898. Albany: J. Munsell's Sons.
80pp—GE4-BH21206--Vendor #D1555

709 - HISTORY OF ALISON OR ALLISON FAMILY IN EUROPE AND AMERICA
....by Leonard Allison Morrison. 1893. Boston, MA: Damrell & Upham.
372pp—GE4-OP45883--Vendor #D1555

710 - LINEAGE AND BIOGRAPHIES OF NORRIS FAMILY IN AMERICA FROM
1640 TO 1892....by Leonard Allison Morrison. 1892. Boston, MA:
Dambrell & Upham.
266pp—GE4-BH15530--Vendor #D1555

711 GENEALOGICAL REGISTER OF DESCENDANTS OF...PURITANS...
GROUT, GOULDING, AND BRIGHAM by Abner Morse. 1861. Boston:
Pr. of H. W. Dutton & Son.
376pp—GE4-BH21412--Vendor #D1555

712 - MORTONS AND THEIR KIN. GENEALOGY...COMPILED BETWEEN
YEARS 1880-1920, 2 vols., by Daniel Morton. 1920. St. Joseph, MO.
915pp—GE4-OP69397--Vendor #D1555

713 - SOME DESCENDANTS OF JOHN MOULTON AND WILLIAM MOULTON
...1592-1892 compiled by Augustus Freedom Moulton. n.d., n.p.
99pp—GE4-OP62908--Vendor #D1555

714 - HISTORY AND GENEALOGICAL RECORD OF MOUNT AND FLIPPIN
FAMILIES by Julius Allen Mount. 1954. n.p.
125pp—GE4-OP17162--Vendor #D1555

715 - GENEALOGY OF THE MORR FAMILY by Calvin Fisher Moyer and Mary
E. Morr. 1896. Ashland, OH: Pr. by Sun Pub. Co.
294pp—GE4-BH06334--Vendor #D1555

716 - MR. WILLIAM SAUNDERS AND MRS. SARAH FLAGG SAUNDERS...
FAMILY RECORD AND GENEALOGY by William Saunders and Sarah Flagg
Saunders. n.p. 1872.
54pp—GE4-BH19006--Vendor #D1555

717 - MUNSON RECORD, 1637-1887. GENEALOGICAL AND BIOGRAPHICAL
...CAPTAIN THOMAS MUNSON...., Vol. I by Myron Andrews Munson.

1895. New Haven: Tuttle, Morehouse ¢ Taylor.
708pp—GE4-BH15520--Vendor #D1555

718 - GENEALOGY OF MUSICK FAMILY AND SOME KINDRED LINES by
Grover Cleveland Musick. 1964. Meadow Bridge, WV.
192pp—GE4-OP43898--------------------------------------Vendor #D1555

719 - NANCE MEMORIAL; HISTORY OF NANCE FAMILY IN GENERAL by
George Washington Nance. 1904. Bloomington, IL: J. E. Burke.
374pp—GE4-OP16672--------------------------------------Vendor #D1555

720 - NASH FAMILY; OR, RECORDS OF DESCENDANTS OF THOMAS NASH
...CONNECTICUT, 1640 compiled by Sylvester Nash. 1853. Hartford:
Case, Tiffany.
328pp—GE4-OP30258--------------------------------------Vendor #D1555

721 - HOFEISCHE KULTUR by Hans Naumann and Guenther Mueller. 1929.
Halle, Saale, Niemeyer.
164pp—GE4-OP17313--------------------------------------Vendor #D1555

722 - NEEL-DICKSON GENEALOGY. REVISED TO JANUARY 1, 1949, 2nd
ed., by William Trent Neel. 1953? Bryn Mawr, PA.
776pp—GE4-CD00389--------------------------------------Vendor #D1555

723 - FAIRFAXES OF ENGLAND AND AMERICA IN SEVENTEENTH AND
EIGHTEENTH CENTURIES....by Edward Duffield Neill. 1868. Albany,
NY: J. Munsell.
254pp—GE4-BH21146--------------------------------------Vendor #D1555

724 - FAMILY RECORD OF DESCENDANTS OF THOMAS NELSON AND JOAN,
HIS WIFE by Nelson. 1868. Haverhill: E. G. Frothingham, Pr.
34pp—GE4-BH21298--------------------------------------Vendor #D1555

725 - JOSIAH HORNBLOWER AND THE FIRST STEAM ENGINE IN AMERICA
by William Nelson. 1883. Newark, NJ: Daily Adv. Pr. Hse.
82pp—GE4-OP36648--------------------------------------Vendor #D1555

726 - MAREEN DUVALL OF MIDDLE PLANTATION by Harry Wright Newman.
1952. Washington.
626pp—GE4-OP66698--------------------------------------Vendor #D1555

727 - SMOOTS OF MARYLAND AND VIRGINIA; GENEALOGICAL HISTORY
OF WILLIAM SMUTE....by Harry Wright Newman. 1936. Wash.,DC.
238pp—GE4-OP65962--------------------------------------Vendor #D1555

728 - HOGE, NICHOLS AND RELATED FAMILIES, BIOGRAPHICAL—HISTO-
RICAL;...OF GENEALOGICAL DATA by William D. Nichols. 1969. n.p.
313pp—GE4-OP65352--------------------------------------Vendor #D1555

729 - DANIEL AND MARY STRICKLER...PENNSYLVANIA DUTCH PIONEERS
OF 1839, WAYNE COUNTY, INDIANA....by Kenneth J. Nicholson and
Frances Fouts Wilson. 1964. Flagstaff, AZ.
273pp—GE4-CD00381--------------------------------------Vendor #D1555

730 - NOAH BROWN AND HIS DESCENDANTS. n.p., n.d.
21pp—GE4-BH21277--------------------------------------Vendor #D1555

731 - GENEALOGICAL COLLECTIONS RELATING TO FAMILIES OF NOBLET,
NOBLAT, NOBLOT AND NOBLETS....compiled by John Hyndman Noblit.
1906. Pr. for priv. circ. by Ferris & Leach.
449pp—GE4-OP70628--------------------------------------Vendor #D1555

732 - DOWN THE CENTURIES WITH THE NOBLITTS, 1180-1955, GENEAL-
OGY, BIOGRAPHY....compiled by Loren Scott Noblitt and Minnie Walls
Noblitt. 1956. Greenfield, IN: Mitchl-Fleming Pr.
216pp—GE4-OP69200--------------------------------------Vendor #D1555

733 - NORTHRUP-NORTHROP GENEALOGY, RECORD OF THE KNOWN
DESCENDANTS OF JOSEPH NORTHRUP by Ansel Judd Northrup.
ca. 1908. NY: Grafton Pr.
479pp—GE4-OP69201--------------------------------------Vendor #D1555

734 - GENEALOGICAL RECORD OF SOME NOYES DESCENDANTS OF JAMES
NICHOLAS AND PETER NOYES, 2 vols., compiled by Henry Erastus

Noyes. 1904. Boston, MA.

Vol. 1 589pp—Vol. 2 437pp—GE4-OP67383--------------------Vendor #D1555

735 - DESCENDANTS OF REVEREND WILLIAM NOYES...ENGLAND, 1568...
ALLIED FAMILIES OF STANTON, LORD, SANFORD, CODDINGTON,
THOMPSON, FELLOWS, HOLDREDGE, BERRY, SAUNDERS, CLARKE,
JESSUP, STUDWELL, RUNDLE, FERRIS, LOCKWOOD compiled by Horace
True Currier. 1900. Chicago, IL: L. W. Noyes.
138pp—GE4-BH21181--Vendor #D1555

736 - OAK-OAKS-OAKES, FAMILY REGISTER, NATHANIEL OAK OF MARL-
BOROUGH....by Henry Loebbeus Oak. 1906. Los Angeles.
102pp—GE4-OP55394--Vendor #D1555

737 - QUAKER OGDENS IN AMERICA: DAVID OGDEN...HIS DESCENDANTS,
1682-1897 by Charles Burr Ogden. 1898. Philadelphia: J. B. Lippincott.
329pp—GE4-OP60726--Vendor #D1555

738 - DESCENDANTS OF VIRGINIA CALVERTS compiled by Ella Foy O'Gorman. 1947. Los Angeles.
796pp—GE4-OP56667--Vendor #D1555

739 - OLDS (OLD, OULD) FAMILY IN ENGLAND AND AMERICA by Edson
Baldwin Olds and Susan Sophia Gascoyne Old. 1915. Washington.
375pp—GE4-OP40181--Vendor #D1555

740 - COMPLETE RECORD OF JOHN OLIN FAMILY...AMERICA IN YEAR
A.D. 1678....by Chauncey C. Olin. 1893. Indianapolis: Baker-Rand-
olph Co. Prs.
458pp—GE4-BH19180--Vendor #D1555

741 - GENEALOGY OF OLMSTED FAMILY IN AMERICA compiled by Henry
King Olmsted. 1914. NY: A. T. De La Mare.
Suppl. 68pp—Text 740pp—GE4-OP17170---------------------Vendor #D1555

742 - GENEALOGY OF DESCENDANTS OF THOMAS OLNEY...WHO CAME
FROM ENGLAND IN 1635 by James H. Olney. 1889. Providence,RI:
Pr. of E. L. Freeman & Son.
318pp—GE4-OP54241--Vendor #D1555

743 - ONE LINE OF THE PHELPS FAMILY. n.p., n.d.
56pp—GE4-BH21287--Vendor #D1555

744 - OP DYCK GENEALOGY, CONTAINING OPDYCK-OPDYCKE-OPDYKE-
UPDIKE AMERICAN DESCENDANTS....by Leonard Eckstein Opdycke.
1889. Albany, NY: Pr. for Charles W. Opdyke, Leonard E. Opdycke
& Wm. S. Opdyke, by Weed, Parsons & Co.
717pp—GE4-OP47032--Vendor #D1555

745 - HENRY TOMLINSON, AND HIS DESCENDANTS IN AMERICA...LATER
FROM ENGLAND by Samuel Orcutt. 1891. New Haven, CT: Pr. of Price,
Lee & Adkins Co.
260pp—GE4-BH21410--Vendor #D1555

746 - ORIGIN AND HISTORY OF NAME ANDREWS WITH BIOGRAPHIES...
NOTED PERSONS.... 1904. Chicago, IL: American Pub. Assn.
127pp—GE4-BH21278--Vendor #D1555

747 - ORIGIN AND HISTORY OF NAME BALDWIN WITH BIOGRAPHIES...
NOTED PERSONS.... 1905. Chicago, IL: American Pub. Assn.
120pp—GE4-BH21279--Vendor #D1555

748 - ORIGIN AND HISTORY OF NAME OF BAILEY, WITH BIOGRAPHIES...
NOTED PERSONS.... 1904. Chicago: American Pub. Assn.
142pp—GE4-BH21170--Vendor #D1555

749 - ORIGIN AND HISTORY OF NAME OF BAKER, WITH BIOGRAPHIES...
NOTED PERSONS.... 1905. Chicago, IL: American Pub. Assn.
140pp—GE4-BH21453--Vendor #D1555

750 - ORIGIN AND HISTORY OF NAME OF BENNETT, WITH BIOGRAPHIES
...NOTED PERSONS.... 1905. Chicago, IL: American Pub. Assn.
132pp—GE4-BH21128--Vendor #D1555

751 - ORIGIN AND HISTORY OF NAME OF BLACK, WITH BIOGRAPHIES...
NOTED PERSONS.... 1905. Crescent Family Record. Chicago, IL:
American Publishers Assn.
120pp—GE4-BH21454--Vendor #D1555

752 - ORIGIN AND HISTORY OF NAME OF BOYD WITH BIOGRAPHIES...
NOTED PERSONS.... 1905. Crescent Family Record. Chicago, IL:
American Pub. Assn.
124pp—GE4-BH21126--Vendor #D1555

753 - ORIGIN AND HISTORY OF NAME OF BROOKS, WITH BIOGRAPHIES...
NOTED PERSONS.... 1905. Crescent Family Record. Chicago, IL:
American Pub. Assn.
132pp—GE4-BH21127--Vendor #D1555

754 - ORIGIN AND HISTORY OF NAME OF BUTLER, WITH BIOGRAPHIES...
NOTED NAMES.... 1905. Crescent Family Record. Chicago, IL:
American Pub. Assn.
134pp—GE4-BH19067--Vendor #D1555

755 - ORIGIN AND HISTORY OF NAME OF DAVIS, WITH BIOGRAPHIES...
NOTED PERSONS.... 1902. Crescent Family Record. Chicago, IL:
American Pub. Assn.
112pp—GE4-OP44327--Vendor #D1555

756 - ORIGIN AND HISTORY OF NAME OF THOMPSON, WITH BIOGRAPHIES
...NOTED PERSONS.... 1902. Crescent Family Record. Chicago, IL:
American Pub. Assn.
124pp—GE4-BH19096--Vendor #D1555

757 - BRIEF SKETCH OF GENEALOGY OF CAPTAIN THOMAS ORR...FRANK-
LIN COUNTY, PENNSYLVANIA....compiled by James P. Orr and John
G. Orr. 1923. n.p.
24pp—GE4-OP63618--Vendor #D1555

758 - ACCOUNT OF DESCENDANTS OF THOMAS ORTON OF WINDSOR,
CONNECTICUT, 1641....by Edward Francis Baxter Orton. 1896.
Colubmus, OH: Pr. of Nitschke Bros.
222pp—GE4-OP43246--Vendor #D1555

759 - HISTORICAL AND GENEALOGICAL ACCOUNT OF ANDREW ROBESON
OF SCOTLAND by Kate Hamilton Osborne. 1916. PA: Pr. of J. B.
Lippincott Co.
829pp—GE4-OP64133--Vendor #D1555

760 - GENEALOGICAL AND HISTORICAL MEMOIR OF OTIS FAMILY IN
AMERICA by William Augustus Otis. 1924. Chicago.
947pp—GE4-OP57440--Vendor #D1555

761 - OVERMYER HISTORY AND GENEALOGY FROM 1680 TO 1905 by Barnhart B. Overmyer and John Calvin Overmyer. 1905. Freemont, OH:
C. S. Beelman, pr.
410pp—GE4-OP43868--Vendor #D1555

762 - GENEALOGY OF LACEY FAMILY by Thomas McAdory Owen. 1900.
Carrolton, AL: West Alabamian Pr.
7pp—GE4-OP55042--Vendor #D1555

763 - WHAT DOES AMERICA MEAN TO YOU. HISTORY AND GENEALOGY...
GENEALOGICAL MATERIAL ON ECKLES AND CREIGHS...ALLIED
FAMILIES OF WINSTON AND CHISWELL by Evelyn Jeanette (Miller)
Ownbey. 1942. Chicago: n.p.
218pp—GE4-OP63781-- Vendor #D1555

764 - GENEALOGY OF PAGE FAMILY IN VIRGINIA...NELSON, WALKER,
PENDLETON, AND RANDOLPH FAMILIES...., 2nd ed., by Richard
Channing Moore Page. 1893. NY: Publishers Pr. Co.
286pp—GE4-OP67321--Vendor #D1555

765 - PALMER RECORDS...MEMORIAL VOLUME OF FIRST PALMER FAMILY
REUNION...1881...., Vol. 1, edited by Noyes Fink Palmer. 1881.
Brooklyn: Brooklyn Union-Argus.
434pp—GE4-OP63798--Vendor #D1555

766 - THE PAINE FAMILY REGISTER, NUMBERS 1-3, 5-8 by Henry D. Pane. 1857-1897. Albany, NY.
74pp—GE4-BH21288--Vendor #D1555

767 - ANCESTRY OF LORENZO ACKLEY AND HIS WIFE, EMMA ARABELLA BOSWORTH compiled by Nathan Grier Parke. Donald Lines Jacobus, ed. 1960. Woodstock, VT.
396pp—GE4-OP66717--Vendor #D1555

768 - BARKER GENEALOGY: GIVING NAMES AND DESCENDANTS OF SEV- ERAL DESCENDANTS...1776....by James Clark Parshall. 1897. Middletown?, NY.
50pp—GE4-BH19068--—Vendor #D1555

769 - HISTORY OF PARSHALL FAMILY, FROM CONQUEST OF ENGLAND BY WILLIAM....by James Clark Parshall. 1903. Cooperstown, NY: Pr. of Crist, Scott & Parshall.
390pp—GE4-OP41515--Vendor #D1555

770 - PARSONS FAMILY; DESCENDANTS OF CORNET JOSEPH PARSONS, SPRINGFIELD, 1636-NORTHAMPTON, 1655, 2 Vols., by Henry Parsons. ca. 1912-20. NY: Frank Allaben Gen. Co.
Vol. 1 533pp—Vol. 2 693pp—GE4-CD00234--------------------Vendor #D1555

771 - GENEALOGY OF PARTHEMORE FAMILY, 1744-1885 by E. Winfield Scott Parthemore. 1885. Harrisburg, PA: L. S. Hart, pr.
254pp—GE4-BH16661--Vendor #D1555

772 - JOHN STODDARD OF WETHERSFIELD, CONNECTICUT, AND HIS DE- SCENDANTS by Williams Patterson. 1873. NY: Newark Valley.
96pp—GE4-OP65994--Vendor #D1555

773 - MARSHALL FAMILY...DESCENDANTS OF JOHN MARSHALL AND ELIZA- BETH MARKHAM, HIS WIFE....by William McClung Paxton. 1885. Cincinnati: R. Clarke.
470pp—GE4-OP50833--Vendor #D1555

774 - PAXTONS; THEIR ORIGIN IN SCOTLAND, AND THEIR MIGRATIONS THROUGH ENGLAND AND IRELAND....by William McClung Paxton. 1903. Platte City, MO: Landmark Pr.
571pp—GE4-OP46399--Vendor #D1555

775 - THE PAYNES OF VIRGINIA by Brooke Payne. 1937. Richmond: Wm. Byrd Pr., Inc.
566pp—GE4-OP61704--Vendor #D1555

776 - PEABODY (PAYBODY, PABODY, PABODIE) GENEALOGY compiled by Selim Hobart Peabody. Charles Henry Pope, ed. 1909. Boston, MA: Charles H. Pope.
623pp—GE4-OP66592--Vendor #D1555

777 - EARLY HISTORY OF PEASE FAMILIES IN AMERICA by Austin Spencer Pease. 1869. Springfield, MA: S. Bowles.
116pp—GE4-OP37829--Vendor #D1555

778 - GENEALOGICAL AND HISTORICAL RECORD OF DESCENDANTS OF JOHN PEASE by David Pease and Austin S. Pease. 1869. Springfield, MA: S. Bowles.
498pp—GE4-OP37675--Vendor #D1555

779 - ACCOUNT OF DESCENDANTS OF JOHN PEASE, WHO LANDED AT MARTHA'S VINEYARD....by Frederick Salmon Pease. 1847. Albany: J. Munsell.
56pp—GE4-OP41020--Vendor #D1555

780 - BELLOWS GENEALOGY; OR, JOHN BELLOWS, BOY EMIGRANT OF 1635....by Thomas Bellows Peck. 1898. Keene, NH: Sentinel Pr. Co.
799pp—GE4-OP42163--Vendor #D1555

781 - CONTRIBUTIONS BIOGRAPHICAL, GENEALOGICAL AND HISTORICAL by Ebenezer Weaver Peirce. 1874. Boston: pr. for author, by D. Clapp & Son.
980pp—GE4-BH19189--Vendor #D1555

782 - WILLS OF SMITH FAMILIES OF NEW YORK AND LONG ISLAND, 1664-1794....by William Smith Pelletreau. 1898. NY: F. P. Harper.
154pp—GE4-BH21166--Vendor #D1555

783 - THAT THE NEXT GENERATION MAY KNOW: KELLY'S OF VIRGINIA AND KENTUCKY compiled by Anita Ball Pendergrass. ca. 1973. Keokee, VA. s.n.
198pp—GE4-AU00103--Vendor #D1555

784 - THE PENNYPACKER REUNION, OCTOBER 4, 1877 by Samuel Whitaker Pennypacker. 1877. Philadelphia: Bavis & Pennypacker, prs.
66pp—GE4-BH11678--Vendor #D1555

785 - A PRIVATE PROOF...THE BOSTON BRANCH OF THE PERKINS FAMILY by Augustus Thorndike Perkins. 1890. Boston: T. R. Marvin & Sons.
126pp—GE4-BH21121--Vendor #D1555

786 - GENEALOGY OF THE PERRIN FAMILY by Glover Perrin. 1885. St. Paul: Pioneer Pr. Co.
236pp—GE4-BH21246--Vendor #D1555

787 - DANIEL PERRINE...DESCENDANTS IN AMERICA...SURNAMES, PERRINE, PERINE, AND PRINE, 1665-1910 by Howland Delano Perrine. 1910. South Orange, NJ: T. A. Wright.
648pp—GE4-OP22150--Vendor #D1555

788 - GENEALOGY OF OTHNIEL PHELPS, ESQ. OF AYLMER, CANADA WEST by Oliver Seymour Phelps. 1862. St. Catharines: H. F. Leavenworth's "Hearld" Power Pr.
45pp—GE4-OP54213--Vendor #D1555

789 - PHELPS FAMILY OF AMERICA AND THEIR ENGLISH ANCESTORS...VALUABLE RECORDS, 2 Vols., by Oliver Seymour Phelps. 1899. Pittsfield, MA: Eagle Pub. Co.
Vol. 1 889pp—Vol. 2 1064pp—GE4-OP52337--------------------Vendor #D1555

790 - PHELPS FAMILY IN AMERICA. n.p., n.d.
17pp—GE4-BH21296--Vendor #D1555

791 - PEDIGREE OF FAMILY OF FINCH. COPIED...EARL OF WINCHILSEA AND NOTTINGHAM by John Philipot. 1872. London: Taylor & Co.,prs.
30pp—GE4-BH21123--Vendor #D1555

792 - DESCENDANTS OF JOHN PHOENIX, AN EARLY SETTLER IN KITTERY, MAINE by Stephen Whitney Phoenix. 1867. NY: Priv. pr. [Bradstreet]
150pp—GE4-BH21228--Vendor #D1555

793 - FAMILY EMPIRE IN JERSEY IRON: THE RICHARDS ENTERPRISES...PINE BARRENS by Arthur Dudley Pierce. ca. 1964. New Brunswick, NJ: Rutgers Univ. Pr.
312pp—GE4-2050626--Vendor #D1555

794 - FIELD GENEALOGY...RECORD OF ALL FIELD FAMILY IN AMERICA...1700, 2 Vols., by Frederick Clifton Pierce. 1901. Chicago: W. B. Conkey.
Vol. 1 690pp—Vol. 2 717pp—GE4-OP31122--------------------Vendor #D1555

795 - FORBES AND FORBUSH GENEALOGY; DESCENDANTS OF DANIEL FORBUSH by Frederick Clifton Pierce. 1892. Rand McNally & Co.
224pp—GE4-OP52338--Vendor #D1555

796 - PEARCE GENEALOGY;...RICHARD PEARCE AN EARLY INHABITANT OF PORTSMOUTH, IN RHODE ISLAND....by Frederick Clifton Pierce.
152pp—GE4-OP46180--Vendor #D1555

797 - WHITNEY, DESCENDANTS OF JOHN WHITNEY, WHO COME FROM LONDON...1635 by Frederick Clifton Pierce. 1895. Chicago: the author, Pr. of W. B. Conkey Co.
612pp—GE4-BH21215--Vendor #D1555

798 - GENEALOGY OF PIERSON FAMILY, MARSH FAMILY, CLARK FAMILY, BAKER FAMILY by Arthur Newton Pierson. 1946. n.p.
40pp—GE4-OP66736--Vendor #D1555

799 - PIERSON GENEALOGICAL RECORDS compiled by Lizzie Benedict
Pierson. 1878. Albany, NY: John Munsell Pr.
105pp—GE4-OP65852--Vendor #D1555

800 - HISTORICAL SKETCHES OF CAMPBELL, PILCHER AND KINDRED
FAMILIES by Margaret Hamilton Campbell Pilcher. 1911. Nashville, TN.
445pp—GE4-OP02165--Vendor #D1555

801 - PILLSBURY FAMILY;...HISTORY OF WILLIAM AND DOROTHY PILLS-
BURY (OR PILSBERY)....compiled by David Brainard Pilsbury and
Emily A. Getchell. 1898. Everett, MA: Massachusetts Pub. Co.
344pp—GE4-BH03182--Vendor #D1555

802 - THE BLACKMANS, DARROWS, BOOSES, JONESES, COLLINGSES,
STEARNES, STRAWS, PLUMBS, HYDES by Henry Blackman Plumb. 1894.
Wilkesbarre?, PA.
60pp—GE4-BH21169--Vendor #D1555

803 - POLK FAMILY AND KINSMEN by William Harrison Polk. 1912. Louis-
Ville: Bradley & Gilbert Co.
772pp—GE4-OP40732--Vendor #D1555

804 - POMEROY, ROMANCE AND HISTORY OF ELTWEED POMEROY'S AN-
CESTORS IN NORMANDY AND ENGLAND by Albert Alonzo Pomeroy.
1909? Toledo, OH: Pr. of Franklin Pr. & Engraving Co.
92pp—GE4-OP42327--Vendor #D1555

805 - COLLECTION OF FAMILY RECORDS FROM BARTHOLOMEW, BOTSFORD
AND WINSTON LINES....by Sarah Annis Winston Pond. 1899. Hartford,
CT: Hartford Pr.
56pp—GE4-BH19065--Vendor #D1555

806 - THE HAVERHILL EMERSONS, 2 parts, by Charles Henry Pope. 1913-
1916. Boston: Murray & Emery.
Part 1 110pp—Part 2 266pp—GE4-OP17255---------------------Vendor #D1555

807 - MERRIAM GENEALOGY IN ENGLAND AND AMERICA, INCLUDING THE
"GENEALOGICAL MEMORANDA"....by Charles Henry Pope. 1906.
Boston: C. H. Pope.
564pp—GE4-OP40640--Vendor #D1555

808 - HOOPER GENEALOGY compiled by Charles Henry Pope and Thomas
Hooper. 1908. Boston, MA: H. Pope.
340pp—GE4-OP44050--Vendor #D1555

809 - THE MARTIN FAMILY, 1680-1934 by Mrs. Anne Carrington (Martin)
Porcher. ca. 1935. Brooklyn.
75pp—GE4-OP66769--Vendor #D1555

810 - CONCERNING PRESIDENT GARFIELD'S ANCESTRY. A COMMUNICA-
TION FROM REVEREND EDWARD G. PORTER....by Edward Griffin
Porter. 1881. Cambridge: J. Wilson & Son.
30pp—GE4-BH21417--Vendor #D1555

811 - THE POST FAMILY by Marie Caroline de Trobriand Post. 1905.
NY: S. Potter.
380pp—GE4-OP62376--Vendor #D1555

812 - GENEALOGY OF THE FAMILY OF JOHN WAIT POTTER compiled by
Albert Potter and Isaac M. Potter. 1885. Providence, RI: Island Pr. Co.
14pp—GE4-BH21282--Vendor #D1555

813 - HISTORICAL COLLECTIONS RELATING TO POTTS FAMILY IN GREAT
BRITAIN AND AMERICA by Thomas Maxwell Potts. 1901. Canonsburg,
PA.
940pp—GE4-OP61795--Vendor #D1555

814 - AUTHENTIC GENEALOGICAL MEMORIAL HISTORY OF PHILIP POWELL,
OF MIFFLIN COUNTY, PENNSYLVANIA...., Vol. 1, by John Powell.
1880. Dayton, OH: pub. for author.
466pp—GE4-BH13691--Vendor #D1555

815 - FAMILY RECORDS OF POWELLS AND GRIFFITHS, WITH...WRITINGS
OF JOHN POWELL....by Rachel Powell. 1866. Philadelphia: J. A.
Wagenseller.
120pp—GE4-BH13689--Vendor #D1555

816 - POWERS FAMILY: GENEALOGICAL AND HISTORICAL RECORD OF
WALTER POWER...NINTH GENERATION by Amos H. Powers. 1884.
Chicago: Fergus Pr. Co.
218pp—GE4-OP44312--Vendor #D1555

817 - SUPPLEMENT TO HISTORY ENTITLED THE PRATT FAMILY...LIEUT.
WILLIAM PRATT....by Frank Everett Pratt. 1916. NY. n.p.
66pp—GE4-OP61647--Vendor #D1555

818 - ALLIED FAMILIES OF READ, CORBIN, LUTTRELL, BYWATERS compiled by Armstead Mead Prichard. 1930. Stanton, VA.
292pp—GE4-OP64934--Vendor #D1555

819 - MEADE RELATIONS: MEAD, BROWN, POWELL, KEYSER, KELLY,
TRUMBO, AUSTIN, TOLER, PRICHARD compiled by Armstead Mead
Prichard. 1933. Staunton, VA. n.p.
265pp—GE4-OP64132--Vendor #D1555

820 - NOTES GENEALOGICAL, BIOGRAPHICAL AND BIBLIOGRAPHICAL,
OF THE PRIME FAMILY by Edward Dorr Griffin Prime. 1888. Cambridge, MA: pr. for priv. use by Univ. Pr.
140pp—GE4-BH19066--Vendor #D1555

821 - MEMORIALS OF THE THACKERAY FAMILY by Jane Townley Pryme
and Alicia Bayne. 1879. London: Spattiswoode & Co.
525pp—GE4-OP69230--Vendor #D1555

822 - GENEALOGICAL NOTES OF THE PROVOST FAMILY OF NEW YORK
compiled by Edwin Ruthven Purple. 1875. NY: Priv. pr.
46pp—GE4-BH21187--Vendor #D1555

823 - GENEALOGICAL NOTES RELATING TO LIEUT.-GOV. JACOB LEISLER,
AND HIS FAMILY....compiled by Edwin Ruthven Purple. 1877. NY:
Priv. pr.
36pp—GE4-BH21188--Vendor #D1555

824 - HISTORY OF PUTNAM FAMILY IN ENGLAND AND AMERICA by Eben
Putnam. 1891. Salem: Salem Pr. Pub. & Pr. Co.
530pp—GE4-OP66546--Vendor #D1555

825 - THE PUTNAM LINEAGE by Eben Putnam. 1907. Salem: Salem Pr. Co.
621pp—GE4-OP66547--Vendor #D1555

826 - GENEALOGICAL MEMORANDA OF QUISENBERRY FAMILY AND OTHER
FAMILIES by Anderson Chenault Quisenberry. 1897. Washington, DC:
Hartman & Cadick Prs.
211pp—GE4-OP64161--Vendor #D1555

827 - MEMORIALS OF QUISENBERRY FAMILY IN GERMANY, ENGLAND AND
AMERICA by Anderson Chenault Quisenberry. 1900. Washington, DC:
Gibson Bros. Prs.
147pp—GE4-OP70873--Vendor #D1555

828 - HISTORY OF "RAILEYS AND KINDRED FAMILIES" by William Edward
Railey. 1929. Frankfort, KY: Roberts Pr. Co.
178pp—GE4-OP16826--Vendor #D1555

829 - RANDALL AND ALLIED FAMILIES; WILLIAM RANDALL (1609-1693) OF
SCITUATE....by Frank Alfred Randall. 1943. Chicago: Raveret-
Weber Pr. Co.
596pp—GE4-CD00382--Vendor #D1555

830 - GENEALOGY OF A BRANCH OF RANDALL FAMILY, 1666 TO 1879....
by Paul King Randall. 1879. Norwich, NY: Pr. at ofc. of Chenango Un.
289pp—GE4-OP65113--Vendor #D1555

831 - FITZ RANDOLPH TRADITIONS: A STORY OF A THOUSAND YEARS
by Lewis Van Syckel Fitz Randolph. 1907. New Jersey Hist. Soc.
170pp—GE4-OP60085--Vendor #D1555

832 - THE RAULSTONS OF RED RIVER COUNTY by Clarence M. Raulston, Jr. 1973. Ft. Worth, TX: Historical Pubs.
87pp—GE4-AU00129--Vendor #D1555

833 - GENEALOGIES OF RAYMOND FAMILIES OF NEW ENGLAND, 1630-1 TO 1886...ORIGIN, ETC. by Samuel Raymond. 1886. NY: Pr. of J. J. Little & Co.
312pp—GE4-OP45854---------------------------------------Vendor #D1555

834 - GENEALOGY OF REBER FAMILY DESCENDED FROM JOHAN BERNHARD REBER, 1738 by Morris Byron Reber. 1901. Reading, PA.
60pp—GE4-OP17716--Vendor #D1555

835 - A RECORD OF FAMILY OF ISAAC PACKARD AND EUNICE RAWSON, HIS WIFE. n.p., n.d.
4pp—GE4-BH21284---Vendor #D1555

836 - REED GENEALOGY; DESCENDANTS OF WILLIAM READE OF WEYMOUTH, MASSACHUSETTS...1902 by John Ludovicus Reed. 1901. Lord Baltimore Pr.
850pp—GE4-BH21408---------------------------------------Vendor #D1555

837 - SEVENTEEN HUNDRED TO 1900, ANCESTRY AND POSTERITY OF JOHNSON REEVES by Francis Brewer Reeves. 1900. Philadelphia: Allen, Lane & Scott.
108pp—GE4-BH21281---------------------------------------Vendor #D1555

838 - REICHNER AND AIKEN GENEALOGIES compiled and edited by Louis Irving Reichner. n.p., n.d.
239pp—GE4-OP66593---------------------------------------Vendor #D1555

839 - THE FAMILY OF REQUA; 1678-1898 by Amos Conklin Requa. 1898. Peekskill, NY.
162pp—GE4-BH21186---------------------------------------Vendor #D1555

840 - REUNION OF DICKINSON FAMILY, AT AMHERST, MASSACHUSETTS, AUGUST 8TH...,1883. 1884. Binghamton, NY: Binghamton Pub. Co.
218pp—GE4-OP37833---------------------------------------Vendor #D1555

841 - THE BUCHANAN AND ALLIED FAMILIES by Clara Elliot Buchanan Rex. 1931. Norristown, PA.
117pp—GE4-OP67378---------------------------------------Vendor #D1555

842 - GENEALOGICAL HISTORY...ARTHUR REXFORD...MARRIED ELIZA-BETH STEVENS, OF NEW HAVEN, CONNECTICUT, IN 1702 by John De Witt Rexford. 1891. Janesville, WI: Gazette Pr. Co., prs.
114pp—GE4-BH21195---------------------------------------Vendor #D1555

843 - HISTORY AND SOME DESCENDANTS OF ROBERT AND MARY REY-NOLDS by Marion Hobart Reynolds. 1931. Brooklyn, NY: Reynolds Family Assn.
252pp—GE4-OP15884---------------------------------------Vendor #D1555

844 - ANCESTORS AND DESCENDANTS OF WILLIAM AND ELIZABETH REYNOLDS OF NORTH KINGSTOWN, R. I. by Thomas A. Reynolds and William A. Reynolds. Alfred C. Willits, ed. 1903. Philadelphia: pr. by J. B. Lippincott Co.
58pp—GE4-BH19071--Vendor #D1555

845 - THE REMY FAMILY IN AMERICA, 1650-1942 compiled by Bonnelle William Rhamy. 1942. Ft. Wayne, IN.
536pp—GE4-OP65963---------------------------------------Vendor #D1555

846 - GENEALOGY OF BUCK FAMILY WHICH SETTLED IN CAMBRIDGE... WOBURN, MASSACHUSETTS...1635 by Elizabeth Frances Smith Richards. 1913. Reading, PA: Eagle Book & Job Pr.
182pp—GE4-OP41731---------------------------------------Vendor #D1555

847 - RECORDS OF ANGLO-NORMAN HOUSE OF GLANVILLE FROM A.D. 1050 TO 1880 by William Urmstons Searle Glanville Richards. 1882. London: Mitchell & Hughes.
271pp—GE4-OP62266---------------------------------------Vendor #D1555

848 - SUPPLEMENT TO RICHARDSON MEMORIAL by Isaac Richardson and Franklin Richardson. 1898. Portland, ME: Thurston Print.
56pp—GE4-BH21185--Vendor #D1555

849 - GENEALOGICAL AND BIOGRAPHICAL SKETCH OF...RICHARDSON:
FROM YEAR 1720 TO YEAR 1860 by Jeffrey Richardson, Jr. 1860.
Boston: Pr. by A. Mudge & Son for author.
44pp—GE4-BH21226--—Vendor #D1555

850 - RICHMOND FAMILY 1594-1896, AND PRE-AMERICAN ANCESTORS,
1040-1594...DOCUMENTS compiled by Joshua Bailey Richmond. 1897.
Boston.
716pp—GE4-BH21222--—Vendor #D1555

851 - AUTOBIOGRAPHY OF PETER D. RIDENOUR WITH...RIDENOUR AND
BEATTY FAMILIES by Peter Darcuss Ridenour. 1908. Kansas City:
Hudon Pr.
372pp—GE4-OP70606--—Vendor #D1555

852 - DESCENT OF RIDGWAY-RIDGEWAY FAMILY IN ENGLAND AND AMER-
ICA, 2nd ed., by George C. Ridgway. 1926. Evansville, IN. n.p.
146pp—GE4-OP66772--—Vendor #D1555

853 - DESCENDANTS AND ANCESTORS OF WILLIAM JACKSON AND...
RACHEL TOMLINSON JACKSON by Mayburt Stephenson Riegel. 1940.
Ann Arbor, MI: Edwards Bros., Inc.
172pp—GE4-OP67207--—Vendor #D1555

854 - RIGGS FAMILY OF MARYLAND: A GENEALOGICAL AND HISTORICAL
RECORD....by John Beverely Riggs. 1939. Baltimore: Lord Baltimore Pr.
601pp—GE4-OP47463--—Vendor #D1555

855 - A HISTORY OF THE RING FAMILY, 1631-1928 by Clark Lombard Ring.
1928.
10pp—GE4-OP34849--—Vendor #D1555

856 - GENEALOGY OF DESCENDANTS OF JERE FOSTER RING AND PHEBE
ELLIS....by Harry Philander Ring. 1931. Wilton, NH.
58pp—GE4-OP36855--—Vendor #D1555

857 - HISTORY AND GENEALOGY OF THE RIX FAMILY OF AMERICA compiled
by Gay S. Rix. 1906. NY: Grafton Pr.
259pp—GE4-OP66811--—Vendor #D1555

858 - ANCESTRY OF CLARENCE V. ROBERTS AND FRANCES A. (WALTON)
ROBERTS by Clarence Vernon Roberts. 1940. Philadelphia, PA.
361pp—GE4-OP70631--—Vendor #D1555

859 - EMERA ALTIZER AND HIS DESCENDANTS WITH SKETCHES OF CON-
NECTED FAMILIES by Ruby Altizer Roberts and Mrs. Rosa Altizer Bray.
n.p., n.d.
268pp—GE4-OP63258--—Vendor #D1555

860 - POCAHONTAS, ALIAS MATOAKA,...JOHN ROLFE...INCLUDING NAMES
OF ALFRIEND, ARCHER, BENTLEY, BERNARD, BLAND, BOLLING,
BRANCH, CABELL, CATLETT, CARY, DANDRIDGE, DIXON, DOUGLAS,
DUVAL, ELDRIDGE, ELLETT, FERGUSON, FIELD, FLEMING, GAY,
GORDON, GRIFFEN, GRAYSON, HARRISON, HUBARD, LEWIS, LOGAN,
MARKHAM, MEADE, McRAE, MURRAY, PAGE, POYTHRESS, RANDOLPH,
ROBERTSON, SKIPWITH, STANARD, TAZEWELL, WALKE, WEST,
WHITTLE....by Wyndham Robertson. 1887. Richmond: J. W. Randolph
& English.
110pp—Ge4-BH21136--—Vendor #D1555

861 - THE HAZARD FAMILY OF RHODE ISLAND, 1635-1894 by Caroline Elizabeth Rodman Robinson. 1895. Boston. n.p.
332pp—GE4-OP64169--—Vendor #D1555

862 - WELD COLLECTIONS: GENEALOGICAL STUDY OF WELD FAMILY IN
AMERICA by Charles Frederick Robinson. 1938. Ann Arbor, MI:
Edwards Bros.
272pp—GE4-OP57325--—Vendor #D1555

863 - BREWER GENEALOGY compiled by Harriet Augusta Robinson. 1903.n.p.
50pp—GE4-OP36438--—Vendor #D1555

864 - RODMAN FAMILY OF PENNSYLVANIA. n.p., n.d.
24pp—GE4-BH21293--—Vendor #D1555

865 - GENEALOGICAL MEMOIRS OF JOHN KNOX AND OF FAMILY OF KNOX
by Charles Rogers. 1879. London: Pr. for Grampian Club.
200pp—GE4-BH21243--Vendor #D1555

866 - THE STAMM FAMILY OF OHIO AND KENTUCKY by Edward J. Ronsheim.
1954. Anderson, IN.
25pp—GE4-OP67382--Vendor #D1555

867 - ROOT GENEALOGICAL RECORDS, 1600-1870...ROOT AND ROOTS
FAMILIES IN AMERICA by James Pierce Root. 1870. NY: R. C. Root,
Anthony & Co.
548pp—GE4-OP53627--Vendor #D1555

868 - ROSENKRANS FAMILY IN EUROPE AND AMERICA compiled by Allen
Rosenkrans. 1900. Newton, NJ: Herald Pr.
409pp—GE4-OP47402--Vendor #D1555

869 - OUR ROUTH FAMILY: DESCENDANTS OF JACOB ROUTH (1745-1827)
by Ross Holland Routh. 1983. El Paso, TX: R. H. Routh.
408pp—GE4-AU00263--Vendor #D1555

870 - THE ROUTH FAMILY IN AMERICA, A GENEALOGY by Ross Holland
Routh. 1976. El Paso, TX. s.n.
727pp—GE4-AU00011--Vendor #D1555

871 - ROUTH FAMILY REVISITED: A GENEALOGY by Ross Holland Routh.
1978. El Paso, TX: Pr. for subscribers by Copyprint.
810pp—GE4-AU00046--Vendor #D1555

872 - STEPHEN ROUTH, 1797-1871, AND SOME DESCENDANTS: A GENEAL-
OGY compiled and published by Ross H. Routh. 1980. El Paso, TX.
501pp—GE4-AU00147--Vendor #D1555

873 - WILLIAM WROE (1670-1730) AND SOME DESCENDANTS: A GENEALOGY
compiled and published by Ross H. Routh. 1980. El Paso, TX.
351pp—GE4-AU00114--Vendor #D1555

874 - BIOGRAPHICAL SKETCH OF SAMUEL ROWELL...GENEALOGY FOR
SEVEN GENERATIONS, 1754-1898 by Roland Rowell. 1898. Manchester,
NH: Pr. by W. E. Moore.
338pp—GE4-BH19179--Vendor #D1555

875 - MY FATHER'S FAMILY; DOUGLAS, HADEN, CHURCHILL, BLAKEY,
GEORGE, PERKINS, OGLESBY, ATTKISSON,...by Edith Attkisson
Rudder. 1947. n.p.
120pp—GE4-OP65939--Vendor #D1555

876 - GENEALOGY OF RUNNELS AND REYNOLDS FAMILIES IN AMERICA...
EARLIEST ANCESTORS by Moses Thurston Runnels. 1873. Boston:
Alfred Mudge & Son.
392pp—GE4-OP65381--Vendor #D1555

877 - HISTORICAL AND GENEALOGICAL ACCOUNT OF THE RUSH FAMILY
by Sylvester R. Rush. 1925. Omaha: Festner Pr. Co.
201pp—GE4-OP62900--Vendor #D1555

878 - DESCENDANTS OF WILLIAM RUSSELL, CAMBRIDGE, MASSACHUSETTS,
ABOUT 1640...MARCH 1, 1900 by Hezekiah Stone Russell. 1900. Pittsfield, MA: Eagle Pub. Co.
66pp—GE4-BH21192--Vendor #D1555

879 - FAMILY RECORDS AND EVENTS. COMPILED...MANUSCRIPTS IN THE
RUTHERFORD COLLECTION by Livingston Rutherfurd. 1894. NY:
pr. at DeVinne Pr.
474pp—GE4-BH21249--Vendor #D1555

880 - THREE BRANCHES OF FAMILY OF WENTWORTH. I. WENTWORTH OF
NETTLESTEAD, SUFFOLK....by William Loftie Rutton. 1891. Oxfordshire, London: Mitchell & Hughes, prs.
364pp—GE4-BH19037--Vendor #D1555

881 - SHORT SKETCH OF LIFE OF MRS. AZUBAH FREEMAN RYDER...DE-
SCENDANTS by John Henry Ryder. 1888. Boston: J. H. Ryder.
62pp—GE4-BH19070--Vendor #D1555

882 - NORFOLK FAMILIES, PART 1-5 by Walter Rye. 1911-13. Norwich:
Goose & Son.
1132pp—GE4-OP57536--Vendor #D1555

883 - HISTORY AND GENEALOGY OF VAN DEUSENS OF VAN DEUSEN
MANOR, GREAT BARRINGTON,...MASSACHUSETTS by Louis Hasbrouck
Sahler. 189-. Great Barrington: Berkshire Courier Co.
46pp—GE4-BH21103--Vendor #D1555

884 - FAMILY-MEMORIALS...FAMILIES OF SALISBURY, ALDWORTH-EL-
BRIDGE, SEWALL, PLYDREN-DUMMER, WALLEY, QUINCY, GOOKIN,
WENDELL, BREESE, CHEVALIER-ANDERSON, AND PHILLIPS....,2 Parts
by Edward Elbridge Salisbury. 1885. New Haven: Pr. of Tuttle,
Morehouse & Taylor.
Part 1 440pp—Part 2 412pp—GE4-BH21106--------------------Vendor #D1555

885 - HISTORY OF THE SALMANS FAMILY by Levi Brimmer Salmans. 1936.
Guanajuato.
234pp—GE4-OP65860---Vendor #D1555

886 - KITH AND KIN...FOR THE CHILDREN OF MR. AND MRS. JOHN
RUSSELL SAMPSON....by Anne Eliza Woods Sampson. 1922. Richmond,
VA: Wm. Byrd Pr., Inc.
263pp—GE4-OP47634---Vendor #D1555

887 - GENEALOGY OF FAMILY OF SAMBORNE OR SANBORN IN ENGLAND
AND AMERICA by Victor Channing Sanborn. 1899. Concord, NH:
Rumford Pr.
837pp—GE4-OP52386---Vendor #D1555

888 - SANBORN FAMILY IN UNITED STATES...LIFE OF JOHN B. SANBORN
by Victor Channing Sanborn. 1887. St. Paul: H. M. Smyth Pr. Co.
80pp—GE4-BH21299--Vendor #D1555

889 - THOMAS SANFORD, EMIGRANT TO NEW ENGLAND: ANCESTRY,
LIFE AND DESCENDANTS, 1632-4, 2 vols., by Carlton Elisha Sanford.
1911. Rutland, VT: Tuttle co. Prs.
Vol. 1 842pp—Vol. 2 867pp—GE4-OP35844--------------------Vendor #D1555

890 - SARGENT RECORD. WILLIAM SARGENT OF IPSWICH,...AND OTHER
SARGENT BRANCHES by Edwin Everett Sargent. 1899. St. Johnsbury,
VT: Caledonian Co.
348pp—GE4-BH21247---Vendor #D1555

891 - FAMILY OF JOHN SAVAGE OF MIDDLETOWN, CONNECTICUT, 1652
by James Francis Savage. 1894. Boston: D. Clapp & Son prs.
106pp—GE4-BH19011---Vendor #D1555

892 - SAYWARD FAMILY...GENEALOGY OF HENRY SAYWARD OF YORK,
MAINE...AMERICA by Charles Augustus Sayward. 1890. Ipswich,
MA: Independent Pr., E. G. Hull.
200pp—GE4-BH19099---Vendor #D1555

893 - HISTORY OF DESCENDANTS OF JOHN GEORGE AND REGINA DOROTHEA
SCHOFER by Henry Morris Schofer. 1897? E. Greenville, PA.
108pp—GE4-BH21292---Vendor #D1555

894 - CONTRIBUTIONS TO A FAMILY TREE OF SCHOLL FAMILY IN SWABIA
compiled by Carl Gustav Albert Scholl. translated...by John Wm. Scholl.
1920. Ann Arbor. s.n.
74pp—GE4-AU00068---Vendor #D1555

895 - GENEALOGY OF COFFINBERRY FAMILY,...GEORGE LEWIS COFFIN-
BERRY...WIFE ELIZABETH (LITTLE) COFFINBERRY...RELATED
FAMILIES: COFFENBERRY, GILKISON, KEASEY, PLATT by Beatrice
Berman Scott. 1952. Cleveland: F. A. Myers.
65pp—GE4-OP63744---Vendor #D1555

896 - SCOTCH-IRISH AND CHARLES SCOTT'S DESCENDANTS AND RELATED
FAMILIES by Orion Cotton Scott. 1917. Berwyn, IL: J. H. Watson.
168pp—GE4-OP40736---Vendor #D1555

897 - GENTLEMAN JOHN PERKINS by William Walter Scott. n.d. Lenoir,
NC: Lenoir News-Topic.
97pp—GE4-OP51263--Vendor #D1555

898 - GENEALOGY, BIOGRAPHY, AND HISTORY...SEAGRAVE FAMILY...
JOHN AND SARAH SEAGRAVE....by Daniel Seagrave. 1881. Worchester:
Pr. by Tyler & Seagrave.
98pp—GE4-OP45790--Vendor #D1555

899 - RECORD OF SEARIGHT FAMILY, (ALSO WRITTEN SEAWRIGHT)...
LANCASTER COUNTY, PENNSYLVANIA, ABOUT 1740....by James Allison Searight. 1893. Uniontown, PA.
237pp—GE4-OP46944---Vendor #D1555

900 - HOLCOMB(E) GENEALOGY; GENEALOGY, HISTORY...OF HOLCOMB(E)S
OF THE WORLD...OTHERS by Jesse Seaver. 1925. Philadelphia, PA:
American Historica-Genealogical Soc.
313pp—GE4-OP70632---Vendor #D1555

901 - BELL FAMILY RECORDS by Jesse Montgomery Seaver. 1929. Philadelphia: American Historical-Genealogical Soc.
36pp—GE4-OP64056--Vendor #D1555

902 - GENEALOGY...OF KNOWN DESCENDANTS OF COLONEL BENJAMIN
SEAWELL, SR. AND LUCY HICKS by Benjamin Lee Seawell. 1935.
South Pasadena, CA.
143pp—GE4-OP60669---Vendor #D1555

903 - SEVERANCE GENEALOGY: BENJAMIN, CHARLES, AND LEWIS LINES
OF THE SEVENTH GENERATION compiled by Henry Ormal Severance.
1927. Columbia, MO: Lucas Bros.
30pp—GE4-OP69345--Vendor #D1555

904 - THE SEVERANS GENEALOGICAL HISTORY by John Franklin Severance.
1893. Chicago: R. R. Donnelley & Sons Co.
178pp—GE4-BH19082---Vendor #D1555

905 - THE SEVERANS GENEALOGICAL HISTORY. [BOUND WITH SEAVERNS
GENEALOGICAL HISTORY....] by John Franklin Severance. 1893.
Chicago: R. R. Donnelley & Sons Co.
165pp—GE4-CD00571---Vendor #D1555

906 - SHARPE GENEALOGY AND MISCELLANY by William Carvosso Sharpe.
1880. Seymour, CT: Record Pr.
176pp—GE4-BH11684---Vendor #D1555

907 - WASHBURN FAMILY. DESCENDANTS OF JOHN OF PLYMOUTH, MASSA-
CHUSETTS, AND WILLIAM....by William Carvosso Sharpe. 1892. Seymour, CT: Record Pr.
30pp—GE4-BH19168--Vendor #D1555

908 - GOVERNOR WILLIAM BRADFORD, AND HIS SON, MAJOR WILLIAM
BRADFORD by James Shepard. 1900. New Britain, CT.
102pp—GE4-OP34573---Vendor #D1555

909 - ISAAC A. SHEPPARD: A BRIEF ACCOUNT OF HIS ANCESTORS...
RELATIVES....by Isaac Applin Sheppard. 1897. Philadelphia: Priv.
pr. for use of his family.
50pp—GE4-BH21201--Vendor #D1555

910 - ANCESTRY OF EDWARD CARLETON AND ELLEN NEWTON, HIS WIFE
by Walter Lee Sheppard. 1978. Havertown, PA. Best copy available.
1410pp—GE4-AU00085--Vendor #D1555

911 - DESCENDANTS OF SAMUEL SHERILL by Charles Hitchcock Sherrill.
1894. NY.
156pp—GE4-OP70617---Vendor #D1555

912 - THE SHERILL GENEALOGY, 2nd ed. rev., by Charles Hitchcock
Sherrill. Ed. & comp. by Louis Effingham de Forest. ca. 1932. New
Haven: Tuttle, Morehouse & Taylor Co.
394pp—GE4-OP70702---Vendor #D1555

913 - HISTORY OF SHINN FAMILY IN EUROPE AND AMERICA by Josiah
Hazen Shinn. 1903. Chicago: Genealogical & Historical Pub. Co.
435pp—GE4-OP44476--Vendor #D1555

914 - STEMMATA SHIRLEIANA; OR THE ANNALS OF THE SHIRLEY FAMILY,
2nd ed., by Evelyn Philip Shirley. 1873. Westminister: Nicholas & Sons.
449pp—GE4-OP62871--Vendor #D1555

915 - ANNALS OF OUR COLONIAL ANCESTORS AND THEIR DESCENDANTS;
...SHOTWELL FAMILY...NATHAN AND PHEBE B. (GARDNER) SHOTWELL
by Ambrose Milton Shotwell. 1897. Lansing, MI: R. Smith & Co.
346pp—GE4-OP43971--Vendor #D1555

916 - THE SHOUSE FAMILY by Thomas R. Shouse. 1928. Liberty, MO.
63pp—GE4-OP65961---Vendor #D1555

917 - GENEALOGY OF DESCENDANTS OF JOHN SILL...CAMBRIDGE,
MASSACHUSETTS IN 1637 by George Griswold Sill. 1859. Albany, NY:
Munsell & Rowland.
108pp—GE4-OP54649--Vendor #D1555

918 - GRAHAM-GRIMES GENEALOGY WITH COGNATE BRANCHES...1756-
1926 by Sara Frances Grimes Sitherwood. 1926? n.p.
242pp—GE4-OP71543--Vendor #D1555

919 - THROCKMORTON FAMILY HISTORY by Sara Frances Grimes Sitherwood. 1929. Bloomington, IL: Pantagraph Pr. & Stationery Co.
476pp—GE4-OP70703--Vendor #D1555

920 - SLACK FAMILY...FAMILY OF ELIPHALET SLACK AND HIS WIFE
ABIGAIL CUTTER....compiled by Rev. William Samuel Slack. 1930.
Alexandria, LA: Standard Pr. Co.
256pp—GE4-CD00233--Vendor #D1555

921 - HISTORY OF SLAYTON FAMILY. BIOGRAPHICAL AND GENEALOGI-
CAL by Asa Walker Slayton. 1898. Grand Rapids, MI: Pr. by Dean
Pr. Co.
336pp—GE4-OP41536--Vendor #D1555

922 - RESOLVED WALDRON'S DESCENDANTS compiled by James Henry
Slipper. 1910. n.p.
90pp—GE4-OP64955---Vendor #D1555

923 - HISTORY AND GENEALOGY OF SLONAKER DESCENDANTS IN AMERI-
CA SINCE EARLY 1700 compiled and edited by James Rollin Slonaker.
1941. Los Angeles: Lyday Pr. Co.
734pp—GE4-OP65960--Vendor #D1555

924 - THE THIGPEN TRIBE by Alice Whitley Smith. Ed. by Casey Thigpen.
ca. 1961. Rev. Yanceyville?, NC., 1963.
534pp—GE4-OP69272--Vendor #D1555

925 - ANCESTORS OF HENRY MONTGOMERY SMITH AND CATHERINE FOR-
SHAEE by Anne Morrill Smith. 1921. Brooklyn, NY: pub. by author.
144pp—GE4-OP65983--Vendor #D1555

926 - SOME ACCOUNT OF SMITHS OF EXETER AND THEIR DESCENDANTS
by Arthur Morton Smith. 1896. Exeter: W. Pollard & Co.
61pp—GE4-OP62367---Vendor #D1555

927 - THE SMITH-JARRATT GENEALOGY by Austin Wheeler Smith. 1941.
Cookeville, TN.
212pp—GE4-OP50861--Vendor #D1555

928 - FAMILY REGISTER OF DESCENDANTS OF NATHANIEL SMITH, JR....
HIS ANCESTORS by Harvey Douglass Smith. 1849. Utica: D. Bennett.
50pp—GE4-BH19008---Vendor #D1555

929 - PEDIGREE OF TURNER FAMILY, AND ITS REPRESENTATIVES IN
1871...SOURCES compiled by Hubert Smith. Arranged and ed. by
Richard Woof. 1871. London: Taylor & Co., prs. priv. pr.
22pp—GE4-BH21209---Vendor #D1555

930 - GENEALOGY OF ROBERT SMITH, OF BUCKINGHAM, BUCKS COUNTY, PENNSYLVANIA, 1719 by Josiah B. Smith. 1885. Newtown, PA.
80pp—GE4-BH21207--Vendor #D1555

931 - GENEALOGY OF WILLIAM SMITH, OF WRIGHTSTOWN, BUCKS COUNTY, PENNSYLVANIA, 1684 by Josiah B. Smith. 1883. Newton, PA. [Philadelphia, PA: Collins Pr. House].
140pp—GE4-BH21208---Vendor #D1555

932 - GENEALOGICAL MEMORANDA—STOUFFER, A.D. 1630-A.D. 1903 compiled by Kate S. Snively. Greencastle, PA. n.d.
112pp—GE4-BH21291---Vendor #D1555

933 - GENEALOGICAL MEMORANDA: SNIVELY, A.D. 1659-A.D. 1882 compiled by William Andrew Snively. Brooklyn. n.d.
78pp—GE4-OP57490--Vendor #D1555

934 - RECORD OF BLAKES OF SOMERSETSHIRE...WILLIAM BLAKE, OF DORCHESTER, MASSACHUSETTS....by Horatio Gates Somerby. 1881. Boston: Priv. Pr.
68pp—GE4-OP01008--Vendor #D1555

935 - SPALDING MEMORIAL: GENEALOGICAL HISTORY OF EDWARD SPALDING, OF MASSACHUSETTS BAY....by Samuel Jones Spalding. 1872. Boston: A. Mudge & Son, prs.
676pp—GE4-BH19191---Vendor #D1555

936 - ANNALS OF FAMILIES OF CASPAR, HENRY, BALTZER AND GEORGE SPENGLER....by Edward Webster Spangler. 1896. York, PA: York Daily Pub. Co., pr.
744pp—GE4-BH21064---Vendor #D1555

937 - DESCENDANTS OF SAMUEL SPARE by John Spare. 1884. New Bedford, MA: P. Howland, Jr., pr. & engraver.
78pp—GE4-BH19086--Vendor #D1555

938 - RECORD AND MEMORIALS OF THE SPEED FAMILY by Thomas Speed. 1892. Louisville, KY: Courier Journal Job Pr. Co.
236pp—GE4-OP65805---Vendor #D1555

939 - ALPHEUS BEEDE STICKNEY, HIS DESCENDANTS....BEEDE, BERKEY, BOULTER, PRESCOTT, SHAW, SWAINE, WIGGIN, SLEEPER, STICKNEY by Emily Stickney Spencer. 1965. Cleveland.
47pp—GE4-OP70715--Vendor #D1555

940 - SPENCER FAMILY HISTORY AND GENEALOGY by Robert Closson Spencer. 1889. Milwaukee, WI.
40pp—GE4-BH21232--Vendor #D1555

941 - FRAGMENTS OF SPILLER FAMILY HISTORY AND GENEALOGY researched and compiled by Wayne Spiller and Dorothy (Spiller) Moffat. With index, update...by Ivie (Reavis) Spiller. n.p., n.d.
332pp—GE4-AU00059---Vendor #D1555

942 - FAMILY RECORD OF DESCENDANTS OF JOHN SPOFFORD...ROWLEY, ESSEX COUNTY, MASSACHUSETTS....2nd ed., by Jeremiah Spofford. 1869. Haverhill: E. G. Frothingham, pr.
140pp—GE4-BH19083---Vendor #D1555

943 - GENEALOGY...SPRAGUE FAMILIES IN AMERICA AS DESCENDED FROM EDWARD SPRAGUE OF ENGLAND...., rev. ed., with corrections and additions, compiled by Augustus Brown Reed Sprague. 1905. Worcester, MA: pub. by compiler.
62pp—GE4-BH19094--Vendor #D1555

944 - BOONE FAMILY—GENEALOGICAL HISTORY OF DESCENDANTS OF GEORGE AND MARY BOONE....by Ella Hazel Atterbury Spraker. 1922. Tuttle.
654pp—GE4-OP34950---Vendor #D1555

945 - GENEALOGICAL TABLE AND HISTORY OF SPRINGER FAMILY IN EUROPE AND NORTH AMERICA by Moses C. Springer. Rev. and additions by E. L. Springer. 1917. Amesbury, MA: Guild & Cameron.
182pp—GE4-CD00231---Vendor #D1555

946 - THE STANDISHES OF AMERICA by Myles Standish. 1895. Boston,
MA: priv. pr. for author by S. Usher.
182pp—GE4-BH19010--Vendor #D1555

947 - RECORD, GENEALOGICAL, BIOGRAPHICAL, STATISTICAL, OF
THOMAS STANTON, OF CONNECTICUT...1635-1891 by William Alonzo
Stanton. 1891. Albany, NY: J. Munsell's Sons.
630pp—GE4-BH21120---------------------------------------Vendor #D1555

948 - DIRECT ANCESTRY OF THE LATE JACOB WENDELL OF PORTSMOUTH,
NEW HAMPSHIRE by James Rindge Stanwood. 1882. Boston: David
Clapp & Son.
57pp—GE4-BH21295--—Vendor #D1555

949 - AARON STARK FAMILY, SEVEN GENERATIONS OF DESCENDANTS OF
AARON STARK....by Charles Rathbone Stark. 1927. Boston, MA:
Wright & Potter.
150pp—GE4-OP65305---------------------------------------Vendor #D1555

950 - BRIEF GENEALOGICAL HISTORY OF ROBERT STARKWEATHER...
DESCENDANTS IN VARIOUT LINES, 1640-1898 by Carlton Lee Starkweather. 1904. Auburn, NY: Pr. of Kanpp, Peck & Thomson.
416pp—GE4-BH19004--------------------------------------Vendor #D1555

951 - NEWBERRY FAMILY OF WINDSOR, CONNECTICUT...CLARINDA (NEW-
BERRY) GOODWIND...1634-1866 compiled by Frank Farnsworth Starr
for James J. Goodwin. 1898. Hartford, CT: Cambridge Univ. Pr., J.
Wilson & Son.
94pp—GE4-BH19166---------------------------------------Vendor #D1555

952 - ROBERTS FAMILY OF SIMSBURY, CONNECTICUT...CAPTAIN LEMUEL
ROBERTS, 1741-1789 compiled by Frank Farnsworth Starr for James
Junius Goodwin. 1896. Hartford, CT: Cambridge, J. Wilson & Son.
78pp—GE4-BH19005---------------------------------------Vendor #D1555

953 - THOMAS SPENCER FAMILY OF HARTFORD, CONNECTICUT...SAMUEL
SPENCER...1744-1818 compiled by Frank Farnsworth Starr for James J.
Goodwin. 1896. Hartford, CT: Cambridge, J. Wilson & Son.
84pp—GE4-BH21110--------------------------------------Vendor #D1555

954 - STEARNS FAMILY RECORD by John Peck Stearns. 1894. Santa
Barbara, CA.
26pp—GE4-BH19093---------------------------------------Vendor #D1555

955 - STEPHENS FAMILY GENEALOGIES; PETER—JOSHUA—WILLIAM—ALEX-
ANDER, 1690-1938, rev. ed., by Dan Voorhees Stephens. 1940. Fremont, NE: Hammond & Stephens Co.
743pp—GE4-CD00222-------------------------------------—Vendor #D1555

956 - STETSON FAMILY...FAMILY ORIGIN...BIOGRAPHICAL SKETCH OF
DESCENDANTS OF SIMEON STETSON by Isaiah Kidder Stetson. 1892.
Bangor: Bangor Pub. Co.
102pp—GE4-BH19060-------------------------------------—Vendor #D1555

957 - ANCESTRAL GENEALOGICAL RECORD AND HISTORY OF STEVENS
FAMILY, OF NORFOLK, CONNECTICUT by Nathaniel Benjamin Stevens.
1896. Winsted, CT.
68pp—GE4-BH19087--------------------------------------Vendor #D1555

958 - GALLOWAY RECORDS by Macleod Stewart. n.d., n.d.
416pp—GE4-OP31752---------------------------------------Vendor #D1555

959 - STICKNEY. SPAULDING. LAWRENCE. by Alvah Franklin Stickney.
1910. West Townsend?, MA.
12pp—GE4-OP71441---------------------------------------Vendor #D1555

960 - JESSE DENNIS OF SUSSEX COUNTY, NEW JERSEY AND HIS DESCEN-
DANTS...STATE by Charles E. Stickney. 1904. Sussex (Deckertown):
Wantage Recorder Office.
114pp—GE4-BH21124-------------------------------------Vendor #D1555

961 - STICKNEY GENEALOGY by Charles Perham Stickney. 1920. n.p.
32pp—GE4-OP71440--------------------------------------Vendor #D1555

962 - STICKNEY FAMILY:...DESCENDANTS OF WILLIAM AND ELIZABETH STICKNEY...TO 1869 by Matthew Adams Stickney. 1869. Salem, MA: Essex Inst. Pr.
545pp—GE4-OP70608--Vendor #D1555

963 - NOTES ON DESCENDANTS OF NICHOLAS STILLWELL...STILLWELL FAMILY IN AMERICA by William Henry Stillwell. 1883. NY: E. W. Nash.
78pp—GE4-BH21111--Vendor #D1555

964 - A HISTORY OF THE STOCKTON FAMILY by John Wishart Stockton. 1881. Philadelphia: Pr. of Patterson & White.
70pp—GE4-OP36735--Vendor #D1555

965 - STOCKTON FAMILY OF NEW JERSEY AND OTHER STOCKTONS by Thomas Coates Stockton. 1911. Washington, DC: Carnahan Pr.
460pp—GE4-OP35606--Vendor #D1555

966 - BOOK TWO OF THE FAMILY OF JOHN STONE...DESCENDANTS OF RUSSELL, BILLE, TIMOTHY AND EBER STONE by Truman Lewis Stone. 1898. Buffalo, NY: C. W. Moulton.
404pp—GE4-BH21251--Vendor #D1555

967 - STARIN FAMILY IN AMERICA. DESCENDANTS OF NICHOLAS STER (STARIN)...FORT ORANGE by William Leete Stone. 1892. Albany, NY: J. Munsell's Sons.
246pp—GE4-CD00390--Vendor #D1555

968 - THE DeLAUNCEYS, A ROMANCE OF A GREAT FAMILY by D. A. Story. 1931. London: T. Nelson.
196pp—GE4-OP40371--Vendor #D1555

969 - A STOUFFER LINE OF DESCENT THAT ORIGINATED IN LANCASTER COUNTY, PENNSYLVANIA. 1951. n.p. For priv. dist. among families of the line.
64pp—GE4-OP72045--Vendor #D1555

970 - BOOK OF STRATTONS; BEING A COLLECTION OF STRATTON RECORDS FROM ENGLAND AND SCOTLAND....compiled by Harriet Russell Stratton. 1908. NY: Grafton Pr.
435pp—GE4-OP63793--Vendor #D1555

971 - SOME GENEALOGIES AND FAMILY RECORDS compiled by Albert Y. Straw. 1931. Clearfield, PA: Pr. of Clearfield Republican.
294pp—GE4-OP56225--Vendor #D1555

972 - THE STREET GENEALOGY by Mary Evarts Anderson Street. 1895. Exeter, NH: John Templeton, The News Letter Pr.
579pp—GE4-OP64831--Vendor #D1555

973 - SAMUEL GRIFFIN OF NEW CASTLE COUNTY ON DELAWARE, PLANTER; ...SEVENTH GENERATION by Thomas Hale Streets. 1905. Philadelphia, PA.
250pp—GE4-BH19197--Vendor #D1555

974 - STRIEBY GENEALOGY AND HISTORY 1726-1967 compiled by Byard B. Strieby, B. Beatrice Strieby and Irene M. Strieby. 1967. Des Moines. Text 265pp—Suppl. 64pp—GE4-AU00030----------------------Vendor #D1555

975 - THE STRUTT FAMILY OF TERLING, 1650-1873 by Charles R. Strutt. 1939. Priv. Pr.
141pp—GE4-OP35530--Vendor #D1555

976 - GENEALOGICAL RECORD OF THE STRYCKER FAMILY by William Scudder Stryker. 1887. Camden, NJ: S. Chew.
112pp—GE4-OP25001--Vendor #D1555

977 - GENEALOGY OF STURM FAMILY...JACOB STURM OF SHARPSBURG, MARYLAND...1936 compiled by Lloyd Elmer Sturm. Ed. by Margaret H. Sturm. 1938. n.p.
330pp—GE4-OP65319--Vendor #D1555

978 - ANCESTRY OF EDWARD WALES BLAKE AND CLARISSA MATILDA GLIDDEN...ALLIED FAMILIES by Edith Bartlett Sumner. 1948. CA.
328pp—GE4-OP65862--Vendor #D1555

979 - HISTORY OF AMERICAN AND PURITANICAL FAMILY OF SUTLIFF OR
SUTLIFFE by Samuel Milton Sutliff. 1909. Downers Grove, IL: Kelms-
cott Pr.
233pp—GE4-OP67327--Vendor #D1555

980 - GENEALOGY OF SUTCLIFF-SUTLIFFE FAMILY IN AMERICA IN AMERI-
CA...1903 by Bennett Hurd Sutliffe. n.d. Hartford, CT: R. S. Peck
& Co. Prs. &Engravers.
262pp—GE4-OP67328--Vendor #D1555

981 - SWAIN AND ALLIED FAMILIES, INCLUDING TILLEY, HOWLAND, CHIP-
MAN, HALE, BARRETT, GILBERT, FOX, BRAYTON, EGERTON, HUNT-
INGTON, ST. JOHN, KEYES compiled by William Chester Swain. 1896.
Milwaukee, WI: Pr. of Swain & Tate Co.
146pp—GE4-OP63228--Vendor #D1555

982 - HISTORY OF THE SWANDER FAMILY by John I. Swander. n.d. T.
S. Falkner & H. D. Pittenger Comm.
172pp—GE4-OP22397--Vendor #D1555

983 - BYBERRY WALTONS; AN ACCOUNT OF FOUR ENGLISH BROTHERS:
NATHANIEL & THOMAS & CANIEL & WILLIAM WALTON....compiled by
Norman Walton Swayne. 1958. Philadelphia: pr. by Stephenson-Bros.
834pp—GE4-OP66847--Vendor #D1555

984 - FAMILY HISTORICAL REGISTER by Henry Hartwell Swearingen. 1884.
Washington: C. W. Brown.
130pp—GE4-OP22982--Vendor #D1555

985 - THE MacKENNAS OF TRUAGH: [INCLUDES 1980 SUPPLEMENT], 2nd ed.
by C. Eugene Swezey. 1977. Huntington, NY: Swezey.
220pp—GE4-AU00222--Vendor #D1555

986 - THE SWEZEYS OF HUNTINGTON by C. Eugene Swezey. 1969.
92pp—GE4-AU00187--Vendor #D1555

987 - WILLIAM SWYFT OF SANDWITCH AND SOME OF HIS DESCENDANTS,
1637-1899 by George Henry Swift. 1900. Millbrook, NY: Round Table Pr.
278pp—GE4-OP57316--Vendor #D1555

988 - HISTORY OF SWOPE FAMILY AND THEIR CONNECTIONS, 1678-1896
edited by Gilbert Ernest Swope. 1896. Lancaster, PA: Cochran.
396pp—GE4-OP47014--Vendor #D1555

989 - THE FAMILY OF SYNGE OR SING by Katherine Charlotte Swan Synge.
1938. Southampton: G. F. Wilson.
111pp—GE4-OP47072--Vendor #D1555

990 - TALCOTT PEDIGREE IN ENGLAND AND AMERICA FROM 1558 TO
1876 by Sebastian Visscher Talcott. 1876. Albany: Weed, Parsons & Co.
476pp—GE4-BH17393--Vendor #D1555

991 - GENEALOGY OF DESCENDANTS OF THOMAS TANNER, SR. OF CORN-
WALL, CONNECTICUT....by Rev. Elias F. Tanner. 1893. Lansing,
MI: D. D. Thorp, pr.
130pp—GE4-CD00442--Vendor #D1555

992 - SKETCH OF THE LIFE OF REV. DANIEL DANA TAPPAN...TAPPAN
FAMILY....by Daniel Dana Tappan. 1890. Boston: Pr. of Samuel Usher.
29pp—GE4-BH21276--Vendor #D1555

993 - TAPPAN-TOPPAN GENEALOGY;...ABRAHAM TOPPAN OF NEWBURY,
MASSACHUSETTS, 1606-1672 by Daniel Langdon Tappan. 1915. Arlington, MA: Daniel Langdon Tappan.
182pp—GE4-OP43605--Vendor #D1555

994 - THE TARLETON FAMILY compiled by Charles William Tarleton. 1900.
Concord, NH: I. C. Evans.
280pp—GE4-OP31595--Vendor #D1555

995 - SOME ACCOUNTS OF ANCESTORS, RELATIVES AND FAMILY OF
HENRY BOARDMAN TAYLOR....by Henry Boardman Taylor. 1892. n.p.
90pp—GE4-BH19108--Vendor #D1555

996 - SOME TEMPLE PEDIGREES...DESCENDANTS OF ABRAHAM TEMPLE ...SALEM, MASSACHUSETTS, IN 1636....by Levi Daniel Temple. 1900. Boston: pr. by D. Clapp & Son.
342pp—GE4-BH11235--Vendor #D1555

997 - ANCESTORS OF ADELBERT P. THAYER, FLORIENE THAYER McCRAY AND GEO. BURTON THAYER....compiled by George Burton Thayer. 1894. Hartford, CT: Pr. of Plimpton Mfg. Co.
198pp—GE4-BH19079--Vendor #D1555

998 - THE BOWMANS; A HISTORY OF HANS DIETERICK BAUMAN AND HIS DESCENDANTS by Augusta Dillman Thomas. ca. 1934. Allentown, PA: Schlechters, prs.
474pp—GE4-OP45095--Vendor #D1555

999 - THE BOARMAN'S by Cornelius Francis Thomas. 1934. Washington.
89pp—GE4-OP35345--Vendor #D1555

1000 - BRIEF HISTORY OF FAMILY THOMASON IN ENGLAND AND THE UNITED STATES by Robert Stewart Thomason. 1938-40. New York City: Scribner Pr.
139pp—GE4-OP72160--Vendor #D1555

1001 - THOMPSON AND GIVEN FAMILIES WITH THEIR ANCESTRAL LINES AND PRESENT BRANCHES by Samuel Findley Thompson. 1898. Hamilton, OH: Brown & Whitaker.
273pp—GE4-OP70781--Vendor #D1555

1002 - THRELKELD GENEALOGY by Hansford Lee Threlkeld. 1932. Morganfield, KY.
350pp—GE4-OP63174--Vendor #D1555

1003 - GENEALOGICAL AND HISTORICAL ACCOUNT OF THROCKMORTON FAMILY IN ENGLAND AND THE UNITED STATES....by Charles Wickliffe Throckmorton. 1930. Richmond, VA: Old Dominion Pr., Inc.
634pp—GE4-OP56867--Vendor #D1555

1004 - THE DOINGS...THURSTONS AT NEWBURYPORT, MASSACHUSETTS, JUNE 24, 25, 1885 by Brown Thurston. 1885. Portland, ME: B. Thurston.
86pp—GE4-OP37671--Vendor #D1555

1005 - THURSTON GENEALOGIES, 2nd ed., by Brown Thurston. 1892. Portland: B. Thurston.
804pp—GE4-OP37659--Vendor #D1555

1006 - THE TIFFANYS OF AMERICA, HISTORY AND GENEALOGY by Nelson Otis Tiffany. 1903. Buffalo, NY: Matthews, Northrup.
343pp—GE4-OP62057--Vendor #D1555

1007 - PARTIAL RECORD OF DESCENDANTS OF JOHN TEFFT...JOHN TIFFT...RECORDS by Mrs. Maria Elizabeth (Maxon) Tifft. 1896. Buffalo, NY: Peter Paul Book Co.
336pp—GE4-BH21250--Vendor #D1555

1008 - SPES ALIT AGRICOLAM (HOPE SUSTAINS THE FARMER)/STEPHEN FREDERICK TILLMAN, 4th rev. ed., by Stephen Frederick Tillman. 1962. Chevy Chase, MD.
332pp—GE4-2050385--- Vendor #D1555

1009 - THE WISWALL FAMILY OF AMERICA. FOUR GENERATIONS by Anson Titus. 1886. Boston.
8pp—GE4-BH19076--- Vendor #D1555

1010 - YOUR LOVING ANNA: LETTERS FROM THE ONTARIO FRONTIER by Louis Tivy. ca. 1972. Toronto: Univ. of Toronto Pr.
128pp—GE4-2016092-- Vendor #D1555

1011 - GENERAL HISTORY OF THE BURR FAMILY...FROM 1193 TO 1902 by Charles Burr Todd. 1902. NY: Knickerbocker Pr.
741pp—GE4-OP57382-- Vendor #D1555

1012 - WINSTON OF VIRGINIA AND ALLIED FAMILIES by Clayton Torrence. 1927. Richmond, VA: Whittet & Shepperson.
670pp—GE4-OP06912-- Vendor #D1555

1013   - DAVID ROE OF FLUSHING, LONG ISLAND AND SOME OF HIS DE-
SCENDANTS....by Clarence Almon Torrey. 1926. Terrytown, NY:
Roe Pr. Co.
55pp—GE4-OP70633---Vendor #D1555

1014   - THE TORREY FAMILIES AND THEIR CHILDREN IN AMERICA, 2 vols.
by Frederic Crosby Torrey. 1924. Lakeburst, NJ.
Vol. 1 414pp—Vol. 2 501pp—GE4-OP63723------------------—Vendor #D1555

1015   - TO THE MEMORY OF JOSEPH MASON STONE, SUSAN F. STONE....
n.p., n.d.
91pp—GE4-BH21289---Vendor #D1555

1016   - TOWER GENEALOGY: ACCOUNT OF DESCENDANTS OF JOHN TOWER,
OF HINGHAM, MASSACHUSETTS by Charlemagne Tower. 1891. Cambridge, England: John Wilson & Son.
704pp—GE4-OP13601---Vendor #D1555

1017   - DESCENDANTS OF WILLIAM TOWNE...1630 AND SETTLED IN SALEM,
MASSACHUSETTS by Edwin Eugene Towne. 1901. Newtonville, MA.
449pp—GE4-OP61268---Vendor #D1555

1018   - DIRECT ANCESTRY AND POSTERITY OF JUDGE CHARLES TOWN-
SEND...TOWNSEND FAMILY by Charles Townsend. 1897. Orange,
NJ.
80pp—GE4-BH21137---Vendor #D1555

1019   - THE TOWNSEND'S by Malcolm Townsend. 1895. NY: Pr. of Mooney
& Co.
122pp—GE4-BH21141---Vendor #D1555

1020   - TROGDON FAMILY HISTORY by Willard Franklin Trogdon. ca. 1926.
n.p.
122pp—GE4-OP53081---Vendor #D1555

1021   - INDEX TO ALVERDO HAYWARD MASON'S GENEALOGY OF SAMPSON
MASON FAMILY compiled by Vivian L. Tubbs. 1979. Hillsdale, MI.
62pp—GE4-AU00200---Vendor #D1555

1022   - GENEALOGY OF THE TUCKER FAMILY by Ephraim Tucker. ca.
1895. Worcester, MA: Pr. of F. S. Blanchard & Co.
451pp—GE4-OP67205---Vendor #D1555

1023   - GENEALOGY OF DESCENDANTS OF HUMPHREY TURNER, WITH
FAMILY RECORDS. IN TWO PARTS. by Jacob Turner. 1852.
Boston: David Turner, Jr.
76pp—GE4-OP55556---Vendor #D1555

1024   - FAMILY MEETING OF DESCENDANTS OF JOHN TUTHILL...AUGUST
28TH, 1867 by William Henry Tuthill. 1867. Sag-Harbor, NY: Express
Pr.
100pp—GE4-BH19000---Vendor #D1555

1025   - TWINING FAMILY. (REVISED EDITION). DESCENDANTS OF WILL-
IAM TWINING, SR. OF EASTHAM, MASSACHUSETTS....by Thomas
Jefferson Twining. 1905. Ft. Wayne, IN: T. J. Twining.
280pp—GE4-BH19102---Vendor #D1555

1026   - THE FAMILY OF HOGE; A GENEALOGY compiled by James Hoge
Tyler. Ed. by James Fulton Hoge. 1927. Greensboro, NC: J. J.
Stone.
170pp—GE4-OP34125---Vendor #D1555

1027   - GENEALOGICAL HISTORY OF TYRRELLS SOMETIME OF THE FRENCH
VEXIN, POIX....by Joseph Henry Tyrrell. 1904. n.p.
258pp—GE4-OP37789---Vendor #D1555

1028   - GENEALOGY OF RICHMOND AND WILLIAM TYRREL OR TERRELL...
VIRGINIA IN SEVENTEENTH CENTURY by Joseph Henry Tyrrell.
1910. Priv. pr.
32pp—GE4-OP35269---Vendor #D1555

1029 - ARMSTRONG, BRANYON, BRYSON, AND ALLIED FAMILIES OF THE
SOUTH by Ethel S. Updike. ca. 1967. Salt Lake City: Hobby Pr.
425pp—GE4-OP71551--Vendor #D1555

1030 - UPTON FAMILY RECORDS: BEING GENEALOGICAL COLLECTIONS
FOR AN UPTON FAMILY HISTORY by William Henry Upton. 1893.
London: Mitchell & Hughes. priv. pr.
550pp—GE4-BH21212---Vendor #D1555

1031 - GENEALOGICAL AND HISTORICAL RECORD OF THE CARPENTER
FAMILY by James Usher. ca. 1883. NY.
76pp—GE4-OP50373---Vendor #D1555

1032 - HISTORY AND GENEALOGY OF THE UTTERBACK FAMILY IN
AMERICA, 1622-1937 by William Irvin Utterback. 1937. Huntington:
Gentry Bros. Pr. Co.
521pp—GE4-OP14685--Vendor #D1555

1033 - THE VALENTINES IN AMERICA 1644-1874 by Thomas Weston Valentine. 1874. NY: Clark & Maynard.
328pp—GE4-BH21219--Vendor #D1555

1034 - VAN DEUSEN FAMILY, 2 vols., by Albert Harrison Van Deusen.
ca. 1912. NY: Frank Allaben Gen. Co.
Vol. 1 396pp—Vol. 2 489pp—GE4-CD00384-------------------Vendor #D1555

1035 - GENEALOGY OF THE VAN DUZEE FAMILY by Frederic Pierce Van
Duzee. 1964. Resada?, CA: Chedwato Serv.
59pp—GE4-OP46125---Vendor #D1555

1036 - KNISS AND ALLIED FAMILIES by Frederic Pierce Van Duzee. 1965.
Vermont: Chedwato Serv.
61pp—GE4-OP50065---Vendor #D1555

1037 - THE VAN NEXX HERITAGE AND ALLIED GENEALOGIES, 1546-1960
by Lottye Gray Van Ness. 1960. Elizabeth, NJ: Tribro Pr.
183pp—GE4-OP63208--Vendor #D1555

1038 - HISTORY OF THE VAN SICKLE FAMILY IN THE UNITED STATES OF
AMERICA by John W. Van Sickle. repr. of 1880 ed. 1968. Sioux
City, IA: D. W. Verstegen, Inc.
238pp—GE4-OP65986--Vendor #D1555

1039 - GENEALOGY OF VAN VOORHEES FAMILY IN AMERICA...STEVEN
COERTE VAN VOORHEES OF HOLLAND, AND FLATLANDS by Elias
William Van Voorhis. 1888. L. I., NY: G. P. Putnam's Sons.
738pp—GE4-OP47736--Vendor #D1555

1040 - GENEALOGY OF VAN WINKLE FAMILY;...SETTLEMENT IN THIS
COUNTRY WITH DATA, 1630-1913 by Daniel Van Winkle. 1913. Jersey City: Datz Pr.
446pp—GE4-OP44601--Vendor #D1555

1041 - ANNALS OF A CLERICAL FAMILY...WILLIAM VENN, VICAR OF
OTTERTON by John Venn. 1904. Devon, 1600-1621. London:
Macmillan.
380pp—GE4-OP26765--Vendor #D1555

1042 - VIELE, 1659-1909. TWO HUNDRED AND FIFTY YEARS WITH A
DUTCH FAMILY OF NEW YORK by Kathlyne Knickerbocker Viele.
1909. NY: T. A. Wright.
168pp—GE4-CD00487--Vendor #D1555

1043 - ANCESTORS OF LOUIS BEVIER VOORHEES by Louis Bevier Voorhees. 1600? n.p.
8pp—GE4-BH21275--Vendor #D1555

1044 - ROBERT VOSE AND HIS DESCENDANTS compiled by Ellen Frances
Vose. 1932. Boston, MA.
733pp—GE4-OP66817--Vendor #D1555

1045 - TWO HUNDRED AND FIFTY YEARS OF THE WADSWORTH FAMILY IN
AMERICA by Horace Andrew Wadsworth. 1883. Lawrence, Hass,
Eagle, Steam Job Pr. Rooms.
286pp—GE4-OP26048--Vendor #D1555

1046 - FAMILY RECORDS OF DESCENDANTS OF THOMAS WAIT, OF PORTS-
MOUTH, RHODE ISLAND by John Cassan Wait. 1904. NY?: J. C. Wait.
60pp—GE4-BH19081--Vendor #D1555

1047 - GENEALOGICAL SKETCH OF A BRANCH OF THE WAIT OR WAITE
FAMILY OF AMERICA by Dennis Byron Waite. 1893. Canadice, NY.
44pp--GE4-BH19088--Vendor #D1555

1048 - WAKEFIELD MEMORIAL...HISTORICAL, GENEALOGICAL AND BIO-
GRAPHICAL REGISTER...FAMILY OF WAKEFIELD by Homer Wakefield. 1897. Bloomington, IL.
379pp—GE4-OP65996---Vendor #D1555

1049 - WAKEMAN GENEALOGY, 1630-1889...DESCENDANTS OF SAMUEL
WAKEMAN, OF HARTFORD, CONNECTICUT....by Robert Peel Wakeman. 1900. Meriden, CT: pr. by Journal Pub. Co.
588pp—GE4-BH19036---Vendor #D1555

1050 - BENSON FAMILY HISTORY by Claudia Louise Walker. 1959.
San Francisco?
119pp—GE4-CD00385---Vendor #D1555

1051 - STORY OF MY ANCESTORS IN AMERICA by Edwin Sawyer Walker.
1895. Chicago: D. Oliphant, pr.
78pp—GE4-BH21105--Vendor #D1555

1052 - WALKERS OF YESTERDAY...., 2 parts, by Ernest George Walker.
ca. 1937. Washington, DC: Ransdell, Inc.
175pp—GE4-OP67325---Vendor #D1555

1053 - MEMORIAL OF WALKERS OF OLD PLYMOUTH COLONY...DESCEND-
ANTS FROM 1620 TO 1860 by James Bradford Richmond Walker. 1861.
Northampton, MA: Metcalf & Co. Prs.
538pp—GE4-BH13675---Vendor #D1555

1054 - MEMORIAL OF WALKERS OF OLD PLYMOUTH COLONY...DESCEND-
ANTS FROM 1620 TO 1860 by James Bradford Richmond Walker. 1861.
Northampton, MA: Metcalf & Co. Prs.
750pp—GE4-BH19098---Vendor #D1555

1055 - GENEALOGY OF JOHN WALKER FROM IRELAND 1720...DESCEND-
ANTS IN AMERICA by Robert Walton Walker. 1900-34. Ft. Worth, TX.
106pp—GE4-OP63169---Vendor #D1555

1056 - THE ABBE GENEALOGY by F. J. A. Wallace. 19--? Frankford,
PA: Martin & Allardyce.
20pp—GE4-BH19164--Vendor #D1555

1057 - WALLACE: ...DESCENDANTS OF PETER WALLACE AND ELIZABETH
WOODS, HIS WIFE compiled by George Selden Wallace. 1927. Char-
lottesville, VA: Michie Co.
282pp—GE4-OP62117---Vendor #D1555

1058 - GENEALOGY OF THE RIGGS FAMILY by John Hankins Wallace. 1901.
NY.
158pp—GE4-OP51503---Vendor #D1555

1059 - GENEALOGY OF WALLACE FAMILY, DESCENDED FROM ROBERT
WALLACE OF BALLYMENA, IRELAND by John Hankins Wallace. 1902.
NY: pub. for the author.
74pp—GE4-OP51541--Vendor #D1555

1060 - WANDERER-WANDER FAMILY OF BOHEMIA, GERMANY AND AMER-
ICA, 1450-1951 by Alwin Eugene John Wanderer. 1951. Ann Arbor:
Edwards Bros.
178pp—GE4-OP36661---Vendor #D1555

1061 - HISTORY OF WANZER FAMILY IN AMERICA FROM SETTLEMENT IN
NEW AMSTERDAM....by William David Wanzer. 1920. Medford
Mercury Pr.
152pp—GE4-OP56856---Vendor #D1555

1062 - GENEALOGICAL HISTORY OF RICE FAMILY: DESCENDANTS OF
DEACON EDMUND RICE....by Andrew Henshaw Ward. 1858. Boston:
C. Benjamin Richardson.
388pp—GE4-OP65863--Vendor #D1555

1063 - GENEALOGY OF THE WARDLAW FAMILY by Joseph George Wardlaw.
n.p., n.d.
231pp—GE4-OP53965--Vendor #D1555

1064 - GENEALOGY OF WARDLAW FAMILY: WITH SOME ACCOUNT OF
OTHER FAMILIES....by Joseph George Wardlaw. 1929. York, SC.s.n.
223pp—GE4-BH06668--Vendor #D1555

1065 - GENEALOGY OF WITHERSPOON FAMILY, WITH SOME ACCOUNT OF
OTHER FAMILIES....by Joseph George Wardlaw. 1910. Yorkville,SC.
251pp—GE4-OP66631--Vendor #D1555

1066 - ONE OF THE WARNER FAMILY IN AMERICA by Andrew Ferdinando
Warner. 1892. Hartford, CT: Pr. for J. J. Warner by the Case,
Lockwood & Brainard Co.
62pp—GE4-BH19085--Vendor #D1555

1067 - DESCENDANTS OF ANDREW WARNER by Lucien Calvin Warner and
Mary Josephine (Genung) Nichols. 1919. New Haven, CT: Tuttle,
Morehouse ¢ Taylor Co.
812pp—GE4-OP13704--Vendor #D1555

1068 - GENEALOGY OF ONE BRANCH OF WARREN FAMILY WITH ITS INTER-
MARRIAGES, 1637-1890....by Mary Parker Warren. Emily Wilder
Leavitt, ed. 1890. Boston: A. Mudge & Son.
80pp—GE4-BH19181--Vendor #D1555

1069 - WARREN: GENEALOGY OF DESCENDANTS OF JAMES WARREN...
KITTERY, MAINES, 1652-1656 compiled by Orin Warren. 1902. Haverhill, MA: Chase Pr.
154pp—GE4-BH21109--Vendor #D1555

1070 - GENEALOGICAL NOTES ON WASHBURN FAMILY...DESCENDANTS OF
ISRAEL WASHBURN OF RAYNHAM, 1755-1841 by Julia Constantia
Chase Washburn. 1898. Lewiston, ME: Pr. of Journal Co.
124pp—GE4-BH19069--Vendor #D1555

1071 - MY SEVEN SONS by Lilian Washburn. 1940. Portland, ME: Falmouth Pub. House.
157pp—GE4-OP61276--Vendor #D1555

1072 - CATALOGUE OF DESCENDANTS OF THOMAS WATKINS OF CHICKA-
HOMONY VIRGINIA by Francis N. Watkins. 1852. NY: J. F. Trow,Pr.
50pp—GE4-OP62030--Vendor #D1555

1073 - A ROYAL LINEAGE: ALFRED THE GREAT, 901-1901 by Annah
Walker Robinson Watson. 1901. Richmond, VA: Whittet & Shepperson.
142pp—GE4-OP55484--Vendor #D1555

1074 - GEORGE WAY AND HIS DESCENDANTS...CONNECTION WITH THE
EARLY PENOBSCOT (PEJEPSCOT)....by Charles Granville Way. 1887.
Boston: Pr. by E. P. Whitcomb.
27pp—GE4-OP47077--Vendor #D1555

1075 - HISTORY AND GENEALOGY OF BRANCH OF WEAVER FAMILY by
Lucius Egbert Weaver. 1928. Rochester, NY.
743pp—GE4-OP00119--Vendor #D1555

1076 - GENEALOGY OF FENTON FAMILY, DESCENDANTS OF ROBERT
FENTON...WINDHAM, CONNECTICUT, (NOW MANSFIELD) by William
L. Weaver. 1867. Willimantic, CT.
56pp—GE4-BH21122--Vendor #D1555

1077 - GENEALOGY OF SOUTHWORTHS (SOUTHARDS) DESCENDANTS OF
CONSTANT SOUTHWORTH...FAMILY IN ENGLAND by Samuel Gilbert
Webber. 1905. Boston: Fort Hill Pr., S. Usher.
516pp—GE4-OP45045--Vendor #D1555

1078   - HARRIS AND ULRICH FAMILY HISTORY by Hazel Harris Webster.
1966. s.l.: s.n.
109pp—GE4-AU00106--Vendor #D1555

1079   - THE TROGDON HISTORY BOOK NUMBER TWO by Hazel Harris
Webster. n.p., n.d.
102pp—GE4-OP66702--Vendor #D1555

1080   - MEMORIAL POEMS AND BRIEF ANCESTRAL RECORD OF WEBSTER
FAMILY AND DESCENDANTS by John Clough Webster. 1904. Hartford, CT: Pr. of Hartford Pr. Co.
102pp—GE4-BH19044--Vendor #D1555

1081   - GENEALOGY OF ONE BRANCH OF WEBSTER FAMILY, FROM THOMAS
WEBSTER OF ORMESBY....by Prentiss Webster. 1894. Lowell, MA:
pr. by E. T. Rowell.
50pp—GE4-BH19061--Vendor #D1555

1082   - WEDGWOOD PEDIGREES: BEING AN ACCOUNT OF THE COMPLETE
FAMILY...RECORDS by Josiah Clement Wedgwood(baron) and Joshua
George English Wedgwood. 1925. Kendal, Titus Wilson & Sons, Prs.
392pp—GE4-OP53913--Vendor #D1555

1083   - GEORGE WEEKES, GENEALOGY OF FAMILY OF GEORGE WEEKES, OF
DORCHESTER, MASSACHUSETTS, PART TWO....by Robert Dodd
Weekes. 1892. Newark, NJ: Pr. of L. J. Hardham.
220pp—GE4-BH19045--Vendor #D1555

1084   - DESCENDANTS OF ANDREW WEEKS compiled by De Witt Clinton
Weeks. 1896. NY: Angell's Pr. Office.
138pp—GE4-BH19001--Vendor #D1555

1085   - THE NEW ENGLAND KEMPS by Arthur James Weise. 1904.
202pp—GE4-OP66752--Vendor #D1555

1086   - SWARTWOUT CHRONICLES, 1338-1899 AND KETELHUYN CHRONICLES,
1451-1899 by Arthur James Weise. 1899. NY: Trow Directory, Pr. &
Bookbinding Co.
790pp—GE4-OP51453--Vendor #D1555

1087   - SAGA OF A PEOPLE; HISTORY OF JOHANNE ROHRER...HIS
DESCENDANTS....by Lister Oliver Weiss and Noah Rohrer Getz.
1939. Mount Joy, PA: Bulletin.
53pp—GE4-OP44315--Vendor #D1555

1088   - HISTORICAL AND GENEALOGICAL RECORD OF DESCENDANTS...
RICHARD AND JOAN BORDEN....compiled by Hattie Lovisa Borden
Weld. 1899? Los Angeles?, CA.
434pp—GE4-OP45369--Vendor #D1555

1089   - ANCESTRAL COLONIAL FAMILIES: GENEALOGY OF WELSH AND
HYATT FAMILIES...THEIR KIN by Luther Winfield Welsh. 1928.
Independence, MO: Lambert Moon Pr. Co.
215pp—GE4-OP65855--Vendor #D1555

1090   - HISTORY OF DESCENDANTS OF NICHOLAS BEERY by Joseph H.
Wenger. 1911. n.p.
496pp—GE4-OP62568--Vendor #D1555

1091   - THE GARRETT SNUFF FORTUNE by Clinton Alfred Weslager. 1965.
Wilmington, DE: Knebels Pr.
199pp—GE4-AU00035--Vendor #D1555

1092   - GENEALOGY OF WESTERVELT FAMILY by Walter Tallman Westervelt. Wharton Dickinson, ed. 1905. NY: T. A. Wright.
198pp—GE4-OP17874--Vendor #D1555

1093   - SACKETTS OF AMERICA, THEIR ANCESTORS AND DESCENDANTS,
1630-1907 by Charles H. Weygant. 1907. Newburgh, NY: Journal Pr.
555pp—GE4-OP47797--Vendor #D1555

1094   - GENEALOGY OF WHARTON FAMILY OF PHILADELPHIA, 1664 TO
1880 by Anne Hollingsworth Wharton. 1880. Philadelphia: Collins,pr.
158pp—GE4-BH09843--Vendor #D1555

1095 - GENEALOGY OF WHEATLEY OR WHEATLEIGH FAMILY...IN ENGLAND
AND AMERICA by Hannibal Parish Wheatley. 1902. Farmington, NH:
E. H. Thomas.
206pp—GE4-OP56962---Vendor #D1555

1096 - GENEALOGY OF WHIPPLE-WRIGHT, WAGER, WARD-PELL, McLEAN-
BURNET FAMILIES, TOGETHER WITH RECORDS OF ALLIED FAMILIES
by Charles Henry Whipple. 1917. Los Angeles: Pr. of Commercial
Pr. House.
187pp—GE4-OP71444---Vendor #D1555

1097 - BRIEF GENEALOGY OF WHIPPLE FAMILIES, WHO SETTLED IN RHODE
ISLAND. 1873. Providence: A. C. Greene, pr.
61pp—GE4-OP70638---Vendor #D1555

1098 - GENEALOGY OF SOME DESCENDANTS OF THOMAS DEW, COLONIAL
VIRGINIA PIONEER IMMIGRANT....compiled by Ernestine Dew White.
1937. Greenville, SC.: s.n.
358pp—GE4-2051583---Vendor #D1555

1099 - GENEALOGICAL RECORD OF FAMILY OF WHITE...OF EAST KILLING-
LY, CONNECTICUT by John Bartlett White. 1878. Danielsonville,
Greenslitt & Hamilton, prs.
56pp—GE4-BH19058---Vendor #D1555

1100 - JENNINGS, DAVIDSON AND ALLIED FAMILIES...JOHN JENNINGS...
AND JOHN DAVISON by Lillie Pauline White. 1944. Seattle, WA:
Sherman Pr. & Binding Co.
270pp—GE4-OP71447---Vendor #D1555

1101 - GEORGE WIGHTMAN OF QUIDNESSETT, RHODE ISLAND, (1632-
1721-2) AND DESCENDANTS compiled by Mary Ross Whitman. 1939.
Chicago, IL. n.p.
489pp—GE4-OP51421---Vendor #D1555

1102 - NOTES ON WHITMORES OF MADELEY, ENGLAND, AND THE FARRARS
AND BREWERS...MASSACHUSETTS by William Henry Whitmore. 1875.
Boston: D. Clapp & Son, prs.
76pp—GE4-BH19035---Vendor #D1555

1103 - RECORD OF DESCENDANTS OF CAPTAIN JOHN AYRES, OF BROOK-
FIELD, MASSACHUSETTS by William Henry Whitmore. 1870. Boston:
T. R. Marvin & Son.
66pp—GE4-BH21115---Vendor #D1555

1104 - MICHAEL HILLEGAS AND HIS DESCENDENTS by Emma St. Clair
Nichols Whitney. 1891. Pottsville, PA: Pr. of M. E. Miller.
120pp—GE4-OP46170---Vendor #D1555

1105 - SOME OF DESCENDANTS OF JOHN AND ELINOR WHITNEY...WATER-
TOWN, MASSACHUSETTS, IN 1635 by William Lebbeus Whitney. 1890.
Pottsville, PA: M. E. Miller.
118pp—GE4-BH19002---Vendor #D1555

1106 - ANCESTRY AND DESCENDANTS OF JOHN PRATT OF HARTFORD,
CONNECTICUT compiled by Charles B. Whittelsey by authority of
Walter Wilcox Pratt. 1900. Hartford, CT: Hartford Pr.
220pp—GE4-BH21428---Vendor #D1555

1107 - GENEALOGY OF WHITTELSEY-WHITTLESEY FAMILY by Charles
Barney Whittelsey. 1898. Hartford, CT: Case, Lockwood & Brainard.
471pp—GE4-OP50353---Vendor #D1555

1108 - ANCESTRAL LINE OF STEPHEN MOTT WRIGHT FROM NICHOLAS
WRIGHT, THE COLONIAL ANCESTOR by Henry Whittemore. 1899?NY.
40pp—GE4-BH21139---Vendor #D1555

1109 - THE VROOMAN FAMILY IN AMERICA by Grace Elizabeth Vrooman
Wickersham. 1949. Dallas?
341pp—GE4-OP00645---Vendor #D1555

1110 - THE WIDENERS IN AMERICA by Howard Hamlin Widener. 1904.
NY: C. A. Nichols, Jr.
332pp—GE4-OP64183---Vendor #D1555

1111 - THE WIGHT FAMILY: MEMOIR OF THOMAS WIGHT OF DEDHAM, MASSACHUSETTS....by Danforth Phipps Wight. 1848. Boston: Pr. of T. R. Marvin.
119pp—GE4-OP53928---Vendor #D1555

1112 - THE WIGHTS, RECORD OF THOMAS WIGHT OF DEDHAM AND MEDFIELD....by William Ward Wight. 1890. Milwaukee: Swain & Tate.
369pp—GE4-OP37899---Vendor #D1555

1113 - ANNEKE JANS BOGARDUS AND HER NEW AMSTERDAM ESTATE, PAST AND PRESENT compiled by Thomas Bentley Wikoff. 1924. Indianapolis, IN.
276pp—GE4-OP64154---Vendor #D1555

1114 - DESCENDANTS OF WILLIAM WILCOXSON, VINCENT MEIGS, AND RICHARD WEBB by Reynold Webb Wilcox. 1893. NY: T. A. Wright.
100pp—GE4-BH21230---Vendor #D1555

1115 - BOOK OF THE WILDERS. A CONTRIBUTION TO THE HISTORY OF THE WILDERS....by Moses Hale Wilder. 1878. NY: Pr. by E. O. Jenkins for the compiler.
422pp—GE4-BH11679---Vendor #D1555

1120 - ISAAC WILLEY OF NEW LONDON, CONNECTICUT, AND HIS DESCENDANTS by Henry Willey. 1888. New Bedford, MA.
195pp—GE4-OP62126---Vendor #D1555

1121 - GENEALOGICAL NOTES OF WILLIAMS AND GALLUP FAMILIES...AND CAPT. JOHN GOLLOP, SR.....by Charles Fish Williams. 1897. Hartford, CT: Pr. of Case, Lockwood & Brainard Co.
145pp—GE4-BH21252---Vendor #D1555

1122 - LASHER GENEALOGY by Charles Selwyn Williams. 1904. NY: C. S. Williams.
316pp—GE4-OP64960---Vendor #D1555

1123 - ROBERT WILLIAMS OF ROXBURY, MASSACHUSETTS, AND HIS DESCENDANTS. FOUR GENERATIONS. by Edward Higginson Williams. 1891. Newport, RI.
50pp—GE4-BH21429---Vendor #D1555

1124 - THE WILLIAMS FAMILY (IN THE HISTORY OF NEW LONDON COUNTY, CONNECTICUT) by Ephraim Williams. n.p., n.d.
10pp—GE4-BH21294---Vendor #D1555

1125 - WILLIAMS FAMILY, TRACING DESCENDANTS OF THOMAS WILLIAMS OF ROXBURY, MASSACHUSETTS....by George Huntington Williams. 1880. Boston: pr. for priv. dist.
30pp—GE4-BH19032---Vendor #D1555

1126 - KLOCK-CLOCK GENEALOGY, rev. ed., by Helen Laura Clock Williams. 1966. Cleveland: Bell & Howell Co. Best copy available.
231pp—GE4-BH10968---Vendor #D1555

1127 - GENEALOGY OF HISTORY OF FAMILY OF WILLIAMS IN AMERICA...ROBERT WILLIAMS OF ROXBURY by Stephen West Williams. 1847. Greenfield: Merriam & Mirick.
474pp—GE4-OP47622---Vendor #D1555

1128 - LETTERS RESPECTING THE WATT FAMILY by George Williamson. 1840. Greenock: W. Johnston & Son.
85pp—GE4-OP62571---Vendor #D1555

1129 - SKETCH OF WILLIS FAMILY OF VIRGINIA...WITH...READES, WARNERS, LEWISES, BYRDS, CARTERS, CHAMPES, BASSETS, MADISONS, DANGERFIELDS, THORNTONS,BURRELLS, TALIAFERROS, TAYLOES, SMITHS, AND AMBLERS by Byrd Charles Willis and Richard Henry Willis. n.d. Richmond, VA: Whittet & Shepperson, prs.
170pp—GE4-BH21221---Vendor #D1555

1130 - GENEALOGY OF FAMILY OF ELIHU PARSONS WILSON OF KITTERY, MAINE BORN 1769...by Fred Allan Wilson. 1894. Nahant, MA.
78pp—GE4-BH21430---Vendor #D1555

1131 - JOHN GIBSON OF CAMBRIDGE, MASSACHUSETTS AND HIS DE-
SCENDANTS, 1634-1899 by Mehitarle Calef Coppenhagen Wilson.
1900. n.p.
547pp—GE4-OP65333--Vendor #D1555

1132 - MEMOIR OF PHILLIPPE MATON WILTSEE AND HIS DESCENDANTS
by Jerome Wiltsee. 1908. n.p. PT1.
303pp—GE4-OP61218--Vendor #D1555

1133 - WINANS FAMILY IN AMERICA: 1939 MINUS 1664 EQUALS 275 YEARS,
2nd ed., by Charles Augustus Winans. 1939. Patterson, NJ.
59pp—GE4-OP57275--Vendor #D1555

1134 - PERRY FAMILY OF HERTFORD COUNTY, NORTH CAROLINA by
Benjamin Brodie Winborne. 1909. Raleigh: Edwards & Broughton Pr.
66pp—GE4-OP63724--Vendor #D1555

1135 - HISTORICAL AND GENEALOGICAL REGISTER OF JOHN WING...
DESCENDANTS, 1631-1888, 2nd ed., by Conway Phelps Wing. 1888.
NY: De Vinne Pr.
612pp—GE4-CD00277--Vendor #D1555

1136 - THE WINTERMUTE FAMILY HISTORY compiled by Jacob Perry Wintermute. 1900. Delaware, OH.
376pp—GE4-OP62003--Vendor #D1555

1137 - A SHORT ACCOUNT OF THE WINTHROP FAMILY by Robert Charles
Winthrop, Jr. 1887. Cambridge: J. Wilson.
32pp—GE4-BH19055--Vendor #D1555

1138 - WISEMAN GENEALOGY AND BIOGRAPHY by Benjamin Winfield Scott
Wiseman. 1910. Culver, IN.
134pp—GE4-OP34881--Vendor #D1555

1139 - AN UNFINISHED HISTORY OF THE WITHERS FAMILY IN KANSAS
CITY, MISSOURI, 2 parts, by Webster Withers. 1932. Kansas City:
Webb Printing Shop.
Part 1 44pp—Part 2 358pp—GE4-OP00422-------------------Vendor #D1555

1140 - WOLFES OF FORENAGHS, BLACKHALL, BARONRATH...AND TFE
WOLFES OF DUBLIN, 2nd ed., by Robert Thomas Wolfe. 1893. Guilford: W. Matthews.
128pp—GE4-BH19047--Vendor #D1555

1141 - BRIEF HISTORY OF DESCENDANTS OF THOMAS WOOD AND ANN,
HIS WIFE by Amasa Wood. 1884. Worcester, MA: pr. by D. Seagrave.
26pp—GE4-BH19046--Vendor #D1555

1142 - HISTORY AND GENEALOGY OF DESCENDANTS OF ABINAH WOOD
AND SUSANNAH HUMPHREYS by Percy Ashton Wood. 1903. Andover,
OH: Pr. of the Citizen.
98pp—GE4-BH19030--Vendor #D1555

1143 - RUCKER FAMILY GENEALOGY WITH THEIR ANCESTORS, DESCEND-
ANTS AND CONNECTIONS by Sudie Rucker Wood. 1932. Richmond,
VA: Old Dominion Pr., Inc.
602pp—GE4-OP61266--Vendor #D1555

1144 - BEAMAN AND CLARK GENEALOGY...DESCENDANTS OF GAMALIEL
BEAMAN AND SARAH CLARK....by Emily Beaman Wooden. 1909. n.p.
222pp—GE4-OP51588--Vendor #D1555

1145 - WOODS-McAFEE MEMORIAL...JOHN WOODS AND JAMES McAFEE OF
IRELAND....by Rev. Neander M. Woods. 1905. Louisville, KY:
Courier-Journal Job Pr. Co.
544pp—GE4-CD00311--Vendor #D1555

1146 - HISTORICAL GENEALOGY OF WOODSONS AND THEIR CONNECTIONS
compiled by Henry Morton Woodson. 1915. Columbia, MO: pr. of
E. W. Stephens Pub. Co.
879pp—GE4-OP67253--Vendor #D1555

1147 - GENEALOGY OF WOODWARD FAMILY OF CHESTER COUNTY, PENN-
SYLVANIA...THE UNITED STATES by Lewis Woodward. 1879. Wilming-

ton, DE: pr. by Ferris Bros.
116pp—GE4-BH11675--Vendor #D1555

1148 - DESCENDANTS OF ROBERT AND JOHN POAGE (PIONEER SETTLERS IN AUGUSTA COUNTY, VIRGINIA)...., 2 vols., edited by Robert Bell Woodworth. 1954. Staunton, VA: McClure Pr. Co.
Vol. 1 1428 pp—Vol. 2 245pp—GE4-OP65399------------------Vendor #D1555

1149 - DESCENDANTS OF WALTER WOODWORTH OF SCITUATE, MASSA-CHUSETTS by William Atwater Woodworth. 1898. White Plains, NY.
130pp—GE4-CD00447--Vendor #D1555

1150 - SOME RECORDS OF PERSONS BY NAMES OF WORDEN...JOHN AND ELIZABETH WORDEN....by Oliver Norton Worden. 1868. Lewisburg, PA: Pr. of J. R. Cornelius.
168pp—GE4-BH11683--Vendor #D1555

1151 - RECORD OF DESCENDANTS OF ISAAC ROSS AND JEAN BROWN... FAMILIES OF ALEXANDER, CONGER, HARRIS, HILL, KING, KILINGS-WORTH, MacKEY, MOORES, SIMS, WADE, ETC. by Anne Julia Mims Wright. 1911. Jackson, MS: Consumers Stationery & Pr. Co.
380pp—GE4-OP66599--Vendor #D1555

1152 - REED-READ LINEAGE. CAPTAIN JOHN REED OF PROVIDENCE, RHODE ISLAND...1660-1901 by Ella Frances Reed Wright. 1909. Waterbury, CT: Mattatuck Pr., Inc.
835pp—GE4-OP69033--Vendor #D1555

1153 - ANDREWS GENEALOGY AND ALLIANCES by Mrs. Clara Louise (Berry) Wyker. 1917. Decatur, AL: Mrs. John D. Wyker.
175pp—GE4-OP00896--Vendor #D1555

1154 - BIRD GENEALOGY by William Bird Wylie. 1903. St. Louis, MO.
28pp—GE4-BH19103--Vendor #D1555

1155 - HISTORY OF GWYDIR FAMILY by Sir John Wynn. 1827. Ruthin: R. Jones.
150pp—GE4-OP17494--Vendor #D1555

1156 - BRIEF HISTORY OF YEAGER, BUFFINGTON, CREIGHTON, JACOBS, LEMON, HOFFMAN, AND WOODSIDE FAMILIES....by James Martin Yeager. 1912. Lewistown, PA.
291pp—GE4-OP57973--Vendor #D1555

1157 - BERKELEYS OF BARN ELMS by Frances Campbell Berkeley Young. 1964. Hamden, CT: Archon Books.
141pp—GE4-2050368--Vendor #D1555

1158 - GENEALOGICAL NARRATIVE OF THE HART FAMILY IN THE UNITED STATES by Sarah Simpson Smith Young. 1882. Memphis: S. C. Toof.
270pp—GE4-OP30223--Vendor #D1555

1159 - GENEALOGY AND BIOGRAPHICAL SKETCHES OF THE YOUNGMAN FAMILY by David Youngman. 1882. Boston: Pr. of G. H. Ellis.
40pp—GE4-BH21107--Vendor #D1555

1160 - YOUNGS FAMILY. VICAR CHRISTOPHER YONGES, HIS ANCESTORS IN ENGLAND AND DESCENDANTS IN AMERICA....by Selah Youngs. 1907. NY.
486pp—GE4-OP71539--Vendor #D1555

1161 - THE ZARTMAN FAMILY, 1692-1942, rev. & enl. ed., by Rufus Calvin Zartman. 1942. Rutland, VT: Tuttle Pub. Co., Inc.
533pp—Suppl. 22pp—GE4-OP69203------------------------Vendor #D1555

1162 - ANCESTRY AND KINDRED OF W. P. ZUBER, TEXAS VETERAN by William Physick Zuber. 1905. Iola?, TX.
32pp—GE4-BH19029--Vendor #D1555

1163 - ABBE-ABBEY GENEALOGY, IN MEMORY OF JOHN ABBE AND HIS DESCENDANTS by Cleveland Abbe and Josephine Genung Nichols. Repr. of 1916 ed. New Haven, CT.
Cloth—$79.00—Paper—$69.00—525pp------------------------ Vendor #D1842

1164 - GENEALOGICAL REGISTER OF DESCENDANTS OF GEORGE ABBOT OF ANDOVER...CONNECTICUT by Abiel Abbot and Ephraim Abbot. Repr. of 1847 ed. Boston.
Paper—$32.50—217pp------------------------------------- Vendor #D1842

1165 - THE ABEEL AND ALLIED FAMILIES by Henry Whittemore. Repr. of 1899 ed. New York.
Paper—$5.00—24pp-------------------------------------- Vendor #D1842

1166 - GENEALOGY OF THE ADAMS FAMILY OF KINGSTON, MASSACHU- SETTS by George Adams. Repr. of 1861 ed.
Paper—$12.50—64pp-------------------------------------- Vendor #D1842

1167 - GENEALOGICAL HISTORY OF ROBERT ADAMS OF NEWBURY, MASSACHUSETTS...1675-1900 by Andrew Adams. Repr. of 1900 ed.
Cloth—$84.50—Paper—$74.50—564pp----------------------- Vendor #D1842

1168 - HISTORY OF THOMAS ADAMS AND THOMAS HASTINGS FAMILIES OF AMHERST, MASSACHUSETTS by Herbert Baxter Adams. Repr. of 1880 ed. Amherst.
Paper—$12.50—$12.50------------------------------------- Vendor #D1842

1169 - HISTORY OF THE ADAMS FAMILY by Henry Whittemore. Repr. of 1893 ed. NY.
Paper—$15.00—84pp-------------------------------------- Vendor #D1842

1170 - DESCENDANTS OF JAMES AND WILLIAM ADAMS OF LONDONDERRY, NOW DERRY, NEW HAMPSHIRE by Andrew N. Adams. Repr. of 1894 ed. Rutland.
Paper—$15.00—87pp-------------------------------------- Vendor #D1842

1171 - GENEALOGY AND HISTORY OF PART OF THE NEWBURY ADAMS FAMILY....by Smith Adams. Repr. of 1895 ed. Calais, ME.
Paper—$12.50—61pp-------------------------------------- Vendor #D1842

1172 -REV. AMOS ADAMS (1728-1775) OF ROXBURY, MASSACHUSETTS, ...AMERICAN ANCESTRY by Robert Means Lawrence. Repr. of 1912 ed. Boston.
Paper—$4.50—17pp-------------------------------------- Vendor #D1842

1173 - HISTORY OF ADDINGTON FAMILY IN UNITED STATES AND ENG- LAND by H. M. Addington. Repr. of 1931 ed.
Paper—$20.00—101pp------------------------------------- Vendor #D1842

1174 - GENEALOGY OF THE AINSWORTH FAMILIES IN AMERICA by Francis J. Parker. Repr. of 1894 ed. Boston.
Paper—$32.00—212pp------------------------------------- Vendor #D1842

1175 - ANCESTORS AND DESCENDANTS OF ISAAC ALDEN AND IRENE SMITH...1599-1903 by Harriet Chapin Fielding. Repr. of 1903 ed.
Paper—$21.50—144pp------------------------------------- Vendor #D1842

1176 - DESCENDANTS OF DANIEL ALDEN...SIXTH IN DESCENT FROM JOHN ALDEN, THE PILGRIM by Frank Wentworth Alden. Repr. of 1923 ed.
Paper—$17.00—113pp------------------------------------- Vendor #D1842

1177 - ALDWORTH-ELBRIDGE FAMILIES 1590-1811 by E. E. Salisbury. Repr. of 1885 ed.
Paper—$8.00—40pp-------------------------------------- Vendor #D1842

1178 - ALEXANDER FAMILY RECORDS by W. M. Clemens. Repr. of 1914 ed.
Paper—$5.00—20pp-------------------------------------- Vendor #D1842

1179 - GENEALOGICAL HISTORY OF FAMILY OF THOMAS ALGER OF TAUNTON AND BRIDGEWATER by A. M. Alger. Repr. of 1876 ed.
Paper—$12.00—60pp-------------------------------------- Vendor #D1842

1180 -GENEALOGICAL SKETCHES OF ALLEN FAMILY OF MEDFIELD...
GERSHOM AND ABIGAIL (ALLEN) ADAMS by Joseph Allen. Repr. of
1869 ed. Boston.
Paper—$15.00—88pp-------------------------------------- Vendor #D1842

1181 - GENEALOGY OF SAMUEL ALLEN OF WINDSOR, CONNECTICUT, AND
...HIS DESCENDANTS by Willard S. Allen. Repr. of 1876 ed. Boston.
Paper—$14.00—76pp-------------------------------------- Vendor #D1842

1182 - GENEALOGY OF ALLEN FAMILY OF MANCHESTER, MASSACHUSETTS,
TO 1886 by John Price. Repr. of 1888 ed. Salem.
Paper—$9.50—47pp-------------------------------------- Vendor #D1842

1183 - GENEALOGICAL HISTORY OF THE ALLEN FAMILY AND SOME OF
THEIR CONNECTIONS by Mrs. Frances M. Stoddard. Repr. of 1891
ed. Boston.
Paper—$20.00—136pp------------------------------------- Vendor #D1842

1184 - PHINEHAS ALLEN'S DESCENDANTS, OF LINCOLN, MASSACHUSETTS
1745;...ASHBY, MASSACHUSETTS, 1777 by George Henry Allen.
Repr. of 1898 ed. Boston.
Paper—$5.50—27pp-------------------------------------- Vendor #D1842

1185 - CHARLES ALLEN OF PORTSMOUTH, NEW HAMPSHIRE, 1657, AND
SOME OF HIS DESCENDANTS by Frank W. Allen. Repr. of 1902 ed.
Boston.
Paper—$3.00—7pp-------------------------------------- Vendor #D1842

1186 - HISTORY OF THE ALLERTON FAMILY IN THE UNITED STATES
1585-1885....by Allerton and Currier. Repr. of 1900 ed.
Paper—$30.00—149pp------------------------------------ Vendor #D1842

1187 - ALLERTONS OF NEW ENGLAND AND VIRGINIA by Isaac J. Greenwood. Repr. of 1890 ed. Boston.
Paper—$3.00—7pp-------------------------------------- Vendor #D1842

1188 - HISTORY OF THE ALLISON FAMILY OF PENNSYLVANIA, 1750-1912
by J. L. Allison. Repr. of 1912 ed.
Paper—$22.50—115pp------------------------------------ Vendor #D1842

1189 - HISTORY OF THE ALISON OR ALLISON FAMILY IN EUROPE AND
AMERICA, 1135-1893 by Leonard Allison Morrison. Repr. of 1893 ed.
Boston.
Cloth—$49.00—Paper—$39.00—328pp---------------------- Vendor #D1842

1190 - MATTHEW ALLYN OF CAMBRIDGE, MASSACHUSETTS by C. C.
Baldwin. Repr. of 1882 ed.
Paper—$7.50—20pp-------------------------------------- Vendor #D1842

1191 - AMBROSE FAMILY RECORDS by W. M. Clemens. Repr. of 1925 ed.
Paper—$3.00—7pp-------------------------------------- Vendor #D1842

1192 - SOME GENEALOGICAL NOTES (AMES AND OTHERS) by Pelham W.
Ames. Repr. of 1900 ed. San Francisco.
Paper—$6.50—32pp-------------------------------------- Vendor #D1842

1193 - GEN. MEM. OF DESCENDANTS OF SAMUEL AMES OF CANTERBURY,
NEW HAMPSHIRE by J. Kimball. Repr. of 1890 ed.
Paper—$11.00—55pp------------------------------------- Vendor #D1842

1194 - ANDERSONS OF GOLDMINE, HANOVER COUNTY, VIRGINIA by E.
L. Anderson. Repr. n.d.
Paper—$7.00—36pp-------------------------------------- Vendor #D1842

1195 - ANDERSON & CHEVALIER FAMILIES OF VIRGINIA 1678-1847 by E.
E. Salisbury. Repr. of 1885 ed.
Paper—$6.00—28pp-------------------------------------- Vendor #D1842

1196 - GENEALOGY IN PART, OF THE ANDERSON-OWEN-BEALL FAMILIES
by Grant James Anderson. Repr. of 1909 ed. Richmond, VA.
Paper—$24.00—159pp------------------------------------ Vendor #D1842

1197 - GENEALOGY OF THE ANDREWS OF TAUNTON AND STOUGHTON,
MASSACHUSETTS...1656-1886 by George Andrews. Repr. of 1887
ed.
Paper—$17.50—86pp-------------------------------------- Vendor #D1842

1198 - LT. JOHN ANDREWS OF CHEBACCO, MASSACHUSETTS, 1637-1708
by H. F. Andrews. Repr. of 1909 ed.
Paper—$4.00—17pp-- Vendor #D1842

1199 - GENEALOGICAL HISTORY OF JOHN AND MARY ANDREWS...FARM-
INGTON, CONNECTICUT, 1640....by Alfred Andrews. Repr. of
1872 ed. Chicago.
Cloth—$98.00—Paper—$88.00—652pp----------------------- Vendor #D1842

1200 - HISTORY OF THE ANDREWS FAMILY...ROBERT ANDREWS AND
HIS DESCENDANTS, 1635-1890 by H. Franklin Andrews. Repr. of
1890 ed. Audubon, IA.
Paper—$35.00—234pp------------------------------------- Vendor #D1842

1201 - ANCESTRY OF HENRY L. AND JOHN C. ANDREWS, WOBURN,
MASSACHUSETTS, 2nd ed. by Henry L. and John C. Andrews.
Repr. of 1914 ed. Woburn, MA.
Paper—$4.50—19pp-- Vendor #D1842

1202 - GENEALOGY OF DESCENDANTS OF THOMAS ANGELL, WHO SETTLED
IN PROVIDENCE, 1636 by A. A. Angell. Repr. of 1872 ed.
Paper—$37.50—210pp------------------------------------- Vendor #D1842

1203 - CENTENNIAL CELEBRATION OF THE ANNIN FAMILY...STONE HOUSE
IN SOMERSET COUNTY, NEW JERSEY, 1866. Repr. Philadelphia.
Paper—4.50—17pp-- Vendor #D1842

1204 - GENEALOGY OF DESCENDANTS OF LAWRENCE AND MARY ANTISELL
OF NORWICH AND WILLINGTON, CONNECTICUT....by Mary Elizabeth
Tisdel Wyman. 1908. Painesville, OH.
Cloth—$50.00—Paper—$40.00—335pp----------------------- Vendor #D1842

1205 - MONUMENTAL MEMORIALS OF THE APPLETON FAMILY by J. A.,
i. e., John Appleton. Repr. of 1867 ed. Boston.
Paper—$6.00—30pp-- Vendor #D1842

1206 - THE FAMILY OF ARMISTEAD OF VIRGINIA by W. S. Appleton.
Repr. of 1899 ed. Boston.
Paper—$5.00—23pp-- Vendor #D1842

1207 - GENEALOGICAL RECORD OF THE ARMS FAMILY...DESCENDANTS
OF WILLIAM FIRST by Edward W. Arms. Repr. of 1877 ed. Troy, NY.
Paper—$10.00—57pp--------------------------------------- Vendor #D1842

1208 - DESCENDANTS OF WILLIAM ARNOLD OF HINGHAM, MASSACHUSETTS,
WITH COOKE, HARRIS AND MOWRY FAMILIES by E. Richardson.
Repr. of 1876 ed.
Paper—$10.00—69pp--------------------------------------- Vendor #D1842

1209 - JOHN ARNOT OF SCOTLAND AND ALBANY, NEW YORK AND
DESCENDANTS by Spooner. Repr. of 1914 ed.
Paper—$4.00—12pp-- Vendor #D1842

1210 - THE ASHLEY GENEALOGY. HISTORY OF DESCENDANTS OF
ROBERT ASHLEY OF SPRINGFIELD, MASSACHUSETTS by Francis
Bacon Trowbridge. 1896. New Haven.
Cloth—$72.50—Paper—$62.50—483pp----------------------- Vendor #D1842

1211 - ASHMEAD FAMILY OF PENNSYLVANIA, DESCENDANTS OF JOHN
ASHMEAD. Repr. n.d.
Paper—$3.00—5pp--- Vendor #D1842

1212 - THE ASPINWALL GENEALOGY by Algernon Aikin Aspinwall.
Repr. of 1901 ed. Rutland, VT.
Paper—$39.00—262pp------------------------------------- Vendor #D1842

1213 - JOSEPH ATKINS, THE STORY OF A FAMILY by Francis Higginson Atkins. Repr. of 1891 ed.
Paper—$24.50—164pp--- Vendor #D1842

1214 - GENEALOGICAL RECORD OF ATLEE FAMILY OF LANCASTER COUNTY, PENNSYLVANIA by E. A. Barber. Repr. of 1884 ed.
Paper—$26.00—130pp--- Vendor #D1842

1215 - GENEALOGICAL REGISTER OF DESCENDANTS IN THE MALE LINE OF DAVID ATWATER....by Edward E. Atwater. Repr. of 1873 ed.
Paper—$12.50—64pp-- Vendor #D1842

1216 - GENEALOGY OF THE ATWELL FAMILY OF NEW LONDON, CONNECTICUT by C. B. Atwell. Repr. of 1896 ed.
Paper—$3.00—11pp--- Vendor #D1842

1217 - FAMILY HISTORY AND GENEALOGY OF DESCENDANTS OF ROBERT AUGUR OF NEW HAVEN COLONY by Edwin P. Augur. Repr. of 1904 ed.
Paper—$39.00—260pp--- Vendor #D1842

1218 - ANCESTRY OF JEREMIAH AUSTIN OF CHARLESTOWN, RHODE ISLAND by J. O. Austin. Repr. n.d.
Paper—$5.00—26pp--- Vendor #D1842

1219 - GENEALOGICAL RECORD OF DEDHAM BRANCH OF THE AVERY FAMILY IN AMERICA by Jane G. (Avery) Carter and Susie P. Holmes. Repr. of 1893 ed.
Cloth—$55.00—Paper—$45.00----------------------------------- Vendor #D1842

1220 - AVERY NOTES AND QUERIES. A QUARTERLY MAGAZINE DEVOTED ...GROTON AVERYS, NUMBERS 1-18 edited by E. M. Avery. Repr. of 1898-1902 editions (all published).
Paper—$37.00—246pp--- Vendor #D1842

1221 - THE AVERY, FAIRCHILD AND PARK FAMILIES OF MASSACHUSETTS, CONNECTICUT AND RHODE ISLAND by Samuel Putnam Avery. Repr. of 1919 ed.
Paper—$25.00—169pp--- Vendor #D1842

1222 - THE WARREN, LITTLE, LOTHROP, PARK, DIX, WHITMAN, FAIRCHILD, PLATT, WHEELER, LANE AND AVERY PEDIGREES...by Samuel Putnam Avery. Repr. of 1925 ed.
Cloth—$44.00—Paper—$34.00—292pp---------------------------- Vendor #D1842

1223 - AXTELL RECORD, DESCENDANTS OF AXTELL, OF MORRIS COUNTY, NEW HAMPSHIRE by E. S. Axtell. Repr. of 1886 ed.
Paper—$14.00—68pp-- Vendor #D1842

1224 - RECORD OF DESCENDANTS OF CAPT. JOHN AYRES OF BROOKFIELD, MASSACHUSETTS by W. H. Whitmore. Repr. of 1870 ed.
Paper—$10.00—55pp-- Vendor #D1842

1225 - GEN. OF THE AYRES FAMILY OF FAIRFIELD COUNTY, CONNECTICUT by J. N. States. Repr. of 1916 ed.
Paper—$25.00—127pp--- Vendor #D1842

1226 - GENEALOGICAL RECORD OF NATHANIEL BABCOCK, SIMEON MAIN, ISAAC MINER, EZEKIEL MAIN by Cyrus H. Brown. Repr. of 1909 ed.
Cloth—$54.00—Paper—$44.00—362pp---------------------------- Vendor #D1842

1227 BABCOCK AND ALLIED FAMILIES by Louis Effingham de Forest. Repr. of 1928 ed.
Paper—$20.50—137pp--- Vendor #D1842

1228 - GEN. NOTES ON BACK & WALLIS FAMILIES by H. E. Back. Repr. of 1911 ed.
Paper—$3.75—12pp--- Vendor #D1842

1229 - GEN. MEMOIR OF THE BACKUS FAMILY...PRIVATE JOURNAL OF JAMES BACKUS....by William Backus. 1889.
Cloth—$58.00—Paper—$48.00—392pp---------------------------- Vendor #D1842

1230 - BACON GENEALOGY. MICHAEL BACON OF DEDHAM, 1640, AND HIS DESCENDANTS by Thomas W. Baldwin. Repr. of 1915 ed.
Cloth—$44.00—Paper—$34.00—422pp---------------------------- Vendor #D1842

1231   - THE FAMILY OF BADCOCK OF MASSACHUSETTS by W. S. Appleton.
        Repr. of 1881 ed.
        Paper—$3.50—11pp--- Vendor #D1842

1232   - GILES BADGER AND HIS DESCENDANTS by J. C. Badger. Repr. of
        1909 ed.
        Paper—$12.50—64pp-- Vendor #D1842

1233   - RECORDS OF THE BAILEY FAMILY, DESCENDANTS OF WILLIAM
        BAILEY OF NEWPORT, RHODE ISLAND....by Hannah C. Hopkins.
        Repr. of 1895 ed.
        Paper—$31.00—207pp-------------------------------------- Vendor #D1842

1234   - ANCESTRY OF JOSEPH TROWBRIDGE BAILEY OF PHILADELPHIA
        AND CATHERINE GODDARD WEAVER....by Joseph Trowbridge
        Bailey. Repr. of 1892 ed.
        Paper—$10.00—54pp--------------------------------------- Vendor #D1842

1235   - GEN. OF THE DESCENDANTS OF EDWARD BAKER OF LYNN, MASSA-
        CHUSETTS, 1630 by Nelson M. Baker. Repr. of 1867 ed.
        Paper—$13.00—99pp--------------------------------------- Vendor #D1842

1236   - SHORT NOTES ON THE BAKER FAMILY by C. C. Baker. Repr. of
        1896 ed.
        Paper—$4.00—$12pp--------------------------------------- Vendor #D1842

1237   - ANCESTRY OF PRISCILLA BAKER, WIFE OF ISAAC APPLETON OF
        IPSWICH by William S. Appleton. Repr. of 1870 ed.
        Paper—$21.50—143pp------------------------------------- Vendor #D1842

1238   - GENEALOGY OF THE FAMILY OF DEACON SMITH BAKER OF LITCH-
        FIELD, MAINE, 1874 by Smith Baker. Repr. of 1874 ed.
        Paper—$4.50—18pp-- Vendor #D1842

1239   - GENEALOGY OF THE BALCH FAMILIES IN AMERICA by Galusha B.
        Balch. Repr. of 1897 ed.
        Cloth—$87.00—Paper—$77.00—585pp----------------------- Vendor #D1842

1240   - BALCH GENEALOGICA by Thomas Willing Balch. Repr. of 1907 ed.
        Cloth—$63.00—Paper—$53.00—420pp----------------------- Vendor #D1842

1241   - GENEALOGY OF THE BALKCOM (BALCOM) FAMILY OF ATTLEBORO,
        MASSACHUSETTS by D. Jillison. Repr.
        Paper—$4.00—16pp-- Vendor #D1842

1242   - THE BALDWIN GENEALOGY, 1500-1881 by Charles C. Baldwin. 1881.
        Cloth—$146.00—Paper—136.00—974pp---------------------- Vendor #D1842

1243   - THE BAALDWIN GENEALOGY, SUPPLEMENT by Charles C. Baldwin.
        Repr. of 1889 ed.
        Cloth—$60.00—Paper—$50.00—498pp----------------------- Vendor #D1842

1244   - GENEALOGY OF THE FAMILIES OF PETER & JOSIAH BALL by J. G.
        Ball. Repr. of 1894 ed.
        Paper—$3.00—8pp--- Vendor #D1842

1245   - BALL FAMILY RECORDS,...BALL FAMILIES OF GREAT BRITAIN,
        IRELAND, & AMERICA by Rev. William B. Wright. Repr. of 1908 ed.
        Cloth—$42.00—Paper—$32.00—284pp----------------------- Vendor #D1842

1246   - HISTORY OF THE BALL FAMILY...NEW HAVEN BRANCH: ALLEN
        BALL...DESCENDANTS, 1638-1864 by Leonard Abram Bradley.
        Repr. of 1916 ed.
        Paper—$10.00—59pp--------------------------------------- Vendor #D1842

1247   - BALLARD GENEALOGY, WILLIAM BALLARD (1603-1639) OF LYNN,
        MASSACHUSETTS...DESCENDANTS by Charles F. Farlow; edited by
        Charles H. Pope. Repr. of 1911 ed.
        Paper—$30.00—203pp-------------------------------------- Vendor #D1842

1248   - AN ELABORATE HISTORY AND GENEALOGY OF THE BALLOUS IN
        AMERICA by Adin Ballou. Repr. of 1888 ed.
        Cloth—$200.00—Paper—$180.00—1338pp-------------------- Vendor #D1842

1249   - HISTORY AND GENEALOGY OF THE BANGS FAMILY IN AMERICA
       ...PLYMOUTH AND EASTHAM by Dean Dudley. Repr. of 1896 ed.
       Cloth—$54.00—Paper—$44.00-------------------------------- Vendor #D1842

1250   - PARTIAL HISTORY AND GENEALOGICAL RECORD OF BANKER OR
       BANKOR FAMILIES.... Repr. of 1909 ed.
       Cloth—$68.00—$58.00—458pp------------------------------- Vendor #D1842

1251   - GENEALOGICAL AND BIOGRAPHICAL RECORDS OF BANNING AND
       ALLIED FAMILIES by the American Historical Society. Repr. of 1924 ed.
       Paper—$24.00—161pp------------------------------------- Vendor #D1842

1252   - A FRISIAN FAMILY, BANTA GENEALOGICAL DESCENDANTS OF
       EPKE JACOBSE...NEW AMSTERDAM....by Theodore M. Banta.
       Repr. of 1893 ed.
       Cloth—$64.00—Paper—$54.00—427pp------------------------ Vendor #D1842

1253   - GENEALOGY OF BARBER FAMILY. DESCENDANTS OF ROBERT
       BARBER OF...PENNSYLVANIA by Edwin A. Barber. Repr. of
       1890 ed.
       Paper—$25.00—166pp------------------------------------- Vendor #D1842

1254   - RECORD OF ANCESTRY AND DESCENDANTS OF EDWARD BARBER
       OF HOPKINTON, RHODE ISLAND by D. W. Matteson. Repr. of 1892 ed.
       Paper—$16.00—80pp-------------------------------------- Vendor #D1842

1255   - BARBER GENEALOGY. SECTION 1. DESCENDANTS OF THOMAS
       BARBER OF WINDSOR, CONNECTICUT....,2 Sections by John Barber
       White; edited by Lillian May Wilson. Repr. of 1909 ed.
       Cloth—$124.00—Paper—$114.00—826pp--------------------- Vendor #D1842

1256   - BARCLAYS OF NEW YORK: WHO THEY ARE AND WHO THEY ARE
       NOT....by R. Burnham Moffat. Repr. of 1904 ed.
       Cloth—$72.00—Paper—$62.00—481pp----------------------- Vendor #D1842

1257   - BARCROFT FAMILY RECORDS...DESCENDANTS OF AMBROSE
       BARCROFT, EMIGRANT OF SOLEBURY, PENNSYLVANIA by Emma T.
       Runk. Repr. of 1910 ed.
       Cloth—$50.00—Paper—$40.00—334pp----------------------- Vendor #D1842

1258   - THE BARGER JOURNAL, BARGERS AND ALLIED KINDRED by A. L.
       Barger. Repr. of 1924 ed.
       Paper—$29.00—144pp------------------------------------- Vendor #D1842

1259   - ...ANCESTRY AND DESCENDANTS OF JONATHAN BARLOW AND
       PLAIN ROGERS...NEW YORK by George Barlow. Repr. of 1891 ed.
       Cloth—$76.00—Paper—$66.00—508pp----------------------- Vendor #D1842

1260   - BARNES GENEALOGY...ANCESTRY, GENEALOGY, AND FAMILY
       RECORDS...OF BARNES PEOPLE by Rev. George N. Barnes. Repr.
       of 1903 ed.
       Paper—$34.00—226pp------------------------------------- Vendor #D1842

1261   - BARNES FAMILY OF EASTHAMPTON, LONG ISLAND, NEW YORK
       by R. Wynkoop. Repr. of 1906 ed.
       Paper—$6.00—25pp--------------------------------------- Vendor #D1842

1262   - HISTORY OF BARR FAMILY, BEGINNING WITH...ROBERT BARR
       AND MARY WILLS....by Rev. William B. Barr. Repr. of 1901 ed.
       Paper—$32.00—216pp------------------------------------- Vendor #D1842

1263   - THOMAS BARRETT OF BRAINTREE, WILLIAM BARRETT OF CAM-
       BRIDGE AND THEIR EARLY DESCENDANTS by J. H. Barrett.
       Repr. of 1888 ed.
       Paper—$3.00—8pp-- Vendor #D1842

1264   - NAME AND FAMILY OF BARROW WITH LINE OF DESCENDANTS by
       A. S. Johnson. Repr. of 1941 ed.
       Paper—$25.00—115pp------------------------------------- Vendor #D1842

1265   - RECORD OF BARTHOLOMEW FAMILY, HISTORY, GENEALOGY,
       AND BIOGRAPHY by George W. Bartholomew, Sr. Repr. of 1885 ed.
       Cloth—$115.00—Paper—$105.00—769pp--------------------- Vendor #D1842

1266 - THE BARTLETTS...AMERICAN PROGENITORS OF BARTLETT FAMILY
      ...DESCENDANTS OF JOHN BARTLETT....by Thomas E. Bartlett.
      Repr. of 1892 ed.
      Paper—$17.00—112pp--- Vendor #D1842

1267 - GENEALOGICAL AND BIOGRAPHICAL SKETCHES...BARTLETT
      FAMILY IN ENGLAND AND AMERICA by Levi Bartlett. Repr. of
      1876 ed.
      Paper—$17.00—114pp--- Vendor #D1842

1268 - DESCENDANTS OF SAMUEL COLCORD BARTLETT AND ELEANOR
      PETTENGILL...SALISBURY, NEW HAMPSHIRE....by Edwin J.
      Bartlett. Repr. of 1909 ed.
      Paper—$4.00—11pp--- Vendor #D1842

1269 - LIEUTENANT WILLIAM BARTON OF MORRIS COUNTY, NEW JERSEY
      AND HIS DESCENDANTS by William Eleazar Barton. Repr. of 1900 ed.
      Paper—$22.00—148pp--- Vendor #D1842

1270 - BARTOW GENEALOGY: PARTS 1 AND 2 AND SUPPLEMENT by E. B.
      (i.e., Evelyn Bartow). Repr. of 1878-9 ed.
      Cloth—$48.00—Paper—$38.00—318pp------------------------------ Vendor #D1842

1271 - GENEALOGICAL RECORD OF THOS. BASCOM AND HIS DESCENDANTS
      by E. Harris. Repr. of 1870 ed.
      Paper—$16.00—79pp-- Vendor #D1842

1272 - ANCESTORS OF MOSES BELCHER BASS, 1735-1817:...TWO WIVES
      ELIZABETH WIMBLE AND MARGARET SPRAGUE by Susan A. Smith.
      Repr. of 1896 ed.
      Paper—$4.00—14pp--- Vendor #D1842

1273 - BATCHELDER, BATCHELLER, DESCENDANTS OF REV. STEPHEN
      BACHILAR OF ENGLAND...NEW HAMPTON, NEW HAMPSHIRE....by
      Frederick C. Pierce. Repr. of 1898 ed.
      Cloth—$93.50—Paper—$83.50—623pp------------------------------ Vendor #D1842

1274 - ANCESTRY AND DESCENDANTS OF DEACON DAVID BATCHELDER
      OF HAMPTON FALLS, NEW HAMPSHIRE by Mary J. Greene. Repr. of
      1902 ed.
      Paper—$12.50—80pp-- Vendor #D1842

1275 - GENEALOGY OF DESCENDANTS OF EDWARD BATES OF WEYMOUTH,
      MASSACHUSETTS by Samuel A. Bates; edited by Frank A. Bates.
      Repr. of 1900 ed.
      Paper—$22.00—145pp--- Vendor #D1842

1276 - BATES AND FLETCHER GENEALOGICAL REGISTER by Theodore C.
      Bates. Repr. of 1892 ed.
      Paper—$12.50—60pp-- Vendor #D1842

1277 - BATES, BEARS, AND BUNKER HILL by Edward Deacon. Repr. of
      1911 ed.
      Paper—$15.00—90pp-- Vendor #D1842

1278 - ENGLISH ANCESTRY OF THE FAMILIES OF BATT AND BILEY by
      J. Henry Lea. Repr. N. E. Hist. & Gen. Register, 1897 ed.
      Paper—$5.00—26pp--- Vendor #D1842

1279 - BATTELLE GENEALOGICAL RECORD by L. Battelle. Repr. of
      1889 ed.
      Paper—$5.00—21pp--- Vendor #D1842

1280 - DESCENDANTS OF THOMAS BEACH OF MILFORD, CONNECTICUT
      by Mary E. Beach. Repr. of 1912 ed.
      Paper—$10.00—51pp-- Vendor #D1842

1281 - JOHN BEAL OF HINGHAM, AND ONE LINE OF HIS DESCENDANTS
      by N. B. S., i.e., Nathaniel Bradstreet Shurtleff. Repr. of 1865 ed.
      Paper—$4.00—8pp-- Vendor #D1842

1282 - JOSHUA BEAN OF EXETER, BRENTWOOD AND GILMANTON, NEW
      HAMPSHIRE AND...DESCENDANTS by Josiah H. Drummond. Repr.
      of 1903 ed.
      Paper—$17.00—116pp--- Vendor #D1842

1283   - A GENEALOGY OF THE BEAR FAMILY AND BIOGRAPHICAL...
      DESCENDANTS OF JACOB BEAR by Walter S. Bear. Repr. of 1906 ed.
      Paper—$32.00—216pp------------------------------------- Vendor #D1842

1284   - GENEALOGY OF DESCENDANTS OF WIDOW MARTHA BEARD OF
      MILFORD, CONNECTICUT by R. Beard. Repr. of 1915 ed.
      Paper—$15.00—99pp-------------------------------------- Vendor #D1842

1285   - WILLIAM BEARDSLEY OF STRATFORD, CONNECTICUT AND
      DESCENDANTS by H. F. Johnston. Repr. typescript.
      Paper—$20.00—108pp------------------------------------ Vendor #D1842

1286   - GENEALOGY OF BEARSE OR BEARSS FAMILY IN AMERICA 1618-
      1871 by J. B. Newcomb. Repr. of 1871 ed.
      Paper—$4.00—16pp-------------------------------------- Vendor #D1842

1287   - GENEALOGICAL RECORD OF FAMILIES OF BEATTY, EGLE, MULLER,
      MARRAY, OUTH AND THOMAS by William H. Egle. Repr. of 1886 ed.
      Paper—$19.00—129pp----------------------------------- Vendor #D1842

1288   - KARL BECHTEL OF HANAU, GERMANY AND SOME OF HIS DESCEND-
      ANTS by J. W. Hook. Repr. of 1936 ed.
      Paper—$7.50—30pp-------------------------------------- Vendor #D1842

1289   - HISTORY OF THE BECK FAMILY TOGETHER WITH...ALLEYNES
      AND CHASES....by Charlotte R. Conover. Repr. of 1907 ed.
      Paper—$39.00—259pp----------------------------------- Vendor #D1842

1290   - GENEALOGY OF BECKHAM FAMILY IN VIRGINIA, KENTUCKY,
      TENNESSEE, PENNSYLVANIA, WEST VIRGINIA by J. M. Beckham.
      Repr. of 1910 ed.
      Paper—$20.00—98pp------------------------------------- Vendor #D1842

1291   - "THE BECKWITHS" by Paul Beckwith. Repr. of 1891 ed.
      Cloth—$57.50—Paper—$47.50—384pp----------------------- Vendor #D1842

1292   - DESCENDANTS OF JOHN BEDELL OF PASSAIC VALLEY, NEW JERSEY
      by E. Bedell. Repr. of 1885 ed.
      Paper—$6.00—29pp-------------------------------------- Vendor #D1842

1293   - MONOGRAPH OF DESCENDANTS OF FAMILY OF BEEBE by C. Beebe.
      Repr. of 1904 ed.
      Paper—$25.00—127pp----------------------------------- Vendor #D1842

1294   - ADDITIONAL MISCELLANEOUS BEEBE DATA (SAME FAMILY) by
      F. S. Whelan. Repr. of 1949 ed.
      Paper—$3.50—11pp-------------------------------------- Vendor #D1842

1295   - BOOK OF BEGGS, GENEALOGICAL STUDY OF BEGGS FAMILY IN
      AMERICA by R. & C. Beggs. Repr. of 1928 ed.
      Paper—$27.50—135pp----------------------------------- Vendor #D1842

1296   - GENEALOGICAL RECORD OF DESCENDANTS OF JACOB BEIDLER...
      BUCKS COUNTY, PENNSYLVANIA by Rev. A. J. Fretz. Repr. of
      1903 ed.
      Cloth—$84.50—Paper—$74.50—565pp----------------------- Vendor #D1842

1297   - RECORD OF THE DESCENDANTS OF ANDREW BELCHER by W. H.
      Whitemore. Repr. N.E. Hist. & Gen. Register, 1873 ed.
      Paper—$4.00—8pp--------------------------------------- Vendor #D1842

1298   - CONCERNING SOME ANCESTORS AND DESCENDANTS OF ROYAL
      DENISON BELDEN AND OLIVE CADWELL BELDEN by Jessie Perry
      Van Zile Belden. Repr. of 1898 ed.
      Paper—$37.00—248pp----------------------------------- Vendor #D1842

1299   - ENGLISH ANCESTRY OF ABRAHAM BELKNAP, WHO SETTLED IN
      LYNN, MASSACHUSETTS, 1635 by Henry Wyckoff Belknap. Repr.
      N. E. Hist. & Gen. Register, 1914 ed.
      Paper—$5.00—20pp-------------------------------------- Vendor #D1842

1300   - BELL FAMILY IN AMERICA by W. Clemens. Repr. of 1913 ed.
      Paper—$7.50—45pp-------------------------------------- Vendor #D1842

1301 - BELLS IN THE REVOLUTION by W. M. Clemens. Repr. of 1916 ed.
Paper—$4.00—16pp--- Vendor #D1842

1302 - JOHN BELL OF LONDONDERRY, NEW HAMPSHIRE AND HIS SCOTTISH
ANCESTORS by L. Bell. Repr. of 1920 ed.
Paper—$4.50—19pp--- Vendor #D1842

1303 - FOUNDERS OF THE BELL FAMILY IN PENNSYLVANIA by R. M. Bell.
Repr. of 1929 ed.
Paper—$4.00—18pp--- Vendor #D1842

1304 - PARENTAGE OF EZRA BELLOWS OF MASSACHUSETTS AND VERMONT
by T. B. Peck. Repr. of 1902 ed.
Paper—$3.00— 9pp--- Vendor #D1842

1305 - BELLOWS GENEALOGY: OR, JOHN BELLOS...1635 AND HIS DESCEND-
ANTS by Thomas Bellows Peck. Repr. of 1898 ed.
Cloth—$100.00—Paper—$90.00—673pp---------------------- Vendor #D1842

1306 - BEMIS FAMILY IN MAINE by C. N. Sinnett. Repr. of 1922 ed.
Paper—$4.00—6pp-- Vendor #D1842

1307 - BEMIS HISTORY AND GENEALOGY,...DESCENDANTS OF JOSEPH
BEMIS OF WATERTOWN, MASSACHUSETTS by Thomas Wain-Morgan
Draper. Repr. of 1900 ed.
Cloth—$44.00—Paper—$34.00—395pp---------------------- Vendor #D1842

1308 - GENEALOGY OF THE BENJAMIN FAMILY IN USA 1632-1898 by E. B.
Baker. Repr. of 1898 ed.
Paper—$17.50—88pp--------------------------------------- Vendor #D1842

1309 - THE BENNET FAMILY OF IPSWICH, MASSACHUSETTS by John M.
Bradbury. Repr. N. E. Hist. & Gen. Register, 1875 ed.
Paper—$4.00—8pp--- Vendor #D1842

1310 - ORIGIN AND HISTORY OF THE NAME BENNETT, WITH BIOGRAPHIES
...NOTED PERSONS OF THE NAME. Repr. of 1905 ed.
Paper—$20.00—112pp-------------------------------------- Vendor #D1842

1311 - THE BENNETT FAMILY, 1628-1910 by Edgar B. Bennett. Repr. of
1910 ed.
Paper—$10.00—50pp--------------------------------------- Vendor #D1842

1312 - BENNETT AND ALLIED FAMILIES. ADDENDA TO BULLARD
AND ALLIED FAMILIES by Edgar J. Bullard. Repr. of 1931 ed.
Paper—$10.00—43pp--------------------------------------- Vendor #D1842

1313 - JACOB BENSON, PIONEER AND HIS DESCENDANTS IN DOVER
AND AMENIA, NEW YORK by A. T. Benson. Repr. of 1915 ed.
Paper—$26.00—130pp-------------------------------------- Vendor #D1842

1314 - THE BENSON FAMILY RECORDS by Fred H. Benson. Repr. of
1920 ed.
Paper—$31.00—207pp-------------------------------------- Vendor #D1842

1315 - BENT FAMILY IN AMERICA,...DESCENDANTS OF JOHN BENT...
SUDBURY, MASSACHUSETTS IN 1638 by Allen H. Bent. Repr. of
1900 ed.
Cloth—$47.00—Paper—$37.00—313pp---------------------- Vendor #D1842

1316 - BENTLEY FAMILY, GENEALOGICAL RECORD OF OHIO BENTLEYS
by C. R. Brinkerhoff. Repr. of 1897 ed.
Paper—$4.25—20pp-- Vendor #D1842

1317 - BENTLEY GLEANINGS, BY JULIA HARRISON LOBDELL: FAMILY OF
JOHN WITHERSTINE by William Witherstine. Repr. of 1905 ed.
Paper—$19.00—128pp-------------------------------------- Vendor #D1842

1318 - SAMUEL BLADE BENTON, HIS ANCESTORS AND DESCENDANTS,
1620-1901 by Josiah Henry Benton, Jr. Repr. of 1901 ed.
Cloth—$55.00—Paper—$45.00—366pp---------------------- Vendor #D1842

1319 - BERGEN FAMILY: OR, THE DESCENDANTS OF HANS HANSEN
BERGEN OF NEW YORK AND BROOKLYN....by Teunis G. Bergen.
Repr. of 1876 ed.
Cloth—$98.00—Paper—$88.00—658pp----------------------- Vendor #D1842

1320 - HISTORY OF PETER AND MARY BEST AND FAMILY by N. R. Best.
Repr. of 1897 ed.
Paper—$3.75—15pp--- Vendor #D1842

1321 - THOMAS BETTS AND HIS DESCENDANTS by C. W. and F. H. Betts.
Repr. of 1888 ed.
Paper—$27.50—136pp-------------------------------------- Vendor #D1842

1322 - HISTORY AND GENEALOGY OF THE BICKNELL FAMILY...OF
NORMANDY, GREAT BRITAIN AND AMERICA by Thomas Williams
Bicknell. Repr. of 1913 ed.
Cloth—$93.00—Paper—$83.00—620pp----------------------- Vendor #D1842

1323 - A SKETCH OF OWEN BIDDLE...ACCOUNT OF THE PARKE FAMILY,
...HIS DESCENDANTS by Henry D. Biddle. Repr. of 1892 ed.
Paper—$17.50—87pp--------------------------------------- Vendor #D1842

1324 - GENEALOGY TO THE SEVENTH GENERATION OF BIDWELL FAMILIES
IN AMERICA by E. M. Bidwell. Repr. of 1884 ed.
Paper—$25.00—123pp-------------------------------------- Vendor #D1842

1325 - GENEALOGY OF SOME DESCENDANTS OF WILLIAM BILLING(S) OF
STONINGTON, CONNECTICUT by F. Billings. Repr., n.d.
Paper—$10.00—49pp--------------------------------------- Vendor #D1842

1326 - GENEALOGY OF BINGHAM FAMILY IN THE UNITED STATES,
ESPECIALLY OF CONNECTICUT by Theodore A. Bingham. Repr.
of 1898 ed.
Cloth—$43.00—Paper—$33.00—288pp----------------------- Vendor #D1842

1327 - GENEALOGICAL SKETCH OF BIRD FAMILY OF HARTFORD by I.
Bird. Repr. of 1855 ed.
Paper—$6.00—24pp-- Vendor #D1842

1328 - FAMILY RECORDS OF SOME DESCENDANTS OF THOMAS BESBEDGE
(BISBEE) OF SCITUATE, MASSACHUSETTS, 1634 by William B. Lap-
ham. Repr. of 1876 ed.
Paper—$10.00—48pp--------------------------------------- Vendor #D1842

1329 - BLACK FAMILY MARRIAGES by W. M. Clemens. Repr. of 1916 ed.
Paper—$6.50—32pp-- Vendor #D1842

1330 - BLACKSTONE FAMILY:...BIOGRAPHICAL AND GENEALOGICAL OF
WILLIAM BLACKSTONE AND HIS DESCENDANTS by Lucius Manlius
Sargent. Repr. of 1857 ed.
Paper—$10.00—43pp--------------------------------------- Vendor #D1842

1331 - BLAIR FAMILY OF NEW ENGLAND by E. W. Leavitt. Repr. of 1900 ed.
Cloth—$40.00—Paper—$30.00—197pp----------------------- Vendor #D1842

1332 - BLAKE FAMILY. A GENEALOGICAL HISTORY OF WILLIAM BLAKE OF
DORCHESTER....by Samuel Blake. Repr. of 1857 ed.
Paper—$21.00—140pp-------------------------------------- Vendor #D1842

1333 - INCREASE BLAKE OF BOSTON, ANCESTORS AND DESCENDANTS;
WILLIAM BLAKE OF DORCHESTER....by Francis E. Blake. Repr. of
1898 ed.
Paper—$22.00—147pp-------------------------------------- Vendor #D1842

1334 - ANCESTRY AND ALLIED FAMILIES OF NATHAN BLAKE, 3RD, AND
SUSAN (TORREY) BLAKE OF EAST CORINTH, VERMONT by Almira
Torrey Blake Fenno-Gendrot. Repr. of 1916 ed.
Paper—$32.00—212pp-------------------------------------- Vendor #D1842

1335 - BLAKENEYS IN AMERICA, WITH REFERENCE TO ENGLISH-IRISH
FAMILY by J. O. Blakeney. Repr. of 1928 ed.
Paper—$20.00—103pp-------------------------------------- Vendor #D1842

1336 - SAMUEL BLAKESLEY OF NEW HAVEN, CONNECTICUT, AND HIS
DESCENDANTS by James Shepard. Repr. N. E. Hist. & Gen. Register,
1902 ed.
Paper—$4.00—15pp-- Vendor #D1842

1337 - GENEALOGY OF THE BLETHEN FAMILY by A. J. Blethen. Repr. of
1911 ed.
Paper—$20.00—108pp-- Vendor #D1842

1338 - BLOSS GENEALOGY by J. C. Bloss. Repr. of 1887 ed.
Paper—$4.00—19pp-- Vendor #D1842

1339 - BLOUNT AND BLUNT FAMILY RECORDS by J. H. Wheeler, chart.
Repr. of 1884 ed.
Paper—$4.00—10pp-- Vendor #D1842

1340 - BOARDMAN GENEALOGY, 1525-1895 by Charlotte Goldthwaite. Repr.
of 1895 ed.
Cloth—$118.50—Paper—108.50—791pp---------------------- Vendor #D1842

1341 - THE BOARDMAN FAMILY IN TOPSFIELD, MASSACHUSETTS by Miss
H. Rosa Towne. Repr. Topsfield Hist. Coll., 1902 ed.
Paper—$6.00—29pp-- Vendor #D1842

1342 - ANCESTRY OF WILLIAM FRANCIS JOSEPH BOARDMAN, HARTFORD,
CONNECTICUT by William F. J. Boardman. Repr. of 1906 ed.
Cloth—$63.00—Paper—$53.00—419pp---------------------- Vendor #D1842

1343 - GENEALOGY OF THE BOLLES FAMILY IN AMERICA by John A.
Bolles. Repr. of 1865 ed.
Paper—$14.00—71pp-- Vendor #D1842

1344 - FAMILY RECORDS OF PETER BOLTON by T. L. Boston. Repr. of
1923 ed.
Paper—$6.00—28pp-- Vendor #D1842

1345 - BOLTONS OF OLD AND NEW ENGLAND, WITH...DESCENDANTS OF
WILLIAM BOLTON OF READING, MASSACHUSETTS, 1720 by Charles
Knowles Bolton. Repr. of 1889 ed.
Paper—$17.50—98pp-- Vendor #D1842

1346 - FAMILY OF BOLTON IN ENGLAND AND AMERICA, 1100-1894....
by Henry Carrington Bolton and Reginald Pelham Bolton. Repr. of
1895 ed.
Cloth—$81.00—Paper—$17.00—540pp---------------------- Vendor #D1842

1347 - AUTOBIOGRAPHICAL REMINISCENCES OF REV. ALVAN BOND, D.D.,
1793-1882...AND SARAH RICHARDSON....by Henry R. Bond. Repr.
of 1896 ed.
Paper—$32.00—214pp-- Vendor #D1842

1348 - ANCESTRY OF DANIEL BONTECOU OF SPRINGFIELD, MASSA-
CHUSETTS by J. E. Morris. Repr. of 1887 ed.
Paper—$6.00—29pp-- Vendor #D1842

1349 - ANNALS OF THE BOODEYS IN NEW ENGLAND, WITH LESSONS FROM
JOHN ELIOT by Robert Boodey Caverly. Repr. of 1880 ed.
Cloth—$44.50—Paper—$34.50—297pp---------------------- Vendor #D1842

1350 - BOONE, MAYFIELD, SHORT AND TATE FAMILY HISTORY (VIRGINIA)
by R. N. Mayfield. Repr. of 1902 ed.
Paper—$4.00—6pp-- Vendor #D1842

1351 - GENEALOGY OF THE BOOTH FAMILY IN ENGLAND AND UNITED
STATES by W. S. Booth. Repr. of 1892 ed.
Paper—$5.00—25pp-- Vendor #D1842

1352 - HISTORY OF BORNEMAN FAMILY IN AMERICA SINCE FIRST SETTLERS
1721-1878 by J. H. Borneman. Repr. of 1881 ed.
Paper—$22.50—114pp-- Vendor #D1842

1353 - GENEALOGICAL REGISTER OF THE NAME OF BOSTWICK 1668-1850
by E. Bostwick. Repr. of 1851 ed.
Paper—$10.00—50pp-- Vendor #D1842

1354 - SOME ACCOUNT OF THE BOWDOIN FAMILY, WITH...FAMILIES OF
       PORDAGE, LYNDE, NEWGATE, ERVING, 2ND EDITION by Temple
       Prime. Repr. of 1894 ed.
       Paper—$10.00—52pp-------------------------------------- Vendor #D1842

1355 - SOME ACCOUNT OF THE BOWDOIN FAMILY, WITH...THE ERVING
       FAMILY, 3RD EDITION by Temple Prime. Repr. of 1900 ed.
       Paper—$4.50—18pp-------------------------------------- Vendor #D1842

1356 - LINEAGE OF THE BOWENS OF WOODSTOCK, CONNECTICUT by
       Edward Augustus Bowen. Repr. of 1897 ed.
       Paper—$37.50—251pp----------------------------------- Vendor #D1842

1357 - RECORD OF DESCENDANTS OF CHARLES BOWLER, ENGLAND—
       1740—AMERICA,...NEWPORT, RHODE ISLAND by N. P. Bowler and
       Cora Bowler Malone. Repr. of 1905 ed.
       Cloth—$44.50—Paper—$34.50—298pp----------------------- Vendor #D1842

1358 - THOMAS BOYDEN AND HIS DESCENDANTS by Wallace C. Boyden,
       Merrill N. Boyden and Amos J. Boyden. Repr. of 1901 ed.
       Cloth—$40.00—Paper—$30.00—267pp----------------------- Vendor #D1842

1359 - AMERICAN BOYNTON DIRECTORY...ALL KNOWN BOYNTONS, BOY-
       INGTONS, AND BYINGTONS IN THE UNITED STATES AND BRITISH
       DOMINIONS by John Farnham Boynton. Repr. of 1884 ed.
       Paper—$22.00—147pp----------------------------------- Vendor #D1842

1360 - BRACE LINEAGE by J. S. Brace. Repr. of 1927 ed.
       Cloth—$40.00—Paper—$30.00—224pp----------------------- Vendor #D1842

1361 - DESCENDANTS OF ANTHONY BRACKETT OF PORTSMOUTH, NEW
       HAMPSHIRE by Alpheus L. Brackett. Repr. of 1897 ed.
       Paper—$4.00—8pp-------------------------------------- Vendor #D1842

1362 - BRACKETT GENEALOGY. DESCENDANTS OF ANTHONY BRACKETT
       OF PORTSMOUTH, AND CAPTAIN RICHARD BRACKETT....by Herbert
       I. Brackett. Repr. of 1907 ed.
       Cloth—$93.50—Paper—$83.50—624pp----------------------- Vendor #D1842

1363 - ONE BRANCH OF THE BRADFORD FAMILY, OR, DESCENDANTS OF
       CAPT. GAMALIEL BRADFORD by Horace Standish Bradford. Repr.
       of 1898 ed.
       Paper—$6.00—27pp-------------------------------------- Vendor #D1842

1364 - GOVERNOR WILLIAM BRADFORD AND HIS SON MAJOR WILLIAM
       BRADFORD by James Shepard. Repr. of 1900 ed.
       Paper—$15.00—103pp----------------------------------- Vendor #D1842

1365 - HISTORY OF THE BRADLEE FAMILY...DESCENDANTS OF NATHAN
       BRADLEY OF DORCHESTER, MASSACHUSETTS by Samuel Bradlee
       Doggett. Repr. of 1878 ed.
       Paper—$9.00—45pp-------------------------------------- Vendor #D1842

1366 - GENEALOGY. FAMILY OF AARON AND SARAH BRADLEY OF GUIL-
       FORD, CONNECTICUT by A. P. Lloyd. Repr. of 1879 ed.
       Paper—$9.00—46pp-------------------------------------- Vendor #D1842

1367 - FAMILY NOTES RESPECTING THE BRADLEY FAMILY OF FAIRFIELD
       ...COLLATERAL ANCESTORS....by Joseph P. Bradley, edited by
       Charles Bradley. Repr. of 1894 ed.
       Paper—$12.50—69pp----------------------------------- Vendor #D1842

1368 - DESCENDANTS OF ISAAC BRADLEY OF CONNECTICUT, 1650-1898
       WITH...BRADLEY FAMILIES IN NEW ENGLAND by Leonard Abram
       Bradley. Repr. of 1917 ed.
       Paper—$25.50—171pp----------------------------------- Vendor #D1842

1369 - GENEALOGY OF THE BRAINERD FAMILY IN THE UNITED STATES:
       WITH SKETCHES OF INDIVIDUALS by David D. Field. Repr. of 1857 ed.
       Cloth—$45.50—Paper—$35.50—303pp----------------------- Vendor #D1842

1370 - CASPER BRANNER OF VIRGINIA AND HIS DESCENDANTS by John
       Casper Branner. Repr. of 1913 ed.
       Cloth—$71.50—Paper—$61.50—477pp----------------------- Vendor #D1842

1371 - BRECKS OF SHERBORN AND GARDNER, MASSACHUSETTS by A. H.
Bent. Repr. of 1902 ed.
Paper—$7.50—16pp-- Vendor #D1842

1372 - GENEALOGY OF BRECK FAMILY, DESCENDED FROM EDWARD OF
DORCHESTER...AMERICA by Samuel Breck. Repr. of 1889 ed.
Cloth—$42.00—Paper—$32.00—281pp----------------------- Vendor #D1842

1373 - PERSONAL REMINISCENCES, WITH A GENEALOGICAL SKETCH OF
THE AMERICAN BRANCH OF THE BREESE FAMILY by J. E. Montgomery.
Repr. of 1884 ed.
Paper—$15.00—73pp-- Vendor #D1842

1374 - BREESE FAMILY OF ENGLAND AND AMERICA, 1709-1875 by E. E.
Salisbury. Repr. of 1885 ed.
Paper—$12.00—61pp-- Vendor #D1842

1375 - GENEALOGY OF LUDWIG BRETZ FAMILY, 1750-1890 by E. Parthemore. Repr. of 1890 ed.
Paper—$30.00—149pp--------------------------------------- Vendor #D1842

1376 - AN ACCOUNT OF THE DESCENDANTS OF JOHN BRIDGE, CAMBRIDGE,
1632 by William Frederick Bridge. Repr. of 1884 ed.
Paper—$18.00—122pp--------------------------------------- Vendor #D1842

1377 - GENEALOGY OF BRIDGMAN FAMILY, DESCENDANTS OF JAMES
BRIDGMAN, 1636-1894 by Burt Nichols Bridgman and J. C. Bridgman.
Repr. of 1894 ed.
Paper—$25.00—168pp--------------------------------------- Vendor #D1842

1378 - THE BRIGHTS OF SUFFOLK, ENGLAND, (AND) DESCENDANTS OF
HENRY BRIGHT, JR....WATERTOWN, MASSACHUSETTS by J. B.
Bright. Repr. of 1858 ed.
Cloth—$54.50—Paper—$44.50—365pp----------------------- Vendor #D1842

1379 - DESCENDANTS OF JOHN BROCKETT OF NEW HAVEN COLONY by
Edward J. Brockett, assisted by John B. Koetteritz and Francis E.
Brockett. Repr. of 1905 ed.
Cloth—$40.00—Paper—$30.00—266pp----------------------- Vendor #D1842

1380 - GENEALOGY OF BRANCH OF DESCENDANTS OF WOLSTON BROCK-
WAY, WHO SETTLED IN LYME, CONNECTICUT, 1660 by B. Brockway.
Repr. of 1887 ed.
Paper—$5.00—22pp--- Vendor #D1842

1381 - BROCKWAY FAMILY, DESCENDANTS OF WOLSTON BROCKWAY by
D. W. Patterson. Repr. of 1890 ed.
Paper—$34.00—167pp--------------------------------------- Vendor #D1842

1382 - THE BROMFIELDS by Daniel Denison Slade. Repr. N. E. Hist. &
Gen. Register, 1872 ed.
Paper—$5.00—19pp--- Vendor #D1842

1383 - BROMLEY GENEALOGY,...DESCENDANTS OF LUKE BROMLEY OF
WARWICK, RHODE ISLAND, AND STONINGTON, CONNECTICUT by
Viola A. Bromley. Repr. of 1911 ed.
Cloth—$67.50—Paper—$57.50—362pp----------------------- Vendor #D1842

1384 - BROOKE FAMILY OF WHITCHURCH, HAMPSHIRE, ENGLAND;...
ROBERT BROOKE OF MARYLAND AND COL. NINIAN BEALL....by
Thomas Willing Balch. Repr. of 1899 ed.
Paper—$12.50—69pp--------------------------------------- Vendor #D1842

1385 - TIMOTHY BROOKS OF MASSACHUSETTS AND HIS DESCENDANTS
by Robert Peacock Brooks. Repr. of 1927 ed.
Paper—$8.00—40pp--- Vendor #D1842

1386 - GENEALOGICAL RECORD OF DESCENDANTS OF JOHN BROWNELL,
1773-1903 by S. Brownell. Repr. of 1903 ed.
Paper—$11.00—53pp--------------------------------------- Vendor #D1842

1387 - GENEALOGY OF BROWNINGS IN AMERICA FROM 1621 to 1908 by
Edward Franklin Browning. Repr. of 1903 ed.
Cloth—$147.00—Paper—$137.00—982pp-------------------- Vendor #D1842

1388 - BUCHANAN FAMILY RECORDS by W. M. Clemens. Repr. of 1914 ed.
Paper—$4.00—15pp--- Vendor #D1842

1389 - BUCK, HISTORY OF A PART OF THE FAMILY AND NEAR CONNEC-
TIONS, BUCK AND WASHBURN. Repr. of 1906 ed.
Paper—$6.00—20pp--- Vendor #D1842

1390 - BUCKINGHAM FAMILY; OR, DESCENDANTS OF THOMAS BUCKING-
HAM OF MILFORD, CONNECTICUT by F. W. Chapman. Repr. of
1872 ed.
Cloth—$57.50—Paper—$47.50—384pp------------------------ Vendor #D1842

1391 - RECORD OF DESCENDANTS OF JOHN AND ELIZABETH BULL,
EARLY SETTLERS IN PENNSYLVANIA by James H. Bull. Repr. of
1919 ed.
Cloth—$58.00—Paper—$48.00—387pp------------------------ Vendor #D1842

1392 - GENEALOGICAL SKETCH OF DR. ARTEMAS BULLARD OF SUTTON,
MASSACHUSETTS AND HIS DESCENDANTS by W. S. Barton. Repr.
of 1878 ed.
Paper—$5.00—22pp--- Vendor #D1842

1393 - BULLARD AND ALLIED FAMILIES: AMERICAN ANCESTORS OF
GEORGE NEWTON BULLARD AND MARY ELIZABETH BULLARD by
Edgar J. Bullard. Repr. of 1930 ed.
Cloth—$50.50—Paper—$40.50—337pp------------------------ Vendor #D1842

1394 - BULLARD AND ALLIED FAMILIES...SUPPLEMENT: OTHER BULLARDS,
A GENEALOGY. Repr. of 1928 ed.
Paper—$16.00—86pp-- Vendor #D1842

1395 - CONTRIBUTION TO THE GENEALOGY OF BURBANK AND BURBANCK
FAMILIES IN THE UNITED STATES by G. T. Ridlon. Repr. of 1880 ed.
Paper—$5.00—24pp--- Vendor #D1842

1396 - AN ACCOUNT OF JOHN BURBEEN, WHO SETTLED AT WOBURN,
MASSACHUSETTS, ABOUT 1660....by Joseph Burbeen Walker. Repr.
of 1892 ed.
Paper—$10.00—52pp-- Vendor #D1842

1397 - BURGESS GENEALOGY. MEMORIAL OF FAMILY OF THOMAS AND
DOROTHY BURGESS...SANDWICH, PLYMOUTH COLONY, 1637 by E.
Burgess. Repr. of 1865 ed.
Paper—$31.50—212pp--------------------------------------- Vendor #D1842

1398 - BURKE AND ALVORD MEMORIAL...DESCENDANTS OF RICHARD
BURKE OF SUDBURY, MASSACHUSETTS by John Alonzo Boutelle.
Repr. of 1864 ed.
Paper—$35.00—239pp--------------------------------------- Vendor #D1842

1399 - GENEALOGY OF THE BURLEY OR BURLEIGH FAMILY OF AMERICA by
C. Burleigh. Repr. of 1880 ed.
Cloth—$40.00—Paper—$30.00—200pp------------------------ Vendor #D1842

1400 - THE BURNAP—BURNETT GENEALOGY by Henry Wyckoff Belknap.
Repr. of 1925 ed.
Cloth—$52.50—Paper—$42.50—351pp------------------------ Vendor #D1842

1401 - BURNHAM FAMILY; OR GENEALOGICAL RECORDS OF DESCENDANTS
OF THE FOUR EMIGRANTS...IN AMERICA by Roderick H. Burnham.
Repr. of 1869 ed.
Cloth—$81.50—Paper—$71.50—546pp------------------------ Vendor #D1842

1402 - REPORT OF BOARD OF TRUSTEES OF BURNHAM ASSOCIATION OF
AMERICA, INCLUDING REPORT OF EDWARD PAYSON. Repr. of 1873 ed.
Paper—$4.50—16pp--- Vendor #D1842

1403 - GENERAL HISTORY OF THE BURR FAMILY, 1193-1891, 2nd ed., by
Charles Burr Todd. Repr. of 1891 ed.
Cloth—$85.50—Paper—$75.50—572pp------------------------ Vendor #D1842

1404 - BURRAGE MEMORIAL...DESCENDANTS OF JOHN BURRAGE, WHO
SETTLED IN CHARLESTOWN, MASSACHUSETTS, IN 1637 by Alvah A.
Burrage. Repr. of 1877 ed.
Paper—$39.50—265pp--------------------------------------- Vendor #D1842

1405 - BURRILL FAMILY OF LYNN DURING THE COLONIAL AND PROVINCIAL
PERIODS...DESCENDANTS....by Ellen Mudge Burrill. Repr. of 1907 ed.
Paper—$10.00—54pp-- Vendor #D1842

1406 - QUISENBERRY-BURRIS FAMILY OF VIRGINIA by J. H. Ray. Repr.
of 1938 ed. (in Haggard Family)
Paper—$3.50—10pp-- Vendor #D1842

1407 - EARLY DAYS IN NEW ENGLAND. LIFE AND TIMES OF HENRY BURT
...DESCENDANTS by Henry M. Burt and Silas W. Burt. Repr. of 1893 ed.
Cloth—$93.00—Paper—$83.00—620pp------------------------ Vendor #D1842

1408 - GENEALOGY OF DESCENDANTS OF JOHN M. BUSH AND JANE OSTER-
HOUDT OF KINGSTON, ULSTER COUNTY, NEW YORK, 1791-1914 by
B. Bush. Repr. of 1914 ed.
Paper—$12.50—63pp-- Vendor #D1842

1409 - HISTORICAL SKETCH OF NICHOLAS BUSBY THE EMIGRANT by
A. C. Kingsbury. Repr. of 1924 ed.
Paper—$5.00—26pp-- Vendor #D1842

1410 - BOOK OF THE FAMILY AND LINEAL DESCENDANTS OF MEDAD
BUTLER by William Allen Butler. Repr. of 1887 ed.
Paper—$12.50—61pp-- Vendor #D1842

1411 - BUTLER GENEALOGY. DEDICATION OF MONUMENT TO DEACON
JOHN BUTLER, PELHAM, NEW HAMPSHIRE, 1886. Repr. of 1887 ed.
Paper—$8.00—36pp-- Vendor #D1842

1412 - BUTLER FAMILY IN AMERICA by William David Butler, John Cromwell
Butler and Joseph Marion Butler. Repr. of 1909 ed.
Cloth—$44.50—Paper—$34.50—306pp------------------------ Vendor #D1842

1413 - TALES OF OUR KINSFOLK PAST AND PRESENT. STORY OF OUR
BUTLER ANCESTORS...1602 TO 1919 by Henry Langdon Butler. Repr.
of 1919 ed.
Cloth—$82.50—Paper—$72.50—552pp------------------------ Vendor #D1842

1414 - GENEALOGICAL REGISTRY OF BUTTERS FAMILY,...WILLIAM BUTTER
OF WOBURN, MASSACHUSETTS, 1665....by George Butters. Repr. of
1896 ed.
Cloth—$71.00—Paper—$61.00—476pp------------------------ Vendor #D1842

1415 - OUTLINE SKETCH OF EARLIEST DESCENDANTS OF MATTHIAS BUT-
TON...SALEM, MASSACHUSETTS IN 1628 by A. Button. Repr. of
1889 ed.
Paper—$4.00—16pp-- Vendor #D1842

1416 - OUTLINE SKETCH OF EARLIEST DESCENDANTS OF MATTHIAS BUT-
TON...SALEM, MASSACHUSETTS IN 1628, 2nd ed. Repr. of 1903 ed.
(addition to 1st ed., does not duplicate)
Paper—$4.00—18pp-- Vendor #D1842

1417 - JOHN BUTTS, HIS ANCESTORS AND SOME OF HIS DESCENDANTS
by Allison Butts. Repr. of 1898 ed.
Paper—$22.50—153pp-- Vendor #D1842

1418 - ABBY BYRAM AND HER FATHER, THEIR ANCESTORS AND DE-
SCENDANTS by J. M. McElroy. Repr. of 1898 ed.
Paper—$12.50—65pp-- Vendor #D1842

1419 - LIST OF 115 COLONIAL ANCESTORS OF CORNELIUS CADLE OF
MUSCATINE, IOWA by C. F. Cadle. Repr., n.d.
Paper—$3.00—12pp-- Vendor #D1842

1420 - SOME NOTES ON NICHOLAS CADY OF WATERTOWN AND DESCEND-
ANTS edited by H. F. Johnston. Repr., typescript.
Paper—$3.00—4pp-- Vendor #D1842

1421 - HISTORY OF THE CAHOON FAMILY by I. M. Cahoon. Repr., n.d.
Paper—$10.00—47pp-- Vendor #D1842

1422 - JOHN CALDWELL AND SARAH DILLINGHAM CALDWELL...IPSWICH,
MASSACHUSETTS, ...1654-1900 by Augustine Caldwell and Mrs.
Summer Kimball. Repr. of 1904 ed.
Cloth—$48.00—Paper—$38.00—318pp----------------------- Vendor #D1842

1423 - CALDWELL RECORDS. JOHN AND SARAH (DILLINGHAM) CALDWELL,
IPSWICH, MASSACHUSETTS, AND THEIR DESCENDANTS....by Aug-
ustine Caldwell. Repr. of 1873 ed.
Paper—$16.00—82pp------------------------------------- Vendor #D1842

1424 - WILLIAM COALDWELL, CALDWELL OR COLDWELL; AND RECORD OF
HIS DESCENDANTS by Charles T. Caldwell. Repr. of 1910 ed.
Paper—$16.00—82pp------------------------------------- Vendor #D1842

1425 - ROBERT CALEF OF BOSTON AND ROXBURY AND SOME OF HIS
DESCENDANTS by W. W. Lunt. Repr. of 1928 ed.
Paper—$14.00—68pp------------------------------------- Vendor #D1842

1426 - CALHOUN FAMILY OF SOUTH CAROLINA by A. S. Salley. Repr.,n.d.
Paper—$8.50—42pp------------------------------------- Vendor #D1842

1427 - GENEALOGICAL HISTORY OF THE CALL FAMILY IN UNITED STATES
by S. T. Call. Repr. of 1908 ed.
Paper—$11.00—52pp------------------------------------- Vendor #D1842

1428 - AN ACCOUNT OF THE CAVENDISH, CANDISH, OR CANDAGE
FAMILY by R. G. F. Candage. Repr. Bangor, Maine Hist. Mag., 1889 ed.
Paper—$4.00—9pp------------------------------------- Vendor #D1842

1429 - HISTORY OF THOMAS CANFIELD AND MATTHEW CANFIELD...
DESCENDANTS IN NEW JERSEY by Frederick A. Canfield. Repr. of
1897 ed.
Paper—$34.00—228pp------------------------------------- Vendor #D1842

1430 - ANDREW CANNON AND HIS DESCENDANTS, 1651-1912 by C. S.
Williams. Repr. of 1912 ed., typescript.
Paper—$17.50—54pp------------------------------------- Vendor #D1842

1431 - CANTRELL FAMILY...DESCENDANTS OF ZEBULON CANTRELL...
WITH...FAMILIES...BY MARRIAGE, 1700-1898 by Carmi G. Cantrell.
Repr. of 1898 ed.
Paper—$23.00—156pp------------------------------------- Vendor #D1842

1432 - GENEALOGY OF DESCENDANTS OF BANFIELD CAPRON FROM A.D.
1660-A.D. 1859 by Frederic A. Holden. Repr. of 1859 ed.
Paper—$39.00—263pp------------------------------------- Vendor #D1842

1433 - DESCENDANTS OF THOMAS CARHART by M. Dusenbury. Repr. of
1880 ed.
Paper—$30.00—142pp------------------------------------- Vendor #D1842

1434 - GENEALOGICAL AND HISTORICAL RECORD OF CARPENTER FAMILY
...OF WEYMOUTH AND REHOBOTH, MASSACHUSETTS...PROVIDENCE,
RHODE ISLAND...PENNSYLVANIA...LONG ISLAND by James Usher.
Repr. of 1883 ed.
Paper—$12.00—70pp------------------------------------- Vendor #D1842

1435 - CARR FAMILY RECORDS...FIRST FAMILY WHO SETTLED IN AMER-
ICA AND THEIR DESCENDANTS....by Edison C. Carr. Repr. of 1894
ed.
Cloth—$81.00—Paper—$71.00—540pp----------------------- Vendor #D1842

1436 - HOUSE OF CARR, HISTORICAL SKETCH OF CARR FAMILY 1450-
1926 by W. L. Watson. Repr. of 1926 ed.
Paper—$12.00—58pp------------------------------------- Vendor #D1842

1437 - GENEALOGY OF...CARRUTH FAMILY: OR DESCENDANTS OF JAMES
CARRUTH OF PHILLIPSTON by Arthur Jay Carruth. Repr. of 1926 ed.
Paper—$12.50—67pp------------------------------------- Vendor #D1842

1438 - BI-CENTENARY MEMORIAL OF JEREMIAH CARTER...PROVINCE OF
PENNSYLVANIA IN 1682...HIS DESCENDANTS by Thomas M. Potts.
Repr. of 1883 ed.
Cloth—$46.00—Paper—$36.00—304pp----------------------- Vendor #D1842

1439   - CARTER...DESCENDANTS OF SAMUEL AND THOMAS, SONS OF
REV. SAMUEL CARTER, 1640-1886 by Mrs. Clara A. & Sarah A. Carter.
Repr. of 1886 ed.
Cloth—$41.00—Paper—$31.00—272pp----------------------- Vendor #D1842

1440   - THE CARY FAMILY IN ENGLAND by Henry Grosvenor Cary. Repr.
of 1906 ed.
Paper—$16.00—105pp------------------------------------- Vendor #D1842

1441   - CARY FAMILY IN AMERICA, BY HENRY GROSVENOR CARY: APPEN-
DIX, JONATHAN CARY YE THIRD by Isaac Harris Cary. Repr. of
1907 ed.
Paper—$17.00—120pp------------------------------------- Vendor #D1842

1442   - JOHN CARY, THE PLYMOUTH PILGRIM by Seth C. Cary. Repr. of
1911 ed.
Cloth—$41.00—Paper—$31.00—274pp----------------------- Vendor #D1842

1443   - THE VIRGINIA CARYS; AN ESSAY IN GENEALOGY by Fairfax
Harrison. Repr. of 1919 ed.
Paper—$33.00—223pp------------------------------------- Vendor #D1842

1444   - JOHN CASE OF CONNECTICUT by A. P. Case. Repr.
Paper—$5.00—24pp-------------------------------------- Vendor #D1842

1445   - JONATHAN CASE OF ONTARIO COUNTY, NEW YORK by C. R. Case.
Repr. of 1915 ed.
Paper—$20.00—104pp------------------------------------ Vendor #D1842

1446   - EARLY FAMILY OF CASEY IN RHODE ISLAND by T. L. Casey. Repr.
of 1893 ed.
Paper—$9.00—45pp-------------------------------------- Vendor #D1842

1447   - CASTOR FAMILY, HOLMESBURG BRANCH by R. A. Martin. Repr.
of 1909 ed.
Paper—$3.00—11pp-------------------------------------- Vendor #D1842

1448   - CATE-CATES FAMILY OF NEW ENGLAND by Cates and Sanborn.
Repr. of 1904 ed.
Paper—$10.00—52pp------------------------------------- Vendor #D1842

1449   - GENEALOGY OF THE CAVERLY FAMILY, 1161-1880 by Robert B.
Caverly. Repr. of 1880 ed.
Paper—$33.00—201pp------------------------------------ Vendor #D1842

1450   - RECORD OF THE CAVERNO FAMILY by A. Caverno. Repr. of 1874 ed.
Paper—$7.00—30pp-------------------------------------- Vendor #D1842

1451   - HOUSE OF CESSNA by H. Cessna. Repr. of 1903 ed., charts.
Paper—$25.00—120pp------------------------------------ Vendor #D1842

1452   - GENEALOGICAL RECORD OF CHASE AND HATHAWAY FAMILIES,
1630-1900 by C. V. Case. Repr. of 1900 ed.
Paper—$8.00—42pp-------------------------------------- Vendor #D1842

1453   - ONE BRANCH OF DESCENDANTS OF THOMAS CHAMBERLAIN OF
WOBURN, 1644 by George W. Chamberlain. Repr. of 1897 ed.
Paper—$4.50—16pp-------------------------------------- Vendor #D1842

1454   - JAMES CHAMBLIN OF SOUTH CAROLINA AND HIS CHILDREN.
Repr. of 1914 ed. (in Anderson-Denny gen.)
Paper—$4.00—16pp-------------------------------------- Vendor #D1842

1455   - CHAMPION GENEALOGY, HISTORY OF DESCENDANTS OF HENRY
CHAMPION OF SAYBROOK AND LYME, CONNECTICUT....by Francis
B. Trowbridge. Repr. of 1891 ed.
Cloth—$86.00—Paper—$76.00—575pp----------------------- Vendor #D1842

1456   - CHANDLER FAMILY, DESCENDANTS OF WILLIAM AND ANNIS CHAN-
DLER...ROXBURY, MASSACHUSETTS, 1637 by George Chandler.
Repr. of 1883 ed.
Cloth—$198.00—Paper—$178.00—1323pp-------------------- Vendor #D1842

1457 - ANCESTRY OF LYDIA MEHITABLE CHANDLER by F. W. Goding.
Repr. of 1904 ed.
Paper—$3.00—11pp--- Vendor #D1842

1458 - CHANDLER OF OARE COUNTY, WILTS., ENGLAND...JOHN AND
GEORGE CHANDLER WHO SAILED TO PENNSYLVANIA IN 1686 by
Chandler and Glenn. Repr. of 1913 ed.
Paper—$6.00—23pp--- Vendor #D1842

1459 - CHANDLER FAMILY; GENEALOGY OF A BRANCH by Mrs. A. M.
Pickford. Repr. Dedham Hist. Register, 1903 ed.
Paper—$5.50—33pp--- Vendor #D1842

1460 -A SKETCH OF THE CHANDLER FAMILY IN WORCESTER, MASSA-
CHUSETTS by Mrs. E. O. P. Sturgis. Repr. of 1903 ed.
Paper—$5.50—37pp--- Vendor #D1842

1461 - CHAPINS WHO SERVED IN THE FRENCH AND INDIAN WARS 1754-
1764...AND OTHERS by G. W. Chapin. Repr. of 1895 ed.
Paper—$10.00—47pp--- Vendor #D1842

1462 - CHAPIN GATHERING. PROCEEDINGS AT THE MEETING OF THE
CHAPIN FAMILY IN SPRINGFIELD, MASSACHUSETTS...1862. Repr.
of 1862 ed.
Paper—$15.00—97pp--- Vendor #D1842

1463 - CHAPIN GENEALOGY...DESCENDANTS OF DEA. SAMUEL CHAPIN
...SPRINGFIELD, MASSACHUSETTS, IN 1642 by Orange Chapin.
Repr. of 1862 ed.
Cloth—$56.00—Paper—$46.00—374pp----------------------- Vendor #D1842

1464 - CHAPMAN FAMILY, OR THE DESCENDANTS OF ROBERT CHAPMAN,
...BENJAMIN CHAPMAN, OF SOUTHINGTON, CONNECTICUT by Rev.
F. W. Chapman. Repr. of 1854 ed.
Cloth—$62.00—Paper—$52.00—414pp----------------------- Vendor #D1842

1465 - A GENEALOGY, EDWARD CHAPMAN OF IPSWICH, MASSACHUSETTS,
1642-1678...DESCENDANTS by Jacob Chapman. Repr. of 1893 ed.
Paper—$22.00—147pp--- Vendor #D1842

1466 - EDWARD CHAPMAN, OF IPSWICH, MASSACHUSETTS, IN 1644, AND
SOME OF HIS DESCENDANTS by Jacob Chapman and W. B. Lapham.
Repr. of 1878 ed.
Paper—$6.50—36pp--- Vendor #D1842

1467 - GENEALOGICAL HISTORY OF CHAPPELL, DICKIE, AND OTHER
KINDRED FAMILIES OF VIRGINIA, 1635-1900, rev. ed., by Phil E.
Chappell. Repr. of 1900 ed.
Cloth—$57.00—Paper—$47.00—384pp----------------------- Vendor #D1842

1468 - GENEALOGY OF THE ANCESTORS AND DESCENDANTS OF JOSEPH
CHASE WHO DIED IN SWANZEY.... Repr. of 1874 ed.
Paper—$13.00—86pp--- Vendor #D1842

1469 - GENEALOGICAL MEMOIR OF CHASE FAMILY OF CHESHAM, BUCKS,
IN ENGLAND...DESCENDANTS by George B. Chase. Repr. Heraldic
Journal, 1869 ed.
Paper—$5.00—19pp--- Vendor #D1842

1470 - RECORDS OF DESCENDANTS OF REV. NATHANIEL CHASE OF BUCK-
FIELD, MAINE....by William B. Lapham. Repr. of 1878 ed.
Paper—$5.00—18pp--- Vendor #D1842

1471 - REMINISCENSES OF FAMILY OF MOODY CHASE OF SHIRLEY, MASSA-
CHUSETTS...ANCESTRY by William Moody Chase. Repr. of 1888 ed.
Paper—$6.00—32pp--- Vendor #D1842

1472 - GENEALOGY OF CHAMPION SPALDING CHASE AND MARY SOPHRONIA
BUTTERFIELD, HIS WIFE....by Champion Spalding Chase. Repr. of
1894 ed.
Paper—$5.00—19pp--- Vendor #D1842

1473 - CHATFIELD FAMILY OF NAUGATUCK VALLEY, CONNECTICUT by W.
C. Sharpe. Repr. of 1896 ed.
Paper—$6.50—32pp--- Vendor #D1842

1474 - MEMORIALS OF THE CHAUNCEYS, INCLUDING PRESIDENT CHAUN-
CEY, HIS ANCESTORS AND DESCENDANTS by William C. Fowler.
Repr. of 1858 ed.
Cloth—$56.00—Paper—$46.00—377pp------------------------ Vendor #D1842

1475 - BARTHOLOMEW AND RICHARD CHEEVER, AND SOME OF THEIR
DESCENDANTS by John T. Hassam. Repr. N.E. Hist. & Gen. Reg.,
1882 ed.
Paper—$4.00—11pp--- Vendor #D1842

1476 - EZEKIEL CHEEVER AND SOME OF HIS DESCENDANTS, Second Part,
by John T. Hassam. Repr. N. E. Hist. & Gen. Reg., 1884 ed.
Paper—$5.00—26pp--- Vendor #D1842

1477 - EZEKIEL CHEEVER; ADDITIONAL NOTES by John T. Hassam. Repr.
N. E. Hist. & Gen. Reg., 1887 ed.
Paper—$4.00—6pp-- Vendor #D1842

1478 - THE CHEEVER FAMILY by John T. Hassam. Repr. of 1896 ed.
Paper—$10.00—54pp-- Vendor #D1842

1479 - THE CHENEY GENEALOGY by Charles Henry Pope. Repr. of 1897 ed.
Cloth—$87.00—Paper—$77.00—582pp------------------------ Vendor #D1842

1480 - GENEALOGY AND CHART OF THE CHENOWETH AND CROMWELL FAMI-
LIES OF MARYLAND AND VIRGINIA by A. C. Chenoweth. Repr. of
1894 ed. 10 charts.
Paper—$10.00—35pp-- Vendor #D1842

1481 - GENEALOGY OF CHESMAN FAMILY, IN THE UNITED STATES, FROM
1713 TO 1893....by Samuel Chessman. Repr. of 1893 ed.
Paper—$16.00—109pp--------------------------------------- Vendor #D1842

1482 - DESCENDANTS OF LESTER CHESTER OF WETHERSFIELD, CONNEC-
TICUT by Edward Strong. Repr. of 1868 ed.
Paper—$3.00—8pp-- Vendor #D1842

1483 - GENEALOGICAL NOTES OF THE FAMILY OF CHESTER (ENGLAND
AND CONNECTICUT) by R. E. C. Waters. Repr. of 1886 ed. chart.
Paper—$7.50—31pp--- Vendor #D1842

1484 - DESCENDANTS OF CHRISTOPHER CHESTER, 1796-1896 by Arthur
Herbert Chester. Repr. of 1896 ed.
Paper—$4.00—11pp--- Vendor #D1842

1485 - CHICKERING-ALLEYNE FAMILIES OF DEDHAM by W. F. Cheney.
Repr. of 1927 ed.
Paper—$5.00—25pp--- Vendor #D1842

1486 - GENEALOGY OF THE CHILD, CHILDS, AND CHILDE FAMILY...1630-
1881 by Elias Child. Repr. of 1881 ed.
Cloth—$128.00—Paper—$118.00—856pp--------------------- Vendor #D1842

1487 - CHIPMANS IN MAINE, A GENEALOGY by Alberto L. Chipman. Repr.
of 1897 ed.
Paper—$7.50—44pp--- Vendor #D1842

1488 - THE CHIPMAN LINEAGE, PARTICULARLY AS IN ESSEX COUNTY,
MASSACHUSETTS by R. Manning Chipman. Repr. Essex Inst. Hist.
Coll., 1872 ed.
Paper—$11.00—59pp-- Vendor #D1842

1489 - CHIPMANS OF AMERICA by Alberto Lee Chipman. Repr. of 1904 ed.
Paper—$34.50—232pp--------------------------------------- Vendor #D1842

1490 - CHISOLM GENEALOGY; BEING A RECORD OF THE NAME FROM 1254,
...ALLIED FAMILIES by William Garnett Chisolm. Repr. of 1914 ed.
Paper—$17.50—101pp--------------------------------------- Vendor #D1842

1491 - CHITTENDEN FAMILY, WILLIAM CHITTENDEN OF GUILFORD, CON-
NECTICUT AND HIS DESCENDANTS, NEW YORK by Alvon Talcott.
Repr. of 1882 ed.
Paper—$39.00—263pp------------------------------------- Vendor #D1842

1492 - CHOATES IN AMERICA, 1643-1896, JOHN CHOATE AND HIS DE-
SCENDANTS...MASSACHUSETTS by E. O. Jameson. Repr. of 1896 ed.
Cloth—$65.00—Paper—$55.00—474pp----------------------- Vendor #D1842

1493 - (CHOUTEAU) CREOLES OF ST. LOUIS by Paul Beckwith. Repr. of
1893 ed.
Paper—$26.00—174pp----------------------------------- Vendor #D1842

1494 - THE HISTORY OF THE CHURCH FAMILY by Oliver Chase, Edward
H. French, and Vernon Wade; edited by James. N. Arnold. Repr. of
1887 ed.
Paper—$21.00—144pp----------------------------------- Vendor #D1842

1495 - DESCENDANTS OF CAPTAIN SAMUEL CHURCH OF CHURCHVILLE
by Etta A. Emens. Repr. of 1920 ed.
Paper—$14.00—80pp------------------------------------ Vendor #D1842

1496 - FACTS CONCERNING THE ANCESTRY AND DESCENDANTS OF
ASAPH. CHURCHILL OF MILTON by G. A. Churchill. Repr. of 1887 ed.
Paper—$4.00—18pp------------------------------------- Vendor #D1842

1497 - THE CHURCHILL FAMILY IN AMERICA by Gardner A. Churchill and
Nathaniel W. Churchill; edited by Rev. George M. Bodge. Repr. of
1904 ed.
Cloth—$108.00—Paper—$98.00—722pp----------------------- Vendor #D1842

1498 - CILLEY FAMILY, DESCENDANTS OF ROBERT SEELY by J. P. Cilley.
Repr. of 1878 ed.
Paper—$10.00—47pp------------------------------------ Vendor #D1842

1499 - RECORDS OF DESCENDANTS OF HUGH CLARK OF WATERTOWN,
MASSACHUSETTS, 1640-1866 by John Clark. Repr. of 1866 ed.
Paper—$39.00—261pp----------------------------------- Vendor #D1842

1500 - RECORD OF DESCENDANTS OF JOHN CLARK OF FARMINGTON,
CONNECTICUT by Julius Gay. Repr. of 1882 ed.
Paper—$15.00—94pp------------------------------------ Vendor #D1842

1501 - RECORDS OF SOME OF THE DESCENDANTS OF THOMAS CLARKE OF
PLYMOUTH, 1623-1697 by Samuel C. Clarke. Repr. of 1869 ed.
Paper—$4.50—43pp------------------------------------- Vendor #D1842

1502 - CLARKE'S KINDRED GENEALOGIES...JOSEPH CLARKE...DENICE
DARLING, EDWARD GRAY AND WILLIAM HORNE by Augustus Peck
Clarke. Repr. of 1896 ed.
Paper—$17.50—185pp----------------------------------- Vendor #D1842

1503 - RICHARD CLARKE OF ROWLEY, MASSACHUSETTS...TIMOTHY
CLARK OF ROCKINGHAM, VERMONT, 1638-1904 by Thomas Bellows
Peck. Repr. of 1905 ed.
Paper—$15.00—93pp------------------------------------ Vendor #D1842

1504 - ANCESTRY OF JEREMY CLARKE OF RHODE ISLAND, AND DUNGAN
GENEALOGY by Alfred Rudulph Justice. Repr. of 1922 ed.
Cloth—$80.50—Paper—$70.50—538pp----------------------- Vendor #D1842

1505 - CLASON, CLAWSON, CLASSON, CLOSSON, CLAUSON; STEPHEN
CLASON OF STAMFORD, CONNECTICUT....collected by Oliver B.
Clason, by William B. Lapham. Repr. of 1892 ed.
Paper—$24.00—160pp----------------------------------- Vendor #D1842

1506 - GENEALOGY AND HISTORY OF THE CLAY FAMILY by Hiland H.
Clay. Repr. of 1916 ed., n.p.
Paper—$24.00—159pp----------------------------------- Vendor #D1842

1507 - CLEMENS FAMILY CHRONOLOGY, BIRTHS, MARRIAGES, DEATHS
by W. M. Clemens. Repr. of 1914 ed.
Paper—$12.50—63pp------------------------------------ Vendor #D1842

1508 - ROBERT CLEMENTS OF HAVERHILL, MASSACHUSETTS, AND SOME
OF HIS DESCENDANTS by A. W. Greely. Repr. Essex Inst. Hist.
Coll., 1911 ed.
Paper—$5.00—18pp--- Vendor #D1842

1509 - THE CLEMENS FAMILY OF DOVER, NEW HAMPSHIRE by John Scales.
Repr. of 1923 ed., n.p.
Paper—$5.00—18pp--- Vendor #D1842

1510 - ANCESTORS AND DESCENDANTS OF ROBERT CLEMENTS OF LEI-
CESTERSHIRE AND WARWICKSHIRE, ENGLAND...., 2 Volumes, by
Percival Wood Clements. Repr. of 1927 ed.
Cloth—$163.50—Paper—$153.50—1092pp--------------------- Vendor #D1842

1511 - THE CLEIVELANDS OF LEICESTERSHIRE, ENGLAND by H. G.
Cleveland. Repr. N. E. Hist. & Gen. Register, 1885 ed.
Paper—$4.00—7pp--- Vendor #D1842

1512 - THOMAS COATES, ENGLAND TO PENNSYLVANIA 1683, AND THE
COATES FAMILY...1785-1901. Repr.
Paper—$7.50—43pp-------------------------------------- Vendor #D1842

1513 - RECORD OF THE COE FAMILY by D. B. Coe. Repr. of 1856 ed.
Paper—$4.00—18pp--- Vendor #D1842

1514 - ROBERT COE, PURITAN, HIS ANCESTORS AND DESCENDANTS,
1340-1910...COE FAMILIES by J. Gardner Bartlett. Repr. of 1911 ed.
Cloth—$99.50—Paper—$89.50—664pp---------------------- Vendor #D1842

1515 - THOMAS COFFEY AND DESCENDANTS by L. H. Coffey. Repr. of
1931 ed.
Paper—$15.00—102pp--- Vendor #D1842

1516 - GENEALOGY OF EARLY GENERATIONS OF THE COFFIN FAMILY IN
NEW ENGLAND by Sylvanus J. Macy. Repr. N. E. Hist. & Gen.
Register, 1870 ed.
Paper—$4.50—17pp-------------------------------------- Vendor #D1842

1517 - COFFIN FAMILY, ITS ARMORIAL BEARINGS AND ORIGIN OF THE
NAME by John Coffin Jones Brown. Repr. N. E. Hist. & Gen. Register,
1881 ed.
Paper—$4.00—8pp--- Vendor #D1842

1518 - COFFIN FAMILY. THE LIFE OF TRISTRAM COFFYN OF NANTUCKET,
MASSACHUSETTS....by Allen Coffin. Repr. of 1881 ed.
Paper—$12.50—64pp--- Vendor #D1842

1519 - EARLY WILLS ILLUSTRATING ANCESTRY OF HARRIOT COFFIN,
WITH GENEALOGICAL AND BIOGRAPHICAL NOTES by William S.
Appleton. Repr. of 1893 ed.
Paper—$14.50—89pp--------------------------------------- Vendor #D1842

1520 - GATHERINGS TOWARD A GENEALOGY OF THE COFFIN FAMILY by
W. S. Appleton. Repr. of 1896 ed.
Paper—$10.00—53pp--------------------------------------- Vendor #D1842

1521 - A SERMON DELIVERED AT THE FUNERAL OF DOCTOR WILLIAM
COGSWELL OF ATKINSON, NEW JERSEY, 1831 by John Kelly (with
Cogswell genealogical appendix). Repr., n.d.
Paper—$4.00—16pp--------------------------------------- Vendor #D1842

1522 - COIT FAMILY: OR, DESCENDANTS OF JOHN COIT, SALEM, MASSA-
CHUSETTS, IN 1638....by F. W. Chapman. Repr. of 1874 ed.
Cloth—$51.00—Paper—$41.00—341pp---------------------- Vendor #D1842

1523 - DESCENDANTS OF ISAAC COLBURN, JR. OF WEST DEDHAM, MASSA-
CHUSETTS by E. J. Cox. Repr., chart.
Paper—$7.50—28pp-------------------------------------- Vendor #D1842

1524 - GENEALOGY OF DESCENDANTS OF EDWARD COLBURN, COLBURN
CAME FROM ENGLAND, 1635 by George A. Gordon and Silas R. Coburn.
Repr. of 1913 ed.
Cloth—$71.00—Paper—$61.00—474pp---------------------- Vendor #D1842

1525 - COLBY FAMILY (OF COLBY COLLEGE), SOMETHING OF ITS HISTORY
IN EUROPE AND AMERICA. Repr. of 1931 ed.
Paper—$3.00—24pp--- Vendor #D1842

1526 - GENEALOGY OF DESCENDANTS OF ABRAHAM COLBY AND ELIZA-
BETH BLAISDELL, HIS WIFE,....by Harrison Colby. Repr. of 1895 ed.
Paper—$22.50—152pp--- Vendor #D1842

1527 - COLCORD GENEALOGY, DESCENDANTS OF EDWARD COLCORD OF
NEW HAMPSHIRE by C. B. Colcord. Repr. of 1908 ed.
Paper—$20.00—166pp--- Vendor #D1842

1528 - ISAAC KOOL (COOL OR COLE) AND CATHERINE SERVEN, MARRIED
1764 AT TAPPAN, NEW YORK....by David Cole. Repr. of 1876 ed.
Cloth—$40.00—Paper—30.00—269pp----------------------- Vendor #D1842

1529 - EARLY GENEALOGIES OF THE COLE FAMILIES IN AMERICA (INCLUD-
ING COLES AND COWLES) by Frank T. Cole. Repr. of 1887 ed.
Cloth—$51.00—Paper—$41.00—340pp----------------------- Vendor #D1842

1530 - DESCENDANTS OF JAMES COLE OF PLYMOUTH, 1633...LIEUTENANT
THOMAS BURNHAM...EDWARD WINSHIP...SIMON HUNTINGTON....
by Ernest Byron Cole. Repr. of 1908 ed.
Cloth—$67.00—Paper—$57.00—448pp--------------------- Vendor #D1842

1531 - GENEALOGY OF WILLIAM COLEMAN OF GLOUCESTER by J. C. Coleman. Repr. of 1906 ed.
Cloth—$40.00—Paper—$30.00—240pp----------------------- Vendor #D1842

1532 - COLEMAN FAMILY. DESCENDANTS OF THOMAS COLEMAN, IN LINE
OF OLDEST SON by Edwin Stearns, edited by L. Coleman. Repr. of
1867 ed.
Paper—$5.00—24pp--- Vendor #D1842

1533 - FAMILY OF PRUDDEN AND COLEY OF CONNECTICUT (IN GOODWIN
GENEALOGY) by Starr and Goodwin. Repr. of 1915 ed.
Paper—$3.00—8pp--- Vendor #D1842

1534 - GENEALOGY OF DESCENDANTS OF ANTHONY COLLAMER OF SCITUATE
MASSACHUSETTS by Charles Hatch. Repr. of 1915 ed.
Paper—$30.00—198pp--- Vendor #D1842

1535 - COLLINS FAMILY, DESCENDANTS OF FRANCIS OF LONDON WHO
EMIGRATED TO NEW JERSEY by George Haines. Repr. of 1902 ed.
Extracted from Haines Gen.
Paper—$6.00—24pp--- Vendor #D1842

1536 - HENRY COLLINS OF LYNN AND SOME OF HIS DESCENDANTS...
NEW HAMPSHIRE by A. Collins and C. Pope. Repr. of 1916 ed.
Paper—$4.50—21pp--- Vendor D1842

1537 - ADDRESS DELIVERED BY DR. S. C. BEANE AT COLLINS FAMILY
GATHERING 1892 edited with notes by L. W. Collins. Repr. of 1898 ed.
Paper—$6.50—34pp--- Vendor #D1842

1538 - COLVER-CULVER GENEALOGY, DESCENDANTS OF EDWARD COLVER
...MASSACHUSETTS...CONNECTICUT, 1635-1909 by Frederic Lathrop
Colver. Repr. of 1910 ed.
Cloth—$40.50—Paper—$30.50—271pp----------------------- Vendor #D1842

1539 - COMEY-COMEE FAMILY IN AMERICA. DESCENDANTS OF DAVID
COMEY OF CONCORD, MASSACHUSETTS...MALTMAN FAMILY by
Allen H. Bent. Repr. of 1896 ed.
Paper—$10.00—50pp--- Vendor #D1842

1540 - CONANT GENEALOGY by Frederick Odell Conant. Repr., n.t.-p.
Paper—$10.00—44pp--- Vendor #D1842

1541 - HISTORY AND GENEALOGY OF CONANT FAMILY IN ENGLAND AND
AMERICA, 1520-1887 by Frederick Odell Conant. Repr. of 1887 ed.
Cloth—$98.00—Paper—$88.00—654pp--------------------- Vendor #D1842

1542 - SOME ACCOUNT OF THE CONE FAMILY IN AMERICA...HADDAM, CONNECTICUT, IN 1662 by William Whitney Cone. Repr. of 1903 ed. Cloth—$82.00—Paper—$72.00—547pp------------------------ Vendor #D1842

1543 - ONE HUNDRED THIRTY-EIGHT GENERATIONS FROM ADAM; A PEDIGREE....TO PRESENT TIME by George Edward Congdon. Repr. of 1910 ed. Paper—$10.00—55pp-------------------------------------- Vendor #D1842

1544 - THE CONGDON CHRONICLE, NUMBERS 1-18 by G. E. Congdon. Repr. of 1921-1934 eds. Paper—36.00—240pp------------------------------------- Vendor #D1842

1545 - SALEM, MASSACHUSETTS AND THE CONKLING FAMILY by F. J. Conkling. Repr. of 1894 ed. Paper—$3.00—11pp-- Vendor #D1842

1546 - HISTORY AND GENEALOGY OF AUTHOR'S BRANCH OF THE CONNET FAMILY by A. Connet. Repr. of 1905 ed. Paper—$10.00—53pp-------------------------------------- Vendor #D1842

1547 - SOME ANCESTORS AND DESCENDANTS OF SAMUEL CONVERSE, JR., MAJOR JAMES CONVERS, HON. HEMAN ALLEN, CAPTAIN JONATHAN BIXBY, SR., 2 Volumes, by Charles Allen Converse. Repr. of 1905 ed. Cloth—$148.00—Paper—$128.00—988pp---------------------- Vendor #D1842

1548 - RECORD OF DESCENDANTS OF WILLIAM COOLBAUGH 1765-1918. Repr. Paper—$10.00—40pp-------------------------------------- Vendor #D1842

1549 - GENEALOGY OF SOME DESCENDANTS OF JOHN COOLIDGE OF WATER-TOWN 1630. Repr. of 1892 ed. Paper—$6.00—32pp--------------------------------------- Vendor #D1842

1550 - THOMAS COOPER OF BOSTON AND HIS DESCENDANTS by F. Tucherman. Repr. of 1890 ed. Paper—$3.50—13pp--------------------------------------- Vendor #D1842

1551 - COOPER FAMILY, HISTORY AND GENEALOGY 1681-1931 by M. R. Cooper. Repr. of 1931 ed. Paper—$22.50—116pp------------------------------------- Vendor #D1842

1552 - DESCENDANTS OF PETER COOPER OF ROWLEY, MASSACHUSETTS by Albion K. P. Cooper. Repr. Maine Hist. & Gen. Record, 1885 ed. Paper—$4.00—11pp-- Vendor #D1842

1553 - GENEALOGY OF THE CORBETT FAMILY by E. C. Corbett. Repr. of 1917 ed. Paper—$17.50—85pp-------------------------------------- Vendor #D1842

1554 - HISTORY AND GENEALOGY OF DESCENDANTS OF CLEMENT CORBIN OF MUDDY RIVER (BROOKLINE), MASSACHUSETTS....by Harvey M. Lawson. Repr. of 1905 ed. Cloth—$56.50—Paper—$46.50—378pp------------------------ Vendor #D1842

1554 - WILLIAM CORDER OF BARBOUR COUNTY, WEST VIRGINIA by H. B. Grant. Repr. of 1934 ed. Paper—$5.00—14pp-- Vendor #D1842

1555 - COREY FAMILY OF SOUTHAMPTON AND SOUTHOLD, LONG ISLAND, 1644-1779 by Lucy Dubois Akerly. Repr. N.Y. Gen. & Biog. Record, 1900 ed. Paper—$4.00—12pp-- Vendor #D1842

1556 - GENEALOGICAL RECORD OF CORLISS FAMILY OF AMERICA, 1st. ed. by Augustus W. Corliss and others. Repr. of 1875 ed. Cloth—$51.00—Paper—41.00—343pp------------------------ Vendor #D1842

1557 - SAMUEL CORNING OF BEVERLY, MASSACHUSETTS AND HIS NOVA SCOTIA DESCENDANTS by G. S. Brown. Repr. of 1897 ed. Paper—$4.50—15pp-- Vendor #D1842

1558 - CORNISH GENEALOGY by C. N. Sinnett. Repr. of 1922 ed.,
typescript.
Paper—$6.00—26pp--------------------------------------- Vendor #D1842

1559 - HISTORY AND GENEALOGY OF THE CORNISH FAMILIES IN AMERICA
by Joseph E. Cornish. Repr. of 1907 ed.
Cloth—$51.50—Paper—$41.50—353pp----------------------- Vendor #D1842

1560 - CORWIN GENEALOGY (CURWIN, CURWEN, CORWINE) IN THE UNITED
STATES by Edward Tanjore Corwin. Repr. of 1872 ed.
Cloth—$47.50—Paper—$37.50—318pp----------------------- Vendor #D1842

1561 - COTTON FAMILY OF PORTSMOUTH, NEW HAMPSHIRE by F. E.
Cotton. Repr., n.d.
Paper—$5.00—26pp--------------------------------------- Vendor #D1842

1562 - ENGLISH ANCESTRY OF REV. JOHN COTTON OF BOSTON by H. G.
Somerby. Repr. of 1868 ed.
Paper—$4.00—12pp--------------------------------------- Vendor #D1842

1563 - COURSENS FROM 1612 TO 1917, WITH THE STATEN ISLAND BRANCH
by P. G. Ullman. Repr. of 1917 ed.
Paper—$18.00—88pp-------------------------------------- Vendor #D1842

1564 - COVERT ANCES by Jones and Horton. Repr. of 1906 ed.
Paper—$5.00—20pp--------------------------------------- Vendor #D1842

1565 - COWDREY-COWDERY-COWDRAY GENEALOGY; WILLIAM COWDERY
OF LYNN, MASSACHUSETTS, 1630....by Mary Bryant Alverson
Mehling. Repr. of 1911 ed.
Cloth—$67.50—Paper—$57.50—451pp----------------------- Vendor #D1842

1566 - THE CRAFTS FAMILY. GENEALOGICAL AND BIOGRAPHICAL HISTORY
OF DESCENDANTS OF GRIFFIN AND ALICE CRAFT....by James M.
Crafats and William F. Crafts. Repr. of 1893 ed.
Cloth—$121.00—Paper—$111.00—807pp--------------------- Vendor #D1842

1567 - GENEALOGY OF THE CRAGIN FAMILY by C. H. Cragin. Repr. of
1860 ed.
Paper—$8.50—42pp--------------------------------------- Vendor #D1842

1568 - CRAIG FAMILY OF PENNSYLVANIA 1708-1895 by W. M. Clemens.
Repr. of 1921 ed.
Paper—$3.50—12pp--------------------------------------- Vendor #D1842

1569 - ANCESTRY OF LEANDER HOWARD CRALL,...CRALL, HAFF, BEATTY
(AND OTHER) FAMILIES by Frank Allaben. Repr. of 1908 ed.
Cloth—$63.50—Paper—$53.50—426pp----------------------- Vendor #D1842

1570 - GENEALOGY OF ELDER JOHN CRANDALL AND HIS DESCENDANTS
by A. P. Crandall. Repr. of 1888 ed.
Paper—$12.50—62pp-------------------------------------- Vendor #D1842

1571 - HENRY CRANE OF MILTON, MASSACHUSETTS, 1654, AND SOME OF
HIS DESCENDANTS by Emily Wilder Leavitt. Repr. of 1893 ed.
Paper—$5.00—29pp--------------------------------------- Vendor #D1842

1572 - CRAWFORD FAMILY RECORDS by W. M. Clemens. Repr. of 1914 ed.
Paper—$6.00—30pp--------------------------------------- Vendor #D1842

1573 - CRENSHAW FAMILY RECORDS (IN VALENTINE PAPERS). Repr.
Paper—$14.00—70pp-------------------------------------- Vendor #D1842

1574 - GENEALOGY OF CRESSEY FAMILY, DESCENDANTS OF MIGHILL
CRESSEY (MIGHEL CRESSE)...MASSACHUSETTS by George Brainard
Blodgette. Repr. N. E. Hist. & Gen. Register, 1877 ed.
Paper—$4.50—13pp--------------------------------------- Vendor #D1842

1575 - CROSBY ANCESTORS, ROBERT, JONAH AND JOEL CROSBY OF MAINE
by M. A. Crosby. Repr. of 1939 ed.
Paper—$12.50—70pp-------------------------------------- Vendor #D1842

1576 - CROSBY FAMILY. JOSIAH CROSBY, SARAH FITCH, AND THEIR
DESCENDANTS by Nathan Crosby. Repr. of 1877 ed.
Paper—$21.00—143pp------------------------------------- Vendor #D1842

1577 - SIMON CROSBY, EMIGRANT; HIS ANCESTRY AND SOME OF HIS
AMERICAN DESCENDANTS by Eleanor Davis Crosby. Repr. of 1914 ed.
Paper—$27.00—183pp-- Vendor #D1842

1578 - MY CHILDREN'S ANCESTORS; DATA CONCERNING NEW ENGLAND
ANCESTORS OF ROSELLE THEODORE CROSS...by R. T. Cross.
Repr. of 1913 ed.
Paper—$31.50—212pp--- Vendor #D1842

1579 - ISAAC CUMMINGS OF TOPSFIELD, MASSACHUSETTS AND SOME OF
HIS DESCENDANTS by Marietta Clark and others. Repr. of 1899 ed.
Paper—$7.50—39pp--- Vendor #D1842

1580 - CUMMINGS GENEALOGY. ISAAC CUMMINGS, 1601-1677, OF IPSWICH
IN 1638....by Albert Oren Cummings. Repr. of 1904 ed.
Cloth—$99.00—Paper—$89.00—661pp----------------------- Vendor #D1842

1581 - GENEALOGICAL MEMOIR OF THE CUNNABELL, CONABLE, OR CON-
NABLE FAMILY 1650-1886 by Connable and Newcomb. Repr. of 1886 ed.
Paper—$37.50—187pp-- Vendor #D1842

1582 - ANDREW CUNNINGHAM OF BOSTON AND SOME OF HIS DESCENDANTS
by Henry Winchester Cunningham. Repr. N. E. Hist. & Gen. Register,
1901 ed.
Paper—$4.50—16pp-- Vendor #D1842

1583 - ADDRESS OR HISTORICAL SKETCH DELIVERED AT A CURRIER
FAMILY REUNION, TOLEDO, OHIO, 1910 by Edwin M. Currier.
Repr. of 1913 ed.
Paper—$4.50—19pp-- Vendor #D1842

1584 - THE FAMILY OF HENRY CURTIS OF SUDBUDY, MASSACHUSETTS
by Henry Ernest Woods. Repr. N. E. Hist. & Gen. Register, 1907 ed.
Paper—$4.00—10pp-- Vendor #D1842

1585 - GENEALOGY OF THE CURTISS FAMILY...ELIZABETH CURTIS, WHO
SETTLED IN STRATFORD, CONNECTICUT, 1639-40 by Frederic Haines
Curtiss. Repr. of 1903 ed.
Cloth—$42.00—Paper—$32.00—283pp----------------------- Vendor #D1842

1586 - GENEALOGY OF THE CUSHING FAMILY by L. Cushing. Repr. of
1877 ed.
Paper—$23.50—117pp-- Vendor #D1842

1587 - GENEALOGY OF THE CUSHING FAMILY; ANCESTORS AND DESCEND-
ANTS OF MATTHEW CUSHING...1638 by James S. Cushing. Repr. of
1905 ed.
Cloth—$100.00—Paper—$90.00—678pp---------------------- Vendor #D1842

1588 - PROCEEDINGS AT THE CUSHMAN CELEBRATION AT PLYMOUTH,
MASSACHUETTS, 1855...ELDER THOMAS CUSHMAN by Nathaniel B.
Shurtleff and Henry W. Cushman. Repr. of 1855 ed.
Paper—$15.00—84pp--- Vendor #D1842

1589 - THE CUSTER FAMILY by Milo Custer. Repr. of 1912 ed.
Paper—$6.50—27pp-- Vendor #D1842

1590 - THE CUTHBERTS, BARONS OF CASTLE HILL, AND THEIR DE-
SCENDANTS IN SOUTH CAROLINA AND GEORGIA by J. Bulloch.
Repr. of 1908 ed.
Paper—$20.00—100pp--------------------------------------- Vendor #D1842

1591 - GENEALOGICAL RECORD OF SEVERAL FAMILIES BEARING THE NAME
OF CUTLER IN THE UNITED STATES by Abner Morse. Repr. of 1867 ed.
Paper—$15.00—80pp--- Vendor #D1842

1592 - A CUTLER MEMORIAL AND GENEALOGICAL HISTORY by Nahum S.
Cutler. Repr. of 1889 ed.
Cloth—$99.50—Paper—$89.50—665pp----------------------- Vendor #D1842

1593 - DAILEY FAMILY, BIOGRAPHICAL HISTORY AND GENEALOGICAL OF
DESCENDANTS OF EBENEZER DAILEY....by E. D. Fox. Repr. of 1939
ed.
Paper—$30.00—186pp--------------------------------------- Vendor #D1842

1594   - THE NAME OF DALRYMPLE, WITH GENEALOGY OF ONE BRANCH IN
THE UNITED STATES by W. H. Dalrymple. Repr. of 1878 ed.
Paper—$14.00—68pp-- Vendor #D1842

1595   - DALRYMPLE, AN HISTORICAL AND GENEALOGICAL ACCOUNT, THE
EARL OF STAIR, ETC. (IN SCOTS' PEERRAGE) edited by J. B. Paul.
Repr. of 1911 ed.
Paper—$10.00—50pp-- Vendor #D1842

1596   - GENEALOGY OF THE DAME FAMILY FOR TEN GENERATIONS IN
AMERICA by E. and M. Estes. Repr. of 1890 ed.
Paper—$6.00—16pp-- Vendor #D1842

1597   - DAMON MEMORIAL by Brazil Monroe Damon. Repr. of 1897 ed.
Paper—$12.50—60pp--------------------------------------- Vendor #D1842

1598   - MEMORANDA OF SOME OF THE DESCENDANTS OF RICHARD DANA
OF CAMBRIDGE by J. J. Dana. Repr. of 1865 ed.
Paper—$12.50—64pp--------------------------------------- Vendor #D1842

1599   - DANFORTH GENEALOGY, NICHOLAS DANFORTH, OF FRAMINGHAM,
ENGLAND...AND THEIR DESCENDANTS by John J. May. Repr. of
1902 ed.
Cloth—$74.00—Paper—$64.00—492pp----------------------- Vendor #D1842

1600   - GENEALOGY OF THE DARBY FAMILY, GEORGE DARBY (1726-1788) OF
MONTGOMERY COUNTY, MARYLAND by R. C. Darby. Repr., n.d.
Paper—$35.00—172pp-------------------------------------- Vendor #D1842

1601   - BENJAMIN DARLING OF CASCO BAY, MAINE AND DESCENDANTS by
C. N. Sinnett. Repr. of 1923 ed., typescript.
Paper—$4.00—14pp-- Vendor #D1842

1602   - GATHERING OF CLAN DARLINGTON, WITH DESCENDANTS OF ABRA-
HAM DARLINGTON, ET AL. Repr. of 1853 ed.
Paper—$9.00—52pp-- Vendor #D1842

1603   - LEWIS DARY OF NORTON, MASSACHUSETTS AND SOME OF HIS DE-
SCENDANTS by G. A. Dary. Repr. of 1903 ed.
Paper—$5.00—25pp-- Vendor #D1842

1604   - SKETCH OF MILITARY CAREER OF CAPTAIN JOHN DAVES OF NORTH
CAROLINA CONTINENTAL LINE....by Graham Daves. Repr. of 1892 ed.
Paper—$4.50—16pp-- Vendor #D1842

1605   - JOHN DAVIS OF CHEBACCO (IPSWICH) PLUS SOME OF HIS DESCEND-
ANTS by E. A. Davis. Repr. of 1934 ed.
Paper—$5.00—24pp-- Vendor #D1842

1606   - DOLAR DAVIS, A SKETCH OF HIS LIFE, WITH RECORD OF HIS
EARLIER DESCENDANTS by H. Davis. Repr. of 1881 ed.
Paper—$9.50—46pp-- Vendor #D1842

1607   - HISTORY OF THE DAVIS FAMILY, DESCENDANTS OF JOHN DAVIS,
...LONG ISLAND, IN 1705....by Albert H. Davis. Repr. of 1888 ed.
Paper—$30.00—199pp-------------------------------------- Vendor #D1842

1608   - GENEALOGY OF JEFFERSON DAVIS; ADDRESS DELIVERED OCT. 9,
1908,...RICHMOND, VIRGINIA by William H. Whitsitt. Repr. of 1908 ed.
Paper—$4.50—16pp-- Vendor #D1842

1609   - GENEALOGY OF DESCENDANTS OF COLONEL JOHN DAVIS, OF
OXFORD, CONNECTICUT....by George T. Davis. Repr. of 1910 ed.
Cloth—$50.50—Paper—$40.50—338pp----------------------- Vendor #D1842

1610   - ONE LINE OF DESCENDANTS FROM DOLAR DAVIS AND RICHARD
EVERETT by Mrs. William Sumner Crosby. Repr. of 1911 ed.
Paper—$12.50—59pp--------------------------------------- Vendor #D1842

1611   - GENEALOGICAL RECORD OF THE DAVISON, DAVIDSON, DAVISSON
FAMILY OF NEW ENGLAND by H. R. Remson Coles. Repr. of 1899 ed.
Paper—$21.00—143pp-------------------------------------- Vendor #D1842

1612   - DAVISON FAMILY by A. A. Davison. Repr. of 1905 ed.
Paper—$15.00—78pp-------------------------------------- Vendor #D1842

1613   - RECORD OF THE DESCENDANTS OF ROBERT DAWSON...INCLUDING
BARNES, BATES AND THIRTY-ONE OTHER FAMILIES by Charles C.
Davidson. Repr. of 1874 ed.
Paper—$18.00—119pp------------------------------------- Vendor #D1842

1614   - GENEALOGICAL REGISTER OF DESCENDANTS IN MALE LINE OF
ROBERT DAY...1648, 2nd Edition. Repr. of 1848 ed.
Paper—$19.00—129pp------------------------------------- Vendor #D1842

1615   - SOME CHRONICLES OF THE DAY FAMILY by E. D. P. (i.e., Ellen
Day Putnam). Repr. of 1893 ed.
Paper—$23.50—159pp------------------------------------- Vendor #D1842

1616   - DESCENDANTS OF ANTHONY DAY OF GLOUCESTER, MASSACHU-
SETTS, 1645 by John Alphonso Day. Repr. of 1902 ed.
Paper—$4.50—11pp-------------------------------------- Vendor #D1842

1617   - GENEALOGICAL STORY, DAYTON AND TOMLINSON FAMILIES by
Laura D. Fessenden. Repr. of 1902 ed.
Paper—$34.50—230pp------------------------------------ Vendor #D1842

1618   - DESCENT OF FAMILY OF DEACON OF ELSTOWE AND LONDON...
ALLIED FAMILIES by Edward Deacon. Repr. of 1898 ed.
Cloth—$63.00—Paper—$53.00—420pp---------------------- Vendor #D1842

1619   - GENEALOGY OF DEAN FAMILY, DESCENDANTS OF EZRA DEAN OF
PLAINFIELD, CONNECTICUT AND CRANSTON, RHODE ISLAND by
A. D. Dean. Repr. of 1903 ed.
Paper—$30.00—158pp------------------------------------ Vendor #D1842

1620   - GENEALOGY OF DESCENDANTS OF JAMES DEAN, ONE OF FIRST
SETTLERS OF OAKHAM, MASSACHUSETTS by Gardner Milton Dean.
Repr. of 1889 ed.
Paper—$5.00—29pp-------------------------------------- Vendor #D1842

1621   - GENEALOGY OF ISAAC DEAN OF GRAFTON, NEW HAMPSHIRE...
JOHN DEAN OF TAUNTON edited by Josiah H. Drummond. Repr. of
1902 ed.
Paper—$7.50—35pp-------------------------------------- Vendor #D1842

1622   - DESCENDANTS OF THOMAS DEANE OF MASSACHUSETTS AND NEW
HAMPSHIRE by John Ward Dean. Repr. of 1883 ed.
Paper—$4.00—12pp-------------------------------------- Vendor #D1842

1623   - DEARBORNS OF HAMPTON, NEW HAMPSHIRE. DESCENDANTS OF
GODFREY DEARBORN OF EXETER AND HAMPTON by Joseph Dow.
Repr. from his History of Hampton, N.H., 1893 ed.
Paper—$4.50—16pp-------------------------------------- Vendor #D1842

1624   - DeCAMP GENEALOGY, LAURENT DeCAMP OF NEW UTRECHT, NEW
YORK 1664 AND HIS DESCENDANTS by G. A. Morrison. Repr. of
1900 ed.
Paper—$16.00—77pp------------------------------------- Vendor #D1842

1625   - HISTORY OF THE DeHAVEN FAMILY, 4th Edition, by H. D. Ross.
Repr. of 1929 ed., chart.
Paper—$10.00—43pp------------------------------------- Vendor #D1842

1626   - GENEALOGY OF DESCENDANTS OF LE MAITRE (DELAMATER) WHO
CAME FROM FRANCE...IN 1652 by La Fayette De La Mater. Repr. of
1832 ed.
Paper—$34.00—229pp------------------------------------ Vendor #D1842

1627   - EARLY OCCURENCES OF THE FAMILY NAME DeLONG IN EUROPE AND
AMERICA by I. H. DeLong. Repr. of 1924 ed.
Paper—$4.00—17pp-------------------------------------- Vendor #D1842

1628   - THE DE LOTBINIERES. A BIT OF CANADIAN ROMANCE AND
HISTORY by I. J. Greenwood. Repr. N. E. Hist. & Gen. Register,
1896 ed.
Paper—$4.00—8pp--------------------------------------- Vendor #D1842

1629   - DeMARANVILLE GENEALOGY, DESCENDANTS OF LOUIS DEMARAN-
VILLE by G. L. Randall. Repr. of 1921 ed.
Paper—$30.00—152pp-- Vendor #D1842

1630   - GENEALOGY OF DESCENDANTS OF JOHN DEMING OF WETHERSFIELD,
CONNECTICUT, WITH HISTORICAL NOTES by Judson K. Deming.
Repr. of 1904 ed.
Cloth—$105.00—Paper—$95.00—702pp----------------------- Vendor #D1842

1631   - RECORD OF THE DESCENDANTS OF CAPTAIN GEORGE DENISON, OF
STONINGTON, CONNECTICUT by John D. Baldwin and William Clift.
Repr. of 1881 ed.
Cloth—$63.50—Paper—$53.50—424pp----------------------- Vendor #D1842

1632   - DENISON MEMORIAL, IPSWICH, MASSACHUSETTS, 1883,...MAJOR-
GENERAL DANIEL DENISON...D. D. SLADE...AUGUSTINE CALDWELL.
Repr. of 1882 ed.
Paper—$10.00—52pp-- Vendor #D1842

1633   - DENMAN FAMILY HISTORY by H. N. Harris. Repr. of 1913 ed.
Paper—$17.50—80pp-- Vendor #D1842

1634   - GENEALOGY OF THE DENNISON FAMILY FROM GEORGE DENNISON
1725. Repr. of 1880 ed.
Paper—$4.50—15pp--- Vendor #D1842

1635   - GENEALOGY OF THE DENNY FAMILY IN ENGLAND AND AMERICA.
DESCENDANTS OF JOHN DENNY....by C. C. Denny. Repr. of 1886 ed.
Cloth—$40.00—Paper—$30.00—267pp----------------------- Vendor #D1842

1636   - DERBY GENEALOGY: RECORD OF JOHN DARBY OF MARBLE-
HEAD (10 GEN.) by W. D. Derby. Repr., n.d.
Paper—$5.00—22pp--- Vendor #D1842

1637   - DERBY GENEALOGY, BEING A RECORD OF DESCENDANTS OF
THOMAS DERBY OF STOW, MASSACHUSETTS by Viola A. Derby
Bromley. Repr. of 1905 ed.
Paper—$21.00—141pp--- Vendor #D1842

1638   - GENEALOGY OF THE DeVEAUX FAMILY by Thomas F. Devoe. Repr.
of 1885 ed.
Cloth—$45.00—Paper—$35.00—302pp----------------------- Vendor #D1842

1639   - DESCENDANTS OF ANDREW DEWING OF DEDHAM, MASSACHUSETTS
WITH...ENGLISH FAMILY OF THE NAME by Benjamin F. Dewing.
Repr. of 1904 ed.
Paper—$25.00—173pp--- Vendor #D1842

1640   - DeWITT FAMILY OF ULSTER COUNTY, NEW YORK by T. G. Evans.
Repr. of 1886 ed.
Paper—$5.00—18pp--- Vendor #D1842

1641   - CHARLES D'WOLF OF GUADALUPE..."RHODE ISLAND D'WOLF'S"...
FROM BALTHASAR deWOLF, OF LYME, CONNECTICUT, 1668 by Rev.
C. B. Perry. Repr. of 1902 ed.
Cloth—$49.00—Paper—$39.00—325pp----------------------- Vendor #D1842

1642   - DEXTER GENEALOGY, 1642-1904, HISTORY OF DESCENDANTS OF
RICHARD DEXTER OF MALDEN, MASSACHUSETTS by O. P. Dexter.
Repr. of 1904 ed.
Cloth—$41.50—Paper—$31.50—279pp----------------------- Vendor #D1842

1643   - GENEALOGY OF THE DEXTER FAMILY IN AMERICA, DESCENDANTS
OF THOMAS DEXTER....by William A. Warden and Robert L. Dexter.
Repr. of 1905 ed.
Cloth—$53.00—Paper—$43.00—353pp----------------------- Vendor #D1842

1644   - DEXTER GENEALOGY; BEING A RECORD OF FAMILIES DESCENDED
FROM REV. GREGORY DEXTER....by S. C. Newman. Repr. of 1859 ed.
Paper—$16.00—108pp--- Vendor #D1842

1645   - GENEALOGY OF THE DICKEY FAMILY by John Dickey. Repr. of
1898 ed.
Cloth—$48.00—Paper—$38.00—322pp----------------------- Vendor #D1842

1646 - GENEALOGY OF DIMOND OR DIMON FAMILY OF FAIRFIELD, CONNEC-
TICUT...DIMON OR DYMONT FAMILY....by Edwin R. Dimond. Repr.
of 1891 ed.
Paper—$26.50—179pp-- Vendor #D1842

1647 - DINGS FAMILY IN AMERICA GENEALOGY, MEMOIRS AND COMMENTS
by Myron Dings. Repr. of 1927 ed.
Paper—$25.00—182pp-- Vendor #D1842

1648 - DINKINS AND SPRINGS FAMILIES by J. Dinkins. Repr. of 1908 ed.
Paper—$5.00—24pp-- Vendor #D1842

1649 - DINSMORE GENEALOGY FROM ABOUT 1620 TO 1925 by Mrs. Marita
Houghton Savage. Repr. of 1927 ed.
Paper—$22.00—141pp-- Vendor #D1842

1650 - HISTORY AND GENEALOGY OF DIMSMOOR-DINSMORE FAMILY OF
SCOTLAND, IRELAND, AND AMERICA 1600-1891....by L. M. Morrison.
Repr. of 1891 ed.
Paper—$9.00—48pp-- Vendor #D1842

1651 - DINWIDDIE OF LAKE COUNTY, VIRGINIA FAMILY RECORDS by T. H.
Ball. Repr. of 1884 ed.
Paper—$3.50—8pp--- Vendor #D1842

1652 - BORDER OR RIDING CLANS FOLLOWED BY HISTORY OF THE CLAN
DICKSON...FAMILY OF AUTHOR by B. Hower Dixon. Repr. of 1889 ed.
Paper—$33.50—223pp-- Vendor #D1842

1653 - HISTORY OF CHARLES DIXON, ONE OF EARLY ENGLISH SETTLERS
OF SACKVILLE, N. B. by James D. Dixon. Repr. of 1891 ed.
Paper—$30.50—204pp-- Vendor #D1842

1654 - DOAK FAMILY by B. E. Hanes. Repr. of 1931 ed.
Paper—$25.00—100pp-- Vendor #D1842

1655 - DOANE FAMILY: I. DEACON JOHN DOANE, OF PLYMOUTH; II,
DOCTOR JOHN DONE, OF MARYLAND....by Alfred A. Doane. Repr.
of 1902 ed.
Cloth—$83.00—Paper—$73.00—554pp------------------------- Vendor #D1842

1656 - GENEALOGY OF MALE DESCENDANTS OF DANIEL DOD, OF BRANFORD,
CONNECTICUT...1646-1863 by Betheul L. Dodd and John R. Burnet.
Repr. of 1864 ed.
Paper—$33.00—221pp-- Vendor #D1842

1657 - ANCESTORS AND DESCENDANTS OF LEWIS DODD AND ELIZABETH
(BALDWIN) DODD by Bethuel Lewis Dodd. Repr., n.d.
Paper—$4.50—19pp-- Vendor #D1842

1658 - GENEALOGY AND HISTORY OF DODDS FAMILY by L. Colby. Repr.
of 1929 ed.
Paper—$35.00—177pp-- Vendor #D1842

1659 - TRISTRAM DODGE AND HIS DESCENDANTS IN AMERICA...BLOCK
ISLAND AND COW NECK, LONG ISLAND....by Robert Dodge. Repr.
of 1886 ed.
Paper—$37.00—248pp-- Vendor #D1842

1660 - GENEALOGY OF THE DODGE FAMILY OF ESSEX COUNTY, MASSA-
CHUSETTS, 1629-1894 by Joseph T. Dodge. Repr. of 1894 ed.
Cloth—$68.00—Paper—$58.00—456pp------------------------- Vendor #D1842

1661 - GENEALOGY OF THE DODGE FAMILY OF ESSEX COUNTY, MASSA-
CHUSETTS, SECOND PART, 1629-1898 by Joseph T. Dodge. Repr. of
1898 ed.
Paper—$33.00—218pp-- Vendor #D1842

1662 - ANCESTRY OF NATHAN DANE DODGE AND HIS WIFE, SARAH
(SHEPARD) DODGE...by Mary A. Parson. Repr. of 1896 ed.
Paper—$11.50—76pp--- Vendor #D1842

1663   - DODGE GENEALOGY, DESCENDANTS OF TRISTRAM DODGE by
       Theron R. Woodward. Repr. of 1904 ed.
       Paper—$36.00—241pp-------------------------------------- Vendor #D1842

1664   - EARLY RECORDS OF THE DODGE FAMILY IN AMERICA by R. R.
       Dodge. Repr. of 1879 ed.
       Paper—$4.00—12pp------------------------------------- Vendor #D1842

1665   - REPORT, FULL, AUTHENTIC, AND COMPLETE...FIRST REUNION
       OF DODGE FAMILY IN AMERICA, AT SALEM, MASSACHUSETTS, 1879
       by Robert Dodge. Repr. of 1879 ed.
       Paper—10.00—53pp-------------------------------------- Vendor #D1842

1666   - GENEALOGICAL HISTORY OF ONE BRANCH OF THE DODGE FAMILY
       by Thomas H. Dodge. Repr. of 1880 ed.
       Paper—$5.00—20pp-------------------------------------- Vendor #D1842

1667   - _____ THE DODGE LANDS AT COW NECK; AN APPENDIX by Richard
       Despard Dodge. Repr. of 1896 ed.
       Paper—$6.00—32pp-------------------------------------- Vendor #D1842

1668   - DODGE FAMILY OF ESSEX COUNTY, MASSACHUSETTS, FIRST
       THREE GENERATIONS by Joseph Thompson Dodge. Repr. N. E. Hist.
       & Gen. Register, 1892 ed.
       Paper—$4.00—11pp-------------------------------------- Vendor #D1842

1669   - A FEW FACTS RELATING TO ORIGIN AND HISTORY OF JOHN DOL-
       BEARE OF BOSTON....by Arthur Dimon Osborne. Repr. of 1893 ed.
       Paper—$6.00—32pp-------------------------------------- Vendor #D1842

1670   - ABRAHAM DOOLITTLE AND SOME OF HIS DESCENDANTS by Allen.
       Repr. of 1893 ed.
       Paper—$7.50—38pp-------------------------------------- Vendor #D1842

1671   - DOOLITTLE FAMILY IN AMERICA by William F. Doolittle. Repr. of
       1901-1908 ed.
       Cloth—$109.00—Paper—$99.00—730pp----------------------- Vendor #D1842

1672   - RECORDS OF DORLAND FAMILY IN AMERICA...BRANCHES DORLAND,
       DORLAN, DURLAND, DARLING...AND CANADA by John D. Cremer.
       Repr. of 1898 ed.
       Cloth—$48.00—Paper—38.00—320pp------------------------- Vendor #D1842

1673   - DORRANCE FAMILY IN THE UNITED STATES by A. A. Dorrance.
       Repr. of 1901 ed.
       Paper—$5.00—24pp-------------------------------------- Vendor #D1842

1674   - DORRANCE INSCRIPTIONS. OLD STERLING TOWNSHIP BURYING
       GROUND, ONECO, CONNECTICUT by Emma Finney Welch. Repr. of
       1909 ed.
       Paper—$10.00—24pp------------------------------------- Vendor #D1842

1675   - DOTY FAMILY HISTORY AND GENEALOGY by E. E. VanSant. Repr.
       of 1935 ed.
       Paper—$20.00—104pp------------------------------------ Vendor #D1842

1676   - DOTY-DOTEN FAMILY IN AMERICA. DESCENDANTS OF EDWARD
       DOTY...1620, 2 Vols., by Ethan Allen Doty. Repr. of 1897 ed.
       Cloth—$155.00—Paper—$135.00—1035pp------------------- Vendor #D1842

1677   - GENEALOGICAL AND BIOGRAPHICAL ACCOUNT OF FAMILY OF
       DRAKE IN AMERICA by Samuel Gardner Drake. Repr. of 1845 ed.
       Paper—$10.00—51pp------------------------------------- Vendor #D1842

1678   - ACCOUNT OF SILVER WEDDING OF MR. AND MRS. F. P. DRAPER
       ...DRAPER AND PRESTON FAMILIES. Repr. of 1871 ed.
       Paper—$6.00—32pp-------------------------------------- Vendor #D1842

1679   - THE DRAPERS IN AMERICA, BEING A HISTORY AND GENEALOGY OF
       ...THAT NAME AND CONNECTION by Thomas Waln-Morgan Draper.
       Repr. of 1892 ed.
       Cloth—$48.50—Paper—$38.50—324pp----------------------- Vendor #D1842

1680 - JOHN DRESSER OF ROWLEY, MASSACHUSETTS AND SOME OF HIS
DESCENDANTS by F. S. Kinsey. Repr., n.d.
Paper—$4.00—12pp--- Vendor #D1842

1681 - DRESSER FAMILY IN AMERICA by C. H. and W. S. Dresser. Repr.
of 1925 ed.
Paper—$4.00—14pp--- Vendor #D1842

1682 - DRINKER FAMILY IN AMERICA by H. D. Biddle. Repr. of 1893 ed.
Paper—$7.00—30pp--- Vendor #D1842

1683 -- DRINKWATER, ANCESTORS AND DESCENDANTS OF MICAJAH DRINK-
WATER OF NORTHFORD, MAINE, 1620-1825 by J. S. Fernald. Repr.,n.d.
Paper—$6.00—29pp--- Vendor #D1842

1684 - FAMILY OF DRINKWATER OF CHESHIRE, LANCASHIRE, ETC. IN
ENGLAND by Drinkwater and Fletcher. Repr. of 1920 ed.
Paper—$22.50—112pp--------------------------------------- Vendor #D1842

1685 - DRIVER FAMILY; GENEALOGICAL MEMOIR OF DESCENDANTS OF
ROBERT AND PHEBE DRIVER OF LYNN, MASSACHUSETTS....by Harriet
Ruth (Waters) Cooke. Repr. of 1889 ed.
Cloth—$83.00—Paper—73.00—556pp------------------------- Vendor #D1842

1686 - THE DUDLEY GENEALOGIES AND FAMILY RECORDS by Dean Dudley.
Repr. of 1848 ed.
Paper—$22.50—150pp--------------------------------------- Vendor #D1842

1687 - THE SUTTON-DUDLEYS OF ENGLAND AND DUDLEYS OF MASSA-
CHUSETTS IN NEW ENGLAND....by George Adlard. Repr. of 1862 ed.
Paper—$27.50—186pp--------------------------------------- Vendor #D1842

1688 - SKETCH OF FAMILY OF DUMARESQ, WITH ADDED REMINISCENCES
OF JAMES DUMARESQ. Repr. of 1863 ed.
Paper—$5.00—23pp--- Vendor #D1842

1689 - DUNCAN AND GIBSON FAMILIES by H. W. Duncan. Repr. of 1905 ed.
Paper—$9.00—44pp--- Vendor #D1842

1690 - ANCESTORS AND DESCENDANTS OF RICHARD DUNHAM OF PENN-
SYLVANIA AND HIS WIFE LAURA by Allen J. Crary. Repr. of 1916 ed.
Paper—$20.00—102pp--------------------------------------- Vendor #D1842

1691 - GENEALOGY OF THE DUNNELL-DWINELL FAMILY OF NE. by H. G.
Dunnel. Repr. of 1862 ed.
Paper—$17.50--- Vendor #D1842

1692 - GENEALOGICAL NOTES ON THE DUNNING FAMILY IN AMERICA
by M. B. Dunning. Repr. of 1915 ed.
Paper—$6.00—30pp--- Vendor #D1842

1693 - HENRY DUNSTER AND HIS DESCENDANTS by Samuel Dunster.
Repr. of 1876 ed.
Cloth—$51.00—Paper—41.00—343pp------------------------- Vendor #D1842

1694 - GENEALOGY OF THE DURAND, WHALLEY, BARNES, AND YALE
FAMILIES by F. B. Hewitt. Repr. of 1912 ed.
Paper—$23.00—115pp--------------------------------------- Vendor #D1842

1695 - GENEALOGY OF DUTTON FAMILY OF PENNSYLVANIA...THE
DUTTONS OF CONNECTICUT by Gilbert Cope. Repr. of 1871 ed.
Paper—$16.50—112pp--------------------------------------- Vendor #D1842

1696 - PRELIMINARY GENEALOGY OF DYAR FAMILY by H. G. Dyar.
Repr. of 1903 ed.
Paper—$6.50—32pp--- Vendor #D1842

1697 - THE DYER SETTLEMENT, FORT SEYBERT, WEST VIRGINIA MASSACRE
by M. Talbot. Repr. of 1937 ed.
Paper—$12.00—64pp--- Vendor #D1842

1698 - SOME RECORDS OF THE DYER FAMILY by Cornelia C. Joy-Dyer.
Repr. of 1884 ed.
Paper—$19.50—130pp--------------------------------------- Vendor #D1842

1699 - GENEALOGY OF ONE BRANCH OF THOMAS EAMES FAMILY...DEDHAM,
MASSACHUSETTS IN 1640 by Moses Eames. Repr. of 1887 ed.
Paper—$6.50—34pp-- Vendor #D1842

1700 - ROBERT EAMES OF WOBURN, MASSACHUSETTS AND SOME OF HIS
DESCENDANTS by Arthur G. Loring. Repr. of 1908 ed.
Paper—$3.00—17pp-- Vendor #D1842

1701 - THE EARLE FAMILY. RALPH EARLE AND HIS DESCENDANTS by
Pliny Earle. Repr. of 1888 ed.
Cloth—$77.00—Paper—$67.00—516pp------------------------ Vendor #D1842

1702 - HISTORY OF THE FAMILY OF EARLY IN AMERICA;...DESCENDANTS
OF JEREMIAH EARLY by Samuel Stockwell Early, arranged by Robert
Stockwell Hatcher. Repr. of 1896 ed.
Paper—$10.50—53pp--- Vendor #D1842

1703 - GENEALOGY OF THE EASTMAN FAMILY, FOR THE FIRST FOUR
GENERATIONS by Rev. Lucius R. Eastman. Repr. of 1867 ed.
Paper—$3.50—11pp-- Vendor #D1842

1704 - HISTORY AND GENEALOGY OF EASTMAN FAMILY OF AMERICA,
CONTINUED BIOGRAPHICAL SKETCHES....by Guy S. Rix. Repr. of
1901 ed.
Cloth—$150.00—Paper—$130.00—1000pp--------------------- Vendor #D1842

1705 - DESCENDANTS OF JOSEPH EASTON, HARTFORD, CONNECTICUT,
1636-1899 by William S. Easton. Repr. of 1899 ed.
Paper—$38.50—257pp-- Vendor #D1842

1706 - THE EATON FAMILY OF NOVA SCOTIA, 1760-1929 by Arthur W. H.
Eaton. Repr. of 1929 ed.
Paper—$38.00—253pp-- Vendor #D1842

1707 - HISTORY OF THE EBERHARTS IN GERMANY AND THE UNITED
STATES, FROM 1265-1890....by Rev. Urian Eberhart. Repr. of 1891 ed.
Paper—$39.50—263pp-- Vendor #D1842

1708 - MEMOIR OF COLONEL JONATHAN EDDY OF EDDINGTON, MAINE,
...PENOBSCOT RIVER by Joseph W. Porter. Repr. of 1877 ed.
Paper—$14.00—73pp--- Vendor #D1842

1709 - EDGERTON GENEALOGY 1762-1927 by J. Edgerton. Repr. of 1927 ed.
Paper—$6.00—29pp-- Vendor #D1842

1710 - GENEALOGY OF THE EDSONS by Jarvis B. Edson. Repr. of 1903 ed.
Paper—$30.00—184pp-- Vendor #D1842

1711 - NATHAN EDSON AND HIS DESCENDANTS by G. T. Edson. Repr. of
1926 ed.
Paper—$10.00—48pp--- Vendor #D1842

1712 - GENEALOGICAL ACCOUNT OF THE EDSONS, EARLY SETTLED IN
BRIDGEWATER, WITH APPENDICES by Theodore Edson. Repr. of
1864 ed.
Paper—$12.00—62pp--- Vendor #D1842

1713 - SEVERAL ANCESTRAL LINES OF JOSIAH EDSON AND HIS WIFE,
SARAH PINNEY....by Harriette Hyde Wells and Harry Weston Van
Dyke. Repr. of 1901 ed.
Paper—$15.00—98pp--- Vendor #D1842

1714 - TIMOTHY AND RHODA OGDEN EDWARDS OF STOCKBRIDGE, MASSA-
CHUSETTS, AND THEIR DESCENDANTS by William H. Edwards. Repr.
of 1903 ed.
Paper—$26.00—172pp-- Vendor #D1842

1715 - A CONDENSED GENEALOGY OF ONE BRANCH OF EDWARDS FAMILY OF
CONCORD AND ACTON, MASSACHUSETTS....by John Harrington Ed-
wards. Repr. of 1907 ed.
Paper—$6.00—28pp--- Vendor #D1842

1716 - OUR PATRONYMICS, EDWARDS, PARSONS, CLEVELAND AND ALLIED
FAMILIES by E. E. Gifford. Repr. of 1886 ed.
Paper—$6.00—28pp--- Vendor #D1842

1717 - GENEALOGY OF ELA FAMILY, DESCENDANTS OF ISRAEL ELA OF
HAVERHILL, MASSACHUSETTS by David Hough Ela. Repr. of 1896 ed.
Paper—$9.00—44pp--- Vendor #D1842

1718 - GENEALOGY OF DAVID ELDER AND MARGERY STEWART by T. A.
Elder. Repr. of 1905 ed.
Paper—$10.00—52pp-- Vendor #D1842

1719 - JOHN ELDERKIN, A FOUNDER OF CONNECTICUT AND SOME OF HIS
DESCENDANTS by J. Elderkin. Repr. of 1896 ed.
Paper—$4.00—19pp--- Vendor #D1842

1720 - EELS FAMILY OF DORCHESTER, MASSACHUSETTS...WITH NOTES
ON THE LENTHALL FAMILY by Frank F. Star. Repr. of 1903 ed.
Paper—$33.50—224pp--------------------------------------- Vendor #D1842

1721 - A SKETCH OF THE ELIOT FAMILY by Walter G. Eliot. Repr. of
1887 ed.
Paper—$25.00—177pp--------------------------------------- Vendor #D1842

1722 - THE JOHN ELLIOT FAMILY OF BOSCAWEN, NEW HAMPSHIRE by
Henry Ames Kimball. Repr. of 1918 ed.
Paper—$20.00—132pp--------------------------------------- Vendor #D1842

1723 - GENEALOGY OF DESCENDANTS OF JOHN ELIOT, "APOSTLE TO THE
INDIANS," 1598-1905 by Willimena H. Emerson. Repr. of 1905 ed.
Cloth—$53.60—Paper—$43.60—356pp------------------------- Vendor #D1842

1724 - THE ELLIS FAMILY by Mrs. Katherine S. Foos. Repr. of 1900 ed.
Paper—$19.00—128pp--------------------------------------- Vendor #D1842

1725 - BIOGRAPHICAL SKETCHES OF RICHARD ELLIS, FIRST SETTLER OF
ASHFIELD, MASSACHUSETTS...by E. R. Ellis. Repr. of 1888 ed.
Cloth—$72.50—Paper—$62.50—483pp------------------------- Vendor #D1842

1726 - GENEALOGY OF ELLIS FAMILY 1632-1920 AND COBURN FAMILY 1618-
1911 by H. W. and A. S. Ellis. Repr. of 1920 ed., chart.
Paper—$6.00—12pp--- Vendor #D1842

1727 - JAMES ELLISON MEMORIAL 1778-1820, WITH ELLISON GENEALOGY
by M. H. Curran. Repr. of 1903 ed.
Paper—$4.00—19pp--- Vendor #D1842

1728 - ELMER-ELMORE GENEALOGY by W. W. Johnson. Repr. of 1899 ed.
Paper—$20.00—96pp-- Vendor #D1842

1729 - FAMILY MEMORIALS, HISTORY AND GENEALOGY OF ELMORE FAMILY
by T. J. Elmore. Repr. of 1880 ed.
Paper—$8.00—40pp--- Vendor #D1842

1730 - HISTORY OF ELY RE-UNION HELD AT LYME, CONNECTICUT, JULY
10TH, 1878 by Mrs. Margaret Elizabeth Dunbar Stuart. Repr. of 1879 ed.
Paper—$23.50—158pp--------------------------------------- Vendor #D1842

1731 - ELWELL FAMILY IN AMERICA; GENEALOGY OF ROBERT ELWELL OF
MASSACHUSETTS by Jacob Thomas Elwell, revised by Charles Henry
Pope. Repr. of 1899 ed.
Paper—$6.00—30pp--- Vendor #D1842

1732 - HISTORICAL NARRATIVE OF ELY, REVELL AND STACYE FAMILIES,
OF TRENTON AND BURLINGTON, WEST JERSEY....by Reuben Pownall
Ely, et al. Repr. of 1910 ed.
Cloth—$66.50—Paper—$56.50—445pp------------------------- Vendor #D1842

1733 - THE IPSWICH EMERSONS, 1636-1900...WITH SOME ACCOUNT OF HIS
ENGLISH ANCESTRY by Benjamin Kendall Emerson. Repr. of 1900 ed.
Cloth—$81.50—Paper—$71.50—544pp------------------------- Vendor #D1842

1734 - THE HAVERHILL EMERSONS, PART 1 by Charles Henry Pope. Repr.
of 1913 ed.
Paper—$15.00—106pp--------------------------------------- Vendor #D1842

1735   - THE HAVERHILL EMERSONS, PART 2 by Charles Henry Pope. Repr.
         of 1916 ed.
         Paper—$37.00—248pp------------------------------------- Vendor #D1842

1736   - D'AMERIE-EMERY-AMORY by J. W. Thornton. Repr. N. E. Hist. &
         Gen. Register, 1869 ed.
         Paper—$3.50—6pp--- Vendor #D1842

1737   - EMERY. FOUR GENERATIONS OF DESCENDANTS OF JOHN EMERY,
         SENATOR, OF NEWBURY, MASSACHUSETTS....by Rufus Emery, et al.
         Repr. of 1889 ed.
         Paper—$4.50—22pp--------------------------------------- Vendor #D1842

1738   - GENEALOGICAL RECORDS OF DESCENDANTS OF JOHN AND ANTHONY
         EMERY OF NEWBURY, MASSACHUSETTS, 1590-1890 by Rufus Emery.
         Repr. of 1890 ed.
         Cloth—$93.00—Paper—$83.00—621pp----------------------- Vendor #D1842

1739   - MATERIALS TOWARD A GENEALOGY OF THE EMMERTON FAMILY by
         James A. Emmerton. Repr. of 1881 ed.
         Paper—$37.00—248pp------------------------------------- Vendor #D1842

1740   - EMMONS FAMILY GENEALOGY. THOMAS EMMONS OF NEWPORT,
         RHODE ISLAND...1639 TO 1905 by Edward Neville Emmons. Repr. of
         1905 ed.
         Cloth—$43.00—Paper—$33.00—287pp----------------------- Vendor #D1842

1741   - THE ENO FAMILY, NEW YORK BRANCH by H. L. Eno. Repr. of
         1920 ed.
         Paper—$7.00—35pp--------------------------------------- Vendor #D1842

1742   - THE ERSKINE FAMILY OF BRISTOL, MAINE by Frank Ernest Wood-
         ward. Repr. of 1920 ed.
         Paper—$6.00—31pp--------------------------------------- Vendor #D1842

1743   - ERWIN FAMILY RECORD by F. Brandt. Repr. of 1895 ed.
         Paper—$3.50—8pp-- Vendor #D1842

1744   - GENEALOGY OF ESTABROOK FAMILY,...ESTERBROOK AND EASTER-
         BROOKS IN THE UNITED STATES by William Booth Estabrook. Repr.
         of 1891 ed.
         Cloth—$54.00—Paper—$44.00—359pp----------------------- Vendor #D1842

1745   - ESTES GENEALOGY 1097-1893 by Charles Estes. Repr. of 1894 ed.
         Cloth—$62.50—Paper—$52.50—417pp----------------------- Vendor #D1842

1746   - ISAAC ESTY OF TOPSFIELD AND SOME OF HIS DESCENDANTS by
         Gay Esty Bangs. Repr. Essex Inst. Hist. Coll., 1900 ed.
         Paper—4.00—12pp-- Vendor #D1842

1747   - GENEALOGY OF THE EUSTIS FAMILY by Henry Lawrence Eustis.
         Repr. N. E. Hist. & Gen. Register, 1878 ed.
         Paper—$5.00—27pp--------------------------------------- Vendor #D1842

1748   - THE EVANS FAMILY by Samuel Evans. Repr. of 1895 ed.
         Paper—$4.50—21pp--------------------------------------- Vendor #D1842

1749   - EVANS FAMILY, DESCENDANTS OF WILLIAM OF WALES...BURLING-
         TON COUNTY, NEW JERSEY by George Haines. Extracted from Haines
         Gen. Repr. of 1902 ed.
         Paper—$4.50—20pp--------------------------------------- Vendor #D1842

1750   - EVELYNS IN AMERICA COMPILED FROM FAMILY PAPERS AND SOURCES,
         1608-1805 by G. D. Scull. Repr. of 1881 ed.
         Cloth—$60.50—Paper—$50.50—404pp----------------------- Vendor #D1842

1751   - DESCENDANTS OF RICHARD EVERETT OF DEDHAM, MASSACHUSETTS
         by Edward F. Everett. Repr. of 1902 ed.
         Cloth—$58.00—Paper—$48.00—389pp----------------------- Vendor #D1842

1752   - EVES FAMILY, DESCENDANTS OF THOMAS OF LONDON WHO EMI-
         GRATED TO BURLINGTON, NEW JERSEY IN 1677 by George Haines.
         Repr. of 1902 ed. Extracted from Haines Gen.
         Paper—$4.00--- Vendor #D1842

1753 - SKETCHES OF THE FAMILY OF THOMAS, WILLIAM, AND JAMES EWING
AND THEIR DESCENDANTS by J. L. Ewing. Repr. of 1910 ed.
Paper—$25.00—123pp-------------------------------------- Vendor #D1842

1754 - THE EWING GENEALOGY WITH COGNATE BRANCHES by P. K. and
M. E. Ewing. Repr. of 1919 ed.
Paper—$36.50—244pp-------------------------------------- Vendor #D1842

1755 - SOME DESCENDANTS OF JONATHAN FABENS OF MARBLEHEAD by
George A. Perkins. Repr. Essex Inst. Hist. Coll., 1881 ed.
Paper—$5.00—26pp-- Vendor #D1842

1756 - GENEALOGY OF FAIRBANKS FAMILY IN AMERICA, 1633-1897 by
Lorenzo Sayles Fairbanks. Repr. of 1897 ed.
Cloth—$145.00—Paper—$125.00—967pp---------------------- Vendor #D1842

1757 - DESCENDANTS OF JOHN FAIRMAN OF ENFIELD, CONNECTICUT,
1638-1898 by O. P. Allen. Repr. of 1898 ed.
Paper—$8.00—38pp-- Vendor #D1842

1758 - FALES FAMILY OF BRISTOL, RHODE ISLAND: ANCESTRY OF HALI-
BURTON FALES OF NEW YORK by De Coursey Fales. Repr. of 1919 ed.
Cloth—$50.00—Paper—$40.00—332pp----------------------- Vendor #D1842

1759 - HISTORY OF THE FANNING FAMILY, A GENEALOGICAL RECORD TO
1900 OF DESCENDANTS OF EDMUND FANNING....by Walter F. Brooks.
Repr. of 1905 ed.
Cloth—$131.00—Paper—$121.00—872pp---------------------- Vendor #D1842

1760 - HISTORY OF THOMAS AND ANNE (BILLOPP) FARMAR AND SOME OF
THEIR DESCENDANTS by C. F. Billopp. Repr. of 1907 ed.
Paper—$25.00—137pp-------------------------------------- Vendor #D1842

1761 - FARNSWORTH MEMORIAL. BEING A RECORD OF MATTHIAS FARNS-
WORTH AND HIS DESCENDANTS IN AMERICA by Moses Franklin Farns-
worth. Repr. of 1897 ed.
Cloth—$77.00—Paper—$67.00—514pp----------------------- Vendor #D1842

1762 - MY ANCESTORS AND THEIR DESCENDANTS, THE FAULKNER FAMILY
by W. L. Brown. Repr., n.d.
Paper—$8.00—38pp-- Vendor #D1842

1763 - FAVILL FAMILY by S. Favill. Repr. of 1899 ed.
Paper—$9.00—44pp-- Vendor #D1842

1764 - FAY GENEALOGY, JOHN FAY OF MARLBOROUGH AND HIS DESCEND-
ANTS by Orlin P. Fay. Repr. of 1898 ed.
Cloth—$63.00—Paper—$53.00—420pp----------------------- Vendor #D1842

1765 - MEMORIAL HISTORY OF FELCH FAMILY IN AMERICA AND WALES,
1641-1881, 3 parts in 1 Vol., by W. Farrnad Felch. Repr. of 1881 ed.
Paper—$15.00—82pp--------------------------------------- Vendor #D1842

1766 - GENEALOGY OF FELL FAMILY IN AMERICA DESCENDED FROM
JOSEPH FELL...BUCKS COUNTY, PENNSYLVANIA, 1705 by Sarah M.
Fell. Repr. of 1891 ed.
Cloth—$77.00—Paper—$67.00—515pp----------------------- Vendor #D1842

1767 - GENEALOGY OF FELLOS-CRAIG AND ALLIED FAMILIES FROM 1619
TO 1919 by Frank H. Craig. Repr. of 1919 ed.
Paper—$22.50—151pp-------------------------------------- Vendor #D1842

1768 - THE FELT GENEALOGY, A RECORD OF DESCENDANTS OF GEORGE
FELT OF CASCO BAY by John E. Morris. Repr. of 1893 ed.
Cloth—$85.00—Paper—$75.00—568pp----------------------- Vendor #D1842

1769 - A BRIEF ACCOUNT OF SOME OF THE DESCENDANTS OF NATHANIEL
AND MARY FELTON....by Cyrus Felton. Repr. of 1877 ed.
Paper—$4.50—19pp-- Vendor #D1842

1770 - GENEALOGICAL HISTORY OF THE FELTON FAMILY...WHO CAME TO
SALEM, MASSACHUSETTS, 1633 by Cyrus Felton. Repr. of 1886 ed.
Paper—$39.00—260pp-------------------------------------- Vendor #D1842

1771 - GENEALOGY OF FENTON FAMILY, DESCENDANTS OF ROBERT FEN-
TON OF WINDHAM, CONNECTICUT by W. L. Weaver. Repr. of 1867 ed.
Paper—$7.50—34pp-- Vendor #D1842

1772 - THE FENTON FAMILY OF AMERICA AND GREAT BRITAIN by Thomas
Astley Atkins. Repr. of 1912 ed.
Paper—$23.00—154pp-------------------------------------- Vendor #D1842

1773 - THOMAS FERRIER AND SOME OF HIS DESCENDANTS by E. E. Lane.
Repr. of 1906 ed.
Paper—$10.00—56pp--------------------------------------- Vendor #D1842

1774 - PARTIAL GENEALOGY OF THE FERRIS FAMILY by C. E. Crowell.
Repr. of 1899 ed.
Paper—$12.00—60pp--------------------------------------- Vendor #D1842

1775 - RECORD OF THE FAMILY OF THE LATE REV. DAVID D. FIELD,
D. D. OF STOCKBRIDGE, MASSACHUSETTS by Henry M. Field. Repr.
of 1880 ed.
Paper—$22.00—147pp-------------------------------------- Vendor #D1842

1776 - FIELD GENEALOGY, BEING THE RECORD OF ALL OF THE FIELD
FAMILIES IN AMERICA...PRIOR TO 1700, 2 Vols., by Frederick C.
Pierce. Repr. of 1901 ed.
Cloth—$179.00—Paper—$159.00—1196pp--------------------- Vendor #D1842

1777 - BRISTOL BRANCH OF THE FINNEY FAMILY by F. C. Clark. Repr.
of 1906 ed.
Paper—$4.00—13pp-- Vendor #D1842

1778 - GENEALOGY OF JOSEPH FISHER AND HIS DESCENDANTS...ALLIED
FAMILIES OF FARLEY, FARLEE, FEHERMAN, PITNER, REEDER, AND
SHIPMAN by Clarence W. Fisher. Repr. of 1890 ed.
Paper—$36.50—243pp-------------------------------------- Vendor #D1842

1779 - FISHER GENEALOGICAL RECORD OF THE DESCENDANTS OF JOSHUA,
ANTHONY AND CORNELIUS FISHER....by Philip H. Fisher. Repr.
of 1898 ed.
Cloth—$86.00—Paper—$76.00—474pp------------------------ Vendor #D1842

1780 - THE FISKE FAMILY...WILLIAM FISKE, SENATOR, OF AMHERST, NEW
HAMPSHIRE, WITH...OTHER BRANCHES, 2nd Ed., by Albert A. Fiske.
Repr. of 1867 ed.
Paper—$32.50—210pp-------------------------------------- Vendor #D1842

1781 - FISKE AND FISH FAMILIES, DESCENDANTS OF SYMOND FISKE,
LORD OF THE MANOR....by Frederick C. Pierce. Repr. of 1896 ed.
Cloth—$99.00—Paper—$89.00—660pp------------------------ Vendor #D1842

1782 - GENEALOGY OF THE FITCH FAMILY IN NORTH AMERICA by John G.
Fitch. Repr. of 1886 ed.
Paper—$17.50—116pp-------------------------------------- Vendor #D1842

1783 - FITCH GENEALOGY. RECORD OF SIX GENERATIONS OF DESCEND-
ANTS OF DEACON ZACHARY FITCH....by Ezra S. Stearns. Repr.
N. E. Hist. & Gen. Register, 1902 ed.
Paper—$4.50—23pp-- Vendor #D1842

1784 - FAMILY RECORDS OF DESCENDANTS OF GERSHOM FLAGG OF
LANCASTER, MASSACHUSETTS....by Norman Gershom Flagg and Lucius
C. S. Flagg. Repr. of 1907 ed.
Paper—$26.00—173pp-------------------------------------- Vendor #D1842

1785 - THE FLANDERS FAMILY by William Prescott. Repr. N. E. Hist. &
Gen. Register, 1873 ed.
Paper—$3.50—8pp--- Vendor #D1842

1786 - FLETCHER GENEALOGY; AN ACCOUNT OF DESCENDANTS OF ROBERT
FLETCHER OF CONCORD, MASSACHUSETTS by Edward H. Fletcher.
Repr. of 1871 ed.
Cloth—$42.00—Paper—$32.00—279pp------------------------ Vendor #D1842

1787 - GENEALOGY IN PART OF FLETCHER-CROWDER-TUCKER FAMILIES
by Grant James Anderson. Repr. of 1909 ed.
Paper—$15.00—92pp------------------------------------- Vendor #D1842

1788 - FLETCHER GENEALOGY, ACCOUNT OF DESCENDANTS OF ROBERT
FLETCHER OF CONCORD, MASSACHUSETTS by Edward H. Fletcher.
Repr. of 1871 ed.
Cloth—$42.00—Paper—$32.00—279pp----------------------- Vendor #D1842

1789 - GENEALOGICAL REGISTER OF DESCENDANTS OF THOMAS FLINT,
OF SALEM by John Flint and John H. Stone. Repr. of 1860 ed.
Paper—$22.50—150pp------------------------------------- Vendor #D1842

1790 - BIOGRAPHICAL GENEALOGY OF THE VIRGINIA-KENTUCKY FLOYD
FAMILY by J. J. Floyd. Repr. of 1912 ed.
Paper—$20.00—113pp------------------------------------- Vendor #D1842

1791 - THE FOGG FAMILY OF AMERICA. REUNIONS OF THE FOGG FAM-
ILIES...1902-1906 (1907) edited by Mrs. A. J. Fogg and J. L. M. Willis.
Repr. of 1907 ed.
Paper—$21.00—141pp------------------------------------- Vendor #D1842

1792 - GENEALOGY OF THE FOGG FAMILY DESCENDANTS OF SAMUEL FOGGE
by Mrs. Horace Fogg. Repr. of 1903 ed.
Paper—$8.50—49pp-------------------------------------- Vendor #D1842

1793 - FOLLETT-DEWEY, FASSETT-SAFFORD ANCESTRY OF CAPTAIN
MARTIN DEWEY FOLLETT...PERSIS FASSETT (1767-1849) by Harry
Parker Ward. Repr. of 1896 ed.
Paper—$37.00—249pp------------------------------------- Vendor #D1842

1794 - GENEALOGY OF THE FOLSOM FAMILY. JOHN FOLSOM AND HIS
DESCENDANTS, 1615-1882 by Jacob Chapman. Repr. of 1882 ed.
Paper—$35.00—297pp------------------------------------- Vendor #D1842

1795 - FORBES AND FORBUSH GENEALOGY, DESCENDANTS OF DANIEL
FORBUSH...MARLBOROUGH, MASSACHUSETTS, IN 1675 by Frederick
C. Pierce. Repr. of 1892 ed.
Paper—$30.00—199pp------------------------------------- Vendor #D1842

1796 - FORD GENEALOGY, AN ACCOUNTING OF SOME OF THE FORDS...
MARTIN-MATHEW FORD OF BRADFORD, ESSEX COUNTY, MASSA-
CHUSETTS by Eliakin R. Ford. Repr. of 1916 ed.
Paper—$37.00—249pp------------------------------------- Vendor #D1842

1797 - FOREMAN-FARMAN-FORMAN GENEALOGY. DESCENDANTS OF WILLIAM
FOREMAN...ANNAPOLIS, MARYLAND by Elbert Eli Farman. Repr. of
1911 ed.
Paper—$34.50—232pp------------------------------------- Vendor #D1842

1798 - FORMAN GENEALOGY. DESCENDANTS OF ROBERT FORMAN OF
KENT COUNTY, MARYLAND...MONMOUTH COUNTY, NEW JERSEY by
Miss Anne S. Dendridge. Repr. of 1903 ed.
Paper—$23.00—151pp------------------------------------- Vendor #D1842

1799 - HISTORY OF ANTECEDENTS AND DESCENDANTS OF WILLIAM AND
DOROTHY WORTHEN FORREST....by Lucy R. H. Cross. Repr. of
1897 ed.
Paper—$22.00—145pp------------------------------------- Vendor #D1842

1800 - PEDIGREE AND DESCENDANTS OF JACOB FORSTER, SENATOR, OF
CHARLESTOWN, MASSACHUSETTS by Edward Jacob Forster. Repr.
of 1870 ed.
Paper—$5.50—25pp-------------------------------------- Vendor #D1842

1801 - A GENEALOGICAL RECORD. FORSYTH OF NYDIE by Forsyth de
Fronsac (Frederic Gregory Forsyth). Repr. of 1888 ed.
Paper—$5.50—29pp-------------------------------------- Vendor #D1842

1802 - MEMORIAL OF FAMILY OF FORSYTH de FRONSAC by Frederic
Gregory de Fronsac. Repr. of 1903 ed., chart.
Paper—$18.50—104pp------------------------------------- Vendor #D1842

1803 - FOSDICK FAMILY, OYSTER BAY BRANCH 1583-1891...SAMUEL FOS-
DICK OF OYSTER BAY by L. I. Fosdick. Repr. of 1891 ed.
Paper—$26.50—137pp-------------------------------------- Vendor #D1842

1804 - FOSTER FAMILY. ONE LINE OF DESCENDANTS OF WILLIAM FOSTER,
...IPSWICH, MASSACHUSETTS by Perley Derby. Repr. of 1872 ed.
Paper—$7.00—35pp-------------------------------------- Vendor #D1842

1805 - GRANDCHILDREN OF COLONEL JOSEPH FOSTER OF IPSWICH AND
GLOUCESTER, MASSACHUSETTS, 1730-1804 by Joseph Foster. Repr.
of 1885 ed.
Paper—$6.00—32pp-------------------------------------- Vendor #D1842

1806 - FOSTER GENEALOGY. A RECORD OF THE POSTERITY OF REGINALD
FOSTER...AMERICAN FOSTERS by Frederick C. Pierce. Repr. of
1899 ed.
Cloth—$162.00—Paper—$142.00—1081pp--------------------- Vendor #D1842

1807 - WILLIAM FOWLER, THE MAGISTRATE, AND ONE LINE OF HIS DE-
SCENDANTS by W. C. Fowler. Repr., n.d.
Paper—$7.50—41pp-------------------------------------- Vendor #D1842

1808 - A GENEALOGICAL MEMOIR OF DESCENDANTS OF AMBROSE FOWLER
...WILLIAM FOWLER OF NEW HAVEN, CONNECTICUT. Repr. of 1857 ed.
Paper—$5.50—27pp-------------------------------------- Vendor #D1842

1809 - DANIEL FOX OF EAST HADDAM, CONNECTICUT AND SOME OF HIS
DESCENDANTS. Repr. of 1890 ed.
Paper—$6.00—29pp-------------------------------------- Vendor #D1842

1810 - HISTORY OF...FOX FAMILY DESCENDED FROM THOMAS FOX OF
CAMBRIDGE, MASSACHUSETTS by N. M. Fox. Repr. of 1899 ed.
Paper—$36.00—240pp-------------------------------------- Vendor #D1842

1811 - FOX FAMILY MARRIAGES by W. M. Clemens. Repr. of 1916 ed.
Paper—$9.00—44pp-------------------------------------- Vendor #D1842

1812 - DESCENDANTS OF ROBERT FRANCIS OF WETHERSFIELD, CONNEC-
TICUT, GENEALOGICAL RECORDS...CONNECTICUT ORIGEN by Charles
E. Francis. Repr. of 1906 ed.
Paper—$34.00—226pp-------------------------------------- Vendor #D1842

1813 - FREEMAN GENEALOGY, PART I: MEMORIAL OF EDMUND FREEMAN
OF SANDWICH AND HIS DESCENDANTS; II: SAMUEL FREEMAN....,
2nd ed., by Frederick Freeman. Repr. of 1875 ed.
Cloth—$68.00—Paper—$58.00—457pp----------------------- Vendor #D1842

1814 - HISTORY OF THE MATTHEW FRANK FAMILY by H. L. Nelson.
Repr. of 1921 ed.
Paper—$5.00—24pp-------------------------------------- Vendor #D1842

1815 - THE FAMILY, ANCESTORS AND DESCENDANTS OF CAPTAIN JOHN
FRENCH, OF STOUGHTON, MASSACHUSETTS by Sidney French.
Repr. of 1870 ed.
Paper—$4.00—12pp-------------------------------------- Vendor #D1842

1816 - JOHN FRENCH OF BRAINTREE, MASSACHUSETTS...FRANCE, ENG-
LAND, IRELAND, SCOTLAND, AND THE UNITED STATES by A. D.
Weld French. Repr. of 1885 ed.
Paper—$4.00—15pp-------------------------------------- Vendor #D1842

1817 - FROST GENEALOGY by A. A. Doane. Repr. of 1910 ed.
Paper—$7.50—3.50-------------------------------------- Vendor #D1842

1818 - FROST GENEALOGY IN FIVE FAMILIES by Norman Seaver Frost.
Repr. of 1926 ed.
Cloth—$61.50—Paper—$51.50—410pp----------------------- Vendor #D1842

1819 - THE FROTHINGHAM GENEALOGY by Thomas Bellows Wyman, edited
by Thomas Goddard Frothingham. Repr. of 1916 ed.
Paper—$25.50—170pp-------------------------------------- Vendor #D1842

1820 - MEMOIR OF COLONEL JOSHUA FRY OF VIRGINIA...AND ALLIED
LINES by P. Slaughter. Repr., n.d.
Paper—$23.50—113pp-------------------------------------- Vendor #D1842

1821 - FRYE GENEALOGY by Ellen Frye Barker. Repr. of 1920 ed.
Paper—$30.00—194pp------------------------------------- Vendor #D1842

1822 - FRYE GENEALOGY. ADRIAN OF KITTERY, MAINE; JOHN OF AND-
OVER, MASSACHUSETTS....by Ellen F. Barker. Repr. of 1920 ed.
Paper—$29.00—194pp------------------------------------- Vendor #D1842

1823 - HISTORICAL NOTICES OF THOMAS FULLER OF MIDDLETON, MASSA-
CHUSETTS AND HIS DESCENDANTS by Fuller and Dean. Repr. of
1859 ed.
Paper—$4.00—17pp--------------------------------------- Vendor #D1842

1824 - DESCENDANTS OF ENS. THOMAS FULLER OF DEDHAM by F. Fuller.
Repr. of 1894 ed.
Paper—$5.00—24pp--------------------------------------- Vendor #D1842

1825 - ALDEN-FULLER RECORD. RECORD OF DESCENDANTS OF LEMUEL
FULLER, SR. by M. Percy Black. Repr. of 1896 ed.
Paper—$13.50—74pp-------------------------------------- Vendor #D1842

1826 - A BRIEF SKETCH OF THOMAS FULLER AND HIS DESCENDANTS, WITH
HISTORICAL NOTES by Jesse Franklin Fuller. Repr. of 1896 ed.
Paper—$10.00—47pp-------------------------------------- Vendor #D1842

1827 - FULTON-HAYDEN-WARNER ANCESTRY IN AMERICA by Clarence
Ettienne Leonard. Repr. of 1923 ed.
Cloth—$94.50—Paper—$84.50—629pp----------------------- Vendor #D1842

1828 - FULLER GENEALOGY, RECORD OF JOSEPH FULLER...WOBURN AND
MIDDLETON, MASSACHUSETTS by Elizabeth Abercrombie. Repr. of
1897 ed.
Paper—$15.00—101pp------------------------------------- Vendor #D1842

1829 - NEW ENGLAND ANCESTRY OF LYMAN J. GAGE by Arthur E. Gage.
Repr. N. E. Hist. & Gen. Register, 1899 ed.
Paper—$3.50—8pp-- Vendor #D1842

1830 - RECORD OF PIERCE GAGE AND HIS DESCENDANTS by G. N. Gage.
Repr. of 1894 ed.
Paper—$12.50—62pp-------------------------------------- Vendor #D1842

1831 - GAGE FAMILY: JOHN GAGE OF IPSWICH AND THOMAS OF YAR-
MOUTH;...AND ROVERT IN IRELAND by Rev. William Gage. Repr. of
1922 ed.
Paper—$12.50—65pp-------------------------------------- Vendor #D1842

1832 - GALE FAMILY RECORDS IN ENGLAND AND THE UNITED STATES,
AND TOTTINGHAM FAMILY...BOGARDUS, WALDON AND YOUNG
FAMILIES OF NEW YORK by George Gale. Repr. of 1866 ed.
Paper—$38.00—254pp------------------------------------- Vendor #D1842

1833 - GENEALOGICAL HISTORY OF THE GALLUP FAMILY IN THE UNITED
STATES....by John D. Gallup. Repr. of 1893 ed.
Cloth—$65.00—Paper—$55.00—329pp----------------------- Vendor #D1842

1834 - DESCENDANTS OF JOHN GAMAGE OF IPSWICH, MASSACHUSETTS by
Anabella L. G. Morton. Repr. of 1906 ed.
Paper—$12.50—83pp-------------------------------------- Vendor #D1842

1835 - 1599-1890, LION GARDINER AND HIS DESCENDANTS by Curtiss C.
Gardiner. Repr. of 1890 ed.
Paper—$29.00—195pp------------------------------------- Vendor #D1842

1836 - GARDINERS OF NARRAGANSETT...THE DESCENDANTS OF GEORGE
GARDINER, COLONIST, 1638 by Caroline E. Robinson. Repr. of 1919 ed.
Cloth—$48.00—Paper—$38.00—320pp----------------------- Vendor #D1842

1837 - GARLAND GENEALOGY, DESCENDANTS OF PETER GARLAND...
CHARLESTOWN, MASSACHUSETTS, IN 1637 by James G. Garland.
Repr. of 1897 ed.
Paper—$33.00—219pp------------------------------------- Vendor #D1842

1838 - GARY GENEALOGY, DESCENDANTS OF ARTHUR GARY OF ROXBURY, MASSACHUSETTS...STEPHEN GARY OF CHARLESTOWN....by Lawrence Brainerd. Repr. of 1908 ed.
Paper—$35.00—235pp-------------------------------------- Vendor #D1842

1839 - SILAS GATES OF STOW, MASSACHUSETTS AND...PAUL GATES OF ASHBY, MASSACHUSETTS by Julius Kendall Gates and Samuel Pearly Gates. Repr. of 1907 ed.
Paper—$22.00—147pp-------------------------------------- Vendor #D1842

1840 - STEPHEN GATES OF HINGHAM AND LANCASTER, MASSACHUSETTS AND HIS DESCENDANTS by Charles O. Gates. Repr. of 1898 ed.
Cloth—$55.00—Paper—$45.00—370pp------------------------ Vendor #D1842

1841 - THE GEDNEY AND CLARKE FAMILIES OF SALEM, MASSACHUSETTS by Henry F. Waters. Repr. of 1880 ed.
Paper—$10.00—52pp-------------------------------------- Vendor #D1842

1842 - GENEALOGY OF THE GEER FAMILY IN AMERICA FROM 1635-1914 by Walter Geer and Florence E. Youngs. Repr. of 1914 ed.
Paper—$38.00—256pp-------------------------------------- Vendor #D1842

1843 - GENTRY FAMILY IN AMERICA; 1676 TO 1909...CLAIBOURNE HARRIS, SHARP AND TWELVE OTHER FAMILIES by Richard Gentry. Repr. of 1909 ed.
Cloth—$61.00—Paper—$51.00—406pp------------------------ Vendor #D1842

1844 - HEINRICH GERNHARDT AND HIS DESCENDANTS by Jeremiah M. M. Gernerd. Repr. of 1904 ed.
Cloth—$47.00—Paper—$37.00—315pp------------------------ Vendor #D1842

1845 - GENEALOGY OF THE FAMILY OF GAMALIEL GEROULD...PROVINCE OF LANGUEDOC, FRANCE by Samuel L. Gerould. Repr. of 1885 ed.
Paper—$17.00—85pp-------------------------------------- Vendor #D1842

1846 - FAMILY OF SAMUEL GETCHELL OF SALISBURY, MASSACHUSETTS by E. and F. Getchell. Repr. of 1909 ed.
Paper—$3.50—10pp-------------------------------------- Vendor #D1842

1847 - FAMILY NOTICES COLLECTED BY WILLIAM GIBBS. Repr. of 1845 ed.
Paper—$3.50—8pp-------------------------------------- Vendor #D1842

1848 - JOHN GIBSON OF CAMBRIDGE, MASSACHUSETTS AND HIS DE-SCENDANTS, 1634-1899 by Mehitable C. C. Wilson. Repr. of 1900 ed.
Cloth—$82.00—Paper—$72.00—547pp------------------------ Vendor #D1842

1849 - GIDDINGS FAMILY...FROM ST. ALBANS, ENGLAND, TO IPSWICH, MASSACHUSETTS, IN 1635 by Minot S. Giddings. Repr. of 1882 ed.
Paper—$34.00—227pp-------------------------------------- Vendor #D1842

1850 - GIFFORD GENEALOGY 1626-1896, DESCENDANTS OF WILLIAM GIFFORD OF SANDWICH, MASSACHUSETTS, 1650 by H. E. Gifford. Repr. of 1896 ed.
Paper—$20.00—101pp-------------------------------------- Vendor #D1842

1851 - GILES MEMORIAL. GENEALOGICAL MEMOIRS OF FAMILIES BEAR-ING NAMES OF GILES, GOULD, HOLMES....by John Adams Vinton. Repr. of 1864 ed.
Cloth—$91.00—Paper—$81.00—608pp------------------------ Vendor #D1842

1852 - NOTES HISTORIQUES SUR L'ORIGINE DE LA FAMILLE GILL DE SAINT-FRANCOIS DU LAC ET SAINT-THOMAS DE PIERREVILLE.... par Charles Gill. Repr. of 1887 ed.
Paper—$15.00—96pp-------------------------------------- Vendor #D1842

1853 - THE GILMERS IN AMERICA by John G. Speed. Repr. of 1897 ed.
Paper—$31.00—208pp-------------------------------------- Vendor #D1842

1854 - GILMORE ANCESTORS, DESCENDANTS OF JOHN GILMORE OF MASSA-CHUSETTS, DOWN TO PASCAL P. GILMORE, ET AL. by P. P. Gilmore. Repr. of 1928 ed.
Paper—$5.00—25pp-------------------------------------- Vendor #D1842

1855 - GIST FAMILY by C. T. Cockey. Repr. of 1885 ed.
Paper—$4.00—12pp--- Vendor #D1842

1856 - DESCENDANTS OF RICHARD GOULD OF CHATHAM, MASSACHUSETTS
1788-1871 by Ames and Sawyer. Repr. of 1902 ed.
Paper—$6.00—31pp--- Vendor #D1842

1857 - GENEALOGICAL HISTORY OF GOTTSHALL FAMILY, DESCENDANTS
OF JACOB GOTTSHALL by N. B. Grubb. Repr. of 1924 ed.
Paper—$22.50—112pp--- Vendor #D1842

1858 - DANIEL GOTT, MT. DESERT PIONEER, HIS ANCESTORS AND DE-
SCENDANTS by W. O. Sawtelle. Repr., n.d.
Paper—$6.00—28pp--- Vendor #D1842

1859 - GOSS FAMILY, AN HISTORICAL ROMANCE by W. H. Boomer. Repr.
of 1886 ed. (incl. 9th Reunion)
Paper—$5.00—27pp--- Vendor #D1842

1860 - GOSNOLD AND BACON, THE ANCESTORS OF BARTHOLOMEW GOSNOLD;
A COLLECTION by J. Henry Lea. Repr. of 1904 ed.
Paper—$7.00—36pp--- Vendor #D1842

1861 - BRIEF GENEALOGY OF THE GORE FAMILY by W. H. Whitmore. Repr.
of 1875 ed.
Paper—$3.00—7pp-- Vendor #D1842

1862 - GOOKIN FAMILY OF ENGLAND AND AMERICA, 1400-1831 by E. E.
Salisbury. Repr. of 1885 ed.
Paper—$17.00—84pp-- Vendor #D1842

1863 - GENEALOGY OF THE GOODYEAR FAMILY by Grace G. Kirkman.
Repr. of 1899 ed.
Paper—$37.50—250pp--- Vendor #D1842

1864 - GOODWINS OF DELAWARE GAP, PENNSYLVANIA AND TOMPKINS
COUNTY, NEW YORK by John S. Goodwin. Repr. of 1898 ed.
Paper—$3.00—10pp--- Vendor #D1842

1865 - THE GOODWINS OF KITTERY, YORK COUNTY, MAINE by John S.
Goodwin. Repr. of 1898 ed.
Paper—$19.00—125pp--- Vendor #D1842

1866 - THE GOODWIN FAMILY IN AMERICA by John S. Goodwin. Repr. of
1897 ed.
Paper—$30.00—200pp--- Vendor #D1842

1867 - GOODWINS WITH HARTFORD, CONNECTICUT DESCENDANTS OF
WILLIAM AND OZIAS GOODWIN by James J. Goodwin and Frank F.
Starr. Repr. of 1891 ed.
Cloth—$121.00—Paper—$111.00—809pp--------------------- Vendor #D1842

1868 - GOODRIDGE GENEALOGY. DESCENDANTS OF WILLIAM GOODRIDGE
...FROM BURY ST. EDMUNDS, ENGLAND IN 1636 by Edwin A.
Goodridge. Repr. of 1918 ed.
Cloth—$47.00—Paper—$37.00—313pp----------------------- Vendor #D1842

1869 - GOODRIDGE MEMORIAL. DESCENDANTS OF ANCESTORS OF MOSES
GOODRIDGE OF MARBLEHEAD, MASSACHUSETTS....by Sidney Perley.
Repr. of 1884 ed.
Paper—$17.00—87pp-- Vendor #D1842

1870 - GOODRICH FAMILY IN AMERICA. GENEALOGY OF THE DESCEND-
ANTS OF JOHN AND WILLIAM GOODRICH....by Lafayette W. Case.
Repr. of 1889 ed.
Cloth—$63.50—Paper—$53.50—423pp----------------------- Vendor #D1842

1871 - DESCENDANTS OF EDMUND GOODNOW IN THE LINE OF DANIEL
GOODNOW....by J. L. Seward. Repr. of 1904 ed.
Paper—$4.00—11pp--- Vendor #D1842

1872 - HISTORY AND GENEALOGY OF GOODHUE FAMILY IN ENGLAND AND
AMERICA TO THE YEAR 1890 by Rev. Jonathan E. Goodhue. Repr. of
1891 ed.
Cloth—$60.00—Paper—$50.00—398pp----------------------- Vendor #D1842

1873 - GOLDTHWAITE GENEALOGY. DESCENDANTS OF THOMAS GOLD-
        THWAITE, EARLY SETTLER OF SALEM, MASSACHUSETTS....by
        Charlotte Goldthwaite. Repr. of 1899 ed.
        Cloth—$63.00—Paper—$53.00—418pp----------------------- Vendor #D 1842

1874 - GENEALOGY OF THE GODING FAMILY by Frederic Webster Goding.
        Repr. of 1906 ed.
        Paper—$26.00—176pp------------------------------------- Vendor #D 1842

1875 - GLOVER MEMORIALS AND GENEALOGY, AN ACCOUNT OF JOHN
        GLOVER OF DORCHESTER...AND OTHER PLACES by Anna Glover.
        Repr. of 1867 ed.
        Cloth—$92.00—Paper—$82.00—612pp----------------------- Vendor #D 1842

1876 - GENEALOGY OF DESCENDANTS OF THOMAS GLEASON OF WATER-
        TOWN, MASSACHUSETTS, 1607-1909 edited by Lillian May Wilson.
        Repr. of 1909 ed.
        Cloth—$100.00—Paper—$90.00—672pp---------------------- Vendor #D 1842

1877 - THE GLADDING BOOK, HISTORICAL RECORD AND GENEALOGICAL
        CHART OF THE GLADDING FAMILY....by Henry C. Gladding. Repr.
        of 1901 ed.
        Paper—$28.00—189pp------------------------------------- Vendor #D 1842

1878 - GENEALOGY OF SAMUEL GOURLEY AND HIS DESCENDANTS,
        1784-1909 by C. T. Heydecker. Repr. of 1909 ed.
        Paper—$6.00—32pp--------------------------------------- Vendor #D 1842

1879 - THE GOVE BOOK; HISTORY AND GENEALOGY OF THE AMERICAN
        FAMILY OF GOVE...EUROPEAN GOVES by William Henry Gove. Repr.
        of 1922 ed.
        Cloth—$104.00—Paper—$94.00—692pp---------------------- Vendor #D 1842

1880 - LAUNCELOT GRANGER OF NEWBURY, MASSACHUSETTS AND SUF-
        FIELD, CONNECTICUT. A GENEALOGICAL HISTORY by James N.
        Granger. Repr. of 1893 ed.
        Cloth—$88.00—Paper—$78.00—587pp----------------------- Vendor #D 1842

1881 - HISTORY OF GRANNIS FAMILY IN AMERICA 1630-1901 by S. S.
        Grannis. Repr. of 1901 ed.
        Paper—$10.00—49pp-------------------------------------- Vendor #D 1842

1882 - DESCENDANTS OF EDWARD GRANNIS, WHO WAS IN NEW HAVEN, CON-
        NECTICUT...1719 by Frederick Augustus Strong. Repr. of 1927 ed.
        Cloth—$43.00—Paper—$33.00—288pp----------------------- Vendor #D 1842

1883 - THE GRANT FAMILY. A GENEALOGICAL HISTORY OF DESCEND-
        ANTS OF MATTHEW GRANT...1601-1898 by Arthur H. Grant. Repr.
        of 1892 ed.
        Cloth—$104.00—Paper—$94.00—692pp---------------------- Vendor #D 1842

1884 - GENEALOGICAL NOTES-1. AMERICAN ANCESTRY OF U. S. GRANT
        by H. E. Robinson. Repr. of 1885 ed.
        Paper—$4.50—17pp--------------------------------------- Vendor #D 1842

1885 - GRAVES FAMILY OF MAINE by C. N. Sinnet. Repr. of 1922 ed.
        Paper—$6.00—32pp--------------------------------------- Vendor #D 1842

1886 - NOTES ON ANCESTRY AND CONNECTIONS OF "REAR ADMIRAL"
        THOMAS GRAVES OF CHARLESTOWN, MASSACHUSETTS by Eben Put-
        nam. Repr. Essex Inst. Hist. Coll., 1895 ed.
        Paper—$4.50—17pp--------------------------------------- Vendor #D 1842

1887 - GENEALOGY OF THE GRAVES FAMILY IN AMERICA, VOLUME 1 by
        John Card Graves. Repr. of 1896 ed.
        Cloth—$82.00—Paper—$72.00—546pp----------------------- Vendor #D 1842

1888 - JOSHUA GRAY OF YARMOUTH, MASSACHUSETTS, AND HIS DE-
        SCENDANTS by Julia Edgar Thacher. Repr. of 1914 ed.
        Paper—$20.00—136pp------------------------------------- Vendor #D 1842

1889 - AN ACCOUNT OF PERCIVAL AND ELLEN GREEN AND SOME OF
THEIR DESCENDANTS by Samuel Abbott Green. Repr. of 1876 ed.
Paper—$12.50—67pp--- Vendor #D1842

1890 - GENEALOGICAL SKETCH OF DESCENDANTS OF ROBERT GREENE OF
WALES, MASSACHUSETTS by R. Greene. Repr. of 1885 ed.
Paper—$12.50—64pp--- Vendor #D1842

1891 - GREENE FAMILY AND ITS BRANCHES FROM 861 TO 1904 by Lora S.
La Mance, together with poems...by Mrs. Attie A. Stowe. Repr. of
1904 ed.
Cloth—$46.00—Paper—$36.00—305pp------------------------- Vendor #D1842

1892 - A GENEALOGY OF THE GREENLEAF FAMILY by Jonathan Greenleaf.
Repr. of 1854 ed.
Paper—$16.00—116pp-- Vendor #D1842

1893 - GENEALOGY OF THE GREENLEAF FAMILY by James Edward Greenleaf.
Repr. of 1896 ed.
Cloth—$84.50—Paper—$74.50—564pp------------------------- Vendor #D1842

1894 - ANCESTRY OF JANE MARIA GREENLEAF, WIFE OF WILLIAM F. J.
BOARDMAN, HARTFORD, CONNECTICUT by William F. J. Boardman.
Repr. of 1906 ed.
Paper—$20.00—133pp-- Vendor #D1842

1895 - NOTES UPON THE ANCESTRY OF EBENEZER GREENOUGH, 1783-1847,
AND OF HIS WIFE, ABIGAIL ISRAEL....by Franklin Platt. Repr. of
1895 ed.
Paper—$8.00—38pp-- Vendor #D1842

1896 - BIOGRAPHICAL AND HISTORICAL SKETCHES OF GRESHAMS OF
AMERICA AND OVERSEAS by A. Strange. Repr. of 1913 ed.
Paper—$10.00—53pp--- Vendor #D1842

1897 - GENEALOGY OF DESCENDANTS OF JASPER GRIFFING by Clara J.
Stone. Repr. of 1881 ed.
Paper—$30.00—194pp-- Vendor #D1842

1898 - GENEALOGY OF THE GRIGGS FAMILY by W. S. Griggs. Repr. of
1926 ed.
Paper—$22.50—116pp-- Vendor #D1842

1899 - GENEALOGY OF THE GRIGGS FAMILY by Walter S. Griggs. Repr.
of 1926 ed.
Paper—$16.00—116pp-- Vendor #D1842

1900 - GENEALOGY OF THE GRIGSBY FAMILY by W. H. Grigsby. Repr. of
1878 ed.
Paper—$3.50—8pp--- Vendor #D1842

1901 - GRISWOLD FAMILY by E. E. Salisbury. Repr. of 1884 ed., charts.
Paper—$16.50—82pp--- Vendor #D1842

1902 - CAPTAIN JOHN GROUT OF WATERTOWN AND SUDBURY, MASSA-
CHUSETTS AND SOME OF HIS DESCENDANTS by Elizabeth E. Boice
Jones. Repr. of 1922 ed.
Paper—$18.50—124pp-- Vendor #D1842

1903 - HISTORY AND GENEALOGY OF THE GROVES FAMILY IN AMERICA,
...BEVERLY, MASSACHUSETTS by William T. Groves. Repr. of 1915 ed.
Paper—$10.00—56pp--- Vendor #D1842

1904 - JOHN GROW OF IPSWICH. JOHN GROO (GROW) OF OXFORD by
George W. Davis. Repr. of 1913 ed.
Cloth—$41.00—Paper—$31.00—274pp------------------------- Vendor #D1842

1905 - GENEALOGY OF THE DESCENDANTS OF JOHN GUILD, DEDHAM,
MASSACHUSETTS by Calvin Guild. Repr. of 1867 ed.
Paper—$20.00—132pp-- Vendor #D1842

1906 - GENEALOGY AND HISTORY OF THE GUILD, GUILE AND GILE FAMILY
by Charles Burleigh. Repr. of 1887 ed.
Cloth—$57.00—Paper—$47.00—381pp------------------------- Vendor #D1842

1907   - GENEALOGY OF DESCENDANTS OF HUGH GUNNISON OF BOSTON,
      MASSACHUSETTS, 1610-1876 by George W. Gunnison. Repr. of 1880 ed.
      Paper—$33.00—222pp------------------------------------- Vendor #D1842

1908   - BRIEF HISTORY OF A BRANCH OF THE GUTHRIE FAMILY by S.
      Guthrie. Repr. of 1889 ed.
      Paper—$12.50—62pp----------------------------------- Vendor #D1842

1909   - GENEALOGICAL RECORD OF WILLIAM GUY, 1634 by A. Guy. Repr.
      of 1898 ed.
      Paper—$4.00—18pp------------------------------------- Vendor #D1842

1910   - A HISTORY AND GENEALOGY OF THE HABERSHAM FAMILY, ALSO
      CLAY, STILES, CUMMING...by Joseph G. B. Bulloch. Repr. of 1901 ed.
      Paper—$37.50—228pp----------------------------------- Vendor #D1842

1911   - GENEALOGICAL RECORD OF DESCENDANTS OF MOSES HADLEY AND
      REBECCA PAGE, OF HUDSON, NEW HAMPSHIRE....by Samuel P.
      Hadley. Repr. of 1887 ed.
      Paper—$15.00—88pp------------------------------------- Vendor #D1842

1912   - NOTES ON THE QUAKER FAMILY OF HADLEY by C. Hadley. Repr.
      of 1916 ed.
      Paper—$12.00—59pp------------------------------------- Vendor #D1842

1913   - DEACON SAMUEL HAINES OF WESTBURY, WILTSHIRE, ENGLAND,
      AND HIS DESCENDANTS IN AMERICA, 1635-1901 by Andrew M. and
      Thomas V. Haines. Repr. of 1902 ed.
      Cloth—$60.00—Paper—$50.00—400pp--------------------- Vendor #D1842

1914   - ORIGINAL PAPERS RELATING TO SAMUEL HAINES AND HIS DE-
      SCENDANTS by Andrew Mack Haines. Repr. N. E. Hist. & Gen.
      Register, 1869 ed.
      Paper—$6.00—29pp------------------------------------- Vendor #D1842

1915   - ANCESTRY OF HAINES, SHARP, COLLINS (AND OTHER) FAMILIES...
      GEORGE HAINES, WITH SOME ADDITIONS by Richard Haines. Repr.
      of 1902 ed.
      Cloth—$68.40—Paper—$58.50—456pp---------------------- Vendor #D1842

1916   - DEACON SAMUEL HAINES OF WESTBURY, WILTSHIRE, ENGLAND,
      ...AND EDITORIAL WORK by Thomas Vanburen Haines. Repr. of 1902 ed.
      Cloth—$60.00—Paper—$50.00—400pp---------------------- Vendor #D1842

1917   - HAKES FAMILY by Harry Hakes. Repr. of 1886 ed.
      Paper—$17.50—87pp------------------------------------- Vendor #D1842

1918   - THE HAKES FAMILY, 2nd ed., by Harry Hakes. Repr. of 1889 ed.
      Paper—$33.00—220pp----------------------------------- Vendor #D1842

1919   - THOMAS HALE, THE GLOVER, OF NEWBURY, MASSACHUSETTS
      (1635) AND HIS DESCENDANTS by Robert S. Hale. Repr. N.E.
      Hist. & Gen. Register, 1877 ed.
      Paper—$4.00—19pp------------------------------------- Vendor #D1842

1920   - THE HALE FAMILY OF CONNECTICUT by Seymour Morris. Repr. of
      1907 ed.
      Paper—$4.00—13pp------------------------------------- Vendor #D1842

1921   - GENEALOGY OF DESCENDANTS OF THOMAS HALE OF WALTON,
      ENGLAND AND OF NEWBURY, MASSACHUSETTS by Robert S. Hale,
      Repr. of 1889 ed.
      Cloth—$64.00—Paper—$54.00—427pp---------------------- Vendor #D1842

1922   - DESCENDANTS OF MAJOR SAMUEL HALE by Elizabeth H. Smith.
      Repr. of 1902 ed.
      Paper—$18.50—123pp----------------------------------- Vendor #D1842

1923   - THE HALLS OF NEW ENGLAND. GENEALOGICAL AND BIOGRAPH-
      ICAL by David B. Hall. Repr. of 1883 ed.
      Cloth—$120.00—Paper—$110.00—800pp-------------------- Vendor #D1842

1924 - HALL ANCESTRY. A SERIES OF SKETCHES OF THE LINEAL AN-
CESTRY OF THE CHILDREN OF SAMUEL HOLDEN PARSONS HALL...
EMELINE BULKELEY....by Charles S. Hall. Repr. of 1896 ed.
Cloth—$77.50—Paper—$67.50—517pp------------------------ Vendor #D1842

1925 - JOHN HALL OF WALLINGFORD, CONNECTICUT. A MONOGRAPH
(WITH GENEALOGY) by James Shepard. Repr. of 1902 ed.
Paper—$12.00—61pp------------------------------------- Vendor #D1842

1926 - RECORD OF A BRANCH OF THE HALLOWELL FAMILY, INCLUDING
THE LONGSTRETH, PENROSE AND NORWOOD BRANCHES by William
Powell Hallowell. Repr. of 1893 ed.
Paper—$37.00—246pp----------------------------------- Vendor #D1842

1927 - GENEALOGICAL RECORD OF THE HAMBLETON FAMILY DESCENDANTS
OF JAMES HAMBLETON OF BUCKS COUNTY, PENNSYLVANIA....by
Chalkey J. Hambleton. Repr. of 1887 ed.
Paper—$17.00—108pp----------------------------------- Vendor #D1842

1928 - THE GENEALOGY OF THE HAMILTON FAMILY FROM 1716-1894 by
Salome Hamilton. Repr. of 1894 ed.
Paper—$20.00—133pp----------------------------------- Vendor #D1842

1929 - THE HAMILTONS OF WATERBOROUGH (YORK COUNTY, MAINE)
THEIR ANCESTORS AND DESCENDANTS by Samuel K. Hamilton. Repr.
of 1912 ed.
Cloth—$63.50—Paper—$53.50—423pp------------------------ Vendor #D1842

1930 - HAMLIN FAMILY; GENEALOGY OF CAPTAIN GILES HAMIL OF MIDDLE-
TOWN, CONNECTICUT, 1654-1900 by H. Franklin Andrews. Repr. of
1900 ed.
Cloth—$72.00—Paper—$62.00—479pp------------------------ Vendor #D1842

1931 - SWANZEY HAMMOND GENEALOGY by Joseph Hammond. Repr. of
1890 ed.
Paper—$4.00—17pp-------------------------------------- Vendor #D1842

1932 - A CONTRIBUTION TO THE GENEALOGY OFTHE HANDERSON FAMILY
by H. E. Handerson. Repr. of 1885 ed.
Paper—$14.00—80pp------------------------------------- Vendor #D1842

1933 - SAMUEL HANDY OF SOMERSET COUNTY, MARYLAND AND SOME
OF HIS DESCENDANTS by H. D. Neill. Repr. of 1875 ed.
Paper—$4.00—8pp--------------------------------------- Vendor #D1842

1934 - HANEY FAMILY by J. L. Haney. Repr. of 1930 ed.
Paper—$10.00—46pp------------------------------------- Vendor #D1842

1935 - DESCENDANTS OF REV. THOMAS HANFORD OF CONNECTICUT by
A. C. Golding. Repr. of 1936 ed.
Paper—$30.00—153pp----------------------------------- Vendor #D1842

1936 - GENEALOGY OF THE HANNUM FAMILY DESCENDED FROM JOHN AND
MARGERY HANNUM. Repr. of 1911 ed.
Cloth—$105.00—Paper—$95.00—702pp---------------------- Vendor #D1842

1937 - ANNALS OF THE HARBAUGH FAMILY IN AMERICA, 1736-1856 by
H. Harbaugh. Repr. of 1856 ed.
Paper—$30.00—148pp----------------------------------- Vendor #D1842

1938 - A NARRATIVE HISTORY OF THE HARDING FAMILY by Anne K. Holdt.
Repr. of 1904 ed.
Paper—$21.00—142pp----------------------------------- Vendor #D1842

1939 - THE HARDINGS IN AMERICA. A GENEALOGICAL REGISTER OF DE-
SCENDANTS OF JOHN HARDING....by Wilbert J. Harding. Repr. of
1925 ed.
Paper—$31.00—209pp----------------------------------- Vendor #D1842

1940 - RECORD OF ONE HUNDRED YEARS OF THE HARDY FAMILY by J.
Hardy. Repr. of 1877 ed.
Paper—$5.00—12pp-------------------------------------- Vendor #D1842

1941 - HARMAN GENEALOGY (SOUTHERN BRANCH) WITH BIOGRAPHICAL
SKETCHES 1700-1924 by John N. Harman, Sr. Repr. of 1925 ed.
Cloth—$56.00—Paper—$46.00—376pp------------------------ Vendor #D1842

1942 - HARMAN-HARMON GENEALOGY AND BIOGRAPHY, WITH HISTORICAL
NOTES, 19 B.C. TO 1928 A.D. by John W. Harman. Repr. of 1928 ed.
Cloth—$70.50—Paper—$60.50—471pp----------------------- Vendor #D1842

1943 - THE HARMON GENEALOGY, COMPRISING ALL BRANCHES IN NEW
ENGLAND by Artemas C. Harmon. Repr. of 1920 ed.
Cloth—$57.50—Paper—$47.50—383pp----------------------- Vendor #D1842

1944 - THE HARRINGTON FAMILY IN AMERICA by Eugene W. Harrington.
Repr. of 1907 ed.
Paper—$19.00—127pp------------------------------------- Vendor #D1842

1945 - HARRIS GENEALOGY. A HISTORY OF JAMES HARRIS OF NEW LON-
DON, CONNECICUT...1640 TO 1878 by Nath'l Harris Morgan. Repr.
of 1878 ed.
Cloth—$76.00—Paper—$66.00—239pp----------------------- Vendor #D1842

1946 - ROBERT HARRIS AND DESCENDANTS WITH NOTICES OF MOREY AND
METCALF FAMILIES by L. M. Harris. Repr. of 1861 ed.
Paper—$9.00—56pp-------------------------------------- Vendor #D1842

1947 - HARRIS'S IN BOSTON BEFORE 1700 by R. B. Jones. Repr.
Paper—$6.00—30pp-------------------------------------- Vendor #D1842

1948 - ARIS SONIS FOCISQUE; BEING A MEMOIR OF AN AMERICAN FAMILY,
HARRISONS OF SKIMINO edited by Fairfax Harrison from material coll.
by Francis Burton Harrison. Repr. of 1910 ed.
Cloth—$63.00—Paper—$53.00—437pp----------------------- Vendor #D1842

1949 - BRIEF HISTORY OF THE FIRST HARRISONS OF VIRGINIA,
DESCENDANTS OF CUTHBERT HARRISON (1600-1915) by H. T. Harri-
son. Repr. of 1915 ed.
Paper—$8.00—40pp-------------------------------------- Vendor #D1842

1950 - JOSEPH HART AND HIS DESCENDANTS by C. C. Hart. Repr. of
1901 ed.
Paper—$22.50—124pp------------------------------------ Vendor #D1842

1951 - THE HARTWELL FAMILY...DESCENDANTS OF WILLIAM HARTWELL
OF CONCORD, MASSACHUSETTS, 1636-1895 by L. W. Densmore. Repr.
of 1895 ed.
Paper—$26.50—176pp------------------------------------ Vendor #D1842

1952 - DESCENDANTS OF ELISHA HARVEY FROM 1719 TO 1914 by J. William
Knappenberger. Rerp. of 1914 ed., n.p.
Paper—$10.00—44pp------------------------------------- Vendor #D1842

1953 - ANCESTRY OF COLONEL JOHN HARVEY OF NORTHWOOD, NEW
HAMPSHIRE by John Harvey Treat. Repr. of 1907 ed.
Paper—$10.00—47pp------------------------------------- Vendor #D1842

1954 - A SHORT ACCOUNT OF THE DESCENDANTS OF WILLIAM HASKELL
OF GLOUCESTER, MASSACHUSETTS by Ulysses G. Haskell. Repr.
Essex Inst. Hist. Coll., 1896 ed.
Paper—$12.50—62pp------------------------------------- Vendor #D1842

1955 - THE HASSAM FAMILY by J. T. Hassam. Repr. of 1896 ed.
Paper—$3.50—11pp-------------------------------------- Vendor #D1842

1956 - GENEALOGICAL HISTORY OF HARWOOD FAMILIES...RESIDED IN
CHELMSFORD, MASSACHUSETTS by Watson H. Harwood. Repr. of
1879 ed.
Paper—$8.00—33pp-------------------------------------- Vendor #D1842

1957 - THE HASTINGS MEMORIAL...DESCENDANTS OF THOMAS HASTINGS
OF WATERTOWN, MASSACHUSETTS....by Lydia Nelson (Hastings)
Buckminster. Repr. of 1866 ed.
Paper—$27.50—183pp------------------------------------ Vendor #D1842

1958 - THOMAS HATCH OF BARNSTABLE AND SOME OF HIS DESCENDANTS
       by Charles Lathrop Pack. Repr. of 1930 ed.
       Cloth—$54.50—Paper—363pp-------------------------------- Vendor #D1842

1959 - DESCENDANTS OF WILLIAM HATCH OF SCITUATE, MASSACHUSETTS
       by P. Derby. Repr. of 1874 ed.
       Paper—$5.00—23pp-------------------------------------- Vendor #D1842

1960 - MAJOREY TIMOTHY HATCH OF HARTFORD AND HIS DESCENDANTS
       by E. H. Fletcher. Repr. of 1879 ed.
       Paper—$7.50—36pp-------------------------------------- Vendor #D1842

1961 - DESCENDANTS OF JOSEPH AND ANNA HATFIELD OF NEW JERSEY
       AND OHIO by S. K. Stephenson. Repr. of 1897 ed.
       Paper—$4.00—12pp-------------------------------------- Vendor #D1842

1962 - GENEALOGY OF DESCENDANTS OF RICHARD HAVEN OF LYNN,
       ETC. by J. Adams. Repr. of 1849 ed.
       Paper—$20.00—94pp------------------------------------- Vendor #D1842

1963 - RICHARD HAWES OF DORCHESTER, MASSACHUSETTS, AND SOME
       OF HIS DESCENDANTS by Frank Mortimer Hawes. Repr. of 1932 ed.
       Paper—$39.50—263pp------------------------------------ Vendor #D1842

1964 - EDMOND HAWES OF YARMOUTH, MASSACHUSETTS, AN EMIGRANT
       TO AMERICA IN 1635....by James William Hawes. Repr. of 1914 ed.
       Paper—$34.50—231pp------------------------------------ Vendor #D1842

1965 - BICENTENNIAL GATHERING OF DESCENDANTS OF HENRY HAYES
       AT UNIONVILLE, PENNSYLVANIA.... Repr. of 1906 ed. Index.
       Paper—$10.00—89pp------------------------------------- Vendor #D1842

1966 - WALTER HAYNES OF SUTTON MANDEVILLE, WILTSHIRE, ENGLAND,
       AND SUDBURY, MASSACHUSETTS...1583-1928 by Frances Haynes.
       Repr. of 1929 ed.
       Paper—$35.00—235pp------------------------------------ Vendor #D1842

1967 - ANCESTORS AND DESCENDANTS OF JOHN RUSSEL HAYNES (IN-
       CLUDING HAINES, COTTON, BRADSTREET, DUDLEY, HUBBARD,
       AND BRAINERD FAMILIES) by G. W. Burch. Repr. of 1924 ed.
       Paper—$30.00—151pp------------------------------------ Vendor #D1842

1968 - GENEALOGY OF THE HAWLEY FAMILY OF MARBLEHEAD, 1st & 2nd
       eds., by W. D. Hawley. Repr. of 1897 ed.
       Paper—$4.00—12pp-------------------------------------- Vendor #D1842

1969 - JAMES HAYWARD, BORN APRIL 4, 1750,...WITH GENEALOGICAL
       NOTES RELATING TO THE HAYWARDS by William Frederick Adams.
       Repr. of 1911 ed.
       Paper—$9.00—58pp-------------------------------------- Vendor #D1842

1970 - THE HAZARD FAMILY OF RHODE ISLAND, 1635-1894...DESCENDANTS
       OF THOMAS HAZARD by C. E. Robinson. Repr. of 1895 ed.
       Cloth—$44.50—Paper—$34.50—298pp----------------------- Vendor #D1842

1971 - GENEALOGICAL SKETCHES OF ROBERT AND JOHN HAZELTON,
       AND SOME OF THEIR DESCENDANTS....by William B. Lapham.
       Repr. of 1892 ed.
       Cloth—$55.00—Paper—$45.00—368pp----------------------- Vendor #D1842

1972 - GENEALOGICAL RECORD OF ONE BRANCH OF HEATH, CLARK AND
       CONE FAMILIES by D. Stilwell. Repr. of 1905 ed.
       Paper—$8.00—42pp-------------------------------------- Vendor #D1842

1973 - THE MASSACHUSETTS HEMENWAY FAMILY, DESCENDANTS OF
       RALPH HEMENWAY OF ROXBURY 1634 by M. and C. Newton. Repr.
       of 1912 ed.
       Paper—$11.00—56pp------------------------------------- Vendor #D1842

1974 - HENDERSON CHRONICLES, DESCENDNATS OF ALEXANDER HEN-
       DERSON OF SCOTLAND by J. N. McCue. Repr. of 1915 ed.
       Paper—$22.50—113pp------------------------------------ Vendor #D1842

1975 - ANCESTORS AND DESCENDANTS OF LT. JOHN HENDERSON OF
GREENBRIAR COUNTY, VIRGINIA....by J. L. Miller. Repr. of 1902 ed.
Paper—$8.00—37pp-- Vendor #D1842

1976 - NOTES ON THE MESSENGER AND HENDRICKSON FAMILIES AND
DESCENDANTS by M. P. Ferris. Repr. of 1916 ed.
Paper—$17.50—79pp--- Vendor #D1842

1977 - HISTORY OF THE HENRY FAMILY (KENTUCKY) by J. F. Henry.
Repr. of 1900 ed.
Paper—$20.00—125pp-- Vendor #D1842

1978 - RECORD OF THE DESCENDANTS OF SIMON, HENRY, 1766-1854, AND
RHODA PARSONS (1774-1847)....by Frederick Augustus Henry. Repr.
of 1905 ed.
Paper—$13.00—65pp--- Vendor #D1842

1979 - HERKIMERS AND SCHUYLERS...WHO SETTLED IN THE MOHAWK
VALLEY, NEW YORK, IN 1721 by Phoebe Strong Cowen. Repr. of
1903 ed.
Paper—$22.00—147pp-- Vendor #D1842

1980 - GENEALOGICAL REGISTER OF THE NAME AND FAMILY OF HERRICK,
...SALEM, MASSACHUSETTS, 1629 TO 1846 by Jedediah Herrick.
Repr. of 1846 ed.
Paper—$13.00—60pp--- Vendor #D1842

1981 - HERRICK GENEALOGY. GENEALOGICAL REGISTER OF THE NAME
AND FAMILY OF HERRICK...SALEM, MASSACHUSETTS, 1629 TO 1846,
REVISED...1885 by Lucius C. Herrick. Repr. of 1885 ed.
Cloth—$79.00—Paper—$69.00—527pp----------------------- Vendor #D1842

1982 - FAMILY RECORD OF THE HESS FAMILY FROM THE FIRST IMMIGRANT
by J. H. Hess. Repr. of 1880 ed.
Paper—$15.00—73pp--- Vendor #D1842

1983 - LIEUTENANT JOSHUA HEWES, A NEW ENGLAND PIONEER, AND
SOME OF HIS DESCENDANTS by Eben Putnam. Repr. of 1913 ed.
Cloth—$101.00—Paper—$91.00—673pp---------------------- Vendor #D1842

1984 - HEYDONS IN ENGLAND AND AMERICA, A FRAGMENT OF FAMILY
HISTORY by W. B. Hayden. Repr. of 1877 ed.
Paper—$9.00—46pp-- Vendor #D1842

1985 - GENEALOGY OF HIBBARD FAMILY WHO ARE DESCENDANTS OF
ROBERT HIBBARD OF SALEM, MASSACHUSETTS by Augustine George
Hibbard. Repr. of 1901 ed.
Cloth—$64.00—Paper—$54.00—428pp----------------------- Vendor #D1842

1986 - FAMILY MEMORIAL—HICKS AND ALLIED FAMILIES by E. H. Johnson. Repr. of 1894 ed.
Paper—$10.00—56pp--- Vendor #D1842

1987 - GENEALOGY OF HIESTER FAMILY by V. E. C. Hill. Repr. of
1903 ed.
Paper—$10.00—64pp--- Vendor #D1842

1988 - THOMAS JUDD AND HIS DESCENDANTS by S. Judd. Repr. of
1856 ed.
Paper—$23.00—112pp-- Vendor #D1842

1989 - KASTNER OR CASTNER FAMILY OF PENNSYLVANIA by S. Castner.
Repr. of 1901 ed.
Paper—$6.50—31pp-- Vendor #D1842

1990 - JOHN KEEP OF LONGMEADOW, MASSACHUSETTS, 1660-1676, AND
HIS DESCENDANTS by Frank E. Best. Repr. of 1899 ed.
Paper—$39.50—263pp-- Vendor #D1842

1991 - HISTORY OF CAPTAIN JOHN KATHAN OF DUMMERSTON, VERMONT
by D. L. Mansfield. Repr. of 1902 ed.
Paper—$30.00—147pp-- Vendor #D1842

1992   - GENEALOGICAL RECORD OF THE KECK FAMILY by Keck and
      Grasselli. Repr. of 1905 ed.
      Paper—$12.50—66pp-- Vendor #D1842

1993   - GENEALOGY OF THE ISBELL FAMILY by Mary Isbell Scott. Repr.
      of 1929 ed., n.p.
      Paper—$38.50—256pp--------------------------------------- Vendor #D1842

1994   - KEESE FAMILY HISTORY AND GENEALOGY 1690-1911 by W. T.
      Keese. Repr. of 1911 ed.
      Paper—$10.00—48pp--------------------------------------- Vendor #D1842

1995   - NOTES ON SOME OF THE DESCENDANTS OF JOSEPH KELLOGG OF
      HADLEY by Justin P. Kellogg. Repr. of 1898 ed.
      Paper—$5.50—27pp--------------------------------------- Vendor #D1842

1996   -_____A SUPPLEMENT, CONTAINING NOTES ON THE FAMILIES OF
      TERRY, WHITE, AND WOODBURY. Repr. of 1899 ed.
      Paper—$10.00—45pp--------------------------------------- Vendor #D1842

1997   - TWO CENTURIES OF KEMMERER FAMILY HISTORY, 1730-1929 by
      W. A. Backenstoe. Repr. of 1929 ed.
      Paper—$30.00—152pp--------------------------------------- Vendor #D1842

1998   - KENDALL FAMILY RECORD, DESCENDANTS OF EDWARD KENDALL
      OF WESTMINSTER, MASSACHUSETTS by E. S. Kendall. Repr. of
      1880 ed.
      Paper—$3.50—11pp--------------------------------------- Vendor #D1842

1999   - KENDALL FAMILY IN AMERICA by W. M. Clemens. Repr. of 1919 ed.
      Paper—$5.00—24pp--------------------------------------- Vendor #D1842

2000   - MEMORIAL OF JOSIAH KENDALL, ONE OF THE FIRST SETTLERS OF
      STERLING, MASSACHUSETTS....by Oliver Kendall. Repr. of
      1884 ed.
      Paper—$25.00—153pp--------------------------------------- Vendor #D1842

2001   - KENT GENEALOGY, DESCENDANTS OF ABSALOM KENT OF ENGLAND
      AND VIRGINIA by A. S. Kent. Repr. of 1933 ed.
      Paper—$20.00—101pp--------------------------------------- Vendor #D1842

2002   - GENEALOGIES OF DIFFERENT FAMILIES BEARING THE NAME OF
      KENT IN THE UNITED STATES...,1295-1898 by L. Vernon Briggs.
      Repr. of 1898 ed.
      Cloth—$52.00—Paper—$42.00—340pp---------------------- Vendor #D1842

2003   - KERLEY AND ALLIED FAMILIES OF THE SOUTH by W. C. Carley.
      Repr. of 1945 ed., typescript.
      Paper—$25.00—128pp--------------------------------------- Vendor #D1842

2004   - GENEALOGY. ROBERT KEYES OF WATERTOWN, MASSACHUSETTS,
      1633, SOLOMON KEYES...DESCENDANTS by Asa Keyes. Repr. of
      1880 ed.
      Cloth—$49.00—Paper—320pp----------------------------- Vendor #D1842

2005   - HISTORY AND ANTIQUITIES OF THE NAME AND FAMILY OF KIL-
      BOURN....by Payne Kenyon Kilbourne. Repr. of 1856 ed.
      Cloth—$66.50—Paper—444pp----------------------------- Vendor #D1842

2006   - ACCOUNT OF THE KEIM FAMILY by H. M. Keim. Repr. of 1874 ed.
      Paper—$5.00—26pp--------------------------------------- Vendor #D1842

2007   - GENEALOGY OF DESCENDANTS OF BENJAMIN KEITH THROUGH
      TIMOTHY, SON OF REV. JAMES KEITH by Ziba C. Keith. Repr. of
      1889 ed.
      Paper—$16.00—114pp--------------------------------------- Vendor #D1842

2008   - GENEALOGY OF THE KILLAM FAMILY OF ESSEX COUNTY, MASSA-
      CHUSETTS by Sidney Perley. Repr. Essex Inst. Hist. Coll., 1913 ed.
      Paper—$6.00—29pp--------------------------------------- Vendor #D1842

2009   - CHILDREN OF WILLIAM AND DOROTHY KING OF SALEM by Henry
      F. Waters. Repr. Essex Inst. Hist. Coll., 1880 ed.
      Paper—$3.50--------------------------------------- Vendor #D1842

2010 – KING FAMILY OF SUFFIELD, CONNECTICUT, ITS ENGLISH ANCES-
TRY, 1389-1662...1662-1908 by C. H. King. Repr. of 1908 ed.
Cloth—$98.00—Paper—$88.00—655pp----------------------- Vendor #D1842

2011 – DESCENDANTS OF HENRY KINGMAN. SOME EARLY GENERATIONS
OF KINGMAN FAMILY by Bradford Kingman. Repr. of 1912 ed.
Paper—$15.00—102pp------------------------------------ Vendor #D1842

2012 – KINSEY, A FAMILY HISTORY by G. S. Kinsey. Repr., n.d.
Paper—$7.00—35pp------------------------------------- Vendor #D1842

2013 – HISTORICAL NOTES OF FAMILY OF KIP OF KIPSBURG AND KIPS
BAY, NEW YORK by W. I. Kip. Repr. of 1871 ed.
Paper—$10.00—49pp------------------------------------ Vendor #D1842

2014 – HISTORIC GENEALOGY OF THE KIRK FAMILY...ROGER KIRK, WHO
SETTLED AT NOTTINGHAM, CHESTER COUNTY, PENNSYLVANIA....
by C. H. Stubbs. Repr. of 1872 ed.
Cloth—$40.00—Paper—$30.00—252pp----------------------- Vendor #D1842

2015 – BRIEF HISTORY OF KIRKBRIDE FAMILY...DESCENDANTS OF
DAVID KIRKBRIDE 1775-1830 by S. A. Kirkbride. Repr. of 1918 ed.
Paper—$12.50—64pp------------------------------------ Vendor #D1842

2016 – KNAPP FAMILY IN AMERICA. GENEALOGY OF DESCENDANTS OF
WILLIAM KNAPP....by Arthur Mason Knapp. Repr. of 1909 ed.
Paper—$13.00—76pp------------------------------------ Vendor #D1842

2017 – SEVEN CENTURIES IN THE KNEELAND FAMILY by Stillman Foster
Kneeland. Repr. of 1897 ed.
Cloth—$87.50—Paper—$77.50—583pp----------------------- Vendor #D1842

2018 – KNEISLY GENEALOGY by H. Kneisly. Repr. of 1932 ed.
Paper—$9.00—46pp------------------------------------- Vendor #D1842

2019 – GENEALOGY OF KNEPPER FAMILY OF UNITED STATES 1681-1911
by M. Knepper. Repr. of 1911 ed.
Paper—$27.50—132pp----------------------------------- Vendor #D1842

2020 – THE KNIGHT FAMILY by J. C. Martindale. Repr. of 1911 ed.
Paper—$4.00—16pp------------------------------------- Vendor #D1842

2021 – HISTORY AND GENEALOGY OF KNOWLTONS OF ENGLAND AND
AMERICA by Charles Henry Wright Stocking. Repr. of 1897 ed.
Cloth—$91.50—Paper—$81.50—610pp----------------------- Vendor #D1842

2022 – _____ERRATA AND ADDENDA: WITH A COMPLETE INDEX TO BOTH
BOOKS by George Henry Knowlton. Repr. of 1903 ed.
Paper—$36.00—239pp----------------------------------- Vendor #D1842

2023 – A BRIEF HISTORY OF JOHN VALENTINE KRATZ...GENEALOGICAL
FAMILY REGISTER by A. J. Fretz. Repr. of 1892 ed.
Cloth—$47.00—Paper—$37.00—315pp----------------------- Vendor #D1842

2024 – PARTIAL HISTORY OF KYLE, KILE, COYLE FAMILY IN AMERICA
by O. M. Kile. Repr. of 1958 ed.
Paper—$35.00—186pp----------------------------------- Vendor #D1842

2025 – THE LADD FAMILY. DESCENDANTS OF DANIEL OF HAVERHILL,
MASSACHUSETTS...CHARLES CITY COUNTY, VIRGINIA by Warren
Ladd. Repr. of 1890 ed.
Cloth—$64.00—Paper—$54.00—425pp----------------------- Vendor #D1842

2026 – LAMB FAMILY MARRIAGES by W. M. Clemens. Repr. of 1916 ed.
Paper—$8.00—40pp------------------------------------- Vendor #D1842

2027 – GENEALOGY OF THE LAKE FAMILY OF GREAT EGG HARBOR, NEW
JERSEY...STATEN ISLAND BRANCHES by A. Adams and S. Risley.
Repr. of 1915 ed.
Cloth—$58.00—Paper—$48.00—386pp----------------------- Vendor #D1842

2028 – LAMBERT FAMILY OF SALEM, MASSACHUSETTS...WIFE OF THOMAS
LORD OF HARTFORD, CONNECTICUT by Henry W. Belknap. Repr.
Essex Inst. Hist. coll., 1918 ed.
Paper—$10.00—48pp------------------------------------ Vendor #D1842

2029 - GENEALOGY OF THE LAMBORN FAMILY by Samuel Lamborn. Repr. of 1894 ed.
Cloth—$73.00—Paper—$63.00—487pp------------------------ Vendor #D1842

2030 - GENEALOGY OF THE LAMBORN FAMILY, WITH EXTRACTS FROM HISTORY, BIOGRAPHIES, ANECDOTES, ETC. by Samuel Lamborn. Repr. of 1894 ed.
Cloth—$73.00—Paper—$63.00—487pp------------------------ Vendor #D1842

2031 - MEMORIAL OF ELDER EBENEZER LAMSON OF CONCORD, MASSA- CHUSETTS...1635-1908 by Otis and Frank Lamson. Repr. of 1908 ed.
Paper—$19.00—125pp------------------------------------- Vendor #D1842

2032 - DESCENDANTS OF WILLIAM LAMSON OF IPSWICH, MASSACHUSETTS, 1634-1917 by William Lamson. Repr. of 1917 ed.
Cloth—$62.00—Paper—$52.00—414pp----------------------- Vendor #D1842

2033 - SKETCH OF THE LAMPTON FAMILY IN AMERICA 1740-1914 by C. Keith. Repr. of 1914 ed.
Paper—$12.00—59pp-------------------------------------- Vendor #D1842

2034 - LANCASTER FAMILY. THOMAS AND PHEBE LANCASTER OF BUCKS COUNTY, PENNSYLVANIA...1711-1902 by H. L. Lancaster. Repr. of 1902 ed.
Cloth—$45.00—Paper—$35.00—302pp----------------------- Vendor #D1842

2035 - JOSEPH LANCASTER OF AMESBURY AND SOME OF HIS DESCEND- ANTS by J. S. Ware. Repr. of 1933 ed.
Paper—$20.00—125pp------------------------------------- Vendor #D1842

2036 - MEMORANDA RELATING TO LANE, REYNER, AND WHIPPLE FAMILIES, YORKSHIRE AND MASSACHUSETTS by W. H. Whitmore. Repr. N. E. Hist. & Gen. Register, 1857 ed.
Paper—$5.00—24pp--------------------------------------- Vendor #D1842

2037 - LANDIS FAMILY OF LANCASTER COUNTY by D. B. Landis. Repr. of 1888 ed.
Paper—$17.50—90pp-------------------------------------- Vendor #D1842

2038 - LAPHAM FAMILY REGISTER;...THOMAS LAPHAM OF SCITUATE, MASSACHUSETTS, IN 1635 by William B. Lapham. Repr. of 1873 ed.
Paper—$6.00—31pp--------------------------------------- Vendor #D1842

2039 - LASHER GENEALOGY by Charles Rich. Repr. of 1904 ed.
Cloth—$40.00—Paper—$30.00—270pp----------------------- Vendor #D1842

2040 - GENEALOGY OF LATHAM-HILL-MONTFORD-LITTLEJOHN-McCULLOCH- CAMPBELL-BROWNRIGG FAMILIES by W. H. Bailey. Repr. of 1899 ed.
Paper—$12.50—66pp-------------------------------------- Vendor #D1842

2041 - GENEALOGICAL MEMOIR OF THE LO—LATHROP FAMILY. DESCEND- ANTS OF REV. JOHN LATHROP...MASSACHUSETTS by E. B. Hunt- ington. Repr. of 1884 ed.
Cloth—$70.00—Paper—$60.00—464pp----------------------- Vendor #D1842

2042 - A GENEALOGICAL CHART OF THE DESCENDANTS OF CHRISTIAN LAUFFER, THE PIONEER (PENNSYLVANIA, OHIO) by Joseph A. Lauffer, et al. Repr. of 1906 ed.
Paper—$35.00—188pp------------------------------------- Vendor #D1842

2043 - LAUGHLIN HISTORY 1807-1907 by J. W. Laughlin. Repr. of 1907 ed.
Paper—$12.50—64pp-------------------------------------- Vendor #D1842

2044 - FAMILIES OF LAWRENCE-COSS-POMROY by J. Lawrence. Repr. of 1881 ed.
Paper—$16.50—92pp-------------------------------------- Vendor #D1842

2045 - GENEALOGY OF FAMILY OF JOHN LAWRENCE OF WISSET IN SUFFOLK, ENGLAND, AND...MASSACHUSETTS by John Lawrence. Repr. of 1869 ed.
Cloth—$50.00—Paper—$40.00—332pp----------------------- Vendor #D1842

2046 - DESCENDANTS OF MAJOR SAMUEL LAWRENCE OF GROTON, MASSA-
CHUSETTS...ALLIED FAMILIES by Robert Means Lawrence. Repr. of
1904 ed.
Cloth—$53.00—Paper—$43.00—355pp------------------------ Vendor #D1842

2047 - HISTORICAL GENEALOGY OF THE LAWRENCE FAMILY, 1635-1858
by Thomas Lawrence. Repr. of 1858 ed.
Paper—$36.00—240pp-------------------------------------- Vendor #D1842

2048 - LAWRENCE LEACH OF SALEM, MASSACHUSETTS AND SOME OF HIS
DESCENDANTS by L. Phelps Leach. Repr. of 1924-1926 ed.
Cloth—$52.00—Paper—$42.00—344pp------------------------ Vendor #D1842

2049 - LEADBETTER RECORDS by J. E. Ames. Repr. of 1917 ed.
Cloth—$48.00—Paper—$38.00—317pp------------------------ Vendor #D1842

2050 - EDWARD LEATHERS AND HIS DESCENDANTS by A. H. Quint.
Repr. Dover Inquirer, 1891 ed.
Paper—$4.00—13pp-------------------------------------- Vendor #D1842

2051 - LEAVENS NAME, ITS ORIGIN AND TRACK THRU NEW ENGLAND TO
NORTHERN VERMONT by P. F. Leavens. Repr. of 1889 ed.
Paper—$6.00—29pp-------------------------------------- Vendor #D1842

2052 - GENEALOGY OF THE LEAVENWORTH FAMILY IN THE UNITED STATES
by Elias Warner Leavenworth. Repr. of 1873 ed.
Cloth—$56.50—Paper—$46.50—376pp------------------------ Vendor #D1842

2053 - THE LEAVENS NAME, INCLUDING LEVINGS, 1632-1903 by P. F.
Leavens. Repr. of 1903 ed.
Paper—$30.00—152pp------------------------------------ Vendor #D1842

2054 - DESCENDANTS OF FRANCIS LE BARON OF PLYMOUTH, MASSA-
CHUSETTS by Mary Le Baron Stockwell. Repr. of 1904 ed.
Cloth—$78.00—Paper—$68.00—521pp------------------------ Vendor #D1842

2055 - LEE FAMILY QUARTER—MILLENNIAL GATHERING OF DESCENDANTS
AND KINSMEN OF JOHN LEE...HARTFORD, CONNECTICUT, 1884 by
William Wallace Lee. Repr. of 1885 ed.
Paper—$19.50—128pp------------------------------------ Vendor #D1842

2056 - LEE FAMILY OF HOUNSFIELD, NEW YORK AND ALLIED FAMILIES
by W. J. Coates. Repr. of 1941 ed.
Paper—$20.00—102pp------------------------------------ Vendor #D1842

2057 - LEE OF VIRGINIA by J. Henry Lea. Repr. N. E. Hist. & Gen.
Register, 1892 ed.
Paper—$5.00—23pp-------------------------------------- Vendor #D1842

2058 - JOHN LEE OF FARMINGTON, HARTFORD COUNTY, CONNECTICUT
AND HIS DESCENDANTS by Sarah Marsh Lee. Repr. of 1878 ed.
Paper—$27.00—182pp------------------------------------ Vendor #D1842

2059 - LEEDS: A NEW JERSEY FAMILY; ITS BEGINNING AND A BRANCHLET
by Clara Louise Humeston. Repr. of 1900 ed.
Paper—$4.00—20pp-------------------------------------- Vendor #D1842

2060 - 1637-1897. THE LEFFINGWELL RECORD. GENEALOGY OF THE DE-
SCENDANTS OF LIEUTENANT THOMAS LEFFINGWELL....by Albert
Leffingwell and Charles Wesley Leffingwell. Repr. of 1897 ed.
Paper—$39.00—261pp------------------------------------ Vendor #D1842

2061 - LEIGHTON GENEALOGY. ACCOUNT OF THE DESCENDANTS OF
CAPTAIN WILLIAM LEIGHTON OF KITTERY, MAINE....by Tristram
Frost Jordan. Repr. of 1885 ed.
Paper—$19.00—127pp------------------------------------ Vendor #D1842

2062 - LELAND MAGAZINE; OR, A GENEALOGICAL RECORD OF HENRY
LELAND AND HIS DESCENDANTS, 1653-1850 by Sherman Leland.
Repr. of 1859 ed.
Cloth—$42.00—Paper—$32.00—279pp------------------------ Vendor #D1842

2063 - BRIEF HISTORY OF THE LEMON FAMILY by J. M. Yeager. Repr.
of 1912 ed.
Paper—$4.00—19pp--- Vendor #D1842

2064 - MEMORIAL: GENEALOGICAL, HISTORICAL, AND BIOGRAPHICAL OF
SOLOMON LEONARD, 1637, OF DUXBURY....by Manning Leonard.
Repr. of 1896 ed.
Cloth—$68.00—Paper—$58.00—454pp----------------------- Vendor #D1842

2065 - A GENEALOGICAL MEMOIR OF THE FAMILY OF ELDER THOMAS
LEVERETT OF BOSTON by Nathaniel B. Shurtleff. Repr. of 1850 ed.
Paper—$3.50—20pp--------------------------------------- Vendor #D1842

2066 - A MEMOIR, BIOGRAPHICAL AND GENEALOGICAL, OF SIR JOHN
LEVERETT, KNT.....by Charles Edward Leverett. Repr. of 1856 ed.
Paper—$30.50—203pp------------------------------------- Vendor #D1842

2067 - EDMUND LEWIS OF LYNN, MASSACHUSETTS, AND SOME OF HIS
DESCENDANTS by George Harlan Lewis. Repr. Essex Inst. Hist.
Coll., 1908 ed.
Paper—$27.00—181pp------------------------------------- Vendor #D1842

2068 - RANDALL LEWIS OF HOPKINTON, RHODE ISLAND, AND DELAWARE
COUNTY, NEW YORK,...DESCENDANTS by Frank Pardee Lewis and
Edward Chester Lewis. Repr. of 1929 ed.
Paper—$30.00—200pp------------------------------------- Vendor #D1842

2069 - MAJOR JOHN LILLIE, 1755-1801. LILLIE FAMILY OF BOSTON, 1663-
1896, Rev. Ed., by Edward Lillie Pierce. Repr. of 1896 ed.
Paper—$18.00—122pp------------------------------------- Vendor #D1842

2070 - HISTORY OF THE LINCOLN FAMILY;...SAMUEL LINCOLN OF HING-
HAM, MASSACHUSETTS, 1637-1920 by Waldo Lincoln. Repr. of 1923 ed.
Cloth—$109.00—Paper—$99.00—728pp---------------------- Vendor #D1842

2071 - NOTES ON THE LINCOLN FAMILIES OF MASSACHUSETTS...FAMILY
OF ABRAHAM LINCOLN by Solomon Lincoln. Repr. N. E. Hist. & Gen.
Register, 1865 ed.
Paper—$4.00—10pp--------------------------------------- Vendor #D1842

2072 - THE LINDSAYS OF AMERICA. A GENEALOGICAL NARRATIVE AND
FAMILY RECORD by Margaret Isabella Lindsay. Repr. of 1889 ed.
Cloth—$44.00—Paper—$34.00—293pp---------------------- Vendor #D1842

2073 - DESCENDANTS OF GEORGE LITTLE WHO CAME TO NEWBURY,
MASSACHUSETTS, IN 1640 by George Thomas Little. Repr. of 1882 ed.
Cloth—$95.50—Paper—$85.50—638pp---------------------- Vendor #D1842

2074 - THE LIVERMORE FAMILY OF AMERICA by Walter Eliot Thwing.
Repr. of 1902 ed.
Cloth—$72.00—Paper—$62.00—479pp---------------------- Vendor #D1842

2075 - SIMON LOBDELL—1646 OF MILFORD, CONNECTICUT AND HIS DE-
SCENDANTS by Julia Harrison Lobdell; NICHOLAS LOBDEN (LOB-
DELL)—1635...DESCENDANTS. Repr. of 1907 ed.
Cloth—$63.50—Paper—$53.50—425pp---------------------- Vendor #D1842

2076 - DESCENDANTS OF BALTHASER AND SUSANA LOESCH by W. W.
Lesh. Repr. of 1914 ed.
Paper—$13.50—68pp------------------------------------- Vendor #D1842

2077 - DESCENDANTS (BY THE FEMALE BRANCHES) OF JOSEPH LOOMIS...
SETTLED IN WINDSOR, CONNECTICUT, IN 1639, 2 Vols., by Elias
Loomis. Repr. of 1880 ed.
Cloth—$160.00—Paper—$150.00—1132pp-------------------- Vendor #D1842

2078 - ANCESTORS AND DESCENDANTS OF DANIEL LOTHROP, SR., 1545-
1901 by George David Read Hubbard. Repr. of 1901 ed.
Paper—$4.50—37pp--------------------------------------- Vendor #D1842

2079 - THE LOVEJOY GENEALOGY WITH BIOGRAPHIES AND HISTORY,
1460-1930 by Clarence Earle Lovejoy. Repr. of 1930 ed.
Cloth—$70.50—Paper—$60.50—470pp---------------------- Vendor #D1842

2080   - THE ANCESTORS OF THE JOHN LOWE FAMILY CIRCLE AND THEIR
DESCENDANTS by Ellen M. Merriam. Repr. of 1901 ed.
Paper—$28.00—189pp-- Vendor #D1842

2081   - SOME ACCOUNT OF THE LOWER FAMILY IN AMERICA by J. L. Lower.
Repr. of 1913 ed.
Paper—$28.50—144pp-- Vendor #D1842

2082   - LOWNDES FAMILY OF SOUTH CAROLINA by G. B. Chase. Repr.
of 1876 ed.
Paper—$7.50—38pp-- Vendor #D1842

2083   - LUDWIG GENEALOGY. SKETCH OF JOSEPH LUDWIG...SETTLED AT
"BROAD BAY," 'WALDOBORO', 1753 by M. R. Ludwig. Repr. of 1866 ed.
Paper—$33.50—223pp-- Vendor #D1842

2084   - EDWARD LUMAS OF IPSWICH, MASSACHUSETTS, AND SOME OF HIS
DESCENDANTS by George Harlan Lewis from notes of Elisha S. Loomis
with additions by Charles A. Lummus. Repr. Essex Inst. Hist. Coll.,
1917 ed.
Paper—$9.50—43pp-- Vendor #D1842

2085   - FRANCES LYFORD OF BOSTON AND EXETER, AND SOME OF HIS
DESCENDANTS by William Lewis Welch. Repr. Essex Inst. Hist. Coll.,
1902 ed.
Paper—$14.00—88pp--- Vendor #D1842

2086   - GENEALOGY OF LYMAN FAMILY IN GREAT BRITAIN AND AMERICA;
...RICHARD LYMAN,...ENGLAND, 1631 by Lyman Coleman. Repr. of
1872 ed.
Cloth—$82.00—Paper—$72.00—549pp----------------------- Vendor #D1842

2087   - RICHARD HIGGINS, RESIDENT AND PIONEER SETTLER AT PLY-
MOUTH AND EASTHAM, MASSACHUSETTS....by Mrs. Katherine
Chapin Higgins. Repr. of 1918 ed.
Cloth—$120.00—Paper—$110.00—799pp---------------------- Vendor #D1842

2088   - DESCENDANTS OF THE REVEREND FRANCIS HIGGINSON by Thomas
Wentworth Higginson. Repr. of 1910 ed., n.p.
Paper—$12.50—84pp--- Vendor #D1842

2089   - JOHN HILL OF DOVER IN 1649, AND SOME OF HIS DESCENDANTS
by W. B. Lapham. Repr. of 1889 ed.
Paper—$4.00—16pp-- Vendor #D1842

2090   - JOHN HILL OF DORCHESTER, MASSACHUSETTS, 1663, AND FIVE
GENERATIONS OF HIS DESCENDANTS....by J. Gardner Bartlett.
Repr. of 1904 ed.
Paper—$15.00—103pp-- Vendor #D1842

2091   - GENEALOGICAL DATA, ANCESTORS AND DESCENDANTS OF WILLIAM
HILLS, ENGLISH EMIGRANT...JOSEPH HILLS IN 1638 by W. and T.
Hills. Repr. of 1902 ed.
Paper—$30.00—148pp-- Vendor #D1842

2092   - HILLS FAMILY IN AMERICA; ANCESTRY AND DESCENDANTS OF
WILLIAM HILLS, 1632, JOSEPH HILLS, 1638....by William Sanford
Hills, edited by Thomas Hills. Repr. of 1906 ed.
Cloth—$110.00—Paper—$100.00—734pp--------------------- Vendor #D1842

2093   - HILTON FAMILY GENEALOGY by J. T. Hassam. Repr. of 1896 ed.
Paper—$5.00—24pp-- Vendor #D1842

2094   - HISTORY AND GENEALOGY OF THE HINDS FAMILY by Albert Henry
Hinds. Repr. of 1899 ed.
Cloth—$59.00—Paper—$49.00—394pp----------------------- Vendor #D1842

2095   - HISTORY OF THE HINMANS, WITH RECORD OF KINDRED FAMILIES
by A. V. Hinman. Repr. of 1907 ed.
Paper—$15.00—75pp--- Vendor #D1842

2096   - THOMAS HINSHAW AND OTHERS by J. E. Hinshaw. Repr. of 1911 ed.
Paper—$10.00—49pp--- Vendor #D1842

2097 - HINSHAW-HENSHAW FAMILY by W. Hinshaw and M. Custer. Repr. of 1911 ed.
Paper—$13.00—66pp--- Vendor #D1842

2098 - CHRONICLES OF THE HINSDALE FAMILY by Albert Hinsdale. Repr. of 1883 ed.
Paper—$6.00—31pp--- Vendor #D1842

2099 - HOADLEY GENEALOGY. HISTORY OF DESCENDANTS OF WILLIAM HOADLEY OF BRANFORD, CONNECTICUT....by Francis Bacon Trowbridge. Repr. of 1894 ed.
Cloth—$44.00—Paper—$34.00—295pp----------------------- Vendor #D1842

2100 - GENEALOGY OF THE HITCHCOCK FAMILY...MATTHIAS HITCHCOCK OF EAST HAVEN, CONNECTICUT....by Mrs. Edward Hitchcock, Sr., arranged by Dwight W. Marsh. Repr. of 1894 ed.
Cloth—$84.50—Paper—$74.50—563pp----------------------- Vendor #D1842

2101 - HOAR FAMILY IN AMERICA AND ITS ENGLISH ANCESTRY:...MADE BY GEORGE FRISBIE HOAR by Henry Stedman Nourse. Repr. N. E. Hist. & Gen. Register, 1899 ed.
Paper—$8.00—37pp--- Vendor #D1842

2102 - WILLIAM HOBART, HIS ANCESTORS AND DESCENDANTS by L. Smith Hobart. Repr. of 1886 ed.
Paper—$28.00—187pp-------------------------------------- Vendor #D1842

2103 - GENEALOGY OF HOBSON FAMILY OF BUXTON, MAINE by J. M. Bailey. Repr. of 1875 ed.
Paper—$4.00—15pp--- Vendor #D1842

2104 - HODGE GENEALOGY FROM THE FIRST OF THE NAME IN THIS COUNTRY...by Orlando John Hodge. Repr. of 1900 ed.
Cloth—$68.00—Paper—$58.00—455pp----------------------- Vendor #D1842

2105 - GENEALOGICAL RECORD OF THE HODGES FAMILY IN NEW ENGLAND, 1633-1853 by Almon D. Hodges. Repr. of 1853 ed.
Paper—$13.50—71pp--------------------------------------- Vendor #D1842

2106 - GENEALOGY OF THE HODGKINS FAMILY OF MAINE by E. B. Hodgkins. Repr. of 1927 ed.
Paper—$20.00—98pp--------------------------------------- Vendor #D1842

2107 -GENEALOGY OF DESCENDANTS OF NICHOLAS HODSDON (HODGDON) 1635-1904 by A. L. White. Repr. of 1904 ed.
Paper—$30.00—164pp-------------------------------------- Vendor #D1842

2108 - THE HOLCOMBS SOME ACCOUNTING OF THEIR ORIGIN SETTLEMENT AND SCATTERMENT...REUNIONS, 1879 AND 1886. Repr. of 1887 ed.
Paper—$7.50—33pp--- Vendor #D1842

2109 - THE HOLDERS OF HOLDERNESS. HISTORY...CHRISTOPHER HOLDER, PIONEER QUAKER MINISTER IN NEW ENGLAND (1656) by Charles Frederick Holder. Repr. of 1902 ed.
Cloth—$54.00—Paper—$44.00—358pp----------------------- Vendor #D1842

2110 - HOLLINGSWORTH GENEALOGICAL MEMORANDA IN THE UNITED STATES, FROM 1682 TO 1884 by William B. Hollingsworth. Repr. of 1884 ed.
Paper—$21.50—144pp-------------------------------------- Vendor #D1842

2111 - HOLLISTER FAMILY OF AMERICA; LIEUTENANT JOHN HOLLISTER OF WETHERSFIELD, CONNECTICUT....by Lafayette Wallace Case. Repr. of 1886 ed.
Cloth—$120.50—Paper—$110.50—805pp--------------------- Vendor #D1842

2112 - ANCESTORS AND DESCENDANTS OF ASHBELL HOLLISTER by H. Hollister. Repr. of 1885 ed.
Paper—$3.50—10pp--- Vendor #D1842

2113 - HOLLISTER FAMILY by S. V. Talcott. Repr. of 1916 ed.
Paper—$4.00—20pp--- Vendor #D1842

2114 - BRIEF ACCOUNT OF FAMILY OF HOMER OR de HOMERE OF ETTING-
SHALL, COUNTY STAFFORD, ENGLAND....by Benjamin Homer Dixon.
Repr. of 1889 ed.
Paper—$6.00—27pp--- Vendor #D1842

2115 - GENEALOGICAL HISTORY OF HOLT FAMILY IN THE UNITED STATES;
...NICHOLAS HOLT...WILLIAM HOLT OF NEW HAVEN, CONNECTICUT
by Daniel S. Durrie. Repr. of 1864 ed.
Cloth—$55.00—Paper—$45.00—367pp----------------------- Vendor #D1842

2116 - JOHN HOOD OF LYNN, MASSACHUSETTS, AND SOME OF HIS DE-
SCENDANTS by Jennie (Hood) Bosson. Repr. Essex Inst. Hist. Coll.,
1909 ed.
Paper—$10.00—46pp--- Vendor #D1842

2117 - BIOGRAPHICAL SKETCH OF EIGHT GENERATIONS OF HOOPERS IN
AMERICA; WILLIAM HOOPER 1635....by Mrs. Sumner Crosby. Repr.
of 1906 ed.
Paper—$9.00—42pp--- Vendor #D1842

2118 - HOOPER GENEALOGY by Charles Henry Pope and Thomas Hooper.
Repr. of 1908 ed.
Cloth—$48.00—Paper—$38.00—321pp----------------------- Vendor #D1842

2119 - STEPHEN AND GILES HOPKINS, MAYFLOWER DESCENDANTS, AND
SOME OF THEIR DESCENDANTS by J. W. Hawes. Repr. of 1915 ed.
Paper—$5.00—27pp--- Vendor #D1842

2120 - HOPKINS FAMILY MARRIAGES by W. M. Clemens. Repr. of 1916 ed.
Paper—$10.00—48pp--- Vendor #D1842

2121 - ONE BRANCH OF THE HOPKINS FAMILY (DESCENDANTS OF STEPHEN
AND GILES) by A. B. Raymond. Repr., n.d., typescript.
Paper—$4.00—16pp--- Vendor #D1842

2122 - NOTES ON THE THOMAS HOPKINS FAMILY OF RHODE ISLAND by
A. Holbrook. Repr. of 1889 ed.
Paper—$4.00—19pp--- Vendor #D1842

2123 - A CHAPTER OF HOPKINS GENEALOGY, 1735-1905 by Ella Harrison.
Repr. of 1905 ed.
Cloth—$60.00—Paper—$50.00—396pp----------------------- Vendor #D1842

2124 - ONE BRANCH OF THE HOPKINS FAMILY (FROM JOHN HOPKINS OF
HARTFORD 1633) by S. M. Hopkins. Repr. of 1898 ed.
Paper—$3.00—6pp--- Vendor #D1842

2125 - HORTON GENEALOGY AND HISTORY, DESCENDANTS OF RICHARD
HORTON AND NATHANIEL HORTON....by G. W. Alloway. Repr. of
1929 ed.
Paper—$25.00—141pp--- Vendor #D1842

2126 - ANCESTORS OF HORACE EBENEZER AND EMMA (BABCOCK) HORTON
by H. E. Horton. Repr. of 1920 ed.
Paper—$22.50—117pp--- Vendor #D1842

2127 - ANCESTORS AND DESCENDANTS OF ISAAC HORTON OF LIBERTY,
NEW YORK by B. B. Horton. Repr. of 1912 ed.
Paper—$12.50—52pp--- Vendor #D1842

2128 - HISTORY OF ISAAC HOWARD OF FOSTER, RHODE ISLAND, AND
HIS DESCENDANTS by D. Howard. Repr. of 1901 ed.
Paper—$35.00—168pp--- Vendor #D1842

2129 - REPORT TO THE HOUGHTON ASSOCIATION, UNITED STATES OF
AMERICA, MADE BY COLUMBUS SMITH, 1869.... Repr. of 1869 ed.
Paper—$12.50—60pp--- Vendor #D1842

2130 - HOWARD GENEALOGY...DESCENDANTS IN THIS COUNTRY OF
THOMAS AND SUSANNA HOWARD by Jarvis Cutler Howard. Repr.
of 1884 ed.
Paper—$35.50—238pp--- Vendor #D1842

2131 - ANCESTORS AND DESCENDANTS OF JACOB HOW(E) OF ROWLEY, MASSACHUSETTS, BRIDGTON AND PARIS, MAINE by F. Howe. Repr. of 1905 ed.
Paper—$4.00—20pp--- Vendor #D1842

2132 - GENEALOGY OF THE HOWES FAMILY IN AMERICA. DESCENDANTS OF THOMAS HOWES...1637-1892 by Joshua Crowell Howes. Repr. of 1892 ed.
Paper—$31.00—209pp------------------------------------- Vendor #D1842

2133 - A BRIEF GENEALOGICAL...HISTORY OF ARTHUR, HENRY AND JOHN HOWLAND, AND THEIR DESCENDANTS, 1st Ed., by Franklyn Howland. Repr. of 1885 ed.
Cloth—$69.50—Paper—$59.50—463pp----------------------- Vendor #D1842

2134 - THE HOWLAND HEIRS; BEING THE STORY OF A FAMILY AND A FORTUNE....FOR MRS. BETTY H. R. GREEN by William M. Emery. Repr. of 1919 ed.
Cloth—$73.50—Paper—$63.50—491pp----------------------- Vendor #D1842

2135 - GENEALOGICAL HISTORY OF THE HOYT, HAIGHT AND HIGHT FAMILIES...AMESBURY, MASSACHUSETTS by David W. Hoyt. Repr. of 1871 ed.
Cloth—$104.50—Paper—$94.50—698pp---------------------- Vendor #D1842

2136 - RECORD OF THE HOYT FAMILY MEETING, 1866 by D. W. Hoyt. Repr. of 1866 ed.
Paper—$10.00—64pp--- Vendor #D1842

2137 - HOYT FAMILY, A GENEALOGICAL HISTORY OF JOHN HOYT OF SALISBURY...DESCENDANTS by D. W. Hoyt. Repr. of 1857 ed.
Paper—$25.00—144pp------------------------------------ Vendor #D1842

2138 - ONE THOUSAND YEARS OF HUBBARD HISTORY, 866 TO 1895 by Edward Warren Day. Repr. of 1895 ed.
Cloth—$76.50—Paper—$66.50—512pp----------------------- Vendor #D1842

2139 - THE HUBBARD THOMPSON MEMORIAL;...ANCESTORS AND DE-SCENDANTS OF EBENEZER HUBBARD AND MARY THOMPSON, HIS WIFE by Lillian Kimball Stewart. Repr. of 1914 ed.
Cloth—$63.50—Paper—$53.50—423pp----------------------- Vendor #D1842

2140 - HUCKINS FAMILY, ROBERT HUCKINS OF THE DOVER COMBINA-TION...HIS DESCENDANTS by H. W. Hardon. Repr. of 1916 ed., maps.
Cloth—$40.00—Paper—$30.00—195pp----------------------- Vendor #D1842

2141 - RECORDS OF SOME DESCENDANTS OF RICHARD HULL, NEW HAVEN, 1639-1662 by Samuel C. Clarke. Repr. of 1869 ed.
Paper—$4.00—20pp--- Vendor #D1842

2142 - RECORD OF THE DESCENDANTS OF RICHARD HULL OF NEW HAVEN, 260 YEARS IN AMERICA by Puella Follett (Hull) Mason. Repr. of 1894 ed.
Paper—$14.00—78pp-- Vendor #D1842

2143 - REV. JOSEPH HULL AND SOME OF HIS DESCENDANTS by Amy Eleanor E. Hull. Repr. of 1904 ed.
Paper—$12.50—64pp-- Vendor #D1842

2144 - HUNTER FAMILY RECORDS by W. M. Clemens. Repr. of 1914 ed.
Paper—$4.00—17pp--- Vendor #D1842

2145 - JOHN HUNTLEY OF LYME, CONNECTICUT AND HIS DESCENDANTS by H. F. Johnston. Repr. of 1949 ed., typescript.
Paper—$15.00—72pp-- Vendor #D1842

2146 - GENEALOGY OF THE NAME AND FAMILY OF HUNT by T. B. Wyman, Jr. Repr. of 1862-63 ed.
Cloth—$64.50—Paper—$54.50—430pp----------------------- Vendor #D1842

2147 - GENEALOGICAL MEMOIR OF THE HUNTINGTON FAMILY...DESCEND-ANTS OF SIMON AND MARGARET HUNTINGTON by E. B. Huntgington. Repr. of 1863 ed.
Cloth—$64.00—Paper—$54.00—428pp----------------------- Vendor #D1842

2148 - HURLBUT GENEALOGY;...DESCENDANTS OF THOMAS HURLBUT OF SAYBROOK AND WETHERSFIELD, CONNECTICUT by Henry H. Hurlbut. Repr. of 1888 ed.
Cloth—$79.00—Paper—$69.00—545pp------------------------ Vendor #D1842

2149 - PHILIP HUNTON AND HIS DESCENDANTS by Daniel T. V. Huntoon. Repr. of 1881 ed.
Paper—$17.00—113pp----------------------------------- Vendor #D1842

2150 - HUTCHINS GENEALOGY by Charles Hutchins. Repr. of 1885 ed.
Paper—$4.00—16pp------------------------------------- Vendor #D1842

2151 - GENEALOGY OF THE HUTCHINSON FAMILY OF YORKSHIRE... RICHARD HUTCHINSON OF SALEM, MASSACHUSETTS by Joseph Lemuel Chester. Repr. N. E. Hist. & Gen. Register, 1868 ed.
Paper—$7.00—33pp------------------------------------- Vendor #D1842

2152 - BRIEF GENEALOGY OF DESCENDANTS OF WILLIAM HUTCHINSON AND THOMAS OLIVER by W. H. Whitmore. Repr. of 1865 ed.
Paper—$7.50—38pp------------------------------------- Vendor #D1842

2153 - HUTCHINSON FAMILY; OR, DESCENDANTS OF BERNARD HUTCHINSON OF COWLAM, ENGLAND by Perley Derby. Repr. of 1870 ed.
Paper—$15.00—107pp----------------------------------- Vendor #D1842

2154 - SOME OF THE DESCENDANTS OF SAMUEL HURLBUT OF CHATHAM, CONNECTICUT by H. Hurlbut. Repr. of 1861 ed.
Paper—$5.00—24pp------------------------------------- Vendor #D1842

2155 - THE HUNTING OR HUNTTING FAMILY IN AMERICA by T. D. Huntting. Repr. of 1888 ed.
Paper—$14.00—83pp------------------------------------ Vendor #D1842

2156 - HUNTER FAMILY OF VIRGINIA by S. M. Culbertson. Repr. of 1934 ed., extract.
Paper—$4.00—22pp------------------------------------- Vendor #D1842

2157 - A BRIEF SKETCH OF THE HUTCHINSON FAMILY OF NEW HAMPSHIRE by Frank Allen Hutchinson. Repr. of 1896 ed.
Paper—$4.50—23pp------------------------------------- Vendor #D1842

2158 - GENEALOGY AND HISTORY OF THE INGALLS FAMILY...EDMUND INGALLS...LYNN, MASSACHUSETTS, IN 1629 by Charles Burleigh. Repr. of 1903 ed.
Cloth—$48.50—Paper—$38.50—324pp-------------------- Vendor #D1842

2159 - THE INGERSOLLS OF HAMPSHIRE...LINE OF JOHN INGERSOLL OF WESTFIELD, MASSACHUSETTS by Charles Stedman Ripley. Repr. of 1893 ed.
Paper—$15.00—107pp----------------------------------- Vendor #D1842

2160 - SOME ACCOUNTING OF THE IRELAND FAMILY OF LONG ISLAND 1644-1880 by J. N. Ireland. Repr. of 1880 ed.
Paper—$10.00—51pp------------------------------------ Vendor #D1842

2161 - A GENEALOGY OF THE INGERSOLL FAMILY IN AMERICA, 1629-1925 by Lillian Drake Avery. Repr. of 1926 ed.
Cloth—$89.00—Paper—$79.00—596pp-------------------- Vendor #D1842

2162 - GENEALOGY OF IRELAND FAMILY IN ENGLAND, IRELAND AND AMERICA by W. M. Taylor. Repr. of 1863 ed.
Paper—$3.50—10pp------------------------------------- Vendor #D1842

2163 - SKETCH OF THE IRELAND FAMILY by J. B. Ireland. Repr. of 1907 ed.
Paper—$8.00—41pp------------------------------------- Vendor #D1842

2164 - SKETCH OF GENERAL JAMES IRISH OF GORHAM, MAINE WITH FAMILY RECORDS by L. Oak. Repr. of 1898 ed.
Paper—$14.00—70pp------------------------------------ Vendor #D1842

2165 - ISBELL AND KINGMAN FAMILIES, ROBERT ISBELL AND HENRY KINGMAN AND THEIR DESCENDANTS by L. Kingman. Repr. of 1889 ed.
Paper—$7.50—30pp------------------------------------- Vendor #D1842

2166 - GENEALOGY OF THE ISBELL FAMILY by Mary Isbell Scott. Repr. of 1929 ed., n.p.
Paper—$38.50—256pp--- Vendor #D1842

2167 - GENEALOGY OF THE JENKS FAMILY OF NEWPORT, NEW HAMPSHIRE by George E. Jenks. Repr. of 1888 ed., n.p.
Paper—$3.50—12pp--- Vendor #D1842

2168 - JENKINS FAMILY BOOK by R. E. Jenkins. Repr. of 1904 ed.
Paper—$35.00—244pp------------------------------------- Vendor #D1842

2169 - JELKE AND FRAZIER AND ALLIED FAMILIES by L. E. DeForest. Repr. of 1931 ed.
Paper—$18.50—93pp------------------------------------- Vendor #D1842

2170 - A BRANCH OF THE JACKSON CORRELATED FAMILY, 1730-1911 by S. Jackson. Repr. of 1911 ed.
Paper—$12.50—60pp------------------------------------- Vendor #D1842

2171 - JAMESONS IN AMERICA, 1647-1900. GENEALOGICAL RECORDS AND MEMORANDA by E. O. Jameson. Repr. of 1901 ed.
Cloth—$92.00—Paper—$82.00—615pp---------------------- Vendor #D1842

2172 - JANES FAMILY. GENEALOGY AND BRIEF HISTORY OF DESCEND-ANTS OF WILLIAM JANES...1637 by Frederic Janes. Repr. of 1868 ed.
Cloth—$63.00—Paper—$53.00—419pp---------------------- Vendor #D1842

2173 - GENEALOGY OF THE JAQUETT FAMILY, Rev. Ed., by Edwin Jaquett Sellers. Repr. of 1907 ed.
Paper—$34.00—226pp------------------------------------- Vendor #D1842

2174 - JAY FAMILY OF LaROCHELLE AND NEW YORK PROVINCE AND STATE by L. J. Wells. Repr. of 1938 ed.
Paper—$12.50—64pp------------------------------------- Vendor #D1842

2175 - JEWELL REGISTER, DESCENDANTS OF THOMAS JEWELL OF BRAIN-TREE by P. and J. Jewell. Repr. of 1860 ed.
Paper—$17.50—104pp------------------------------------- Vendor #D1842

2176 - THE JOHNES FAMILY OF SOUTHAMPTON, LONG ISLAND, 1629-1886 by Edward R. Johnes. Repr. of 1886 ed.
Paper—$9.50—46pp------------------------------------- Vendor #D1842

2177 - JACOB JOHNSON OF HARPSWELL, MAINE AND HIS DESCENDANTS by C. N. Sinnett. Repr. of 1907 ed.
Paper—$26.00—132pp------------------------------------- Vendor #D1842

2178 - JOHNSON GENEALOGY...JOHN JOHNSON OF IPSWICH AND AND-OVER, MASSACHUSETTS, 1635-1892....by William W. Johnson. Repr. of 1892 ed.
Paper—$30.00—200pp------------------------------------- Vendor #D1842

2179 - THE NEW HAVEN AND WALLINGFORD (CONNECTICUT) JOHNSONS by James Shepard. Repr. N. E. Hist. & Gen. Register, 1902 ed.
Paper—$3.50—11pp------------------------------------- Vendor #D1842

2180 - ANCESTORS OF SARAH JOHNSON, WIFE OF JOSEPH NEAL, OF LITCHFIELD, MAINE by W. G. Davis. Repr. of 1960 ed.
Paper—$17.50—104pp------------------------------------- Vendor #D1842

2181 - GENEALOGICAL RECORD OF PETER JOHNSTON, WITH HISTORY OF CLAN by C. E. Johnston. Repr. of 1900 ed.
Paper—$22.50—118pp------------------------------------- Vendor #D1842

2182 - SOME DESCENDANTS OF LEWIS AND ANN JONES OF ROXBURY, MASSACHUSETTS....by William Blake Trask. Repr. of 1878 ed.
Paper—$14.00—83pp------------------------------------- Vendor #D1842

2183 - CAPTAIN ROGER JONES OF LONDON AND VIRGINIA. SOME OF HIS ANTECEDENTS AND DESCENDANTS....by L. H. Jones. Repr. of 1891 ed.
Cloth—$44.00—Paper—$34.00—295pp---------------------- Vendor #D1842

2184 - GENEALOGY OF FAMILY OF CERENO UPHAM JONES OF WEYMOUTH, NOVA SCOTIA (....LEWIS JONES OF ROXBURY, MASSACHUSETTS, 1640) by Mary E. R. Jones. Repr. of 1905 ed.
Paper—$8.00—38pp-------------------------------------- Vendor #D1842

2185 - THE JORDAN MEMORIAL. FAMILY RECORDS OF THE REV. ROBERT JORDAN...IN AMERICA by Tristram Frost Jordan. Repr. of 1882 ed.
Cloth—$74.00—Paper—$64.00—495pp----------------------- Vendor #D1842

2186 - A BRIEF HISTORY OF THE JOY FAMILY, BY ONE OF THEM by Cornelia C. Joy Dyer. Repr. of 1876 ed.
Paper—$7.50—37pp------------------------------------- Vendor #D1842

2187 - THOMAS JOY AND HIS DESCENDANTS by J. R. Joy. Repr. of 1900 ed.
Paper—$37.50—225pp----------------------------------- Vendor #D1842

2188 - ENGLISH ANCESTRY AND ROYAL DESCENT OF THE JOY FAMILY OF AMERICA by A. A. G. Repr. of 1902 ed.
Paper—$3.50—13pp------------------------------------- Vendor #D1842

2189 - McCLANAHAN FAMILY, DESCENDANTS OF ROBERT OF IRELAND AND VIRGINIA by H. White. Repr. of 1894 ed.
Paper—$9.00—43pp------------------------------------- Vendor #D1842

2190 - FOUR GENERATIONS OF THE McCLARY FAMILY FROM ANDREW McCLARY OF ULSTER 1726 by H. P. McClary. Repr. of 1896 ed.
Paper—$10.00—52pp----------------------------------- Vendor #D1842

2191 - McCLURE FAMILY RECORDS by W. M. Clemens. Repr. of 1914 ed.
Paper—$4.00—14pp------------------------------------- Vendor #D1842

2192 - McCLURE FAMILY GENEALOGY by J. A. McClure. Repr. of 1914 ed.
Paper—$35.00—232pp----------------------------------- Vendor #D1842

2193 - McCONNELL MARRIAGE GENEALOGY, ANCESTORS, DESCENDANTS, MARRIAGES OF A VIRGINIA FAMILY by H. and M. Addington. Repr. of 1929 ed.
Paper—$8.00—36pp------------------------------------- Vendor #D1842

2194 - GENEALOGY OF THE McCULLOUGH FAMILY AND OTHER SKETCHES by J. McCullough. Repr. of 1912 ed.
Paper—$20.00—100pp----------------------------------- Vendor #D1842

2195 - McDANIEL FAMILY RECORD by C. G. Harris. Repr. of 1929 ed.
Paper—$30.00—161pp----------------------------------- Vendor #D1842

2196 - DESCENDANTS OF DANIEL McFARLAND, ONE OF THE SCOTCH PRESBYTERIANS...WORCESTER, MASSACHUSETTS by Ellery B. Crane. Repr. of 1907 ed.
Paper—$5.50—28pp------------------------------------- Vendor #D1842

2197 - GENEALOGY OF THE McFARLAND FAMILY OF HANCOCK COUNTY, MAINE by Daniel Y. McFarland. Repr. of 1910 ed.
Paper—$12.00—58pp----------------------------------- Vendor #D1842

2198 - HISTORY OF THE CLAN MacFARLANE (MACFARLANE), MacFARLAN, MacFARLAND, MacFARLIN by Mrs. C. M. Little. Repr. of 1893 ed.
Paper—$38.00—254pp----------------------------------- Vendor #D1842

2199 - THE McGUIRE FAMILY IN VIRGINIA by W. G. Stannard. Repr. of 1926 ed.
Paper—$25.00—126pp----------------------------------- Vendor #D1842

2200 - GENEALOGICAL RECORDS OF DESCENDANTS OF DAVID MACK TO 1879 by Sophia Smith and Charles S. Smith. Repr. of 1879 ed.
Paper—$15.00—81pp----------------------------------- Vendor #D1842

2201 - GENEALOGY OF HUGH McKAY AND HIS LINEAL DESCENDANTS, 1788-1895 by William L. Kean. Repr. of 1895 ed.
Paper—$14.50—76pp----------------------------------- Vendor #D1842

2202 - SCOTCH ANCESTORS OF WILLIAM McKINLEY, PRESIDENT OF THE UNITED STATES by Edward A. Claypool. Repr. of 1897 ed.
Paper—$10.00—46pp----------------------------------- Vendor #D1842

2203 - GENEALOGY OF HUGH McKAY AND HIS LINEAL DESCENDANTS by
W. L. Kean. Repr. of 1894 ed.
Paper—$16.00—76pp-- Vendor #D1842

2204 - GENEALOGY OF THE McKINSTRY FAMILY...THE SCOT-IRISH IMMI-
GRATIONS TO AMERICA by W. Willis. Repr. of 1866 ed.
Paper—$10.00—46pp-- Vendor #D1842

2205 - THE MacQUEENS, BEING A BRIEF HISTORY OF THE ORIGIN OF
THE MacQUEEN FAMILY by James Archibald Nydegger. Repr. of 1928 ed.
Paper—$15.50—111pp--- Vendor #D1842

2206 - HISTORY OF DESCENDANTS OF DAVID McKEE by J. Y. McKee.
Repr. of 1892 ed.
Paper—$22.50—112pp--- Vendor #D1842

2207 - TALES OF OUR FOREFATHERS...FAMILIES ALLIED TO THOSE OF
McPIKE, GUEST AND DUMONT by Eugene F. McPike. Repr. of 1898 ed.
Paper—$27.00—181pp--- Vendor #D1842

2208 - MALTBY-MALTBIE FAMILY HISTORY by Dorothy Maltby Verril.
Repr. of 1916 ed.
Cloth—$65.00—Paper—$55.00—435pp----------------------- Vendor #D1842

2209 - MAN FAMILY by R. W. Lloyd. Repr. of 1932 ed.
Paper—$6.00—24pp-- Vendor #D1842

2210 - MANN MEMORIAL...MANN FAMILY IN AMERICA...DESCENDANTS
OF RICHARD MAN OF SCITUATE, MASSACHUSETTS by George S.
Mann. Repr. of 1884 ed.
Paper—$37.50—251pp--- Vendor #D1842

2211 - GENEALOGY OF THE JOHN MARSH OF SALEM, AND HIS DESCEND-
ANTS, 1633-1888 collected by Lucius B. Marsh, revised and edited by
Dwight W. Marsh. Repr. of 1888 ed.
Paper—$30.00—283pp--- Vendor #D1842

2212 - GENEALOGY OF THE MARSH FAMILY. OUTLINE FOR FIVE GENERA-
TIONS...LAKE PLEASANT IN 1886 edited by D. W. Marsh. Repr. of
1886 ed.
Paper—$12.00—60pp-- Vendor #D1842

2213 - MEMOIRS OF THE MARSTONS OF SALEM...SOME OF THEIR DE-
SCENDANTS by John L. Watson, Repr. N. E. Hist. & Gen. Register,
1873 ed.
Paper—$9.50—48pp--- Vendor #D1842

2214 - MARSH GENEALOGY...DESCENDANTS OF JOHN MARSH OF HART-
FORD, CONNECTICUT, 1636-1895 by Dwight Whitney Marsh. Repr.
of 1895 ed.
Cloth—$87.50—Paper—$77.50—585pp----------------------- Vendor #D1842

2215 - THE MARCY FAMILY by C. D. Paige. Repr. of 1902 ed.
Paper—$4.00—16pp--- Vendor #D1842

2216 - MARSTON ENGLISH ANCESTRY WITH SOME ACCOUNT OF THE
AMERICAN IMMIGRANTS OF THE NAME by M. L. Holman. Repr. of
1929 ed., chart.
Paper—$8.00—41pp--- Vendor #D1842

2217 - NOTES ON THE MANNING FAMILY OF COUNTY KENT, ENGLAND
...WATERS, PROCTOR AND WHITFIELD FAMILIES by Henry F.
Water. Repr. N. E. Hist. & Gen. Register, 1897 ed.
Paper—$7.00—35pp--- Vendor #D1842

2218 - THE MARSTON GENEALOGY, IN TWO PARTS by Nathan Washington
Marston. Repr. of 1888 ed.
Cloth—$91.00—Paper—$81.00—607pp----------------------- Vendor #D1842

2219 - NOTICES GENEALOGICAL AND HISTORICAL OF THE MARTIN FAMILY
OF NEW ENGLAND....by Henry J. Martin. Repr. of 1880 ed.
Cloth—$53.50—Paper—$43.50—358pp----------------------- Vendor #D1842

2220 – GENEALOGICAL SKETCH OF THE DESCENDANTS OF REINOLD AND MATTHEW MARVIN...NEW ENGLAND IN 1635 by T. R. Marvin.
Repr. of 1848 ed.
Paper—$10.50—56pp--- Vendor #D1842

2221 – A RECORD OF THE DESCENDANTS OF ROBERT MASON, OF ROXBURY, MASSACHUSETTS by William L. Mason. Repr. of 1891 ed.
Paper—$7.50—39pp--- Vendor #D1842

2222 – GENEALOGY OF DESCENDANTS OF JOHN MAY WHO CAME FROM ENGLAND TO ROXBURY IN AMERICA, 1640 by Samuel May, et al.
Repr. of 1878 ed.
Paper—$31.50—210pp--- Vendor #D1842

2223 – JOHN MAYNARD OF SUDBURY, MASSACHUSETTS AND DESCENDANTS by W. E. Gould. Repr. of 1914 ed.
Paper—$8.00—38pp--- Vendor #D1842

2224 – BRIEF MEMOIR OF MAYNARD FAMILY, ETC. by C. P. Stevens.
Repr. of 1916 ed.
Paper—$13.00—64pp--- Vendor #D1842

2225 – ROBERT MEANS AND DESCENDANTS by C. N. Sinnett. Repr. of 1929 ed.
Paper—$4.00—14pp--- Vendor #D1842

2226 – MEEK GENEALOGY, WITH SKETCHES OF ADAM MEEK AND HIS DESCENDANTS, 1640-1902 by H. Meek. Repr. of 1902 ed.
Paper—$10.00—54pp--- Vendor #D1842

2227 – SOME MERIAMS AND THEIR CONNECTION WITH OTHER FAMILIES by Rufus N. Meriam. Repr. Worcester Soc. of Antiquity, Proc., 1888 ed.
Paper—$10.00—52pp--- Vendor #D1842

2228 – A CONTRIBUTION TO THE GENEALOGY OF THE MERRILL FAMILY IN AMERICA....by Frederick J. H. Merrill. Repr. of 1899 ed.
Paper—$4.50—20pp--- Vendor #D1842

2229 – WALTER MERRYMAN OF HARPSWELL, MAINE, AND HIS DESCENDANTS by Charles Nelson Sinnett. Repr. of 1905 ed.
Paper—$18.50—123pp--- Vendor #D1842

2230 – THE FAMILY OF MERRIAM OF MASSACHUSETTS by W. S. Appleton.
Repr. of 1892 ed.
Paper—$4.00—15pp--- Vendor #D1842

2231 – JOHN MILES OF CONCORD, MASSACHUSETTS AND HIS DESCENDANTS by J. M. Miles. Repr. of 1920 ed.
Paper—$10.00—48pp--- Vendor #D1842

2232 – GENEALOGY OF THE MESSINGER FAMILY by George W. Messinger.
Repr. of 1863 ed.
Paper—$4.00—14pp--- Vendor #D1842

2233 – THE MESSINGER FAMILY IN EUROPE AND AMERICA by George Washington Messinger. WITH A MEMOIR OF HON. DANIEL MESSINGER OF BOSTON by John Ward Dean. Repr. N. E. Hist. & Gen. Register, 1882 ed.
Paper—$3.50—12pp--- Vendor #D1842

2234 – DESCENDANTS OF CAPTAIN JOSEPH MILLER OF WEST SPRINGFIELD, MASSACHUSETTS, 1698-1908 by C. S. Williams. Repr. of 1908 ed.
Paper—$8.00—39pp--- Vendor #D1842

2235 – MILLS FAMILY MARRIAGES by W. M. Clemens. Repr. of 1916 ed.
Paper—$10.00—52pp--- Vendor #D1842

2236 – GENEALOGICAL RECORD OF THE MINOT FAMILY IN AMERICA AND ENGLAND by Joseph Grafton Minot. Repr. of 1897 ed.
Paper—$10.50—55pp--- Vendor #D1842

2237 – MOFFATANA BULLETIN. GENEALOGICAL NOTES ON MOFFAT 1907-15. Repr.
Paper—$10.00—44pp--- Vendor #D1842

2238 - LUDWIG MOHLER AND HIS DESCENDANTS 1696-1921 by C. G. Dunning. Repr. of 1921 ed.
Paper—$12.50—63pp-- Vendor #D1842

2239 - MEETING OF THE MONTAGUE FAMILY AT HADLEY, MASSACHUSETTS, 1882 edited by Richard Montague. Repr. of 1882 ed.
Paper—$15.50—107pp--- Vendor #D1842

2240 - THE PORTSMOUTH, NEW HAMPSHIRE RACE OF MONSONS, MUNSONS, MANSONS; RICHARD MONSON AND HIS DESCENDANTS by M. A. Munson. Repr. of 1910 ed., chart.
Paper—$18.50—89pp--- Vendor #D1842

2241 - GENEALOGICAL HISTORY OF THE FAMILY OF MONTGOMERY by T. H. Montgomery. Repr. of 1863 ed.
Paper—$35.00—170pp-- Vendor #D1842

2242 - MOOAR (MOORS) GENEALOGY. ABRAHAM MOOAR OF ANDOVER AND HIS DESCENDANTS by George Mooar. Repr. of 1901 ed.
Paper—$15.00—97pp--- Vendor #D1842

2243 - GENEALOGY OF ONE BRANCH OF MOREY FAMILY 1631-1890 by E. W. Leavitt. Repr. of 1890 ed.
Paper—$7.50—36pp-- Vendor #D1842

2244 - HISTORY OF DESCENDANTS OF DAVID MORGAN IN AMERICA... MORGAN AND HOWARD FAMILIES by William Allen Daily. Repr. of 1909 ed.
Paper—$4.00—11pp-- Vendor #D1842

2245 - FAMILY OF MORGAN, STANLEY AND BLATCHLEY by A. S. Blatchley. Repr. of 1929 ed.
Paper—$8.50—43pp-- Vendor #D1842

2246 - MORGAN GENEALOGY. HISTORY OF JAMES MORGAN OF NEW LONDON, CONNECTICUT, AND HIS DESCENDANTS, 1607-1869.... by Nathaniel H. Morgan. Repr. of 1869 ed.
Cloth—$42.00—Paper—$32.00—281pp---------------------- Vendor #D1842

2247 - ANCESTRY OF DANIEL MORRELL OF HARTFORD, WITH HIS DESCENDANTS AND...FAMILIES by Francis V. Morrell. Repr. of 1916 ed.
Paper—$20.00—132pp--------------------------------------- Vendor #D1842

2248 -AMERICAN ANCESTRY OF BENJAMIN MORRILL AND HIS WIFE, MIRIAM PECKER MORRILL...TO 1901 by Horace Edwin Morrill. Repr. of 1903 ed.
Paper—$4.50—21pp-- Vendor #D1842

2249 - MORRILL KINDRED IN AMERICA...DESCENDANTS OF ABRAHAM MORRILL OF SALISBURY, MASSACHUSETTS, 1631-1662, 2 Vols., by Annie Morrill Smith. Repr. of 1914-1931 ed.
Cloth—$88.00—Paper—$78.00----------------------------- Vendor #D1842

2250 - MEMORANDA OF DESCENDANTS OF AMOS MORRIS OF EAST HAVEN, CONNECTICUT by E. L. Hart and O. Street. Repr. of 1853 ed.
Paper—$15.00—103pp--------------------------------------- Vendor #D1842

2251 - MEMORIAL OF THE FAMILY OF MORSE by Henry Dutch Lord. Repr. of 1896 ed,
Cloth—$85.00—Paper—$75.00—556pp---------------------- Vendor #D1842

2252 - HISTORICAL SKETCHES OF JOHN MOSES OF PLYMOUTH...WINDSOR, AND SIMSBURY...PORTSMOUTH...DESCENDANTS by Zebina Moses. Repr. of 1890-1907 ed.
Cloth—$44.50—Paper—$34.50—298pp---------------------- Vendor #D1842

2253 - MORTON FAMILY RECORD FROM 1668-1881 (SETTLED HATFIELD, MASSACHUSETTS) by C. Morton. Repr. of 1881 ed.
Paper—$10.00—48pp--- Vendor #D1842

2254 - GEORGE MORTON OF PLYMOUTH COLONY AND SOME OF HIS DESCENDANTS by John K. Allen. Repr. of 1908 ed.
Paper—$10.00—46pp--- Vendor #D1842

2255 - ORIGIN AND HISTORY OF MOSHER FAMILY, WITH GENEALOGY OF
ONE BRANCH...FROM 1660-1898 by W. C. Mosher. Repr. of 1898 ed.
Paper—$10.00—48pp-- Vendor #D1842

2256 - GENEALOGY OF MOSELEY FAMILY, SKETCH OF ONE BRANCH by
E. S. Mosely. Repr. of 1878 ed.
Paper—$11.50—56pp-- Vendor #D1842

2257 - HISTORICAL SKETCHES OF JOHN MOSES OF PLYMOUTH, PORTS-
MOUTH, WINDSOR AND SIMSBURY by Z. Moses. Repr. of 1890 ed.
Paper—$27.50—138pp--- Vendor #D1842

2258 - MOTT, STRIKER FAMILIES by H. S. Mott. Repr. of 1898 ed., chart.
Paper—$4.00—18pp--- Vendor #D1842

2259 - SOME DESCENDANTS OF JOHN MOULTON AND WILLIAM MOULTON
OF HAMPTON, NEW HAMPSHIRE, 1592-1892 by Augustus F. Moulton.
Repr. of 1892 ed., n.p.
Paper—$15.00—99pp-- Vendor #D1842

2260 - JAMES MOTT OF DUTCHESS COUNTY, NEW YORK, AND HIS DE-
SCENDANTS by Edward Doubleday Harris. Repr. of 1911 ed.
Paper—$12.50—62pp-- Vendor #D1842

2261 - GENEALOGICAL REGISTER OF SOME DESCENDANTS OF JOHN
MOULTON OF HAMPTON....by Thomas Moulton. Repr. of 1873 ed.
Paper—$9.00—44pp--- Vendor #D1842

2262 - MOWER GENEALOGY 1690-1897 by E. Mower. Repr.
Paper—$3.50—11pp--- Vendor #D1842

2263 - HISTORY OF THE MOULTON FAMILY...JAMES MOULTON OF SALEM
AND WENHAM, MASSACHUSETTS...TO 1905 by Eban Hobson Moulton
and Henry A. Moulton. Repr. of 1905 ed.
Paper—$11.00—56pp-- Vendor #D1842

2264 - RICHARD MOWER OF LYNN AND SOME OF HIS DESCENDANTS by
Edward L. Smith. Repr. of 1904 ed.
Paper—$4.00—16pp--- Vendor #D1842

2265 - A FAMILY HISTORY. RICHARD MOWRY OF UXBRIDGE, MASSACHU-
SETTS...AND HIS DESCENDANTS by William A. Mowry. Repr. of
1878 ed.
Paper—$36.00—239pp--- Vendor #D1842

2266 - DESCENDANTS OF JOHN MOWRY OF RHODE ISLAND by William A.
Mowry. Repr. of 1909 ed.
Cloth—$44.00—Paper—$34.00—292pp------------------------- Vendor #D1842

2267 - MEMORIALS: BEING A GENEALOGICAL...MUDGE IN AMERICA,
FROM 1638 TO 1868 by Alfred Mudge. Repr. of 1868 ed.
Cloth—$68.50—Paper—$58.50—457pp------------------------- Vendor #D1842

2268 - THE MUNROE GENEALOGY by J. G. Locke. Repr. of 1853 ed.
Paper—$4.00—15pp--- Vendor #D1842

2269 - TRADITIONS CONCERNING THE ORIGIN OF THE AMERICAN MUN-
SONS by Myron A. Munson. Repr. of 1897 ed.
Paper—$3.00—6pp-- Vendor #D1842

2270 - MURDOCHS ALONG THE SUSQUEHANNA, DESCENDANTS OF ROBERT
MURDOCH by L. C. Russell. Repr. of 1917 ed.
Paper—$4.00—9pp-- Vendor #D1842

2271 - HISTORICAL NOTICE OF JOSEPH MYGATT OF CAMBRIDGE...RECORD
OF HIS DESCENDANTS by F. T. Mygatt. Repr. of 1853 ed.
Paper—$15.00—116pp--- Vendor #D1842

2272 - NASH FAMILY FROM THOMAS NASH, 1638 by Nash and Noble.
Repr. of 1850 ed.
Paper—$4.00—16pp--- Vendor #D1842

2273 - THE NEAL RECORD...DESCENDANTS OF JOHN NEALE...EARLY
SETTLERS OF SALEM, MASSACHUSETTS by Theodore Augustus Neal.
Repr. of 1856 ed.
Paper—$6.00—30pp--- Vendor #D1842

2274   - NELL FAMILY IN THE UNITED STATES by R. B. Nell. Repr. of
1929 ed.
Paper—$20.00—104pp--------------------------------------- Vendor #D1842

2275   - A FAMILY RECORD OF DESCENDANTS OF THOMAS NELSON AND
JOAN, HIS WIFE, BY ONE OF THEM. Repr. of 1868 ed.
Paper—$5.00—32pp--- Vendor #D1842

2276   - DESCENT OF JOHN NELSON...NOTES ON THE FAMILIES OF TAILER
AND STOUGHTON, 2nd Ed., by Temple Prime. Repr. of 1894 ed.
Paper—$7.00—61pp--- Vendor #D1842

2277   - NEWBERRY FAMILY OF WINDSOR, CONNECTICUT, IN THE LINE OF
CLARINDA (NEWBERRY) GOODWIN....by Frank Farnsworth Starr.
Repr. of 1898 ed.
Paper—$13.50—70pp--------------------------------------- Vendor #D1842

2278   - THOMAS NEWELL, WHO SETTLED IN FARMINGTON, CONNECTICUT,
1632, AND HIS DESCENDANTS by Mary A. (Newell) Hall. Repr. of
1878 ed.
Paper—$40.00—268pp------------------------------------- Vendor #D1842

2279   - THE RECORD OF MY ANCESTRY by Charles L. Newhall. Repr. of
1899 ed.
Paper—$33.00—222pp------------------------------------- Vendor #D1842

2280   - DESCENDANTS OF SAMUEL NEWMAN OF REHOBOTH, MASSACHU-
SETTS by S. C. Newman. Repr. of 1860 ed.
Paper—$3.50—14pp-------------------------------------- Vendor #D1842

2281   - GENEALOGICAL NOTES CONCERNING DESCENDANTS OF THOMAS
NEWTON...AND HENRY WALLBRIDGE...by W. G. Wallbridge. Repr.
of 1896 ed.
Paper—$8.00—39pp-------------------------------------- Vendor #D1842

2282   HISTORY OF NEWTON FAMILIES OF COLONIAL AMERICA, WITH AMER-
ICAN HISTORY OF FAMILY INTEREST...., Vol. 1, by Clair Alonzo
Newton. Repr. of 1927 ed.
Paper—$14.00—96pp------------------------------------- Vendor #D1842

2283   - SERGEANT FRANCIS NICHOLLS OF STRATFORD, CONNECTICUT,
1639...HIS SON CALEB NICHOLLS by Walter Nicholls. Repr. of 1909 ed.
Paper—$15.00—101pp------------------------------------ Vendor #D1842

2284   - NICHOLS FAMILIES IN AMERICA by L. N. Nichols. Repr. of 1919 ed.
Paper—$5.00—16pp-------------------------------------- Vendor #D1842

2285   - ANCESTORS OF WILLARD ATHERTON NICHOLS...MILITARY AFFAIRS
OF THE AMERICAN COLONIES by Willard Atherton Nichols. Repr. of
1911 ed.
Paper—$14.00—77pp------------------------------------- Vendor #D1842

2286   - CHRISTOPHER NOBLE OF PORTSMOUTH, NEW HAMPSHIRE, AND
SOME OF HIS DESCENDANTS by F. S. Davis. Repr.
Paper—$9.00—45pp-------------------------------------- Vendor #D1842

2287   - JONATHAN AND TAMESIN NORRIS OF MAINE, THEIR ANCESTORS
AND DESCENDANTS by H. M. Norris. Repr. of 1906 ed.
Paper—$12.00—60pp------------------------------------- Vendor #D1842

2288   - NORRIS FAMILY OF MARYLAND by T. M. Myers. Repr. of 1916 ed.
Paper—$22.50—119pp------------------------------------ Vendor #D1842

2289   - JOHN NORTH OF FARMINGTON, CONNECTICUT, AND HIS DESCEND-
ANTS, WITH...NORTH FAMILIES by Dexter North. Repr. of 1921 ed.
Cloth—$50.00—Paper—$40.00—334pp--------------------- Vendor #D1842

2290   - DESCENDANTS OF EZEKIEL NORTHEND OF ROWLEY by W. D. Northend. Repr. Essex Inst. Hist. Coll., 1874 ed.
Paper—$4.00—16pp-------------------------------------- Vendor #D1842

2291   - THE NORTHRUP-NORTHROP GENEALOGY...ORIGINAL SETTLERS OF
MILFORD, CONNECTICUT, IN 1639 by A. Judd Northrup. Repr. of
1908 ed.
Cloth—$71.00—Paper—$61.00—473pp--------------------- Vendor #D1842

2292 - GENEALOGICAL ACCOUNT OF THE NOYES FAMILY...DIKE FAMILY,
      AND FULLER AND EDSON FAMILIES by Jacob Noyes. Repr. of 1861 ed.
      Paper—$4.00—13pp--- Vendor #D1842

2293 - NOYES GENEALOGY...DESCENDANTS OF REV. JAMES NOYES, NEW-
      BURY, 1634-1656 by Horatio N. Noyes. Repr. of 1889 ed.
      Paper—$6.00—32pp--- Vendor #D1842

2294 - NUNN FAMILY, SKETCH OF JOHN MILTON NUNN AND SALLY HEIS-
      TON NUNN...AND DESCENDANTS by C. & H. Nunn. Repr. of 1939 ed.
      Paper—$14.00—64pp-- Vendor #D1842

2295 - NUTTING GENEALOGY. A RECORD...JOHN NUTTING OF GROTON,
      MASSACHUSETTS by John Keep Nutting. Repr. of 1908 ed.
      Cloth—$41.50—Paper—$31.50—278pp------------------------ Vendor #D1842

2296 - THE O'BRIENS OF MACHIAS, MAINE...TOGETHER WITH A SKETCH
      OF THE CLAN O'BRIEN by A. M. Sherman and T. H. Murray. Repr.
      of 1904 ed.
      Paper—$15.00—87pp-- Vendor #D1842

2297 - OAKS-OAKES FAMILY REGISTER, NATHANIEL OAK OF MARLBORO,
      MASSACHUSETTS...HIS DESCENDANTS by H. L. Oak. Repr. of 1906 ed.
      Paper—$18.50—90pp-- Vendor #D1842

2298 - THE OGDENS OF SOUTH JERSEY. DESCENDANTS OF JOHN OGDEN
      ...BORN 1673; DIED, 1745 by W. O. Sheeler and E. D. Halsey.
      Repr. of 1894 ed.
      Paper—$7.00—36pp--- Vendor #D1842

2299 - THE QUAKER OGDENS IN AMERICA. DAVID OGDEN...AND HIS
      DESCENDANTS, 1682-1897 by Charles Ogden. Repr. of 1898 ed.
      Paper—$37.00—245pp--- Vendor #D1842

2300 - OGDEN FAMILY HISTORY IN THE LINE OF LIEUTENANT BENJAMIN
      OGDEN...WIFE, RACHEL WESTERVELT by Anna Vermilve. Repr. of
      1906 ed.
      Paper—$18.00—119pp-- Vendor #D1842

2301 - OGDEN-PRESTON GENEALOGY. ANCESTORS...CAPTAIN BENJAMIN
      STRATTON OGDEN AND...NANCY (PRESTON) OGDEN by Josie Powell
      Stone and William Ogden Powell. Repr. of 1914 ed.
      Paper—$6.00—31pp--- Vendor #D1842

2302 - DESCENDANTS OF THOMAS OLCOTT, ONE OF THE FIRST SETTLERS
      OF HARTFORD, CONNECTICUT, Rev. Ed., by Nathaniel Goodwin,
      with additions by Henry S. Olcott. Repr. of 1874 ed.
      Paper—$18.50—124pp-- Vendor #D1842

2303 - OLCOTT FAMILY OF HARTFORD, CONNECTICUT...EUNICE (OL-
      COTT) GOODWIN, 1639-1807 by Frank Farnsworth Starr. Repr. of
      1899 ed.
      Paper—$14.50—84pp--- Vendor #D1842

2304 - A COMPLETE RECORD OF THE JOHN OLIN FAMILY, 1678-1893 by
      C. C. Olin. Repr. of 1893 ed.
      Cloth—$48.50—Paper—$38.50—324pp------------------------ Vendor #D1842

2305 - HISTORY OF THE OLIVER, VASSALL AND ROYALL HOUSES IN
      DORCHESTER, CAMBRIDGE AND MEDFORD by Robert Tracy Jackson.
      Repr. Genealogical Magazine, 1907 ed.
      Paper—$4.00—17pp--- Vendor #D1842

2306 - ANCESTRY OF MARY OLIVER 1640-1698, WIFE OF SAMUEL APPLE-
      TON....by William Appleton. Repr. of 1867 ed.
      Paper—$5.00—29pp--- Vendor #D1842

2307 - ABRIDGED GENEALOGY OF OLMSTEAD FAMILY OF NEW ENGLAND
      by E. L. Thomas. Repr. of 1869 ed.
      Paper—$6.00—30pp--- Vendor #D1842

2308 - SOME HISTORICAL NOTICES OF THE O'MEAGHERS OF IBERRIN by
      Joseph C. O'Meagher. Repr. of 1890 ed.
      Paper—$32.00—216pp-- Vendor #D1842

2309 - GENEALOGY OF DESCENDANTS OF THOMAS OLNEY...WHO CAME
FROM ENGLAND IN 1635 by James H. Olney. Repr. of 1889 ed.
Cloth—$44.50—Paper—$34.50—298pp------------------------ Vendor #D1842

2310 - GENEALOGY OF THE ONDERDONK FAMILY IN AMERICA by Elmer
and Andrew Onderdonk. Repr. of 1910 ed.
Cloth—$56.00—Paper—$46.00—374pp------------------------ Vendor #D1842

2311 - SHORT ACCOUNT OF FAMILY OF ORMSBY OF PITTSBURGH, PENN-
SYLVANIA by O. O. Page. Repr. of 1892 ed.
Paper—$10.00—48pp--------------------------------------- Vendor #D1842

2312 - A SHORT ACCOUNT OF THE FAMILY OF ORMSBY OF PITTSBURGH
by Oliver Ormsby Page. Repr. of 1892 ed.
Paper—$10.00—48pp--------------------------------------- Vendor #D1842

2313 - AN ACCOUNT OF DESCENDANTS OF THOMAS ORTON OF WINDSOR,
CONNECTICUT, 1641 by Edward Orton. Repr. of 1896 ed.
Paper—$33.00—220pp-------------------------------------- Vendor #D1842

2314 - A HISTORY OF THE ORVIS FAMILY IN AMERICA by Francis W.
Orvis. Repr. of 1922 ed.
Paper—$30.00—203pp-------------------------------------- Vendor #D1842

2315 - ACCOUNT OF AZARAIH ORTON OF FARMINGTON, ILLINOIS AND
DESCENDANTS by E. Orton. Repr. of 1900 ed.
Paper—$5.00—23pp-- Vendor #D1842

2316 - GENEALOGY OF DESCENDANTS OF JOHN, CHRISTOPHER AND
WILLIAM OSGOOD WHO SETTLED IN NEW ENGLAND....by Ira Osgood.
Repr. of 1894 ed.
Cloth—$74.00—Paper—$64.00—491pp------------------------ Vendor #D1842

2317 - GENEALOGICAL AND HISTORICAL MEMOIR OF THE OTIS FAMILY
IN AMERICA by William A. Otis. Repr. of 1924 ed.
Cloth—$109.00—Paper—$99.00—729pp----------------------- Vendor #D1842

2318 - GENEALOGICAL MEMOIR OF THE FAMILY OF RICHARD OTIS, AND
...FAMILIES OF BAKER, VARNEY, WALDRON....by Horatio N. Otis.
Repr. of 1851 ed.
Paper—$10.00—50pp--------------------------------------- Vendor #D1842

2319 - CELEBRATION OF THE TWO HUNDRED AND FIFTIETH ANNIVERSARY
OF THE LANDING OF SAMUEL PACKARD.... issued by the Packard
Memorial Assn. Repr. of 1888 ed., n.p.
Paper—$14.00—72pp--------------------------------------- Vendor #D1842

2320 - HISTORY AND GENEALOGY OF THE PAGE FAMILY 1257-1911 (WITH
NASH AND PECK FAMILIES) by D. N. Page. Repr. of 1911 ed.
Paper—$27.50—143pp-------------------------------------- Vendor #D1842

2321 - STORY OF OUR FORBEARS, PAGE, BRADBURY, FESSENDEN AND
PERLEY FAMILIES by R. P. Reed. Repr. of 1903 ed.
Paper—$20.00—154pp-------------------------------------- Vendor #D1842

2322 - PAGE DESCENT FROM NICHOLAS PAGE OF ENGLAND by C. L.
Peirson. Repr. of 1915 ed.
Paper—$4.00—18pp-- Vendor #D1842

2323 - HISTORY AND DESCRIPTION OF THE GREAT PAGE ESTATE by C.
N. Page. Repr. of 1917 ed.
Paper—$5.00—31pp-- Vendor #D1842

2324 - GENEALOGICAL NOTES ON THE PAINE FAMILY OF WORCESTER,
MASSACHUSETTS by Nathaniel Paine. Repr. of 1878 ed.
Paper—$5.50—27pp-- Vendor #D1842

2325 - THE DISCOVERY OF A GRANDMOTHER...EIGHT GENERATIONS OF
AN IPSWICH-PAINE FAMILY by H. H. Carter. Repr. of 1920 ed.
Cloth—$51.00—Paper—41.00—343pp------------------------- Vendor #D1842

2326 - PAINE FAMILY RECORDS. A JOURNAL...AMERICAN FAMILIES OF
PAYNE, PAINE, PAYN, ETC., 2 Vols. in 1, edited by H. D. Paine.
Repr. of 1880-1883 ed.
Cloth—$78.00—Paper—$68.00—522pp------------------------ Vendor #D1842

2327 - PALGRAVE FAMILY MEMORIALS by Charles and Stephen Parker.
Repr. of 1878 ed.
Paper—$31.00—208pp-------------------------------------- Vendor #D1842

2328 - PAINE ANCESTRY. THE FAMILY OF ROBERT TREAT PAINE, THE
SIGNER OF THE DECLARATION OF INDEPENDENCE....by Sarah Cush-
ing Paine, edited by Charles Henry Pope. Repr. of 1912 ed.
Cloth—$50.50—Paper—$40.50—336pp----------------------- Vendor #D1842

2329 - GENEALOGICAL RECORD OF DESCENDANTS OF JOHN AND MARY
PALMER OF CONCORD...SONS-IN-LAW, WILLIAM AND JAMES TRIMBLE
by Lewis Palmer. Repr. of 1875 ed.
Cloth—$71.00—Paper—$61.00—474pp----------------------- Vendor #D1842

2330 - BIOGRAPHICAL SKETCH OF THE PARK FAMILY OF WASHINGTON
COUNTY, PENNSYLVANIA by W. J. Park. Repr. of 1880 ed.
Paper—$24.00—121pp----------------------------------- Vendor #D1842

2331 - GENEALOGY OF THE PARKE FAMILIES OF CONNECTICUT...PARKE,
PARK, PARKS, ETC. WHO FOUGHT IN THE REVOLUTION by Frank S.
Parks. Repr. of 1906 ed.
Cloth—$50.00—Paper—$40.00—333pp----------------------- Vendor #D1842

2332 - PARKER IN AMERICA, 1630-1910, GENEALOGICAL, BIOGRAPHICAL,
AND HISTORICAL by Augustus Parker. Repr. of 1911 ed.
Cloth—$91.00—Paper—$81.00—608pp----------------------- Vendor #D1842

2333 - FAMILY RECORDS. PARKER-POND-PECK, 1636-1892 by Edwin Pond
Parker. Repr. of 1892 ed.
Paper—$10.00—51pp------------------------------------- Vendor #D1842

2334 - GLEANINGS FROM PARKER RECORDS, 1271 TO 1893 by William
Thornton Parker. Repr. of 1894 ed.
Paper—$10.00—51pp------------------------------------- Vendor #D1842

2335 - GLANCES AT THE ANCESTORS OF JOHN PARKER (BORN 1807,
DIED 1891) by Harry Parker Ward. Repr. of 1895 ed.
Paper—$4.00—16pp-------------------------------------- Vendor #D1842

2336 - JOHN PARKHURST, HIS ANCESTORS AND DESCENDANTS by G. H.
Parkhurst. Repr. of 1897 ed.
Paper—$10.00—51pp------------------------------------- Vendor #D1842

2337 - THE PARLIN GENEALOGY. DESCENDANTS OF NICHOLAS OF CAM-
BRIDGE, MASSACHUSETTS by Frank E. Parlin. Repr. of 1913 ed.
Cloth—$43.00—Paper—$33.00—289pp----------------------- Vendor #D1842

2338 - THE PARRISH FAMILY (PHILADELPHIA)...FAMILIES OF COX, DIL-
LINGER, ROBERTS, CHANDLER, MITCHELL, PAINTER AND PUSEY
by Susanna Wharton and Dillinger Parrish. Repr. of 1925 ed.
Cloth—$50.00—Paper—$40.00—336pp----------------------- Vendor #D1842

2339 - JAMES PARSHALL AND HIS DESCENDANTS by James C. Parshall.
Repr. of 1900 ed.
Paper—$8.00—42pp-------------------------------------- Vendor #D1842

2340 - GENEALOGICAL RECORD OF THE FAMILY OF PARSONS AND LEON-
ARD OF WEST SPRINGFIELD, MASSACHUSETTS by S. L. Parsons.
Repr. of 1867 ed.
Paper—$7.00—36pp-------------------------------------- Vendor #D1842

2341 - GENEALOGY OF THE PARTHEMORE FAMILY, 1744-1885 by E. W. S.
Parthemore. Repr. of 1885 ed.
Paper—$37.50—250pp------------------------------------ Vendor #D1842

2342 - DESCENDANTS OF JOHN PARTRIDGE OF MEDFIELD, MASSACHU-
SETTS by G. H. Partridge. Repr. of 1904 ed.
Paper—$10.00—46pp------------------------------------- Vendor #D1842

2343 - WILLIAM PARTRIDGE OF MEDFIELD AND HIS DESCENDANTS by
G. H. Partridge. Repr. of 1909 ed.
Paper—$3.50—10pp-------------------------------------- Vendor #D1842

2344 - DESCENDANTS OF GEORGE PARTRIDGE OF DUXBURY, MASSACHU-
SETTS by G. H. Partridge. Repr. of 1915 ed.
Paper—$10.00—46pp--- Vendor #D1842

2345 - PATTEN GENEALOGY. WILLIAM PATTEN OF CAMBRIDGE, 1635,
AND HIS DESCENDANTS by Thomas W. Baldwin. Repr. of 1908 ed.
Cloth—$45.00—Paper—$35.00—300pp----------------------- Vendor #D1842

2346 - PEABODY (PAYBODY, PABODY, PABODIE) GENEALOGY by Selim
H. Peabody. Repr. of 1909 ed.
Cloth—$92.00—Paper—$82.00—614pp----------------------- Vendor #D1842

2347 - GENEALOGY OF THE PEABODY FAMILY, WITH A PARTIAL RECORD
OF THE RHODE ISLAND BRANCH by C. M. Endicott. Repr. of 1867 ed.
Paper—$11.00—65pp--- Vendor #D1842

2348 - GENEALOGY OF DESCENDANTS OF MOSES AND HANNAH (FOSTER)
PEABODY by Mary Ellen Perley. Repr. of 1904 ed.
Paper—$10.00—47pp--- Vendor #D1842

2349 - PEARCE GENEALOGY...RICHARD PEARCE, AN EARLY INHABITANT
OF PORTSMOUTH, RHODE ISLAND by Frederick C. Pierce. Repr. of
1888 ed.
Paper—$22.50—150pp--- Vendor #D1842

2350 - PEASE FAMILY OF ENGLAND AND NEW ENGLAND by F. S. Pease.
Repr. of 1849 ed.
Paper—$7.00—34pp-- Vendor #D1842

2351 - THE PEASLEES AND OTHERS OF HAVERHILL, (MASSACHUSETTS)
AND VICINITY by E. A. Kimball. Repr. of 1899 ed.
Paper—$12.00—72pp--- Vendor #D1842

2352 - GENEALOGICAL HISTORY OF DESCENDANTS OF JOSEPH PECK, WHO
EMIGRATED IN 1638....by Ira Peck. Repr. of 1868.
Cloth—$66.00—Paper—$57.00—443pp----------------------- Vendor #D1842

2353 - PEIRCE GENEALOGY. THE RECORD OF JOHN PERS OF WATER-
TOWN (MASSACHUSETTS)...FAMILIES OF PEIRCE, PIERCE, PEARSE,
ETC. by Frederick C. Peirce. Repr. of 1880 ed.
Cloth—$42.00—Paper—$32.00—283pp----------------------- Vendor #D1842

2354 - PEIRCE FAMILY RECORD 1687-1893. NEW EDITION REVISED...
HARDY, GRAFTON, GARDENER, DAWES, LATHROP, CORDIS, RUS-
SELL, HASWELL, GRAY, CHIPMAN, BLANCHARD, HOLLAND, MAY,
WEST, WYMAN, COBIN, ETC. by E. W. West. Repr. of 1894 ed.
Paper—$15.00—101pp--- Vendor #D1842

2355 - PEIRCE FAMILY OF THE OLD COLONY...DESCENDANTS OF ABRA-
HAM PEIRCE...1623 by Ebenezer W. Peirce. Repr. of 1870 ed.
Cloth—$76.50—Paper—$66.50—510pp----------------------- Vendor #D1842

2356 - THOMAS PEMBER OF NEW LONDON, CONNECTICUT AND DESCEND-
ANTS. Repr. of 1916 ed., n.a.
Paper—$4.00—13pp-- Vendor #D1842

2357 - THE RECORDS OF THE PEMBERTON FAMILY by Olive Smith (Cady)
Babcock. Repr. of 1890 ed., n.p.
Paper—$5.00—26pp-- Vendor #D1842

2358 - HISTORY OF JUDGE JOHN PENCE AND DESCENDANTS by K. A.
Pence. Repr. of 1912 ed.
Paper—$25.00—126pp--- Vendor #D1842

2359 - PENN FAMILY OF VIRGINIA by W. N. Clemens. Repr. of 1915 ed.
Paper—$4.00—16pp-- Vendor #D1842

2360 - MEMOIR OF THE PENHALLOW FAMILY; WITH COPIES OF LETTERS
AND PAPERS....by Pearce W. Penhallow. Repr. N. E. Hist. & Gen.
Register, 1878 ed.
Paper—$4.50—22pp-- Vendor #D1842

2361 - GENEALOGICAL RECORD OF THE DESCENDANTS OF THOMAS PENNEY OF NEW GLOUCESTER, MAINE by J. W. Penney. Repr. of 1897 ed.
Paper—$25.00—167pp-- Vendor #D1842

2362 - THE PENNYPACKER REUNION, OCTOBER 4, 1877 by Samuel Whitaker Pennypacker. Repr. of 1878 ed.
Paper—$10.50—55pp-- Vendor #D1842

2363 - PERKINS FAMILIES IN THE UNITED STATES IN 1790 by D. W. Perkins. Repr. of 1911 ed.
Paper—$10.00—48pp-- Vendor #D1842

2364 - PERKINS FAMILY IN YE OLDEN TIMES...LETTERS BY MANSFIELD PARKYNS, ESQUIRE edited by D. W. Perkins. Repr. of 1916 ed.
Paper—$14.50—88pp-- Vendor #D1842

2365 - THE FAMILY OF JOHN PERKINS OF IPSWICH, MASSACHUSETTS by George A. Perkins. Repr. of 1880 ed.
Cloth—$75.00—Paper—$65.00—499pp------------------------ Vendor #D1842

2366 - GENEALOGY OF THE PERRIN FAMILY by Glover Perrin. Repr. of 1885 ed.
Paper—$34.00—224pp--- Vendor #D1842

2367 - DAVID PERRIN, "THE HUGUENOT,"...SURNAMES PERRINE, PERINE, AND PRINE, 1665-1910 by Howland D. Perrine. Repr. of 1910 ed.
Cloth—$83.00—Paper—$73.00—553pp------------------------ Vendor #D1842

2368 - GENEALOGY OF THE PERRIN FAMILY by Laphem and Bowen. Repr. of 1942 ed.
Paper—$5.00—20pp--- Vendor #D1842

2369 - THE PERSHING FAMILY IN AMERICA. A COLLECTION OF HISTORI-CAL AND GENEALOGICAL DATA by Edgar Pershing. Repr. of 1924 ed.
Cloth—$65.00—Paper—$55.00—434pp------------------------ Vendor #D1842

2370 - A PETERS LINEAGE...DESCENDANTS OF DR. CHARLES PETERS OF HEMPSTEAD by Martha Flint. Repr. of 1896 ed.
Paper—$26.00—175pp--- Vendor #D1842

2371 - PETERS OF NEW ENGLAND. A GENEALOGICAL AND FAMILY HISTORY by Edward and Eleanor Peters. Repr. of 1903 ed.
Cloth—$70.00—Paper—$60.00—470pp------------------------ Vendor #D1842

2372 - A PETTINGELL GENEALOGY by John M. and Charles Pope. Repr. of 1906 ed.
Cloth—$89.00—Paper—$79.00—596pp------------------------ Vendor #D1842

2373 - GENEALOGY OF THE PHILBRICK AND PHILBROOK FAMILIES... THOMAS PHILBRICK, 1583-1667 by Jacob Chapman. Repr. of 1886 ed.
Paper—$30.00—202pp-- Vendor #D1842

2374 - PHILLIPS FAMILY OF ENGLAND AND NEW ENGLAND, 1593-1877 by E. E. Salisbury. Repr. of 1885 ed.
Paper—$8.50—43pp-- Vendor #D1842

2375 - PHILLIPS GENEALOGY INCLUDING FAMILY OF GEORGE PHILLIPS, FIRST MINISTER OF WATERTOWN, MASSACHUSETTS....by Albert M. Phillips. Repr. of 1885 ed.
Paper—$37.50—245pp-- Vendor #D1842

2376 - FAMILY OF JOHN PHILLIPS, SR. OF DUXBURY AND MARSHFIELD by A. Ames. Repr. of 1903 ed.
Paper—$8.50—43pp-- Vendor #D1842

2377 - DESCENDANTS OF JOHN PHOENIX, AN EARLY SETTLER IN KITTERY, MAINE by S. Whitney Phoenix. Repr. of 1867 ed.
Paper—$10.00—59pp-- Vendor #D1842

2378 - ANCESTORS AND DESCENDANTS OF SHERWOOD AND PICKEL FAMI-LIES, UNITED EMPIRE LOYALISTS....by W. U. Pickel. Repr. of 1948 ed.
Paper—$12.50—62pp-- Vendor #D1842

2379 - GENEALOGICAL DATA RESPECTING JOHN PICKERING OF PORTS-
MOUTH, NEW HAMPSHIRE...DESCENDANTS by R. H. E., i.e., Robert
Henry Eddy. Repr. of 1884 ed.
Paper—$6.50—36pp--- Vendor #D1842

2380 - PIERREPONT GENEALOGIES. ESPECIALLY THE LINE FROM HEZE-
KIAH PIERPONT...OF NEW HAVEN by Hattie M. Pierpont. Repr. of
1913 ed.
Paper—$32.00—211pp-- Vendor #D1842

2381 - PIERSON GENEALOGICAL RECORD by L. B. Pierson. Repr. of
1878 ed.
Paper—$20.00—106pp-- Vendor #D1842

2382 - DESCENDANTS OF STEPHEN PIERSON OF SUFFOLK COUNTY, ENG-
LAND AND NEW HAVEN AND DERBY, CONNECTICUT by F. L. Pier-
son. Repr. of 1895 ed.
Paper—$7.00—33pp--- Vendor #D1842

2383 - DESCENDANTS OF JOHN PITMAN, FIRST OF THE NAME IN RHODE
ISLAND by C. M. Thurston. Repr. of 1868 ed.
Paper—$10.00—48pp-- Vendor #D1842

2384 - RICHARD PINKHAM OF OLD DOVER, NEW HAMPSHIRE, AND HIS
DESCENDANTS by Charles Nelson Sinnett. Repr. of 1908 ed.
Cloth—$45.00—Paper—$35.00—308pp------------------------- Vendor #D1842

2385 - GENEALOGY OF THE FAMILY OF SOLOMON PIPER OF DUBLIN, NEW
HAMPSHIRE by Solomon Piper. Repr. of 1849 ed.
Paper—$4.50—20pp--- Vendor #D1842

2386 - MEMORIAL OF THE LIVES AND SERVICES OF JAMES PITTS AND
HIS SONS....by Daniel Goodwin, Jr. Repr. of 1882 ed.
Paper—$13.00—69pp-- Vendor #D1842

2387 - LT. ROGER PLAISTED OF KITTERY, MAINE AND SOME OF HIS
DESCENDANTS by M. F. King. Repr. of 1904 ed.
Paper—$13.00—66pp-- Vendor #D1842

2388 - THE PLUMBS, 1635-1800, 2nd Ed., by H. B. Plumb. Repr. of 1893
ed.
Paper—$15.00—102pp--------------------------------------- Vendor #D1842

2389 - THE PLUMMER SYSTEM...LINEAGE OF MR. FRANCIS PLUMER, NEW-
BURY, MASSACHUSETTS, 1635 by Alvin Plummer. Repr. of 1904 ed.
Paper—$12.50—64pp-- Vendor #D1842

2390 - POLLOCK. A RECORD OF DESCENDANTS OF JOHN, JAMES, CHARLES
AND SAMUEL POLLOCK....by Horace Edwin Hayden. Repr. of 1884 ed.
Paper—$5.00—16pp--- Vendor #D1842

2391 - FAMILY OF SELAH POMROY OF QUEBEC AND NORTHAMPTON,
MASSACHUSETTS by J. Lawrence. Repr. of 1881 ed.
Paper—$4.00—12pp--- Vendor #D1842

2392 - PONDS OF MILFORD AND BRANFORD, CONNECTICUT by N. G.
Pond. Repr., n.d.
Paper—$5.00—16pp--- Vendor #D1842

2393 - GENEALOGICAL RECORDS OF SAMUEL POND AND HIS DESCEND-
ANTS by D. S. Pond. Repr. of 1875 ed.
Paper—$25.00—126pp--------------------------------------- Vendor #D1842

2394 - A GENEALOGICAL RECORD OF DANIEL POND AND HIS DESCEND-
ANTS by Edward Doubleday Harris. Repr. of 1873 ed.
Paper—$31.50—210pp--------------------------------------- Vendor #D1842

2395 - HISTORY OF EDWARD POOLE OF WEYMOUTH, MASSACHUSETTS
(1635) AND HIS DESCENDANTS by Murray Edward Poole. Repr. of
1893 ed.
Paper—$24.50—164pp--------------------------------------- Vendor #D1842

2396 - A MEMOIR AND GENEALOGY OF JOHN POORE. TEN GENERATIONS,
1615-1880 by Alfred Poore. Repr. of 1881 ed.
Cloth—$50.00—Paper—$40.00—333pp------------------------- Vendor #D1842

2397 - HISTORY OF THE DORCHESTER POPE FAMILY, 1634-1888. WITH
...POPE IN ENGLAND AND AMERICA by Charles Henry Pope. Repr.
of 1888 ed.
Cloth—$51.00—Paper—$41.00—340pp------------------------ Vendor #D1842

2398 - GENEALOGY OF THOMAS POPE (1608-1683) AND SOME OF HIS DE-
SCENDANTS by Franklin Leonard Pope. Repr. N. E. Hist. & Gen.
Register, 1888 ed.
Paper—$4.50—22pp-- Vendor #D1842

2399 - GENEALOGY OF DESCENDANTS OF RICHARD PORTER, WHO SETTLED
AT WEYMOUTH, MASSACHUSETTS, 1635....by Joseph W. Porter.
Repr. of 1878 ed.
Cloth—$51.50—Paper—$41.50—344pp----------------------- Vendor #D1842

2400 - PORTER FAMILY. PROCEEDINGS AT THE REUNION OF DESCEND-
ANTS OF JOHN PORTER...JULY 17TH, 1895. Repr. of 1897 ed.
Paper—$14.00—72pp--------------------------------------- Vendor #D1842

2401 - A PORTER PEDIGREE...SAMUEL AND MARTHA (PERLEY) PORTER
OF CHESTER, NEW HAMPSHIRE by Miss Juliet Porter. Repr. of 1907 ed.
Paper—$24.00—161pp------------------------------------- Vendor #D1842

2402 - POWERS FAMILY...WALTER POWERS AND SOME OF HIS DESCEND-
ANTS TO THE NINTH GENERATION by A. H. Powers. Repr. of 1884 ed.
Paper—$35.00—199pp------------------------------------- Vendor #D1842

2403 - THE PRATT FAMILY; OR, DESCENDANTS OF LIEUTENANT WILLIAM
PRATT,...OF HARTFORD AND SAY-BROOK....by F. W. Chapman.
Repr. of 1864 ed.
Cloth—$63.00—Paper—$53.00—421pp----------------------- Vendor #D1842

2404 - SKETCH OF THE LIFE OF SAMUEL F. PRATT, WITH...EARLY HISTO-
RY OF THE PRATT FAMILY....by William P. Letchworth. Repr. of
1874 ed.
Paper—$31.50—211pp------------------------------------- Vendor #D1842

2405 - THE PRATT FAMILY. GENEALOGICAL RECORD OF MATHEW PRATT
OF WEYMOUTH, MASSACHUSETTS...1623-1889 by Francis G. Pratt, Jr.
Repr. of 1890 ed.
Paper—$34.00—226pp------------------------------------- Vendor #D1842

2406 - 1538-1900. THE ANCESTRY AND DESCENDANTS OF JOHN PRATT
OF HARTFORD, CONNECTICUT by Charles B. Whittelsey. Repr. of
1900 ed.
Paper—$30.50—204pp------------------------------------- Vendor #D1842

2407 - PHINEHAS PRATT AND SOME OF HIS DESCENDANTS. A MONO-
GRAPH by Eleazer Franklin Pratt. Repr. of 1897 ed.
Paper—$24.50—164pp------------------------------------- Vendor #D1842

2408 - GENEALOGICAL SKETCH OF THE PREBLE FAMILIES RESIDENT IN
PORTLAND, MAINE, 1850 by William P. Preble. Repr. of 1850 ed.
Paper—$5.50—28pp--------------------------------------- Vendor #D1842

2409 - JOHN PREBLE OF MACHIAS (1771-1841) AND HIS DESCENDANTS by
William Preble Jones. Repr. of 1929 ed.
Paper—$6.00—32pp--------------------------------------- Vendor #D1842

2410 - HISTORY AND GENEALOGY OF THE PRENTICE OR PRENTISS FAMILY
IN NEW ENGLAND...., 2nd Ed., by C. J. F. Binney. Repr. of 1883 ed.
Cloth—$68.00—Paper—$58.00—453pp----------------------- Vendor #D1842

2411 - THE PRESCOTT MEMORIAL. A GENEALOGICAL MEMOIR OF THE
PRESCOTT FAMILIES IN AMERICA by William Prescott. Repr. of 1870 ed.
Cloth—$100.00—Paper—$90.00—667pp---------------------- Vendor #D1842

2412 - MEMORANDA OF THE PRESTON FAMILY by Orlando Brown. Repr.
of 1864 ed.
Paper—$5.00—26pp--------------------------------------- Vendor #D1842

2413 - PRESTON GENEALOGY; TRACING THE HISTORY OF THE FAMILY
FROM ABOUT 1040 edited by L. A. Wilson, under the direction of
William Bowker Preston. Repr. of 1900 ed.
Cloth—$56.00—Paper—$46.00—374pp----------------------- Vendor #D1842

2414 - DESCENDANTS OF WILLIAM PRICHARD by A. M. Prichard. Repr.
of 1912 ed.
Paper—$12.00—61pp-- Vendor #D1842

2415 - SOME ACCOUNT OF THE FAMILY OF PRIME OF ROWLEY, MASSA-
CHUSETTS, WITH...PLATTS, JEWETT, AND HAMMOND by Temple
Prime. Repr. of 1887 ed.
Paper—$8.00—40pp-- Vendor #D1842

2416 - ELDER JOHN PRINCE OF HULL, MASSACHUSETTS. A MEMORIAL
BIOGRAPHICAL AND GENEALOGICAL by George Prince. Repr. of
1888 ed., n.t.-p.
Paper—$6.50—32pp-- Vendor #D1842

2417 - THE PROCTOR GATHERING IN COMMEMORATION...MR. JOSEPH
PROCTER AND MISS ELIZABETH EPES.... Repr. of 1868 ed.
Paper—$10.00—46pp-- Vendor #D1842

2418 - ANCESTORS AND DESCENDANTS OF JONATHAN PULSIFER OF
POLAND AND SUMNER, MAINE by W. E. Pulsifer. Repr. of 1928 ed.
Paper—$14.00—71pp-- Vendor #D1842

2419 - DESCENDANTS OF SAMUEL SHERRILL OF EASTHAMPTON, NEW
YORK by C. H. Sherrill. Repr. of 1894 ed., charts.
Paper—$27.50—132pp-- Vendor #D1842

2420 - PYLDREN-DUMMER FAMILIES, 1100-1884 by E. E. Salisbury.
Repr. of 1885 ed.
Paper—$14.00—70pp-- Vendor #D1842

2421 - THE HONORABLE SAMUEL PUTNAM AND SARAH (GOOLL) PUTNAM,
WITH...DESCENDANTS by Elizabeth Cabot Putnam and Harriet Sil-
vester Tapley. Repr. Danvers Hist. Coll., 1922 ed.
Paper—$8.00—42pp-- Vendor #D1842

2422 - RECORD OF THE PYNCHON FAMILY IN ENGLAND AND AMERICA
by Pynchon and Adams. Repr. of 1898 ed.
Paper—$5.00—24pp-- Vendor #D1842

2423 - RECORD OF LINE OF DESCENDANTS FROM ROBERT QUINBY TO
BENJAMIN QUINBY (QUIMBY)....by S. E. Quimby. Repr. of 1910 ed.
Paper—$6.00—29pp-- Vendor #D1842

2424 - QUINCY FAMILY IN ENGLAND AND AMERICA, 1559-1877 by E. E.
Salisbury. Repr. of 1885 ed.
Paper—$16.00—81pp-- Vendor #D1842

2425 - GENEALOGY OF THE RAGLAND FAMILY AND ...WHOM THEY HAVE
INTERMARRIED by Margaret Strong. Repr. of 1928 ed.
Paper—$19.00—129pp-- Vendor #D1842

2426 - THE RAINBOROWE FAMILY. Gleanings by Henry Waters, with annotations by Isaac J. Greenwood. Repr. N. E. Hist. & Gen. Register,
1886 ed.
Paper—$4.00—16pp-- Vendor #D1842

2427 - BIOGRAPHICAL HISTORY OF ROBERT RANDALL AND HIS DE-
SCENDANTS, 1608-1909 by William L. Chaffin. Repr. of 1909 ed.
Cloth—$40.00—Paper—$30.00—267pp---------------------- Vendor #D1842

2428 - A GENEALOGY OF THE RAND FAMILY IN THE UNITED STATES by
Florence Rand. Repr. of 1898 ed.
Cloth—$40.00—Paper—$30.00—269pp---------------------- Vendor #D1842

2429 - GENEALOGY OF A BRANCH OF THE RANDALL FAMILY, 1666 TO
1879 by Paul K. Randall. Repr.
Cloth—$43.00—Paper—$33.00—389pp---------------------- Vendor #D1842

2430 - NOTES RELATING TO RAWLINS, OR ROLLINS, WITH NOTICES OF
EARLY SETTLERS....by John R. Rollins. Repr. of 1870 ed.
Paper—$14.00—84pp-- Vendor #D1842

2431   - THE RAWSON FAMILY. A REVISED MEMOIR OF EDWARD RAWSON,
SECRETARY OF THE COLONY OF MASSACHUSETTS BAY....by E. B.
Crane. Repr. of 1875 ed.
Cloth—$52.00—Paper—$42.00—350pp----------------------- Vendor #D1842

2432   - ANCESTORS OF EDWARD RAWSON by E. B. Crane. Repr. of 1887 ed.
Paper—$10.00—54pp------------------------------------- Vendor #D1842

2433   - MEMOIR OF EDWARD RAWSON, WITH GENEALOGICAL NOTICES OF
HIS DESCENDANTS by S. S. Rawson. Repr. of 1849 ed.
Paper—$30.00—148pp------------------------------------ Vendor #D1842

2434   - GENEALOGY OF RAYMOND FAMILY OF NEW ENGLAND 1630 TO 1886,
...RAYMONDS OF EARLY TIMES by Samuel Raymond. Repr. of 1886 ed.
Cloth—$46.00—Paper—$36.00—304pp----------------------- Vendor #D1842

2435   - READ GENEALOGY OF THE BROTHERS AND SISTERS AND FAMILY
OF ISRAEL...AND NATHANIEL READ by Henry M. Dodd. Repr. of
1912 ed.
Cloth—$45.00—Paper—$35.00—301pp----------------------- Vendor #D1842

2436   - DANIEL REA OF DANVERS AND SOME OF HIS DESCENDANTS by F.
M. Ray. Repr. of 1881 ed.
Paper—$3.00—9pp--------------------------------------- Vendor #D1842

2437   - GENEALOGICAL AND BIOGRAPHICAL MEMOIRS OF THE READING,
HOWELL, YERKES, WATTS, LATHAM, AND ELKINS FAMILIES by
Josiah Leach. Repr. of 1898 ed.
Cloth—$44.00—Paper—$34.00—296pp----------------------- Vendor #D1842

2438   - GENEALOGICAL HISTORY OF THE REDFIELD FAMILY IN THE UNITED
STATES...REVISION AND EXTENSION OF...1839, BY WILLIAM C.
REDFIELD by John H. Redfield. Repr. of 1860 ed.
Cloth—$52.00—Paper—$42.00—345pp----------------------- Vendor #D1842

2439   - JOHN REDINGTON OF TOPSFIELD, MASSACHUSETTS...WITH NOTES
ON THE WALES FAMILY by Cornelia M. Redington Carter, edited by
Josiah Granville Leach. Repr. of 1909 ed.
Paper—$15.00—94pp------------------------------------- Vendor #D1842

2440   - REED-READ LINEAGE. CAPTAIN JOHN REED OF PROVIDENCE,
RHODE ISLAND....1660-1909 by Ella Reed-Wright. Repr. of 1909 ed.
Cloth—$117.00—Paper—$107.00—796pp-------------------- Vendor #D1842

2441   - HISTORY OF THE REED FAMILY IN EUROPE AND AMERICA by
Jacob W. Reed. Repr. of 1861 ed.
Cloth—$89.00—Paper—$79.00—596pp----------------------- Vendor #D1842

2442   - THE REED GENEALOGY, DESCENDANTS OF WILLIAM READE OF
WEYMOUTH, MASSACHUSETTS FROM 1635-1902 by John L. Reed.
Repr. of 1901 ed.
Cloth—$115.00—Paper—$105.00—786pp--------------------- Vendor #D1842

2443   - RENWICK GENEALOGY by H. H. McIver. Repr. of 1924 ed.
Paper—$5.00—23pp-------------------------------------- Vendor #D1842

2444   - GENEALOGICAL HISTORY AND PATERNAL LINE OF DESCENDANTS
FROM ARTHUR REXFORD OF ENGLAND AND CONNECTICUT by J. D.
Rexford. Repr. of 1891 ed.
Paper—$16.00—77pp------------------------------------- Vendor #D1842

2445   - HISTORY AND DESCENDANTS OF JOHN AND SARAH REYNOLDS
(1630?-1923) OF WATERTOWN, MASSACHUSETTS....by Marion H.
Reynolds. Repr. of 1924 ed.
Cloth—$76.50—Paper—$66.50—509pp----------------------- Vendor #D1842

2446   - ANCESTORS AND DESCENDANTS OF WILLIAM AND ELIZABETH
REYNOLDS OF NORTH KINGSTOWN, RHODE ISLAND by Thomas A.
Reynolds. Repr. of 1903 ed.
Paper—$8.00—42pp-------------------------------------- Vendor #D1842

2447   - ANCESTRAL LINEAGES OF NELSON OSGOOD RHOADES AND
FRANCIS (BROWN) RHOADES by N. O. Rhoades. Repr. of 1920 ed.
Paper—$4.00—21pp-------------------------------------- Vendor #D1842

2448 - GENEALOGICAL HISTORY OF THE RICE FAMILY AND DESCENDANTS OF DEACON EDWARD RICE...1638 by Andrew H. Rice. Repr. of 1858 ed. Cloth—$58.00—Paper—$48.00—387pp----------------------- Vendor #D1842

2449 - BY THE NAME OF RICE. AN HISTORICAL SKETCH OF DEACON EDMUND RICE...HIS DESCENDANTS by Charles Elmer Rice. Repr. of 1911 ed. Paper—$15.00—99pp--------------------------------------- Vendor #D1842

2450 - GENEALOGY AND BIOGRAPHICAL STUDY OF THE NAME AND FAMILY OF RICHARDSON FROM 1720 TO 1860 by J. Richardson. Repr. of 1860 ed. Paper—$6.00—30pp--------------------------------------- Vendor #D1842

2451 - THE RICHARDSON MEMORIAL...POSTERITY OF THE THREE BROTH- ERS, EZEKIEL, SAMUEL AND THOMAS RICHARDSON by John A. Ainton. Repr. of 1876 ed. Cloth—$14 ;.00—Paper—$134.00—959pp---------------------- Vendor #D1842

2452 - RICHARDSON-DePRIEST FAMILY by Robert Douglas Roller. Repr. of 1905 ed. Paper—$10.00—50pp--------------------------------------- Vendor #D1842

2453 - DESCENDANTS OF DANIEL RICKERT AND BARBARA (ROSENBERGER) RICKERT OF PENNSYLVANIA by A. Fretz. Repr. of 1906 ed. Paper—$4.00—13pp--------------------------------------- Vendor #D1842

2454 - WILLIAM RICKETSON, WILLIAM RICKETSON, JR. AND THEIR DE- SCENDANTS by Grace Williamson Edes. Repr. of 1917 ed. Paper—$19.00—127pp-------------------------------------- Vendor #D1842

2455 - THE RICHMOND FAMILY, 1594-1896, AND PRE-AMERICAN ANCES- TORS, 1040-1594 by Joshua B. Richmond. Repr. of 1897 ed. Cloth—$95.00—Paper—$85.00—633pp----------------------- Vendor #D1842

2456 - HISTORY AND GENEALOGY OF THE RICK FAMILY OF AMERICA by Guy S. Rix. Repr. of 1908 ed. Paper—$27.50—184pp-------------------------------------- Vendor #D1842

2457 - HISTORY OF THE ANCIENT RYEDALES...FROM 860-1914, COMPRIS- ING FAMILIES OF RIDDELL, RIDDLE, RIDLON, RIDLEY, ETC. by G. T. Ridlon. Repr. of 1884 ed. Cloth—$119.00—Paper—$109.00—796pp---------------------- Vendor #D1842

2458 - DESCENDANTS OF RIDGWAY-RIDGEWAY FAMILIES IN ENGLAND AND AMERICA by G. Ridgway. Repr. of 1926 ed. Paper—$27.50—130pp-------------------------------------- Vendor #D1842

2459 - GENEALOGY OF RIGGS FAMILY, DESCENDANTS OF EDWARD RIGGS OF ENGLAND AND ROXBURY, MASSACHUSETTS (B. 1590) by J. H. Wallace. Repr. of 1901 ed. Paper—$30.00—147pp-------------------------------------- Vendor #D1842

2460 - GENEALOGY OF A PART OF THE RIPLEY FAMILY by H. W. Ripley. Repr. of 1867 ed. Paper—$8.00—48pp--------------------------------------- Vendor #D1842

2461 - HISTORY AND GENEALOGY OF THE RIX FAMILY OF AMERICA by Guy S. Rix. Repr. of 1906 ed. Paper—$38.00—253pp-------------------------------------- Vendor #D1842

2462 - MEMOIR OF THE REV. WILLIAM ROBINSON OF SOUTHINGTON, CON- NECTICUT...COUNTRY by Edward Robinson. Repr. of 1859 ed. Paper—$34.00—226pp-------------------------------------- Vendor #D1842

2463 - GENEALOGY OF THE ROBERDEAU FAMILY, INCLUDING A BIOGRA- PHY OF GENERAL DANIEL ROBERDEAU....by Roberdaux Buchanan. Repr. of 1876 ed. Paper—$29.00—196pp-------------------------------------- Vendor #D1842

2464 - THE ROBERTS FAMILY OF SIMSBURY, CONNECTICUT...CAPTAIN SAMUEL ROBERTS, 1742-1789 by Frank Starr. Repr. of 1896 ed. Paper—$9.00—54pp--------------------------------------- Vendor #D1842

2465 - RECOLLECTIONS OF OLDER TIMES; ROWLAND ROBINSON OF NAR-
RAGANSETT...ROBINSON AND HAZARD FAMILIES OF RHODE ISLAND
....by Thomas Hazard. Repr. of 1879 ed.
Cloth—$40.00—Paper—$30.00—264pp---------------------- Vendor #D1842

2466 - ROBINSON GENEALOGY. DESCENDANTS OF THE REV. JOHN ROB-
INSON, PASTOR OF THE PILGRIMS, Vol. 1 by Charles Edson Robin-
son. Repr. of 1928 ed.
Cloth—$61.50—Paper—$51.50—410pp---------------------- Vendor #D1842

2467 - THE ROCKWELL FAMILY IN ONE LINE OF DESCENT by Francis
Williams Rockwell. Repr. of 1924 ed.
Paper—$36.00—241pp------------------------------------ Vendor #D1842

2468 - GENEALOGY OF THE RODMAN FAMILY, 1620 TO 1886 by Charles
Henry Jones. Repr. of 1886 ed.
Cloth—$43.50—Paper—$33.50—291pp---------------------- Vendor #D1842

2469 - HISTORICAL RECORDS OF AN OLD FAMILY, ROE FAMILY by F. A.
Roe. Repr. of 1890 ed.
Paper—$4.00—16pp------------------------------------- Vendor #D1842

2470 - GENEALOGICAL MEMOIR OF THE FAMILY OF REV. NATHANIEL
ROGERS OF IPSWICH....by Augustus D. Rogers. Repr. N. E. Hist.
& Gen. Register, 1851 ed., n.t.-p.
Paper—$10.00—48pp------------------------------------ Vendor #D1842

2471 - JAMES ROGERS OF NEW LONDON, CONNECTICUT, AND HIS DE-
SCENDANTS by James Swift Rogers. Repr. of 1902 ed.
Cloth—$77.00—Paper—514pp------------------------------ Vendor #D1842

2472 - ROOT GENEALOGICAL RECORDS, 1600-1870, COMPRISING...ROOT
AND ROOTS FAMILIES IN AMERICA by James Pierce Root. Repr. of
1870 ed.
Cloth—$80.00—Paper—$70.00—533pp---------------------- Vendor #D1842

2473 - THE ROPERS OF STERLING AND RUTLAND by Ella E. Roper. Repr.
of 1904 ed.
Cloth—$71.00—Paper—$61.00—473pp---------------------- Vendor #D1842

2474 - GENEALOGY OF THE ROSS FAMILY, DESCENDANTS OF ZEBULON
ROSS (SCOTLAND TO...NEW YORK) by Griffith and Palston. Repr.
of 1885 ed.
Paper—$4.00—15pp------------------------------------- Vendor #D1842

2475 - LIEUTENANT HERMAN ROWLEE (1746-1818) AND HIS DESCENDANTS
by Willard Rowlee. Repr. of 1907 ed.
Paper—$21.00—138pp----------------------------------- Vendor #D1842

2476 - DESCENDANTS OF MOSES ROWLEY OF CAPE COD (CIRCA 1715) by
H. S. Russell. Repr. of 1908 ed.
Paper—$7.50—33pp------------------------------------- Vendor #D1842

2477 - THE NEW ENGLAND ROYALLS by Edward Doubleday Harris. Repr.
of 1885 ed.
Paper—$5.50—27pp------------------------------------- Vendor #D1842

2478 - HISTORY OF CHRISTOPHER ROYER AND HIS POSTERITY by A. K.
Gift. Repr. of 1909 ed.
Paper—$8.50—40pp------------------------------------- Vendor #D1842

2479 - THE RUGGLES LINEAGE. FIVE GENERATIONS by Henry Stoddard
Ruggles. Repr. of 1896 ed., n.p.
Paper—$4.00—14pp------------------------------------- Vendor #D1842

2480 - GENEALOGY OF THOMAS RUGGLES OF ROXBURY, 1637, TO THOMAS
RUGGLES...ALITHEAH SMITH...AND GENEALOGY OF DESCENDANTS
...SAMUEL LADD....by Franklin Ladd Bailey. Repr. of 1896 ed., n.p.
Paper—$9.50—44pp------------------------------------- Vendor #D1842

2481 - RUNKLE FAMILY...RUNKLES IN EUROPE AND THEIR DESCENDANTS
IN AMERICA by Ben Lisker. Repr. of 1899 ed.
Cloth—$55.50—Paper—$45.50—366pp---------------------- Vendor #D1842

2482   - A GENEALOGY OF THE RUNNELS AND REYNOLDS FAMILIES IN
        AMERICA by M. T. Runnels. Repr. of 1873 ed.
        Cloth—$56.00—Paper—$46.00—371pp------------------------ Vendor #D1842

2483   - DESCENDANTS OF JOHN RUSSELL OF WOBURN, MASSACHUSETTS
        by J. R. Bartlett. Repr. of 1879 ed.
        Paper—$35.00—212pp-------------------------------------- Vendor #D1842

2484   - AN ACCOUNT OF SOME OF THE DESCENDANTS OF JOHN RUSSELL
        ...ALLIED FAMILIES OF WADSWORTH, TUTTLE AND BERESFORD by
        Gurdon Wadsworth Russell, edited by Edwin Stanley Welles. Repr.
        of 1910 ed.
        Cloth—$47.50—Paper—$37.50—318pp------------------------ Vendor #D1842

2485   - GENEALOGICAL REGISTER OF DESCENDANTS OF ROBERT AND
        AGNES (LEITCH) RUSSELL...PIONEER EXPERIENCES by Nelson and
        Robert F. Flint. Repr. of 1923 ed.
        Paper—$9.50—44pp--------------------------------------- Vendor #D1842

2486   - THE RUST FAMILY, DESCENDANTS OF HENRY RUST OF HINGHAM,
        MASSACHUSETTS by G. S. Brown. Repr. of 1909 ed.
        Paper—$3.00—9pp-- Vendor #D1842

2487   - RECORD OF THE RUST FAMILY...WHO CAME FROM ENGLAND AND
        SETTLED IN HINGHAM, MASSACHUSETTS, 1634-1635 by Albert D.
        Rust. Repr. of 1891 ed.
        Cloth—$81.50—Paper—$71.50—542pp------------------------ Vendor #D1842

2488   - SKETCH OF LIFE OF AZUBAH (FREEMAN) RYDER, WITH A LIST OF
        HER IMMEDIATE ANCESTORS AND DESCENDANTS by J. H. Ryder.
        Repr. of 1888 ed.
        Paper—$9.00—45pp--------------------------------------- Vendor #D1842

2489   - THE RYERSON GENEALOGY...KNICKERBOCKER FAMILIES OF RYER-
        SON, RYERSE, RYERSS: ALSO ANDRIANCE AND MARTENSE FAMILIES:
        ...REYERSZ (REYERSZEN), OF AMSTERDAM, HOLLAND by Albert
        Winslow Ryerson, edited by Alfred L. Holman. Repr. of 1916 ed.
        Cloth—$67.00—Paper—$57.00—449pp------------------------ Vendor #D1842

2490   - THE SABIN FAMILY OF AMERICA. THE FOUR EARLIEST GENERA-
        TIONS by Anson Titus, Jr. Repr. N. E. Hist. & Gen. Register, 1882 ed.
        Paper—$4.00—11pp--------------------------------------- Vendor #D1842

2491   - THE SACKETTS OF AMERICA, THEIR ANCESTORS AND DESCENDANTS,
        1630-1907 by Charles Weygant. Repr. of 1907 ed.
        Cloth—$83.00—Paper—$73.00—553pp------------------------ Vendor #D1842

2492   - NOTES ON GENEALOGY OF SADOWSKI FAMILY by A. C. Sandusky.
        Repr. of 1937 ed.
        Paper—$6.00—31pp--------------------------------------- Vendor #D1842

2493   - GENEALOGICAL RECORD OF DESCENDANTS OF DAVID SAGE...
        MIDDLETON, CONNECTICUT, 1652 by Elisha L. Saage. Repr. of
        1878 ed.
        Paper—$14.50—82pp-------------------------------------- Vendor #D1842

2494   - HISTORY OF SAGE AND SLOCUM FAMILIES OF ENGLAND AND
        AMERICA, INCLUDING...MONTAGUE, WANTON (AND OTHERS) by
        Henry Whittemore. Repr. of 1908 ed.
        Paper—$15.00—95pp-------------------------------------- Vendor #D1842

2495   - FAMILY OF GENERAL ARTHUR ST. CLAIR by J. G. Maginess.
        Repr. of 1897 ed.
        Paper—$6.50—32pp--------------------------------------- Vendor #D1842

2496   - GENEALOGY OF THE SAHLERS OF THE UNITED STATES AND OF
        THEIR KINSMEN, THE GRASS FAMILY by Louis Sahler. Repr. of 1895 ed.
        Paper—$7.50—38pp--------------------------------------- Vendor #D1842

2497   - SALISBURY FAMILY OF ENGLAND AND AMERICA by E. E. Salisbury.
        Repr. of 1885 ed.
        Paper—$27.50—188pp------------------------------------- Vendor #D1842

2498 - ANCESTRY AND DESCENDANTS OF SIR RICHARD SALTONSTALL...
PATENTEE OF CONNECTICUT by Leverett Saltonstall. Repr. of 1897 ed.
Cloth—$41.50—Paper—$31.50—277pp------------------------ Vendor #D1842

2499 - GENEALOGY OF THE SANBORN FAMILY by Nathan Sanborn. Repr.
N. E. Hist. & Gen. Register, 1856 ed.
Paper—$4.00—21pp--------------------------------------- Vendor #D1842

2500 - THE ST. JOHN GENEALOGY, DESCENDANTS OF MATTHIAS OF DOR-
CHESTER, MASSACHUSETTS, 1634....by Orline Alexander. Repr.
of 1907 ed.
Cloth—$96.00—Paper—$86.00—639pp----------------------- Vendor #D1842

2501 - THE AMERICAN AND ENGLISH SANBORNES by V. C. Sanborn.
Repr. of 1895 ed.
Paper—$5.00—25pp-------------------------------------- Vendor #D1842

2502 - GENEALOGY OF THE FAMILY OF SANBORNE OR SANBORN IN ENG-
LAND AND AMERICA, 1194-1898 by V. C. Sanborn. Repr. of 1899 ed.
Cloth—$106.00—Paper—$96.00—709pp---------------------- Vendor #D1842

2503 - THE SAMPSON FAMILY...ARRIVAL OF THE MAYFLOWER IN 1620 TO
THE PRESENT TIME by John A. Vinton. Repr. of 1864 ed.
Paper—$21.00—140pp------------------------------------- Vendor #D1842

2504 - GENEALOGY OF THE CORTLAND COUNTY, NEW YORK BRANCH OF
THE SANDERS FAMILY by Joshua Sanders. Repr. of 1908 ed.
Paper—$17.00—111pp------------------------------------- Vendor #D1842

2505 - DESCENT OF COMFORT SANDS...FAMILIES OF RAY, THOMAS,
GUTHRIE (AND OTHERS) by Temple Prime. Repr. of 1886 ed.
Paper—$15.00—91pp-------------------------------------- Vendor #D1842

2506 - SANFORD GENEALOGY; THE BRANCH OF WILLIAM OF MADISON,
NEW YORK, OF THE SIXTH AMERICAN GENERATION by Herman
Howes Sanford. Repr. of 1894 ed.
Paper—$13.50—70pp-------------------------------------- Vendor #D1842

2507 - SARGENT RECORD. WILLIAM SARGENT OF NEW ENGLAND...AND
OTHER SARGENT BRANCHES by Edwin Everett Sargent. Repr. of
1899 ed.
Cloth—$49.50—Paper—$39.50—331pp---------------------- Vendor #D1842

2508 - HISTORY OF THE SAPP FAMILY by Sapp and Stanley. Repr. of
1910 ed.
Paper—$20.00—102pp------------------------------------- Vendor #D1842

2509 - EARLY SARGENTS OF NEW ENGLAND by Winthrop Sargent. Repr.
of 1922 ed.
Paper—$10.00—53pp-------------------------------------- Vendor #D1842

2510 - SARGENT GENEALOGY, HUGH SARGENT OF COURTEENHALL, NORTH-
HAMPTONSHIRE...AND HIS DESCENDANTS IN AMERICA by John S.
Sargent. Repr. of 1895 ed.
Paper—$33.00—218pp------------------------------------- Vendor #D1842

2511 - MR. WILLIAM SAUNDERS AND MRS. SARAH FLAGG SAUNDERS,
LATE OF CAMBRIDGE, WITH...GENEALOGY. Repr. of 1872 ed.
Paper—$8.00—39pp-------------------------------------- Vendor #D1842

2512 - FAMILY OF JOHN SAVAGE OF MIDDLETOWN, CONNECTICUT, 1652
by James Francis Savage. Repr. of 1894 ed.
Paper—$5.00—25pp-------------------------------------- Vendor #D1842

2513 - GENEALOGICAL AND BIOGRAPHICAL RECORD OF THE SAVERY
FAMILIES (SAVORY AND SAVARY)...SEVERY FAMILY, (SEVERIT,
SAVERY, SAVORY, AND SAVARY)...NEW ENGLAND AND PHILADEL-
PHIA by A. W. Savary. Repr. of 1893 ed.
Cloth—$43.00—Paper—$33.00—286pp---------------------- Vendor #D1842

2514 - SAWIN: SUMMARY NOTES CONCERNING JOHN SAWIN AND HIS
POSTERITY by Thomas E. Sawin. Repr. of 1866 ed.
Paper—$10.00—48pp-------------------------------------- Vendor #D1842

2515 - _____ (SAWIN) SUPPLEMENT by A. W. Savary. Repr. of 1905 ed.
Paper—$10.50—58pp-- Vendor #D1842

2516 - SAWYERS IN AMERICA, OR A HISTORY OF THE IMMIGRANT SAW-
YERS...NEW ENGLAND by Amory Carter. Repr. of 1883 ed.
Paper—$18.00—120pp-- Vendor #D1842

2517 - SAYRE FAMILY, LINEAGE OF THOMAS SAYRE, A FOUNDER OF
SOUTHAMPTON by Theodore Banta. Repr. of 1901 ed.
Cloth—$116.00—Paper—$106.00—774pp---------------------- Vendor #D1842

2518 - DESCENDANTS OF JOHN CHRISTIAN SCHELL AND JOHN SCHELL OF
NEW YORK STATE by C. Denissen. Repr. of 1896 ed.
Paper—$20.00—98pp--- Vendor #D1842

2519 - THE REV. WILLIAM SCHENK, HIS ANCESTRY AND HIS DESCENDANTS
by A. D. Schenck. Repr. of 1883 ed.
Paper—$25.00—163pp-- Vendor #D1842

2520 - DESCENDANTS OF JOHN PETER SCHOLL AND HIS WIFE ANNA A. D.
SCHOLL...AND DESCENDANTS by A. G. Scholl. Repr. of 1903 ed.
Paper—$15.00—87pp--- Vendor #D1842

2521 - THE SHEARER-AKERS FAMILY, COMBINED WITH "THE BRYAN LINE"
...SEVENTH GENERATION by James William Shearer. Repr. of 1915 ed.
Paper—$25.50—171pp-- Vendor #D1842

2522 - DANIEL SHED GENEALOGY; ANCESTRY AND DESCENDANTS OF
DANIEL SHED OF BRAINTREE, MASSACHUSETTS, 1327-1920 by Frank
E. Shedd, with English ancestry by J. Gardner Bartlett. Repr. of 1921 ed.
Cloth—$119.50—Paper—$109.50—812pp--------------------- Vendor #D1842

2523 - A GENEALOGICAL HISTORY OF WILLIAM SHEPARD, OF FOSSECUT,
NORTHAMPTONSHIRE, ENGLAND...by George L. Shepard. Repr. of
1886 ed.
Paper—$12.50—63pp--- Vendor #D1842

2524 - SHERMAN GENEALOGY INCLUDING FAMILIES OF ESSEX, SUFFOLK
AND NORFOLK, ENGLAND by Thomas Townsend Sherman. Repr. of
1920 ed.
Cloth—$73.50—Paper—$63.50—490pp---------------------- Vendor #D1842

2525 - DESCENDANTS OF JAMES SKIFF OF LONDON, ENGLAND AND SAND-
WICH, MASSACHUSETTS by F. L. Pierson. Repr. of 1895 ed.
Paper—$5.00—24pp-- Vendor #D1842

2526 - HISTORY OF THE SINCLAIR FAMILY IN EUROPE AND AMERICA FOR
ELEVEN HUNDRED YEARS by Leonard Allison Morrison. Repr. of
1896 ed.
Cloth—$68.00—Paper—$58.00—453pp---------------------- Vendor #D1842

2527 - DOCTOR HENRY SKILTON AND HIS DESCENDANTS by John Davis
Skilton. Repr. of 1921 ed.
Cloth—$61.50—Paper—$51.50—412pp---------------------- Vendor #D1842

2528 - HISTORY OF THE SHINN FAMILY IN EUROPE AND AMERICA by
Josiah H. Shinn. Repr. of 1903 ed.
Cloth—$65.00—Paper—$55.00—434pp---------------------- Vendor #D1842

2529 - LUTHER SISSON OF EASTON, MASSACHUSETTS, HIS ANCESTORS
AND DESCENDANTS by A. A. Wood. Repr. of 1909 ed.
Paper—$4.00—13pp-- Vendor #D1842

2530 - SIMPSONS OF TYE TOP, CUMBERLAND VALLEY, PENNSYLVANIA
by E. S. Bladen. Repr. of 1905 ed.
Paper—$7.50—34pp-- Vendor #D1842

2531 - MEMORIAL OF JOHN SLAFTER, WITH A GENEALOGICAL ACCOUNT
OF HIS DESCENDANTS by Edmund F. Slafter. Repr. of 1869 ed.
Paper—$25.00—165pp-- Vendor #D1842

2532 - GENEALOGY OF ORIGINAL SIMPSON FAMILY OF YORK AND HAN-
COCK COUNTIES, MAINE by J. S. Emery. Repr. of 1891 ed.
Paper—$10.00—51pp--- Vendor #D1842

2533   - A SHORT HISTORY OF THE SLOCUMS, SLOCUMBS AND SLOCOMBS
       OF AMERICA...FROM 1637 TO 1881 by Charles Elihu Slocum. Repr.
       of 1882 ed.
       Cloth—$96.50—Paper—$86.50—644pp----------------------- Vendor #D1842

2534   -   SUPPLEMENT, VOL. 2 Repr. of 1908 ed.
       Cloth—$84.00—Paper—$74.00—559pp----------------------- Vendor #D1842

2535   - THE SKIPWITHS OF AMERICA, DESCENDANTS OF THE BARONETS
       OF PRESTWOULD by F. Skipwith. Repr. of 1878 ed.
       Paper—$4.00—8pp-- Vendor #D1842

2536   - GENEALOGICAL NOTES ON THE SMOCK FAMILY IN AMERICA by
       J. C. Smock. Repr. of 1922 ed.
       Paper—$10.00—47pp--- Vendor #D1842

2537   - SNOW GENEALOGY, DESCENDANTS OF NICHOLS SNOW OF PLYMOUTH
       COLONY by M. Alder. Repr. of 1897 ed.
       Paper—$5.00—24pp-- Vendor #D1842

2538   - WILLIAM SNOW FAMILY WHO LANDED AT PLYMOUTH IN 1635 by
       E. H. Snow. Repr. of 1908 ed.
       Paper—$12.50—64pp--- Vendor #D1842

2539   - MONOGRAPHS ON THE SOUTHGATE FAMILY OF SCARBOROUGH,
       MAINE...ANCESTORS AND DESCENDANTS by Leonard B. Chapman.
       Repr. of 1907 ed.
       Paper—$14.00—68pp--- Vendor #D1842

2540   - GENEALOGICAL MEMORANDA; SNIVELY, 1659-1882 by William Andrew
       Snively. Repr. of 1883 ed.
       Paper—$14.00—77pp--- Vendor #D1842

2541   - GENEALOGY OF DESCENDANTS OF LAWRENCE AND CASSANDRA
       SOUTHWICK OF SALEM, MASSACHUSETTS by James. M. Caller and
       Mrs. M. A. Ober. Repr. of 1881 ed.
       Cloth—$92.00—Paper—$82.00—616pp----------------------- Vendor #D1842

2542   - GENEALOGY OF THE SOUTHWORTHS (SOUTHARDS), DESCENDANTS
       OF CONSTANT SOUTHWORTH...ENGLAND by Samuel G. Webber.
       Repr. of 1905 ed.
       Cloth—$73.50—Paper—$63.50—492pp----------------------- Vendor #D1842

2543   - RECORDS AND MEMORIALS OF THE SPEED FAMILY by Thomas Speed.
       Repr. of 1892 ed,
       Paper—$31.00—206pp-- Vendor #D1842

2544   - THE MAINE SPENCERS. A HISTORY AND GENEALOGY, 1596-1898
       by W. D. Spencer. Repr. of 1898 ed.
       Paper—$37.00—247pp-- Vendor #D1842

2545   - MATERIALS FOR A GENEALOGY OF THE SPARHAWK FAMILY IN
       NEW ENGLAND by Cecil Hampden Cutts Howard. Repr. Essex Inst.
       Hist. Coll., 1892 ed.
       Paper—$16.00—113pp-- Vendor #D1842

2546   - SPALDING MEMORIAL AND PERSONEL REMINISCENCES by Phineas
       Spalding and LIFE AND SELECTED POEMS OF CAROLINE A. SPALDING
       by George B. Spalding. Repr. of 1887 ed.
       Cloth—$48.00—Paper—$38.00—324pp----------------------- Vendor #D1842

2547   - GENEALOGY OF THE SPOTSWOOD FAMILY IN SCOTLAND AND VIR-
       GINIA by Charles Campbell. Repr. of 1868 ed.
       Paper—$9.00—44pp-- Vendor #D1842

2548   - GENEALOGY OF THE SPRAGUE'S IN HINGHAM, COUNTING FROM
       WILLIAM SPRAGUE...FROM ENGLAND, IN 1628 by Hosea Sprague.
       Repr. of 1828 ed.
       Paper—$12.50—68pp--- Vendor #D1842

2549   - THE SPRAGUES OF MALDEN, MASSACHUSETTS by George Walter
       Chamberlain. Repr. of 1923 ed.
       Cloth—$48.50—Paper—$38.50—325pp----------------------- Vendor #D1842

2550 - GENEALOGICAL TABLE AND HISTORY OF THE SPRINGER FAMILY
        IN EUROPE AND NORTH AMERICA, Vol. 1, by M. C. Springer,
        revisions and additions by E. L. Scribner. Repr. of 1917 ed.
        Paper—$23.00—154pp------------------------------------- Vendor #D1842

2551 - HISTORY AND GENEALOGY OF THE STACKPOLE FAMILY, 2nd ed.,
        by Everett S. Stackpole. Repr. of 1920 ed.
        Cloth—$52.50—Paper—$42.50—352pp----------------------- Vendor #D1842

2552 - A CONTRIBUTION TO THE GENEALOGY OF THE STAFFORD FAMILY
        IN AMERICA by H. M. Benedict. Repr. of 1870 ed.
        Paper—$7.50—27pp-------------------------------------- Vendor #D1842

2553 - THE STANDISHES OF AMERICA by Myles Standish. Repr. of 1895 ed.
        Paper—$23.00—153pp------------------------------------ Vendor #D1842

2554 - THE STANLEY FAMILIES OF AMERICA AS DESCENDED FROM JOHN,
        ...HARTFORD, CONNECTICUT, 1636 by Israel P. Warren. Repr. of
        1887 ed.
        Cloth—$52.50—Paper—$42.50—352pp----------------------- Vendor #D1842

2555 - A RECORD, GENEALOGICAL...OF THOMAS STANTON OF CONNECTI-
        CUT...1635-1891 by William A. Stanton. Repr. of 1891 ed.
        Cloth—$92.00—Paper—$82.00—613pp----------------------- Vendor #D1842

2556 - THE STARIN FAMILY IN AMERICA. DESCENDANTS OF NICHOLAS
        STER (ATARIN)...FORT ORANGE (ALBANY, NEW YORK) by William
        L. Stone. Repr. of 1892 ed.
        Paper—$35.00—233pp------------------------------------ Vendor #D1842

2557 - THE AARON STARK FAMILY, SEVEN GENERATIONS...AARON STARK,
        OF GROTON, CONNECTICUT by Charles R. Stark. Repr. of 1927 ed.
        Paper—$22.00—148pp------------------------------------ Vendor #D1842

2558 - A BRIEF GENEALOGICAL HISTORY OF ROBERT STARKWEATHER
        OF ROXBURY AND IPSWICH, MASSACHUSETTS...1640-1898 by Carlton
        Lee Starkweather. Repr. of 1904 ed.
        Cloth—$53.00—Paper—$43.00—356pp----------------------- Vendor #D1842

2559 - A GENEALOGICAL RECORD OF THE START FAMILY IN AMERICA
        by William A. Start. Repr. of 1894 ed.
        Paper—$6.00—30pp-------------------------------------- Vendor #D1842

2560 - GENEALOGICAL RECORD OF DESCENDANTS OF HENRY STAUFFER,
        AND OTHER STAUFFER PIONEERS by A. J. Fretz. Repr. of 1899 ed.
        Cloth—$55.50—Paper—$45.50—371pp----------------------- Vendor #D1842

2561 - GENEALOGY OF THE STEARNS, LANES, HOLBROOK AND WARREN
        FAMILIES by Mary L. Brook. Repr. of 1898 ed.
        Paper—$10.00—59pp------------------------------------- Vendor #D1842

2562 - GENEALOGY AND MEMOIRS OF CHARLES AND NATHANIEL STEARNS,
        AND THEIR DESCENDANTS by Avis Van Wagenen. Repr. of 1901 ed.
        Cloth—$80.00—Paper—$70.00—531pp----------------------- Vendor #D1842

2563 - GENEALOGY AND MEMOIRS OF ISAAC STEARNS AND HIS DESCEN-
        DANTS by Mrs. Avis Van Wagenen. Repr. of 1901 ed.
        Cloth—$112.00—Paper—$102.00—746pp---------------------- Vendor #D1842

2564 - MEMORANDA OF THE STEARNS FAMILY INCLUDING RECORDS OF
        MANY OF THE DESCENDANTS. Repr. of 1901 ed.
        Paper—$25.50—173pp------------------------------------ Vendor #D1842

2565 - ARCHIBALD STEELE AND HIS DESCENDANTS by Newton Chambers
        Steele. Repr. of 1900 ed.
        Paper—$21.50—143pp------------------------------------ Vendor #D1842

2566 - STEELE FAMILY. GENEALOGICAL HISTORY OF JOHN AND GEORGE
        STEELE (SETTLERS OF HARTFORD, CONNECTICUT)....by Daniel
        Steele Durrie. Repr. of 1859 ed.
        Paper—$23.00—159pp------------------------------------ Vendor #D1842

2567 - THE STERLING GENEALOGY, 2 Vols., by Albert Mack Sterling.
        Repr. of 1909 ed.
        Cloth—$212.50—Paper—$192.50—1418pp-------------------- Vendor #D1842

2568 - GENEALOGY AND BIOGRAPHICAL SKETCH OF NAME AND FAMILY OF STETSON 1634-1847 by J. S. Barry. Repr. of 1847 ed.
Paper—$25.00—116pp--------------------------------------- Vendor #D1842

2569 - ERASMUS STEVENS, BOSTON, MASSACHUSETTS, 1674-1690, AND HIS DESCENDNATS by Eugene R. Stevens, rev. by William Plumb Bacon. Repr. of 1914 ed.
Paper—$17.00—116pp--------------------------------------- Vendor #D1842

2570 - GENEALOGY OF THE STEVENS FAMILY 1635-1891 by F. S. Stevens. Repr. of 1891 ed.
Paper—$12.50—63pp-- Vendor #D1842

2571 - THOMAS STEVENSON OF LONDON, ENGLAND, AND HIS DESCENDANTS by John R. Stevenson. Repr. of 1902 ed.
Paper—$27.00—181pp--------------------------------------- Vendor #D1842

2572 - GENEALOGY AND BIOGRAPHY OF DESCENDANTS OF WALTER STEWART OF SCOTLAND...SETTLED IN LONDERRY, NEW HAMPSHIRE by B. Frank Severance. Repr. of 1905 ed.
Paper—$34.00—226pp--------------------------------------- Vendor #D1842

2573 - THE STICKNEY FAMILY, GENEALOGY OF THE DESCENDANTS OF WILLIAM AND ELIZABETH, 1637-1869 by M. A. Stickney. Repr. of 1869 ed.
Cloth—$80.00—Paper—$70.00—534pp----------------------- Vendor #D1842

2574 - STILES FAMILY IN AMERICA. GENEALOGIES OF THE MASSACHU-SETTS FAMILY, AND THE DOVER, NEW HAMPSHIRE FAMILY by Mrs. Mary Stiles Guild. Repr. of 1892 ed.
Cloth—$103.00—Paper—$93.00—689pp---------------------- Vendor #D1842

2575 - CONTRIBUTIONS TOWARDS A GENEALOGY OF THE (MASSACHU-SETTS) FAMILY OF STILES....by Henry R. Stiles. Repr. of 1863 ed.
Paper—$10.00—48pp-- Vendor #D1842

2576 - HISTORY OF THE KENTUCKY-MISSOURI STILES, WITH...NEW JERSEY AND OTHER KINDRED by L. S. Pence. Repr. of 1896 ed.
Paper—$10.00—47pp-- Vendor #D1842

2577 - 1654-1903. HISTORY AND GENEALOGY OF GEORGE STILLMAN 1ST, AND HIS DESCENDANTS....by Edgar Stillman. Repr. of 1903 ed.
Paper—$14.00—76pp-- Vendor #D1842

2578 - NOTES ON DESCENDANTS OF NICHOLAS STILLWELL, THE...STILL-WELL FAMILY IN AMERICA by W. H. Stillwell. Repr. of 1883 ed.
Paper—$12.50—62pp-- Vendor #D1842

2579 - HISTORY AND GENEALOGICAL RECORD OF ONE BRANCH OF STILL-WELL FAMILY by DeWitt Stilwell, with introduction and contributions by Lamont Stilwell. Repr. of 1914 ed.
Paper—$15.00—94pp-- Vendor #D1842

2580 - EARLY MEMOIRS OF THE STILWELL FAMILY...LIFE AND TIMES OF NICHOLAS STILWELL....by Benjamin Marshall Stilwell. Repr. of 1878 ed.
Cloth—$43.00—Paper—$33.00—289pp----------------------- Vendor #D1842

2581 - JOHN STODDARD OF WETHERSFIELD, CONNECTICUT, AND HIS DESCENDANTS, 1462-1872....by D. Williams Patterson. Author's ed. Repr. of 1873 ed.
Paper—$15.00—96pp-- Vendor #D1842

2582 - JOHN STODDARD OF NEW LONDON, CONNECTICUT AND HIS DE-SCENDANTS by Stoddard and Shappee. Repr.
Paper—$20.00—96pp-- Vendor #D1842

2583 - GENEALOGY OF STIMPSON FAMILY OF CHARLESTOWN, MASSACHU-SETTS, AND ALLIED LINES by Charles Collyer Whittier. Repr. of 1907 ed.
Paper—$31.00—206pp--------------------------------------- Vendor #D1842

2584 - ANTHONY STODDARD AND HIS DESCENDANTS by C. and E. Stod-dard. Repr. of 1865 ed.
Paper—$17.50—95pp-- Vendor #D1842

2585 - SOME ANCESTORS OF RODMAN STODDARD, OF WOODBURY, CON-
NECTICUT, AND DETROIT, MICHIGAN by Edward Deacon. Repr. of
1893 ed.
Paper—$14.50—86pp-- Vendor #D1842

2586 - SOUVENIR OF A PART OF THE DESCENDANTS OF GREGORY AND
LYDIA COOPER STONE, 1634-1892 by Mrs. John Livingston Stone.
Repr. of 1892 ed.
Paper—$14.50—78pp-- Vendor #D1842

2587 - THE FAMILY OF JOHN STONE, ONE OF THE FIRST SETTLERS OF
GUILFORD, CONNECTICUT by William L. Stone, 2d. Repr. of 1888 ed.
Paper—$29.00—192pp--- Vendor #D1842

2588 - BOOK II, OF THE FAMILY OF JOHN STONE...NAMES OF ALL DE-
SCENDANTS OF RUSSELL, BILLE, TIMOTHY AND EBER STONE by
Truman Lewis Stone. Repr. of 1898 ed.
Cloth—$54.00—Paper—$44.00—360pp----------------------- Vendor #D1842

2589 - GENEALOGIES OF THE STRANAHAN, JOSSELYN, FITCH AND DOW
FAMILIES IN NORTH AMERICA by H. R. S., e.e., Henry R. Stiles.
Repr. of 1868 ed.
Paper—$19.00—126pp--- Vendor #D1842

2590 - GENEALOGICAL HISTORY OF DESCENDANTS OF STEPHEN AND
URSULA STREETER OF GLOUCESTER, MASSACHUSETTS, 1642....
by Milford B. Streeter. Repr. of 1896 ed.
Cloth—$54.00—Paper—$44.00—360pp----------------------- Vendor #D1842

2591 - WILLIAM STROTHER OF VIRGINIA AND HIS DESCENDANTS by T. M.
Owen. Repr. of 1898 ed.
Paper—$5.00—25pp-- Vendor #D1842

2592 - GENEALOGY. STROBRIDGE MORRISON OR MORISON STRAWBRIDGE
by Mrs. Mary Stiles (Paul) Guild. Repr. of 1891 ed.
Cloth—$47.50—Paper—$37.50—318pp----------------------- Vendor #D1842

2593 - THE STROUDS. A COLONIAL FAMILY OF ENGLISH DESCENT by
A. B. Stroud. Repr. of 1919 ed.
Paper—$39.50—263pp--- Vendor #D1842

2594 - GENEALOGICAL HISTORY OF THE DUNCAN STUART FAMILY IN
AMERICA by Joseph A. Stuart. Repr. of 1894 ed.
Paper—$27.50—183pp--- Vendor #D1842

2595 - GENEALOGY OF STURGES AND COLMAN FAMILIES by A. W. Sturges.
Repr. of 1898 ed.
Paper—$4.00—16pp-- Vendor #D1842

2596 - STURGES FAMILY OF MAINE by A. W. Sturges. Repr. of 1900 ed.
Paper—$8.00—41pp-- Vendor #D1842

2597 - SOLOMON STURGES AND HIS DESCENDANTS by E. Buckingham.
Repr. of 1907 ed., charts.
Paper—$16.50—84pp--- Vendor #D1842

2598 - EDWARD STURGIS OF YARMOUTH, MASSACHUSETTS, 1613-1695,
AND HIS DESCENDANTS edited by Roger Faxton Sturgis. Repr. of
1914 ed.
Paper—$15.00—88pp--- Vendor #D1842

2599 - THE SULLIVAN FAMILY OF SULLIVAN, MAINE, WITH SOME AC-
COUNTING OF THE TOWN by J. Emery. Repr. of 1891 ed.
Paper—$5.00—22pp-- Vendor #D1842

2600 - RECORD OF DESCENDANTS OF WILLIAM SUMNER OF DORCHESTER,
MASSACHUSETTS by W. S. Appleton, 1881-1902, additional notes and
corrections to original. Repr. of 1879 ed.
Paper—$8.00—40pp-- Vendor #D1842

2601 - MEMOIR OF INCREASE SUMNER, GOVERNOR OF MASSACHUSETTS
by William H. Sumner, WITH A GENEALOGY OF THE SUMNER FAMILY
by William B. Trask. Repr. of 1854 ed.
Paper—$14.00—70pp--- Vendor #D1842

2602   - SUTPHEN FAMILY, GENEALOGY AND BIOGRAPHICAL NOTES by
L. L. DeBoar. Repr. of 1926 ed.
Paper—$27.50—132pp--- Vendor #D1842

2603   - SUTHERLAND RECORDS by D. Merritt. Repr. of 1918 ed.
Paper—$15.00—76pp--- Vendor #D1842

2604   - SWAIN AND ALLIED FAMILIES by William C. Swain. Repr. of 1896 ed.
Paper—$20.50—137pp-- Vendor #D1842

2605   - SWAIN FAMILY, JEREMIAH SWAIN OF READING, MASSACHUSETTS,
DESCENDANTS by W. C. Swain. Repr. of 1896 ed.
Paper—$10.00—52pp--- Vendor #D1842

2606   - GENEALOGY OF THE SURDAM FAMILY by Charles Edward Surdam.
Repr. of 1909 ed.
Cloth—$40.00—Paper—$30.00—266pp------------------------- Vendor #D1842

2607   - SILAS SWEET OF NEW BEDFORD, MASSACHUSETTS AND BRADFORD,
VERMONT, AND HIS DESCENDANTS by C. Johnson. Repr. of 1898 ed.
Paper—$5.00—21pp-- Vendor #D1842

2608   -FAMILY REGISTER OF GERRET VAN SWERINGEN AND DESCENDANTS,
BY A MEMBER OF THE FAMILY, 2nd ed., by Henry Hartwell Swearin-
gen. Repr. of 1894 ed.
Paper—$15.00—85pp--- Vendor #D1842

2609   - SWETT GENEALOGY, DESCENDANTS OF JOHN SWETT OF NEWBURY,
MASSACHUSETTS by Everett S. Stackpole. Repr., n.d.
Paper—$18.50—123pp-- Vendor #D1842

2610   - MEMENTOS OF THE SWETT FAMILY by John Wingate Thornton. Repr.
of 1851 ed.
Paper—$5.00—26pp-- Vendor #D1842

2611   - THE SYMMES MEMORIAL by J. A. Vinton. Repr. of 1873 ed.
Paper—$27.50—184pp-- Vendor #D1842

2612   - TABER GENEALOGY, DESCENDANTS OF THOMAS, SON OF PHILLIP
TABER by George L. Randall. Repr. of 1924 ed.
Cloth—$78.00—Paper—$68.00—518pp----------------------- Vendor #D1842

2613   - THE TAFT KIN by Anson Titus. Repr. Boston Evening Transcript,
1909 ed.
Paper—$4.00—8pp--- Vendor #D1842

2614   - THE ENGLISH ANCESTRY OF PETER TALBOT OF DORCHESTER,
MASSACHUSETTS by J. G. Bartlett. Repr. of 1917 ed.
Paper—$17.00--116pp--- Vendor #D1842

2615   - TALCOTT PEDIGREE IN ENGLAND AND AMERICA FROM 1558-1876
by S. V. Talcott. Repr. of 1876 ed.
Cloth—$47.00—Paper—$37.00—316pp----------------------- Vendor #D1842

2616   - HISTORY OF THE TALLEY FAMILY ON THE DELAWARE AND THEIR
DESCENDANTS FROM 1686 by George A. Talley. Repr. of 1899 ed.
Paper—$38.00—252pp-- Vendor #D1842

2617   - THE TALMADGE, TALLMADGE AND TALMAGE GENEALOGY, BEING
THE DESCENDANTS OF THOMAS TALMADGE OF LYNN, MASSACHU-
SETTS....by Arthur Talmadge. Repr. of 1909 ed.
Cloth—$58.00—Paper—$48.00—385pp----------------------- Vendor #D1842

2618   - GENEALOGY OF TANKERSLEY FAMILY IN UNITED STATES by C. W.
Tankersley. Repr. of 1950 ed.
Paper—$7.00—31pp-- Vendor #D1842

2619   - GENEALOGY OF DESCENDANTS OF THOMAS TANNER, SR., OF
CORNWALL, CONNECTICUT...ALLIED FAMILIES by Rev. Elias Tanner.
Repr. of 1893 ed.
Paper—$19.00—129pp-- Vendor #D1842

2620   - WILLIAM TANNER OF NORTH KINGSTOWN, RHODE ISLAND, AND
HIS DESCENDANTS by Rev. George C. Tanner. Repr.
Paper—$32.00—216pp-- Vendor #D1842

2621 - THE FAMILY RECORDS OF JAMES AND NANCY DUNHAM TAPPAN...
MIDDLESEX COUNTY, NEW JERSEY by Peter B. Good. Repr. of 1884 ed.
Paper—$20.00—136pp-------------------------------------- Vendor #D1842

2622 - GENEALOGY OF THE TAPLEY FAMILY by Harriet Tapley. Repr. of
1900 ed.
Cloth—$41.00—Paper—$31.00—275pp----------------------- Vendor #D1842

2623 - TAPPAN-TOPPAN GENEALOGY. ANCESTORS AND DESCENDANTS
OF ABRAHAM TOPPAN...1606-1672 by Daniel Tappan. Repr. of 1915 ed.
Paper—$25.00—169pp-- Vendor #D1842

2624 - THE TARLETON FAMILY by C. W. Tarleton. Repr. of 1900 ed.
Paper—$36.50—244pp-- Vendor #D1842

2625 - HISTORY OF JOHN TAYLOR OF HADLEY, MASSACHUSETTS, AND
...HIS DESCENDANTS by Rev. Elvert Taylor. Repr. of 1903 ed.
Paper—$16.50—111pp-- Vendor #D1842

2626 -DESCENDANTS OF ROBERT TAYLOR OF PENNSYLVANIA by A. R.
Justice. Repr. of 1925 ed.
Paper—$23.50—113pp-- Vendor #D1842

2627 - TEALL GENEALOGICAL RECORDS IN ENGLAND AND AMERICA by
E. Dunn. Repr. of 1926 ed.
Paper—$12.50—59pp--- Vendor #D1842

2628 - GENEALOGY OF THE TENNEY FAMILY (VERMONT, OHIO), AND
THE KENT FAMILY (VERMONT) by H. A. Tenney. Repr. of 1875 ed.
Paper—$14.00—76pp--- Vendor #D1842

2629 - THE TENNEY FAMILY, OR DESCENDANTS OF THOMAS TENNEY OF
ROWLEY, MASSACHUSETTS, 1638-1904 by M. J. Tenney. Repr. of
1904 ed.
Cloth—$103.50—Paper—$93.50—691pp---------------------- Vendor #D1842

2630 - GENEALOGY OF TERRELL FAMILY by C. M. Terrell. Repr. of 1906 ed.
Paper—$3.50—8pp--- Vendor #D1842

2631 - GENEALOGICAL LINE OF TYRRELL, TERRELL, TERRILL FAMILY OF
VIRGINIA AND TEXAS by R. L. Terrell. Repr. of 1934 ed.
Paper—$3.50—11pp-- Vendor #D1842

2632 - NOTES OF TERRY FAMILY IN THE UNITED STATES. MAINLY DE-
SCENDANTS FROM SAMUEL OF SPRINGFIELD, MASSACHUSETTS....
by Stephen Terry. Repr. of 1887 ed.
Cloth—$52.50—Paper—$42.50—351pp---------------------- Vendor #D1842

2633 - AN OLD FAMILY (THACHER), AMERICAN DESCENDANTS OF PETER
OF SALISBURY, MASSACHUSETTS, ORANGE, NEW JERSEY. Repr.
of 1882 ed.
Paper—$8.00—48pp--- Vendor #D1842

2634 - GENEALOGICAL RECORDS AND SKETCHES OF DESCENDANTS OF
WILLIAM THOMAS OF HARDWICK, MASSACHUSETTS by A. R. Thomas.
Repr. of 1891 ed.
Paper—$35.00—232pp--------------------------------------- Vendor #D1842

2635 - THOMAS FAMILY OF TALBOT COUNTY, MARYLAND by R. P.
Spencer. Repr. of 1914 ed.
Paper—$8.00—40pp--- Vendor #D1842

2636 - THE THOMAS BOOK, GIVING GENEALOGIES OF SIR RHYS ap THOMAS,
K.G., THE THOMAS FAMILY....by Lawrence Buckley Thomas. Repr.
of 1896 ed.
Cloth—$97.00—Paper—$87.00—648pp---------------------- Vendor #D1842

2637 - OUR THOMPSON FAMILY IN MAINE, NEW HAMPSHIRE AND THE
WEST by Charles N. Sinnett. Repr. of 1907 ed.
Cloth—$44.00—Paper—$34.00—293pp---------------------- Vendor #D1842

2638 - MEMORIAL OF JAMES THOMPSON OF CHARLESTOWN, MASSACHU-
SETTS, 1630-1643, AND WOBURN, MASSACHUSETTS....by Rev.
Leander Thompson. Repr. of 1887 ed.
Paper—$27.50—246pp--------------------------------------- Vendor #D1842

2639 - HISTORY OF THE THOMPSON FAMILY OF ENGLAND AND NEW YORK
by G. Thompson. Repr. of 1937 ed.
Paper—$17.50—87pp--- Vendor #D1842

2640 - EIGHT GENERATIONS FROM WILLIAM THORNE OF DORSETSHIRE,
ENGLAND, AND LYNN, MASSACHUSETTS by Joseph Middleton and
Alan McLean Taylor. Repr. of 1913 ed.
Paper—$3.50—10pp-- Vendor #D1842

2641 - THURBER GENEALOGY. DESCENDANTS OF JOHN THURBER by
A. E. Thurber, Jr. Repr. of 1954 ed.
Paper—$8.00—39pp-- Vendor #D1842

2642 - ANCESTRY OF WALTER M. THURSTON...FAMILIES OF CARROLL,
De BEAUFORT (AND OTHERS) by John H. and Walter M. Thurston.
Repr. of 1894 ed.
Paper—$15.00—95pp--- Vendor #D1842

2643 - GENEALOGY OF CHARLES THURSTON AND RACHEL PITMAN AND
DESCENDANTS by C. M. Thurston. Repr. of 1865 ed.
Paper—$15.00—80pp--- Vendor #D1842

2644 - DESCENDANTS OF EDWARD THURSTON, THE FIRST OF THE NAME
IN THE COLONY OF RHODE ISLAND by Charles M. Thurston. Repr.
of 1868 ed.
Paper—$12.00—70pp--- Vendor #D1842

2645 - 1655-1892. THURSTON GENEALOGY, 2nd Ed., by Brown Thurston.
Repr. of 1892 ed.
Cloth—$114.00—Paper—$104.00—760pp---------------------- Vendor #D1842

2646 - THWING: A GENEALOGY, BIOGRAPHY AND HISTORICAL ACCOUNT
OF THE FAMILY by Walter E. Thwing. Repr. of 1883 ed.
Paper—$32.00—216pp-- Vendor #D1842

2647 - A PARTIAL HISTORY OF THE TICHENOR FAMILY IN AMERICA...
SPELLING THE NAME TEACHENOR edited by Richard B. Teachenor.
Repr. of 1918 ed.
Paper—$6.50—32pp-- Vendor #D1842

2648 - TIFFANY FAMILY GENEALOGY by E. F. Wright. Repr. of 1904 ed.
Paper—$20.00—92pp--- Vendor #D1842

2649 - A PARTIAL RECORD OF THE DESCENDANTS OF JOHN TEFFT OF
PORTSMOUTH, RHODE ISLAND....by Maria E. (Maxon) Tifft. Repr.
of 1896 ed.
Paper—$24.00—159pp-- Vendor #D1842

2650 - GENEALOGY OF THE TILLEY FAMILY by R. H. Tilley. Repr. of
1878 ed.
Paper—$16.00—79pp--- Vendor #D1842

2651 - TILSON GENEALOGY FROM EDMUND TILSON AT PLYMOUTH,...
WATERMAN, MURDOCK, BARTLETT, TURNER, WINSLOW, STURTE-
VANT, KEITH AND PARRIR FAMILIES by Mercer Tilson. Repr. of
1911 ed.
Cloth—$91.50—Paper—$81.50—610pp---------------------- Vendor #D1842

2652 - HISTORY OF THE TILTON FAMILY IN AMERICA, Volume 1, Numbers
1-8, by Francis Theodore Tilton. Repr. of 1927-1930 eds.
Paper—$38.00—256pp-- Vendor #D1842

2653 - GENEALOGY OF ISRAEL (TISDALE) AND HIS DESCENDANTS by
E. F. Tisdale. Repr. of 1909 ed.
Paper—$16.50—82pp--- Vendor #D1842

2654 - TOBEY (TOBIE, TOBY) GENEALOGY. THOMAS OF SANDWICH AND
JAMES OF KITTERY....by Rufus B. Tobey and C. H. Pope. Repr. of
1905 ed.
Cloth—$52.50—Paper—$42.50—350pp---------------------- Vendor #D1842

2655 - TODD GENEALOGY OR REGISTER OF DESCENDANTS OF ADAMS TODD
OF THE NAMES OF TODD, WHETTEN....by Richard Greene. Repr.
of 1867 ed.
Paper—$24.00—160pp--- Vendor #D1842

2656 - THE NEEDHAM (MASSACHUSETTS) BRANCH OF THE TOLMAN FAM-
ILY by Anna Maria Pickford. Repr. of 1894 ed.
Paper—$5.50—29pp--- Vendor #D1842

2657 - HENRY TOMLINSON AND HIS DESCENDANTS IN AMERICA WITH
...BRANCHES OF TOMLINSONS by Rev. Samuel Orcott. Repr. of
1891 ed.
Paper—$36.50—244pp--- Vendor #D1842

2658 - RECORD OF ANCESTRY AND KINDRED OF CHILDREN OF EDWARD
TOMPKINS, SR...., Preliminary Ed., by Edward Thompkins, Jr.
Repr. of 1893 ed.
Paper—$13.00—65pp--- Vendor #D1842

2659 - TOPPANS OF TOPPAN'S LANE (NEWBURY, MASSACHUSETTS), THEIR
DESCENDANTS AND RELATIONS by J. Coffin. Repr. of 1862 ed.
Paper—$5.50—28pp--- Vendor #D1842

2660 - JOHN AND THOMAS TOTMAN (TATMAN) AND THEIR DESCENDANTS
by R. N. Meriam. Repr. of 1895 ed.
Paper—$6.00—31pp--- Vendor #D1842

2661 - TOWER GENEALOGY. AN ACCOUNT OF DESCENDANTS OF JOHN
TOWER OF HINGHAM, MASSACHUSETTS by Charlemagne Tower.
Repr. of 1891 ed.
Cloth—$105.00—Paper—$95.00—701pp----------------------- Vendor #D1842

2662 - DESCENDANTS OF JONATHAN TOWLE, 1747-1822, OF HAMPTON AND
PITTSFIELD, NEW HAMPSHIRE by Alvin Towle, et al. Repr. of 1903 ed.
Cloth—$47.00—Paper—$37.00—312pp----------------------- Vendor #D1842

2663 - ANCESTRY OF LIEUTENANT AMOS TOWNE OF KENNEBUNKPORT,
MAINE by W. G. Davis. Repr. of 1927 ed.
Paper—$16.00—81pp--- Vendor #D1842

2664 - THE TOWNE FAMILY MEMORIAL by Edwin Hubbard. Repr. of 1880 ed.
Paper—$195.00—130pp-- ---------------------------------- Vendor #D1842

2665 - DESCENDANTS OF WILLIAM TOWNE...1630 AND SETTLED IN
SALEM, MASSACHUSETTS by Edwin Eugene Towne. Repr. of 1901 ed.
Cloth—$57.00—Paper—$47.00—379pp----------------------- Vendor #D1842

2666 - NOTES ON THE TOWNSEND FAMILY by Henry F. Waters. Repr.
of 1883 ed.
Paper—$8.50—43pp--- Vendor #D1842

2667 - TOWNSHEND FAMILY OF LYNN, IN ENGLAND AND NEW ENGLAND,
3d Ed., by C. H. Townshend. Repr. of 1884 ed.
Paper—$17.50—138pp--- Vendor #D1842

2668 - THE TOWNSHEND FAMILY by Charles Hervey Townsend. Repr.
N. E. Hist. & Gen. Register, 1875 ed.
Paper—$4.00—15pp--- Vendor #D1842

2669 - TRACY GENEALOGY. ANCESTORS AND DESCENDANTS OF LIEU-
TENANT THOMAS TRACY OF NORWICH....by Evert E. Tracy. Repr.
of 1898 ed.
Cloth—$44.00—Paper—$34.00—294pp----------------------- Vendor #D1842

2670 - DESCENDANTS OF HENRY TRAVERS OF ENGLAND AND NEWBURY,
MASSACHUSETTS by N. H. Daniels. Repr. of 1903 ed.
Paper—$25.00—147pp--- Vendor #D1842

2671 - DOWN SEVEN GENERATIONS. A RESCRIPT OF TREADWELL AND
PLATT GENEALOGY by Mrs. A. C. Maltbie. Repr. of 1883 ed.
Paper—$7.50—36pp--- Vendor #D1842

2672 - THE TREAT FAMILY. A GENEALOGY OF TROTT, TRATT AND
TREAT FOR FIFTEEN GENERATIONS....by John Harvey Treat. Repr.
of 1893 ed.
Cloth—$97.00—Paper—$87.00—649pp------------------------ Vendor #D1842

2673 - SOME ACCOUNTING OF THE TREE FAMILY AND ITS CONNECTIONS
IN ENGLAND AND AMERICA by J. Leach. Repr. of 1908 ed.
Paper—$22.50—116pp-------------------------------------- Vendor #D1842

2674 - HISTORICAL ACCOUNTING OF THE TREGO FAMILY by A. T. Shert-
zer. Repr. of 1884 ed.
Paper—$28.50—144pp-------------------------------------- Vendor #D1842

2675 - HISTORY OF THE TRUBEE FAMILY 1275-1894 by H. T. Garlick.
Repr. of 1894 ed.
Paper—$30.00—151pp-------------------------------------- Vendor #D1842

2676 - CONTRIBUTIONS TO A TRUMBULL GENEALOGY, FROM GLEANINGS
IN ENGLISH FIELDS by J. Henry Lea. Repr. N. E. Hist. & Gen. Reg-
ister, 1895 ed.
Paper—$5.50—27pp-- Vendor #D1842

2677 - TUCK GENEALOGY. ROBERT TUCK OF HAMPTON, NEW HAMPSHIRE,
AND HIS DESCENDANTS, 1638-1877 by Joseph Dow. Repr. of 1877 ed.
Paper—$22.00—146pp-------------------------------------- Vendor #D1842

2678 - GENEALOGY OF THE TUCKER FAMILY, FROM VARIOUS AUTHENTIC
SOURCES by Ephraim Tucker. Repr. of 1895 ed.
Cloth—$62.00—Paper—$52.00—414pp------------------------ Vendor #D1842

2679 - TUCKER GENEALOGY. A RECORD OF GILBERT RUGGLES AND
EVELINA CHRISTINA (SNYDER) TUCKER....by Tyler Seymour Morris.
Repr. of 1901 ed.
Cloth—$55.00—Paper—$45.00—305pp------- ----------------- Vendor #D1842

2680 - GENEALOGY AND HISTORICAL ACCOUNT OF DESCENDANTS OF
HENRY TUCKER by G. H. Tucker. Repr. of 1851 ed.
Paper—$10.00—45pp--- Vendor #D1842

2681 - TULEY FAMILY. MEMOIRS, HISTORY, BIOGRAPHY, AND GENEAL-
OGY...FLOYD FAMILY CONNECTIONS IN VIRGINIA, KENTUCKY,
AND INDIANA by W. F. Tuley. Repr. of 1906 ed.
Paper—$15.00—75pp-------------------------------------- Vendor #D1842

2682 - GENEALOGY OF DESCENDANTS OF HUMPHREY TURNER, WITH
FAMILY RECORDS by Jacob Turner. Repr. of 1852 ed.
Paper—$12.50—64pp-------------------------------------- Vendor #D1842

2683 - SKETCH OF THE JAMES TWEED FAMILY OF WILMINGTON, MASSA-
CHUSETTS by B. Walker. Repr. of 1887 ed.
Paper—$6.00—30pp--------------------------------------- Vendor #D1842

2684 - GENEALOGY...ONE BRANCH OF TYER FAMILY, DESCENDED FROM
JOHN TYER by E. T. Savery. Repr. of 1894 ed.
Paper—$7.50—35pp--------------------------------------- Vendor #D1842

2685 - GENEALOGY OF THE UHLER FAMILY 1735-1901 by G. H. Uhler.
Repr. of 1901 ed.
Paper—$7.00—35pp--------------------------------------- Vendor #D1842

2686 - NOTICES OF JOHN UPHAM AND DESCENDANTS by A. G. Upham.
Repr. of 1845 ed.
Paper—$18.00—92pp-------------------------------------- Vendor #D1842

2687 - GENEALOGY AND FAMILY HISTORY OF UPHAMS OF CASTINE,
MAINE...BROOKS, KIDDER AND OTHER FAMILIES by F. K. Upham.
Repr. of 1887 ed.
Paper—$14.00—68pp-------------------------------------- Vendor #D1842

2688 - GLEANINGS FROM UPTON FAMILY RECORDS by P. E. Hamilton.
Repr. of 1916 ed.
Paper—$6.00—31pp--------------------------------------- Vendor #D1842

2689   - URANN FAMILY OF NEW ENGLAND by C. C. Whittier. Repr. of
1910 ed.
Paper—$12.00—59pp-------------------------------------- Vendor #D1842

2690   - A BRIEF GENEALOGY OF THE USHER FAMILY OF NEW ENGLAND
by W. H. Whitmore. Repr. of 1869 ed.
Paper—$3.50—11pp------------------------------------- Vendor #D1842

2691   - GENEALOGY OF THE VAN BRUNT FAMILY OF NEW YORK, 1653-1867.
Repr.
Paper—$16.50—79pp------------------------------------- Vendor #D1842

2692   - LAMBERT JANSE VAN ALSTYNE AND SOME OF HIS DESCENDANTS
by L. Van Alstyne. Repr. of 1897 ed.
Paper—$30.00—142pp----------------------------------- Vendor #D1842

2693   - THE VALENTINES IN AMERICA, 1644-1874 by T. W. Valentine.
Repr. of 1874 ed.
Paper—$38.00—254pp----------------------------------- Vendor #D1842

2694   - HISTORY OF JAN VAN CLEEF OF NEW UTRECHT, LONG ISLAND,
NEW YORK, AND SOME OF HIS DESCENDANTS by M. E. Poole. Repr.
of 1909 ed.
Paper—$3.75—14pp-------------------------------------- Vendor #D1842

2695   - VANDERLIP, VAN DERLIP, VANDER LIPPE FAMILY IN AMERICA...
VON DER LIPPE FAMILY OF LIPPE, GERMANY by C. E. Booth. Repr.
of 1914 ed.
Cloth—$40.00—Paper—$30.00—194pp----------------------- Vendor #D1842

2696   - GENEALOGY OF THE VAN HOOSEAR FAMILY, DESCENDANTS OF
RINEAR VAN HOOSEAR, AN OFFICER....by D. H. VanHoosear.
Repr. of 1902 ed.
Paper—$20.00—96pp------------------------------------- Vendor #D1842

2697   - AN HISTORICAL RECORD OF VanHORNE FAMILY IN AMERICA by
A. VanHorne. Repr. of 1888 ed.
Paper—$16.00—80pp------------------------------------- Vendor #D1842

2698   - THE VAN KLEECK FAMILY OF POUGHKEEPSIE, NEW YORK by F.
VanKleeck. Repr. of 1900 ed.
Paper—$12.00—59pp------------------------------------- Vendor #D1842

2699   - VAN NORDEN FAMILY 1623-1925 by T. L. Van Norden. Repr. of
1923 ed.
Paper—$15.00—74pp------------------------------------- Vendor #D1842

2700   - GENEALOGICAL RECORD OF VAN PATTEN FAMILY 1641-1922. Repr.
of 1922 ed.
Paper—$6.00—27pp-------------------------------------- Vendor #D1842

2701   - GENEALOGY OF VAN WAGENEN FAMILY 1650-2884 by G. H.
VanWagenen. Repr. of 1884 ed.
Paper—$17.50—83pp------------------------------------- Vendor #D1842

2702   - THE VARNUMS OF DRACUT (IN MASSACHUSETTS). A HISTORY OF
GEORGE VARNUM....by John Marshall Varnum. Repr. of 1907 ed.
Cloth—$47.00—Paper—$37.00—314pp---------------------- Vendor #D1842

2703   - VASSALLS OF NEW ENGLAND AND THEIR IMMEDIATE DESCENDANTS
by E. D. Harris. Repr. of 1862 ed.
Paper—$6.50—26pp-------------------------------------- Vendor #D1842

2704   - ABRAHAM VAUGHAN OF KENTUCKY AND DESCENDANTS, A FAMILY
TREE by N. V. Ragland. Repr., n.d.
Paper—$10.00—55pp------------------------------------- Vendor #D1842

2705   - REMINISCENCES OF THE VAUGHAN FAMILY, AND MORE PARTICU-
LARLY OF BENJAMIN VAUGHAN, LL.D. by John H. Sheppard; with
a few additions, a genealogy and notes. Repr. of 1865 ed.
Paper—$8.00—40pp-------------------------------------- Vendor #D1842

2706 - REMINISCENCES AND GENEALOGICAL RECORD OF THE VAUGHAN
FAMILY OF NEW HAMPSHIRE by George E. Hogdon. SUPPLEMENTED
BY...VAUGHANS OF SOUTH WALES....by Thomas W. Hancock. Repr.
of 1918 ed.
Paper—$27.00—179pp-------------------------------------- Vendor #D1842

2707 - AMERICAN LINEAGES OF VEACH AND STOVER FAMILIES by R. S.
Veach. Repr. of 1913 ed.
Paper—$26.50—134pp-------------------------------------- Vendor #D1842

2708 - VENABLES OF VIRGINIA by E. M. Venable. Repr. of 1925 ed.
Cloth—$40.00—Paper—$30.00—228pp------------------------ Vendor #D1842

2709 - VEBLEN GENEALOGY by A. A. Veblen. Repr. of 1925 ed.
Paper—$30.00—156pp-------------------------------------- Vendor #D1842

2710 - GENEALOGY OF DESCENDANTS OF PETER VILAS by C. H. Vilas.
Repr. of 1875 ed.
Paper—$35.00—221pp-------------------------------------- Vendor #D1842

2711 - FAMILY OF VINCENT, HISTORY, GENEALOGY AND BIOGRAPHICAL
NOTICES by B. Vincent. Repr., n.d.
Paper—$30.00—158pp-------------------------------------- Vendor #D1842

2712 - GENEALOGICAL SKETCHES OF DESCENDANTS OF JOHN VINTON OF
LYNN, 1648....by John Adams Vinton. Repr. of 1858 ed.
Paper—$38.00—252pp-------------------------------------- Vendor #D1842

2713 - VOUGHT FAMILY, DESCENDANTS OF SIMON AND CHRISTINA VOUGHT
by W. VerPlanck. Repr. of 1907 ed.
Paper—$6.50—27pp--------------------------------------- Vendor #D1842

2714 - THE WADE GENEALOGY...PEDIGREES OF FAMOUS ENGLISHMEN OF
THE NAME:...FAMILIES IN MASSACHUSETTS AND NEW JERSEY by
Stuart C. Wade. Repr. of 1900 ed.
Cloth—$57.50—Paper—$47.50—384pp------------------------ Vendor #D1842

2715 - WADHAM GENEALOGY by Harriet Stevens. Repr. of 1913 ed.
Cloth—$100.00—Paper—$90.00—664pp----------------------- Vendor #D1842

2716 - 250 YEARS OF THE WADSWORTH FAMILY IN AMERICA...REUNION
AT DUXBURY, MASSACHUSETTS AND A GENEALOGY REGISTER by
Horace A. Wadsworth. Repr. of 1883 ed.
Paper—$38.50—257pp-------------------------------------- Vendor #D1842

2717 - HISTORY OF THE WAGENSELLER FAMILY IN AMERICA WITH KIN-
DRED BRANCHES by George W. Wagenseller. Repr. of 1898 ed.
Paper—$34.00—225pp-------------------------------------- Vendor #D1842

2718 - FAMILY RECORDS OF DESCENDANTS OF THOMAS WAIT OF PORTS-
MOUTH, RHODE ISLAND by John C. Wait. Repr. of 1904 ed.
Paper—$12.50—58pp-------------------------------------- Vendor #D1842

2719 - NOTES ON THE FAMILY OF WAGER, WIRTZ, HOUSER, ET AL., OF
PHILADELPHIA by T. A. Glenn. Repr. of 1900 ed.
Paper—$4.00—13pp--------------------------------------- Vendor #D1842

2720 - GENEALOGICAL SKETCH OF A BRANCH OF THE WAIT OR WAITE
FAMILY OF AMERICA by D. Byron Waite. Repr. of 1893 ed.
Paper—$5.50—28pp--------------------------------------- Vendor #D1842

2721 - THE WAITE FAMILY OF MALDEN, MASSACHUSETTS by Deloraine P.
Corey. Repr. of 1913 ed.
Paper—$19.50—129pp-------------------------------------- Vendor #D1842

2722 - THE WALCOTT BOOK. HISTORY AND GENEALOGY OF THE AMERI-
CAN FAMILY OF WALCOTT...ENGLISH WALCOTTS by Arthur Stuart
Walcott. Repr. of 1925 ed.
Cloth—$43.00—Paper—$33.00—286pp------------------------ Vendor #D1842

2723 - WAKEFIELD MEMORIAL, AN HISTORICAL, GENEALOGICAL, AND
BIOGRAPHICAL REGISTER OF THE NAME AND FAMILY by Homer
Wakefield. Repr. of 1897 ed.
Cloth—$55.00—Paper—$45.00—367pp------------------------ Vendor #D1842

2724 - GENEALOGY AND BIOGRAPHAY OF THE WALDOS OF AMERICA, FROM 1650 TO 1883 by Joseph D. Hall, Jr. Repr. of 1883 ed.
Paper—$22.00—145pp-------------------------------------- Vendor #D1842

2725 - GENEALOGY OF FREDK. WALDRON FROM SETTLEMENT OF NEW AMSTERDAM THRU THE WALDRONS, WHITNEYS AND RIGGES by F. H. Waldron. Repr. of 1909 ed.
Paper—$6.00—32pp-- Vendor #D1842

2726 - GENEALOGY OF DESCENDANTS OF TIMOTHY WALES OF CONNECTI-CUT by W. H. Whittemore. Repr. of 1875 ed.
Paper—$12.00—56pp--------------------------------------- Vendor #D1842

2727 - MEMORIAL OF THE WALKERS OF THE OLD PLYMOUTH COLONY... AND OF THEIR DESCENDANTS by J. B. R. Walder. Repr. of 1861 ed.
Cloth—$72.00—Paper—$62.00—479pp----------------------- Vendor #D1842

2728 - LEWIS WALKER OF CHESTER VALLEY AND HIS DESCENDANTS, 1686-1896 by Priscilla W. Streets. Repr. of 1896 ed.
Cloth—$67.00—Paper—$57.00—446pp----------------------- Vendor #D1842

2729 - GENEALOGY OF DESCENDANTS OF JOHN WALKER OF WIGTON, SCOTLAND...HISTORY OF VIRGINIA, 1600-1902 by Emma S. White. Repr. of 1902 ed.
Cloth—$113.00—Paper—$103.00—752pp--------------------- Vendor #D1842

2730 - GENEALOGY OF WALLACE FAMILY OF PENNSYLVANIA by J. H. Wallace. Repr. of 1902 ed.
Paper—$12.50—60pp--------------------------------------- Vendor #D1842

2731 - DESCENDANTS OF HENRY WALLBRIDGE WHO MARRIED ANNA AMOS ...ALLIED FAMILIES OF BRUSH, FASSETT, DEWEY, FOBES, GAGER, LEHMAN, MEECH, STAFFORD, SCOTT by William G. Wallbridge. Repr. of 1898 ed.
Cloth—$45.00—Paper—$35.00—369pp----------------------- Vendor #D1842

2732 - ADAMS, DESCENDANTS OF JAMES AND WILLIAM ADAMS OF LONDON-DERRY, NOW DERRY, NEW HAMPSHIRE by Andrew Adams. Repr. of 1894 ed.
Paper—$12.50—87pp--------------------------------------- Vendor #D1842

2733 - DESCENDANTS OF GEORGE ABBOTT OF ROWLEY, MASSACHUSETTS AND GEORGE ABBOTT, SR. OF ANDOVER, MASSACHUSETTS by Lemuel A. Abbott. Repr. of 1906 ed.
Cloth—$175.00—Paper—$165.00—1232pp-------------------- Vendor #D1842

2734 - GENEALOGY HISTORY OF HENRY ADAMS OF BRAINTREE, MASSA-CHUSETTS...JOHN ADAMS OF CAMBRIDGE by Andrew Adams. Repr. of 1898 ed.
Cloth—$175.00—Paper—$165.00—1238pp-------------------- Vendor #D1842

2735 - HENRY ADAMS OF SOMERSETSHIRE, ENGLAND AND BRAINTREE, MASSACHUSETTS; HIS ENGLISH ANCESTRY....by J. Gardner Bartlett. Repr. of 1927 ed.
Cloth—$35.00—Paper—$25.00—185pp----------------------- Vendor #D1842

2736 - GENEALOGICAL AND HISTORICAL SKETCHES OF THE ALLEN FAMILY OF DEDHAM...1637-1890 by Frank Allen Hutchinson. Repr. of 1896 ed.
Paper—$15.00—80pp--------------------------------------- Vendor #D1842

2737 - GENEALOGY OF THE APPLETON FAMILY by W. S. Appleton. Repr. of 1874 ed.
Paper—$10.00—54pp--------------------------------------- Vendor #D1842

2738 - YE ATTE WODE (ATWOOD) ANNALS by Elijah F. Atwood. Repr. of 1928 ed.
Paper—$15.00—90pp--------------------------------------- Vendor #D1842

2739 - INVESTIGATIONS CONCERNING THE FAMILY OF BALDWIN OF ASTON CLINTON, BUCKS (ENGLAND) by Joseph Lemuel Chester. Repr. of 1884 ed.
Paper—$5.00—28pp-- Vendor #D1842

2740   - THE DESCENDANTS OF ISRAEL BALLARD AND ALICE FULLER by
Melvin G. Dodge. Repr. of 1942 ed.
Cloth—$56.00—Paper—$46.00—375pp----------------------- Vendor #D1842

2741   - THE BARKER FAMILY OF PLYMOUTH COLONY AND COUNTY by
Barker Newhall. Repr., n.d.
Paper—$15.00—102pp------------------------------------- Vendor #D1842

2742   - THE BARKER ANCESTRY by J. O. Austin. Repr. of 1880 ed.
Paper—$4.50—13pp-------------------------------------- Vendor #D1842

2743   - BARKER GENEALOGY by Elizabeth Frye Barker. Repr. of 1927 ed.
Cloth—$83.00—Paper—$73.00—553pp----------------------- Vendor #D1842

2744   - BARNEY, 1634—HOSMER, 1635 by William Frederick Adams. Repr.
of 1912 ed.
Paper—$18.50—133pp------------------------------------- Vendor #D1842

2745   - THE BARRY FAMILY RECORDS, CAPTAIN CHARLES BARRY AND
DESCENDANTS by Laurence H. Parker. Repr. of 1951 ed.
Paper—$22.00—148pp------------------------------------- Vendor #D1842

2746   - LUCIUS BEEBE OF WAKEFIELD AND SYLENDA MORRIS BEEBE, HIS
WIFE, THEIR FORBEARS AND DESCENDANTS by Louise Beebe Wilder.
Repr. of 1930 ed.
Paper—$38.00—255pp------------------------------------- Vendor #D1842

2747   - BENSON FAMILY OF NEWPORT, RHODE ISLAND...BENSON FAMILIES
IN AMERICA OF ENGLISH DESCENT by Wendell P. Garrison. Repr. of
1872 ed.
Paper—$12.50—65pp-------------------------------------- Vendor #D1842

2748   - A MEMORIAL OF A RESPECTABLE AND RESPECTED FAMILY, AND
ESPECIALLY OF JOSHUA BICKNELL....by Thomas Williams Bicknell.
Repr. of 1880 ed.
Paper—$8.50—48pp-------------------------------------- Vendor #D1842

2749   - REPORT OF THE BIGELOW FAMILY REUNION AT LINCOLN PARK
(WORCESTER, MASSACHUSETTS), 1887 by Gilman Bigelow Howe.
Repr. of 1887 ed.
Paper—$8.50—46pp-------------------------------------- Vendor #D1842

2750   - ANCESTORS OF BENJAMIN FERRIS BLAKENEY AND HIS WIFE STELLA
PERDUNE SABIN. Repr. of 1926 ed.
Cloth—$45.00—Paper—$35.00—309pp----------------------- Vendor #D1842

2751   - DESCENDANTS OF RICHARD BLOOD OF BELLINGHAM AND CHARL-
TON, MASSACHUSETTS by C. W. Barlow. Repr. of 1952 ed.
Paper—$7.50—37pp-------------------------------------- Vendor #D1842

2752   - BOLTON FAMILIES IN IRELAND WITH THEIR ENGLISH AND AMERI-
CAN KINDRED by Charles K. Bolton. Repr. of 1937 ed.
Paper—$15.00—109pp------------------------------------- Vendor #D1842

2753   - ONE BRANCH OF THE BOOTH FAMILY...CONNECTION WITH 100
MASSACHUSETTS BAY COLONISTS by Charles Edwin Booth. Repr.
of 1910 ed.
Cloth—$40.00—Paper—$30.00—270pp----------------------- Vendor #D1842

2754   - ORIGIN OF THE BOTSFORD FAMILY by Otis M. Botsford. Repr.
of 1937 ed.
Paper—$4.50—20pp-------------------------------------- Vendor #D1842

2755   - THE BOWDITCH FAMILY OF SALEM, MASSACHUSETTS. Repr. of
1936 ed.
Paper—$8.00—50pp-------------------------------------- Vendor #D1842

2756   - BETHAM'S HISTORY, GENEALOGY AND BARONETS OF THE BOYNTON
FAMILY IN ENGLAND by John F. Boynton. Repr. of 1884 ed.
Paper—$7.50—40pp-------------------------------------- Vendor #D1842

2757   - BOUTON-BOUGHTON FAMILY. DESCENDANTS OF JOHN BOUTON
OF FRANCE...NORWALK, CONNECTICUT by James Boughton. Repr.
of 1890 ed.
Cloth—$100.00—Paper—$90.00—684pp---------------------- Vendor #D1842

2758 - THE BOYNTON FAMILY. A GENEALOGY OF DESCENDANTS OF
WILLIAM AND JOYN BOYNTON by John Farnham Boynton and Caroline
(Harriman) Boynton. Repr. of 1897 ed.
Cloth—$58.00—Paper—$48.00—386pp------------------------ Vendor #D1842

2759 - THE BREWSTER GENEALOGY, 1566-1907: RECORD OF DESCENDANTS
OF WILLIAM BREWSTER OF THE MAYFLOWER, 2 Vols., by Emma C.
Brewster Jones. Repr. of 1908 ed.
Cloth—$210.00—Paper—$190.00—1493pp--------------------- Vendor #D1842

2760 - THE BRIGGS GENEALOGY WITH ALLIED WHITE LINES by Bertha
Aldridge. Repr. of 1953 ed.
Paper—$15.00—116pp------------------------------------- Vendor #D1842

2761 - THE BROOKFIELDS OF NEW JERSEY, CONNECTICUT, AND N. S. by
Henry M. Brookfield. Repr., n.d.
Paper—$22.00—159pp------------------------------------- Vendor #D1842

2762 - BUNKER GENEALOGY: ANCESTRY AND DESCENDANTS OF BENJA-
MIN BUNKER by Edward C. Moran. Repr. of 1942 ed.
Paper—$34.00—232pp------------------------------------- Vendor #D1842

2763 - THE BURNETT FAMILY WITH COLATERAL BRANCHES by Charles H.
Burnett. Repr. of 1950 ed.
Cloth—$55.00—Paper—$45.00—316pp----------------------- Vendor #D1842

2764 - BURES OF SUFFOLK, ENGLAND, AND BURR OF MASSACHUSETTS
BAY COLONY, NEW ENGLAND by Chauncey Rea Burr. Repr. of 1926
ed.
Paper—$19.50—131pp------------------------------------- Vendor #D1842

2765 - BUTLERS OF N. E. AND N. S. AND RELATED FAMILIES OF OTHER
NAMES, INCLUDING DURKESS by Elmer E. Butler. Repr. of 1944 ed.
Cloth—$63.00—Paper—$53.00—358pp----------------------- Vendor #D1842

2766 - ROBERT CALEF OF BOSTON AND SOME OF HIS DESCENDANTS by
Anne Calef Boardman. Repr. of 1940 ed.
Paper—$30.00—195pp------------------------------------- Vendor #D1842

2767 - CASAVANT. GENEALOGIES Des FAMILLES CASAVANT et RAVENELLE
- LALINE by L'Abbe G. A. Dejordy. Repr. of 1910 ed.
Paper—$6.00—27pp--------------------------------------- Vendor #D1842

2768 - RECORDS OF SOME OF THE DESCENDANTS OF WILLIAM CURTIS,
ROXBURY 1632 by Samuel C. Clarke. Repr. of 1899 ed.
Paper—$6.00—29pp--------------------------------------- Vendor #D1842

2769 - AN ACCOUNT OF THE LINEAGE OF GENERAL MOSES CLEAVELAND
OF CANTERBURY, CONNECTICUT....by H. G. Cleveland. Repr. of
1885 ed.
Paper—$4.00—14pp--------------------------------------- Vendor #D1842

2770 - GENEALOGY OF BENJAMIN CLEVELAND, GREAT-GRANDSON OF
MOSES CLEVELAND, OF WOBURN, MASSACHUSETTS. Repr. of 1879 ed.
Cloth—$39.00—Paper—$29.00—260pp----------------------- Vendor #D1842

2771 - A HISTORY OF THE COBB FAMILY, Parts 1-4, by Philip L. Cobb.
Repr. of 1907-1923 eds.
Paper—$40.00—278pp------------------------------------- Vendor #D1842

2772 - THE CODMANS OF CHARLESTOWN AND BOSTON, 1637-1929 by Cora
Codman Wolcott. Repr. of 1930 ed.
Paper—$14.50—94pp-------------------------------------- Vendor #D1842

2773 - COLE FAMILY OF STARK, NEW HAMPSHIRE, DESCENDANTS OF
SOLOMON COLE OF BEVERLY, MASSACHUSETTS by Henry W. Hardon.
Repr. of 1932 ed.
Paper—$15.00—90pp-------------------------------------- Vendor #D1842

2774 - ANCESTORS OF WILLIAM ADAMS COLLORD AND REBECCA SEVERNS,
HIS WIFE by Isora Collord. Repr. of 1899 ed.
Paper—$8.00—43pp--------------------------------------- Vendor #D1842

2775 - FAMILY HISTORY IN THE LINE OF JOSEPH CONVERSE OF BEDFORD, MASSACHUSETTS, 1759-1828 by John J. Putnam. Repr. of 1897 ed.
Paper—$15.00—97pp------------------------------------- Vendor #D1842

2776 - A SHORT BIOGRAPHY OF THE REV. JOHN COTTON AND A COTTON GENEALOGY OF HIS DESCENDANTS by L. C. Cooley. Repr. of 1945 ed.
Paper—$18.00—125pp----------------------------------- Vendor #D1842

2777 - MEMORIALS OF THE CRANES OF CHILTON WITH A PEDIGREE OF THE FAMILY by William Appleton. Repr. of 1868 ed.
Paper—$15.00—86pp------------------------------------ Vendor #D1842

2778 - GENEALOGY OF THE CRANE FAMILY, DESCENDANTS OF HENRY CRANE OF WETHERSFIELD AND GUILFORD by Ellery B. Crane. Repr. of 1895-1900 ed.
Cloth—$125.00—Paper—$115.00—839pp---------------------- Vendor #D1842

2779 - A GENEALOGY OF THE CREHORE FAMILY by Charles F. Crehore. Repr. of 1887 ed.
Paper—$6.50—32pp-------------------------------------- Vendor #D1842

2780 - THE CROCKETT FAMILY OF NEW ENGLAND, 1632-1943 by Leon Crockett. Repr. of 1943 ed.
Paper—$9.00—41pp-------------------------------------- Vendor #D1842

2781 - THE DENNISON FAMILY OF NORTH YARMOUTH AND FREEPORT, MAINE...1699-1747 by G. M. Rogers and A. L. Dennison. Repr. of 1906 ed.
Paper—$22.00—148pp----------------------------------- Vendor #D1842

2782 - THE DESCENDANTS OF NICHOLAS DOE by Elmer E. Doe. Repr. of 1918 ed.
Cloth—$56.00—Paper—$46.00—375pp---------------------- Vendor #D1842

2783 - THE DESCENDANTS OF HENRY DOUDE (DOWD) WHO CAME FROM ENGLAND IN 1639 by W. W. Dowd. Repr. of 1885 ed.
Cloth—$54.00—Paper—$44.00—362pp---------------------- Vendor #D1842

2784 - THE DOWNERS OF AMERICA by David R. Downer. Repr. of 1900 ed.
Paper—$36.50—244pp----------------------------------- Vendor #D1842

2785 - GENEALOGY OF DEACON JOHN DUNHAM OF PLYMOUTH, MASSA-CHUSETTS, 1589-1669....by Isaac Watson. Repr. of 1907 ed.
Cloth—$57.00—Paper—$47.00—384pp---------------------- Vendor #D1842

2786 - GENEALOGY OF THE DURAND, WHALLEY, BARNES AND YALE FAMILIES by Frances B. Hewitt. Repr. of 1912 ed.
Paper—$17.00—115pp----------------------------------- Vendor #D1842

2787 - HISTORY OF THE FANTON FAMILY by Carl A. Fanton. Repr. of 1935 ed.
Paper—$10.00—55pp------------------------------------ Vendor #D1842

2788 - THE FARRINGTON MEMORIAL; A SKETCH OF THE ANCESTORS AND DESCENDANTS OF DEACON JOHN FARRINGTON. Repr. of 1880 ed.
Paper—$5.00—24pp-------------------------------------- Vendor #D1842

2789 - CAPTAIN JONATHAN FARREN OF AMESBURY AND SOME OF HIS DESCENDANTS by Frank M. Ferrin. Repr. of 1941 ed.
Paper—$33.00—222pp----------------------------------- Vendor #D1842

2790 - GENEALOGY OF THE FIELDS OF PROVIDENCE, RHODE ISLAND by Harriet A. Brownell. Repr. of 1878 ed.
Paper—$12.50—65pp------------------------------------ Vendor #D1842

2791 - GENEALOGY OF A FISKE FAMILY, 1399-1867 by Alfred Poor. Repr. of 1867 ed.
Paper—$4.50—20pp-------------------------------------- Vendor #D1842

2792 - HISTORY OF THE FAMILY OF WILLIAM FISKE, SR. OF AMHERST, NEW HAMPSHIRE, 2nd Ed., by Albert A. Fiske. Repr. of 1867 ed.
Paper—$31.00—209pp----------------------------------- Vendor #D1842

2793 - SIMON FORRESTER OF SALEM AND HIS DESCENDANTS by Henry
W. Belknap. Repr. of 1935 ed.
Paper—$10.00—48pp-- Vendor #D1842

2794 - THE DESCENDANTS OF JEHIEL FOX OF CANAAN, HOOSICK FALLS,
AND CHESTER, NEW YORK by George H. Fox. Repr. of 1931 ed.
Paper—$8.00—37pp-- Vendor #D1842

2795 - DESCENDANTS OF THOMAS FOX OF CONCORD, MASSACHUSETTS
THROUGH HIS FIRST SON ELIPHALET by George H. Fox. Repr. of
1931 ed.
Paper—$10.00—49pp-- Vendor #D1842

2796 - DESCENDANTS OF THOMAS FOX OF CONCORD, MASSACHUSETTS
THROUGH HIS THIRD SON SAMUEL OF NEW LONDON by George H.
Fox. Repr. of 1931 ed.
Paper—$10.00—47pp-- Vendor #D1842

2797 - DESCENDANTS OF THOMAS FOX OF CONCORD, MASSACHUSETTS
THROUGH HIS FOURTH SON, JOHN OF NEW LONDON by George H.
Fox. Repr. of 1931 ed.
Paper—$4.00—18pp-- Vendor #D1842

2798 - DESCENDANTS OF THOMAS FOX OF CONCORD, MASSACHUSETTS
THROUGH HIS SIXTH SON, ISAAC, OF MEDFORD AND NEW LONDON
by George H. Fox. Repr. of 1931 ed.
Paper—$10.00—54pp-- Vendor #D1842

2799 - THE SAXON ORIGIN OF THE FRY FAMILIES by George S. Fry.
Repr. of 1928 ed.
Paper—$5.00—27pp-- Vendor #D1842

2800 - A BRIEF HISTORY OF JOHN AND CHRISTIAN FRETZ...FAMILY
REGISTER by A. J. Fretz. Repr. of 1890 ed.
Cloth—$90.00—Paper—$80.00—607pp----------------------- Vendor #D1842

2801 - NOTES ON THE SURNAMES OF FRANCUS, FRANCEIS, FRENCH, ETC.
IN SCOTLAND by A. D. W. French. Repr. of 1893 ed.
Paper—$15.00—109pp-------------------------------------- Vendor #D1842

2802 - INDEX ARMORIAL OF THE SURNAME OF FRENCH, FRANC, FRANCOIS,
ETC. by A. D. W. French. Repr. of 1892 ed.
Paper—$16.00—115pp-------------------------------------- Vendor #D1842

2803 - GENEALOGY OF THE FULLER FAMILIES DESCENDING FROM ROBERT
FULLER OF SALEM AND REHOBETH, MASSACHUSETTS by Newton
Fuller. Repr. of 1898 ed.
Paper—$10.00—50pp-- Vendor #D1842

2804 - RECORDS OF SOME OF THE DESCENDANTS OF JOHN FULLER, NEW-
TON 1644-1698 by Samuel C. Clarke. Repr. of 1869 ed.
Paper—$4.00—16pp-- Vendor #D1842

2805 - A BRIEF HISTORY OF BISHOP HENRY FUNCK AND OTHER FUNK
PIONEERS by A. J. Fretz. Repr. of 1899 ed.
Cloth—$75.00—Paper—$65.00—874pp----------------------- Vendor #D1842

2806 - OUR AMERICAN ANCESTRY (GATES GENEALOGY) by Frederick T.
Gates. Repr. of 1928 ed.
Cloth—$43.00—Paper—$33.00—289pp----------------------- Vendor #D1842

2807 - THE GIBBS FAMILY OF RHODE ISLAND by George Gibbs. Repr. of
1933 ed.
Paper—$30.00—195pp-------------------------------------- Vendor #D1842

2808 - GENEALOGY OF THE GLOVER CLANS by C. M. Glover. Repr. of
1938 ed.
Paper—$10.00—50pp-- Vendor #D1842

2809 - GOODELL MEMORIAL TABLETS by Isaac Goodell. Repr. of 1892 ed.
Paper—$8.00—38pp-- Vendor #D1842

2810   - GRANBERRY FAMILY AND ALLIED FAMILIES by E. F. Waterman and
D. L. Jacobus. Repr. of 1945 ed.
Cloth—$57.00—Paper—$47.00—383pp------------------------- Vendor #D1842

2811   - THE GOODWINS OF E. ANGLIA by Augustus Jessop. Repr. of 1889 ed.
Paper—$8.00—37pp-- Vendor #D1842

2812   - THE FAMILY OF EZRA GREEN; GENEALOGY AND GENERAL FAMILY
HISTORY by Charles R. Green. Repr. of 1893 ed.
Paper—$15.00—98pp-------------------------------------- Vendor #D1842

2813   - A GENEALOGICAL SKETCH OF THE DESCENDANTS OF THOMAS
GREEN OF MALDEN, MASSACHUSETTS by Samuel S. Green. Repr. of
1958 ed.
Paper—$14.50—80pp-------------------------------------- Vendor #D1842

2814   - GREENES OF WARWICK, RHODE ISLAND IN COLONIAL HISTORY by
H. E. Turner. Repr. of 1877 ed.
Paper—$13.50—68pp-------------------------------------- Vendor #D1842

2815   - ANCESTRY AND DESCENDANTS OF HENRY GREGORY by Grant
Gregory. Repr. of 1938 ed.
Cloth—$60.00—Paper—$50.00—402pp----------------------- Vendor #D1842

2816   - RECORDS OF THE GUTHRIE FAMILY OF PENNSYLVANIA, CONNEC-
TICUT, AND VIRGINIA by H. A. and E. G. Dunn. Repr. of 1898 ed.
Paper—$25.50—170pp------------------------------------- Vendor #D1842

2817   - THE HAKES FAMILY, 2nd Ed., by Harry Hakes. Repr. of 1889 ed.
Paper—$33.00—220pp------------------------------------- Vendor #D1842

2818   - THOMAS HALEY OF WINTER HARBOR AND HIS DESCENDANTS by
W. G. Davis and A. Haley. Repr. of 1930 ed.
Paper—$10.50—55pp-------------------------------------- Vendor #D1842

2819   - BRIEF SKETCH OF THE HALLOCK ANCESTRY by John M. Sherman.
Repr. of 1866 ed.
Paper—$4.00—17pp--------------------------------------- Vendor #D1842

2820   - THE HARRIS FAMILY FROM 1630 IN TWO LINES by D. J. Harris and
N. D. Harris. Repr. of 1909 ed.
Paper—$19.50—131pp------------------------------------- Vendor #D1842

2821   - EDWARD HARRIS AND HIS ANCESTORS 1634-1820 by William Johnston. Repr. of 1899 ed.
Paper—$5.00—26pp--------------------------------------- Vendor #D1842

2822   - ANCESTRY OF LYDIA HARMON, 1755-1836, WIFE OF JOSEPH WATER-
HOUSE OF STANDISH, MAINE by Walter Goodwin Davis. Repr. of 1924 ed.
Paper—$19.00—127pp------------------------------------- Vendor #D1842

2823   - A BRIEF HISTORY OF ELKANAH HASKIN AND DESCENDANTS OF HIS
SON ENOCH 1700-1890 by D. C. Haskin. Repr. of 1890 ed.
Paper—$10.00—53pp-------------------------------------- Vendor #D1842

2824   - GENEALOGICAL HISTORY OF THE CONCORD HARWOODS, DESCEN-
DANTS OF NATHANIEL HARWOOD...LONDON, ENGLAND by Watson
H. Harwood. Repr. of 1912 ed.
Paper—$19.00—129pp------------------------------------- Vendor #D1842

2825   - GENEALOGICAL HISTORY OF THE SALEM HARWOODS, DESCENDANTS
OF HENRY AND ELIZABETH HARWOOD...FROM ENGLAND IN 1630 by
Watson H. Harwood. Repr. of 1912 ed.
Paper—$14.00—93pp-------------------------------------- Vendor #D1842

2826   - SERGT. RICHARD HAVEN, 1620-1703, LYNN, MASSACHUSETTS,
"KING PHILIP'S WAR," AND ONE LINE OF HIS DESCENDANTS by
William Haven. Repr. of 1927 ed.
Paper—$15.00—104pp------------------------------------- Vendor #D1842

2827   - A HISTORY OF THE HEVERLY FAMILY INCLUDING OTHER SPELLINGS
by N. F. Mears. Repr. of 1945 ed.
Cloth—$51.00—Paper—340pp----------------------------- Vendor #D1842

2828 - GENEALOGY OF THE HILL FAMILY FROM 1632...BIOGRAPHICAL
       SKETCH OF JOEL BARLOW by Moses Hill. Repr. of 1879 ed.
       Paper—$5.00—29pp-- Vendor #D1842

2829 - A FAMILY RECORD OF DESCENDANTS OF SGT. EDWARD HINMAN OF
       STRATFORD, CONNECTICUT, 1650 by R. R. Hinman. Repr. of 1856 ed.
       Paper—$12.00—80pp-------------------------------------- Vendor #D1842

2830 - THE HOLDEN GENEALOGY. ANCESTRY AND DESCENDANTS OF
       RICHARD AND JUSTINIAN HOLDEN...RANDALL HOLDEN, 2 Vols.,
       by Eben Putnam. Repr. of 1923-1926 eds.
       Cloth—$147.00—Paper—$137.00----------------------------- Vendor #D1842

2831 - HOOD MEMORIALS OF OUR FATHER AND MOTHER; ALSO A FAMILY
       GENEALOGY by George Hood. Repr. of 1867 ed.
       Cloth—$12.00—64pp-------------------------------------- Vendor #D1842

2832 - DESCENDANTS OF REV. THOMAS HOOKER, HARTFORD, CONNECTI-
       CUT, 1586-1908 by Edward Hooker, edited by Margaret Huntington
       Hooker. Repr. of 1909 ed.
       Cloth—$89.00—Paper—$79.00—594pp---------------------- Vendor #D1842

2833 - YE HORSEFORDE BOOKE, THE HORSFORD—HOSFORD FAMILIES IN
       THE UNITED STATES by Henry T. Hosford. Repr. of 1936 ed.
       Paper—$38.50—256pp------------------------------------- Vendor #D1842

2834 - HOSMER GENEALOGY. DESCENDANTS OF JAMES HOSMER...AMERI-
       CA IN 1635, AND SETTLED IN CONCORD, MASSACHUSETTS by
       George Leonard Hosmer. Repr. of 1928 ed.
       Cloth—$42.00—Paper—$32.00----------------------------- Vendor #D1842

2835 - HISTORY AND GENEALOGY OF THE HOUGHTON FAMILY, CANADA
       by an anonymous author. Repr. of 1896 ed.
       Paper—$15.00—100pp------------------------------------- Vendor #D1842

2836 - THE ALFRED HOVEY FAMILY (ALFRED HOVEY—ABIGAIL HOWARD).
       A MEMORANDUM OF BIRTHS, MARRIAGES, AND DEATHS by an anon-
       ymous author. Repr. of 1893 ed.
       Paper—$6.00—31pp-------------------------------------- Vendor #D1842

2837 - THE HOUGHTON ASSOCIATION REPORT OF THE AGENT TO ENG-
       LAND, CONCERNING WILLS AND PROPERTY. Repr. of 1848 ed.
       Paper—$8.50—43pp-------------------------------------- Vendor #D1842

2838 - WALTHALL FAMILY by E. T. Walthall. Repr. of 1906 ed.
       Paper—$7.50—33pp-------------------------------------- Vendor #D1842

2839 - WALTON FAMILY RECORDS 1598-1898, WITH...OAKES AND EASTONS
       AND THE PROCTOR FAMILY by J. P. Walton. Repr. of 1898 ed.
       Paper—$18.00—88pp------------------------------------- Vendor #D1842

2840 - WALTZ FAMILY HISTORY AND GENEALOGICAL RECORD, DESCEN-
       DANTS OF FREDERICK WALTZ by L. Waltz. Repr. of 1884 ed.
       Paper—$25.00—128pp------------------------------------ Vendor #D1842

2841 - WALWORTHS OF AMERICA, FIVE CHAPTERS OF FAMILY HISTORY,
       WITH...GENEALOGY by C. A. Walworth. Repr. of 1897 ed.
       Cloth—$40.00—Paper—$30.00—202pp---------------------- Vendor #D1842

2842 - HISTORY OF THE WANTON FAMILY OF NEWPORT, RHODE ISLAND
       by J. R. Bartlett. repr. of 1878 ed.
       Paper—$30.00—152pp------------------------------------ Vendor #D1842

2843 - HISTORY OF THE WANZER FAMILY IN AMERICA, SETTLED IN NEW
       AMSTERDAM, 1642-1920 by W. D. Wanzer. Repr. of 1920 ed.
       Paper—$25.00—121pp------------------------------------ Vendor #D1842

2844 - GENEALOGY OF JOHN WARBURTON AND DESCENDANTS by Pennin-
       ton and Warburton. Repr. of 1913 ed.
       Paper—$5.00—21pp-------------------------------------- Vendor #D1842

2845 - WARD FAMILY. DESCENDANTS OF WILLIAM WARD, WHO SETTLED
       IN SUDBURY, MASSACHUSETTS, IN 1639....by Andrew Henshaw Ward.
       Repr. of 1851 ed.
       Cloth—$40.00—Paper—$30.00—265pp---------------------- Vendor #D1842

2846 - BRIEF HISTORY OF WARDELL FAMILY 1734-1910 by G. P. Smith.
Repr. of 1910 ed.
Paper—$20.00—104pp-- Vendor #D1842

2847 - THE ANCESTORS, KIN AND DESCENDANTS OF JOHN WARDEN AND
NARCISSA (DAVIS) WARDEN....by William A. Warden. Repr. of 1901 ed.
Paper—$38.00—256pp--------------------------------------- Vendor #D1842

2848 - SKETCHES OF ANTECEDENTS OF SOLOMON WARDWELL, WITH DE-
SCENDANTS OF TWO SONS, EZRA AND AMOS WARDWELL by E. W.
Stay. Repr. of 1905 ed.
Paper—$5.00—22pp--- Vendor #D1842

2849 - WARE GENEALOGY, ROBERT WARE OF DEDHAM, MASSACHUSETTS
1642-1699, AND HIS LINEAL DESCENDANTS by Miss Emma Ware. Repr.
of 1901 ed.
Cloth—$50.00—Paper—$40.00—335pp----------------------- Vendor #D1842

2850 - WARFIELD FAMILY OF MARYLAND by J. D. Warfield. Repr. of
1898 ed.
Paper—$16.50—81pp--------------------------------------- Vendor #D1842

2851 - GENEALOGY OF THE WARNE FAMILY IN AMERICA, PRINCIPALLY
THE DESCENDANTS OF THOMAS WARNE 1652-1722....by Rev. George
Lobaw. Repr. of 1911 ed.
Cloth—$105.00—Paper—$95.00—701pp---------------------- Vendor #D1842

2852 - GENEALOGY OF THE WARREN FAMILY, FROM RICHARD, WHO CAME
IN THE MAYFLOWER IN 1620, TO 1872. Repr. of 1874 ed.
Paper—$3.50—7pp--- Vendor #D1842

2853 - SOME NOTES ON THE EVESHAM BRANCH OF THE WASHBURNE
FAMILY by E. Barnard. Repr. of 1914 ed.
Paper—$12.00—60pp--------------------------------------- Vendor #D1842

2854 - THE WARRINER FAMILY, OF NEW ENGLAND ORIGIN...WILLIAM
WARRINER OF SPRINGFIELD, MASSACHUSETTS...1638-1898 by Rev.
Edwin Warriner. Repr. of 1899 ed.
Cloth—$43.00—Paper—$33.00—287pp---------------------- Vendor #D1842

2855 - THE PEDIGREE AND HISTORY OF THE WASHINGTON FAMILY, DE-
RIVED FROM ODIN, THE FOUNDER OF SCANDINAVIA, B.C. 70....
by Albert Welles. Repr. of 1879 ed.
Cloth—$63.00—Paper—$53.00—420pp----------------------- Vendor #D1842

2856 - AN EXAMINATION OF THE ENGLISH ANCESTRY OF GEORGE WASH-
INGTON...WASHINGTONS OF SULGRAVE AND BRINGTON by Henry
F. Waters. Repr. N. E. Hist. & Gen. Register, 1889 ed.
Paper—$10.50—53pp--------------------------------------- Vendor #D1842

2857 - WATERHOUSE AND OTHER FAMILIES OF STROUDWATER VILLAGE,
MAINE by L. D. Chapman. Repr. of 1906 ed.
Paper—$6.50—31pp-- Vendor #D1842

2858 - ANCESTRY OF WATERS FAMILY OF MARIETTA, OHIO by W. Waters.
Repr. of 1882 ed.
Paper—$6.50—32pp-- Vendor #D1842

2859 - A GENEALOGICAL HISTORY OF THE WATERS AND KINDRED FAM-
ILIES by Philemon B. Waters. Repr. of 1902 ed.
Paper—$28.00—189pp-------------------------------------- Vendor #D1842

2860 - JOHN WATSON OF HARTFORD, CONNECTICUT, AND HIS DESCEN-
DANTS; A GENEALOGY by Thomas Watson. Repr. of 1865 ed.
Paper—$10.00—47pp--------------------------------------- Vendor #D1842

2861 - CATALOGUE OF THOMAS WATKINS OF CHICKAHOMONY IN VIR-
GINIA by F. N. Watkins. Repr. of 1899 ed.
Paper—$10.00—50pp--------------------------------------- Vendor #D1842

2862 - THE WATTERS FAMILY by D. A. Watters. Repr. of 1915 ed.
Paper—$5.00—23pp-- Vendor #D1842

2863 – WATTS (WATT) IN NEW YORK AND SCOTLAND, ALSO WATTES, WATTYS, WATHES, ETC. IN ENGLAND by A. Welles. Repr. of 1898 ed.
Paper—$10.00—48pp--- Vendor #D1842

2864 – GEORGE WAY AND HIS DESCENDANTS 1628-1821 by C. G. Way. Repr. of 1887 ed.
Paper—$5.00—23pp-- Vendor #D1842

2865 – ENGLISH ANCESTORS OF THE WAYNE FAMILY, OF PENNSYLVANIA by E. J. Sellers. Repr. of 1927 ed.
Paper—$12.00—56pp--- Vendor #D1842

2866 – WEAVER FAMILY MARRIAGES by W. M. Clemens. Repr. of 1916 ed.
Paper—$6.50—32pp-- Vendor #D1842

2867 – GENEALOGICAL NOTES OF THE WEBB FAMILY by Edward Stanley Waters. Repr. Essex Inst. Hist. Coll., 1880 ed.
Paper—$5.00—24pp-- Vendor #D1842

2868 – DESCENDANTS OF ANDREW WEBBER 1763-1845 by L. Webber. Repr. of 1897 ed.
Paper—$11.00—55pp--- Vendor #D1842

2869 – RICHARD WEBBER FAMILY, GENEALOGY FROM THE FIRST SETTLE-MENT IN AMERICA by L. Washburn. Repr. of 1909 ed.
Paper—$6.00—25pp-- Vendor #D1842

2870 – GENEALOGY OF SOME DESCENDANTS OF JOHN WEBSTER, OF IPS-WICH, MASSACHUSETTS, IN 1635, the earlier families compiled by William B. Lapham, and the later by J. O. Webster. Repr. of 1884 ed.
Paper—$4.50—14pp-- Vendor #D1842

2871 – GENEALOGICAL SKETCH OF DESCENDANTS...WEBBER FAMILY, WHO CAME TO NEW YORK AND NEW ENGLAND...SEVENTEENTH CENTURY by A. Button. Repr. of 1878 ed.
Paper—$9.00—42pp-- Vendor #D1842

2872 – GENEALOGY OF ONE BRANCH OF THE WEBSTER FAMILY, FROM THOMAS WEBSTER OF ORMSEBY, COUNTY NORFOLK, ENGLAND by Prentiss Webster. Repr. of 1894 ed.
Paper—$9.00—45pp-- Vendor #D1842

2873 – SOME OF THE DESCENDANTS OF JOHN WEBSTER OF IPSWICH, MASSACHUSETTS, 1634 by John C. Webster. Repr. of 1912 ed.
Paper—$15.00—92pp--- Vendor #D1842

2874 – GENEALOGY OF THE FAMILY OF GEORGE WEEKES, OF DORCHESTER, MASSACHUSETTS, 1635-1650...THOMAS OF HUNTINGTON, LONG ISLAND by Robert D. Weeks. Repr. of 1885 ed.
Cloth—$70.00—Paper—$60.00—468pp------------------------ Vendor #D1842

2875 – LEONARD WEEKS OF GREENLAND, NEW HAMPSHIRE AND DE-SCENDANTS 1639-1888, WITH...FAMILIES CONNECTED by J. Chapman. Repr. of 1889 ed.
Paper—$35.00—202pp-- Vendor #D1842

2876 – ANCESTORS AND DESCENDANTS OF DANIEL WEIS, "GENTLEMAN-AT-ARMS," 1629 by Frederick Lewis Weis. Repr. of 1927 ed.
Paper—$9.00—45pp-- Vendor #D1842

2877 – WEITZEL MEMORIAL, HISTORY AND GENEALOGICAL RECORD OF DESCENDANTS OF PAUL WEITZEL OF LANCASTER, PENNSYLVANIA, 1740 by H. E. Hayden. Repr. of 1883 ed.
Paper—$17.00—81pp--- Vendor #D1842

2878 – A FEW FACTS CONCERNING ROGER WELLINGTON AND SOME OF HIS DESCENDANTS by A. W. Griswold. Repr. of 1892 ed.
Paper—$6.00—26pp-- Vendor #D1842

2879 – GENEALOGY AND HISTORY OF THE WELLMANS OF NEW ENGLAND by J. Wellman. Repr. of 1867 ed.
Paper—$13.00—66pp--- Vendor #D1842

2880 - DESCENDANTS OF THOMAS WELLMAN OF LYNN, MASSACHUSETTS
by Joshua Wyman Wellman. Repr. of 1918 ed.
Cloth—$89.00—Paper—$79.00—596pp------------------------ Vendor #D1842

2881 - GENEALOGY OF WELLS FAMILY OF WELLS, MAINE by C. K. Wells.
Repr. of 1874 ed.
Paper—$16.50—81pp--------------------------------------- Vendor #D1842

2882 - WILLIAM WELLS OF SOUTHOLD AND HIS DESCENDANTS, 1638-1878
by Charles W. Hayes. Repr. of 1878 ed.
Cloth—$45.00—Paper—$35.00—300pp----------------------- Vendor #D1842

2883 - WILLIAM WELLS AND HIS DESCENDANTS, 1755-1909 by Frederic
Wells. Repr. of 1909 ed.
Paper—$17.50—117pp-------------------------------------- Vendor #D1842

2884 - WENDELL FAMILY OF HOLLAND AND AMERICA by E. E. Salisbury.
Repr. of 1885 ed.
Paper—$4.00—15pp-- Vendor #D1842

2885 - DIRECT ANCESTORS OF THE LATE JACOB WENDELL OF PORTS-
MOUTH, NEW HAMPSHIRE...NEW NETHERLAND SETTLEMENT 1614-1664
by J. Stanwood. Repr. of 1882 ed.
Paper—$10.00—49pp--------------------------------------- Vendor #D1842

2886 - RECORD OF DESCENDANTS OF JOHANN JOST WENTZ by R. W.
Wentz. Repr. of 1884 ed.
Paper—$18.50—89pp--------------------------------------- Vendor #D1842

2887 - THE WETMORE FAMILY OF AMERICA AND ITS COLLATERAL BRANCHES
by James C. Wetmore. Repr. of 1861 ed.
Cloth—$101.00—Paper—$91.00—672pp---------------------- Vendor #D1842

2888 - GENEALOGY OF WESTERVELT FAMILY by Westervelt and Dicksinson.
Repr. of 1905 ed.
Paper—$25.00—175pp-------------------------------------- Vendor #D1842

2889 - DESCENDANTS OF EDMUND WESTON OF DUXBURY, MASSACHU-
SETTS FOR FIVE GENERATIONS by Thomas Weston, Jr. Repr. N. E.
Hist. & Gen. Register, 1887 ed.
Paper—$5.00—23pp-- Vendor #D1842

2890 - GENEALOGY OF THE WHEATLEY OR WHEATLEIGH FAMILY...FAMILY
IN ENGLAND AND AMERICA by Hannibal P. Wheatley. Repr. of 1902 ed.
Paper—$23.00—154pp-------------------------------------- Vendor #D1842

2891 - GENEALOGY OF SOME DESCENDANTS OF OBADIAH WHEELER OF
CONCORD, AND THOMAS THAXTER OF HINGHAM by Henry M.
Wheeler. Repr. of 1898 ed.
Paper—$14.00—74pp--------------------------------------- Vendor #D1842

2892 - AMERICAN ANCESTORS OF THE CHILDREN OF JOSEPH AND DANIELLA
WHEELER OF WHOM WE HAVE RECORDS by Joseph and Daniella Wheeler.
Repr. of 1896 ed.
Paper—$5.00—24pp-- Vendor #D1842

2893 - WHEELER AND WARREN FAMILIES, DESCENDANTS OF GEORGE
WHEELER OF CONCORD 1638, AND JOHN WARREN OF BOSTON 1630
by H. Wheeler. Repr. of 1892 ed.
Paper—$24.00—121pp-------------------------------------- Vendor #D1842

2894 - WHEELER FAMILY OF RUTLAND, MASSACHUSETTS, AND SOME OF
THEIR ANCESTORS by Daniel M. Wheeler. Repr. of 1924 ed.
Paper—$24.00—137pp-------------------------------------- Vendor #D1842

2895 - WHEELWRIGHT, A FRONTIER FAMILY by E. M. Wheelwright. Repr.
of 1894 ed.
Paper—$10.00—35pp--------------------------------------- Vendor #D1842

2896 - BRIEF GENEALOGY OF WHIPPLE FAMILY WHO SETTLED IN RHODE
ISLAND by H. E. Whipple. Repr. of 1873 ed.
Paper—$12.50—63pp--------------------------------------- Vendor #D1842

2897 - BRIEF GENEALOGY OF THE WHIPPLE FAMILY by J. A. Boutelle.
      Repr. of 1857 ed.
      Paper—$8.00—36pp-- Vendor #D1842

2898 - GENEALOGICAL RECORD OF ANTIGONISH, NOVA SCOTIA WHIDDEN
      FAMILY by D. G. Whidden. Repr. of 1930 ed.
      Paper—$5.00—24pp-- Vendor #D1842

2899 - DESCENDANTS OF CHASE WHITCHER OF WARREN, NEW HAMPSHIRE,
      ...THOMAS WHITTIER OF SALISBURY (HAVERHILL), MASSACHU-
      SETTS by William F. Whitcher. Repr. of 1907 ed.
      Paper—$20.00—135pp-- Vendor #D1842

2900 - GENEALOGICAL NOTES OF THE WHIPPLE-HILL FAMILIES...RECORDS
      OF OTHER FAMILIES by John Whipple Hill. Repr. of 1897 ed.
      Paper—$20.00—106pp-- Vendor #D1842

2901 - THE WHITCOMB FAMILY IN AMERICA, A BIOGRAPHICAL GENEALOGY
      by Charlotte Whitcomb. Repr. of 1904 ed.
      Cloth—$93.00—Paper—$83.00—621pp------------------------ Vendor #D1842

2902 - GENEALOGY OF WHITE FAMILY by J. Nichols-Vanderpool. Repr.
      of 1899 ed.
      Paper—$20.00—104pp-- Vendor #D1842

2903 - MEMOIRS OF ELDER JOHN WHITE, ONE OF THE FIRST SETTLERS OF
      HARTFORD, CONNECTICUT....by Allyn Kellogg. Repr. of 1860 ed.
      Cloth—$51.00—Paper—$41.00—340pp------------------------ Vendor #D1842

2904 - DESCENDANTS OF THOMAS WHITE OF MARBLEHEAD, AND MARK
      HASKELL OF BEVERLY...COOMBS FAMILY by Perley Derby. Repr.
      of 1872 ed.
      Paper—$14.50—82pp--- Vendor #D1842

2905 - DESCENDANTS OF WILLIAM WHITE, OF HAVERHILL, MASSACHU-
      SETTS....by Daniel Appleton White; ADDITIONAL GENEALOGICAL
      AND BIOGRAPHICAL NOTIES by Annie Frances Richards. Repr. of
      1863/1889 eds.
      Paper—$14.50—80pp--- Vendor #D1842

2906 - 1632-1892. MEMORIALS OF RODERICK WHITE AND HIS WIFE LUCY
      BLAKESLEE, OF PARIS HILL, NEW YORK....by Andrew C. White.
      Repr. of 1892 ed.
      Paper—$6.50—32pp-- Vendor #D1842

2907 - ANCESTRY OF JOHN BARBER WHITE AND OF HIS DESCENDANTS by
      Almira Larkin White. Repr. of 1913 ed.
      Cloth—$53.00—Paper—$43.00—355pp------------------------ Vendor #D1842

2908 - A BRIEF ACCOUNT OF THE FAMILIES OF WHITE AND CLARKE by
      James Clarke White. Repr. of 1915 ed.
      Paper—$7.50—37pp-- Vendor #D1842

2909 - MEMOIR OF JOHN WHITMAN AND HIS DESCENDANTS by E. Whitman.
      Repr. of 1832 ed.
      Paper—$10.00—44pp--- Vendor #D1842

2910 - HISTORY OF THE DESCENDANTS OF JOHN WHITMAN OF WEYMOUTH,
      MASSACHUSETTS by Charles H. Farnam. Repr. of 1889 ed.
      Cloth—$189.00—Paper—$169.00—1261pp---------------------- Vendor #D1842

2911 - WHITMORE GENEALOGY, RECORD OF DESCENDANTS OF FRANCIS
      WHITMORE OF CAMBRIDGE by J. Purdy. Repr. of 1907 ed.
      Paper—$30.00—158pp-- Vendor #D1842

2912 - RECORD OF DESCENDANTS OF FRANCIS WHITMORE OF CAMBRIDGE
      by W. H. Whitmore. Repr. of 1855 ed.
      Paper—$5.00—24pp-- Vendor #D1842

2913 - ANCESTRY OF JOHN WHITNEY, WHO EMIGRATED FROM LONDON IN
      1635, AND SETTLED IN WATERTOWN, MASSACHUSETTS....by Henry
      Melville. Repr. of 1896 ed.
      Cloth—$47.00—Paper—$37.00—313pp------------------------ Vendor #D1842

2914   - WHITNEY. DESCENDANTS OF JOHN WHITNEY, WHO CAME FROM LONDON, ENGLAND, TO WATERTOWN, MASSACHUSETTS, IN 1635 by Frederick Clifton Pierce. Repr. of 1895 ed.
Cloth—$95.00—Paper—$85.00—692pp------------------------ Vendor #D1842

2915   - NOTES ON THE WHITMORES OF MADELEY, ENGLAND, AND THE FARRARS AND BREWERS OF ESSEX COUNTY, MASSACHUSETTS by William Henry Whitmore. Repr. of 1875 ed.
Paper—$9.50—47pp------------------------------------- Vendor #D1842

2916   - GENEALOGY OF THE WHITTELSEY—WHITTLESEY FAMILY by Charles B. Whittelsey. Repr. of 1898 ed.
Cloth—$62.00—Paper—$52.00—414pp------------------------ Vendor #D1842

2917   - GENEALOGY OF SEVERAL BRANCHES OF THE WHITTEMORE FAMILY by B. B. Whittemore. Repr. of 1893 ed.
Paper—$25.00—132pp----------------------------------- Vendor #D1842

2918   - GENEALOGY OF SEVERAL BRANCHES OF THE WHITTEMORE FAMILY, ...BRIEF LINEAGE OF OTHER BRANCHES by B. B. Whittemore. Repr. of 1890 ed.
Paper—$16.00—106pp----------------------------------- Vendor #D1842

2919   - ANCESTORS OF REV. WILLIAMS HOWE WHITTEMORE, BOLTON, CONNECTICUT, 1800—RYE, NEW YORK...WIFE MARIA CLARK....by William Plumb Bacon. Repr. of 1907 ed.
Paper—$20.00—133pp----------------------------------- Vendor #D1842

2920   - MEMORIAL OF THE WHITTLESEY FAMILY IN THE UNITED STATES published by The Whittlesey Assn. Repr. of 1855 ed.
Paper—$20.00—131pp----------------------------------- Vendor #D1842

2921   - GENEALOGY OF THE WHITTELSEY—WHITTLESEY FAMILY by Charles Barney Whittelsey. Repr. of 1898 ed.
Cloth—$62.00—Paper—$52.00—414pp------------------------ Vendor #D1842

2922   - THE WIGHTS. THOMAS WIGHT OF DEDHAM AND MEDFIELD... DESCENDANTS, 1635-1890 by William W. Wight. Repr. of 1890 ed.
Cloth—$55.00—Paper—$45.00—368pp------------------------ Vendor #D1842

2923   - GENEALOGICAL RECORD OF THE WILBUR FAMILY by Asa Wilbur. Repr. of 1871 ed.
Paper—$14.50—89pp------------------------------------- Vendor #D1842

2924   - GENEALOGICAL RECORD OF THE WILBUR FAMILY by Asa Wilbur. Repr. of 1871 ed.
Paper—$14.50—89pp------------------------------------- Vendor #D1842

2925   - BOOK OF THE WILDERS. HISTORY FROM 1497 IN ENGLAND, THE EMIGRATION OF MARTHA...TO MASSACHUSETTS BAY IN 1638.... by Rev. Moses Wilder. Repr. of 1878 ed.
Cloth—$61.50—Paper—$51.50—410pp------------------------ Vendor #D1842

2926   - (WILDES) FAMILY OF ESSEX COUNTY, MASSACHUSETTS by Walter Davis. Repr. of 1906 ed.
Paper—$10.00—61pp------------------------------------- Vendor #D1842

2927   - MEMOIR OF THE WILKINSON FAMILY IN AMERICA...AND THEIR DESCENDANTS 1645-1868 by Rev. Israel Wilkinson. Repr. of 1869 ed.
Cloth—$88.00—Paper—$78.00—589pp------------------------ Vendor #D1842

2928   - GENEALOGY OF THE WILLCOMB FAMILY OF NEW ENGLAND (1665-1902)...IPSWICH, MASSACHUSETTS by Oliver Clifton Willcomb. Repr. of 1902 ed.
Cloth—$45.00—Paper—$35.00—302pp------------------------ Vendor #D1842

2929   - ISAAC WILLEY OF NEW LONDON, CONNECTICUT, AND HIS DE-SCENDANTS by Henry Willey. Repr. of 1888 ed.
Paper—$28.00—189pp----------------------------------- Vendor #D1842

2930   - THE GROVES, AND LAPPAN (MONAGHAN COUNTY, IRELAND)... IN SEARCH OF THE GENEALOGY OF THE WILLIAMS FAMILY by John Fletcher Williams. Repr. of 1889 ed.
Paper—$13.50—68pp------------------------------------- Vendor #D1842

2931 - GENEALOGY AND HISTORY OF THE FAMILY OF WILLIAMS IN AMERI-
CA...ROBERT WILLIAMS OF ROXBURY by Stephen W. Williams.
Repr. of 1847 ed.
Cloth—$63.50—Paper—$53.50—424pp----------------------- Vendor #D1842

2932 - GENEALOGICAL NOTES OF THE WILLIAMS AND GALLUP FAMILIES...
CAPTAIN JOHN GOLLOP, SR. OF BOSTON, MASSACHUSETTS by
Charles Fish Williams. Repr. of 1897 ed.
Paper—$20.50—136pp------------------------------------- Vendor #D1842

2933 - GENEALOGY OF SAMUEL WILLIAMS OF GRAFTON, NEW HAMPSHIRE
...FROM RICHARD WILLIAMS OF TAUNTON by Josiah H. Drummond.
Repr. of 1899 ed.
Paper—$4.50—20pp------------------------------------- Vendor #D1842

2934 - ANCESTORS AND DESCENDANTS OF EZEKIEL WILLIAMS OF WETHERS-
FIELD, 1608-1907 by Mary Dyer (Williams) McLean. Repr. of 1907 ed.
Paper—$15.00—92pp------------------------------------- Vendor #D1842

2935 - DESCENDANTS OF VEACH WILLIAMS OF LEBANON, CONNECTICUT
by A. H. Wright. Repr. of 1887 ed.
Paper—$28.00—186pp------------------------------------- Vendor #D1842

2936 - GENEALOGICAL RECORDS OF WILLIAMSON FAMILY IN AMERICA
by J. A. Williamson. Repr. of 1896 ed.
Paper—$6.00—26pp------------------------------------- Vendor #D1842

2937 - THE WILLIAMSON AND COBB FAMILIES IN THE LINES OF CALEB AND
MARY (COBB) WILLIAMSON....by Frank Farnsworth Starr. Repr. of
1896 ed.
Paper—$12.50—66pp------------------------------------- Vendor #D1842

2938 - SKETCH OF THE WILLIS FAMILY, FREDERICKSBURG BRANCH by
B. C. Willis. Repr. of 1909 ed.
Paper—$22.50—116pp------------------------------------- Vendor #D1842

2939 - WILLISTON GENEALOGY. JOSEPH WILLISTON AND JOSEPH WILLIS-
TON, JR., 1667-1747...WITH ALLIED BRANCHES, 1734-1912 by A.
Lyman Williston. Repr. of 1912 ed.
Paper—$5.50—28pp------------------------------------- Vendor #D1842

2940 - THE WILLOUGHBY FAMILY OF NEW ENGLAND by Isaac J. Greenwood.
Repr. N. E. Hist. & Gen. Register, 1876 ed.
Paper—$4.50—15pp------------------------------------- Vendor #D1842

2941 - ANCESTORS AND DESCENDANTS OF JAMES AND ANN WILLITS OF
LITTLE EGG HARBOR, NEW JERSEY by Alfred C. Willits. Repr. of
1898 ed.
Paper—$6.00—30pp------------------------------------- Vendor #D1842

2942 - GENEALOGY OF THE FAMILY OF ELIHU PARSONS WILSON OF KIT-
TERY, MAINE....by Fred A. Wilson. Repr. of 1894 ed.
Paper—$7.50—38pp------------------------------------- Vendor #D1842

2943 - GENEALOGICAL AND PSYCHOLOGICAL MEMOIR OF PHILIPPE MATON
WILTSEE AND HIS DESCENDANTS...AND ITS COLONIES, PART 1 by
Jerome Wiltsee, Sr. Repr. of 1908 ed.
Cloth—$45.50—Paper—$35.50—304pp----------------------- Vendor #D1842

2944 - THE WINCHELL GENEALOGY. THOSE BORN TO THE WINCHELL
NAME IN AMERICA SINCE 1635...NOTES ON THE WINCOLL FAMILY,
2nd Ed., by Newton and Alexander Winchell. Repr. of 1917 ed.
Cloth—$85.00—Paper—$75.00—566pp----------------------- Vendor #D1842

2945 - JOHN WINCHESTER AND ONE LINE OF HIS DESCENDANTS by G. R.
Presson. Repr. of 1897 ed.
Paper—$9.00—45pp------------------------------------- Vendor #D1842

2946 - WINCHESTER NOTES by Mrs. Fanny Winchester Hotchkiss. Repr.
of 1912 ed.
Cloth—$56.00—Paper—$46.00—375pp----------------------- Vendor #D1842

2947 - JOHN WINCHESTER OF NEW ENGLAND AND SOME OF HIS DESCEN-
DANTS by Henry Winchester Cunningham. Repr. N. E. Hist. & Gen.
Register, 1925 ed.
Paper—$21.00—139pp-------------------------------------- Vendor #D1842

2948 - HISTORICAL AND GENEALOGICAL REGISTER OF JOHN WING OF
SANDWICH, MASSACHUSETTS...1662-1881 by Rev. Conway Wing.
Repr. of 1881 ed.
Cloth—$51.00—Paper—$41.00—340pp----------------------- Vendor #D1842

2949 - HISTORY OF THE WINGATE FAMILY IN ENGLAND AND AMERICA
WITH GENEALOGICAL TABLES by Charles E. Wingate. Repr. of
1886 ed.
Cloth—$44.00—Paper—$34.00—293pp----------------------- Vendor #D1842

2950 - WINSTON OF VIRGINIA AND ALLIED FAMILIES by Clayton Torrence.
Repr. of 1927 ed.
Cloth—$75.00—Paper—$65.00—501pp----------------------- Vendor #D1842

2951 - GENEALOGICAL ACCOUNT OF ANCIENT WINSOR FAMILY IN UNITED
STATES by O. Winsor. Repr. of 1847 ed.
Paper—$3.50—13pp-- Vendor #D1842

2952 - A SHORT ACCOUNT OF THE WINTHROP FAMILY by Robert C. Winthrop, Jr. Repr. of 1887 ed.
Paper—$4.00—16pp-- Vendor #D1842

2953 - SOME ACCOUNT OF THE EARLY GENERATIONS OF THE WINTHROP
FAMILY IN IRELAND by R. C. Winthrop, Jr. Repr. of 1883 ed.
Paper—$5.00—24pp-- Vendor #D1842

2954 - EVIDENCES OF THE WINTHROPS OF GROTON, COUNTY SUFFOLK,
ENGLAND...WITH WHOM THEY INTERMARRIED edited by Joseph James
Muskett, assisted by Robert C. Winthrop, Jr. Repr. of 1894-1896 eds.
Paper—$26.00—174pp------------------------------------- Vendor #D1842

2955 - WOLCOTT GENEALOGY. THE FAMILY OF HENRY WOLCOTT...
SETTLERS OF WINDSOR, CONNECTICUT by Chandler Wolcott. Repr.
of 1912 ed.
Cloth—$72.00—Paper—$62.00—480pp----------------------- Vendor #D1842

2956 - A WISWALL LINE, TEN GENERATIONS IN DESCENDANTS FROM
THOMAS WISWALL OF DORCHESTER 1635 by C. A. Wiswall. Repr. of
1925 ed.
Paper—$12.50—57pp-- Vendor #D1842

2957 - GENEALOGY OF THE LINEAL DESCENDANTS OF WILLIAM WOOD WHO
SETTLED IN CONCORD, MASSACHUSETTS, IN 1638....by Clay W.
Holmes. Repr. of 1901 ed.
Cloth—$54.50—Paper—$44.50—365pp----------------------- Vendor #D1842

2958 - DESCENDANTS OF THE TWIN BROTHERS JOHN AND BENJAMIN WOOD
by James A. Wood. Repr. of 1902 ed.
Paper—$28.00—187pp------------------------------------- Vendor #D1842

2959 - THE WOOD FAMILY, SACKYVILLE, N. B., BEING A GENEALOGY OF
THE LINE OF THOMAS WOOD OF ROWLEY, MASSACHUSETTS....by
James Allen Kibble. Repr. of 1904 ed.
Paper—$9.00—46pp-- Vendor #D1842

2960 - GENEALOGY OF ONE BRANCH OF THE WOOD FAMILY 1638-1870 by
T. W. Valentine. Repr. of 1871 ed.
Paper—$5.00—26pp-- Vendor #D1842

2961 - JOHN WOODBURY AND SOME OF HIS DESCENDANTS...FOUND AMONG
THE MANUSCRIPTS OF THE LATE PERLEY DERBY. Repr. Essex Inst.
Hist. Coll., 1900 ed.
Paper—$5.00—24pp-- Vendor #D1842

2962 - GENEALOGICAL SKETCHES OF THE WOODBURY FAMILY, ITS INTER-
MARRIAGES AND CONNECTIONS by Charles Levi Woodbury, edited by
E. Woodbury. Repr. of 1904 ed.
Paper—$37.50—215pp------------------------------------- Vendor #D1842

2963 - HISTORY OF THE WOODCOCK FAMILY 1692-1912 by W. L. Woodcock.
Repr. of 1913 ed.
Paper—$12.00—62pp--- Vendor #D1842

2964 - THE WOODMANS OF BUXTON, MAINE by Cyrus Woodman. Repr. of
1874 ed.
Paper—$19.50—131pp--- Vendor #D1842

2965 - MATTHEW WOODRUFF OF FARMINGTON, CONNECTICUT 1640, AND
TEN GENERATIONS OF HIS DESCENDANTS by Mackenzie, Stewart, and
Woodruff. Repr. of 1925 ed.
Paper—$6.50—29pp--- Vendor #D1842

2966 - THE WOODRUFFS OF NEW JERSEY, WHO CAME FROM FORDWICH,
KENT, ENGLAND...REVISED...FROM "A BRANCH OF THE WOODRUFF
STOCK" by Francis E. Woodruff. Repr. of 1909 ed.
Paper—$21.50—143pp--- Vendor #D1842

2967 - MATTHEW WOODWELL OF SALEM, MASSACHUSETTS, AND HIS DE-
SCENDANTS by William H. Woodwell. Repr. Essex Inst. Hist. Coll.,
1910 ed.
Paper—$4.50—21pp--- Vendor #D1842

2968 - DESCENDANTS OF WALTER WOODWORTH OF SCITUATE, MASSA-
CHUSETTS by Elijah B. Woodworth. Repr. of 1901 ed.
Paper—$14.00—70pp--- Vendor #D1842

2969 - DESCENDANTS OF RICHARD AND HANNAH HUGGINS WOOLWORTH,
WHO LANDED AT NEWBURY, MASSACHUSETTS, 1678....by Charlotte
R. Woolworth, assisted by Josephine L. Kimpton. Repr. of 1893 ed.
Paper—$31.00—209pp--- Vendor #D1842

2970 - THE WORCESTER FAMILY; OR, DESCENDANTS OF REV. WILLIAM
WORCESTER, WITH...CONNECTICUT WOOSTER FAMILY by J. F.
Worcester. Repr. of 1856 ed.
Paper—$17.00—112pp--- Vendor #D1842

2971 - HISTORY OF THE WRIGHT FAMILY, WHO ARE DESCENDANTS OF
SAMUEL WRIGHT (1722-1789), OF LENOX, MASSACHUSETTS....by
William Henry Wright and Gertrude Wright Ketcham. Repr. of 1913 ed.
Paper—$35.00—235pp--- Vendor #D1842

2972 - WRIGHT FAMILY MEMORIALS by A. E. Matthews. Repr. of 1886 ed.
Paper—$8.50—42pp--- Vendor #D1842

2973 - WRIGHT FAMILY OF CONNECTICUT by S. V. Talcott. Repr. of
1912 ed.
Paper—$4.00—20pp--- Vendor #D1842

2974 - THE GENEALOGY OF THE WYATT FAMILY by Alden H. Wyatt. Repr.
of 1921 ed.
Paper—$7.00—35pp--- Vendor #D1842

2975 - WYNKOOP GENEALOGY IN THE UNITED STATES by R. Wynkoop.
Repr. of 1878 ed.
Paper—$25.00—130pp--- Vendor #D1842

2976 - YALE FAMILY DESCENDANTS OF DAVID YALE by Elihu Yale. Repr.
of 1850 ed.
Paper—$30.00—201pp--- Vendor #D1842

2977 - GENEALOGY OF THE YARDLEY FAMILY, 1402-1881 by Thomas W.
Yardley. Repr. of 1881 ed.
Paper—$38.50—257pp--- Vendor #D1842

2978 - THE YATES BOOK. WILLIAM YATES AND HIS DESCENDANTS...
WILLIAM YATES (1772-1868) OF GREENWOOD, MAINE, AND HIS WIFE,
MARTHA MORGAN....by Edgar Yates. Repr. of 1906 ed.
Paper—$10.00—51pp--- Vendor #D1842

2979 - HISTORY OF THE YEAGER FAMILY OF PENNSYLVANIA by J. M.
Yeager. Repr. of 1912 ed.
Paper—$22.50—110pp--- Vendor #D1842

1498 - Family Genealogies

2980 - CHRONICLE OF THE YERKES FAMILY, WITH NOTES ON THE LEECH
AND RUTTER FAMILIES by Josiah G. Leach. Repr. of 1904 ed.
Cloth—$41.00—Paper—$35.00—274pp---------------------- Vendor #D1842

2981 - YOUNGS FAMILY. VICAR CHRISTOPHER YONGES, HIS ANCESTORS
IN ENGLAND AND HIS DESCENDANTS IN AMERICA by Selah Youngs, Jr.
Repr. of 1907 ed.
Cloth—$58.00—Paper—$48.00—385pp---------------------- Vendor #D1842

2982 - THOMAS YOUNGS OF OYSTER BAY AND HIS DESCENDANTS by Rev.
C. Youngs. Repr. of 1890 ed.
Paper—$21.00—142pp----------------------------------- Vendor #D1842

2983 - MOTLEY ANCESTRAL GLEANINGS by American Motley Association;
Thomas Motley-Freeman, editor.
(Family History and Genealogy Periodical)
A booklet type periodical, averages 20 pages/issue. Complemented by
Kinsfolk (Newsletter). Distributed to Association members. All
Motleys (including variegated spellings) and all allied family members
are cordially invited to join.
Annual membership dues—$8.00; Single copies—$4.00------- Vendor #D0002

2984 - A WILLIAMS CHRONICLE—DESCENDANTS OF THOMAS WILLIAMS OF
SULLIVAN COUNTY, NEW YORK AND JEFFERSON COUNTY, PENNSYL-
VANIA by Frances H. Ehrig. 1970.
Indexed. Surnames Horton, Morris, Hickox, Foster, Elwood, Rice,
Zum Brunnen, Nolph, Crissman, Hastings, Edelblute, McKnight.
Branches in Green County, Wisconsin; Montgomery County, Iowa;
Converse and Niobrara Counties, Wyoming. Photos and maps.
Cloth—$8.00—198pp----------------------------------- Vendor #D0013

2985 - MEEKER FAMILY OF EARLY NEW JERSEY FROM PAPERS OF CHARLES
H. MEEKER by Leroy J. Meeker. 1974.
Paper—$8.00—375pp---------------------------------- Vendor #D0017

2986 - THE WEEKS FAMILY OF SOUTHERN NEW JERSEY by Elmer Garfield
Van Name.
Weeks: A detailed work on the Weeks, Wicks, Wyke families of South
Jersey.
Paper—$2.75—67pp----------------------------------- Vendor #D0019

2987 - LETTERS AND PAPERS OF RICHARD SOMERS by Frank Stewart. 1942.
Somers: Excerpts of Somers' life from his midshipman days of 1798 to
1804 in United States Navy. Somers was from Atlantic County, New
Jersey.
Paper—$1.75—36pp----------------------------------- Vendor #D0019

2988 - THE LEEK FAMILY OF SOUTHERN NEW JERSEY by Helen Leek Mack.
1975.
Leek: South Jersey descendants of Philip Leek, who came to America
in 1640.
Paper—$7.50—200pp---------------------------------- Vendor #D0019

2989 - THE EASTLACK FAMILY by John William Eastlack, Sr. 1982 Repr.
of 1971 ed.
Eastlack: Gloucester County, New Jersey.
Descendants of Francis Estlack of England, who settled in Old Gloucester
County, New Jersey in late 1600's.
Paper—$9.50—138pp---------------------------------- Vendor #D0019

2990 - BRITTON GENEALOGY by Elmer Garfield Van Name. 1964.
Britton: Fine study of the Britton, Britaine, Britten family from
England to Staten Island, New York.
Paper—$2.75—34pp----------------------------------- Vendor #D0019

2991 - THE JOSEPH SMITH FAMILY OF GLOUCESTER AND SALEM COUNTIES
—THE JAMES DYE FAMILY OF GLOUCESTER COUNTY by Elmer Gar-
field Van Name. 1976 repr. of 1964 ed.
Smith: Gloucester County, New Jersey—1762-1841.
Dye: Salem and Gloucester Counties, New Jersey—1742-1835.
Paper—$2.75—32pp----------------------------------- Vendor #D0019

2992 - PIERRE CRESSON, THE HUGUENOT OF STATEN ISLAND, PENNSYL-
VANIA AND NEW JERSEY PROGENY. 1968.
Cresson: France—1609-1657; Delaware (state)—1657-1679;
Long Island—1679-ca 1681.
Paper—$1.75—21pp-- Vendor #D0019

2993 - GENEALOGY OF JOSEPH PAULL 1657-1717 by Elmer Garfield Van Name.
1969.
Paull: England—1657-1685; Pennsylvania—1685-1717.
Paper—$1.75—18pp-- Vendor #D0019

2994 - THE HOUSMAN—(HUYSMAN) SIMONSON FAMILY OF STATEN ISLAND,
NEW YORK by Elmer Garfield Van Name. 1955.
Housman: Staten Island, New York—1700-1850.
Paper—$1.50—10pp-- Vendor #D0019

2995 - ANTHONY NELSON 17TH CENTURY PENNSYLVANIA AND NEW JERSEY
AND SOME OF HIS DESCENDANTS by Elmer Garfield Van Name. 1976
repr. of 1962 ed.
Nielson-Nelson: Gloucester County, New Jersey—1652-1695.
Paper—$3.25—54pp-- Vendor #D0019

2996 - PIERRE BILLIOU FAMILY by Elmer Garfield Van Name. 1960.
Billiou: France—1632-1661; New York (state)—1661-1699.
Paper—$1.50—16pp-- Vendor #D0019

2997 - THE ELWELL FAMILY—17TH AND 18TH CENTURIES SOUTHERN
NEW JERSEY by Elmer Garfield Van Name.
Elwell: Concerns various branches of Elwell family in Southern New
Jersey, founded by Thomas Elwell, born in Massachusetts, in 1654.
Paper—$2.75—40pp-- Vendor #D0019

2998 - JOHN CAWMAN EASTLACK DIARY compiled by Mrs. Walter A. Simpson.
1952.
Eastlack: Gloucester County, New Jersey.
1854-1887 diary of John Eastlack, his family and friends of Gloucester
County, New Jersey. Indexed.
Paper—$3.75—103pp-- Vendor #D0019

2999 - THOMAS KNIGHT OF PENNSYLVANIA AND SOME OF HIS DESCEND-
ANTS by William Beckett Brown, III. 1973.
Knight: South Jersey and Pennsylvania descendants of Thomas
Knight of England from 1687 to present.
Paper—$8.00—78pp-- Vendor #D0019

3000 - THE PAULLIN FAMILY OF SOUTHERN NEW JERSEY by Elmer Garfield
Van Name. 1977 repr. of 1958 ed.
Paper—$2.75—31pp-- Vendor #D0019

3001 - THE BENJAMIN MOORE FAMILY OF BURLINGTON COUNTY by Edmund
J. Moore. 1982.
Hundreds of descendants are traced from 17th Century New Jersey to
the present.
Paper—$16.00—354pp-- Vendor #D0019

3002 - GENEALOGY OF THE CHEW FAMILY by Robert L. Chew. 1982.
A remarkable history and catalog of the Chew family in America for
almost four centuries!
Paper—$18.50—488pp-- Vendor #D0019

3003 - GENEALOGY OF THE MATTSON FAMILY by George P. Walmsley, Sr.
1983.
Three hundred years of Mattson descendants in America.
Paper—$13.00—185pp-- Vendor #D0019

3004 - THE SIMONSON FAMILIES OF STATEN ISLAND, NEW YORK by Elmer
Garfield Van Name. 1981 repr.
Five generations of early Simonsons are traced in this work.
Paper—$1.75—20pp-- Vendor #D0019

3005 - THE PANCOAST FAMILY IN AMERICA by Bennett S. Pancoast. 1981.
This excellent genealogy includes the first seven generations of
Pancoasts in America.
Paper—$18.50—490pp--Vendor #D0019

3006 - AFTER TWELVE GENERATIONS A BROOKS FAMILY SKEIN IS ENDING
by Lillian Brooks Black. 1978.
The male descent of one line from Henry Brooks of the 17th Century
is traced.
Paper—$1.50—38pp---Vendor #D0019

3007 - LIPPINCOTT—FIVE GENERATIONS OF THE DESCENDANTS OF
RICHARD AND ABIGAIL LIPPINCOTT by Judith M. Olsen. 1982.
A superb genealogy! Both male and female lines are detailed for
five generations.
Paper—$18.50—471pp---Vendor #D0019

3008 - THE BOURLANDS IN AMERICA by Carl and May Read. 1978.
Traces the Bourlands from colonial Virginia to the present. All who
bear this rare name in America today are related to each other—
springing from a common Scotch-Irish ancestor. The surname is a
variant of an old name - Bordland. Other corrupt spellings now used
by the family: Bowland, Bouland, Bolin, Borlen and about 25 others.
Cloth—$22.00—450pp-- Vendor #D0022

3009 - THE LOVING FAMILY IN AMERICA by Carl and May Read. 1981.
A comprehensive book about the Loving/Lovan/Lovin/Lovvorn/Lovern
Families in America, yesterday and today.
This family, of Flemish origins in the city of Louvain, now in Belgium,
entered England with William the Conqueror in 1066. The surname was
originally De Louvaine, but variant spellings in use today number in
the dozens, from Lovein to Loven to Lovvorn.
Cloth—$38.00—800pp-- Vendor #D0022

3010 - THE RAYS LOOK BACK by Nordan and McCarley. 1972.
Cloth—$30.00—311pp-- Vendor #D0023

3011 - OUR ANCESTORS: JOHNSON; SMITH; HAMPTON; PAYNE; AND
PACE by Col. (ret.) Glen R. and Delorean R. Johnson. 1979.
The history of Colonel Johnson's paternal ancestry. Duncan Johnson,
a Revolutionary War soldier in North Carolina, was first American
Johnson identified. Michael Smith, the first of that line, was in Vir-
ginia by 1695. Joseph Payne, who was in Franklin County, George in
1780's was the first proven Payne ancestor. Richard Pace founded the
American branch of that line in Jamestown about 1611, and William
Hampton started his line in America just nine years later when he
arrived aboard the Bona Nova, in 1620. Documented; indexed.
Cloth—$15.00—162pp-- Vendor #D0027

3012 - FLOYD MARRIAGES. 1620-1910 MARRIAGES OF PEOPLE NAMED
FLOYD compiled by Anna M. Cartlidge.
Over 5100 Floyd marriages, documented from research all over the
United States. Areas of largest concentration: Georgia, Kentucky,
Virginia, the South and the Mid-West. Price includes tax and postage.
Paper—$17.00-- Vendor #D0033

3013 - ONLY A TWIG—A BRANCH OF THE ZUGS/ZOOKS FROM PENNSYLVANIA
by Lois Ann Zook. 1979.
Paper—$9.00—211pp-- Vendor #D0062

3014 - THE BICKNELL FAMILY (SOUTHERN BRANCH) by Vera Reeve, C.G.
1977.
From Virginia (1750-1780), North Carolina (1770-1830), Kentucky
(from 1808 to now—other migrations to Indiana, Illinois, Iowa, etc.).
No proved connection yet to the New England Bicknells. Contains a
name index and a picture index; spiral bound. It contains material
on the allied lines of: Asbill/Asbell/Azbell, Buckles, Hulan/Hulen/Hulin,
and Kemp.
Paper—$32.00—500pp-- Vendor #D0063

3015 - CONRAD WEISER, 1696-1760: FRIEND OF COLONIST AND MOHAWK
by Paul A. W. Wallace. 1971 repr. of 1945 ed.
Cloth—$27.50—643pp--- Vendor #D0079

3016 - LEWISES, MERIWETHERS AND THEIR KIN by Sarah Travers Lewis
(Scott) Anderson. 1984. Illus.; indexed.
Cloth—$35.00—652pp-- Vendor #D0080

3017 - THE GEORGIANS. GENEALOGIES OF PIONEER FAMILIES by Jeanette
Holland Austin. 1984. Indexed.
Cloth—$30.00—479pp-- Vendor #D0080

3018 - FAMILIES OF EARLY HARTFORD, CONNECTICUT by Lucius Barnes
Barbour. 1982 repr. of 1977 ed. Indexed.
Cloth—$35.00—742pp-- Vendor #D0080

3019 - POCAHONTAS, ALIAS MATOAKA, AND HER DESCENDANTS THROUGH
HER MARRIAGE AT JAMESTOWN, VIRGINIA IN APRIL, 1614 WITH JOHN
ROLFE, GENTLEMAN by Wyndham Robertson and Robert A. Brock.
1982 repr. of 1887 ed.
Cloth—$8.50—84pp-- Vendor #D0080

3020 - THE BOONE FAMILY. A GENEALOGICAL HISTORY OF DESCENDANTS
OF GEORGE AND MARY BOONE WHO CAME TO AMERICA IN 1717 by
Hazel Atterbury Spraker. 1982 repr. of 1922 ed.
Cloth—$30.00—707pp-- Vendor #D0080

3021 - HALE, HOUSE AND RELATED FAMILIES, MAINLY OF THE CONNECTI-
CUT RIVER VALLEY by Donald L. Jacobus and Edgar F. Waterman.
1978 repr. of 1952 ed.
Cloth—$38.50—914pp-- Vendor #D0080

3022 - LEWIS OF WARNER HALL, THE HISTORY OF A FAMILY by Merrow E.
Sorley. 1979 repr. of 1935 ed.
Cloth—$35.00—887pp-- Vendor #D0080

3023 - ....UNTO THE HILLS...SOME HILLMANS AND OTHERS by Belva
Marshall Counts. Repr. of 1979 ed.
A partial genealogy of the Southwest Virginia families of Carrico,
Edwards, Hillman, Newberry, Stallard, Wells and other allied families.
The book includes old family photos, coats of arms, bibliography and
completely indexed.
Carico (Carrico) - Charles County, Maryland; Fairfax, Grayson, Russell,
Washington, Wise Counties, Virginia.
Edwards - North Carolina; Carroll, Grayson, Scott, Wise, Wythe
Counties, Virginia.
Hillman - Somerset County, Maryland; Montgomery, Scott, Russell,
Wise Counties, Virginia.
Newberry - Augusta, Bland, Botetourt, Montgomery, Scott, Wythe
Counties, Virginia; Crawford County, Missouri.
Stallard - Culpeper, Essex (Old Rappahannock), Russell, Scott,
Washington, Wise Counties, Virginia.
Wells - Pennsylvania; Russell, Scott Counties, Virginia; Floyd, John-
son Counties, Kentucky.
LC number 78-74645
Paper—$10.50—161pp-- Vendor #D0083

3024 - OUR NEW ENGLAND HADLEY AND ALLIED FAMILIES—A GENEALOGY
by Elsie E. Kempton. 1979.
Descendants of Benjamin Hadley 1684-1776. Related families include
Andrews, Briggs, Hubbard. Indexed.
Cloth—$17.00—256pp-- Vendor #D0085

3025 - OUR EGGLESTON AND ALLIED FAMILIES—A GENEALOGY by Elsie
E. Kempton. 1975.
Descendants of Bigod Eggleston 1587-1674.
Cloth—$12.00—113pp-- Vendor #D0085

3026 - THE AULLS GENEALOGY by Leslie A. Bryan. 1974.
Cloth—$12.50—162pp-- Vendor #D0088

3027 - THOMAS BRYAN AND SOME OF HIS DESCENDANTS by Leslie A.
Bryan. 1979.
Cloth—$12.50—131pp-------------------------------------- Vendor #D0088

3028 - IMMIGRANT ANCESTORS by Leslie A. Bryan. 1981.
Vital information on 143 immigrant ancestors and their descendants for
two to eight generations of New England and Dutch immigrants.
Surnames: Adams, Alexander, Allyn, Ammerman, Andriessen, Aulls,
Bacus, Babcock, Badie, Barlow, Beach, Belcher, Bill, Bissell, Blake,
Bloetgoet, Bradley, Brown, Bryan, Burr, Burroughs, Burrows, Burt,
Burton, Clapham, Cogswell, Collins, Cool, Coshun, Covert, Crandall,
Crane, Crow, Culver, Denyse, Dewey, Dimon, Dorland, Drake,
Eggleston, Ellis, Evertszen, Fenno, Fenimore, Fletcher, Foote, Ford,
Gaylord, Gelder, Gerritsen, Gilbert, Gilchrist, Godwin, Goodwin,
Goodyear, Graves, Griswold, Groves, Halsey, Haughton, Hawley,
Haynes, Hegeman, Higbee, Hill, Hinman, Hutchinson, Jackson, Jones,
Judson, Leach, Littlefield, Lockwood, Loomis, Lyman, Marsh, Merwin,
Mitchell, Moore, Morehouse, Norman, Oakley, Odell, Oldage, O'Rourke,
Osborn, Parke, Pickney, Polhemius, Porter, Praa, Randall, Rapalje,
Root, Rowlett, Sanford, Sawyer, Scott, Seals, Sherman, Sherwood,
Skidmore, Smith, Snedeker, Sprong, Stanley, Stebbins, Stevens,
Stiles, Tilton, Freeman, Tompson, Treadwell, Tucker, Turney,
Van Arsdalen, Van Couwenhoven, Van der Beeck, Vandervliet, Van Ness,
Van Schouwen, Van Vechten, Van Voorhees, Van Wyck, Verkerk,
Vrelant, Waite, Wakelee, Wakeman, Waldo, Ward, Webster, Wheeler,
White, Willemsen, Witter, Woertman, Woodward, Wyckoff, etc.
Cloth—$15.00—208pp------------------------------------- Vendor #D0088

3029 - ROHRBACH GENEALOGY, VOLUME III by Lewis Bunker Rohrbach,
C.G. 1982.
The West Virginia Rorabaugh, Rohrabaugh, etc. families; descendants
of Johann Reinhart Rohrbach, a 1749 immigrant.
Cloth—$34.95—376pp------------------------------------- Vendor #D0096

3030 - THE PEDENS OF SOUTHWEST VIRGINIA AND SOUTH CENTRAL
KENTUCKY by Henry C. Peden, Jr. 1978.
The Pedens were Scotch-Irish immigrants who settled in Virginia prior
to the American Revolution, and migrated into Kentucky in the early
1800's. This book contains many of the descendants of John Peden
(1734-1815) and Mary Smith, (1734-1806). Geographically it involves
the Virginia counties of Augusta, Botetourt, and Montgomery, and the
Kentucky counties of Barren, Simpson, and Monroe, with mentionings
of related Peden-Pedan-Paden families in Tennessee, North Carolina,
South Carolina, Pennsylvania, and Maryland. Following an historical
review of their settlements in Virginia and Kentucky, an alphabetical
compendium or sketch of each Peden is presented.
Paper—$15.00—126pp----------------------------------- Vendor #D0099

3031 - DULANY-FURLONG AND KINDRED FAMILIES by Roland Dulany
Furlong. 1975.
Dennis Dulany, son of 1709 immigrant, Thomas.
Progenitor of name in Western Pennsylvania, West Virginia and Ohio.
John Furlong, 1816 immigrant to Cambria County, Pennsylvania.
Major families in 9000 name index: Fox, Goughenour, Haines, Headlee,
John, Lemley, Pitcock, Shriver.
Cloth—$25.00—544pp----------------------------------- Vendor #D0101

3032 - HALIFAX COUNTY VIRGINIA HISTORY: VOLUME I, NARRATION;
VOLUME II, DOCUMENTATION by Pocahontas Wight Edmunds. 1978.
Richmond Times Dispatch: "Will doubtless stand as a major document
in Virginia's local history for years to come." Note Volume I is now
scarce so $40.00; Volume II is $20.00. No discounts.
Cloth—Vol. I—$40.00—Vol. II—$20.00—1735pp/set----------- Vendor #D0102

3033 - THE GRAY FAMILY AND ALLIED LINES: BOWMAN, LINDSAY,
MILLIS, DICK, PEEBLES, WILEY, SHANNON, LAMAR, AND McGEE
by Jo White Linn (Mrs. Stahle Linn, Jr.). 1976.
Piedmont section of North Carolina, primarily Guilford and Randolph
Counties.
Cloth—$27.50—660pp----------------------------------- Vendor #D0104

3034   - THE HANES FAMILY OF NORTH CAROLINA by Jo White Linn (Mrs.
Stahle Linn, Jr.). 1980.
Tobacco, hosiery and knitting empire, origins in Rowan, Davie,
Forsyth. Early Moravians from York County, Pennsylvania to
North Carolina by 1774.
--- Vendor #D0104

3035   - DIARY OF ELIZABETH DICK LINDSAY 1837-1861 by Jo White Linn
(Mrs. Stahle Linn, Jr.). 1975.
Facsimilie edition with lineage, maps, illustrations, Guilford County,
North Carolina families.
Cloth—$18.50--- Vendor #D0104

3036   - THE ANCESTRY OF NATHALIE FONTAINE LYONS: LYONS,
NUNES MIRANDA, LURIA, COHEN, HART, CLAYLAND, MAFFITT,
AND BEACH by Jo White Linn (Mrs. Stahle Linn, Jr.). 1981.
Brochure upon receipt of SASE.
Cloth—$25.00—260pp-------------------------------------- Vendor #D0104

3037   - JACOB WOODWARD COLLADAY AND HIS DESCENDANTS by Wayne
V. Jones. 1976.
He was building contractor in Philadelphia, remodeling part Indepen-
dence HALL 1854-55. Descendants all over USA, concentrations in
Illinois, Indiana, California. Biographies of most descendants.
Paper—$5.00—132pp-------------------------------------- Vendor #D0112

3038   - THE RIEKE FAMILY OF BAVENHAUSEN AND AMERICA by Wayne V.
Jones. 1979.
German ancestry in Lippe-Detmold, some to 16th Century, includes
Stapperfenne, Heger, Linneweber, Wehrman, Lehmeÿer, Sandmeÿer,
Meÿer, Brockhausen, Lüdeke-Saak, Freÿtag, Prüssner, and Kluckhohn
families. Extensive accounts of descendants in USA named Rieke,
Kluckhohn, Hauswirth, Prussner and many others.
Cloth—$27.50—593pp------------------------------------- Vendor #D0112

3039   - JAMES TURNER (1758-1826) AND HIS MANY DESCENDANTS by
Mrs. Pauline Turner Fake. 1979.
The book is divided into two parts. Part One contains the Traditional
Ancestors of James Turner, beginning with William Turner, a minister
of the Kirk of Scotland, born in Aberdeenshire, Scotland 1645. The
genealogy continues to Part Two, which begins with James Turner,
born 1758 in Maryland and who later lives in South Carolina and
Georgia; the Turner Family history is clearly written, listing documentation or source through 1978; it contains copies of Documents, abstracts,
family photos and obituaries, with full name index.
Paper—$17.50—74pp------------------------------------- Vendor #D0114

3040   - KEY AND COLLATERAL FAMILIES by Edward S. Key and Irene
T. Sevier. 1972.
Key: North Carolina, 1776-1883; Mississippi, 1833-1860; Texas,
1870-1972. An addendum completed in 1980.
Cloth—$9.50—300pp------------------------------------- Vendor #D0116

3041   - HOUGH AND HUFF FAMILIES OF THE UNITED STATES, 1620-1900,
HOUGH FAMILIES OF THE SOUTH—PART A by Granville W. Hough.
1978.
Census and family data through 1900, Maryland through South Carolina.
Paper—$20.00—251pp------------------------------------ Vendor #D0119

3042   - SOME HUFF FAMILIES OF TENNESSEE by Granville W. Hough. 1983.
Census and family data through 1900.
Paper—$20.00—174pp------------------------------------ Vendor #D0119

3043   - HOUGH, HUFF, AND HOFF FAMILIES OF MISSISSIPPI by Granville
W. Hough. 1985.
Census and family data through 1910.
Paper—$20.00—apx. 250pp------------------------------- Vendor #D0119

3044 - HOUGH AND HUFF FAMILIES OF IOWA by Granville W. Hough. 1984.
Census and family data through 1915.
paper—$20.00—apx. 300pp---------------------------------- Vendor #D0119

3045 - CORBIN—WAITE—COOPER OF BALTIMORE COUNTY AND CITY by
Dorothy Cooper Knoff. 1984.
Beginning in 1671, Nicholas Corbin and his male descendants are followed
for four generations. The Waite and Cooper lines stem from the marriage
of Diana Corbin and Richard Waite in 1772.
Cloth—$17.00—140pp-------------------------------------- Vendor #D0122

3046 - AUSTINS TO WISCONSIN (RICHARD LINE) by Paul R. Austin. 1964.
Austin: Suffield, Connecticut 1674-1783; Shickshinny, Pennsylvania
1779-1804; Ohio 1804-1815; Indiana 1815-1818; Illinois 1818-1846;
Wisconsin 1835-1963.
Woodle: Maryland 1778-1799; Fayette County, Pennsylvania 1799-1836;
Green County, Wisconsin 1836-1970.
Smith (Col. James): Chester County, Pennsylvania 1720-1748;
Franklin County, Pennsylvania 1748-1776; Westmoreland County,
Pennsylvania 1769-1788; Bourbon County, Kentucky 1788-1812.
Cloth—$9.00—99pp--------------------------------------- Vendor #D0124

3047 - KNIGHT LETTER by Merle Ganier. 1984.
Quarterly newsletter for Knight family researchers, subscription $7.00
annually. Volumes I-XVI, 1968-1983 on microfiche $25.00.
Annual subscription—$7.00--------------------------------Vendor #D0127

3048 - THE DESCENDANTS OF HARVEY WILDER AND HIS ANCESTORS TO
1485 IN ENGLAND, WITH A HISTORY OF THE WILDER NAME AND
RELATED FAMILIES OF WARNER, BARNHARD, BENEDICT, HEPWORTH,
POORE, CROCKER AND NEWMAN by Justin E. Wilder. 1974.
Wilder: Massachusetts—1638; Rutland County, Vermont—1787;
Kent and Newaygo Counties, Michigan—1844, 1855.
Cloth—$8.75—271pp------------------------------------- Vendor #D0128

3049 - THE LEES AND KINGS OF VIRGINIA AND NORTH CAROLINA,
1636-1976 by Mrs. Reba S. Wilson and Mrs. Betty S. Glover. 1976.
Fully documented record of two of Virginia's finest first families—Henry
Lee and Michael King—and fifteen generations of their descendants
scattered throughout the United States.
Included are land grants, wills, deeds, inventories, Bible records,
maps and migration routes and background history of the nation's
early growth and development in Virginia and North Carolina. Profusely illustrated, some in color. Seventeen pages of family lineage
charts.
Cloth—$51.50—186pp------------------------------------ Vendor #D0139

3050 - THE BERRYS OF MARYLAND, AN OLD PRINCE GEORGE'S COUNTY
FAMILY by George R. Griffiths. 1977.
Line of James Berry who arrived in Virginia from England about
1633 is traced. In 1652 he migrated to Calvert County, Maryland.
Major line followed to current times was also in Talbot, Dorchester,
and Caroline Counties, Maryland, and Kent County, Delaware, but
primarily in Prince George's County. Other families mentioned:
Bowie, Clagett, Hillary, Jeffries, Keene, Marsh, Pitt, Preston,
Sasscer, Seely, Tarlburtt, Towgood, Williams.
Paper—$5.95—44pp------------------------------------- Vendor #D0146

3051 - THE MATHIAS FAMILY OF HARDY COUNTY, VIRGINIA AND
WEST VIRGINIA by George R. Griffiths. 1977.
Reviews early Mathias/Matthias surnames back to 1651 in Norfolk and
Princess Anne Counties, Virginia; traces descendants of John and
Barbara Mathias from 1779 in Shenandoah County, Virginia, to Hardy
County, West Virginia. Other families mentioned: Bowman, Caldwell,
Crider, Disponet, Fitzwater, Harter, Miller, Sager, See, Shireman,
Snider.
Paper—$5.50—42pp-------------------------------------- Vendor #D0146

3052 - ROBERT GRIFFITH FROM CARNO, WALES, AND HIS DESCENDANTS
by George R. Griffiths. 1981.
Robert Griffith(s) and family came from North Wales between 1837-1842
to Butler County, Ohio. Son Robert W. Griffith moved to Putnam/Allen
Counties, Ohio, in 1857. Some went to Dayton, Ohio; Hocking and
Perry Counties, Ohio; Wright County, Missouri; Oklahoma; Texas.
Related families: Clevenger, Davi(e)s, Edwards, Evans, Roberts,
Watkins, and Williams.
Paper—$14.95—135pp-- Vendor #D0146

3053 - PIONEER LEWIS FAMILIES, VOLUME I AND II (SET) by Michael L.
Cook, C.G. 1984 repr. of 1978 ed.
Lewis families lineage.
Cloth—$131.00/set—2451pp------------------------------------- Vendor #D0150

3054 - PIONEER LEWIS FAMILIES, VOLUME III by Michael L. Cook, C.G.
1984 repr. of 1980 ed.
Lewis families lineage.
Cloth—$27.50—357pp-- Vendor #D0150

3055 - PIONEER LEWIS FAMILIES, VOLUME IV by Michael L. Cook, C.G.
1984.
Lewis families lineage.
Cloth—$79.00—1597pp--------------------------------------- Vendor #D0150

3056 - DESCENDANTS OF NICOLA DALL'AVA INCLUDING RELATED
FAMILIES, VIALE AND ROSSI OF VICENZA, ITALY AND BERKSHIRE
COUNTY, MASSACHUSETTS by Phyllis Walker Johnson. 1977.
Paper—$5.00—60pp--- Vendor #D0155

3057 - EDWARDS—WHO, WAS WHERE, WHEN by Bette Dickson Casteel.
1983.
Information from the Edwards Heirs Publication of 1925-1926 on
hand printed descent charts plus research on early Edwards:
early arrivals, wills, marriages, tax and census data.
1300 Edwards indexed. Ads.
Paper—$17.95—108pp-------------------------------------- Vendor #D0157

3058 - COON—GOHN DESCENDANTS FROM CHANCEFORD TOWNSHIP, YORK
COUNTY, PENNSYLVANIA by Frances Davis McTeer. 1979.
Gohn: Pennsylvania, Berkeley County, West Virginia.
Coon: Washington County, Maryland; Botetourt County, Virginia;
Madison, Ross, Fairfield Counties, Ohio; Coles, Piatt, McLean, Greene
Counties, Illinois; Mercer County, Missouri; Utah; Butte County,
California.
Cloth—$20.00—277pp-------------------------------------- Vendor #D0158

3059 - THE McTEER—MATEER FAMILIES OF CUMBERLAND COUNTY,
PENNSYLVANIA by Frances Davis McTeer. 1975.
McTeer: Cumberland County, Pennsylvania; Tennessee.
Mateer: Armstrong, Mifflin Counties, Pennsylvania; Ohio.
McTier: Georgia.
Cloth—$15.00—232pp-------------------------------------- Vendor #D0158

3060 - SOME DESCENDANTS OF PETER PITTS OF TAUNTON, MASSACHU-
SETTS by Frances Davis McTeer and Julia Bumpus Berndt. 1979.
Pitts: All male lines through five generations, 1643-1850.
Paper—$7.50—72pp--------------------------------------- Vendor #D0158

3061 - HAVENS—AUSTIN GENEALOGY: DESCENDANTS OF LAUREN
HAVENS, CHARLOTTE RANNEY, CHARLES GRANDISON AUSTIN,
AND CATHARINE BLAKEMAN by Esther Deidamia (Littleford)
Woodworth. 1956.
New York, Illinois, and west.
Paper—$10.00—46pp—unbound---------------------------Vendor #D0163

3062 - HULING GENEALOGY: DESCENDANTS OF JAMES AND MARGARET
HULING OF NEWPORT, RHODE ISLAND AND LEWES, DELAWARE by
Esther Littleford Woodworth-Barnes; edited by Jane Fletcher Fiske,
F.A.S.G. 1984.
New York, Vermont, Ohio, Michigan, Illinois, and all states West. Index.
Cloth—$35.00—675+pp----------------------------------- Vendor #D0163

3063   - THE VISTAS AT "EAGLE'S NEST"—THE FITZHUGH—GRYMES FAMILY
HOME, KING GEORGE COUNTY, VIRGINIA by Liza Lawrence (Dow).
Repr. of 1968 ed.
Illustrated (with Fitzhugh-Grymes Family Chart—10 generations).
Paper—$7.50—12pp--- Vendor #D0170

3064   - AUTOGRAPHS 1701/2 CHARLES CITY/PRINCE GEORGE AND SURRY
COUNTIES by Elizabeth Lawrence-Dow. 1976.
The Autographs and biographical information of these 65 prominent
Virginias: Charles City/Prince George—50 Autographs of:
Anderson, Tho.; Baxter, Jno.; Bland, Rich'rd, Gent.; Blighton, Geo.,
Gent.; Bolling, Robt., Gent.; Bradford, Rich'd, Gent.; Byrd, William,
Esq.; Cocke, John; Daniell, Jno.; Daniell, Thomas; Epes, Fra.; Epes,
Jno.; Epes, Jno.; Epes, Littlebury, Gent.; Goodrich, Char., Gent.;
Gudgane, David; Gunn, James; Hamlin, Jno.; Hamlin, Rich'd;
Hardyman, Jno., Gent.; Harwood, Robt.; Harrison, James; Harrison,
Thomas; Higdon, Dan'll; Hill, Edw.; Hunt, Jno.; Jackson, Thomas;
Jones, Peter; Llewellin, Daniel, Gent.; Limbrey, Jno.; Lowe, Micajah,
Sheriff; Madox, Randall; New, Robt.; Pasmore, George; Poythres,
Jno.; Poythres, Jno.; Poythres, Peter; Reekes, Rich'd; Reekes,
Jno., Jr.; Rese, Roger; Simmons, Tho.; Tapley, Adam; Taylor, John;
Thweatt, James; Wickett, Jno.; Woodham, Tho.; Wyatt, Anthony;
Wyatt, Anthony; Wynne, Joshua, Gent.
Surry County—15 Autographs of: Browne, Wm.; Cocke, Wm.; Drew,
Thomas; fflood, Tho.; ffoster, William; Gray, Wm.; Gray, Wm.;
Harrison, Benja.; Harrison, Nath'll; Holt, Tho.; Lancaster, Robt.;
Lane, Tho.; Lucus, Wm.; Rose, Will.; Shelly, Philip
who signed the Oath of Loyalty to King William III on the same day
in March 1701/2 are from original sources only.
The addenda should answer any questions you have about the laws
and customs of that time.
Illustrated, Indexed.
Paper—$12.50—148pp----------------------------------- Vendor #D0170

3065   - DESCENDANTS OF JOHN HANSARD OF AMHERST COUNTY, VIR-
GINIA 1766-1976. SAM L. HANSARD II. 1977.
Hansard: Amherst County, Virginia—1700's; Knox County, Tennessee—
1800's. Related families in Amherst County: Rucker, Cashwell,
Tinsley, Burford, Davis, Garner, and Taylor. Related families in
Knox, Union, and Anderson counties in Tennessee: Vandergriff,
Warwick, Lewis, Petree, Davis, and Henderson. Indexed.
Cloth—$28.00—444pp--------------------------------- Vendor #D0173

3066   - HANSARD—CHRISTIAN FAMILY HISTORY RECORDS by Annie Walker
Burns. 1978 repr. of 1951 (uncertain) ed.
Hansard, William and Christian, Robert—Revolutionary War Soldiers,
Amherst County, Virginia.
Primarily about William Hansard's descendants. After 1806, family
was in Knox County, Tennessee. His children were: John, Lucy,
Mary, Martha Jane, William Christian, Nancy, Robert Christian,
Samuel H., Archibald G. (born 1814), and Abner Christian Hansard.
Completely indexed.
Paper—$37.50—124+pp-------------------------------- Vendor #D0173

3067   - HANSARD MILITARY RECORDS OF THE CIVIL WAR. ALSO SOME
CHEROKEE RECORDS OF THE HANSARD NAME by Annie Walker
Burns. 1978 repr. of 1964 (uncertain date) ed.
Samuel H. Hansard, Cedar County, Missouri—1860.
National Archive Civil War military service and pension records for
Tennessee, Georgia, Missouri, and Ohio Hansards. Completely
indexed.
Paper—$25.50—38+pp-------------------------------- Vendor #D0173

3068   - TODDS IN EARLY LAWRENCE AND MONROE COUNTIES, INDIANA—
A RESEARCH AID by Nancie Todd Weber. 1979.
Related families include Brooks, Conger, Dayton, Fleetwood, Hays,
Helton, Martin, McFarland, McLean, Newton, Pritchett, Ragsdale.
Neither a "proper" genealogy nor necessarily accurate, it compiles a

decade's correspondence. Traditionally, two unrelated Todd clans
(England and Irish) figure in this area's early history.
Paper—$5.00—54pp-- Vendor #D0174

3069   - TODD FAMILY IN INDIANA BY GROVER C. TODD, AN ANALYSIS by
Nancie Todd Weber. 1979.
Grover Todd's 1971 genealogy (descendants of George Todd and wives
Elizabeth Seip and Sarah Brooks), plus accompanying analysis. Indexed.
Paper—$5.00—48pp-- Vendor #D0174

3070   - THE DESCENDANTS OF HENRY AND POLLY MILLER OF BEDFORD,
NEW YORK 1766-1977 by Eric E. Hovemeyer. 1977.
Including over 300 descendants of Griffin Henry Miller. Related
families include Curtis, Dixon, Fancher, Hollister, Hurd, Kellogg,
Reynolds, Silkman.
Paper—$20.00—372pp--------------------------------------- Vendor #D0177

3071   - THE GOLDSBERRY REGISTER edited by Eric E. Hovemeyer. 1980.
Paper—$4.00—42pp-- Vendor #D0177

3072   - THE HOVEMEYER FAMILY IN GERMANY AND AMERICA by Eric E.
Hovemeyer. 1972.
Out of print—photocopies available.
Paper—$5.00—32pp-- Vendor #D0177

3073   - THE TINGLEY FAMILY REVISED, VOLUME I by Marian McCauley
Frye. 1970.
Malden, Massachusetts 1635—Male and female lines, over 800 different
surnames, as: Adams, Allen, Anderson, Arnold, Ball, Barbour,
Baxter, Bennett, Berry, Bishop, Bliss, Briggs, Brown, Burrows,
Carpenter, Carter, Case, Chalker, Chapman, Chase, Clark, Coates,
Coddington, Cole, Collins, Colpitts, Comstock, Cosad, Cox, Crabtree,
Craig, Dary, Davis, Dennis, Dix, Dixon, Dobson, Drake, Draper,
Eldredge, Ellis, Estabrook, Everett, Fillmore, Follet, Fuller, Haddix,
Hall, Harper, Haskell, Holmes, Hunter, Jenckes, Johnson, Keith,
Kennedy, Kinkade, Knox, Lane, Lee, Martin, Mason, Masters, McCully,
McLellan, McMorris, Meek, Mercer, Miller, Mitton, Moore, Morse, Oulton,
Parcel, Parshall, Patterson, Paynter, Peck, Phillips, Potter, Read,
Reade, Reed, Richards, Richardson, Robinson, Runyon, Scott, Sexton,
Shipman, Shotwell, Simpson, Smith, Stearns, Steeves, Sterling, Stewart,
Stiles, Sweet, Taylor, Thompson, Throop, Tiffany, Tower, Trenholm,
Tuttle, Waldo, Walker, Wallace, Wells, West, Wheaton, White, Williams,
Wilmarth, Wilson, Wolfe, Wood, Young, plus many names listed in
volumes below; descendants throughout United States and Canada.
Cloth—$30.00—611pp--------------------------------------- Vendor #D0179

3074   - THE TINGLEY FAMILY REVISED, VOLUME II by Marian McCauley
Frye. 1972.
Continuation Volume I, over 800 different surnames, as: Alward,
Andrews, Ayer, Babcock, Bailey, Barnes, Bowser, Brundage, Buck,
Carey, Chandler, Cochrane, Copp, Crawford, Crossman, Cushman,
Davall, Dean, Dillon, Dunham, Elliott, Estabrooks, Gardner, Goodrich,
Graves, Greene, Hale, Hathaway, Haven, Hicks, Hoar, Hollister,
Hopkins, Hunt, Jenkins, Jones, Lawson, Lewis, Lowerison, McKay,
Merritt, Murray, Nelson, Newton, Packard, Parker, Peckham,
Perkins, Perry, Pierce, Platt, Porter, Powers, Pratt, Randall,
Reynolds, Rhodes, Rider, Rought, Russell, Sears, Sharer, Shaw,
Skinner, Spencer, Stephens, Stevens, Stillman, Stokes, Stuart,
Thatcher, Thayer, Townsend, Trites, Troop, Wheeler, Whipple,
Whiting, Whitney, Wilcox, Wilkinson, Wright, Yeomans, plus most names
listed above and in volumes below.
Cloth—$30.00—609pp--------------------------------------- Vendor #D0179

3075   - THE TINGLEY FAMILY REVISED, VOLUME III by Marian McCauley
Frye. 1974.
Continatuion Volume II, over 850 different surnames, as: Alexander,
Avery, Ayer, Bartlett, Beard, Bell, Benedict, Benjamin, Bigelow,
Black, Bloxham, Bradley, Brownell, Bryant, Burns, Campbell, Carson,
Chamberlain, Chappell, Cinnamon, Constantine, Craft, Crane, Daven-
port, DeMarest, DeMerchant, Dickerson, Dickey, Dickie, Dunn, Fawcett,

Fisher, Foster, Francisco, Frazee, Goodwin, Green, Harris, Hart,
Hartley, Hebbert, Hedden, Hoffman, Holaday, Hull, Irvin, Irwin,
Jackson, Jacobs, James, Johnston, King, Lindley, Lowe, Maguire,
Main, Maxwell, McComb, McCormack, McCormick, McDiarmid, McDonald,
McIntyre, Mills, Miner, Mitchell, Morris, Myers, Nichols, Northrup,
Ogden, Osborn, Page, Partridge, Paterson, Payne, Pickering, Powell,
Rayworth, Reid, Ridgeway, Robertson, Rockwell, Rosendale, Rossbury,
Schmell, Scribner, Sharp, Shawver, Sherwood, Shumaker, Smitley,
Snodgrass, Snyder, Sorenson, Sterns, Stienback, Stone, Tappan,
Torrey, Treat, Trueman, Tucker, Turner, Underwood, Van Barriger,
Van Buskirk, Vaughan, Wade, Weaver, Welsh, Whitaker, Whitman,
Wilder, Womack, plus most names listed in volumes above and below.
Cloth—$30.00—614pp--- Vendor #D0179

3076 - THE TINGLEY FAMILY REVISED, VOLUME IV by Marian McCauley
Frye. 1977.
Continuation plus supplement to first 8 generations, over 950 different
surnames as: Addison, Alvord, Applegate, Austin, Babbitt, Baker,
Baldwin, Barnard, Barrett, Bates, Bayley, Beals, Belcher, Belknap,
Benning, Blandin, Blend, Bloomfield, Bogart, Bonner, Brewer, Bryan,
Bunnell, Burdick, Butler, Byrne, Cahill, Chestnut, Clapper, Cone,
Conrad, Cook, Corse, Crouch, Cure, Dannels, Darling, Darrow,
Dewey, Donaldson, Dunlop, Eaton, Ellsworth, Emley, Empet, Estes,
Everson, Feaster, Forsyth, Fortney, Fox, Freeman, Gates, Gidding,
Giles, Gillett, Gillmore, Gladden, Graham, Gray, Greenwood,
Hamilton, Hammer, Hammond, Harding, Harrington, Harrison,
Hartt, Harvey, Hatfield, Hawkins, Hawley, Heath, Helmuth,
Henderson, Herrington, Hill, Hobbs, Horsman, Howard, Howell,
Ingraham, Jeffers, Jenks, Kagler, Kent, Kinnan, Kinney, Kittle,
Knapp, Loomis, Lott, Lowry, Luse, Lyons, Manzer, March, McClain,
McCollum, Mead, Michaels, Moran, Morgan, Neff, Nichols, Niles,
Norris, Norton, Oakley, O'Blenis, Odell, Olds, Olin, Overholt,
Packer, Palett, Pease, Perkins, Quick, Ramsay, Raught, Rice,
Roberts, Rolls, Rounds, Ryder, Rymond, Sayler, Sheldon, Shepardson,
Shook, Slocum, Snider, Sophia, Staples, Styles, Summers, Sutton,
Tallman, Tweksbury, Thomas, Titus, Tweedie, Tweedy, Van Loan,
Wagner, Walton, Warren, Washburn, Webster, Westphal, Whinery,
Wilbur, Wilkinson, Williamson, Woodworth, Wry, plus most names listed
in preceding volumes.
Cloth—$30.00—620pp--- Vendor #D0179

3077 - THE TINGLEY FAMILY REVISED, VOLUME V by Marian McCauley
Frye. 1980.
Over 900 different surnames, as: Atwood, Averill, Bainbridge,
Baisley, Banks, Beaumont, Bickford, Block, Bosket, Bogman, Bowman,
Boyce, Bryden, Buchanan, Cameron, Cassidy, Chambers, Chappell,
Chumbley, Cobb, Collier, Crabtree, Cunningham, Curtis, Daly,
Dickinson, Dexter, Downey, Douthwright, Duffy, Dunning, Estey,
Eye, Ewings, Fairbanks, Felthoff, Fisher, Fullerton, Galloway, Gammon,
Goodsell, Goodwin, Gordon, Griswold, Grover, Haigh, Hamilton,
Hazard, Helms, Hopper, Hubbard, Jarvis, Jennings, Jordan, Keller,
Kimball, Knowlan, Kyle, Ladner, Laidley, Lake, Landers, Landry,
Larson, Latham, Lauder, Lessor, Lilley, Livingstone, Lockwood, Lutes,
Madison, Mallery, Manning, Maxcy, McArthur, McCauley, McKenzie,
Merrin, Mingo, McLasky, Morrison, Murphy, Nielson, Nisbet, North-
rup, Parks, Phinney, Pollock, Poole, Proctor, Putnam, Ripley, Rowe,
Seabury, Shannon, Shores, Socia, Stout, Teed.
Cloth—$30.00—610pp--- Vendor #D0179

3078 - THE TINGLEY FAMILY REVISED, VOLUME VI by Marian McCauley
Frye. 1984.
Cloth—$30.00—600+pp--------------------------------------- Vendor #D0179

3079 - GENEALOGY AND MEMOIRS OF ISAAC STEARNS AND HIS DESCEN-
DANTS, VOLUME I; CHARLES AND NATHANIEL STEARNS AND THEIR
DESCENDANTS, VOLUME II by Mrs. Avis Stearns Van Wagenen.
1981 repr. of 1901 eds.
Descendants, various surnames found throughout United States and

Canada, as: Adams, Allen, Atwell, Bacon, Baldwin, Ball, Barton, Belding, Blood, Bowers, Brown, Burt, Butterfield, Carlton, Chamberlain, Clark, Coburn, Colburn, Conant, Cook, Corbin, Cummings, Davidson, Davis, Dodgeaton, Edmonds, Emerson, Fairbanks, Farwell, Fletcher, Freeman, French, Gould, Hale, Hawks, Hill, Hobart, Holden, Holmes, Holt, Holton, Houghton, Hovey, Howard, Ireland, Jones, Joslin, Keith, Keyes, Kimball, Lamb, Learned, Locke, Longley, Lovewell, Marcy, Marshall, Mayo, Mellen, Newhall, Page, Parker, Patterson, Pearson, Perham, Pierce, Poole, Powers, Pratt, Rand, Read, Reading, Richardson, Robertson, Sawtell, Shattuck, Shumway, Smith, Snow, Spalding, Sprague, Stevens, Stewart, Stokes, Stone, Thompson, Thurston, Todd, Tucker, Warren, Wentworth, Wetherbee, Wheeler, Whitcomb, White, Wilkins, Wilkinson, Willard, Wilson, Woods, Wright. Would like information from and about descendants, including female lines, please.
Paper—$50.00/Vol.—$75.00/Set—1275pp-------------------- Vendor #D0179

3080   - ISAAC STEARNS AND HIS DESCENDANTS (VOLUME I) compiled by Marian McCauley Frye.
Still planned for future revision. Must wait for records of female lines and their descendants to be incorporated before any of the revisions can be published. Please rush such records to compiler. Thank you.
-- Vendor #D0179

3081   - KNOWING THE BRUNERS by Donald Lewis Osborn. 1968.
Bruner/Brunner: Schifferstadt, Germany—1679-1729; Frederick County, Maryland—1736-1821; other states through 1968.
Cloth—$52.00—240pp--- Vendor #D0189

3082   - GENEALOGY OF EDWARD AND SARAH (BURCHETT) OSBORN OF FLOYD COUNTY, KENTUCKY by Donald Lewis Osborn. 1970.
Paper—$4.50—12pp--- Vendor #D0189

3083   - A FAMILY RECORD: STEPHENS by Donald Lewis Osborn. 1973.
Orange County, Virginia; Boone County, Kentucky; Cass County, Missouri.
Paper—$6.50—20pp--- Vendor #D0189

3084   - THE TANGIER SMITH FAMILY: DESCENDANTS OF COLONEL WILLIAM SMITH OF THE MANOR OF SAINT GEORGE, LONG ISLAND, NEW YORK by Ruth Tangier Smith, M.D. and Henry Bainbridge Hoff. 1978.
Related families include Aspinwall, Brewster, Lawrence, Mount, Muirson, "Bull" Smith, Strong, Woodhull.
Paper—$5.00—102pp--- Vendor #D0190

3085   - ADAMS ADDENDA by Dorothy Amburgey Griffith. 1971-1984.
Now in fourteenth year. Over 100 pages of Adams records. Published March and October. Send SASE for information.
Paper—Current Year—$9.00; All others—$10.00—100+pp------ Vendor #D0192

3086   - WAMPLERS IN AMERICA by Genevieve M. Shouse. 1981.
Book begins with Hans Peter Wampler and his wife, Veronica, who came to America in 1741 and settled in Lancaster County, Pennsylvania. Chapter I concerns the immigrants. Chapter II covers their children: Hans Peter, Jr.; Hans Michael; Anna Magdalena; Anna Veronica and Hans George, including their spouses and children. The remainder of the book deals with son, Hans George Wampler and his wife, Elizabeth Stephan (Steffey), and their descendants, who moved to Montgomery County (now Wythe County), Virginia, in 1783. Fully documented. Includes photos, maps, wills, illustrations, inventoris and an index.
Cloth—$30.00—417+pp-------------------------------------- Vendor #D0195

3087   - RICHARD PATRICK/PARTRICK OF NORWALK, CONNECTICUT AND SOME DESCENDANTS by Patricia Liddle Haslam, C.G.R.S. 1978.
Earliest record 1725 deed, but Richard not the immigrant. Further data needed to support tradition that immigrant was Capt. John Patrick of 1630 Winthrop Fleet, brother to Capt. Daniel, same fleet. 156 related families include: Abbott, Adams, Allen, Allsbrook, Avery, Baker,

Barbaree, Barnes, Barrett, Bates, Beattie, Bedient, Beers, Benedict, Benjamin, Bennett, Bobbins, Botsford, Boyd, Brown, Buffington, Bull, Burt, Burtch, Bushnell, Buttrick, Buys, Camp, Carroll, Chapman, Chase, Chiverton, Clark, Cleveland, Clute, Colvin, Couch, Cowling, Crippen, Crofut, Culver, Dauchy, Davis, Day, Demit, Dickens, Dingess, Drew, Duffy, Dykeman, Edminster, Ekberg, Faircloth, Ferry, Finch, Follett, Fox, Gallagher, Gildersleeve, Godfrey, Goodwin, Green, Gregory, Haines, Hall, Hardison, Hartwell, Henderson, Herring, Hopkins, Hoyt, Hughson, Jaffee, Jennings, Jessup, Johnson, Kasey, Knapp, Lee, Leonard, Lockwood, Ludington, Markus, Martindale, McIntire, McKinstry, Mead, Merritt, Mills, Morse, Mott, Moyer, Nash, Newton, Nickerson, Noe, Nolan, Northrop, Olmsted, Palmer, Parker, Phillips, Pierce, Pike, Post, Quick, Reynolds, Russique, Schoof, Sheehan, Sherwood, St. John, Smalley, Smith, Southard, Sterling, Steuben, Sturtevant, Sullivan, Swarthout, Terwilliger, Tucker, Tuttle, Tyler, Van Hoosear, Van Scoy, Van Waganen, Vermilye, Wallis, Webb, Welsh, Wheeler, Whitehead, Whitney, Williams, Wilson, Wiltsey, Wimberly, Wise, Winters, Wright, Young.
Documented, indexed, illustrations.
Paper—$10.00—129pp--------------------------------------- Vendor #D0196

3088 - BLUE RIDGE MOUNTAIN KINFOLKS—NINE BLUE RIDGE MOUNTAIN FAMILY HISTORIES by Larry King. 1976.
Fisher, Gilbert, Hall, Harrington, Hartley, Hill, King, Kirby, Lawson Families. Grayson—Patrick—Rappahannock—Wythe Counties, Virginia/ Stokes—Surry, North Carolina. Allied Families: Alley, Anders, Anderson, Bartee, Bedwell, Byrd, Cole, Compton, Cornett, Corvin, Crockett, Delp, Eanes, Evans, Funk, Grubb, Hash, Hittle, Huddle, Huff, Jackson, Jenkins, Johnson, Keith, Kilbourne, Martin, Matthews, McKinnon, Miller, Osborne, Poole, Porter, Reynolds, Rhudy, Richardson, Scott, Sexton, Shuler, Snow, Sutherland, Taylor, Thompson, Tipton, Vaughan, Vaught, Waddell, Walker, Williams, Wingate, Wright. Blue cloth, gold lettering/design, 6"x9", typeset, 60 pound paper. 415 photographs, 7500 name index.
Cloth—$25.00—335pp--------------------------------------- Vendor #D0198

3089 - KEITH KINFOLKS—JAMES KEITH, SR. DESCENDANTS FROM 1720 TO 1979 by Larry King. 1979.
Eleven generation biographical genealogy featuring known/proven descendants of James Keith, Sr. who emigrated to Virginia, raised eight children. Today has numerous offspring in 2,075 families, including: Alderman, Bishop, Bolt, Brown, Bruce, Buckner, Chapman, Cole, Daily, Dorsey, Duncan, Eanes, Fitzwater, Gearhart, Grayson, Harman, Harris, Holcomb, Howell, Hylton, Jarvis, Jeffers, Keith, Kincaid, King, Kirby, Knowles, Legg, Logan, Loving, Lunsford, Moles, Moody, Morris, Moseley, Motley, McGaughey, Neal, Rollins, Rountree, Rucker, Semones, Shipman, Slaughter, Slusher, Smith, Sowers, Spence, Sprinkle, Sutphin, Taylor, Tilson, Turman, Weddle, Weeks, Whalen, Williams, Wingate, Woodruff, Woods. Green cloth, gold lettering/design, 7"x10", typeset, 70 pound paper, simple format/numbering, 182 photographs, 16,500 name index. Additional Keith works planned. Send your Keith ancestry for inclusion.
Cloth—$25.00—363pp--------------------------------------- Vendor #D0198

3090 - A BEDWELL FAMILY by Larry King. 1982.
Fourteen generations of Robert Bedwell descendants from London to Old Rappahannock County, Virginia in 1661; 3,760 Bedwell biographies; 2,600 allied families; 15,700 name index; typeset; pictures.
Cloth—$25.00—383pp--------------------------------------- Vendor #D0198

3091 - JOHN JACOB RECTOR/ELIZABETH FISHBACK DESCENDANTS by Larry King. In process (possibly 1 vol. ea. yr.—1984, 1985, 1986, 1987).
From Trupbach, Germany to Germanna, Virginia in 1714. Sons John, Henry, Harmon and Jacob. Beginning in 1984 a record will be published on descendants of each son—possibly four volumes. Contact Vendor #D0198.
--- Vendor #D0198

3092 - THE CIVIL WAR LETTERS OF COLONEL H. C. CAVINS, 14TH
INDIANA by Barbara A. Smith. 1981.
Paper—$17.95—230pp--- Vendor #D0203

3093 - DAVIS FAMILY DATA by Edward F. Nash. 1981.
Paper—$6.95—48pp-- Vendor #D0203

3094 - RECORD OF CARTER JERRELL KELLY by Carter Jerrell Kelly. 1979, repr.
Paper—$9.95—140pp-- Vendor #D0203

3095 - MATTHIAS SCHULTZ AND HIS DESCENDANTS by Carlyle W. Bennett.
1980.
Paper—$11.95—187pp--- Vendor #D0203

3096 - THE AUTOBIOGRAPHY OF ELDER WILSON THOMPSON by Wilson
Thompson (1788-1866). 1979, repr.
Carried the Gospel through Kentucky, Illinois, Missouri, Indiana and
Ohio.
Paper—$19.95—502pp--- Vendor #D0203

3097 - THE HUGHES GENEALOGY, ELLIS HUGHES 1776-1850 by Mrs.
Robert A. Hughes. 1979.
Cloth—$27.95—367pp--- Vendor #D0203

3098 - THE NEAVES STORY by Bettie J. Marsh. 1980.
Paper—$13.95—170pp--- Vendor #D0203

3099 - THE AUTOBIOGRAPHY OF KALOOST NAZARIAN, AN AMERICAN
IMMIGRANT by Kaloost Nazarian; edited by Leland Bibb. 1980 repr.
Cloth—$17.95—132pp--- Vendor #D0203

3100 - PROUD WANDERERS: MY MOTHER'S FAMILY by Virginia Sullivan
Bruch. 1985.
The Helm, Blakemore, Buck, and Neville families of the Shenandoah
Valley of Virginia, Middle Tennessee, and Western Kentucky.
Announced previously, re-scheduled for publication in early 1985.
Paper—apx. $30.00—apx. 400pp-------------------------- Vendor #D0205

3101 - BERNARDUS RYDER AND HIS DESCENDANTS by Kenneth R.
Harms. 1979.
A series of charts showing the known descendants of Bernardus
Ryder, born in Brooklyn, New York in 1744 and Femmetie De Nyse,
his wife. Related families include Bennett, Kouwenhoven, Stillwell,
Stryker, Voorhies. Index and map included.
Paper—$6.00—35pp--- Vendor #D0208

3102 - BRYANS, HORTONS AND ALLIED FAMILIES by Elizabeth Cate Manly.
1978.
Paper—$10.00—110pp-- Vendor #D0218

3103 - McCONNAUGHEY SOCIETY OF AMERICA, INCORPORATED BULLETIN
by Patricia McConnaughay Gregory.
Annual; back issues available; 32 pages 1963—$3.00;
64 pages 1971-1975—$5.00; 64 pages 1976-1977—$7.50;
72 pages 1978—$7.50; 80 pages 1979-1983—$10.00 each;
1984—$17.50 including dues and monthly newsletter.
Paper—$3.00—$17.50--------------------------------------- Vendor #D0221

3104 - McCONNAUGHEYS AND VARIANT SPELLINGS IN THE 1900 CENSUS.
1982.
Alphabetically arranged by first names and by states. 8½"x11¼.
Paper—$10.00—100+pp-------------------------------------- Vendor #D0221

3105 McCONNAUGHHAY by Gerald Born. 1983.
Genealogy of descendants of David McConnaughhay and Martha Ranson
of Pennsylvania and (Nicholas County) Kentucky, approximately
1750-1983.
Paper—$10.00—90+pp-------------------------------------- Vendor #D0221

3106 - REPORT FROM ULSTER, IRELAND, 1979 INCLUDING SUPPLEMENT
THERETO COMPILED BY MARIANNE HERALD McNAIR. 1980.
Up-to-date (in 1979) account of genealogical resources in Ulster,
Ireland, a 'first-hand' report. Some of the names mentioned are
Bovaird, Campbell, Duncan, Graham, Hannah, Lindsay, McConnaughey,
McCloud, McKinley, Platt, Story, Stunkard, Thompson, Walker, and
others. 8½"x11¼, 37 pages total, indexed.
Paper—$7.50—37pp--- Vendor #D0221

3107 - BURTONSVILLE HERITAGE, GENEALOGICALLY SPEAKING by
Elizabeth M. Lord. 1978 repr. of 1976 ed.
Documented indexed genealogies of over 100 settling and related
Maryland families including Aitcheson, Athey, Beall, Becraft, Bergmann,
Brown, Bryan, Burton, Carr, Carroll, Croasdale, Donaldson, Dustin,
Duvall, Harding, Iager, Kruhm, Marlow, Merson, Miles, Milstead,
Oursler, Parsley, Phair, Poole, Renn, Rich, Roby, Soper, Spencer,
Thompson, Turner, Waters, Wilson, Wootten, Wright, Yerkes.
Cloth—$18.00—377pp--- Vendor #D0227

3108 - THE MOSES JEFFRIES FAMILY OF NORTHERN VIRGINIA by Marie
Jeffries Capps. 1976 rev. ed.
This is the history of the family of Moes Jeffries, ca. 1769-1832,
son of James Jeffries of Fauquier County, Virginia and Molly Rector,
ca. 1789-?1879, daughter of Ann and Nathaniel Rector, and their
descendants. The line followed is that of Harrison Jeffries, early
teacher in MaGaheysville, Virginia, and his wives, Margaret Darnell
and Lucy Kyger. The book includes information on Alexander
Jefferies I of Stafford County, who is the founder of most of the
Jeffries families in Fauquier County. This book has been developed
to serve as a sourcebook for other Jeffries people across the country,
and serves this purpose by adding and correcting information as
other researchers share their work.
Paper—$30.00—150pp--- Vendor #D0229

3109 - MORAGNES IN AMERICA AND RELATED FAMILIES by Nell H.
Howard and Bessie W. Quinn. 1973.
A detailed history of the Moragne families descended from Pierre
Moragne and Cecile Bayle who came from France to the Abbeville
District, South Carolina prior to the Revolution. Surviving parts
of Pierre's diary included. Related families are:
Williams—England to Rappahannock County, Virginia, 1650;
Quarles, King William County, Virginia 1695; Read—Virginia 1704;
Whorton—Hall County, Georgia ca. 1800 (Mike Whorton, Attalla,
Alabama has traced this line to the first Lord Wharton, England);
Fulgham—Virginia; Wilson—Etowah County, Alabama; Young—Lincolnton
County, North Carolina 1777; Sutherlin—South Carolina 1787; Forney—
Alsace, France 1721, Pennsylvania and North Carolina 1754; Aber-
nathy—Abernathy, Scotland, 13th Century, Charles City County, Vir-
ginia 1655; Hughes—North Carolina 1840; Thayer—Gloucestershire,
England 13th Century, Boston 1640; Fortune—Kentucky 1798;
Hodges—Essex County, Virginia 1765; South Carolina 1763; Howard—
North Carolina 1730, New Jersey 1777; Yeilding—North Carolina 1705,
Blount County, Alabama 1800's; Hillsman—Amelia County, Virginia
1760; Mynatt—England 1727, Fauquier County, Virginia 1771; Burns—
North Carolina 1780; Dobbins—Granville County, North Carolina 1740,
South Carolina York District 1785.
Most of these families have been followed as they scattered over the
50 states. 62 pages of index.
Cloth—$20.00—566pp--- Vendor #D0238

3110 - THE BRACKIN FAMILY IN THE SOUTHEASTERN UNITED STATES
by Henry B. Brackin, Jr., M.D. 1979.
Related families include Allredge, Angel, Barber, Barker, Benedict,
Berryman, Boren, Boyle, Brown, Butler, Cooper, Faucett, Fine,
Freedle, Graves, Groves, Hall, House, Johnson, Jones, Keen, Kirk-
land, Lewis, Mankins, Meadows, Metcalf, Mills, Myers, McGlothlin,
McKendree, Norwood, Perdue, Smith, Tate, Taylor, Terry, Van Hoose,

Ward, Williams, Young.
This book begins with William Bracken of New Castle County, Delaware, an immigrant from England in 1699, giving data on all of his children and grandchildren. It then follows the descendants of the second son, John, who moved to Orange County, North Carolina in 1763. There are as many as ten generations in some lines, the families spreading over the south and then into the midwest, southwest and far west. Large numbers settled in such places as Rowan, Davie, Wilkes, Orange, Caswell, Transylvania Counties, North Carolina; Pendleton District, Greenville and Anderson Counties, South Carolina; Washington County, Georgia; Henry and Lawrence Counties, Alabama; Sumner, Carroll, Dyer and Obion Counties, Tennessee; Allen, Simpson, Graves, Ohio and Ballard Counties, Kentucky; Washington County, Arkansas; and Marshall County, Mississippi. The book is fully indexed. There is much resource material including wills, deeds, court records, Bible records, marriage lists and census records.
Cloth—$26.50—432pp--- Vendor #D0239

3111   - WILLIAM BRACKEN OF NEW CASTLE COUNTY, DELAWARE AND HIS DESCENDANTS by Henry Martyn Bracken, M.D. 1930, repr.
This book begins with William Bracken of New Castle County, Delaware, an immigrant from England in 1699, giving data on all of his children. It then follows the descendants of his first son, Thomas, and his third son, Henry, for up to seven generations. These families migrated across Pennsylvania, into Ohio, Indiana and on across the midwest. One branch joined the Morman movement and went to Utah. For researchers on the Bracken, Brackin Family this work is indispensible due to its voluminous records, both public and private. It contains interviews of people and letters written 55 to 110 years ago and includes antedotal material and family records long ago otherwise lost. There is a small amount of material on the second son, John. There are letters from people from other Bracken, Brackin families, many of whom were Irish immigrants. The book is well indexed.
Paper—$26.50—592pp------------------------------------- Vendor #D0239

3112   - UNTANGLING SOME OF THE WRIGHTS OF BEDFORD COUNTY, VIRGINIA by Robert N. Grant. 1977.
Thomas Wright (?-1763) and sons John Wright (?-1803) and Joseph Wright (?-1815) and their descendants. Related families include in part: Asberry or Asbury, Brown, Corley, Drake, Greer, Hardy, Holland(?), Hopper, Hurt, Mays or Mayse, McCormack, Meador, McGeorge, Pasley, Pate(?), Scott, Simmons and Wheeler.
John Wright (?-1810) and his descendants. Related families include in part: Bateman, Clayton, Daniel, Hardwicke, Hunter, Mayse, Waugh, and Worley.
John Wright (?-1814) and his descendants. Related families include in part: Bibb(?), Pace or Pierce, Pullen, Watts, and Weekes.
Cloth—$60.00—1000pp--------------------------------- Vendor #D0240

3113   - THE PEAK—PEAKE FAMILY HISTORY by Cyrus H. Peake and Carol J. Snow. 1975 and 1977.
Of value to anyone interested in this surname. Four volumes in one, covering: I—General History (family origins and growth, notable members); II—Branches in Great Britain; III—Branches in United States and Canada (Christopher of Massachusetts, William of Massachusetts and Vermont, John of Maryland); IV—Branches in Australia, New Zealand, and elsewhere. Genealogical and biographical details, including photographs; fully indexed. Price is for combined 1975-1977 edition with binders; however, purchase of individual sections is possible. Inquiries welcome!
Paper—in binders—$39.00—554pp------------------------- Vendor #D0250

3114   - MILLS FAMILY HISTORY, QUAKERS AND OTHER EARLY ARRIVALS by Paul Mills. 1979.
The book starts with John Mills, the immigrant, born about 1660, came to America about 1682. His son John had twelve children and the book brings some of the lines down to 1974. Other related lines are:

Beals, Beeson, Bond, Canaday, Cook, Davis, Hadley, Hammer,
Harrold, Hawkins, Hiatt, Hockett, Hodgson, Hodson, Hunt, Jay,
Jackson, Lewis, Macy, Mendenhall, Morgan, Stanley, Thornburg,
Williams, Wilson and many more. Indexed.
Paper—$9.50—168pp--- Vendor #D0251

3115   - NEWBY FAMILY HISTORY by Paul Mills. 1975.
Starts with William Newby of Virginia and lists his descendants; some
down to 1973. Several pictures. Also an article on early life in
Nebraska.
Paper—$7.50—60pp-- Vendor #D0251

3116   - WALLEN FAMILY HISTORY by Paul Mills. 1975.
Starts with Isaiah Wallen of New Jersey and his eight children. Much
of the book is devoted to Pierson Wallen and his twelve children. Also
contains an article on early life in Nebraska.
Paper—$7.50—48pp-- Vendor #D0251

3117   - HENRY MILLS FAMILY: ANCESTORS AND DESCENDANTS by Paul
Mills. 1966.
Starts with John Mills. Shows that all descendants of Henry have
Mayflower ancestry. Many pictures and articles.
Cloth—$9.50—138pp--------------------------------------- Vendor #D0251

3118   - MILLS AND RELATED LINES by Paul Mills. 1984.
A new book with over 7000 names, indexed. This is the best and
largest Mills book ever published. Related lines: Beals, Beeson,
Bond, Broon, Cook, Cox, Davis, Elliott, Hadley, Harlan, Haworth,
Hester, Hiatt, Hinshaw, Hockett, Hudson, Hoskins, Hunt, Jackson,
Jones, Mendenhall, Morgan, Osborn, Stanbrough, Stanley, Smith,
Thornburg, Williams and many, many more.
Paper—$19.50—662pp-------------------------------------- Vendor #D0251

3119   - GENERATIONS BACK: NORTON AND RELATED LINES compiled
and edited by Sarah Mills Norton. 1977.
Genealogy of Norton—Montgomery County, Virginia, 1790; Pendleton
District, South Carolina, 1793. Related lines include Abney, Burdyne,
Campbell, Cason, Dowtin, Golding (Golden), Grisham (Gresham),
Halbert, Hall, Lawrence, Lesley (Lesly), Madison, Meek, Mills,
Spraggins (Spraggans), Watt. Most of the families were colonial
Virginia settlers, then migrants into North Carolina, the Piedmont
counties of South Carolina, or into Georgia. Descendants now wide-
spread. Family Bible records, burying grounds and epitaphs are
included. Seven family manuscripts (memorabilia or reminiscence)—
earliest is 1846, latest is 1890's. Much is Civil War material. Civil
War Letters and Diary of J. J. Norton of Orr's South Carolina
Regiment (Gen. Gregg's Brigade)—1860 thru Battle of Fredericksburg.
Indexed with complete bibliography, 336 pages, cloth only—$22.00.
Cloth—$22.00—336pp--------------------------------------- Vendor #D0252

3120   - HISTORY OF THE KIMBALL FAMILY IN AMERICA 1634-1897 by
Leonard A. Morrison and Stephen P. Sharples. 1978 repr. of 1897 ed.
Cloth—$35.00—1278pp-------------------------------------- Vendor #D0256

3121   - KIMBALL FAMILY ASSOCIATION QUARTERLY NEWSLETTER by
Kimball Family Association.
Quarterly.
Paper—$5.00/year—6pp------------------------------------- Vendor #D0256

3122   - KIMBALL FAMILY NEWS by Kimball Family Association, January, 1980.
Paper—$5.00/year-- Vendor #D0256

3123   - THE SIMMS FAMILY OF STAFFORD COUNTY, VIRGINIA by William
K. Hall. 1969.
Richard Simms (ca 1720-ca 1812) and Elizabeth Bridwell (-ca 1816)
of Stafford County, Virginia, had three sons who served in Revolu-
tionary War. This book is a genealogy of their descendants. The
sons were:
Richard Simms (1752-1850) married Elizabeth Ashby and settled in
Clay County, Missouri

Presley <u>Simms</u> (ca 1754-1852) married Nancy <u>Bridwell</u> and settled in Montgomery County, Indiana.
Rhodam <u>Simms</u> (1756-1853) married Mary <u>Stark</u> and settled in Ralls County, Missouri.
Completely indexed.
Cloth—$10.00—248pp-- Vendor #D0269

3124   - MASSEY: VOLUME 1, MASSEY GENEALOGY by Judge Frank A. Massey.
Containing Book I, *My Massey Family in England*, and Book II, *Massey Families in America*.
Cloth—$20.00—417pp-- Vendor #D0270

3125   - MASSEY: VOLUME 2, MASSEY GENEALOGY ADDENDUM by Judge Frank A. Massey.
Indexed; also containing index for Book II.
Cloth—$30.00—472pp-- Vendor #D0270

3126   - MASSEY: VOLUME 3, MASSEY ON CENSUSES by Judge Frank A. Massey.
1790-1850, inclusive, plus miscellaneous information including marriages, etc., plus some later census data.
The <u>Massey/Massie</u>, etc. history beginning 1086 in England to the author via his immigrant ancestor in 1636 to which nearly all by the sur-name would connect; and the immigrant ancestors by the sur-name with lines of descent traced where discovered, and with information to aid in tracing back in time from 1850 or later where not already developed by the author.
Cloth—$30.00--- Vendor #D0270

3127   - THE LONDON FAMILY by Opal London Cox. 1976.
200 years of the <u>London</u> Family in America; Bicentennial Edition covers most of the early <u>Londons</u> in America; New Jersey, North Carolina, Pennsylvania, <u>Virginia</u>, Tennessee.
Cloth—$13.50—400pp--- Vendor #D0272

3128   - THE BOATMAN FAMILY by Opal London Cox. 1980.
Descendants of Henry, of Lancaster County, Virginia 1675 Claudis <u>Boatman</u>, Bernard <u>Boatman</u>.
Cloth—$26.50—300pp-- Vendor #D0272

3129   - KINFOLKS by Opal London Cox. 1984.
<u>Thornbury</u>, <u>Yates</u>, <u>McCoy</u>, <u>Cain</u>, <u>Bewley</u>, <u>Holdren</u>, <u>Dowell</u>, <u>Board</u>, in Virginia early then Maryland, Bedford County, <u>Virginia</u>, Hardin, Breckinridge, Meade Counties in Kentucky. Together for over 200 years. In process.
(In process)—Cloth—300pp----------------------------- Vendor #D0272

3130   - SWETT—ALLEN AND ALLIED FAMILIES by R. A. Swett, edited and extended by Susan S. Forrester. 1978.
Genealogies of some contemporary <u>Swetts</u> and <u>Allens</u> whose immigrant ancestors were John <u>Swett</u> (Newbury, Massachusetts, 1642) and Walter <u>Allen</u> (Newbury, Massachusetts, ca 1640). Related families include <u>Andrews</u>, <u>Baldwin</u>, <u>Bixby</u>, <u>Conant</u>, <u>Cook</u>, <u>Dodge</u>, <u>Fuller</u>, <u>Gibson</u>, <u>Healy</u>, <u>Jewett</u>, <u>Moore</u>, <u>Prescott</u>, <u>Putnam</u>, <u>Rice</u>, <u>Richards</u>, <u>Tenney</u>, <u>Terry</u>, <u>Wheeler</u>, <u>Whitman</u>, <u>Wight</u>, <u>Woodbury</u>, among dozens of others. Most families from England and remained in New England until 1900's. Photographs. Large number of entries coded to bibliography of 263 references. Index.
Cloth—$15.00—263pp-- Vendor #D0278

3131   - WARREN AND ETHEL (GARLAND) MARKWITH. THEIR ANCESTORS, DESCENDANTS AND RELATED FAMILIES by Joseph H. Vance. 1982.
Warren Roscoe <u>Markwith</u> (1885 Ohio—1935 Ohio) and Mamie Ethel <u>Garland</u> (1890 Indiana—1975 California); lived Darke County, Ohio; nine children.
Chapter for each of these families with descendants of earliest known progenitors:
Markwith: John C. (1774 Jew Jersey—1836 Ohio) and Elizabeth <u>Muck-ridge</u> (1786 New Jersey—1861 Indiana); Daniel (ca 1779 New Jersey—

1830 New Jersey); Richard J. (1789 New Jersey—1871 Ohio) and Esther, Elizabeth, Rachel Brown (1792—).
Nealeigh: Joseph Nechlich (—1786 Pennsylvania); Henry Nehlich (Nealeigh), Sr. (1767 Pennsylvania—1848 Ohio) and Elizabeth (Wertz?) (1773 Pennsylvania—1855 Ohio).
Brown: Jacob "Wagonmaker" Braun (1731—1808 Tennessee) and Elizabeth.
Langston: Lazarus (1774-1841 Ohio) and Elizabeth Mashburn (1775-1872 Ohio), Southern families.
Sliger: John, Sr. (ca 1740-1818 Tennessee) and Cathrina.
Shields: Daniel, Sr. (1741 Ireland-1833 Ohio) and Mary.
Garland: Joseph (ca 1782 Tennessee—1856 Ohio) and Sarah.
Ferguson: Elisha (1803 Ireland or Vermont—1875 Ohio) and Aba Cora McFlinn, Nancy (1804-1872 Ohio), Huldy.
Albright: Johannes Albrecht (ca 1695 Germany—1752 Pennsylvania) and Anna Barbara.
Burk: Isaac (-1834 Ohio) and Mrs. Esther (Clapp) Albright (1738 Pennsylvania—).
Davis: John (Or William) (ca 1800) and Theranza Walker (ca 1803 Pennsylvania or Ohio—1878 Indiana).
Clapp: George Valentine (1702 Germany—1773 North Carolina) and Barbara; John Ludwig (1704 Germany—1777 North Carolina) and Anna Margaret (Strader?) (1717 Germany—1785 North Carolina).
Historical background, biographical sketches, 180 illustrations, 11 maps, pedigree charts. Every name index, over 11,500 names.
Big 8½"x11" pages. Beautifully printed, offset, heavy paper, perfect binding.
Cloth—$26.50—Paper—$19.50—270pp----------------------- Vendor #D0282

3132   - PHILIP AND ANNA CHRISTINA (CLAPP) ALBRIGHT, THEIR AN-CESTORS AND DESCENDANTS by Joseph H. Vance. 1985.
Philip Albright (1756 North Carolina—1820 Ohio) and Anna Christina ("Christine") Clapp (1756 North Carolina—1817 Ohio). Moved from Guilford County, North Carolina to Campbell County, Tennessee about 1800 and to Ohio in 1805. Lived Preble County, Ohio; buried Roselawn cemetery, Lewisburg, Ohio. Ten children.
This book documents thousands of descendants of Philip and Christine (Clapp) Albright, pioneer Ohio family. Family names among descendants: Albright, Thomas, Sharp, Tillman (Tilman), Chenoweth, Brock, Mote, Richardson, Garland, Osborn, Moser, Emerick, Jefferis, Hercules, Hunt, Nealeigh, Oaks, Penix, Smith, McClure, Silence, Ingraham, Yenter, Garner, Limbert, Ditmer, Krickenberger, Ludy, Hawley, Cole, Murphy, Lukens, Snyder, Baker, Henthorn, Roberts, Bollinger, Dubbs, Cowley, Brannan, Page, Clemens, Meade, Sarver, Tice, McCluen, Delk, John, Fox, Condon, Weider, Loughman, Niles, Stager, Markwith, Myers, Hussey, Kaiser, West, McCauley, Fitzpatrick, Turpin, Brankle, Hobbs, Ballinger, Chambers, Bishop, Willard, Dobbs, Harris, Graham, Barrington, Sheldon, Fernelius, Folkerth, Shrader, Wakefield, Gordon, Randall, Wickersham, Roberts, Heitland, Eggers, Jacobsen, Jones, Benson, Struck, Clock, Wood, Richmond, Thompson, Van Meter, Gilbert, Beasecker, Lensch, Frock, Barton, Fouts, Hemmert—and many, many more.
Philip Albright was grandson of Johannes Albrecht (ca 1695 Germany—1752 Pennsylvania) and Anna Barbara. Christine Clapp was grand-daughter of George Valentine Clapp (1702 Germany—1773 North Carolina) and Barbara.
(In process)--- Vendor #D0282

3133   - CARY ESTES GENEALOGY by Webb Estes. 1981 repr. of 1939 ed.
Cary Family—England; armorial documentation; Miles Cary—Windmill Point, Virginia 1640's; Blairs (Washington, DC): Bell; Bates; Abraham Estes immigrant 1600's Virginia; Este Family—Italy; Folk; Mann; Moody; Snedecor.
(Only 200 books left of 500); $50.00 per set with *Cary Estes Moore.*
Cloth—$30.00—249pp----------------------------------Vendor #D0289

3134 - CARY ESTES MOORE GENEALOGY by Helen Estes Seltzer. 1981.
Up-date—Cary Estes (see above listing); also Shildes Moore—immigrated
Maryland 1725; migrated North Carolina; Major Green Hill (Rev.);
Yates; Menefee; Leake; 117 illustrations.
(Only 200 books left of 500); $50.00 per set with Cary Estes.
Cloth—$35.00—498pp-- Vendor #D0289

3135 - THE NIGHTINGALE GENEALOGY, 1814-1976, WITH ALLIED FAMILIES
by Dorman J. Robinson. 1979.
All of the allied families originated in Lapeer County, Michigan.
Includes Bell, English, Fisher, Gates, Hough, Lavene, McInally,
Mitchell, Richards, Rockwell, Robinson, Soule, and many more. 6"x9".
Cloth—$11.00—150pp------------------------------------- Vendor #D0295

3136 - THE WIATT FAMILY OF VIRGINIA by Alexander L. Wiatt. 1980.
The descendants of John, Jr. (1732-1805) of Gloucester County,
Virginia and his wife Mary Todd are traced with a monograph about
each family member. The work also includes John's lineal descent
from Adam Wiot, who lived in the mid 1300's in Yorkshire, England
through the Rev. Haute Wiat who came to America in 1619. There
is also information on collateral families. These include: Field,
Carter, Todd, Cocke, Ball, Montague, Jones and other Wiatt Families
not descendants of John.
Cloth—$12.50—186pp------------------------------------ Vendor #D0297

3137 - THE ANDREW HICKS AND CHARLES STONE FAMILIES by Lucile
Kaufmann Novak. 1977.
Hicks: Cornwall County, England, to Knox County, Ohio, 1835.
Stone: England to Ohio, 1820's; Richland County, Ohio, 1853.
Related families: Baker, Congdon, Ford, Hobbs, McCullough,
McFarland, McMillan, Scoggan, White. Indexed. Illustrated.
Cloth—$12.50—129pp------------------------------------ Vendor #D0299

3138 - THE JOHN AND MILLEY HESTER FAMILY by Lucile Kaufmann
Novak and Gladis M. Kaufmann. 1977.
Hester: Granville, Stokes Counties, North Carolina—1770's-present;
Shelby County, Indiana—1820's. Related families: Carrell, Crews,
Crim, Fair, Fulp, Linville, Rigsbee, Starbuck, Wicker, Workman.
Indexed. Illustrated.
Cloth—$16.00—339pp------------------------------------ Vendor #D0299

3139 - KAUFMANN FAMILIES FROM GRINDELWALD, SWITZERLAND:
CHRISTIAN AND ULRICH OF HOLMES COUNTY, OHIO; RUDOLPH OF
TETON COUNTY, WYOMING; PETER OF KNOX COUNTY, OHIO by
Lucile Kaufmann Novak and Gladis M. Kaufman. 1982.
Kaufman(n): Grindelwald records 1508-1950; Christian to United
States—1880; Ulrich-ca 1862; Rudolph-1900; Peter-1895. Indexed.
Illustrated.
Related families: Bohren, Durtschi, Inaebnit, Bergundthal.
Cloth—$25.00—282pp------------------------------------ Vendor #D0299

3140 - THE HESTER NEWSLETTER (QUARTERLY) edited by Lucile Novak.
1980—.
Paper—$5.00/yearly—12pp/issue------------------------ Vendor #D0299

3141 - BAKER, WOMACK AND OTHER KIN (BYARS, HALARSONS, ETC.)
compiled by Martha McDaniel Thompson, C.G. 1978.
Paper—$8.00—51pp------------------------------------- Vendor #D0302

3142 - McDANIEL RESEARCH IN VIRGINIA compiled by Martha McDaniel
Thompson, C.G. 1984.
Paper—$10.00—75pp----------------------------------- Vendor #D0302

3143 - McDANIEL RESEARCH IN NORTH CAROLINA compiled by Martha
McDaniel Thompson, C.G. 1984.
Paper—$10.00—75pp----------------------------------- Vendor #D302

3144 - FELAND AND SINGLETON FAMILIES, VIRGINIA, KENTUCKY,
MISSOURI compiled by Martha McDaniel Thompson, C.G.
Paper—$8.00—60pp------------------------------------ Vendor #D0302

3145 - SOME DESCENDANTS OF WILLIAM WOMACK, THE IMMIGRANT compiled by Martha McDaniel Thompson, C.G. Revised 1984. Paper—$15.00—130pp------------------------------------ Vendor #D0302

3146 - GRADELESS GENEALOGY, VOLUME 1: ANCESTORS, RELATIVES AND DESCENDANTS OF NATHANIEL GRADELESS by Donald E. Gradeless. 1973. Paper—$10.00—113pp------------------------------------ Vendor #D0304

3147 - THE MORT FAMILY IN AMERICA, VOLUME 1 by Donald E. Gradeless. 1983. Paper—$15.00—128pp------------------------------------ Vendor #D0304

3148 - THE THOMPSON BROTHERS OF KOSCIUKO COUNTY, INDIANA by Donald E. Gradeless. 1984. Paper—$15.00—55pp------------------------------------- Vendor #D0304

3149 - THE SIMISON, LUCAS, AND WRIGLEY FAMILIES OF KOSCIUSKO COUNTY, INDIANA by Donald E. Gradeless. 1984. Paper—$15.00—55pp------------------------------------- Vendor #D0304

3150 - THE CLENDINEN FAMILY: THOMAS CLENDINEN OF CECIL COUNTY, MARYLAND AND YORK COUNTY, SOUTH CAROLINA. A GENEALOGICAL RECORD OF HIS FAMILY AND DESCENDANTS IN THE SOUTH, 1741-1983 by Anita C. Clendinen Enquist. 1985. Includes the Clendinen family of early Augusta, Greenbrier and Kanawha Counties, Virginia, 1740-1790; Henry and Houston Counties, Alabama, 1846-1983. Family charts, photographs and index included. In Process. (In process)-- Vendor #D0306

3151 - THE BATEMAN CONNECTION, THE KNOWN DESCENDENTS OF WILLIAM BATEMAN OF LONDON, ENGLAND, CHARLESTOWN, AND CONCORD, MASSACHUSETTS, AND FAIRFIELD, CONNECTICUT by Bradley B. Ridge. 1978. *The Bateman Connection* is a painstakingly documented record of the descendants of a distinguished New England family with English antecedents in 1629. It has been researched and assembled by a scholar intimately associated with that family, who brings to the subject a thoroughly grounded knowledge of genealogy and the behavioral sciences. The volume explores the nature and extent of its dispersal in the mainstream of American life from its base points in Concord, Massachusetts, Killingly, Connecticut and Fairfield (Bridgeton), New Jersey. It also provides a list of references to published English sources by shire on the surname Bateman. The volume is composed of three indexes: the first index is a detailed listing by given name of each of the known Bateman descendants of William Bateman. The second index is a list of Bateman wives by first name facilitating research from other family groups. The surname of the wife is included where known. The third index is that of the standard cross reference surname variety which is indispensable in a genealogical reference book. There are some 194 pages of text showing birth, marriage, death and burial dates and places, as well as the available information on names associated with wills, inventories, and administrations. The book shows Revolutionary and Colonial military service and contains pedigree charts. It concludes with a 63-page two-column surname index. References and Bibliography. LC 7963722; ISBN: 9960251804. Cloth—$30.00—291+pp------------------------------------Vendor #D0308

3152 - A BATEMAN DIRECTORY FOR ILLINOIS by Bradley B. Ridge. 1983. -- Vendor #D0308

3153 - THE BAUCOM, BAUCUM, BAWCOM, BAUGHCOM, BALCOMBE, BALCOM, BALKCOM, ETC., FAMILIES IN THE UNITED STATES edited by Banks McLaurin, Jr. 1980, repr. Baucom ancestry from Nicholas Baucom, Baltimore, Maryland, in 1725, in North Carolina in 1742; New England ancestry from Alexander Balcom, b. Sussex, England, first found in Portsmouth, Rhode Island, in 1664. Descendants of all variant spellings of the Baucom names

are included in this book, completely indexed with alphabetical identification code which immediately identifies each individual by generation and family lineage, with over five thousand individual names. Also included are all known census records of Baucoms, regardless of spelling, Revolutionary War records, court records, bibliography. Related families number over five hundred, including Banks, Brewer, Burris, Cooper, Cowdry, Crockett, Curd, Davis, Edwards, Evans, Fowler, Gambill, Gibson, Goodson, Hale, Hamilton, Hays, Hobbs, Huston, Jones, Johnson, Johnston, Kinnington, Lawson, Little, Marx, McLaurin, Mills, Nance, Owen, Owens, Parker, Purser, Railsback, Ramsey, Scott, Sellars, Sheffield, Smith, Sparlin, Stacy, Staton, Thomas, Thompson, Trevathan, Turner, Tyree, Upchurch, Vick, Walston, Wells, West, Williams, Wilson, Winston, Wright, Yates, and Zachary.
Paper—$26.00—loose leaf—apx. 340pp----------------------- Vendor #D0310

3154 - THE SHARK RIVER DISTRICT by George Castor Martin. 1983 repr. of 1914 ed.
Monmouth County genealogies: Chambers, Corlies, Drummond, Morris, Potter, Shafts, Webley, White.
Paper—$7.00—98pp--- Vendor #D0318

3155 - GEORGE WASHINGTON CANTRELL AND HIS WIFE MARTHA ELIZABETH LEA CARVER OF TENNESSEE; THEIR ANCESTRY AND DESCENDANTS by Mildred Sulser Wright. 1983.
Documented information on ancestry as relates to Carver, Swingley, Curd, Price and the Lumpkin-Woodson lineage of Martha Curd; Hardy and McDougle.
Paper—$30.00—80pp-------------------------------------- Vendor #D0326

3156 - WILLIAM HARPER WRIGHT OF STONE'S RIVER, TENNESSEE AND ALLIED FAMILIES by Mildred S. Wright. 1980.
8½"x11". Maps; photos.
Cloth—$35.00—Paper—$25.00—172pp------------------------- Vendor #D0326

3157 - JOSIAH AND LYDIA WILSON AND SLASHAM VALLEY, ST. CLAIR COUNTY, ALABAMA KINFOLK by Mildred S. Wright. 1980.
Cloth—$28.75—Paper—$18.75—100pp----------------------- Vendor #D0326

3158 - JACKSONIANA, A JACKSON FAMILY NEWSLETTER edited and published by Earnest H. Jackson, quarterly.
Free queries with subscription. Subscriber's data is entered into computer and if information is matched subscriber is notified.
Paper—$10.00/annually------------------------------- Vendor #D0338

3159 - OLD TIME TAZEWELL by Mary Ann Hansard (1825-1899), published by Mary Lorena Hansard Wilson. 1979.
The book contains 200 family histories and events of the time in Tazewell, Claiborne County, Tennessee. Author was a long time resident and contemporary of the period (1825-1899). Included in the index of over 600 surnames are such names of early settlers as Atkins, Brown, Burch, Burchfield, Cadle, Campbell, Cardwell, Carr, Carriger, Cloud, Cottrell, Davis, Day, DeBusk, Ely, Epps, Evans, Fugate, Fulkerson, Fultz, Garrett, Goin, Graham, Greer, Hamilton, Hansard, Harmon, Helms, Henderson, Hill, Hodge, Hollingsworth, Hollensworth, Houston, Huddleston, Hunt, Hurst, Janeway, Jennings, Jessee, Johnston, Jones, Kelley, Large, Lewis (Fielding), Margraves, Markhan, Mayes, Meyres, Miller, McBee, McDowell, McNealance, Neil, Niel, Ousley, Owens, Parker, Patterson, Posey, Robinson, Rodgers, Rose, Soard, Saunders, Sewell, Simmons, Skaggs, Stone, Thompson, Townsley, Walker, White, Wiley, Yoakum.
Geographic areas referred to in text are Tennessee Counties: Anderson, Campbell, Claiborne, Carter, Greene, Hawkins, Hancock, Johnson, Jefferson, Knox, Monroe, Union, Washington. Virginia Counties: Lee, Russell, Scott, Tazewell, Washington, Wise and Wythe. Kentucky Counties: Bell, Harlan, Knox, Warren and Whitley. Western North Carolina, Southeast, Indiana, Ohio, Arkansas, Missouri, Texas, Kansas, California. Through sales book placed in 33 states. Cloth $15.00 (includes handling and postage). Tennessee residents add 6% state sales tax.
Cloth—$15.00—289pp-------------------------------------- Vendor #D0342

3160 - DESCENDANTS OF ABRAHAM COLEMAN AND THEIR NEIGHBORS
by Jonathan Coleman.
8"families: Adkins, Blackburn, Goff, Justice,
Kendrick, Slone, Thacker.
Paper—$7.50—108pp--- Vendor #D0349

3161 - McEATHRON (McEACHRON, McEACHRAN, McEACHERN) FAMILY by
Ellsworth D. McEathron. 1983 repr. of 1941 ed.
Paper—$1.50—8pp--- Vendor #D0354

3162 - THE ILIFF GENEALOGIST by George Ely Russell, C.G., F.A.S.G.,
F.N.G.S. 1983.
Richard Iliff of Bucks County, Pennsylvania, Family.
Paper—$9.00—84pp--- Vendor #D0354

3163 - RICHARD TAYLOR, TAILOR, AND SOME OF HIS DESCENDANTS by
James W. Hawes. Repr. of 1914 ed.
Massachusetts, Connecticut, New York.
Paper—$5.00—38pp--- Vendor #D0354

3164 - DESCENDANTS OF ALEXANDER PATON OF FENWICK, AYRSHIRE
by James R. Paton. Repr. of 1903 ed.
Scotland, 1644-1903.
Paper—$3.50—12pp--- Vendor #D0354

3165 - DESCENDANTS OF JAMES PATON (1811) AND JACOBINA WILLS
(OSBORNE) PATON OF GALSTON, SCOTLAND, AND UTAH by Hubert
A. Paton. Repr. of 1959 ed.
Paper—$5.50—48pp--- Vendor #D0354

3166 - CRESSWELL FAMILY AND THE AMERICAN CRISWELLS by Edgar
Golden Criswell. 1983 repr. of 1931 ed.
Paper—$16.00—157pp--- Vendor #D0354

3167 - JOHN AND NANCY GUNTER OF JEMSEG, NEW BRUNSWICK, THEIR
ANCESTORS AND DESCENDANTS by Andrew Gunter. 1969.
Gunter: New York (state)— -1783; New Brunswick, Canada—
1783-1969.
Paper—$2.00—48pp--- Vendor #D0356

3168 - FROM CELTS, FAMINE, AND SAWDUST by Tim Delanty. 1979.
Covers the social-economic history (1790-1928) and Celtic origins of
the Delahanty (Delanty), Tynan, Cummings, and Dunphy families
of Tipperary, Ireland who immigrated to the United States in the
1850's. Illustrated; footnoted; indexed.
Paper—$25.00—373pp--- Vendor #D0357

3169 - AN AMERICAN FAMILY AND ITS ANCESTOR PREDECESSORS by
Vivian Higgins Morse. 1973.
Fourteen generations in America (New England and South) of British
extraction. Genealogical lines down from Roman and Greek Monarchs,
Queen Boadicea of early Druids, two lines down from Adam of the Bible.
It is historical as well as genealogical, has had several complimentary
reviews, is indexed, illustrated, and documented.
Families included: Higgins, Hardy, Bangs, Bray, Booth, Carpenter,
Clarke, Cole, Converse, Curtiss, Doane, Douglas, Greene, Holden,
Hopkins, Howland, Johnson, Knowles, Lancaster, Lovelace, McGlashan,
Paine, Patterson, Phelps, Pitcher, Reed, Sackett, Sandys, Sears,
Smith, Snow, Spencer, Swift, Treat, Waite, Warren, Weaver, Webb,
Welles, Wyman....others.
Cloth—$14.00—181pp--- Vendor #D0362

3170 - THE GENEALOGY OF THE MATTHIAS FRANTZ FAMILY OF BERKS
COUNTY, PENNSYLVANIA by E. Harold Frantz, Reuben F. King,
et al.. 1976 repr. of 1972 ed.
Includes a historical section on European background and colonial
beginnings, with maps, diagrams and pictures, from Christian Frantz,
1685-1738; and a section of genealogical data on all descendants of
Matthias Frantz, 1769-1829. Includes much genealogical information
on Bashore, Brightbill, Bross, Crouse, Darkes, Dubble, Erb,

Firestone, Gibble, Houtz, Hunsicker, King, Lentz, Long, Meyer, Miller, Wenger, Ziegler. Hardbound, 621 pages, (includes 59 page index, 13,500 names) $22.00 postpaid.
Cloth—$22.00—621pp-- Vendor #D0363

3171 - ELDER JACOB MILLER AND DUNKARD KIN, VIRGINIA, OHIO AND INDIANA by Patricia Givens Johnson. 1977.
Miller, Toney, Darst, Lybrook, Moss, Witter, Ritter, Kingery, Petry, Brower, Eikenberry and related families in Iowa; Oregon; California; Preble County, Ohio; Union, Cass, Parke, Wayne Counties, Indiana.
Paper—109pp-- Vendor #D0364

3172 - GENERAL ANDREW LEWIS OF ROANOKE AND GREENBRIER by Patricia Givens Johnson. 1980-81.
Andrew Lewis and his associates in Augusta, Botetourt, Greenbrier, Bath, Roanoke Counties, Virginia; War and land speculation 1740-1780.
Cloth—$13.00—300pp------------------------------------- Vendor #D0364

3173 - JAMES PATTON AND THE APPALACHIAN COLONISTS by Patricia Givens Johnson. 2nd pr., 1983.
James Patton came from Ireland in mid 1700's and was a leader in settlement of Valley of Virginia and Southwestern Virginia. One of his daughters married William Thompson, the other married John Buchanan. William Preston was a nephew.
Cloth—$25.00--- Vendor #D0364

3174 - WILLIAM PRESTON AND THE ALLEGHENY PATRIOTS by Patricia Givens Johnson. 1976.
This is a documented biography of William Preston (1729-1783) of Montgomery County, Virginia. A history of the entire area of Southwest Virginia during the period 1753-1783. Related families include Floyd, Buchanan, Campbell, Smith, Blair, Breckenridge.
Cloth—$12.65—325pp------------------------------------- Vendor #D0364

3175 - THE CONLEY FAMILY—DESCENDANTS OF NICHOLAS by Jean Alonzo Curran, M.D. 1976.
Nicholas arrived Boston 1758. Family moved westward generally to New York, Iowa and Minnesota. Related families include Curran, Engstrom, Hutchins, Loveless.
Cloth—$25.00—Paper—$15.00-------------------------- Vendor #D0365

3176 - TAYLOR FAMILY OF LINCOLNSHIRE, ENGLAND by R. B. Taylor. 1982.
Ninety-eight Taylor families all descendants of John Taylor of Lincoln-shire 1699. Traces family to Nottingham, England, Richmond, Virginia, Macon, Georgia, and many other towns. Chart 10"x24".
Only $2. Satisfaction guaranteed.
Order from: R. B. Taylor, 820 Trotter Circle, Las Vegas, NV 89107-4501
Paper—$2.00--- Vendor #D0367

3177 - FOWLKES FAMILY OF VIRGINIA by R. B. Taylor. 1984.
Thirty Fowlkes families starting with Gabriel Fowlkes from Wales, 1775.
Chart 18"x30". Only $5. Satisfaction guaranteed.
Order from: R. B. Taylor, 820 Trotter Circle, Las Vegas, NV 89107-4501
Paper—$5.00--- Vendor #D0367

3178 - FAMILY HISTORY OF JOHN BISHOP OF WHITBURN, SCOTLAND by Stanley R. Scott and Robert H. Montgomery. 1951.
Cloth—$11.00—148pp-------------------------------- Vendor #D0370

3179 - SOME DESCENDANTS OF NATHANIEL WOODWARD WHO CAME TO BOSTON ABOUT 1630 by Harold Edward Woodward. 1984.
Cloth—$12.50—240pp---------------------------------Vendor #D0370

3180 - DESCENDANTS OF JOHN DEAN OF DEDHAM, MASSACHUSETTS by Marion D. Cooper. 1957.
Paper—$11.00—217pp-------------------------------- Vendor #D0370

3181 - DESCENDANTS OF ANDREW DEWING OF DEDHAM, MASSACHUSETTS by Benjamin Franklin Dewing. 1904.
Cloth—$13.50—165pp-------------------------------------- Vendor #D0370

3182 - DESCENDANTS OF LAWRENCE DOWS by Azro Milton Dows. 1890.
Genealogies of the Masterman, Morse and allied families, 1642-1890.
Cloth—$11.00—348pp-------------------------------------- Vendor #D0370

3183 - DESCENDANTS OF DEACON JOSEPH EASTMAN OF HADLEY, MASSA-CHUSETTS by Guy S. Rix. 1908.
Cloth—$11.00—263pp-------------------------------------- Vendor #D0370

3184 - THE PEDIGREE OF FLETCHER GARRISON HALL by Garrison Kent Hall. 1979.
Cloth—$36.00—400pp-------------------------------------- Vendor #D0370

3185 - MUNROES OF LEXINGTON, MASSACHUSETTS by Richard S. Munroe. 1966.
Cloth—$13.50—468pp-------------------------------------- Vendor #D0370

3186 - NEW ENGLAND PARISH FAMILIES by Roswell Parish. 1938.
Cloth—$11.00—502pp-------------------------------------- Vendor #D0370

3187 - PALMER FAMILIES OF AMERICA: WILLIAM PALMER OF PLYMOUTH AND DUXBURY, MASSACHUSETTS by Horace Wilbur Palmer. 1973.
Cloth—$18.50—231pp-------------------------------------- Vendor #D0370

3188 - DESCENDANTS OF THOMAS PEMBER by John E. Pember. 1939.
Cloth—$18.50—325pp-------------------------------------- Vendor #D0370

3189 - DESCENDANTS OF THE REV. JOHN ROBINSON, PASTOR OF THE PILGRIMS. 1926.
Cloth—$26.00—410pp-------------------------------------- Vendor #D0370

3190 - EARLY HISTORY OF THE STRICKLANDS OF SIZERGH by S. H. Lee Washington. 1942.
Cloth—$18.50—100pp-------------------------------------- Vendor #D0370

3191 - THE ANCESTORS OF LT. THOMAS TRACY OF NORWICH, CONNECTI-CUT by Lt. Charles Stedman Ripley. 1895.
Cloth—$11.00—100pp-------------------------------------- Vendor #D0370

3192 - DESCENDANTS OF NATHANIEL WHITING OF DEDHAM, MASSACHU-SETTS, 1641 by Theodore S. Lazell. 1902.
Cloth—$16.00—80pp-------------------------------------- Vendor #D0370

3193 - JONATHAN BEADLE FAMILY by Walter J. Beadle. 1973.
History and Genealogy of Descendants of Jonathan Beadle who came to Ovid, Seneca County, New York about 1805 from New Jersey, probably Somerset County.
Cloth—$31.00—80pp-------------------------------------- Vendor #D0370

3194 - SAMUEL BEADLE FAMILY by Walter J. Beadle. 1970.
History and Genealogy of Descendants of Samuel Beadle, Planter; who lived in Charlestown, Massachusetts in 1656 and died in Salem, Massa-chusetts in 1664.
Cloth—$31.00—1043pp-------------------------------------- Vendor #D0370

3195 - DESCENDANTS OF JOHN DEAN OF DEDHAM, MASSACHUSETTS by Marion D. Cooper. 1957.
Paper—$11.00—217pp--------------------------------------Vendor #D0370

3196 - THE PEDIGREE OF FLETCHER GARRISON HALL by Garrison Kent Hall. 1980.
Exhaustive treatment of over sixteen generations of Hall family stretching back to the sixteenth century. Also covers collateral lines.
Cloth—$36.00—400pp-------------------------------------- Vendor #D0370

3197 - PALMER FAMILIES IN AMERICA, VOLUME III compiled and arranged by Horace Palmer; edited by Palmer and Wood. 1973.
William Palmer of Plymouth and Duxbury, Massachusetts.
Cloth—$18.50—231pp-------------------------------------- Vendor #D0370

3198   - THE ANCESTORS OF LT. THOMAS TRACY OF NORWICH, CONNECTI-
CUT by Lt. Charles Stedman Ripley. 1895.
Cloth—$11.25—100pp-- Vendor #D0370

3199   - THE JAQUITH FAMILY IN AMERICA by Dr. George Oakes and
Georgetta Jaquith Walker. 1982.
Cloth—$76.00—750pp-- Vendor #D0370

3200   - JOURNAL OF REVEREND JONATHAN SCOTT, WITH ADDITIONAL
NOTES ON THE BASS, MARBURY, RING, SCOTT, AND THWING
FAMILIES edited by Henry E. Scott, Jr. 1980.
Paper—$18.50—140pp-- Vendor #D0370

3201   - RODEN ROOTS: SIX GENERATIONS OF THE DESCENDANTS OF
JEREMIAH RODEN AND SUSANNAH KIRKLAND OF DeKALB COUNTY,
ALABAMA by Leslie R. Waltman. 1979.
Paper—$15.00—102pp-- Vendor #D0383

3202   - ANCESTORS OF CORA BELLE ADAMS 1881-1957—A GENEALOGY
by William Sheperd West.
Adams family members include: John Emory, 1844-1935; Isaac,
1809-1877; Isaac, ca 1790.
Related families include Gordy, Dashiell, Jones, Magee, Mcgee,
Ward, Winder, Wootten primarily in Sussex County, Delaware and
in nearby counties on Maryland's Eastern Shore. Interesting
charts, photographs, etc. planned. Your information welcome.
(In process)—Cloth—$15.00 estimated—200pp estimated------ Vendor #D0387

3203   - ANCESTORS OF CURTIS TURNER DAVIDSON 1864-1924—A GENEALOGY
by William Sheperd West.
Davidson family members include: Samuel, 1817-1870; James, 1784-1854;
James, 1751-1819; William, -1779; James, -1744.
Related families include Coffin, Joseph, Wood primarily in Sussex
County, Delaware and in nearby counties on Maryland's Eastern
Shore. Interesting charts, photographs, etc. planned. Your
information welcome.
(In process)—Cloth—$15.00 estimated—200pp estimated------ Vendor #D0387

3204   - ANCESTORS OF SHEPERD SALISBURY WEST 1876-1937—A GENEALOGY
by William Sheperd West.
West family members include: Samuel Painter 1853-1922; William S.,
1829-1905; Painter, -1832.
Related families include Moore, Timmons, Warren primarily in Sussex
County, Delaware and in nearby counties on Maryland's Eastern
Shore. Interesting charts, photographs, etc. planned Your
information welcome.
(In process)—Cloth—$10.00 estimated—100pp estimated------ Vendor #D0387

3205   - ANCESTORS OF MARGIE WILLEY 1877-1937—A GENEALOGY by
William Sheperd West.
Willey family members include: James, 1836-1911, herein of three
wives and twenty-one children; John, 1806-1877.
Related families include Saterfield, Brown, Higman. Primarily in
Sussex County, Delaware and in nearby counties of Maryland's
Eastern Shore. Your information welcome. Interesting charts,
photographs, etc. planned.
(In process)—Cloth—$10.00 estimated—100pp estimated------ Vendor #D0387

3206   - DESCENDANTS OF JAMES AND AGNES (WILSON) ADAMS WITH
FIFTY-SEVEN ALLIED FAMILIES by Leona Adams Loviska. 1978.
Adams: Lists nine generations of descendants, male and female
lines, beginning in Virginia, with succeeding generations traced
through Kentucky, Arkansas, Missouri, Texas, Oregon, Kansas,
and other states. Allied families include Alden, Allison, Armstrong,
Baity, Barnes, Beeby, Berrell, Burnes, Burroughs, Carter, Cullison,
Delzell, Doddridge, Everley, Fort, Glascoe, Gray, Guay, Harnett,
Hedrick, Hyde, Irwin, Jefferson, Keeter, Kerns, Lambert with
Charlemagnian Line, Lathrop, Loomis, Lyman, McKinney, Marsh,
Merrill, Milton, Morgan, Morris, Morse, Mullins, Nielsen, Paulson,

Pennington, Price, Pyle, Sager, Scoville, Sherbourne, Sherrets, Sidfrid(s), Skinner, Springer, Stalcup, Staples, Steele, Stewart, Tibbs, Walker, Watson, Wilson and Wolf. The allied families are found in many states. Text includes references, wills, Bible records and many photographes. Indexed.
Cloth—$26.50—470pp--- Vendor #D0395

3207   - ALEXANDER STEWART, HIS SCOTS ANCESTRY AND AMERICAN DESCENDANTS WITH FORTY-EIGHT ALLIED AND RELATED FAMILIES by Dorothy Kintigh Sidfrid. 1979.
Stewart: Renfrew, Scotland, 1685-1836; New Jersey, 1836-1845 then to Rock and Sauk Counties, Wisconsin with present generations spread across the nation. Gives male and female lines.
Fulcomer: Begins in Alsace—Lorraine in 1770. Family settled in York County, Pennsylvania. Migration of one branch traced through Ohio, Wisconsin and Kansas.
Pack: Traces descent of two Kansas pioneer half brothers back to the New Jersey Colonist and down to the present generations for some lines. Gives two Royal lines connected by marriage through Draper and Greene lines.
Other allied and related families include Agnew, Anthony, Ashley and Rankin, Barton, Beeby, Buckhout, Buttles and Tindall, Campbell, Carroll and Wollenzein, Clarke, Cook, Crutcher and Sacre, Dwelly, Fine, Flegal, Flynn, Gorton, Gramling (Grumling), Harvey, Hohenschild, Hunter, Hyde, Jackson, Kint, Kintigh, Maplet, Marsh, Moreland, Pennington, Porteous, Prentice, Robertson, Ross, Russell, Shephard, Sidfrid, Slocum, Starkey, Stewart, Tibbs, Tucker and Winters.
Text includes references, wills, Bible records and many photographs. Indexed.
Cloth—$27.50—408pp--- Vendor #D0395

3208   - VANCE PAPERS AND DOCUMENTS by Virginia Vance Lovett. 1981.
--- Vendor #D0401

3209   - SOME DESCENDANTS OF JOHN NICHOLAS BLANKENBEKER, 1717 IMMIGRANT by Virginia Vance Lovett. 1985.
(In process)-- Vendor #D0401

3210   - THE ANCESTORS AND DESCENDANTS OF MATTHEW A. B. HOWARD, GEORGIA—FLORIDA, 1793-1978 by Norma Slater Woodward. 1979.
Huge mass of information organized into concise, effective genealogical chronicle. Over 1000 descendants of subject with sibling and in-law branches. Major families: Clark, Crawford, Davis, Howard; allied families: Bennett, Boatright, Chancey, Drawdy, Hiers, Lyons, O'Berry, Prescott, Spence, Strickland, Sweat, Thomas, Townsend, Waldron, Winn. 2500 name index.
Cloth—$16.50—224pp--- Vendor #D0403

3211   - DESCENDANTS OF RICHARD WOODWARD, NEW ENGLAND, 1589-1982 by Norma Slater Woodward. 1982.
This family history and genealogy covers thirteen generations, in some lines, from the progenitor who was born 1589 and emigrated from England to Boston, 1634. Each line is followed as far as possible. Included are other Woodard/Woodward lines previously recorded in histories, biographies and new, undetermined families of value to anyone interested in Woodward lines originating in New England. Index over 3200 names.
Cloth—$25.00—280pp--- Vendor #D0403

3212   - REYNOLDS—HUGHES—TURNLEY—ISBELL: THE ANCESTORS OF JOHN HUGHES REYNOLDS AND MARY TURNLEY REYNOLDS by Rubyn Reynolds Ogburn. 1976.
Reynolds from 1750, Montgomery, Abington Counties, Virginia; Hawkins, Greene, McMinn, Polk Counties, Tennessee; Floyd County, Georgia.
Hughes from 1745, Augusta County, Virginia; Rowan, Burke Counties, North Carolina; Washington, Greene, Bledsoe, McMinn,

Bradley Counties, Tennessee; Floyd County, Georgia.
Turnley from 1649, England; Wales; Botetourt County, Virginia;
Greene County, North Carolina/Tennessee; Cherokee County,
Alabama.
Isbell from 1747, Albemarle County, Virginia; Wilkes County,
North Carolina; McMinn County, Tennessee; Cherokee County,
Alabama.
Also: Parkes from 1759, Virginia; Wilkes County, North Carolina;
McMinn County, Tennessee. Howard from 1630, Virginia; Anne
Arundel, Frederick Counties, Maryland; Wilkes County, North
Carolina.
Paper—$15.00—146pp-------------------------------------- Vendor #D0409

3213   - OGBURN: A COLLECTION OF GENEALOGICAL INFORMATION ABOUT
THE OGBURN FAMILY by Fielding Ogburn and Patricia D. Ogburn.
1980.
5800 indexed names. Descendants of John Ogborne—1774, Henry
Ogburn, 1754-1831, Little Berry Ogburn 1774-1856, John Ogburn
1784-1841, James Ogburn ca 1786—, John William Ogburn 1813—,
George Thomas Ogburn ca 1819-ca 1884, and Thomas J. Ogburn ca 1845—.
Allied lines include Adams, Anderson, Blackmon, Clark, Davis, Feni-
more, Ferguson, Harrison, Hart, Hill, Jackson, Johnson, Jones, Moore,
Neblett, Palmer, Porter, Powell, Sowell, Stevens, Vest, Williams, and
Young. Sources given for all names, dates, and lineages.
Cites references to Ogburn in 17th and 18th Century official records.
Lists Ogburns appearing in indexes to United States Censuses.
Paper—$16.00—314pp-------------------------------------- Vendor #D0409

3214   - GENEA-BIOGRAPHICAL HISTORY OF THE RITTENHOUSE FAMILY
AND BRANCHES IN AMERICA by Daniel K. Cassel. 1893.
Major families: Rittenhouse, Kulp, Cassel.
Allied: Papen, Brownback, Shimer, Gorgas, Pastorius, Up-de-Graeff,
Henderichs, Streper, Van-Bebber, Howell, Jansen.
Cloth—$37.00—272pp------------------------------------- Vendor #D0416

3215   - THE WENGER BOOK: A FOUNDATION BOOK OF AMERICAN WENGERS
edited by Samuel S. Wenger. 1978.
Major families: Wenger, Groff, Graybill, Horst, Martin, Weaver.
Allied: Zimmerman, Musser, Sensenig, Stauffer, Eby, Gehman,
Nolt, Burkholder, Funk, Hoover, Brenneman, Hershey, Landis.
Cloth—$41.50—1250pp------------------------------------ Vendor #D0416

3216   - DESCENDANTS OF JACOB HOCHSTETLER, THE IMMIGRANT OF
1736 by Harvey Hostetler. 1977 repr. of 1912 ed.
Major families: Hostetler, Keim, Beachy, Byler, Gingerich, Zook.
Allied: Hershberger, Kauffman, Mast, Miller, Yoder, Eash, Brenneman,
Gerber, Gnagey, King, Kurtz, Nissley, Plank, Schlabach, Smucker,
Schrock, Snyder, Stutzman, Swartzentruber, Troyer, Weaver.
Cloth—$23.95—1191pp----------------------------------- Vendor #D0416

3217   - GENEALOGICAL RECORD OF REV. HANS HERR AND HIS DIRECT
DESCENDANTS by Theodore W. Herr. 1980 repr. of 1908 ed.
Major families: Herr, Groff, Baer, Brackbill, Eshleman, Neff.
Allied: Frantz, Kendig, Hoover, Witmer, Forrer, Bowman, Carpenter,
Forney, Hershey, Hess, Kauffman, Hartman, Landis, Martin, Miller,
Shaub, Weaver, Brenneman, Bachman, Harnish, Kreider, Lefever,
Shenk, Stehman.
Cloth—$20.00—792pp------------------------------------- Vendor #D0416

3218   - GENEALOGY AND HISTORY OF THE KAUFFMAN—COFFMAN FAMILIES
OF NORTH AMERICA by Charles Fahs Kauffman. 1980 repr. of 1940 ed.
Major families: Kauffman, Coffman.
Allied: Bear, Correll, Erisman, Hershey, Neff, Shenk, Witmer,
Becker, Brenneman, Brubaker, Frey, Hiestand, Landis, Long,
Martin, Miller, Musselman, Meyers, Nissley, Smith, Snavely,
Snyder, Shirk, Sprenkle.
Cloth—$44.00—776pp------------------------------------- Vendor #D0416

3219 - DESCENDANTS OF BARBARA HOCHSTEDLER AND CHRISTIAN
STUTZMAN by Harvey Hostetler. 1980 repr. of 1938 ed.
Major families: Hochstedler, Eash, Miller, Troyer, Yoder, Zook.
Allied: Beachy, Bontrager, Hoover, Lichty, Long, Martin, Musser,
Myers, Plank, Stutzman, Thomas, Weaver.
Cloth—$25.95—1391pp------------------------------------- Vendor #D0416

3220 - A BICENTENNIAL HISTORY OF ELEVEN PIONEER FAMILIES, A
GENEALOGY by Mary M. Beadles. 1974.
These pioneer families, most of which will be found in the Old South,
are all traced back 200 years. Some are traced back to the immigrant
ancestor and his origin. Names included are: Mottley or (Motley),
Guier, Travis, Tanner, Caldwell, Connerly, Rebsamen or (Turnipseed),
Going, Cook, Collins, Duren—with connecting families of Hammond,
Moore, Rieger, Sellers, Ellington, Creed, Hamiter, Ladmann, Thalmann,
Vogt or (Smith), Schnurrenburger, Ysenring, Rothman, Hood, Love,
Giles, Gayden.
Full name index—offset print—referenced—illustrated—cloth—6"x9".
3,453 names.
Cloth—$19.00—269pp------------------------------------- Vendor #D0418

3221 - A HISTORY OF FOUR JACKSON PURCHASE FAMILIES, A GENEALOGY
by Mary M. Beadles. 1978.
Harris: Harris family of England and Virginia—emigrant John Harris
and his descendants—coat-of-arms of Sir William Harris—Tennessee.
Beadles: Eight generations—Virginia, North Carolina, Tennessee.
Browder: 200 year history of this family—Isham Browder's 150 year
old letters illustrated—Kentucky.
Guerrant: Emigrant Daniel Guerin (Guerrant) Huguenot of France
and Virginia traced from Province of Saintonge, France, as well as
later generations in Virginia and North Carolina, Kentucky;
Huguenot Cross history and illustrated.
Connecting families: Barringer, Cobb, Bard, Warford, Allin, Aydelott,
Baird, Coats, Jackson, Dutoit, Ellington, Kemp, Nunnally, Penick,
Porter, Rowlett, Trabue.
Full name index—separate slave index—bibliography. 4,158 names;
6"x9" offset print.
Cloth—$35.00—352pp------------------------------------- Vendor #D0418

3222 - WILLIAM AND LUCY HAYES AND SOME OF THEIR DESCENDANTS
by Mary Margaret Hayes Boyles. 1979.
Early pioneers to Kentucky from Maryland and Virginia.
Related families: Bradley, Couchman, Gatewood, Goodwin, Graves,
Harris, Redd.
Fayette, Owen and Trigg Counties, Kentucky.
Cloth—$16.50—141pp------------------------------------- Vendor #D0435

3223 - THE BERTRAM BOOK by Luther York and Myrtle B. Dalton.
1985 repr. of 1959 ed.
A picture book containing the photos and short biographical sketches
of approximately 1300 members of the Bertram Family originating in
the vicinity of Sunnybrook, Wayne County, Kentucky. Reprint of
1959 edition with full name index added by Irene Byrer.
79pp--- Vendor #D0441

3224 - THE SMOLA FAMILY HISTORY: A GENEALOGY OF THE MARTIN
SMOLA FAMILY IN AMERICA (1801-1978) by Marvin P. Rezabek. 1979.
Genealogical history of the first Bohemian (Czech) family to settle
in Madison County, Illinois. Included are many of the early Bohemian
families of Madison County and near-by Saint Louis, Missouri.
Eight pictures and five documents included. Book is indexed and
well documented.
Cloth—$20.00—329pp------------------------------------- Vendor #D0447

3225 - OF BUSHES AND STARLINGS: GENEALOGY OF REZABEK AND
SPACEK by Marvin P. Rezabek. 1981.
Genealogical history tracing two Bohemian families from their beginnings
in Czechoslovakia to their growth in America in Madison County,
Illinois; Saint Louis, Missouri; Hanover, Kansas.

Matthias Rezabek Family traced ca 1695–1980; Joseph Spacek Family traced ca 1822–1980. Collateral families: Brinda, Bulan, Hovora (Howard), Koles, Medek, Mraz, Smola, Vlcek. Over 100 pictures, index, and documentation.
Cloth—$30.00—302pp------------------------------------ Vendor #D0447

3226 - OUR SIMMONS FOREFATHERS AND THEIR DESCENDANTS by Bennett L. Smith. 1973.
Contains information on Simmons, Luce, Rhoads, Baker, and Studebaker families.
Cloth—$13.00—450pp------------------------------------ Vendor #D0449

3227 - JAMES DOUGALL OF GLASGOW (1699-1760) AND HIS DESCENDANTS THROUGH DOUGALL AND McDOUGALL LINES IN THE UNITED STATES AND CANADA by Richardson Dougall. 1973.
Dougall, Richardson. *James Dougall of Glasgow (1699-1760) and His Descendants Through Dougall and McDougall Lines in the United States and Canada*, 1973, 464 pages, paper. Traces Dougalls who came to Montreal and Ontario in the early 19th Century, and a McDougall line which came to New York in 1774 and spread to New Jersey, particularly Newark and Morris County. Descents through daughters are traced. Includes name index (51 pages) and geographic index (17 pages) of 49 states and all Canadian provinces. Full bibliography. Related families include Anderson, Baker, Bird, Crane, Dewar, Ferguson, Goble, Harris, Hayward, Henry, Howell, Johnson, Johnston, Jones, King, MacDougall, Mackenzie, McColl, McDougall, Robertson, Smith, Taylor, Van Wagenen, Walker, Wark, Woodruff, Young.
Paper—$15.00—464pp------------------------------------ Vendor #D0456

3228 - ANCESTRAL LINES REVISED: 190 FAMILIES IN ENGLAND, WALES, GERMANY, NEW ENGLAND, NEW YORK, NEW JERSEY AND PENNSYL-VANIA by Carl Boyer, 3rd. 1981.
Lineages have been included for the following families: Abell, Allen, Allright, Allsop, Althouse, Andrews, Anthony, Armington, Avery, Babcock, Baker, Ballard, Barber, Bassett, Battin, Baulstone, Bennett, Bliss, Bonython, Borden, Borton, Bosworth, Bowen, Bowne, Boyer, Brown, Browne, Brownell, Buffington, Bullock, Burton, Butter, Cadman, Campbell, Carpenter, Carr, Chaffee, Chandler, Chase, Cheyney, Chickering, Cobb, Coggeshall, Cooke, Cooper, Cotton, Debozear, Dell, Dodge, Durfee, Eames, Evans, Feake, Feller (Fellows), Ferris, Fish, Fiske, Fones, Fowle, Fowler, Freeborn, Frost, Frye, Fulwater, Gardner, George, Gifford, Griesemer, Haines, Hale, Hancock, Harper, Haskins, A. Hathaway, N. Hathaway, Hazard, Hearne, Hickman, Hicks, Holbrook, Holloway, Holmes, Holzwarth, Howland, Hull, E. Hunt, T. Hunt, Hunter, Hurst, Hyatt, Ingraham, Jefferis, Jenckes, Jones, Kendrick, Kent, Kingsbury, Kirby, Kitchen, Kruse, Kuser, Lawrence, Lawter, Lawton, Leonard, Lilley, Lookermans, Ludwig, Luther, J. Marshall, M. Marshall, Matlack, Mendenhall, Mercer, Metselaer, Mott, Moulton, Owen, A. Paine, S. Paine, Parker, Paul(s), Pawley, Peabody, Pearce, Pennell, Perry, Pitts, Porter, Potter, Prior, J. Read, W. Read(e), Remington, Reynolds, Rown (Rau), Rowning, Russell, Sale (Searles), Segar, Sheever (Shafer), Sheldon, Sherman, Slade, Smedley, H. Smith, J. Smith, Specht, Sprague, Strange, Strode, Talbot, Tallman, Talmadge, Taylor, Tefft, Thomas, Thurston, Tilley, Timberlake, Timm, Tisdale, Titus, Toogood, Tripp, Underhill, Vandenburgh, Vanderbilt, Vandervliet, Van Vranken, Vinhagen, Visscher, Waeger, R. Walker, Widow Walker, Warren, M. Watson, R. Watson, Webb, E. White, W. White, Wilbore, Wilmarth, Winne, Winthrop, Wodell, Wood, J. Wright, N. Wright, and Wynter.
Cloth—$41.20—666pp------------------------------------Vendor #D0457

3229 - NICHOLAS HUTCHINS OF LYNN AND GROTON, MASSACHUSETTS, AND HIS DESCENDANTS by Marvin Clayton Hutchins. 1984.
Cloth—$31.20—apx. 450pp------------------------------ Vendor #D0457

3230 - NEW ENGLAND COLONIAL FAMILIES: BROWN FAMILIES OF BRIS-
TOL COUNTIES, RHODE ISLAND AND MASSACHUSETTS, AND DE-
SCENDANTS OF JARED TALBOT OF DIGHTON, MASSACHUSETTS by
Carl Boyer, 3rd, Helen H. Lane and Elaine Varley. 1982.
Cloth—$21.20—219pp--- Vendor #D0457

3231 - DESCENDANTS OF PHEBE (WALTERS) AND ISAAC LOCKWOOD:
WESTCHESTER, NEW YORK QUAKERS by Nancy Jo Stein. 1976.
Paper—$10.50—94pp-- Vendor #D0459

3232 - DESCENDANTS OF WILLIAM OLIPHANT OF NORTH CAROLINA, rev.
ed., edited by Nancy Jo Stein. 1977, rev. 1983.
To Indiana 1828: Martindale, Burch, Morgan, Hale, Vaughn,
Slough, Crum, Mitchell, King.
Paper—$18.00—308pp--------------------------------------- Vendor #D0459

3233 - OLIPHANT, OLIFANT, OLIPHINT, OLIVANT—OF UNITED STATES,
INDEX AND DOCUMENTATION edited by Nancy Jo Stein. 1981.
Cloth—$24.00—Paper—$18.00—250+pp----------------------- Vendor #D0459

3234 - WALTERS/WATERS OF EIGHTEENTH CENTURY SOUTH EAST NEW
YORK by Nancy Jo Stein. 1980.
Paper—$7.00—60pp-- Vendor #D0459

3235 - MAGREE/MCGREE DIRECTORY by Melvyn D. Magree. 1981.
Not for sale, sent in exchange for additional Magree or McGree
information. Over 500 entries.
Paper-- Vendor #D0460

3236 - ROBERT MCKAY CLAN NEWSLETTER by Wallace and Dorothy Shipp.
Is published once a year for 219 families and friends of the Robert
McKay Clan. Holds annual reunion in June in Virginia. Reports
current news of families and historical articles. Newsletter started
in 1965. First reunion 1946.
Paper—$7.00—8-16pp--------------------------------------- Vendor #D0463

3237 - IN SEARCH OF CALEB—A RESEARCH REPORT OF SOME OF THE
DESCENDANTS OF WILLIAM SHERMAN, THE PILGRIM, OF MARSH-
FIELD, MASSACHUSETTS by Sherman W. Bear. 1980.
Allen, Archer, Bear, Beck (Peck), Briggs, Carroll, Cole, Coverdale,
Crandall, Davis, Eddy (Eady), Faulkner (Forker), Fish, Fritz, Gay,
Grissinger, Hanna, Hargas, Harrison, Hartley, Hidey (Heidy), Hol-
man, Humphreys, Jackson, Jones, Kirby, Lawrence, Little, Maxwell,
McCoy, Mika, Moncton, Patterson, Perry, Pollet, Porter, Rider, Ring,
Shephard, Sherman, Steeves, Swales, Thompson, Trueman, Van Buren,
Ward, Washington, Webster, Westmorland, Wheldon, Williams, Winslow,
Wood, Wortman, Wright. Traces the movements of the Caleb Sherman
family of plymouth, Massachusetts to Nova Scotia in 1761. Reviews
the exchange of properties from vicinity of Fort Cumberland to the
shores of the Petitcodiac River. Highlights the migration of Canadians
to eastern Ohio in 1830. Descendants settled in Maine, Pennsylvania,
Iowa, and Colorado. More than 60 sources documented, index, separate surname index, line of descent from William Sherman 1610-1679
to author.
Paper—$6.00—36pp-- Vendor #D0464

3238 - THE WINE FAMILY IN AMERICA, SECTION THREE by Jacob David
Wine (1881-1968) and Joseph Floyd Wine. 1971.
Wine: Germany—1741-1749; York County, Pennsylvania—1749-1776;
Frederick County, Maryland—1776-1782; Forestville, Shenandoah
County, Virginia—1782—present.
Cloth—$17.50—591pp------------------------------------- Vendor #D0467

3239 - ANTHONY PLYMELL AND HIS DESCENDANTS by Mrs. James H.
Davis. 1977.
Anthony, son of John and Jane (Twiley) Plimell, Madison County,
Ohio, located in Daviess and Harrison Counties, Missouri 1839.
Over 1200 indexed surnames including Salmon, VanMeter, Morris,
Bryant, Cameron, Daniel, Rice, and many more. Maps, wills,
official records and family pictures. Soft-cover, 8½"x11".
Paper—$32.00—527pp--------------------------------------- Vendor #D0481

3240 - MAXWELL GENEALOGY AND HISTORY 12TH AND 14TH by Fay
Maxwell. 1973, 2nd run in 1975.
Begins with Robert, son of Maccus landgrant from King William
28 December 1200, and Robert Thomas Maunsell of Limerick, Maxwell
of Pollock, land office grants 1761-1800 in America, covers Maxwell's
of Ohio, Pennsylvania, Virginia, Indiana, Tennessee, Nebraska,
Kentucky, New Jersey, New Mexico, Ohio census indexes of 1820
through 1840, much on Ohio Maxwell's, wills, courthouse records,
pensions; also related families: Schnebele-Snively, Alexander,
Houstons, Anderson, Hussey's of England and Pennsylvania;
many maps and illustrations. 8½"x11".
Paper—$20.00—170pp------------------------------------- Vendor #D0483

3241 - MAXWELL GENEALOGY AND HISTORY INDEX (to book pub. 1974)
by Fay Maxwell.
Completely alphabetized.
(In process)—Paper—$10.00----------------------------- Vendor #D0483

3242 - LARIMER GENEALOGY AND HISTORY by Fay Maxwell.
(In process)—Paper—$15.00----------------------------- Vendor #D0483

3243 - MAXWELL NAME INDEX by Fay Maxwell.
Ohio Maxwell Names Computer Alphabetized One Liners plus source,
data, also carries other Maxwell names from other states. A good
reference book on Maxwell name.
(In process)—Paper—$15.00----------------------------- Vendor #D0483

3244 - DESCENDANTS OF ISAAC SIMMONS by August and Miriam Simmons.
1981.
Isaac (Fitz) Simmons arrived in America in 1776, dropped Fitz.
Married in Maryland in 1814. Other lines include Bradford, Cotton,
Williams, Daily, Delashmutt, Russell, Kinner, Wortman, Weaver,
Pennington, Shirer, McKinsey, Fairman, McKellip, DuBois, Stillwell,
Hiatt and many other names. Many Ohio lines.
Paper—$12.00—128pp----------------------------------- Vendor .#D0483

3245 - A STRANGE HISTORY by M. Robert Strange. 1977.
A Strange History, by M. Robert Strange, deals with the ancestors
and descendants of William Ambrose Strange (1809-1894), of Martin
County, Indiana. The narrative begins with 1750 and moves from
Charles County, Maryland, through Hardin County, Kentucky to
Martin County, Indiana, and beyond. The family tree section enables
living descendants of William Ambrose Strange to trace their line back
to him. A chapter entitled "Loose Leaves" deals briefly with other
Stranges. The comprehensive index of persons contains more than
1700 names. Among these, besides the Stranges, are the names
Arvin, Flynn, Gootee, Harris, Hopkins, Irvin, Jones, Lewis,
Matthews, McAtee, Miles, Nonte, Norris, O'Brian, O'Maley, O'Neal,
Padgett, Toon, Williams and many others. The lives and activities
of the persons who appear in *A Strange History* take them to the more
than 340 places in the index of places. More than 70 photographs,
made and edited by Wanda Lee Jacobs Strange, enhance the narrative.
Hard bound brown woodgrain. Write to Strange Family History,
1809 Forsythia Drive, Indianapolis, Indiana 46219.
Cloth—$17.75—144pp---------------------------------- Vendor #D0484

3246 - CLARION, IOWA AS IT WAS—1896. 1976 repr. of 1896 ed.
Being the reprint of an 1896 publication, containing pictures and
information about all business, professional men and others in this
county seat town. Indexed.
Paper—64pp--- Vendor #D0487

3247 - BOUCHER FAMILY—BOWSHER, BAUSCHER, BAUSHER, BOUSHER—
A GENEALOGY by Franklin A. Burkhart. 1976 repr. of 1917 ed.
Descendants of Daniel Boucher who landed in America in 1752 and
settled in Berks County, Pennsylvania.
Related families include Ambrose, Arthur, Baker, Barron, Beeler,
Blacker, Brant, Brinker, Burkhardt, Cox, Crider, Critchfield,
Cryder, Daniels, Danner, Davis, DeLong, Dotson, Duck, Ebbert,

Eich, Fantz, Fawner, Forney, Fox, Geiger, Graham, Hammons, Hanaway, Harpster, Henderson, Johnston, Jones, Kimmel, Knable, Knott, Kooser, Lane, Lyons, McClintock, McClure, McConaughey, Mayer, Miller, Moody, Moore, Mort, Mowery, Myers, Neff, Orrison, Parke, Patterson, Phillippi, Pickens, Poyser, Rathburn, Reed, Reeder, Reichelderfer, Ridenour, Ritchie, Rubert, Rubright, Shaffer, Shappell, Shaw, Shumaker, Sims, Smith, Snyder, Soldman, Spangler, Stahl, Stepleton, Stoker, Stump, Straw, Strawn, Tedrow, Teegardin, Trexler, Tripp, Walters, Ward, Weaver, Whipkey, Will, Wilson, Winget, Young.
The reprint is indexed, and contains numerous pictures.
Cloth—$25.00—490pp-------------------------------------- Vendor #D0490

3249   - THE HORACE STOCKING HUBBARD FAMILY HISTORY by Jasper J.
Davis. 1975.
Genealogy 1799 Pennsylvania to present in Wayne County, Illinois,
plus original poems.
Paper—$10.50—washable—89pp---------------------------- Vendor #D0503

3250   - MARTIN LETTERS (1886-1977) by Vera L. Dean. 1977.
Nathaniel Martin (1821-1896) of Wayne County, Tennessee and New-
ton County, Arkansas and his descendants' genealogy.
Related families mostly from Colonial South migrating to Arkansas:
Atkinson, Carter, Cook, Cotton, Curtis, Dean, Dickey, Jones,
other Martin, Ross, Standridge, Thompson, Ward, Whitecotton,
Wilson, Yates. Indexed.
Cloth—$30.00—Paper—$12.00—253pp------------------------ Vendor #D0512

3251   - ROSS AND KIN by Granville J. Ross. 1980.
Related families mostly from Colonial South to Newton, Pope, and
Johnson County, Arkansas: Brown, Freeman, Gunter, Harris,
Howard, Hull, Phillips, Standridge, Sumners, Tumbleston, Yates.
Indexed.
Cloth—$16.00—397pp------------------------------------- Vendor #D0512

3252   - THE WRIGHT BOOK: WORTHY HERITAGE, ENDURING CHALLENGE
by Pauline W. Wright. 1974.
Subtitle: Being the History of Some of the Descendants of John
Wright (1745-1814), Bedford County, Virginia.
Appendices: Schooley Family, Short Family, Tallant Family,
Grant Family.
Cloth—$7.50—251pp------------------------------------- Vendor #D0509

3253   - JOHANN ADAM BRUCKER AND HIS AMERICAN DESCENDANTS by
Wallace Hawn Brucker, Brigadier General, United States Army, retired.
1978.
In addition to the text, this book contains 117 photographs, 2 maps,
82 family charts and full name index. Sources used include church
and civil documents, family chronicles, and oral and written recollections obtained by author. Earliest documented Brucker, Joseph was
born ca 1680. Johann Adam was born in Hesse-Darmstadt 1787, went
to Austria where he married, reared a family and had career as
architect and builder. Three children, Ferdinand in 1849, followed
by Anna and Karl migrated to Michigan. Text includes biographical
sketches of Adam's descendants through successive generations to
present. Related families include Carmichael, Eberly, Elliott, Green,
Gump, Kerr, Lehman, Lever, McNally, Parker, Robertson, Rossiter,
Simmons, Sinclair, Wagner, Wernert. Though mainly in Michigan,
Ohio and California, these families also live in twenty other states.
Cloth—$20.00—264pp------------------------------------ Vendor #D0514

3254   - SOME DESCENDANTS OF LIBORIUS AND THERESIA (WORMER)
BORST OF BRUCHSAL, BADEN, GERMANY by Charles B. Garlet, Jr.
1982.
Two sons settled in Ross County, Ohio. Later descendants went to
Kansas.
Paper—$3.00—8pp--------------------------------------- Vendor #D0519

3255   - JOHN HART, THE BIOGRAPHY OF A SIGNER OF THE DECLARATION
OF INDEPENDENCE by Cleon E. Hammond. 1977.
This award winning biography of the New Jersey Signer includes
meticulously researched information concerning the Hart family plus
extensive descriptions of the political, economic and social climates
of the period. Extensive notes and fully indexed references to innumerable colonial families that migrated to the "frontier" following the
Revolution provide much genealogical and historical information of
general interest beyond New Jersey. The author received the New
Jersey Historical Commission Award "for outstanding services to
public knowledge and preservation of the history of New Jersey."
Cloth—$16.95—357+pp-------------------------------------Vendor #D0520

3256   - DESCENDANTS OF HUGH MOSHER AND REBECCA MAXSON THROUGH
SEVEN GENERATIONS by Mildred Mosher Chamberlain and Laura
McGaffey Clarenbach. 1980.
Related families: Allen, Chase, Davol, Gifford, Macomber, Tripp,
Wilbur, Wilcox, Wood.
Cloth—$22.50—759pp------------------------------------- Vendor #D0535

3257   - KATES KIN NEWSLETTER by Anna Kates Gardner, bimonthly since
March, 1978.
A bimonthly newsletter for Kates/Cates. Gathering material for a
book about the surname Kates/Cates and various spellings. Those
with this name occurring in their ancestry are urged to submit for
inclusion. No cost—and no obligation to buy book.
Paper— 4pp/issue--- Vendor #D0538

3258   - JOHN MASSIE, 1743-c 1830, THE FAMILY OF: REVOLUTIONARY
PATRIOT OF LOUISA COUNTY, VIRGINIA by Mavis P. Kelsey, M.D.
1979.
*John Massie, 1743-c1830, The Family of: Revolutionary Patriot of
Louisa County, Virginia* including early emigrants to Kentucky and
Texas; and related families: Bachman, Baker, Baughan, Bollinger,
Booth, Burrus, Clopton, Duke, Harris, Jackson, Keener, Mills,
Overton, Parrott, Poer, Riddell and Walton. 241 pages with over
4,000 names from all states.
Includes research on early Massies of Virginia and their westward
migration. Some other families included are Bullock, Butler, Christ-
mas, Carnohan, Carpenter, Dickinson, Goodwin, Gunter, Hiter,
Hogan, Holland, Kelsey, Leadbetter, Matthews, Martin, Maynard,
Penick, Reynolds, Swift, Terrell, Timberlake, Thornhill, Watkins,
Walker, Winston, Woolfolk, Wright and many more.
Appendix includes early records on several of these families, including
wills, Bible records and other documents. Fully indexed. Soft $35.00;
hard $40.00. Order from Mavis P. Kelsey, #2 Longbow Lane,
Houston, Texas 77024.
Cloth—$40.00—Paper—$35.00------------------------------ Vendor #D0548

3259   - SAMUEL KELSO/KELSEY 1720-1796, OF CHESTER, SOUTH CAROLINA:
SCOTCH-IRISH IMMIGRANT AND REVOLUTIONARY PATRIOT, HIS
DESCENDANTS AND RELATED FAMILIES by Dr. & Mrs. Mavis P. Kelsey.
1984.
With newly published information of the following families: Gill,
McAlexander, Mills, Moore, Morrow, Pagan, and Wylie.
Also includes Membership List and Cemetery Inscriptions from the
Wesley Chapel Methodist Church and Cemetery of Red Banks, Marshall
County, Mississippi.
The first published genealogy on this large family. Eleven members
of the immediate family participated in the American Revolution.
Over 10,000 names indexed. Order from Mavis P. Kelsey, #2 Longbow
Lane, Houston, Texas 77024.
Cloth—Special Price $50.00 postpaid—700+pp---------------- Vendor #D0548

3260   - DESCENDANTS OF JOHN KNOWLES, 1660-1978 by Virginia Knowles
Hufbauer. 1979.
Hampton, New Hampshire progenitor. Extensive research on New
Hampshire and Maine lines, particularly; also includes migrations and

their descendants in west and midwest. Complete and comprehensive index.
Some allied families: Batchelder, Brown, Dearborn, Dow, Leavitt, Libby, Locke, Marston, Page, Palmer, Pendleton, Philbrick, Sawyer. 8½"x11", hardcover, illustrated. 426 pages. $50.00 ppd.
Available from compiler 2148 Avenida de la Playa, La Jolla, California 92037.
Cloth—$50.00—426pp------------------------------------- Vendor #D0552

3261 - DESCENDANTS OF RICHARD KNOWLES, 1637-1973 by Virginia Knowles Hufbauer. 1974.
Genealogy of one of Cape Cod's earliest families, endorsed by the Eastham, Massachusetts Historical Society. Contains thirteen generations of the Knowles family with many of their sea stories and pioneering adventures. Branch migrations followed to north, west, midwest, Nova Scotia. Complete comprehensive index.
Allied families: Atkins, Atwood, Brewster, Cobb, Cook, Collins, Doane, Farwell, Freeman, Ghen, Godfrey, Harding, Hatch, Higgins, Hopkins, Lombard, Mayo, Merrick, Nickerson, Paine, Prence, Sears, Smith, Snow, Sparrow, Rice, Rogers, Walker, Wells, Young, many others. 8½"x11", hardcover, 1000+ pages, fully illustrated, $60.00 ppd.
Cloth—$60.00—1,000+pp------------------------------- Vendor #D0552

3262 - RONEY FAMILY HISTORY AND GENEALOGY 1690-1972 by Doris Roney Bowers. 1978.
Lines: Hercules Roney, Bucks County, Pennsylvania, emigrant ancestor; Joseph Roney, Virginia and West Virginia; James Roney, 1775-1838, Virginia, Kentucky and Illinois, his fourteen children and their descendants to 1972. Lived Shelby County, Kentucky and Moultrie County, Illinois.
Other lines: Hercules Roney, Wheeling West Virginia; b 1743, County Donegal, Ireland; James Roney, 1711-1765, Virginia, to North Carolina 1740; William Roney, Belfast, Ireland 1786.
Related families include: Bankson, Buchanan, Brown, Carter, Clark, Clay, Cordray, Dalton, Duke, Eakin, Florey, Freeland, Gough, Harding, Henderson, Hinkle, Howard, James, Kinkade, McGuffey, McGuire, Mathias, Means, Mitchell, Moore, Pfeifer, Potts, Purdy, Rhodes, Robertson, Sconce, Sedgwick, Sloan, Smith, Tyler, Underwood, Walker, Ward, Warren, Wright. These families are scattered over most of the fifty states.
Historical section is in narrative form. Genealogical data is well documented. Contains maps, pictures, charts, Scotch-Irish history, geographical place-names index, and every-name index including women's maiden and married names.
Paper—$32.00—933pp------------------------------------- Vendor #D0565

3263 - SUPPLEMENT OF ADDITIONS AND CORRECTIONS TO RONEY FAMILY HISTORY AND GENEALOGY 1690-1972 by Doris Roney Bowers.
Additional births, deaths and marriages 1972-1979, and human interest items from correspondents; newspaper obituaries; wills. Interesting volume; not dry reading.
Paper—$4.70—40pp------------------------------------- Vendor #D0565

3264 - TRUMAN TRIBUTE (FOR TRUEMAN, TREWMAN AND VARIANT SPELLINGS) by Doris Roney Bowers.
A 20-page quarterly began in 1982 for all Truman researchers. Truman data nationwide and abroad; queries; member's ancestor charts; etc.
Paper—$10.00—80pp/yr plus annual index------------------ Vendor #D0565

3265 - BOZARTH BEACON (FOR BOZORTH, BOSWORTH AND VARIANT SPELLINGS) by Doris Roney Bowers.
A 20-page quarterly to begin 1985 for all Bozarth researchers. Genealogical data and history, queries, member's ancestor charts, etc.
Paper—$10.00—80pp/yr plus annual index------------------ Vendor #D0565

3266 - ROBERT THOMAS d. 1768 FAIRFAX COUNTY, VIRGINIA AND HIS
DESCENDANTS WITH PARTICULAR ATTENTION TO MOSES THOMAS
d. 1818 BOURBON COUNTY, KENTUCKY by Betty J. Gilbert. 1983.
By Betty J. Gilbert, 2518 S. E. Faxon, Topeka, Kansas 66605.
1983 printing, 8½"x11", 549 pages, hardback $40.00, available now.
A few related families: Violett, Mitchell, Sutton, Remey, Whaley,
Greenwade, Hutchison, Johnston, Nicholls, Reid, Worster (Wooster),
Evans, Talbot, Linton, Black, Connor, Beall, Hardy.
Cloth—$40.00—549pp-- Vendor #D0566

3267 - ALABAMA KINFOLKS by Louise Milam Julich. 1984.
Reprint of Harselle and Decatur, Alabama Genealogical Columns
listing: Aldridge, Allen, Alexander, Anderson, Archibald, Aycock,
Baker, Bennett, Clark, Freeman, Parker, Vest, Praytor, Summerford,
Walker and many others.
Paper—$35.00—217pp--- Vendor #D0577

3268 - MAMMY BARCLIFT'S SCRAPBOOK compiled by Mammy Barclift,
Frances Caldeonia Woodall (Mrs. W. A. Barclift) 1855-1930; edited
by Frances Lee Burkart. Indexed.
Paper—$25.00—135pp--- Vendor #D0577

3269 - FAMILY HISTORY OF JOHN BISHOP OF SCOTLAND, RELATED AMERI-
CAN FAMILIES AND DESCENDANTS compiled by Stanley R. Scott and
Robert H. Montgomery. 1951, out of print, limited.
Cloth—$10.00—148pp--- Vendor #D0577

3270 - BURGESS FAMILY [FROM JOHN BURGESS, SR. b 1784, VIRGINIA
AND HIS WIFE SARAH SMITH, b 1780....] by Harl Donald Burgess
and Dr. Elbert Felton Johnston (deceased). 1981. Indexed.
Cloth—$25.00—208pp--- Vendor #D0577

3271 - COPELAND FIVE HUNDRED YEARS OF FAMILY HISTORY: ENGLAND,
SCOTLAND, IRELAND, GERMANY, THE NETHERLANDS, AMERICA,
CANADA by Barry A. Copeland. 1981.
Cloth—$35.00—351pp--- Vendor #D0577

3272 - THE CROWDER FAMILY COLLECTION, 1200—1983 by Fredrea Cook.
1983. Indexed.
Cloth—$30.00--- Vendor #D0577

3273 - DEWITT-DUETT ROOTS AND SHOOTS by Avis Williams Dewitt. 1984.
(In process)—Cloth--- Vendor #D0577

3274 - DeMONEY—De MONIA—DeMONEIA—MONET—MONEY—MONNET—LeMOINE
FAMILY FROM FRANCE TO AMERICA, 1676-1981 by Montez Demonia
Jones. 1981. Indexed.
Cloth—$35.00—224pp--- Vendor #D0577

3275 - DOWNINGS OF EUROPE AND AMERICA, 1273-1973, VOLUME I by
Ann Cochrane-Gregath. 1976. Indexed.
Cloth—$40.00—554pp--- Vendor #D0577

3276 - DOWNINGS OF EUROPE AND AMERICA, 1273-1973, VOLUME II by
Ann Cochrane Gregath. 1983. Indexed.
Cloth—$40.00--- Vendor #D0577

3277 - DUNSTON, PONDER, WALKER by Bettina Pearson Higdon. 1981.
Indexed.
Cloth—$40.00—241pp--- Vendor #D0577

3278 - FAITH FAMILY by Loyce Margaret Smith Robbins.
Cloth—$30.00—202pp--- Vendor #D0577

3279 - FOSTER: A FIRST FAMILY IN ALABAMA by Bettina Pearson Higdon.
1983. Indexed.
Cloth—$40.00--- Vendor #D0577

3280 - GAMBLE, SAPP, WILLIAMS: EARLY SETTLERS OF BLOUNT COUNTY,
ALABAMA by Carolina K. Nigg. 1982. Indexed.
Cloth—$30.00—171pp--- Vendor #D0577

3281 - GARDNER, GARDENER, GARDINER, GARDINIER, GARTNER
GENEALOGY AND ALLIED FAMILIES by Marshall Kim Gardner. 1983.
Indexed.
Cloth—$35.00—271pp-- Vendor #D0577

3282 - DESCENDANTS OF REUBEN HAMBY by Betty Dean Hamby Cooper.
1984.
Cloth—$30.00—124pp-- Vendor #D0577

3283 - HART FAMILY ALBUM, WITH ALLIED FAMILIES by Craig Hart. 1982.
Paper—$15.00—110pp-------------------------------------- Vendor #D0577

3284 - THE HERNDON AND INGE FAMILIES by George B. Inge (deceased).
1973. Indexed.
Cloth—$35.00—306pp-------------------------------------- Vendor #D0577

3285 - HIGDON-WHITAKER by Bettina Pearson Higdon. 1982.
Cloth—$40.00—408pp-------------------------------------- Vendor #D0577

3286 - HITE-JOIST (YOST HEYDT) AND SOME OF HIS DESCENDANTS by
Frances Cooper. 1983. Indexed.
Cloth—$30.00—217pp-------------------------------------- Vendor #D0577

3287 - INGRAM FAMILIES AND THEIR DESCENDANTS, MEMORIES THAT
NEVER DIE by Maude Ingram Markee. 1984.
Cloth—$35.00—137pp-------------------------------------- Vendor #D0577

3288 - JONES—REESE AND ALLIED FAMILIES by Montez De Monia Jones.
1982. Indexed.
Cloth—$30.00—215pp-------------------------------------- Vendor #D0577

3289 - KARTER—OTTE FAMILIES by Sister Benedicta Karter, O.S.B.
1982. Indexed.
Cloth—$30.00—196pp-------------------------------------- Vendor #D0577

3290 - KEEL AND RELATED FAMILIES, PART I by Hilda Barnett, Ola John-
son and P. B. Keel; WHITAKER WANDERINGS, PART II by Harold
Whitaker, Two Books in One. 1983. Combined index.
Cloth—$40.00—596pp-------------------------------------- Vendor #D0577

3291 - KENNADAY, THE OTHER KENNADYS PLUS "THAT JINKS," Two Books
In One by Hazel Kennady Lewis.
Cloth—$30.00—176pp-------------------------------------- Vendor #D0577

3292 - LEE LINEAGE [JONATHAN LEE'S FAMILY HISTORY] by Edna Earle Lee
James. 1982. Indexed.
Cloth—$30.00—148pp-------------------------------------- Vendor #D0577

3293 - LUCIA LEE'S CLIPPINGS, A SEQUEL TO MAMMY BARCLIFT'S SCRAP-
BOOK, 2 Volumes. [Vol. I-1877-1950; Vol. II-1950-1977] Indexed.
Cloth—$25.00/Vol.-------------------------------------- Vendor #D0577

3294 - LENDERMANN (LINDERMAN, LENAMOND, LENAMON, LENDEMAN)
LINKS, 1763-1982, 2 Volumes, by Ranelle Hemrick Brown and Margene
Hemrick Black. Indexed.
Cloth—Vol. I $35.00—238pp—Vol. II $35.00—264pp-----------Vendor #D0577

3295 - A LOCKHART FAMILY IN AMERICA (1744-1972) by Ann Cochrane
Gregath. Indexed.
Paper—$10.00—138pp-------------------------------------- Vendor #D0577

3296 JOHN MAINWARING OF NEW JERSEY AND ALLIED FAMILIES by
Charles William Mainwaring. 1982. Indexed.
Cloth—$35.00—290pp-------------------------------------- Vendor #D0577

3297 - THOMAS ALEXANDER MARTIN FAMILY HISTORY by Montez De Monia
Jones. 1982. Indexed.
Cloth—$25.00—135pp-------------------------------------- Vendor #D0577

3298 - PATRIOTS ON PARADE [REVOLUTIONARY WAR FAMILIES OF
BOYLES, CRAWFORD...] by Ann Cochrane Gregath. 1976. Indexed.
Paper—$10.00—50pp-------------------------------------- Vendor #D0577

3299 - PEARSON, SEEK AND YE SHALL FIND by Bettina Pearson Higdon. 1979. Indexed.
Cloth—$40.00—352pp--- Vendor #D0577

3300 - PONDERS OF EUROPE AND AMERICA by Odalene Little Ponder. Indexed.
Cloth—$35.00—300pp--- Vendor #D0577

3301 - THE POPEJOY FAMILY IN AMERICA, 1700-1976 by Charles L. Popejoy. 1976.
Cloth—$30.00—350pp--- Vendor #D0577

3302 - POPEJOY PAST AND PRESENT, 1680-1980 by Charles L. Popejoy. 1982. Indexed.
Cloth—$35.00—483pp--- Vendor #D0577

3303 - GATHERING THE ROSES by Charles M. Rose. 1980. Indexed.
Cloth—$35.00—471pp--- Vendor #D0577

3304 - THE SLACK FAMILY, 1753-1981 by Mary Louise McCarthy Slack. 1981.
Paper—$15.00—53pp--- Vendor #D0577

3305 - JOHN SMITH THE SCOT by Mrs. Loyce Margaret S. Robbins. 1970. Indexed.
Cloth—$25.00—156pp--- Vendor #D0577

3306 - A DRIVE BACK INTO HISTORY, GENEALOGYS OF SMITH, TEXADA, TREVILLION AND CULPEPPER FAMILIES OF LOUISIANA AND MISS-ISSIPPI by Mrs. Loyce Margaret S. Robbins. 1969. Indexed.
Cloth—$35.00—305pp--- Vendor #D0577

3307 - JACKSON JOHNSON SPALDING III by Mrs. Loyce S. Robbins. Indexed.
Cloth—$25.00—108pp--- Vendor #D0577

3308 - STOVALL JOURNAL by Major W. T. Stovall. Indexed.
Cloth—$30.00--- Vendor #D0577

3309 - DANIEL TUBB, 1794-1882 OF SOUTH CAROLINA, TENNESSEE, ALABAMA, AND DESCENDANTS by Dianne Lollar, Bruce Myers (deceased) and Bill Tubbs. 1982. Indexed.
Cloth—$30.00—193pp--- Vendor #D0577

3310 - WILDMAN—HUCKABY (ALL SPELLINGS) by Bettina Pearson Higdon. 1983. Indexed.
Cloth—$40.00—278pp--- Vendor #D0577

3311 - THE STORY OF JOHN AND ELIZABETH WILKES CRANFORD by Willodene Cranford Brumbach.
Paper—$20.00--- Vendor #D0577

3312 - CROW AND STROUP FAMILIES, SOUTH CAROLINA TO ALABAMA, 1818 by Louise Milam Julich. 1984. Indexed.
Cloth—$35.00--- Vendor #D0577

3313 - THE GOOD LIFE by Kay Good Gregath. Indexed.
Cloth—$40.00--- Vendor #D0577

3314 - A JEFFREYS FAMILY, 1765-1984 by Allen Ray Jeffreys. Indexed.
Cloth—$35.00--- Vendor #D0577

3315 - THE SEVEN LOTT SISTERS by Jimmy Lou Golden and Louella Steele. 1984.
Cloth—$30.00—78pp--- Vendor #D0577

3316 - SELF HERITAGE by Larry R. Brown and Edna Earle James. 1984. Indexed.
Cloth—$35.00—217pp--- Vendor #D0577

3317 - MILLWOOD GENEALOGY by Shelia Cochran McCoy. Indexed.
Cloth—$35.00--- Vendor #D0577

3318 - A FAMILY NAMED McCOY FROM EARLIEST TIMES, 1763 TO 1983. THE DESCENDANTS OF JOHN AND MARY EBERMAN McCOY by William K. McCoy. 1984.
Cloth—$35.00—183pp--- Vendor #D0577

3319 - THE STOVALL FAMILY IN AMERICA by Carmae Massey Smith. 1983.
Cloth—$35.00—236pp--- Vendor #D0577

3320 - THE CHARLES BRANCH OF MY SUNSHINE TREE by Sybil Roberts Smith.
Cloth—$35.00—274pp--- Vendor #D0577

3321 - KILGO—KILGORE COUSINS AND KIN by Darrell Blalock. 1984.
Cloth—$35.00—246pp--- Vendor #D0577

3322 - THE ALLENS AND THE HARRISONS OF THE KINGDOM OF CALLAWAY
by Crockett Allen Harrison. 1981.
The author weaves his Allen and Harrison lines into the history of
the period from about 1500 to the present including anywhere from a
few words to chapters on 42 connecting lines. Included are 41 four
generation and family charts with notes plus maps and illustrations.
Connecting lines included are: Addie, Allen (a second line), Arm-
strong, Bailey, Bassett, Beauforest, Billups, Branch, Brighby,
Burton, Casey, Christain, Crockett, deSaix, deVigne, Duncan,
Gamble, Glasscock, Gose, Gouch, Gunnell, Hampton, Harris,
Jennings, Johnson, Lackey, Leech, Lilley, Lorton, Malone, Mann,
Page, Pfeiffer, Sandifer, Sayers, Smith (Va.), Smith (Ky.),
Spangler, Spracher, Stewart, Stovall, Thomson, Wade, Wilson.
Printers type, 748 pages, cloth hard cover. Unusual inspection
and copying terms. $61.50 delivered.
Cloth—$61.50—748pp--- Vendor #D0578

3323 - THE FAMILY HISTORY OF THOMAS MARTIN, SR. A NORTH CAROLIN-
IAN AMERICAN REVOLUTIONARY SOLDIER by Jenny Martin Fagg. 1976.
129 photographs 1870-1975. Index to 565 surnames.
Indexes to: Martin deeds—Carroll County, Georgia 1827-1934, Ruther-
ford County, North Carolina 1802-1884; Martin Estates York County,
South Carolina 1814-1875; Martin and McAfee marriages Cullman County,
Alabama 1886-1939.
Major allied families prior to 1900: Barnette, Bishop, Collins, Ellison,
Entrekin, Gammon, Goforth, Jennings, Lackie, Logan, McAfee, More-
land, Peeler, Pitts, Roach, Sepauch, Thayer, Washburn, Westbrook.
Cloth—$25.00—384pp--- Vendor #D0589

3324 - CARTER HALL AND SOME GENEALOGICAL NOTES ON THE BURWELL
FAMILY OF VIRGINIA by Stuart E. Brown, Jr. 1978.
Burwell Family.
Cloth—$26.00—197pp--- Vendor #D0591

3325 - THE WOLTZ FAMILY by Flora Lee Woltz. Repr. of 1929 ed.
Cloth—$12.50—139pp--- Vendor #D0591

3326 - DATA ON SOME VIRGINIA FAMILIES by Dakota Best Brown. 1979.
Virginia families: Best, Brown, Carlin, Denty [Dentie]-Potter-Dailey,
Ellett, Forloine, Gartrell, Hannon, Harrison-Rust, Hill-Clopton, Janney,
Biles-Baker, Jefferson, Johnson, Kemp [Kempe], Lowell [Lowle], Lunt,
McGeorge, McIlhany, Neale, Robinson, Silver, Slaughter, White and
Whiting.
Cloth—$22.50—287pp--- Vendor #D0591

3327 - THE WASHINGTONS AND THEIR HOMES by John Walter Wayland.
Repr. of 1944 ed.
Cloth—$18.50—385pp--- Vendor #D0591

3328 - COOK—HEARD AND ALLIED LINES: BARTON, BULLOCK, FITZ-
PATRICK, SMITH by Tressie Cook. 1978.
Richard Cooke, Bristol, England. Son *William* emigrated to Isle of Wight
County, Virginia, 1635.
Stephen Heard and Charles Heard, brothers, emigrated from Tyrone
County, Ireland, 1820.
John Bullock, David Barton, John Bailey Smith, Joseph Fitzpatric.
Descendants of above familied moved from Virginia into Georgia and
then into Louisiana.
Cloth—$20.00—195pp--- Vendor #D0606

3329 - ROSEWELL, GARLAND OF VIRGINIA by Claude Lanciano. 1978.
When built the largest mansion in Virginia known as America's grandest
home. Outstanding manor regarded as continents' greatest architec-
tural treasure; one of early America's most interesting landmarks.
With Page genealogy.
Cloth—$12.50—256pp ------------------------------------- Vendor #D0646

3330 - "OUR MOST SKILLFUL ARCHITECT," RICHARD TALIAFERRO AND
ASSOCIATED COLONIAL VIRGINIA CONSTRUCTIONS by Claude
Lanciano. 1982.
Biography and architectural critique authenticating alleged Taliaferro
architectural credits; of value to genealogists, untangling and firming
foundations of Taliaferro family.
Cloth—$15.00—189pp ------------------------------------- Vendor #D0646

3331 - CAPTAIN JOHN SINCLAIR OF VIRGINIA by Claude Lanciano. 1973.
Patriot, privateer and alleged pirate in the early trials of nation.
Contains Sinclair genealogy.
Cloth—$7.50—312pp -- Vendor #D0646

3332 - JOHN GRANBERY, VIRGINIA, 1493-1964 by Julian Hastings Granbery
and Alice Granbery Walter. 1965.
Descendants in England, Bermuda, Virginia, Tennessee, Alabama,
31 states. Generously illustrated, hard cover printed in gold. Over
2,000 descendants. Maps, charts, Name, Place and Numerical Indices.
Foreword by the late E. G. Swem, Williamsburg.
Paper—$40.00—351pp ----------------------------------- Vendor #D0657

3333 - CORNICK FAMILY OF PRINCESS ANNE COUNTY, VIRGINIA 1618-1900s
by Alice Granbery Walter. 1980.
This is a set of 4 charts of Princess Anne County, Virginia with family
connections to: Adams, Anguish, Ashley, Attwood, Bonney, Barlow,
Camp, Cannon, Cartwright, Drewery, Dyer, Edings, Etheridge,
Fitzgerald, Gornto, Hancock, Henley, Herbert, Hoggard, Hogle,
Hunter, Ivy, James, Keeling, Land, Lovett, Martin, Mason, Morse,
Needham, Nimmo, Old, Parker, Porter, Richason, Scott, Shepherd,
Shipp, Steed, Walke, Walker, Walter, West, Wilson, Woodhouse, et als.
Paper—$15.00—4 charts ----------------------------------- Vendor #D0657

3334 - MASON—IVY—GANEY FAMILIES OF LOWER NORFOLK COUNTY,
VIRGINIA 1584-1700s compiled and published by Alice Granbery
Walter. 1980.
A chart. Family connections to: Argent, Cheeseman, Cock, Cornick,
Hobson, Hodges, Needham, Porten, Sanderson, Sayer, Sewell, Sidney,
Thelaball, Thorowgood, Wilson.
Paper—$5.00—chart ----------------------------------- Vendor #D0657

3335 - NIMMO FAMILY OF PRINCESS ANNE COUNTY, VIRGINIA, 1710-1968
9 GENERATIONS by Julian Hastings Granbery and Alice Granbery
Walter. 1980.
A set of 4 charts from James Nimmo, the emmigrant to one or more
generations of these family connections in Virginia and other states.
Becket, Burroughs, Carraway, Ellis, Forrest, Ghiselin, Granbery,
Haak, Hall, Haynes, Henley, Hunter, Jones, Marsden, Mumford,
Old, Parker, Stokes, Styron, Thelaball, Thoroughgood, Tucker,
Walter.
Paper—$12.00—4 charts --------------------------------- Vendor #D0657

3336 - 17TH CENTURY FAMILIES OF JOHN MARTIN AND THOMAS KEELING
OF LOWER NORFOLK COUNTY, VIRGINIA by Alice Granbery Walter.
1978.
Martin: 1635-1700 in Virginia and North Carolina 1704-1716.
Keeling: ca 1635-1691 Lower Norfolk County and 1691-1700's Princess
Anne County.
Giving connections to Bray, Cornick, Dyer, Lawson, Lovett, Needham,
Okeham, Penny, Poole, Richason, Watson, Woodhouse, et als.
Documented, full name and place index. Includes *Offley* and *Thorowgood*
Charts in England.
Paper—$15.00—35pp --------------------------------- Vendor #D0657

3337 - DERIVATION OF THE HERBERT FAMILY, 163-1900s by Alice Granbery Walter. 1979.
From Pippin−1613 to the family in Lower Norfolk County, Virginia 1649.
In England 1424-1700's including Earls of Pembroke, Lords of Chirbury, John Herbert alias Wilkinson in Virginia, and his descendants to 1900's.
Includes a Yates chart in England, British West Indies and Lower Norfolk County, Virginia. Fully documented. Name, Place and Subject Indices.
Paper−$25.00−13 charts−-89pp ---------------------------- Vendor #D0657

3338 - FRANCIS LAND FAMILY OF LOWER NORFOLK AND PRINCESS ANNE COUNTIES, VIRGINIA by Alice Granbery Walter. 1980.
3 charts, 1604-1800−9 generations with family connections to: Bonney, Cornick, Gardner, Gaskins, Haynes, Hoggard, Keeling, Langley, Moseley, Phillips, Rutherford, Salmons, Shepherd, Shipp, Smith, Snaile, West, White, Woodhouse.
Paper−$10.00−3 charts --------------------------------- Vendor #D0657

3339 - IVY IN ENGLAND 1400−LATE 1600s by Alice Granbery Walter. 1980.
An attempt to trace the ancestry of Thomas Ivy born 1604 and died 1653/4 in Lower Norfolk County, Virginia. With connections in England to: Canning, Malet, Winter, Keynes, Hyde, Aileffe, Hinton, Culpeper, et als.
Paper−$7.50−set of charts ----------------------------- Vendor #D0657

3340 - DESCENDANTS OF CAPTAIN ADAM THOROWGOOD AND SARAH OFFLEY 1603-1800s by Alice Granbery Walter. 1980.
7 generations in Lower Norfolk and Princess Anne Counties, Virginia with family connections to: Bray, Calvert, Church, Clouse, Colcough, Conner, Cornick, Daynes, Fowler, Gookin, Hackett, Haynes, Hunter, Kempe, Keeling, Lawson, Lovett, Michael, Moseley, Nicholson, Nimmo, Offley, Overzee, Phripp, Poole, Robinson, Sanford, Sayer, Simmons, Trevethan, Walke, White, Willoughby, Woodhouse, Wright, Yardley, et als.
Paper−$15.00−set of charts ----------------------------Vendor #D0657

3341 - BOUSH−NIMMO 1655-1904−7 GENERATIONS FROM HENRY SNAYLE TO HENRY A. T. GRANBERY compiled and published by Alice Granbery Walter.
This is a chart of Lower Norfolk and Princess Anne Counties, Virginia with family connections to: Ashall, Bennett, Brickhouse, Butt, Dyson, Ewell, Granbery, Haynes, Hollowell, Hunter, Johnson, Land, Mason, McClanahan, Ramsey, Saunders, Sweeny, Thelaball, Thorowgood, Walke, Wilson and Woodhouse.
Paper−$7.00- --- Vendor #D0657

3342 - WALKE FAMILY CONNECTIONS 1662-ca 1800 PRINCESS ANNE COUNTY, VIRGINIA by Alice Granbery Walter. 1976.
3 charts: 5 generations of Walke lines.
Four marriages of Mary Anne Thorowgood/Thorowgood/Walke/Phripp/ Hackett and their issue.
Daynes−Conner−Lawson−Walke−Thorowgood connections.
Includes family connections to: Armistead, Bassett, Boush, Calvert, Clouse, Conner, Hunter, Land, Lawson, McClenahan, Moore, Moseley, Newton, Sanford, Sayer, Thorowgood, Westcott, Williamson, Willoughby, Wright, et als.
Paper−$12.00−3 charts --------------------------------- Vendor #D0657

3343 - ABIGAIL LANGLEY'S JOURNAL 1694-1723, Originally called "John Granbery, His Book." 1983.
Original photo copy of book and commentary by Julian Hastings Granbery. It furnished proof needed to document several generations of the Granbery Family.
"I know of no other journal that is a diary of any Virginia woman of the Colonial Period"−Earl Gregg Swem−29 March 1963.
Paper−$25.00−53pp ----------------------------------- Vendor #D0657

3344 - HOGGARD OF WARWICK AND PRINCESS ANNE COUNTIES, VIRGINIA 1640-1900s, 12 GENERATIONS by Alice Granbery Walter. 1984.
(To be published late 1984.)
Peter, the emigrant to the Thurmer Hoggard Family of Princess Anne, and Poplar Hall the Ancestral Home.
(In process)—Charts-- Vendor #D0657

3345 - THE FFUWELLEN/LLEWELLYN, LLEWELLING FAMILY OF LOWER NORFOLK COUNTY, VIRGINIA, 1600-1700s by Alice Granbery Walter. 1983.
Family connections to: Ballentine, Bunting, Bustin, Dyer, Ewell, Herbert, Horne, Jackson, Johnson, Langley, Luke, Markham, Smith, Thomas, White, Yates.
Paper—$5.00—1 chart------------------------------------- Vendor #D0657

3346 - 4TH—7TH GENERATIONS OF LOVETTS OF LOWER NORFOLK AND PRINCESS ANNE COUNTIES, VIRGINIA 1700-1795 by Alice Granbery Walter. 1982.
Family connections to: Cornick, Cox, Edney, Farrar, Gaskins, Giles, Hayes, Haynes, Henley, Hoggard, Keeling, Kemp, Lamount, Malbone, Moore, Newman, Richason, Stewart, Thorowgood, Ward, Westwood, Woodhouse.
Paper—$5.00—1 chart------------------------------------- Vendor #D0657

3347 - HANCOCK CONNECTIONS OF LOWER NORFOLK, PRINCESS ANNE, HENRICO, BEDFORD AND SURRY COUNTIES, VIRGINIA AND ROTTER-DAM, HOLLAND by Alice Granbery Walter. 1983.
1600—ca 1780—From Gurgany and Hancock to connections to: Ashell, Blackmore, Burnet, Cockroft, Emperor, Fox, Gookin, Gurgany, Guy, Harding, Hargrave, Harris, Hoggard, Jameson, Kemp, Lawson, Lygon, Lyon, Moseley, Piggot, Whishard, Woodson, et als.
Paper—$6.00—1 chart------------------------------------- Vendor #D0657

3348 - WOODHOUSE/WODEHOUSE OF ENGLAND, BERMUDA AND NORFOLK COUNTY, VIRGINIA 1316-1900s by Alice Granbery Walter. 1983.
3 Woodhouse and 1 Bacon Ancestry Charts with connections to:
Ackiss, Adams, Atwood, Bacon, Bonny, Brock, Caesar, Camp, Capps, Cason, Carter, Cartwright, Cheshire, Clark, Clowes, Colt, Cornick, Croft, Dale, Dietrick, Driver, Etheridge, Ewell, Fastolf, Fulcher, Furneaux, Gedding, Gerard, Granbery, Gresham, Haen, Henly, Herbert, Hill, Hobart, Hoggard, James, Jermyn, Keeling, Land, Langley, Lovett, Low, Luke, Luttrel, Malbone, Moore, Morrisett, Morton, Owen, Pallet, Parker, Paynter, Pebworth, Persley, Peters, Petty, Power, Ratcliffe, Repps, Rutherford, Sanford, Sayer, Scott, Skelton, Shepherd, Smith, Snail, Sothern, Spratt, Strathyng, Stuthart, Sweeting, Thorowgood, Tiriel, Townsend, Tuthill, Walke, Walter, Ward, Webb, West, Woodside, Wooten.
Paper—$25.00—4 charts------------------------------------- Vendor #D0657

3349 - TATEM OF BERMUDA AND NORFOLK COUNTY, VIRGINIA 1625-1860s by Alice Granbery Walter. 1983.
Family connections to: Carney, Edgerton, Felgate, Godfrey, Granbery, Herbert, Hoggard, Murden, Nash, Nicholson, Oldner, Portlock, Smith, Teatom (Tatum), Trimingham, Trimble, Turner, Tynes, Underwood, Wainwright, Walter, Williams, Williamson, Wilson, Woodhouse, Wright.
Paper—$10.00—2 charts------------------------------------- Vendor #D0657

3350 - THURMER: ELIZABETH CITY, YORK, AND WARWICK COUNTIES, VIRGINIA 1622-1750s by Alice Granbery Walter. 1983.
Search for ancestors or Robert Thurmer. Connections to: Asson, Elwes, Glanville, Haynes, Hoggard, Jackson, Morecroft, Morgan, Powell, Ramsha, Rice, Tignall, Travers, Waterhouse.
Paper—$6.00—1 chart------------------------------------- Vendor #D0657

3351 - MASON/LANGLEY/THELABALL FAMILIES OF LOWER NORFOLK AND PRINCESS ANNE COUNTIES, VIRGINIA 1566-1800 by Alice Granbery Walter. 1983.
Connections to: Argent, Ballard, Bartee, Boush, Bruce, Butt, Chi-chester, Clements, Cocke, Cornick, Crafford, Dunnock, Ellison,

French, Gayne, Granbery, Hargroves, Hobson, Hodge, Ivy, Jamison, Johnson, Land, Langley, Lewelling, Major, Martin, Mason, Moseley, Newton, Nichalson, Pasteur, Phripp, Porten, Robinson, Sanderson, Sayer, Sewell, Snaile, Thorowgood, Trevethan, Walton, Willoughby, Wilson, Wishard.
Paper—$10.00—4 charts------------------------------------ Vendor #D0657

3352 - RANSHA/RAMSHAW OF WARWICK COUNTY, VIRGINIA 1611-1750s by Alice Granbery Walter. 1983.
Connections to: Cheesman/Cheeseman, Glanville, Haynes, Jackson, Hoggard, Mackintosh, Morgan, Powell, Ramsheir, Renshaw, Smith, Thurmer, Westerhouse, Wills.
Paper—$5.00—1 chart------------------------------------ Vendor #D0657

3353 - PORTLOCK OF NORFOLK COUNTY, VIRGINIA 1650s-1750s by Alice Granbery Walter. 1983.
Connections to: Bacon, Bevan, Butt, Etheredge/Etheridge, Gardner, Hallford, Herbert, Hodges, Jervis, Marrington, Matthais, Mayle, Nash, Robinson, Spivey, Tatem, Whitehurst, Wright.
Paper—$10.00—1 chart------------------------------------ Vendor #D0657

3354 - NASH OF LOWER NORFOLK COUNTY, VIRGINIA 1638-1900 by Alice Granbery Walter. 1983.
Connections to: Dillard, Etheridge/Etheredge, Foster, Francis, Granbery, Robinson, Tatem, Walke, Wallace, Whitehurst.
Paper—$8.00—2 charts------------------------------------ Vendor #D0657

3355 - MOSELEY OF LOWER NORFOLK, PRINCESS ANNE AND HENRICO COUNTIES, VIRGINIA 1600-1800 by Alice Granbery Walter. 1982.
From William Moseley, the Emigrant with connections to: Blackmore, Burgess, Burnet, Butt, Cocke, Conner, Corker, Crowinsheild, Daingerfield, Drewery, Ellegood, Emperor, Gookin, Hack, Hancock, Haynes, Hughlett, Hunter, James, Jameson, Keeling, Kelsick, Lamount, Land, Langley, Lawson, Lovett, Luke, Malbone, McKensie, Moore, Newton, Nimmo, Poole, Robinson, Sayer, Stringer, Thelaball, Thorowgood, Walke, Weblin, Whitehurst, Wiles, Wishart, et als.
Paper—$15.00—8 charts------------------------------------ Vendor #D0657

3356 - MACKENTOSH FAMILY OF NEW POQUOSON, YORK COUNTY, VIRGINIA 1600s-1790s by Alice Granbery Walter. 1983.
Connections to: Burt, Eaton, Johnson, Kiston, Lewis, Mallicote, Noblin, Puryear, Ramsha/Ramshaw, Ridley, Watts, Young.
Paper—$5.00—1 chart------------------------------------ Vendor #D0657

3357 - ETHERIDGE OF LOWER NORFOLK COUNTY, VIRGINIA 4 GENERATIONS 1610-1790 by Alice Granbery Walter. 1983.
Connections to: Blanch, Robinson, Marrington, Nicholas, Norcott, Fenford, Mohan, Murray, Nash, Portlock, Shepherd, Watson, and Yates.
Paper—$5.00—1 chart------------------------------------ Vendor #D0657

3358 - CURLE FAMILY OF ELIZABETH CITY COUNTY, VIRGINIA 1699-1800s by Alice Granbery Walter. 1983.
5 generations of connections to: Armistead, Bridger, Bayley, Barraud, Herbert, Jenkins, Pierce, Ricketts, "Silverfist" Thomas Herbert, Wilson.
Paper—$6.00—1 chart------------------------------------ Vendor #D0657

3359 - MATHAIS FAMILY CHART OF LOWER NORFOLK COUNTY, VIRGINIA 1669-1700s by Alice Granbery Walter. 1983.
5 generations with connections to: Drewery/Drury, Holstead/Halstead, Nash, Portlock.
Paper—$5.00—1 chart------------------------------------ Vendor #D0657

3360 - FAMILY TIES—#1 AND #2 of LOWER NORFOLK COUNTY, VIRGINIA by Alice Granbery Walter. 1983.
Chart #1—Marriages and intermarriages of: Ballantine, Cawson, Church, Dale, Herbert, Horne, Llewellyn, Markham, Sayer, Whiddon, Willoughby, Yeats.
Chart #2—Marriages and intermarriages 1628-1800's of: Cawson,

Nicholson, Smith and Yates to Whiddon, Herbert and Hoggard.
Paper—Chart #1—$10.00—1 chart—Chart #2—$7.00—1 chart--- Vendor #D0657

3361 - GANY/GANEY/GAYNEY OF ELIZABETH CITY COUNTY 1591-1600s
by Alice Granbery Walter. 1983.
Two generation chart: Mason Family connection and Chisman, Cheesman, Thelaball, Baker, Robinson.
Paper—$4.00—1 chart------------------------------------ Vendor #D0657

3362 - MALLICOTE FAMILY OF WARWICK COUNTY, VIRGINIA 1660-1790s
by Alice Granbery Walter. 1983.
Connections to: Atkinson, Batts, Giles, Gray, Hoggard, Lewelling,
Lupo, Mackentosh, Morgan, Patrick, Rowell.
Paper—$6.00—1 chart----------------------------------- Vendor #D0657

3363 - YATES: IN ENGLAND AND IN ENGLAND, WEST INDIES, AND
VIRGINIA by Alice Granbery Walter.
First Chart—1591-1644 with connections to: Bitefield, Bingham,
Phelps, Pirry, Prince and Taylor in England.
Second Chart—British West Indies and Lower Norfolk County, Virginia
—1656-ca 1750: Connections to: Ballentine, Dale, Etheridge, Gater,
Hodges, Horne, Leake, Llewellyn, Lovell, Markham, Smith, Valentine,
Whiddon.
Paper—$9.00—2 charts--------------------------------- Vendor #D0657

3364 - THE HISTORY OF THE DESCENDANTS OF THE JERSEY SETTLERS
OF ADAMS COUNTY, MISSISSIPPI, 2 Volumes, edited by Frances
Preston Mills. 1981.
History of the descendants of the Jersey Settlers of Adams County,
Mississippi (Natchez). The Reverend Samuel Swayze and Richard
Swayze, sons of Judge Samuel of Chester, New Jersey, including
their forebears back to William King and John Swayze, immigrants,
Salem, Massachusetts. History of the founding of Protestantism in
Mississippi by the Jersey Settlers. Genealogy of these Mississippi
pioneers for two hundred and seven years since 1773. (737 pages of
Swayze genealogy.)
Source book for the History of the Jersey Settlement; Accounts of the
Founding of the Jersey Settlement—Kingston including statistical records
of activities of descendants of the Jersey Settlers in Mississippi Terri-
tory; Records—Land Records, Court Records, Will Abstracts including
John Swayze and Samuel King.
Genealogy Sources for the Swayze and King family; King Family Records,
Bible Records; Marriage Records, Census Records, Cemetery Records.
Index. Illustrated with mid-nineteenth century family pictures, cemetery
pictures, facsimilies of old documents and records and pictures of the
only two known heirlooms of the Jersey Settlers. Large fold-in map,
inserted in the book, is an authentic copy of the Spanish division of
the Mandamus lands among the heirs of Samuel and Richard Swayze,
1787. Extensive bibliography.
Contains information pertaining to families of: Swayze, King, Bradley,
Coleman, Griffing, Cory, Luse, Ogden, Carter and allied families.
Cloth—$75.00 Set—2947pp---------------------------- Vendor #D0659

3365 - THE STORY OF THE ARNDTS by John Stover Arndt. 1922.
Cotton, Crane, Dewalt, Foresman, Fry, Houpt, Innes, Jacoby, John-
son, Kessler, King, Kulp, Lombaert, McFall, Miller, Moyer, Nellis,
Reiley, Shoemaker, Springman, Steckel, Stout, Welch, Williams.
Cloth—$17.50—427pp--------------------------------Vendor #D0679

3366 - THE KITH AND KIN OF CAPTAIN JAMES LEEPER AND SUSAN DRAKE
HIS WIFE by Nell McNish Gambill. 1946.
Gambill, Drake, Smith, Criddle, Ewing, Wheless, McNish, Dean,
Stump, Marshall, Descendants of first couple married in Fort Nash-
borough, Tennessee.
Cloth—$10.00—198pp-------------------------------- Vendor #D0679

3367 - MEMOIR AND GENEALOGY OF THE MARYLAND AND PENNSYLVANIA FAMILY OF MAYER by Brantz Mayer. 1968, repr.
Agnew, Atkins, Blackford, Bryan, Cottrell, Dinkle, Ernst, Euston, Fahnestock, Franklin, Houseal, Humphreville, Keim, Lane, Leech, Legett, Logan, McClure, McConkey, Miley, Morris, Randolph, Richey, Righter, Schuler, Shepherd, Stauffer, Steinman, Thomas, Thomson, Weatherill.
Cloth—$10.00—179pp--------------------------------------- Vendor #D0679

3368 - A SAGA OF STRAUDS AND THE STRODES by Octavia Jordan Perry. 1966.
Allied lines: Atwater, Bass, Bryan, Burckley, Goucher, Hall, Hicks, Holeman, Jordan, Key, Strowd, Thompson, Thrift, Wilson and Yount.
Cloth—$10.00—159pp--------------------------------------- Vendor #D0679

3369 - THE VAN TREESE FAMILY NEWSLETTER—" A DECADE OF DIGGING" by Robert V. Van Trees. 1983.
Contains 24 11"x16" fold-out charts of Van Treese and related lines.
Paper—$7.50—42pp--------------------------------------- Vendor #D0679

3370 - CHENOWETH FAMILY HISTORY by Cora Chenoweth Hiatt. 1979, 3d pr. of 1925 ed.
Cloth—$20.00—248pp--------------------------------------- Vendor #D0730

3371 - ARTHUR AYLSWORTH AND DESCENDANTS by Homer S. Aylsworth. Plus 136 page Index.
Cloth—$25.00—496pp--------------------------------------- Vendor #D0730

3372 - EARLY MARRIAGE RECORDS OF THE HOPKINS FAMILY IN THE UNITED STATES 1628-1865 edited by William M. Clemens. 1916, repr.
Index to inter-marriages.
Paper—$5.00—52pp--------------------------------------- Vendor #D0730

3373 - KERR CLAN OF NEW JERSEY BEGINNING WITH WALTER KER OF FREEHOLD AND OTHER RELATED LINES by William C. Armstrong. 1931, repr.
Cloth—$10.00—193pp--------------------------------------- Vendor #D0730

3374 - LEWIS FAMILY, PIONEERS OF EASTERN TENNESSEE AND INDIANA TERRITORY by Maunta G. Miller. 1928, repr.
New index by Dr. Ralph Kirkpatrick.
Paper—$5.50—60pp--------------------------------------- Vendor #D0730

3375 - THE FAMILY OF RICHARD SMITH OF SMITHTOWN, LONG ISLAND: TEN GENERATIONS by Frederick Kinsman Smith. 1967.
Published by the Smithtown Historical Society. The late Dr. Frederick Kinsman Smith of Warren, Ohio devoted more than twenty years, prior to his death in October, 1944, gathering and preserving all available data concerning Richard Smythe, founder of Smithtown, Long Island. This long awaited genealogy is the record of the Smith Family in Smithtown and the part it has played in the early development of Long Island. Through marriage this family has been allied to many of the early families of Long Island. Descendants are numerous and are scattered throughout the United States.
Cloth—$26.00—716pp--------------------------------------- Vendor #D0744

3376 - DESCENDANTS OF SALISBURY BURTON (1769-1813) compiled by Thelma Burton Bootes.
All states; New York—1800, Oneida County; 1810 Steuben County.
(In process)--------------------------------------- Vendor #D0756

3377 - FREDERICK OYER AND HIS DESCENDANTS by Phyllis Smith Oyer. 1977.
Oyer was killed at Oriskany, Revolutionary War. 150 families charted in succession. 200 collateral surnames including Bargy, Clemens, Duhan, Finster, Folts, Frank, Hochstetter, Lints, Pratt, Widrig. Many Herkimer and Cattaraugus County, NYS. Historical and biographical. Many alternate spellings of Oyer, including Auyer.
Three-ring hard cover binder, illustrations and index.
Paper—$9.00—70pp--------------------------------------- Vendor #D0759

3378   - MARTIN FAMILY QUARTERLY, VOL. X, edited by Michal Martin
Farmer. ISSN 0099-1864.
Volume X (May 1984 - February 1985). The first issue was May, 1975,
and it has been published quarterly since that date. Each volume
includes an every name and locality index. The Quarterly is published
in May, August, November and February with a subscription rate of
$15.00 per volume. All subscriptions begin with the May issue. The
magazine is 5¼"x8¼", offset printed and saddle stitched.
Volumes IV - IX are in print and include an average of 135 pages
per volume. The emphasis in Vol. I - IX was Martin families in the
South and Mid-West. Contents of back issues are sent on request.
Queries are published for current subscribers only. Each quarterly
contains documented source material about Martins across the United
States from the earliest settlements to ca 1900, but most records are
before 1850. Included are documented family lineages, wills, census,
marriage records, cemeteries and Bible records on Martin families.
Paper—$15.00—200pp/vol. --Vendor #D0761

3379   - FOUR AMERICAN SETTLERS, THE CHILDREN OF JOHANN GEORG
WECKESSER AND THEIR DESCENDANTS by Miriam Whaley. 1979.
Four children of Johann Georg Weckesser emigrated from Hessen,
Germany from 1852 to 1884. Maria Elisabeth settled in Philadelphia
and married Fiedler. Heinrich settled in Wayne County, Ohio and
married Long. Johannes settled in Whiteside County, Illinois and
married Marzolf. Konrad settled in Fulton County, Ohio and married
Henckel. Over 1,000 direct descendants of Johann Georg are listed
in the genealogy; related names include, among others: Barthelme,
Benedict, Borton, Burkholder, Bushey, Clayton, Cleckner, Collamore,
Davis, Douglass, Eimen, Galehouse, Garwick, Graber, Green, Harms,
Hawkins, Hughes, Jenkins, Johnson, Kandle, Krites, Lauber, Mason,
Maxwell, Miller, Newcombe, Pittenger, Plettner, Radabaugh, Rhine,
Roth, Ruger, Rupp, Schroeder, Smucker, Weaver, Welch, Whaley,
Young, Zaros, Zolman. Heinrich, Johannes, and Konrad all joined
the Mennonite Church. Stories and legends concerning this and
other aspects of the lives of all four original settlers are recorded
by their descendants; nearly 50 photographs and vital documents are
reproduced. Ancestors of Johann Georg in Germany are traced back
to 1666.
Cloth—$22.50—254pp-------------------------------------- Vendor #D0766

3380   - THE MEANS FAMILY OF AMERICA by Elizabeth Cissel Foglesong. 1972.
Very complete documented work in four indexed sections with many wills,
deeds, court records, military records, letters and photographs. Descendants in many states.
Cloth—$35.00—1018pp------------------------------------- Vendor #D0775

3381   - THE GOODRICH GOSPEL—QUARTERLY NEWSLETTER by Goodrich
Family Association. 1980.
The Goodrich Gospel* from the Goodrich Family Association.
Goodnews about the Goodrichs, Quarterly.
Searches, genealogical helps, biographies, membership activities.
Related families include: Allen, Bulkley, Chauncey, Deming, Foote,
Treat, Welles, Wolcott, Wright, and many other N. E. families.
Sample, details, $2.00.
--- Vendor #D0777

3382   - SEARCH-LIGHT, THE LIGHT FAMILY NEWSLETTER by Betty M.
Light Behr.
Published quarterly. Wide circulation. Fun and getting results.
Contact Betty M. Light Behr, Route 8, Carmel, NY 10512.
Paper—$5.00/yr--- Vendor #D0787

3383   - INDEX AND GAZETEER TO THE LIGHT FAMILY IN AMERICA, 1896
[by Moses Light, Manheim, Pennsylvania] by Betty M. Light Behr. 1974.
Indexed by surname, many varients, Maiden names, allied families and
place names where Light families are found.
Paper—$5.25—15pp-- Vendor #D0787

3384   - WORKING WITH PEOPLE, BUGS AND APPLES, LINDLEY M. AND
GRACE SELBY SMITH by Malcolm L. Smith. 1979.
Tells life and work (fruit grower, entomologist, horticulturist, parents
of ten, Illinois Mother of 1952) stories of the Smiths in Ozarks region
of Southern Illinois for 60 years. Relates how they and their forbears
lived in Ohio in the 1800's; that ancestors were in ten original colonies,
most coming from Great Britain; shows ancestry to families of Allen,
Anders, Bailey, Baker, Barrow, Birckhead, Borden, Brainerd, Bundy,
Bunting, Calhoun, Cartwright, Childrey, Clarke, Coffin, Cone, Cranston,
Dennis, Doan, Dutton, Edmundson, Embree, Ewen, Farquhar, Fenwick,
Gard, Gates, Gayer, Hardman, Hines, Hodgin, Howell, Hull, Humphrey,
Johns, Kirk, Knight, Laing, Lambert, Langdon, Large, Latham,
Llewelyn, Lundy, Lyon, Mack, Maddock, Mears, Minor, Moore, Niest,
Olmstead, Peasley, Rardin, Rees, Reynolds, Richardson, Roberts, Rye,
Sayre, Selby, Sharpley, Shotwell, Smith, Spencer, Stanton, Starbuck,
Stevens, Stubbs, Talbott, Thomas, Thurston, Ubrum, Ventres,
Vernon, Washburn, Weston, Willets, and Williams.
Includes source references, charts, indexes, pictures.
Cloth—$11.50—444pp--Vendor #D0798

3385   - THE QUIET ADVENTURERS IN NORTH AMERICA by Marion G. Turk.
1983.
Thousands of American and Canadian family charts and sources,
including Balleine, Bisson, Brehaut, Bubier, Coonier, De Gruchy,
De Quetteville, Durell, Falley, Favor, Hawkins, Henry, Hubbard, etc.
from 1600's on. See *Genealogical Helper*, Sept. 1983.
Cloth—$22.00—700pp--Vendor #D0800

3386   - ALLEN ROBINETT AND HIS DESCENDANTS IN AMERICA by James
M. Robinett.
A comprehensive genealogy of descendants of Allen Robinett from 1682
to present. Paper cover, 10 parts, each $15.00.
Almost all known Robinetts (Robnett, Robinette) are
descendants. All states. Twelve generations.
Paper—$15.00/each—150-200pp/each part--------------------Vendor #D0811

3387   - THE MAXWELLS OF SCOTLAND AND ALLIED FAMILIES: ALLAN,
ADDISON, PHILLIPS, COWIE, LAURIE, MONCREIFF by Ruth Maxwell Graham. 1982.
25 Illustrations; Indexed. 5½"x8½".
Biographical genealogy of major Maxwell branches in Scotland from 1100.
(150 pages.) Genealogy of immigrant (1842) William Maxwell to Illinois
and Kansas, and allied families.
Paper—$30.00—334pp--------------------------------------Vendor #D0812

3388   - PRESCOTTS UNLIMITED by Doris Cline Ward.
Of interest to all Prescotts by name, or descendants of Prescotts of
whatever immigrant to USA or Canada. Clans identified and material
pertinent to many of them in each issue. Co-ordinates research in
England, family gatherings, encourages publishing of further family
genealogy. Free Prescott-related queries to subscribers.
Published quarterly, March, June, September, December.
Subscription—$7.00/yr—16pp-----------------------------Vendor #D0813

3389   - THE PRESCOTT MEMORIAL by William Prescott, M. D. 1983 repr.
of 1870 ed.
A genealogy of the descendants of John Prescott of Lancaster, Massa-
chusetts, and James Prescott of Hampton Falls, New Hampshire.
(From 1600 to 1870)
Cloth—$41.50—653pp--------------------------------------Vendor #D0813

3390   - NORMAN GENEALOGY—ANCESTORS AND DESCENDANTS OF GEORGE
NORMAN, I AND MARTHA MELHUISH NORMAN, SOMERSET, ENGLAND
WITH DESCENDANT AND COLLATERAL FAMILIES OF AMERICA by
William E. Norman. 1976.
It covers a wide sector of Normans; Normans of Canada, Wisconsin,
Minnesota, Illinois, Connecticut, New England, and England. Also
abridged genealogies of the families of Leigh, Wells, and Woodrow
(including lines of Woodrow Wilson, President of the United States,

back to 1550). "Contents of Book" is comprehensive and concise.
Index of Collateral Family Names as they first appear in the main
genealogy. Does not include names in special sections or lists.
The cover is light blue Kroydon Flex, vinyl, Morocco grain, flexible
with outside corners rounded; washable; soil resistant.
Pictures of family Patriarchs and ancestors.
Review from Illinois State Genealogical Society: ...*The book is
absolutely crammed with information about hundreds of Normans and
the relationship between them is coded by a clever numbering system
devised by the author. If you have the NORMAN surname among
your ancestors, you ought to inspect this book.*
Paper—$13.00—267pp------------------------------------ Vendor #D0814

3391 - ROSE FAMILY BULLETIN (QUARTERLY) by Seymour T. and Christine
Rose, Editors.
Paper—$10.00/yearly—apx. 25pp/issue-------------------- Vendor #D0820

3392 - BROTHERS CAPT. LEWIS, MATTHIAS AND MARTIN ROSE, SONS OF
GOBLIEB/GODLOVE ROSE by Christine Rose. 1972.
Paper—$8.00—55pp------------------------------------- Vendor #D0820

3393 - REV. ROBERT ROSE OF SCOTLAND AND VIRGINIA by Christine
Rose. 1972.
Paper—$6.00—55pp------------------------------------- Vendor #D0820

3394 - REV. CHARLES ROSE OF SCOTLAND AND WESTMORELAND COUNTY,
VIRGINIA by Christine Rose. 1976.
Paper—$6.00—34pp------------------------------------- Vendor #D0820

3395 - ANDREW ROSE OF BUCKS AND MERCER COUNTIES, PENNSYLVANIA
by Christine Rose. 1977.
Paper—$10.00—81pp------------------------------------ Vendor #D0820

3396 - FREDERICK ROSE OF VIRGINIA, NORTH CAROLINA AND TENNESSEE
by Christine Rose. 1978.
Paper—$10.00—apx. 80pp------------------------------- Vendor #D0820

3397 - ROBERT ROSE OF WETHERSFIELD AND BRANFORD, CONNECTICUT;
WHO CAME ON THE SHIP FRANCIS FROM IPSWICH, ENGLAND IN 1634
by Christine Rose. 1983.
Robert Rose with his wife Margery and eight children sailed for New
England, the last of April 1634. The Rose family settled in Wethers-
field and Branford, Connecticut, but quickly spread into New Jersey,
western Massachusetts, and later New York, Ohio, Michigan, and
virtually every state. At least one branch was in Hunterdon County,
New Jersey and in Virginia by the 1740's.
This volume includes many additional sources such as census records,
Bible records, unpublished manuscripts, etc. Anyone seeking any
New England connection should not fail to examine the massive index
of this book, for all names including witnesses, bondsmen, etc. have
been indexed.
Many family connections appear including Frisbie, Foote, Hunt, Hale,
Page, Palmer, Seward, and many others.
Illustrated. Fully indexed.
Cloth—$40.00—512pp---------------------------------- Vendor #D0820

3398 - THE LEARNED FAMILY IN AMERICA, 1630-1967 by Eugenia Learned
James, Ph.D. 1967.
A record of the known lineal descendants of William Learned, who
came from Bermondsey, County Surrey, England, to the Massachusetts Bay Colony with Winthrop's fleet in 1630. This book lists fourteen generations of Learneds (spelled also Larned, Larnard, Larnerd,
Leanard, Leanhard, Learnard, Leonard, Lerned). The late Judge
William Law Learned, of the New York State Supreme Court, compiled
two editions of *The Learned Family*, the first in 1882, and second in
1898.
Among the thousands of names of persons who married into the family
(indexed with cross references) are Alden, Austin, Ballard, Bigelow,
Churchill, Cleveland, Colt, Conant, Davis, Farwell, French, Hand,

Kellogg, Lathrop, Lovejoy, Marcy, McMillan, Olds, Packard, Raleigh, Stetson, Shumway, Townsend, Upham, Van Nostrand, Whipple, Youngblood.
This volume includes a full page color reproduction of the coat-of-arms used by the family. A color reproduction of this coat-of-arms, suitable for framing, 10"x14", is now available at $5.00 per copy.
An attractive bound volume, hard cover, red with gold lettering, 5-3/4"x8-3/4".
Cloth—$22.50—406pp-- Vendor #D0822

3399   - HESSELGRAVE FAMILIES IN AMERICA by Ruth A. Hesselgrave and Polly U. Kahler. 1979.
The Hesselgrave surname originated during the thirteenth century in West Riding, Yorkshire, England. An overview of Yorkshire, early family records, and the English ancestry of American Hesselgraves provide background for history and genealogy of six immigrants from Yorkshire to America:

Thomas Hesselgrave	St. Lawrence County, New York	1821
Robert Hesselgrave	St. Lawrence County, New York	1829
Joseph Hesselgrave	Juab County, Utah	1881
Frances H. Foster	Juab County, Utah	1882
William Hesselgrave	Indianapolis, Indiana	1911
Herbert Hesselgrave	Indianapolis, Indiana	1911

Male and female descendants are presented through five generations.
Related families include Armour, Ball, Beckett, Bourne, Boyd, Bradley, Braithwait, Burse, Champion, Chase, Clark, Cockrill, Cooper, Cotton, Coulter, Dalton, Deans, Dixon, Downing, Fellows, Ford, Freeman, Grant, Hammer, Hazelton, Holderness, Howden, Howgate, Johnson, Jones, Kohn, Livingston, Lockwood, Lonie, Main, Marcyes, McCready, McGary, McGill, Millard, Nisbit, Pacy, Pearson, Persons, Pierce, Purves, Randall, Ray, Robinson, Robson, Rutherford, Scrutton, Shampine, Short, Sims, Tait, Talcott, Todd, Tompkins, Veitch, Vroman, Warwick, Wheeler, Woods, Wooley. Maps; charts; bibliography; every-name index.
Cloth—$18.00—532pp-------------------------------------- Vendor #D0840

3400   - PIONEERS by A. Judson Arrick, Thomas S. Cowger and John C. Downey. 1979, repr. of 1941 ed.
A history of the Moore, Downey and Cowger families who pioneered in White County, Indiana, with tracing of their ancestors back to 1641 in Massachusetts. The book includes several sermons by well-known clergymen in the family lineage.
Cloth—$15.00—Paper—$12.00—187pp---------------------- Vendor #D0842

3401   - A BEARD MOSAIC—DAVID BEARD AND HIS DESCENDANTS by Virginia Beard Asterino. 1972.
Includes the descendants of David and Lavina Beard, born in North Carolina. In 1850 they owned land in District #12, Wilson County, Tennessee. They had eight children and 49 grandchildren. The book is divided into eight parts with chapters titled after each grandchild with continuing issue.
The appendix includes data concerning other Beard families who lived in the same area. Includes information for descendants: Andrews, Atkinson, Barrett, Barry, Bass, Beard, Bittelmeyer, Bryan, Cardwell, Charlick, Clark, Eastes, Greenway, Hite, Hollabaugh, Holmes, Huddleston, Jones, Lebo, Litchford, Marks, McCluskey, McDermott, Moffitt, Neal, Odum, Ozment, Patton, Phillips, Pickering, Roberson, Sellars, Taylor, Young, Yows; and non-descendants: Baird, Bass, Beard, Branch, Cartwright, Clark, Floyd, Green, Odum, Phillips, Young.
Illustrations: coat-of-arms, portrait. Includes examples of family letters, census extracts, will abstracts, Quaker records, deed abstracts, tax lists, court minutes, records of orphans and wards.
Brings together large amount of family history and information from secondary sources. Descendant index and non-descendant index.
Cardstock, wrap around cover, 6"x9".
Paper—$16.00—371pp-- Vendor #D0855

3402   - JAMES DAWSON FROM WALES AND HIS DESCENDANTS by Carol
Dawson. 1968.
Cloth—$10.00—204pp-- Vendor #D0858

3403   - DAWSONS IN THE REVOLUTIONARY WAR, VOLUME I by Carol Dawson. 197‹
16 Dawsons.
Cloth—$20.00—170pp-- Vendor #D0858

3404   - DAWSONS IN THE REVOLUTIONARY WAR, VOLUME II by Carol R.
Dawson. 1983.
28 more Dawsons plus additions to Volume I.
Paper—$40.00—404pp-- Vendor #D0858

3405   - ILLINOIS BEERS FAMILIES by Mary Louise Regan. 1980.
Beers: Arranged by counties; over 700 individuals from various Beers
family groups who resided Illinois mostly through 1900 with some
account of their families.
Cloth—$13.00—52pp-- Vendor #D0863

3406   - THE BEERS GENEALOGY, VOLUME II (THE DESCENDANTS OF
ANTHONY BEERS OF FAIRFIELD, CONNECTICUT THROUGH SON
JOHN) by Mary Louise Regan. 1974.
Beers: Newtown, Connecticut (1712-1974); Ithaca, New York (1810-1880);
Chicago, Illinois (1834-1974); Salt Lake City, Utah (1868-1974);
others.
Cloth—$27.50—247pp-- Vendor #D0863

3407   - THE BEERS GENEALOGY, VOLUME III (THE DESCENDANTS OF
ANTHONY BEERS OF FAIRFIELD, CONNECTICUT THROUGH SON
EPHRAIM) by Mary Louise Regan. 1978.
Beers: Weston, Connecticut (1644-1978); Walton (Beerston), New
York (1788-1978); many other states.
Cloth—$31.50—299pp-- Vendor #D0863

3408   - THE BEERS GENEALOGY, VOLUME IV (THE DESCENDANTS OF
ANTHONY BEERS OF FAIRFIELD, CONNECTICUT THROUGH SON
BARNABAS) by Mary Louise Regan. 1982.
Beers: Stratford, Connecticut (1648-1982); New Haven, Connecticut
(1754-1900+); Litchfield County, Connecticut (1750-1942); Addison
and Chittenden Counties, Vermont (1797-1982); Tompkins County,
New York (1811-1982); Huron County, Ohio (1827-1940); Marion
County, Oregon (1837-1982); others.
Cloth—$33.50—198pp-- Vendor #D0863

3409   - BEERS BULLETIN (A NEWSLETTER) edited by Mary Louise Regan.
Beers: Updates information in published Beers Genealogy volumes;
also carries items on unpublished families of the name; published
since 1982.
Subscription: $5.00 per year—4 issues per year.
Subscription—$5.00/yr-- Vendor #D0863

3410   - FESSLER ANCESTRIES by William T. Fessler. 1978.
Foreign origins and family summaries in Pennsylvania, California,
Illinois, Indiana, Iowa, Kansas, Kentucky, North Carolina, Missouri,
Ohio and Virginia.
Paper—$12.50—124pp-- Vendor #D0875

3411   - THIRTY-FOUR FAMILIES OF OLD SOMERSET COUNTY, MARYLAND—
A GENEALOGY by Colonel Woodrow T. Wilson. 1974.
Families include Adams, Boston, Bedsworth, Chelton, Conner, Coul-
bourn, Cullen, Dixon, Garrison, Green, Gunby, Hall, Handy, Horsey,
Johnson, Kellam, Lankford, Lawson, Maddox, Miles, Nelson, Peyton,
Powell, Roach, Sterling, Stevenson, Taylor, Tull, Ward, Whittington,
Williams, Wilson and many others.
cloth—$25.00—655pp-- Vendor #D0876

3412   - CRISFIELD, MARYLAND 1676-1976 by Colonel Woodrow T. Wilson.
1976.
Listing Somerset County Veterans, all wars; Smith, Tangier Islands;
Colonial Homesteads with photographs; 100-year Bicentennial Pyramid

Time Capsule.
Complete genealogy of Wilson, Dennis, Long, Crisfield families;
biographical sketches of over 700 Somerset County families.
106 photographs.
Cloth—$20.00—558pp------------------------------------- Vendor #D0876

3413   - HISTORY AND TALES OF A PIONEER by John S. Blue. 1980.
A historical narrative of western migration covering a period of nearly
one-hundred years extending from Virginia, following the Revolutionary
War, westward to the settlement of that region beyond the Mississippi
River called the Sod House Frontier.
While family characters are employed in relating the migration story as
they moved along the trail and through several frontier communities,
it is not unlike the history of many thousands of others who were a
part of the celebrated pioneer movement across the eastern mountain
ranges into the Ohio Valley and beyond.
It is not only a modest addition to the history of the pioneer movement
but destined to become a unique family document for those descended
from or related to John Blue (1691-1770) the founder of the family in
Hampshire County, Virginia. It should also be of special interest to
the family historian in suggesting ways to enliven genealogical data
by associating family members with local and historic events of the
period.
Illustrated by Dale Fleming; designed by Huron Valley Graphics,
Incorporated and Joanne Kinney.
Illustrated brochure furnished on request.
Cloth—$27.00—194pp------------------------------------- Vendor #D0874

3414   - A NEW JERSEY DUTCH LINEAGE TO CHRISTIAN BARENTSEN VAN
HORNE by Jean Baber. 1975.
Traces all families joining this Van Horne line from 1650 to 1900.
Paper—$20.00—164pp------------------------------------- Vendor #D0887

3415   - BRADLEY GENEALOGY (1637-1850) by Henry Olcott Sheldon and
Martha Sheldon Hutchins. 1976.
First part of a book in H. O. Sheldon's handwriting. Second part—
Indexes by M. S. Hutchins. Names include Bartholomew,
Tillolson, and Sheldon.
Paper—$8.50—apx. 40pp------------------------------------- Vendor #D0917

3416   - DESCENDANTS OF THOMAS OLCOTT, 1630-1874, ONE OF THE FIRST
SETTLERS IN HARTFORD, CONNECTICUT by Nathaniel Goodwin. 1975,
repr. of 1874 ed.
Includes early history of Hartford, Connecticut. Many surnames
given.
Paper—$3.25—124pp------------------------------------- Vendor #D0917

3417   - GREGG LINES by F. Lee Nichols.
Semi-annual newsletter re: Gregg - Hadley - Cooper - Huddleston -
Underwood - Waggoner. Information exchanged.
Paper—$5.00------------------------------------- Vendor #D0924

3418   - HINES AND ALLIED FAMILIES by Benjamin McFarland Hines. 1981.
An authoritative study on the Hines family of Sussex County, Virginia.
Allied families covered are: Watson (Virginia, Mississippi), Shackelford
(Virginia, South Carolina, Georgia), Nisbet (North Carolina, Georgia),
and Kennon (Virginia).
Other surnames included, many covered in detail, are: Avent, Bossard,
Cooper, Cowdrey, Davis, Gregory, Lewis, Macon, Moore, Oliver, Osborn,
Perrin, Price, Ragland, Reade, Serre, Staige, and Warner. Numerous
family letters, memorabilia, and obituaries. Illustrated, indexed,
bibliography.
Cloth—$20.00—259pp------------------------------------- Vendor #D0973

3419   - THE LEEDOM FAMILY by Sara A. L. Eachus. 1982.
Traces two branches of the Leedom family in the United States:
(1) descendants of Richard Leedom (b. Yorkshire, England ca 1675)
who settled in Bucks County, Pennsylvania, and

(2) descendants of Irish-born John Leedom who set out for Redstone County in Western Pennsylvania and later helped settle Adams County, Ohio.
Allied families include Phipps, Twinings, Edgingtons, Clarks, and others. Illustrated, indexed.
Cloth—$20.00—378pp-- Vendor #D0973

3420 - KINDRED: DAVIS—STANSBURY LINES by Helen B. Davis. 1977.
Genealogical study of Davis and Stansbury families in Pennsylvania, Maryland and Virginia. Related families include: Walmsley, Roberts Carr, Paxson, Singley and Searle (Pennsylvania); Utie, Merryman, Gouldsmith, Howard, Parker, and Besson (Virginia); and Hall, Hanslap, Beedle, Reade, Frisby, Carvill, Tolley, and Phillips (Maryland).
Illustrated, indexed.
Cloth—$10.00—327pp-- Vendor #D0973

3421 - WE VEITCHES, VEATCHES, VEACHES, VEECHES by Laurence R. Guthrie and Wanda Veatch Clark. 1974.
An historical treasury of the descendants of James Veitch, the Sheriffe (Maryland 1651).
Cloth—$13.00—937pp-- Vendor #D0974

3422 - JAMES CLIFFORD VEATCH: SCHOLAR, SOLICITOR, STATESMAN AND SOLDIER by William A. Veitch. 1983.
Civil War General.
Paper—$6.00—103pp-- Vendor #D0974

3423 - CUMMINS ANCIENT, CUMMINS NEW by Frances Funk. 1978.
The first history ever published on the Cummin(g)s family of Virginia and Kentucky. Part One deals with the general background of the Cummins family in the Middle Ages. Part Two documents 300 years (thirteen generations) of Cummins lineages with a running narrative.
Milton Rubincam, F.A.S.G., F.N.G.S., F.G.S.P., C.G., says *Mrs. Funk...has written a very good genealogy of her mother's family....[she] gives us more than just a well-documented genealogy... She provides us with the historical background in which her ancestors lived....*
Cloth—$27.00—276pp-- Vendor #D0975

3424 - CUMMINS ANCIENT, CUMMINS NEW, VOLUME 2 by Frances Funk. 1980.
Two generations considered probably connected have now been established, expanding known lineages to fifteen generations in America, beginning at Jamestown in 1622. From further research there has been included much additional intelligence on the period 1623-1639, collateral relationships during the colonial period, and a quantity of lineages furnished by readers of Volume 1.
Cloth—$28.00—ca 232pp-------------------------------------- Vendor #D0975

3425 - JOSEPH FUNK, A BIOGRAPHY by Frances Funk. 1984.
In three parts: (1) Joseph Funk's lineage with an account of significant events in Europe and colonial America; (2) a biography of Joseph, and (3) all descendants of Joseph's youngest child, Benjamin.
The literary reputations of four generations are well documented and thoroughly described. Particular emphasis is placed on the phenomenal musical talent and authority of Joseph, his teaching, writing, translating and composing, his enthusiastic spirit of enterprise, and his pervasive influence upon the South through his schools and publishing business.
Foreword by Phyllis Diller.
Red cloth, gold imprint—$30.00 plus $2.00 mailing—263 pages plus index.
5-1/2"x7-3/4".
Cloth—$32.00—263+pp-------------------------------------- Vendor #D0975

3426 - THE WALTON FAMILY IN AMERICA, 1756-1976 compiled by Joan Walton White. 1976.
Descendants of John Walton of Yorkshire, England and New Hampshire. Contains Walton First Name Index and Surname Index of Allied Lines.
Charts; maps; illustrations; photographs.
Cloth—$13.00—96pp-- Vendor #D0984

3427   - "WALTONOLOGY"-THE STUDY OF WALTONS-AN INDEX TO WALTONS
APPEARING IN AMERICAN RECORDS PRIOR TO 1850 compiled by Joan
Walton White. 1979.
Contains over 1,732 names and 89 Waltonologists. Attempts to bring
together the names of all Waltons which the compiler has "run across"
during her twenty years of research. For each given name she lists
one significant date (birth, marriage, death, census, or other) and
the area(s) in which these records are located. In the absence of a
significant date she has listed some other pertinent fact, such as name
of parent or spouse, if possible.
Table of Contents: Index to Waltons found in American Records prior
to 1850; Index to "Links of Walton History"-reprinted by permission
of the author's daughter; Index to Walton Family in America;
Waltonologists-a list of contributors and their addresses.
Paper-$9.00-40pp-- Vendor #D0984

3428   - THE POE FAMILY LINE by Pauline Mae Brannan. 1974.
Poe Family History, with Allied Lines of Hitt, Corley, Crim/Grimm by
Pauline M. Brannan.
Poe, Samuel-Culpeper County, Virginia 1736-1800; Orange County,
Virginia 1714-1800; Rappahannock County, Virginia 1815-1895;
Warren County, Virginia 1895-1917.
Hitt-Orange County, Virginia 1714-1724; Fauquier County, Virginia
1724-1900.
Corley-Culpeper County, Virginia 1767-1830; Rappahannock County,
Virginia 1830-1922.
Crim/Grimm-Rappahannock County, Virginia 1740-1767; Fauquier
County, Virginia 1767-1810.
Spilman/Spielmann-1525-1700.
Cloth-$35.00-465pp------------------------------------- Vendor #D1020

3429   - SKETCHES AND INCIDENTS by Henry Hoover. With appendix Family
Record by Williard Heiss. 1962.
Indianapolis, Indiana Quaker Records. Bibliography.
Paper-$5.00-60pp-- Vendor #D1024

3430   - THE WHITE HAT, HENRY FREDERICK SCHRICKER by Charles F.
Fleming. 1966.
Paper-$1.00-145pp-------------------------------------- Vendor #D1024

3431   - ERI RICH FAMILY TREE by Everett Eri Thomas. 1963.
Illustrations.
Paper-$7.50-61pp--------------------------------------- Vendor #D1024

3432   - AUTOBIOGRAPHY OF DAVID TATUM: FORMATIVE YEARS....With
genealogical notes compiled by Willard Heiss. 1963.
Paper-$2.50-12pp--------------------------------------- Vendor #D1024

3433   - AUTOBIOGRAPHY OF WILLIAM HOBBS edited by B. C. Hobbs. 1962.
Paper-$3.00-32pp--------------------------------------- Vendor #D1024

3434   - DESCENDANTS OF THOMAS BRUMFIELD OF BERKS COUNTY,
PENNSYLVANIA by Ray C. Brumfield. 1962.
Maps, illustrations, index and appendices.
Cloth-$15.00-493+pp----------------------------------- Vendor #D1024

3435   - A STRECHER-STECKER SAGA by R. Stecher, M.D. 1977.
Cloth-$13.25-209pp------------------------------------ Vendor #D1030

3436   - THE CALLAWAY JOURNAL, VOLUME 4 by The Callaway Association.
Primary records of Callaways in the United States and England-mostly
1700's.
Paper-$10.00-132pp------------------------------------ Vendor #D1048

3437   - THE CALLAWAY JOURNAL, VOLUME 5 by The Callaway Association.
Contains descendants of Joseph Callaway of Virginia (4 generations)
and Peter Callaway of Maryland (5 generations).
Paper-$10.00-80pp------------------------------------- Vendor #D1048

3438 - FAMILY BIBLE RECORDS, 4 Volumes, compiled and indexed by
Stephenie H. Tally-Frost. 1969, 1970, 1970, 1971.
Volume I contains information on the following families:
Bailey, Baker, Ballinger, Bacon, Brame, Barnhart, Baumgardner,
Caswell, Cocke, Copeland, Compton, Crane, Crist, Dickinson, Dunlap,
Dye, Ebbs, Easterling, Evans/Evens, Eagleton, Fannin, Flack, Fisch-
haber, Gerard, Glaze, Grimes, Grubb, Hall, Harper, Heaton, Hecker,
Heimbach, Hicks, Hubbard, Hunt, Hurd, Hoyt, Houx, Huffman, Immel,
Jackson, Jones, Harris, Keach, Kemp, Koontz, Lefever, Leberer,
Lard, Martin, Murdocks, Marshall, May, Morgan, Mayer, McDuffee,
McKinney, McDaniel, Nichols, Morningstar, Paxton, Perigo, Peters,
Proctor, Price, Perrine, Phelps, Richardson, Rodgers, Reed, Stratton,
Scott, Simmons, Smith, Stewhern, Springer, Thompson, Warren, Wells,
Wright, Ward, Watt, White, Whitlock, Wilburn, Wood, Young, Zimmerman
and many others.
Volume II:
Ayres, Armstrong, Barkley, Burkhalter, Boggs, Brown, Blakeney,
Bennet, Baker, Blackwell, Bradshaw, Carmichael, Connor, Call, Collett,
Cooper, Chapman, Cummins, Coody, Curtis, Childress, Durst, Donnell,
Ervin, Evans, Fowler, Fislar, Gresham, Herring, Horn, Hagerty,
Hipple, Holland, Hoffstrom, Hanks, Hays, Hollis, Hughes, Johnston,
Kephart, Kennedy, James, King, Luce, McMillan, Moore, McFadden,
Keach, Lucy, Macon, Nordan/Norden, Odom, O'Bannon, Prigmore,
Pinkston, Purnell, Pilchard, Pistole, Pegues, Patrick, Rogers, Rawlings,
Ray, Ritter, Rutledge, Redden, Riley, Simons, Sanders, Sharp,
Stuart, Sutherland, Smith, Spain, Stell, Stewart, Thornton, Talley,
Trawick, Varnell, Vaughan, Van Duzer, Van Derbilt, Wahl, Watson,
Weaver, Zeller and many others.
Volume III:
Alexander, Aves, Brown, Black, Bowser, Bonnel, Bales, Burleson,
Bell, Brady, Cox, Criner, Carmichael, Craig, Culbertson, Cochran,
Devenport, Dickinson, Cooper, Evans, Frost, Gibbons, Gatlin, Hanna,
Holloway, Halliday, Hodges, Hipple, Haines, Herridge, Hervey,
Houston, Jenkins, Jackson, Kuykendall, Klein, Lumsden, Lindsey,
Linville, Landis, McCain, Merritt, McCollough, Morrison, McCowen,
McBride, Meador, Musser, Nelson, Price, Parks, Pate, Payne, Pollard,
Reagan, Ritter, Richardson, Robbins, Sanford, Snow, Souter,
Stevenson, Street, Shannon, Shelby, Sassenrath, Sybert, Thrash,
Wood, Wright, Wyche, Weidman, Wuesthoff, Young and others.
Volume IV:
Brunson, Blake, Broom, Barten, Bordley, Brooks, Clinton, Craddock,
Cavender, Cook, Craven, Crow, Colver, Dement, Durst, Doggerr,
Ducker, Davidson, Dewey, Dyar, Ericsfon, Ellis, Fesm, Fish, Gunning,
Glough, Hall, Helsley, Hopkins, Harper, Hanna, Heflin, Heard,
Howell, Holbert, Heckel, Haselbusch, Hankinson, Hays, Houk,
Davidge, Harvey, Ingersoll, Jacobs, Jackson, Jamison, Lackey,
Landers, Lantis, McDaniel, McMillan, McElroy, May, Newcombe,
Osbodby, Perkins, Poirrier, Prather, Russell, Roberts, Ross,
Rayner/Reyner, Ripley, Roserance, Rector, Spencer, Seagrave,
Sparks, Spradling, Sneed, Slaughter, Sims, Steger, Seger, Schanck,
Schiffel, Schonnig, Steinkamp, Schackleton, Simpson, Toland, Taylor,
Thompson, Vestergard, Wintermute, Yohnson and others.
For full description see listing number 817, pages 196 through 930, in
the Third Edition, *Genealogical & Local History Books In Print.*
Send large SASE for information.
Paper—$10.00/volume—$27.00/Set—37,43,33,39pp----------- Vendor #D1036

3439 - THE FAMILY HISTORY OF JUDGE ELLSWORTH B. BELDEN AND
COLLATERAL FAMILIES by Stanley R. Belden and Elvera K. Belden.
1980, rev. ed. of 1969 ed.
A sketch of known facts about Richard Belden, the Settler in Wethersfield, Connecticut, and his sons are included. Well documented lineage
of Judge Belden is given through eight generations, from the two sons
of Richard's son John Belden (1630/1-1677), namely John, and Jonathan.
This branch of Beldens migrated to Litchfield County during 1738-1739,
and later generations settled in Ohio, Indiana and Wisconsin.
Collateral families include Bennett and Browns of Massachusetts and

Vermont, Dean (Josiah to children of Asa—1760-1840), Dibble, Farr, Horton, Whitman, Hurlbut, Kellogg, Palmer, Olmsted and Wright. The book contains early history about Racine County, Wisconsin; in particular, Rochester, a township in western Racine County, and the city of Racine. 22 pages of Index; photographs; Census Schedules. Cloth—$25.00—310+pp----------------------------------- Vendor #D1070

3440 - THE TINKLING SPRING, HEADWATER OF FREEDOM, 2nd Ed., by Howard McKnight Wilson, Th.D. 1974, repr. of 1954 ed.
This Scotch-Irish "Triple Forks Congregation" was founded in 1738 within the boundaries of the Beverly Manor Patent in what is now Augusta County among the "Christian Warlike" settlers west of the Blue Ridge Mountains. The Reverend John Craig's installation as pastor in 1740 was the first to legally break the Established Church monopoly in Virginia. In 1785 Zechariah Johnston, a son of Tinkling Spring, was the first Presbyterian to chair the Committee on Religion in the Virginia Assembly. He bore the brunt of the fights for Jefferson's bill "for establishing religious freedom," as well as the state's approval in 1788 of the Federal Constitution. The Craig Autobiography, 882 Baptisms 1740-1749, and the 193 family importation records 1734-1745, begin the more than 4,000 individuals, the descendants of whom are scattered across America today, including: Anderson, Bell, Brown, Caldwell, Campbell, Cathy, Crawford, Davidson, Frazier, Gillaspy, Givens, Hall, Hays, Henderson, Hutchison, Irvine, Johnston, McClure, McDowell, Maxwell, Mills, Mitchell, Moore, Patterson, Robinson, Scott, Smith, Stephenson, Thompson, Wilson. Award of Merit from AASLH in 1955.
Cloth—$16.65—640pp------------------------------------- Vendor #D1093

3441 - THE LEXINGTON PRESBYTERY HERITAGE by Howard McKnight Wilson. 1971.
When the Presbyterian Church formed a Presbytery in 1786 among the Scotch-Irish in Virginia, west of the Blue Ridge, it was called Lexington because of the Appalachian region's significant efforts in the Revolution. The book is illustrated (maps, charts, tables and photographs) with index and blibliography. It fills some of the gaps in the religious history of the Appalachian region and tells of the tremendous odds against which the pioneer churchmen labored. The advance of Presbyterianism from the Blue Ridge to the Ohio River is set forth and it lists thousands of officers and families including: Blair, Breckenridge, Davis, Edmondson, Gibson, Gordon, Graham, Hamilton, Hanger, Harris, Henry, Houston, Jones, Kerr, King, Leech, Lewis, Lockridge, Logan, Lowman, McCue, McCutchen, Martin, Marshall, Miller, Moffett, Morrison, Paxton, Poage, Ramsey, Reid, Taylor, Turk, Waddell, Wade, Walker, Wallace, White, Williams, Woods, Wright, Young.
Received Presbyterian Historical Foundation's Mekamie Award for 1971.
Cloth—$10.00—524pp-------------------------------------- Vendor #D1093

3442 - "CHRIST AND ANNA", DESCENDANTS OF: ANTON BACH, JACOB DAMM, JOHN HARTMAN, GEORGE KREMER, JOHN YOCUM by Patty Dahm Pascoe. 1980.
An account of, generation by generation to the present day, descendants of Anton Bach (1836-1899), Jacob Damm (1832-1899), and John Hartman (1790-1859), George Kremer (1825-1900) and John Yocum (1758-1849). Also includes genealogies and sketches of the families of Breest, Claty, Corso, Knapp, Konzen, McCormick, Schaefer, Shafer, Showalter, Zimmer and allied families by marriage.
Encompasses two states: Ohio (Ashland, Defiance, Erie, Fulton, Henry, Lucas and Tuscawaras Counties) and Pennsylvania (Berks, Chester, Huntingdon, Juniata, Mifflin and Perry Counties).
Includes many photographs, stories and tales of "local history" regarding Sandusky and the Sandusky area of years gone by.
363 original photographs and sketches. 22 "family trees" graphically illustrated, over 3,000 names in the index with the maiden and married name of the females, over 500 listings in the subject and topographical index, and many newspaper articles.
Limited Edition.
Cloth—$35.00—472pp-------------------------------------- Vendor #D1105

3443   - OUR DOLLISON FAMILY IN AMERICA 1752-1984 by Louise Dollison
Marsh. 1984.
8½"x11", single-spaced, 114 photos, 17 maps, hard cover, every name
index. Descendants for eleven generations in both male and female
lines of descent from James Dollison, an emigrant from Scotland to
Fayette County, Pennsylvania, 1752. His three sons removed to
Greene County, Pennsylvania (1790-1814); three of his grandsons
migrated to Guernsey County, Ohio (1830's); a fourth moved to
Wood County, West Virginia (1840's), and changed the spelling to
Dallison. Excursus pages: Barker, Boone, Burroughs, Church,
Glenn, Goodin, Laughlin, Lindsey, Moore, Rowland, Schaff,
Yater/Yeater.
Cloth—$32.50—485pp-- Vendor #D1204

3444   - THE CATLIN GENEALOGY by Louise Catlin Koloson, edited by
Joanne Kirchman. 1981.
Over 5,000 members of Catlin Family are described and indexed; most
are descendants of immigrants John and Thomas who came to Connecti-
cut before 1645; many moved on to New York; includes Indian painter
George Catlin. Names, addresses of some current Catlin researchers
listed.
Paper—$13.65—200pp--- Vendor #D1207

3445   - TRACKING BAREFOOT RUNYAN,—DESCENDANTS OF ISAAC BARE-
FOOT RUNYAN by Marie Runyan Wright. 1980.
A family history of Isaac Barefoot Runyan 1750-1867 and Margaret
Rambo Runyan. Takes into account six of their sons and traces the
path of some of their descendants from the Shenandoah Valley, Virginia
through Tennessee and Alabama on their journey westward. Inter-
marriages include Boyds, Daffords, Lamberts, Masseys, McKnights,
Reagans, Tacketts, Thompsons, Turners and others.
100 photographs; indexed.
Cloth—$26.25—300pp--- Vendor #D1310

3446   - THE SCHROEPFER CONNECTIONS by Cleo Shoen Van Lerberg. 1983.
Franz Schroepfer, Eckstein, Rathman and Shoen Families.
Contains index of over 400 names; over 100 photos.
Vicinity of New Ulm, Minnesota 1865—.
Cloth—$20.00—138pp--- Vendor #D1460

3447   - THOMASSON NOTEBOOKS edited by Mary Morris and Nelle Chesley.
Clearinghouse for research on all Thomasson, Thomason, Thomaston
lines. Census, Bible records, courthouse records, family information,
etc. 28 Volumes now in print. 3 Volumes a year, 100+ pages per
volume, fully indexed.
Paper—for sale or rental.
Paper—$10.00-- Vendor #D1461

3448   - A WRIGHT BRANCH ON THE ROOTS OF ABEL, WITH ALLIED
FAMILIES, GILLIAM, STEWART, SCUDDER by F. G. Wright and
Hazel W. Dishman. 1983.
Abel Wright, Springfield, Massachusetts 1655 down to authors in direct
line by generations. New England States, Illinois, Iowa, Missouri, West.
Four biographies. Several side branches.
Photographs, Map. 12 page Index.
Cloth—$12.00—120pp--- Vendor #D1466

3449   - BALLENGEE TRAILS AND RUSSELL RELATIVES by Judith A.
Richardson.
A History of Ballengees in America. An exchange of genealogical
data for the Russell families. Free queries. 20 pages three times
annually.
Paper—$6.50—60pp-- Vendor #D1467

3450   - CALDWELL—SWEANEY RESEARCHER by Judith A. Richardson.
An Exchange of source materials and genealogies. Free queries.
Three editions annually.
Paper—$6.50—60pp-- Vendor #D1467

3451 - HILDEBRAND—WILLIAMS EXCHANGE by Judith A. Richardson.
An Exchange of source materials and genealogies. Free queries.
Three editions annually.
Paper—$6.50—60pp-------------------------------------- Vendor #D1467

3452 - PHILLIPS—LOONEY TRADER by Judith A. Richardson.
An Exchange of source materials and genealogies. Free queries.
Three editions annually.
Paper—$6.50—60pp-------------------------------------- Vendor #D1467

3453 - McCLUNG FAMILY ASSOCIATION JOURNAL by Judith A. Richardson.
An Exchange of source materials and genealogies. Free queries.
$5.00 includes membership, Journal, and newsletters for one year.
Back issues available.
Paper—$5.00/yr—40pp/annually--------------------------- Vendor #D1467

3454 - SANDIFER, VOLUME I, SOUTH CAROLINA TO MISSISSIPPI AND
WESTWARD compiled by Annie Sandifer Trickett, M.L.S., C.G. 1982.
Lines of John D. Sandifer, ca 1783-1854; Johnson P. Sandifer,
ca 1796-1866; Joseph Sandifer, 1800-1871; Joshua A. Sandifer,
1797-1882; Peter Sandifer, 1771-1844; William Nightingale Sandifer,
? by 1760-1850; William Y. Sandifer, 1792-1870 or later and others.
30 pictures, map, Smyth Sewn. Sources cited, Sixty page Full Name
Index. Articles on Sandifer Families cover 199 pages; over 1,300
Sandifers and Sandifer wives. Some related surnames included:
Barron, Bell, Bridges, Gates, Murphree, Stanfill, Tillman.
Add tax in Texas.
Cloth—$40.00—474pp------------------------------------- Vendor #D1468

3455 - "DOWN IN THE BARNS": THE KECKS OF CLAIBORNE COUNTY,
TENNESSEE by Virginia Billingsley Fletcher. 1983.
Conrad "Coonrod" Keck, John Ousley and Joseph Yadon, Revolutionary
War veterans, were pioneer settlers of East Tennessee. Details their
service; genealogy; and descendants through grandchildren,
John "Guider" and Rebecca (Yadon) Keck, to present generation.
Fully documented, 50 photographs, 4,200 name-index includes:
Beason, Capps, Cole, Collins, England, Ford, Fortner, Francisco,
Goin, Lynch, O'Dell, Pennybaker, Simmons, Williams, many others.
Cloth—$27.00—440pp------------------------------------- Vendor #D1469

3456 - TINNEY—GREEN(E) FAMILY ORGANIZATION NEWSLETTER by Thomas
Milton Tinney, C.G.R.S.
Have records, correspondence from earliest times (B.C. to A.D.):
Teney, Tenne, Tenney, Tenneyson, Tennison, Tiney, Tin, Tinn,
Tinne, Tinney, Tinneyson, Tinning, Tinnison, Tinny, Tyne, Tynney
and variations. Will exchange, publish, correspond, or do research
upon request at $20.00/hour—in English records in British Isles,
America, Australia, South Africa, Canada (plus expenses).
Phone (801) 969-1020
Tinney—Green(e) Family Organization, Post Office Box 27441,
Salt Lake City, Utah 84127-0441
Monthly since 1972 A.D., Xerox of originals.
Paper—$15.00/issue—apx. 40pp/issue---------------------Vendor #D1470

3457 - NELSON JOLLY, SR. AND HIS FAMILY OF BRECKINRIDGE COUNTY,
KENTUCKY by Nellie Fern Baker. 1983.
History and genealogy of the Jolly family from early Bucks County,
Pennsylvania origins to the present. Documented research, includes
tax records, wills and deeds. Allied lines: Baker, Ball, Basham,
Hendrick, Howard, Lyons, Miller, Hardin, McClellan, Pool/Poole,
Walker and others. Indexed.
Cloth—$25.00—256pp------------------------------------- Vendor #D1472

3458 - THE JOHN ROUND FAMILY OF SWANSEA AND REHOBOTH, MASSA-
CHUSETTS: THE FIRST SIX/SEVEN GENERATIONS by H. L. Peter
Rounds, C.G. 1983.
A totally new, heavily-documented, comprehensive treatment of ALL
lines of the John Round family, first recorded at Swansea in 1689.
Full of biographical and historical information scoured from primary
sources and original records. Indexed. 6"x9".
Cloth—$32.00 postpaid—522pp---------------------------Vendor #D1473

3459 - THE ANCESTORS OF GEORGE STEWART, MIDSHIPMAN, H.M.S.
BOUNTY compiled by Barbara Juarez Wilson and Betty Harkness Cain.
1985.
Ancestor charts with armorial illustrations for all major families;
also genealogical data on all known descendants.
Soft cover/spiral bound; 8½"x11". $45.00 plus $2.00 P&H (6% sales
tax for California residents only)
Paper—$47.00—300pp--- Vendor #D1474

3460 - FROM MISSION TO MAJESTY: A GENEALOGY AND HISTORY OF
EARLY CALIFORNIA AND ROYAL EUROPEAN ANCESTORS by Barbara
Juarez Wilson. 1983.
The author has traced her family through the California Mission Era to
Scottish royalty via Tahiti, where one ancestor, Scotsman George
Stewart, midshipman on the Bounty of Mutiny fame, left a daughter who
formed the link connecting California and Scotland. Family trees,
descendancy charts, and mission records abound. California family
names include: Ayala, Dominguez, Eayrs, Feliz, Harkness, Harloe,
Juarez, Olivera, Packard, Porter, Sparks, Trussell. Among the Scottish names are: Douglas, Drummond, Elphinstone, Gordon, Graham,
and many Stewarts including Kings Robert II through James V.
6"x9¼"; $25.00 plus $1.00 P&H (6% sales tax for California residents
only)
Cloth—$26.00—172pp--- Vendor #D1474

3461 - THE BROOKS FAMILY QUERY EXCHANGE edited by Madeline S.
Mills.
Brook, Brooks, Brooke, Brookes researchers. Published quarterly.
100 pages, plus index. $9.00 per volume year.
Subscription—$9.00/yr—100pp---------------------------------Vendor #D1475

3462 - THE PTOMEY FAMILY OF ALABAMA AND THE ALLIED FAMILIES
OF BLANKENSHIP, MELTON, KYSER, AND COWART by Kyser Cowart
Ptomey.
Well documented history of the Virginia and Alabama Ptomey family.
Complete index; illustrated.
John P. Tomey married Elizabeth Jackson May 17, 1785, Augusta
County, Virginia; their son George W. Ptomey married Mary Blanken-
ship (daughter of John Blankenship and Nancy Houchen of Virginia)
February 5, 1824; migrated with infant daughter and John Blanken-
ship (with his children) in a caravan led by Hugh McKee to Wilcox
County, Alabama; settled in or near Pine Apple. Related families
were: Comptons, Meltons, Linams, Adams, Noreds, Grimes and
Kysers.
Paper—$26.50—354pp--- Vendor #D1478

3463 - MEN OF MATADEQUIN: THREE HUNDRED YEARS FROM NEW KENT
COUNTY by June Banks Evans. 1984.
Virginia: Banks, Blackwell, Burnett, Durvin, Gaulding, Goodman,
Lipscomb, McGhee, Parsley, Slaughter, Weisiger, Wood, Zall;
4,000 names, indexed.
Cloth—$23.25—198+pp--- Vendor #D1479

3464 - ANTHONY EVANS OF COLONIAL SOUTHSIDE VIRGINIA: RELATED
LINES; VIRGINIA SOURCEBOOK by June Banks Evans. 1983.
Documented narrative based on court records beginning early 1600's
in Surry, Southampton, Sussex, Brunswick, Lunenburg, Mecklenburg Counties. Nine area maps, 1614-1981; extensive bibliography
and sourcebook. Allied lines: Banks, Bennett, Blackwell, Bugg,
Burnett, Davis, Ellis,Ezell, Fox, Hill, Ingram, Mabry, Mathews,
Peebles, Smith, Taylor, Walker, Watson, Wrenn, and others;
1880—item index includes maiden names.
182pp--- Vendor #D1479

3465 - BLATCHLEY PHYSICIANS AND PIONEERS, DESCENDANTS OF
THOMAS BLATCHLEY 1635-1929 by Shirley Hathaway Stebbings. 1983.
Family History traces early United States Medicine and migrations into
Connecticut, Long Island, New York, New Jersey, Pennsylvania,
Ohio, Indiana, Oregon.

Allied names: Armstrong, Batholomew, Bell, Boyd, Butler, Brown, Carlile, Cooper, Davis, Day, De Janvier, Dye, Guernsey, Hathaway, Hopper, Houser, January, Johnson, Jones, Kirk, Lindley, Lytle, McKinney, Miller, Moot, Morfitt, Morgan, Pond, Seavey, Shinabarger, Simmons, Smith, Soverns, Van Sickle, Wadleigh, and Yates.
Hardcover - documented - indexed.
Cloth—$28.50—265pp------------------------------------- Vendor #D1480

3466 - THE AGEE REGISTER compiled by Louis N. Agee. 1982.
A genealogical record of the direct descendants of Mathieu Agee, a Huguenot refugee to Virginia about 1700. The author spent twenty years updating and correcting information found in two previous publications concerning the Agee family: *Agee Bee* by James W. Agee and *The Agee Family* by Dr. Purl M. Agee. He also collected data on lines not found in the earlier books.
Smythe-sewn and case-bound in buckram. Fully indexed.
Cloth—$30.00—752pp------------------------------------- Vendor #D1482

3467 - THE PENICK FAMILY: DESCENDANTS OF EDWARD PENICK/PENIX/PINIX OF ST. PETER'S PARISH, NEW KENT COUNTY, VIRGINIA by Lyman W. Priest. 1982.
Edward Pinick first appeared on August 15, 1686, at the baptism of his son Edward in St. Peter's Church. In the next 300 years his descendants migrated as far west as California and Washington state and as far south as Louisiana and Texas.
Related families in Virginia include Averett, Barksdale, Boatwright, Fowlkes, Hamblen, Morton, Owen, Price, Tuggle, and Tyree.
6"x9", Indexed.
Cloth—$25.00—330pp------------------------------------- Vendor #D1483

3468 - BROOKS FAMILY HISTORY by Bernice (Brooks) Casey and Robert Brooks Casey. 1982.
Indexed, early ancestors lived in South Carolina, Georgia, Alabama, Louisiana, and Texas. Allied families Adkins, Ferguson, King, Lackey, Lumpkin, Mathis, Nelson, Perkins, Shelburne, Slaughter, Turner, Whittington.
Cloth—$25.00—382pp------------------------------------- Vendor #D1484

3469 - CASEY FAMILY HISTORY by Alvin Harold Casey and Robert Brooks Casey. 1980.
Indexed, Early Ancestors lived in South Carolina, Tennessee, Arkansas.
Cloth—$20.00—195pp------------------------------------- Vendor #D1484

3470 - SEVEN GENERATIONS OF THE DESCENDANTS OF AQUILA AND THOMAS CHASE by John Carroll Chase and George Walter Chamberlain. 1983, repr. of 1928 ed.
Hampton, New Hampshire, Newbury, Massachusetts family of 1600's.
Indexed.
Cloth—$45.00—650pp------------------------------------- Vendor #D1486

3471 - A MERRILL MEMORIAL, 2 Volumes, by Samuel Merrill. 1983, repr. of 1928 ed.
Original publication 26 copies only. Reprint contains corrections and notes of author to his death. Indexed.
Cloth—$75.00/Set—721pp------------------------------------- Vendor #D1486

3472 - THE GENEALOGY OF THE DESCENDANTS OF THOMAS HALE OF WATTON, ENGLAND, AND NEWBURY, MASSACHUSETTS by Robert Safford Hale, LLD. 1983, repr. of 1889 ed.
Indexed.
Cloth—$60.00—415pp------------------------------------- Vendor #D1486

3473 - THE PLUMER GENEALOGY by Sidney Perley. 1983, repr. of 1917 ed.
Indexed.
Cloth—$50.00—259pp------------------------------------- Vendor #D1486

3474 - A HISTORY OF THE LUNT FAMILY IN AMERICA by Thomas S. Lunt. 1983, repr. Indexed.
Cloth—$55.00—292pp------------------------------------- Vendor #D1486

3475 - A MEMOIR AND GENEALOGY OF JOHN POORE by Alfred Poore.
Repr. of 1881 ed. Indexed.
Cloth—$52.00—332pp-------------------------------------- Vendor #D1486

3476 - THE PILLSBURY FAMILY by David B. Pilsbury and Emily A. Getchell.
Repr. of 1898 ed. Indexed.
Cloth—$52.00—340pp-------------------------------------- Vendor #D1486

3477 - GENEALOGICAL RECORD OF SOME OF THE NOYES DESCENDANTS
OF JAMES, NICHOLAS, AND PETER, 2 Volumes, by Henry E. Noyes
and Henrietta E. Noyes. Repr. of 1904 ed. Indexed.
Cloth—$82.50/Set—826pp---------------------------------- Vendor #D1486

3478 - THE DESCENDANTS OF ABEL HUSE OF NEWBURY, MASSACHUSETTS
1602-1690 by Harry Pinckney Huse. Repr. of 1907 ed. Indexed.
Cloth—$62.00—438pp-------------------------------------- Vendor #D1486

3479 - BAILEY GENEALOGY by Hollis R. Bailey. Repr. of 1899 ed.
Indexed.
Cloth—$62.00—479pp-------------------------------------- Vendor #D1486

3480 - A GENEALOGICAL HISTORY OF HENRY ADAMS OF BRAINTREE,
MASSACHUSETTS AND HIS DESCENDANTS; ALSO JOHN ADAMS OF
CAMBRIDGE, MASSACHUSETTS by Andrew N. Adams. Repr. of
1897 ed. Indexed.
Cloth—$87.50—1,248pp------------------------------------ Vendor #D1486

3481 - GATHERINGS TOWARD A GENEALOGY OF THE COFFIN FAMILY by
William S. Appleton. Repr. of 1896 ed.
Five Generations of the Descendants of Tristram Coffin of Newbury
and Nantucket in the line of his son, Tristram Coffin, of Newbury,
Massachusetts. Indexed.
Paper—$12.50—57pp-------------------------------------- Vendor #D1486

3482 - THE HILLS FAMILY IN AMERICA, 2 Volumes, by William S. Hills and
Thomas Hills. Repr. of 1906 ed.
Plus 36 page softbound supplement of 1908.
Cloth—$75.00/Set—713pp--------------------------------- Vendor #D1486

3483 - GENEALOGY OF THE DESCENDANTS OF NATHANIEL CLARKE OF
NEWBURY, MASSACHUSETTS, 2d Ed., by George K. Clarke. Repr.
of 1885 ed.
Ten generations.
Cloth—$35.00—121pp-------------------------------------- Vendor #D1486

3484 - DESCENDANTS OF JOSIAH RISDON AND MARTHA COCHRAN by
Daniel B. Risdon and Robert E. Cook. 1982. 1,800 name index.
Family charts Revolutionary War to present.
Vital information, Biographies, Obituaries, Colonial Records, Photo-
graphs. Descendants emigrated from New England to western states.
Notes on prior ancestry, Beemer, Cushing, Eldridge, Martin, Switzer
and other allied families. California residents add $1.80 sales tax.
Cloth—$30.00—430pp-------------------------------------- Vendor #D1487

3485 - THE McDONALDS OF SOMERSET, OHIO AND THEIR DESCENDANTS by
D. M. Schlegel. 1977.
Families of McDonald, McGahan, Ward, Stine, Fink, Flautt, May,
McKenney, and Clark.
Cloth—$19.95—Paper—$15.95—189pp---------------------- Vendor #D1488

3486 - THE ROUTE OF THE ROOTS by Ferne K. Patterson. 1982.
Descendants of John Roote, Badby, England, who settled in Connecti-
cut, Massachusetts, New York, and West, including Root, Pomeroy,
Gray, Kitson, Churton, Nieman, Hoffman.
Cloth—$21.00—Paper—$16.00—150pp---------------------- Vendor #D1490

3487 - COAN GENEALOGY 1697-1982—PETER AND GEORGE OF EAST HAMPTON,
LONG ISLAND, AND GUILFORD, CONNECTICUT, WITH THEIR DE-
SCENDANTS IN THE COAN LINE AS WELL AS OTHER LINES by Ruth
Coan Fulton. 1983.
Discussion of Palatine Emigration of 1709-1710 as it applied to Peter and

George Coan; traditions and facts on their ancestry. Detailed biographies of descendants. Over 500 illustrations; photographs, deeds, wills, maps, letters, and other documents. Comments on pronunciation of Coan. Documented and indexed.
Cloth—$45.00— 700pp-- Vendor #D1491

3488 - FAMILY CONNECTIONS: HUTCHINS, FEREBEE, HARBIN, NAYLOR, EATON, FROST, BEEMAN, CAIN by Eleanor Cain Blackmore. 1983. Settlers of North Carolina, 30 photographs, family charts.
Cloth—$25.00— 210pp--Vendor #D1492

3489 - THE ORDWAY ODYSSEY: COMPRISING A GENEALOGICAL ACCOUNT OF JAMES[1] ORDWAY, 1634 EMIGRANT TO AMERICA...TO THE PRESENT DAY by Philip M. Ordway. 1985.
Includes variants (Ordiway, etc.), English origins, other United States and foreign lines. Well illustrated and indexed. Numbered, limited edition; send SASE for information.
-- Vendor #D1493

3490 - BAUCOM GENEALOGY by Banks McLaurin, Jr. 1983. Published in one or more issues yearly to supplement the Baucom book by B. E. Bawcom, and increase interest in Baucom, Bawcom, Baughcom, Balcombe, Balkcom genealogy.
Paper—$10.00—100pp------------------------------------- Vendor #D1496

3491 - JOSEPH AND SUSAN (QUARTERMAN) HANOVER, THEIR CHILDREN, AND SOME LATER DESCENDANTS by Ann-jannette Emerson. 1983.
Ca 1750-1850. From Baltimore County, Maryland and York County, Pennsylvania; to Fayette County, Pennsylvania; to Ohio County, (West) Virginia; to Adams and other counties in Ohio. 11"x8½".
Paper—$10.00—44pp------------------------------------- Vendor #D1497

3492 - JACOB EMERSON, 17TH CENTURY GRAND JUROR OF KENT COUNTY, DELAWARE by Ann-jannette Emerson. 1981.
Court, ancient tracts, prominent families. Includes Bedwell, Bishop, Bowman, Edmundson, Hunn, Heathred, Manlove, Needham, Robisson, Rouse, Walker. Indexed. 11"x8½".
Paper—$10.00—65pp------------------------------------- Vendor #D1497

3493 - CHRONOLOGICAL NOTES ON EMERSONS IN MARYLAND, 1650-1850 compiled and edited by Ann-jannette Emerson. 1982.
Documented, statewide entries from county records and recognized publications. Presented by date, name, and county. Full-name index. 11"x8½".
Paper—$10.00—56pp------------------------------------- Vendor #D1497

3494 - JAMES AND MARY (VEATCH) ELLIS, THEIR SONS, AND SOME DESCENDANTS by Ann-jannette Emerson. Spring,1985.
1750 immigrants from Britain. Frederick County, Maryland to Washington County, Pennsylvania. Sons went downstream to Adams County, Ohio ca 1795. Transcripts, review and analysis of the evidence and literature on the first two generations, plus pedigrees of hundreds of living descendants. Indexed. 6"x9".
Cloth—price to be announced—apx 400pp------------------ Vendor #D1497

3495 - CAMPBELL CONTACTS by Frances R. Nelson, Publisher-Editor. Information-exchange, Campbells anytime and anywhere.
Quarterly plus Annual Index issue. ($12.50 outside U.S.)
Subscription—$10.00/yr—36pp/issue---------------------Vendor #D1498

3496 - JONES JOURNEYS by Frances R. Nelson, Publisher-Editor. Information-exchange, Jones's anytime and anywhere.
Quarterly plus Annual Index issue. ($12.50 outside U.S.)
Subscription—$10.00/yr—36pp/issue---------------------Vendor #D1498

3497 - MILLER MONITOR compiled by Frances R. Nelson. Information-exchange, Millers anytime and anywhere.
Quarterly plus Annual Index issue. ($12.50 outside U.S.)
Subscription—$10.00/yr—36pp/issue---------------------Vendor #D1498

3498 - RUSSELL REGISTER by Frances R. Nelson.
Information-exchange, Russells anytime and anywhere.
Quarterly plus Index issue. ($12.50 outside U.S.)
Subscription–$10.00/yr–36pp/issue----------------------- Vendor #D1498

3499 - VANDERPOOL NEWSLETTER by Frances R. Nelson, Publisher-Editor.
Information-exchange, Vanderpools anytime and anywhere.
4 issues annually plus Annual Index issue. ($12.50 outside U.S.)
Subscription–$10.00/yr–120pp/yr------------------------ Vendor #D1498

3500 - NELSON NOTES by Frances R. Nelson.
Information-exchange, Nelsons anytime and anywhere.
Quarterly plus Annual Index issue. ($12.50 outside U.S.)
Subscription–$10.00/yr–36pp/issue----------------------- Vendor #D1498

3501 - THE COPELAND/COPLEN AND ALLIED FAMILIES–IMMIGRANTS TO
VIRGINIA compiled by Herman L. Coplen, Jr. 1983.
William Copeland and Mary, his wife, immigrated to Virginia from Scotland prior to 1650 and settled in Lancaster County. Their descendants
migrated first to Chowan Precinct, North Carolina ca 1712. From there,
family branches migrated west in North Carolina and south and west via
Georgia to Arkansas and Texas. Other family branches migrated further
west via Ohio, Indiana, Illinois to Colorado, Oregon, and Washington.
Ten generations of descendants are traced in this work down to children
with birth dates of ca 1900. Contains 10 pictures and is fully indexed.
Allied families are: Bell, Birks, Bowers, Brown, Buckles, Dranke,
Dubose, Dunn, Edwards, Ferguson, Fisher, French, Gasaway, Girtman,
Green, Hanson, Harrod, Hile, Jones, Lee, Lucas, Morris, Mullins,
Myers, Parkhill, Parks, Payne, Powers, Reeves, Ridgeway, Robinson,
Scroggin, Stanbery, Swanson, Swartz, Trammell, Turner, Van Hook,
Whiteside and Wireman.
Cloth–$20.00–216pp---------------------------------- Vendor #D1499

3502 - THE FAMILY TREE DAVISON by Claude M. Oliver. 1973.
Various spellings: Davison, Davisson, Davidson, etc.
Edward R. Davison, born 1750, Augusta County, Virginia; died
August, 1827, Pickaway County, Ohio. Married 1) Mary ____,
2) Elsia (Eliza/Elizabeth) Stevenson, 3) Elizabeth Ikes (1811).
Well documented; includes several interesting reproductions of wills,
Bible records and deed records. Indexed; 23 pictures.
Paper–$2.50–106pp---------------------------------- Vendor #D1500

3503 - THE FAMILY TREE OF GOLDSBERRY INCLUDING THE SANTEE
BRANCH by Claude M. Oliver. 1982.
Benjamin S. Goldsberry (1785-1859) and his wife Elizabeth (1795-1872);
born in Virginia; settled in Ross County, Ohio.
Children: James H., John M., Hester E.
David L. Goldsberry married Martha Elizabeth Bradberry.
Delay Fletcher Goldsberry (1823-1904) married 1) Sarah J. Fisher
(1825-1861); 2) Nancy (Santee) Cowman.
Well documented; indexed; 40 pictures, including Elijah Santee.
Paper–$14.50–87pp---------------------------------- Vendor #D1500

3504 - THE FAMILY OF JOHN PRICE AND NANCY AGNES MOORE by Elberta
Price Griffiths. 1982.
John, son of Reece Price, Pennsylvania, and Nancy Agnes Moore,
daughter of Jacob and Hannah (Steel), New Castle County, Delaware,
married 1787. Moved from York County, Pennsylvania to Morgan
County, Ohio, with eight children. Descendants scattered over United
States, especially Iowa, Missouri, Kansas. Collateral families:
Armentrout, Bailey, Cook, Dawson, Moody, Warthman, York.
Cloth–$14.95–127pp---------------------------------- Vendor #D1501

3505 - THE JOHN GEORGE WÄBER (WEAVER) FAMILY, OF SHENANDOAH
VALLEY OF VIRGINIA by Dorothy L. Weaver. 1981.
1752, some to present. Allied lines: Denton, Odell, Lichliter,
Stickleman, Persinger, Worley, Kisner, Miller, Hopping, Hess,
Bowers, Bryant, Gilmer, Moubray, Clatterbuck, Jacob Weaver,
Bosserman, Wiseman, Anderson, Hayes.
Paper–$21.00–220pp---------------------------------- Vendor #D1502

3506 - **JOHN LEMMON AND WIFE ELIZABETH MICKEY—PIONEER SETTLERS OF COLONIAL PENNSYLVANIA—ANCESTORS AND DESCENDANTS** by Lawrence Clifton Lemmon. 1983.
The Lemmon family, its arrival in America and settlement in Cumberland County, participation in the Revolution and resettlement in Westmoreland County.
Some allied families: Eicher, Galloway, Kalp, Mickey, Morrison, Overly and Porch.
Cloth—$25.00—456pp--- Vendor #D1503

3507 - **OF THEM THAT LEFT A NAME BEHIND—THE STARNS/STARNES FAMILY HISTORY AND GENEALOGY** by H. Gerald Starnes and Herman Starnes. 1983.
Traces family immigration route from Alzey, a small village in Germany; to Holland, to London, to New York; migration from upstate New York to Virginia, to North Carolina, South Carolina, Kentucky, Tennessee, and Louisiana. Encompasses participation in the making of American Frontier history on several fronts: early wilderness settlements; Indian fighting; militia service in French and Indian, Revolutionary, and 1812 Wars. True documented adventures of ancestors.
Over 200 maps and photographs show where Starnes/Starns lived, fought, farmed, died and are buried from Hudson and Mohawk Valleys in New York to Holston and Clinch Valleys in Tennessee, Tickfaw River in Louisiana. Numerous lines and branches represented in extensive genealogical listings.
Easy to read, enlightening, entertaining narrative with supporting genetic lineages of colorful old family in the annals of American history. With detailed historical accounts and genealogical data contained, most Starnes/Starns descendants might expect to become knowledgeable enough of the family to trace their own line of ancestry. The authors have concentrated on organizing and interpreting sparse, difficult and incomplete early records into a comprehensive format that can serve as a base for further research. Appendices address the unrelated English Stearns/Starns line and the apparently related very early family of Charles Starnes in South Carolina families with those of the Starnes/Starns family of Palatine German origins. Probabilities of direct immigration to Virginia and North Carolina from Europe are discussed as is that via Pennsylvania.
Both co-authors are seventh-generation descendants of the immigrant youth Frederick Staring known as Frederick Starnes on the Virginia frontier in the 1740's. They grew up, lived and researched in areas once occupied by their ancestors; regarded as authorities on family history and lineage.
Cloth—$50.00—800+pp--- Vendor #D1504

3508 - **A HISTORY OF MY PEOPLE AND YOURS: INCLUDING THE FAMILIES OF NICHOLAS LAKE, AND OTHERS** by Claud Nelson McMillan. 1956.
Includes also: The McMillan family; Woods family; Congdon family—the Temple familly; Cramton family—and notes on the Allen family.
Indexed; illustrations (documents); portraits; colonial coat-of-arms.
Cloth—$32.00—822pp--- Vendor #D1506

3509 - **ADAMSON ANCESTRY, VOLUME 4** by John and Judy Dye. 1983.
Indexed.
Paper—$5.63—38pp--- Vendor #D1508

3510 - **DYE DATA, VOLUME 1** by John and Judy Dye. 1983.
Indexed.
Paper—$5.63—45pp--- Vendor #D1508

3511 - **RAMBO REFERENCES, VOLUME 1** by John and Judy Dye. 1983.
Indexed.
Paper—$5.63—41pp--- Vendor #D1508

3512 - **WEBB FAMILY HISTORY AND GENEALOGY "OH HOW I HAVE SEARCHED"** by Earl F. Webb. 1982.
Seven generations of my Webb Heritage and allied families; includes many old and priceless photographs as well as more current and recent

ones. Beginning in Buckingham County, Virginia 1769; Theodoric and Catharine (Mattox) Webb. Also Hawkins County, Tennessee 1800-1900. NOTICE: Due to the limited number of copies of this Webb book printed, orders will only be filled for BONAFIDE DESCENDANTS of Theodoric and Catharine Mattox Webb. Please send evidence (Family Group Sheets) with order. Index.
Cloth—$25.00—80+--- Vendor #D1509

3513   - NOLLE PROSSE,...A HISTORY OF NEW YORK INDIANS AND THE PRINTUP FAMILY....by Printup, II A.D. 1983.
Nolle Prosse; A document which covers a large span of history of the New York Indians and the Printup Family who traveled from Canada into the United States in the 17th Century and to all parts of the United States today. The book involves itself with racial mixing, intermarriages, Indians in the Revolution—the War of 1812 with the Printup surname, Religious backgrounds, Education, Health, Death Rates, Indian Ancestry. Pictures of many of the Six Nation Indian or Iroquois, Part Indians who fled New York and went South and lived as white men, Un-claimed children of members of the same group, Negro/Dutch/Indian ancestry, and Maps of the Reservations of the Tribes of New York which shows the actual residences of the Indians and part-Indians, Telephone list of most Printups in the United States today, Census Records from 1790-1910, many surnames and their racially mixed ancestors and much more!
Nolle Prosse is bound in brown with gold letters, either hard or soft cover, has brown marble parchment as a divider between cover and the text, contains chapter index, appendix, bibliography, and is 8½"x11" with 99 pages. This document took over three years of intensive research to complete and is priced, with discount, direct from the author at the low price of $26.40 for soft cover and $32.70 for hard cover.
Library of Congress Catalogue Card Number: 83-72027 and ISBN: 0-913821-00-4 Hard and 0-913821-01-2 Soft.
NOLLE PROSSE t-47524
P.O. Box 5603
Tacoma, WA 98405
(206)272-7588 Mon-Fri/10a-17p pst.
Cloth—$32.70—Paper—$26.40—99pp------------------------- Vendor #D1510

3514   - THE GILSON FAMILY, FEATURING GEORGE AND MARY GILSON OF BERRIEN COUNTY, MICHIGAN, AND INCLUDING THE RELATED FAMILIES OF LANDON AND KUNZMAN by Ann C. Sherwin. 1983.
Gilson: Middlesex County, Massachusetts, 17th and 18th Centuries; Warren County, Pennsylvania and Chautauqua County, New York, 19th Century.
Landon: Sussex County, New Jersey, 18th Century; Crawford County, Pennsylvania, 19th Century. Index contains 200 related surnames. Author answers inquires.
Paper—$13.50—89pp------------------------------------- Vendor #D1511

3515   - THE HECKATHORN FAMILY: CHARLES HECKATHORN AND NANCY WHITLA OF COLUMBIANA AND CARROLL COUNTIES, OHIO, AND ISABELLA COUNTY, MICHIGAN; THEIR ANCESTORS AND DE-SCENDANTS by Ann C. Sherwin. 1981.
Index contains over 200 related surnames. Author answers inquiries.
Paper—$8.25—77pp------------------------------------- Vendor #D1511

3516   - THE EARLY YANDELLS OF NORTH CAROLINA AND SOME OF THEIR DESCENDANTS, 1737-1982 by Velma Nancyann Yarbrough. 1982.
Believed to be the only published, general genealogy compiled on Yandell name (including all variations of spelling). Delineates in-dividual family lines of first Yandells of record who settled in North Carolina in 1760's and extends migrating lines as far as information allowed into 1900's. Includes copy of original grants, Revolutionary War vouchers, old Bible records, wills, photographs. References. Fully indexed. 8½"x11".
Cloth—$42.00—516pp------------------------------------- Vendor #D1512

3517   - SEVIER FAMILY HISTORY WITH THE LETTERS OF GEN. JOHN
SEVIER, FIRST GOVERNOR OF TENNESSEE, AND 28 COLLATERAL
FAMILY LINEAGES by Cora Bales Sevier and Nancy S. Madden.
1982, repr. of 1961 ed. 75 illustrations. Indexed.
Records begin with Valentine Sevier (1712-1803), a young Huguenot,
who immigrated to the Shenandoah Valley of Virginia by 1740. Of
his five sons, John was the oldest. Two hundred nine letters written
by Gen. John Sevier, and included in the book, virtually tell the
story of his life--as well as much of early Tennessee history in which
all the brothers figured prominently. The letters were written between 1745 and 1815 to Indian Chiefs, Presidents and future Presidents
of the United States, and other interesting figures of the period. Also
included are 46 letters written to General Sevier and 29 letters written
about him or the events in which he figured. The notes of Dr. Lyman
C. Draper who interviewed three of General Sevier's sons and one of
his nieces in 1844 are included.
Family lineage records furnished by more than 500 correspondents
and augmented by research in the National Archives, and in state
and county records, furnish extensive information on the Seviers and
collateral families of Borden, Lt. Col. Richard Campbell, Chambers of
Staunton, Virginia, Chiles, Conway, Capt. Robert Craig of Abingdon,
Virginia, James Davis, Sr., of Abingdon, Virginia, Jonathan Doug-
lass, Kelsey Harris Douglass, Col. George Eskridge, Ewing of Cecil
County, Maryland, and Southwest Virginia, Garoutte, Goad, Goggin,
Harris, Hawkins, Henley, Kenner, King, Love of Charles County,
Maryland, Maloney, Nash, Overstreet, Col. Charles Robertson,
Sawyer, Sherrill, Snow, Warren, Whitley.
There are eight pages of authentic information, collected by the
authors on a special trip to Spain, concerning the Xavier family of
Navarre. Photos of the Xavier Castle are provided, as well as the
Xavier Coats of Arms. 11"x8½".
Cloth—$37.40—576pp------------------------------------- Vendor #D1513

3518   - JAMES BALL AND COLVIN POWELL CONNECTIONS by Grace Powell
Harms. 1983.
Part I concerns James Ball, the Patriot (1751-1834), of Maryland, Ohio
and Indiana and his sons: Daniel, Vachel and James H.
Part II deals with Colvin Powell (1809-1879) of Ohio and Iowa, his wife,
Barbara Ellen Ball, daughter of Daniel Ball, and their descendants:
Norvil, Francis Marion, Levin, John Wesley, Celia Ann (Powell) Artis,
Colvin C., Sarah Caroline (Powell) Bradbury, Nancy J. (Powell)
Ressman and Samuel Fletcher.
Allied families: Bryan, Carothers, Elmore, Ellis, Johnson, Johnston,
LaFortune, Reynolds, Smith, etc. Indexed; 10"x7".
Cloth—$18.50—128pp------------------------------------- Vendor #D1514

3519   - STRONG FAMILY OF VIRGINIA AND OTHER SOUTHERN STATES by
James Robert Rolff. 1983.
Descendants of John Strong of New Kent County, Virginia, born about
1675, probably a grandson of William Strong, who arrived in Virginia
in 1619. This family includes most Strongs of southern states.
Cloth hardbound, 487 pages, indexed, $35.00;
150 page supplement, $12.00.
Cloth—$35.00—487pp------------------------------------- Vendor #D1517

3520   - SOME DESCENDANTS OF STONEBURNER, SPRACKLIN, AUSTIN AND
BROYLES by Helen Cox Tregillis. 1981.
Paper—$10.00—80pp----------------------------------- Vendor #D1528

3521   - SOME WEBSTER COUNTY, KENTUCKY, FAMILIES—BAKER, BASSETT,
GIVENS, JOHNSON, PAYNE, PRICE, RICE AND OTHERS by Minerva
Bone Bassett and Patricia Randle Gillespie. 1983.
7,000 name index, illustrated.
Cloth—$20.00—216pp----------------------------------- Vendor #D1529

3522   - SOME OF THE DESCENDANTS OF PETER CLEAVER by William Jessup
Cleaver. 1983.
Includes 55 pages of index covering six generations with their children
from the Germantown Settler.
Paper—$19.75—332pp----------------------------------- Vendor #D1535

3523 a.- GENEALOGICAL CLASSIFICATION BY FAMILY-GROUP CODING FOR
DESCENT FROM COMMON ANCESTORS by Cameron R. Stewart, 1981.
Progenitors and related families (female descent) include *Stewart*,
John (V.1.) (son of James), b 1796, Perthshire (Dunkeld?), Scotland;
d 1858, Puslinch (Killean), Wellington County, Ontario, Canada; to
Adams, Allen, Armstrong, Auer, Bakken, Bartzen, Brown, Cameron,
Carpenter, Clark, Cosens, Crittenden, Davis, DeGelder, DeLaura,
Duley, Easton, Goldfinch, Grandy, Halpenny, Haman, Hayes, Heapy,
Hickson, Johnson, Katterhagan, Kuhnhenn, Larson, Lawrence, Loken,
McArthur, McCallum, McComb, McDonald, McGivern, MacIntyre,
McMillan, McNaughten, Matheson, Miller, Morey, Moses, Neilans,
O'Leary, Palo, Pennington, Pinning, Reilly, Richardson, Scharmer,
Scott, Severson, Steeves, *Stewart*, Thornton, Trygstad, Vallette,
Wagner, Walsh, Watson, Winthrow, Wood, Wright, and Young.

b. *McAlester—McMaster*, Flora (VI.6.) (daughter of Charles McAlister,
VII.11., of Ballygowan, Shisken), d ae. 84, 4.23.1843, Feorline
(Clachan), Isle of Arran, Scotland; to Adams, Andersen, Armstrong,
Auer, Bakken, Bartzen, Brown, Brundit, Burrows, Caldwell, Cameron,
Carpenter, Champ, Clark, Cloughton, Craig, Crittenden, DeGelder,
DeLaura, Duley, Easton, Foster, Goldfinch, Halpenny, Hamilton, Haugen,
Hayes, Heapy, Hickson, Hutchison, Johnson, Lankester, Larson,
Lawrence, MacAlester, McAlester, McAlister, McBride, McCallum,
McComb, McDonald, McIntosh, McLarty, McLellan, *MacMaster*, *McMaster*,
Miller, Morey, Moses, Neilans, O'Leary, Olness, Ord, Palo, Pennington,
Quinlan, Richardson, Scharmer, Scott, Steeves, *Stewart*, Thomson,
Trygstad, Vallette, Viney, Wagner, Walsh, Watson, Withrow, Wood,
and Young.

c. *Sarles*, William, Sr. (VI.9.), lived in Dutchess County, New York,
until c1800, when he moved to Hastings County, Ontario, Canada
(descendants throughout Canada and parts of United States); to
Armstrong, Bakken, Bartzen, Bell, Bergot, Bird, Bonenfant, Brown,
Carlson, Carson, Cassidy, Chown, Clapp, Clifford, Connor, Crawford,
Crittenden, Dafoe, Davidson, Decker, DeGelder, Dickens, Doncaster,
Donnau, Dowswell, Drake, Duley, Elliot, Fair, Fallis, Farrow, Faulkner,
Fields, Flood, Gall, Gay, Godbout, Goldfinch, Golding, Goldsack,
Gordon, Grant, Green, Hagerman, Haggerty, Hall, Hamilton, Harvey,
Hill, Holmes, Holton, Horton, Hughes, Hughson, Hunt, Irwin, Ivory,
Jackson, Jaycock, Jochmaring, Joynt, Ketcheson, Knapp, Larson, Long,
Lott, McCallum, McGee, McGetbury, McGuire, Manning, Mack, May,
Mikkelsen, Moir, Moorcraft, Moore, Mortson, Mosher, Palmer, Patterson,
Payne, Peterson, Quinlan, Rait, Richardson, Roach, Robins, Robinson,
Sannes, Sansom, *Sarles*, Scharmer, Scheerschmidt, Scott, *Searles*,
Sernyk, Shelly, Simmons, Simon, Sine, Solmes, Stevenson, Stewart,
Tarr, Tatum, Trygstad, Unger, VanLuterin, Voss, Walden, Wagner,
Walter, Wanamaker, Wannamaker, Wannop, Ward, Welch, Wickens, Wilks,
Wilson, Windsor, Winsor, Wojt, and Wood.

d. *Sharrard*, William, Sr. (VI.11.), U.E.L., from England to Dutchess
County, New York, c1760; entered Hastings County, Ontario, Canada,
6.1789; to Allin, Arlidge, Armstrong, Bakken, Barry, Bartzen, Benner,
Birch, Braaten, Bradford, Brooke, Brown, Cameron, Cappon, Carlson,
Churchill, Clarke, Cochrane, Collins, Cowie, Crittenden, DeGelder,
Diamond, Dickinson, Dingman, Dobson, Dotter, Drake, Duley, Dulmage,
Ekstrom, Evans, Farrow, Fields, Finney, Forsythe, Glore, Goldfinch,
Goldsack, Gordon, Gould, Green, Haag, Hall, Ham, Hamilton, Herrick,
Hogle, Holton, Hudson, Hunt, Jochmaring, Johnson, Johnstone, Jones,
Kemmeter, Lake, Larson, Lees, Lillicroppe, Long, McCallum, McGregor,
McIntosh, McLean, McPhail, McRoberts, Madill, Matthews, Mikkelsen,
Milieke, Moir, Morgan, Noll, Otto, Palmer, Patchell, Pearce, Percy,
Peterson, Phillips, Ponach, Proudfoot, Pugh, Richardson, Rogers,
Sannes, Sansom, Sarles, Scharmer, Scott, Searles, Sellars, Sernyk,
Sharrard, Short, Simkins, Sisko, Skene, Springer, Stevenson,
Stewart, Tarrant, Trygstad, Unger, Walden, Wagner, Walker, Walter,
Warrick, Webb, Williams, Williamson, Willson, Wilson, Winterburn, Wixon,
Wojt, Wood, and Woodside.

3523 (cont.)

e. *Bentl(e)y*, William, Sr. (X.193.) (John's son), baptized 1640, Ampthill, Bedfordshire, England; settler in Narragansett Country (Rhode Island), 1678/9, d Kingstown (N.), Rhode Island Colony, 1720 (descendants in Exeter and Greenwich of Rhode Island, in New York and Canada); to Abramson, Alger, Allen, Alsup, Anderson, Anweiler, Arms, Armstrong, Arndt, Babington, Bacon, Badger, Bakken, Baldwin, Bamford, Barton, Bartzen, Beaman(?), Beck, Bell, Bennett, Bentley, Bently, Berg, Berns, Bieri, Birch, Birkett, Bond, Bostwick, Boughton, Bowen, Bowey, Boyles, Bozanic, Braun, Bray, Brien, Brown, Bunnell, Burke, Burnell, Cain, Cameron(?), Capwell, Carlson, Caughron, Caywise, Charles, Chase, Clark, Cleveland, Coldgrove, Conner, Cookson, Coryell, Cowles, Crabtree, Crittenden, Crocker, Cruikshank, Cummings, Dafoe, Daley, Davis, DeCelles, DeGelder, Denmond, Denton, Deputy, DeWan, Dingman, Dorsey, Drake, Duley, Dunham, Eastman, Edwards, Ellsworth, Ensworth, Essex, Evans, Facer, Farrow, Findley, Fish, Fisher, Fishleigh, Flanagan, Fletcher, Frederick, Fuller, Gardiner, Gardner, Gatherer, Gaydon, George, Geppert, Gerard, German, Gibson, Gilbert, Gile, Goldfinch, Goldsack, Gordon, Gosnell, Green, Griffin, Griffiths, Grim, Grommon, Gundlach, Guyett, Hamilton, Hannant, Hanson, Harlow, Hawkman, Hays, Heighton, Hensch, Hensel, Herath, Highberg, Higinbotham, Hill, Hitchcock, Holder, Holton, Hosner, Hotschenbacher, Howman, Hubbard, Hulett, Hunt, Hurdle, Hurst, Hyland, Imes, Inglis, Innes, Ireland, Jackson, Jardine, Jenner, Jensen, Job, Jochmaring, Jones, Keeler, Keller, Kempton, Kenny, Keskitalo, King, Knauss, Knutsen, Korach, Kottmeier, LaDue, Lake, Larson, Lautenslayter, Lawrence, Layton, Lazell, Lecog, L'Ecuyer, Ledger, Leegaard, Levicy, Lewis, Linn, Long, Love, Lund, McAvay, McAvey, McBride, McCall, McCallum, McConnell, McCrady, McKenna, McLellan, McMahon, McMillan, McNeil, Mallory, Malpass, Martin, Marstellar, Mason, Mayo, Mendenhall, Merrick, Meyer, Mikkelsen, Miller, Mills, Mitton, Mix, Moir, Moore, Morris, Mosier, Murphy, Murray, Naeve, Neville, Noble, O'Connor, Olstad, Oltman, Overton, Paine, Parker, Pascoe, Patton, Patterson, Paul, Paxton, Penhall, Perine, Peterson, Pettie, Pettit, Phillips, Piel, Piper, Prutsman, Puffer, Quinn, Quorn, Race, Ramesbotham, Randall(?), Rees, Reynolds, Richardson, Rippitor, Roberts, Robinson, Roest, Rosa, Rosandich, Russell, Salhany, Sanford, Sannes, Sansom, S(e)arles, Sauter, Scharmer, Schied, Schmidt, Schrymaguer, Scott, Scrafford, Sealy, Seiver, Sernyk, Sharrard, Sheaff(?), Shelly, Shenick, Shep(p)ard, Shulver, Sinclair, Skaggs, Skinner, Sisum, Slocum, Smith, Snow, Soland, Sorensen, Sparks, Sperry, Spicer, Spink, Stauffer, Stewart, Stevens, Stevenson, Still, Stuart, Sullivan, Sutherland, Taber, Taylor, Teeples, Tenney, Thirsk, Thomas, Thompson, Tomlinson, Traynor, Trombly, Trygstad, Turner, Tyler, Unger, VanAuken, Vance, VanDevin, Wagner, Wakefield, Walden, Walter, Warren, Waterman, Webster, Wenzel, West, Wheaton, Wheeler, White, Wightman, Wilcox, Wiles, Willis, Wilson, Winmill, Winston, Witherstine(?), Wojt, Wolfly, Wood, Woolridge, Youngman, and Zimmerman, et al.

f. *Shippee*, David (X.197.), married 8.15.1664, Warrick, Rhode Island, Margaret *Scranton* (X.198.), daughter of Thomas and Mary; son Samuel (IX.99.) married 12.29.1702, Ann Litchfield (IX.100.), daughter of Thomas (X.199.) and Mary (X.200.), b. 8.18.1678, Dorchester, Massachusetts, d 1752, East Greenwich, Rhode Island; to *Bentl(e)y*, Bergsten(?), Fish, Fiske, Johnson, Joshlin, Matteson, Quick, Rutenburg, Sarles, *Shippee*, Spink, Stewart, Tarbox, Whitman, Winmill, et al.

g. *Badgerow*, Martinas (VI.15.), son of Francis and a *Gordon*(?), b c1779 (New York—?), (Justin's brother), d 8.23.1853, Markham Township, York County, Ontario County, Ontario, Canada; married Margaret *Sager* (Henry's sister); to Alger, Anderson, Anweiler, Archer, Armstrong, Badgerow plus Badg(e)ro(w)(?), Bailey, Bakken, Bartzen, Bentley, Bergot, Bliss, Boadwin, Bonenfant, Booth, Bowey, Brown, Buchan, Burke, Campbell, Carlson, Carpenter, Castetter, Chapman, Charles, Chatten, Chichester, Collins, Conrad, Coscarelli, Coughran, Crawford, Crittenden, Davidson, Decker, DeFeyter, DeGelder, DeWeese,

3523 (cont.)
DeWitt, Dimma, Doncaster, Dow, Downing, Dowswell, Drake, Duley,
Empringham, Evett, Farrier, Farrow, Ferrier, Ferris, Fields, Gall,
Garver, George, Gerrow, Gibson, Gillies, Goddard, Goldfinch, Golding,
Goldsack, Gordon, Gould, Grant, Hall, Ham, Hamilton, Hanna, Hanson,
Harkness, Hegler, Heighton, Heise, Hester, Holland, Holmes, Holton,
Hood, Hope, Houle, Howman, Hubbard, Hughes, Hughson, Hunt,
Ireland, Irwin, Jaycock, Jochmaring, Johns, Johnson, Knapp, Kuhowski,
Larson, Lautenschlager (Lautenslayter?), Lee, Lenz, Lewis, Long, Lott,
McCallum, McCowan, McGuire, McKay, McKenna, McKnight, McLellan,
McMahon, Manning, Mansell, Martillo, Martin, Mattison, Maurer, May,
Mikkelsen, Millard, Miller, Moir, Morris, Mortson, Mosher, Nevins,
Noble, Nye, O'Connor, Orem, Ormerod, Paine, Paul, Payne, Penhall,
Pennock(?), Peterson, Pipher, Pope, Powell, Provost, Quantz, Rait,
Reeder, Richardson, Roach, Robins, Rosa, Rutherford, Sannes,
Sansom, Sarles, Scharmer, Scheerschmidt, Scholl, Schrymaguer
(Scrommonger?), Scott, Searles, Sernyk, Shepard, Slimmon, Smith,
Stellhorn, Stevenson, Stewart, Stone, Stonehouse, Stump, Sumption,
Sundholm, Swindle, Tarr, Tatum, Taylor, Tilley, Tomlinson, Trygstad,
Tucker, Tyson, Unger, Veit, Vossbeck, Walden, Wagner, Wallace,
Walter, Wannop, Warrener, Webster, Whaley, White, Wilbur, Wiley,
Williams, Wilson, Winmill, Wojt, and Wood.
h. *Gjer(d)e-Trodo (-Traa)*, Gunvor (V.10.), daughter of Anders,
    b 1797, d 1891 in Skulestadmo, Voss, Norway; mother of Anders (IV.5.),
    Iowan immigrant (1860) who was married 1861, Wisconsin to fourth-
    cousin Kari Knutsdtr *Afdal*, also from Voss, Norway (both *Miltzow*
    descendants); to Almo, Andersdtr, Autry, Bergrud, Bernards,
    Brouwer, Brown, Bunke, Carlson, Castello, Chase, Christopherson,
    Clauson, Dahl, Davis, Doering, Edmundson, Ellefson, Everitt, Fossum,
    Garafolo, Gergrud, Geving, Gjerde, Gjere, Gotskalksson, Hansen,
    Headington, Holland, Holstad, Hunt, Jakobsdtr, Johnson, Jokinen,
    Kauri, Kolbo., Lenz, Liljegren, Losen, McCalley, McConnell, Mandal,
    Mann, Martin, Mestad, Miller, Montroy, Morgantini, Murphy, Nelson,
    Nielsen, Olson, Osborn, Perry, Peterson, Richardson, Rist, Roney,
    Roppe, Rowe(?), Rude, St. Mary, Schmidt, Scholten, Scott, Sherburne,
    Sivesind, Skorve, Stenberg, Stevenson, Stewart, Strehlow, Thayer,
    Thompson, Torbjornsdtr, Torbjornsson, Torsteinsdtr, Torsteinsson,
    Traa, Trigg, Trodo, Trones, Vavroch, Vermeer, Wilhelmson, and
    Wilson.
i. *Miltzow*, Henrik (XI.637., XI.765.), Gjert's son (of Norwegian, Dutch,
    and Pomeranian descent), b 10.20.1599, Bergen, Norway, d 11.19.1666,
    Voss, Norway; to Æn, Afdal, Bakke, Berge, Bo, Boe, Brekku, Finne,
    Foster, Gavle, Gjerde, Gjere, Gjerme, Gjoestein, Grevle, Henricksdtr,
    Hoyland, Jernes, Kindem, Knutsdtr, Leiddal, Lunde, Mann, Matzke,
    Melve, Miltzow, Myers, Pechacek, Raudstad, Ringham, Ringheim,
    Rist, Rockne, Rokne, Saeve, Skogstad, Skorve, Steen-Hansen,
    Stewart, Torbjornsdtr, Torbjornsson, Torsteinsdtr, Torsteinsson,
    Traa, Trodo, and Tvinno, et al.
j. *Osmundsdatter-Knutson*, Margit (IV.8.) (*Kvale* descendant), b 1.1.1826,
    Setesdal (Nordgarden), Norway, d 3.25.1891, Bygland, Polk County,
    Minnesota; m 1.21.1847, Knut Knutson Sandnes (and Froysnes, etc.),
    baptized 3.15.1808 ("Sannaes"), Setesdal, Norway; Wisconsin immigrants
    (1859), to Minnesota (1879); to Anderson, Astrup, Austin, Austinson,
    Bauer, Blume, Bray, Cruzan, Daigle, Danielson, Denison, Eben,
    Egeland, Ellefson, Erickson, Ernst, Eubank, Fideldy, Garry, Gullikson,
    Gunderson, Hammargren, Hennagir, Hoffman, Hove, Isakson, Kasper,
    Knudsen, Knudson, Knutson, Larson, Mann, Masters, Nelson, Nomland,
    Nordgarden, Osmundsdatter, Osmundson, and Penne; descendants in
    Minnesota and North Dakota.
k. Among compiler Cameron Ralph Stewart's many identified and classified
    ancestors are Ralph John (baptized John Ralph) Stewart (II.1.), b 1896,
    Drayton, North Dakota; Vinnie M. Gjere (II.1.), b 1899, Hatton, North
    Dakota; John "C." Stewart (III.1.), b 1857, Harriston, Ontario,
    Canada; Sarah Elizabeth Sarles (III.2.), b 1859, Whitby-Ashburn-
    Myrtle, Ontario; Louis Gjer(d)e (III.3.), b 1872, Decorah, Iowa;
    Thea Caroline Knutson (III.4.), b 1870, Waupaca, Wisconsin; Peter

3523 (cont.)

k.   Stewart (IV.1.), b 1825, Perthshire, Scotland; Flora McMaster (IV.2.),
(cont.) b 1825, Feorline, Isle of Arran, Scotland; John Sarles (IV.3.), b 1830,
Ontario; Almira Hannah Bentley (IV.4.), b 1833 ca, Ontario; Anders
Torbjornson Gjer(d)e (IV.5.), b 1832, Voss, Norway; Kari Knutsdatter
Afdal (IV.6.), b 1836, Ytre Afdal, Voss, Norway; Knut Knutson
(Sandnes, Froysnes, etc.) (IV.7.), Christened 1808 in Setesdal, Nor-
way; Margit Osmundsdatter Nordgarden-Froysnes (IV.8.), b 1826,
Norway; John Stewart (V.1.), b ca 1795, Perthshire, Scotland; Jean
McLean (V.2.), b ca 1801, Scotland; Archibald McMaster (V.3.),
b 1785, Scotland; Catherine Cook (V.4.), b Isle of Arran, Scotland;
William Sarles, Junior (V.5.), b ca 1787 (New York?); Eunice Sharrard
(V.6.), b ca 1786 (New York?); Miron Bentley (V.7.), b ca 1799
(New York?); Hannah Badgerow (V.8.), b 1802 (New York?/Ontario?);
Torbjorn Andersson Trodo (Traa) (V.9.), b 1789; Gunnvor Andersdatter
Gjerde (V.10.), b 1797, Voss; Knut Larsson Saude (V.11.), b ca 1805;
Geirtrud Olavsdtr Afdal (V.12.), b 1812; Knut Knutson Skomedal-
Sandnes (V.13.), m 1807; Guro Halvorsdtr Rike-in-Valle (Riige)
(V.14.), Christened 1787, Norway; Osmund Olsen Sandnes (V.15.),
Christened 1802, Sandnes, Bygland, Setesdal, Norway; Berte Isachsdtr
Oustad (V.16.), Christened 1805; James Stewart (VI.1.), b-d Scotland;
Alexander McMaster (VI.5.), b ca 1758, Isle of Arran, Scotland;
Flora McAlester (VI.7.), baptized 1764, Isle of Arran; Cathrine Cook
(VI.8.); William Sarles, Senior (VI.9.); William Sharrard, Senior
(VI.11.), b 1744 (England?), res. New York (ca 1760-89) and Canada
(6.1789, UEL); Reuben Bentley (VI.13.), b ca 1774; Martinas
Badgerow (VI.15.), b ca 1779 (New York?); Margaret Sager (Seager?
Sargier?) (VI.16.), b ca 1772 (New York? Pennsylvania?) (Henry's
daughter?);Anders Eirikson Lono (VI.17.), b 1751; Brita Andersdatter
Gjerde (Lono) (VI.18.), b 1751, Voss, Norway; Anders Halleson Gjerde
(VI.19.), b 1773; Brita Torsteinsdtr Ringheim (VI.20.), b 1769; Lars
Davidson Ringheim (VI.21.), b 1777; Ingebjorg Knutsdtr Gjoastein
(VI.22.), b 1772; Olav (Ole) Nilsson Afdal (VI.23.), b 1787; Kari
Sjursdtr Bo-Dyrvedalen (VI.24.), b 1784, Voss; Halvor Gunderson
Rike-Valle (VI.27.), Christened 1753, Setesdal, Norway; Gunvor
Osmundsdtr Jore-Valle (VI.28.), Christened 1759; Olav (Ole) Tommeson
(Thomeson) Nordgarden (VI.29.), b 1754; Margit (Margrethe)
Knutsdatter Nordgarden (VI.30.), b 1763, Setesdal, Norway; Isak
Larson Austad (VI.31.) ;Svaloug. Aanesdtr (VI.32.); Charles McAlister
(VII.11.), b 1726, resided at Ballygowan, Shisken, Isle of Arran,
Scotland; Niel McCook (VII.13.); Samuel Bentl(e)y, Senior (VII.25.),
b 1746, Exeter, Rhode Island Colony, New England; Anders Halleson
Liɗ (Gjerde) (VII.35.), living ae. 80 y, 1779; Kristi Johannesdtr
Gjerde (VII.36.), b 1715; Torstein Arnfinnson Ullestad-Ringheim
(VII.39.), b 1740; Anna Nilsdtr Finne-Ringheim (VII.40.), b 1739;
David Larsson Saude (VII.41.), b 1746; Sjur Nilsson Gjukestein
(VII.47.), m 1767; Ingjerd Steffasdtr Bo (VII.48.), b 1747 ca, d 1831;
Gunder Biornson Rike (VII.53.); Guro Olavsdtr Aanebjorg (VII.54.),
b 1727, Rike-Bygland, Norway; Osmund Jonson Jore (VII.55.), b 1724;
Targier Taraldsdtr Myrum-Valle (VII.56.); Tommes Olavson Nordgaarden
(VII.57.), b 1728; Targjerd Aasmundsdtr Sandnes (VII.58.), d 1777;
Knut Ellefson Nordgaarden (VII.59.), b 1725; Lars Isakson Austad
(VII.61.); Ronald McAlister (VIII.21.) left Skipness, Kintyre, Scotland,
to settle at Drumadoon, Isle of Arran, Scotland; Benjamin Bentl(e)y
(VIII.49.), b July 5, 1714, Kingstown, Colony of Rhode Island and
Providence Plantations (Narragansett Country), New England; Sarah
Shippee (VIII.50.), b ca 1717, d 1760/61 (smallpox), Exeter, Rhode
Island Colony; Johannes Sverkveson Gjerde (VIII.71.), b 1689, m 1714,
d 1737; Brita Jakobsdtr Hoyland (VIII.72.); Nils Arnfinnson Finne-
Ringheim (VIII.79.), b 1707; Brita Knutsdtr Finne (VII.80.), b 1709;
Lars Davidson Hommedal-Saude (VII.81.), b 1710; Herborg Ivarsdtr
Saude (VII.82.), b 1728; Steffa Mikkjelson Bo-Dyrvedalen (VIII.95.),
b 1699; Kristense Knutsdatter Finne (VIII.96.), b 1705; Jon Pedersen
Jore (VIII.109.); Ragnild Halvorsdtr Kvasager-in-Valle (VIII.110.);
Olav Tommasson Sandnes (VIII.113.), b 1703; Siri Nilsdtr Nordgarden
(VIII.114.); Asmund Tommesen (Osmund Tomasson) Sandnes (VIII.115.),

Family Genealogies - 1567

3523 (cont.)
m. b 1700; Gunnhild Ormsdtr Skomedal (VIII.116.), d 1753; Ellef Ellefsen
Nordgaarden (VIII.117.), d 1739; Mari(the) Olsdtr Nordenaa-in-Bygland
(VIII.118.), Setesdal, Norway; Sgt. Isak Ager Hagen-in-Austad
(VIII.121.), arrived in Austad in 1750; Thomas Bentl(e)y (IX.97.),
b June 19, 1685, d 1778, ae. 92 y, Exeter, Rhode Island; Elizabeth
Chamberl(a)in (IX.98.), m June 6, 1706, Kingstown, Rhode Island
Colony (possibly the daughter of Job of Boston); Samuel Shippee
(IX.99.), d 1740, East Greenwich, Rhode Island; Ann(e) Litchfield
(IX.100.), b August 18, 1678, Dorchester, Massachusetts Bay Colony,
m December 29, 1702, East Greenwich, Rhode Island Colony; Sverkve
Johanneson Gjerde (IX.141.); Knut Nilsson Sonve-Finne (IX.159. and
IX.191.), b 1672 (b 1664-?), d 1739; Margreta Klausdtr Miltzow
(IX.160. and IX.192.); b 1672, d 1763; Havor Knutson Kvasager
(IX.219.); Guroe Osmundsdtr (IX.220.); Tomas Osmundson Sandnes
(IX.225.), b 1634; Anlaug Bjorgulvsdtr Vik (IX.226.); Nils Mikkjelson
Nordgarden (IX.227.), b 1722; Tore Asmundsdtr (IX.228.); Tomes
Asmundsen Sandnes (IX.229.), b ca 1634; Anlaug Bjorgulvsdtr
Vik-in-Birtedalen (IX.230.), m 1699; Ole Knutson Nordena (IX.235.),
m 1698; Joran Tomasdtr Sandnes (IX.236.); William Bentl(e)y (X.193.),
b Amp(t)hill, Bedfordshire, England; Christened September 13, 1640,
Ampthill; lived in Narragansett Country, The Kings Province, The
Southern Part of New England (now Rhode Island), 1678 ca; d 1720,
Kingstown, Rhode Island Colony; David Shippee (X.197.) of Rhode
Island; Margaret Scranton (X.198.) of Prudence Island and Warwick,
m August 15, 1664; Thomas Litchfield (X.199.) of Dorchester and
Boston, Massachusetts, m ca 1677; Mary (unidentified maiden-name)
Long-Litchfield-Hooper (X.200.) was a hostage of the Turks,
Barbary Coast pirates, ca 1680, taken from a ship sailing from
Massachusetts to England; Johannes Sverkveson Seve-Gjerde (X.281.),
Seve farmer in 1635; Klaus Henrikson Miltzow (X.319. and X.383.),
b 1632 (b 1625-?), d 1692; Inger Lauritsdtr Lydvo (X.320. and
X.384.); Osmund Gunnarson Sandnes (X.449.), b ca 1601; Tomas
Osmundson Sandnes (X.471.), b ca 1634; Margit Torbiornsdtr
Birkeland (X.472.), John Bentl(e)y (XI.385.), Christened November
5, 1608, Elstow, Bedfordshire, England, and buried March 25, 1666,
Ampthill; Mary Betts (XI.386.), m October 3, 1630, Ampthill, Bed-
fordshire, England; Henrik Gerdtson Miltzow (XI.637. and XI.765),
b October 20, 1599, Bergen, Norway, became head-minister of Vossa-
kyrkja, Voss, Norway, 1623, d 1666; Kristense Madsdtr (XI.638. and
XI.766.), b 1594, Hardanger, Norway; Laurits Anderson Heiberg
(XI.639.) of Lydvo, tax collector at Voss; Kirsten Jakobsdtr (XI.640.);
Gunnar Jorundson Kvale (XI.897.); Kristi Jensdtr Horsdal-Froland
(XI.898.); Torbjorn Ormson Birkeland (XI.943.), d before 1689;
William Bentl(e)y (XII.769.), paternal-grandfather of the Rhode
Island Bentley progenitor and maternal-grandfather of John Bunyan,
English preacher and author of Pilgrim's Progress; Mary Goodwin
(XII.770.), m May 18/20, 1601, St. Paul's Church, Bedford, Bedford-
shire, England, bur July 1, 1632; Gjert Klausson Miltzow (XII.1273.);
Margreta Ivarsdtr Mork (XII.1274.); Mass (Mads) Jorgensen (Jensen-?)
(XII.1275.) of Hardanger was believed to have been descended from
a Schlesien family; Margrethe Mikkelsdtr (XII.1276.); Anders Lauritsson
Heiberg (XII.1277.), b 1570; Jakob Jorgensen (XII.1279.) of Bergen
and Mel, Norway; Inger Axelsdtr Gyntersberg (XII.1280.); Jorund
Olavson Kvale (XII.1793.); Klaus Henriksson Miltzow (XIII.2545.),
d 1595, Bergen; Anna Adriansdtr Falkoner (XIII.2546.), b Nidaros
(Trondheim), Norway; Jorgen van der Huus (XIII.2549.); Laurits
Andersson (XIII.2553.); Axel Henrikson Gunterbergh (XIII.2559.),
d 1588; Kirstin Trondsdtr Benkestok (XIII.2560.), b 1530, d 1572,
Torget, memorialized on armorial church-epitaphs, the oldest known
in Norway (burned; copies in Royal Archives, Copenhagen, Denmark);
Olav Gunnarson Kvale (XIII.3585.), living 1514-30 in Setesdal; Henrick
Miltzow (XIV.5089.), official of the diocese of Altentreptow-on-the-
Tolense-River, Pomerania (now Mecklenberg, Deutsche Demokratische
Republik, popularly referred to as the Russian Zone of East Germany),
1540-80; Anna Hannemans (XIV.5090.); Adrian Rotker Falkener

3523 (cont.)

n. (XIV.5091.), b The Netherlands, was long-term Mayor of Trondheim,
d ca 1595, ae. 120 y (legend) ; Margrete Petersdtr (XIV.5092.); Anders
from Hessoen (XIV.5105.), d 1620; Henrik Gunterbergh (XIV.5117.),
Mel-in-Kvinnherad, Norway; Kirstin Lavisdtr Foss (XIV.5118.) (?);
Trond Tordson Benkestok (alias Trond Torlefsson Benkestoch-?)
(XIV.5119.), b 1490, Meloy-Joranger-Hannanger; Anna Jonsdtr Haar
(XIV.5120.), d 1569, bur Domkirken, Bergen; Gunnar Sveinson Kvale
(XIV.7169.), lived in 1505; unidentified Benkestok (XV.10237.);
Benkestok's wife (XV.10238.), hypotheses include (1) Adelus Eriksdtr
Kruckow or (2) Sigrid Urup or (3) Anne Bosdtr Flemming; Jon Haar
(XV.10239.), lived ca 1500; unidentified Tjotta (XV.10240.); Asgjerd
Tollefsdtr Kvale (XV.14338.); Trond Tordson Benkestok (XVI.20473.),
"Norges Riksraad," Talgoy-Finnoy-Ryfylke, res. 1444-72; Byrnhild
Torleifsdtr Kjaellingmule(?) (Bergieth-?) (Ingeborg Smor-?) (XVI.20474.)
(correct identity?); uncertain ancestor (XVI.20475.), may be Erik
Kruckow or perhaps Bo Flemming; (unk.) Tjotta (XVI.20479.); (unk.)
Frieland (XVI.20480.); Tollef Torgeirson Kvale (XVI.28675.), lived
in 1434, Bygland, Setesdal, Norway; Tord Benkestok (XVII.40945.),
knighted for protecting his king (legend); (unk.) Kjaellingmule
(XVII.40947.) (?); (unk.) Smor (XVII.40948.) (?); Sir John Hallvardson
Smor (XVIII.81895.)(?), in 1375, was the Crown's Peace Officer in
Bergen, Norway; Halvard Jonsson Smor (XIX.163789.) (?); Hr. Jon
Ragnvaldsson Smor (XX.327577.) (?), "Rigsraad og Ridder,
1295-1305"; and Ragnvald Urka (XXI.655153.) (?), lived in 1263.
Many American, Canadian, Scotch, English, and Norwegian descendants
of the author's selected progenitor—ancestors have been genealogically
classified in this kinship history, well-illustrated with photographs,
charts, drawings, and maps. Evidence has been carefully documented
with relevant dates, places, events, and sources. Two indices include
both stray and enciphered names. Twenty years of research, compiling
and classifying and the cooperation of many others have made this
publication possible. Limited edition, restricted availability; copies
of first-priority to be in leading genealogical libraries in the United
States, Canada, Norway, England, Scotland, France, and Mecklenburg
(DDR).
(In process)-approximately 2000pp------------------------Vendor #C0579

3524 - WILD GARLIC ISLANDS (A GENEALOGICAL ACCOUNT OF THE
RAMSEY FAMILY) by Robert H. Stone. 1982.
Covering general information about the prominent and obscure from
the Scottish Earls of Dalhousie and the British Colonial Governors
of India and Canada, Wild Garlic Islands, gives specific names of the
Ramsay-Ramsey Clan as well as dates when as indentured servants
some were sentenced to transportation to such colonial establishments
as the Barbados and the New World. Births, marriages, deaths, wills,
administrations, census records, etc. recorded in such states as
Pennsylvania, Virginia, Kentucky, Tennessee, Missouri, and Arkansas
are given their place. Specifically the book covers those families
which migrated to Arkansas Territory, and found homes in the Northwestern part of that State.
As well as a listing of Ramseys who served in the Confederate Army
from Arkansas, there is also a record of veterans (and their widows)
who applied for pensions based on such service.
The book is indexed and has pictures, charts, maps, reproduced wills,
marriage records, newspaper clippings, etc. as well as an interesting
account of how the author decided on the name for his book, Wild
Garlic Islands.
Cloth—$22.50—191pp------------------------------------ Vendor #D1516

3525 - THE DESCENDENTS OF THOMAS HUTCHINSON OF SOUTHOLD, NEW
YORK 1666-1982 by Jane Errickson Hutchinson. 1982.
Related families include Case, Conklin(g), Cooper, Davids, Davis,
Dayton, DeLancey, Dickerson, Edwards, Floyd, Goldsmith, Halsey,
Havens, Horton, Jones, Landon, Miller, Moore, Mulford, Nicoll,
Norton, Osborn(e), Overton, Randall, Terry, Thorn(e), Tuthill, Wells,
Worth, Young(s), others. 6"x9".
Cloth—$23.95—350pp------------------------------------ Vendor #D1520

3526 - THE JOSEPH KEMMERER FAMILY by Louise Redfern Pells. 1978.
Joseph Kemmerer (1817-1891) his wife, Elizabeth Matilda Johnson
(1818-1873) were both born in Northampton County, Pennsylvania and
married there. Seven daughters and two sons were born in Pennsylvania. In 1850 the family moved to Summit County, Ohio where three
daughters and three sons were born, and the three oldest daughters
married. In 1864 the family moved to Christian County, Illinois. The
twelve younger children married in Illinois, and the parents died there.
The allied families into which the daughters married: Ephraim Dutton
Austin, Joel Baughman, Thomas Jefferson Deeren, Owen Henshue
(Hanshue), Solomon J. Kryder, John H. Loutzenhiser, Franklin
Miller, James Moser, Nathan Columbus Potts, and Martin Whitesell.
The families then separated and some migrated further west into
Missouri, Nebraska, Montana, and California.
A chapter is devoted to Jonas Kryder, father of "Sol" Kryder.
A brief outline of the Revolutionary War ancestors of Joseph and
Elizabeth (Johnson) Kemmerer is presented.
Indexed; illustrated.
Cloth—$15.50—323pp------------------------------------- Vendor #D1521

3527 - THE FRANCIS REDFEARN FAMILY by Louise Redfern Pells. 1982.
Francis Redfearn (1777-1858) was born in Durham County; his wife,
Ruth Milner (1779-1857) was born in Muker, Yorkshire, England.
They married in Muker and six of their children were born there.
The family came to America in 1830 with three young adult sons
and three teenage daughters. After farming briefly in Wayne County,
Ohio they moved to Hancock County, where five of their children
married.
In the 1840's all the families but the youngest son, Joseph, moved to
Jo Daviess Counth, Illinois and the contiguous Lafayette County,
Wisconsin. Joseph remained in Hancock and Wood Counties, Ohio
all his long life.
The allied families into which the daughters married: Charles
Worthington Goldsborough, Robert L. Levitt, John M. Aten.
Son Peter married Elizabeth Emery; sons Francis and Joseph married
Elizabeth and Ann Phillips (relationship undetermined), both natives
of Pennsylvania.
Descendants are found in Iowa, the Dakotas, Washington and
California.
Since two grandsons of Francis and Ruth Redfearn married two Lash
sisters, one large section of the book is devoted to the ancestors
and descendants of Joseph and Susanna (Greenawalt) Lash of West-
moreland County, Pennsylvania and later Ohio and Nebraska.
Indexed; illustrated.
Cloth—$30.00—810pp------------------------------------- Vendor #D1521

3528 - LETTERS TO A PRAIRIE WIFE compiled by Elizabeth H. Gardner and
Sally H. Sauer. 1978.
A unique view of everyday family life in the Midwest (Ohio, Illinois,
Indiana) from 1850—1878, provided by over 100 letters saved by family
members. Not indexed but genealogy charts, pictures, maps included.
Family names included: Morey, Perham, Perry, Stubbs, Wadleigh,
Whitcomb.
Paper—$8.00—125pp------------------------------------- Vendor #D1526

3529 - ANCESTORS AND DESCENDENTS OF JAMES AND ALTHEA LOOSE
JOHNSTON, AND ALLIED FAMILIES by A. Montgomery Johnston. 1983.
307 photographs, 20 full page genealogy charts, Indexes of 4,000 names
and 600 places. A fascinating combination of family history, photo-
graph album (many more than 100 years old), and genealogy, containing brief biographical and autobiographical sketches, anecdotes,
and genealogies. Full attention has been paid to both matriarchal
and patriarchal lines.
Families included: Bennett of Groton, Massachusetts (back to England
1632); Criss of Clarksburg, West Virginia (back to Ireland 1720);
Gay of Rockbridge County, Virginia (back to Lancaster, Pennsylvania
1720); Johnston of Harrisonburg, and Rockbridge County, Virginia

(back to Lancaster, Pennsylvania 1740); Loose of Berks County,
Pennsylvania (back to Germany 1723); Maitland of Clarendon, Canada
(back to Paisley and Lauderdale, Scotland); Montgomery of Rockbridge
County, Virginia (back to Lancaster, Pennsylvania 1720); Palm of
Palmyra, Pennsylvania (back to Bavaria, Germany 1718); Round of
Manassas, Virginia (back to Conanicutt Island, Rhode Island 1640).
Other frequently mentioned families include: Smith, Lawrence,
Moore, Greene, Dodge, Wilson, Shattuck, Tarbell, Brown, Miesse,
Elliott, and Johnson. Beautifully printed on 70 pound textured paper.
11"x8½".
Cloth—$55.00—Paper—$45.00—420pp----------------------- Vendor #D1530

3530   - LINEAGE OF LIBBIE LUCINDA LEWIS by Alexis Ann Kolb. 1984.
Elizabeth L. (Norton) Lewis 1864-1940. Twelve generations in America.
Surnames: Babcock, Bassett, Bell, Bishop, Bushnell, Champion,
Codman, Cody, Cook, Fanning, Gillett, Griswold, Holocombe, Jordan,
Norton, Owen, Partridge, Peck, Phelps, Post, Rix, Skiff, Sprague,
Stone, Thacher, Tracy, Whitney. Index.
Paper—$18.00—apx. 200pp-------------------------------- Vendor #D1531

3531   - MARTIN SNYDER (SCHNEIDER) AND SOME OF HIS DESCENDANTS
by Mrs. Viola E. Moak. 1982.
Palatine German settler Martin Snyder (Schneider) and descendants
1698 to 1982. Includes maps of old Germany where he came from,
and old Saugerties, Ulster County, New York, where he settled 1726;
illustrations, family pictures, deeds, letters, documents, events of
Revolutionary War, genealogy of many descendants of his fourteen
children, some genealogy of Mackey, Gifford, Lobdell, Norton,
Barkman families married to Snyders.
Documented, Indexed.
Paper—$27.00—205pp------------------------------------- Vendor #D1532

3532   - THE TRUE FAMILY—SOME HENRY TRUE DESCENDANTS IN TEXAS
by Charles W. True, Jr. 1981.
History and genealogy of Ancestors, Descendants and Allied Families
of Margaret Wade and Charles Sumner True of Nueces County, Texas.
320 pages, illustrated, indexed, with 66 pages genealogy including
progenitor Henry True of Salem ca 1633, Salem, Massachusetts, a
brief chronology of early allied families Dudley, Cotton, Gordon,
Blaisdell, Perkins, Pike, Bradbury, Greeley and Ward and later,
Wade, Polk, Spann, Moores, Hines, Watts, Brown, Jung, Lehne,
Kuenemann, Edwards, Sanders, Conger, Strunk, Glover, and
several other lines.
Cloth—$40.00—320pp------------------------------------- Vendor #D1534

3533   - SOME HENRY TRUE DESCENDANTS ON THE FRONTIER by Charles
W. True, Jr. 1984.
Brings together several genealogy collections of the descendants in-
cluding those of Art, Mark and Dr. H. A. True with some exceptions
as those by Lois True, Stephen G. True and Don Lawse. Includes
briefs from journals, memoirs, first hand reports and the Salem
Witch Trials. Brief allied family chronology of Dudley, Cotton,
Bradbury, Brannan, Conger, Gordon, Lehne, March, Pike and
Andrew Ward. Index includes 1,900 surnames and 3,000 descendants
named True.
Cloth—$32.00—366pp------------------------------------- Vendor #D1534

3534   - WILLIAMS NEWSLETTER by Donald E. Ramage.
Published in July and December. $3.00 per issue. Free queries.
National in scope.
Paper—$3.00/issue—8-12pp------------------------------Vendor #D1536

3535   - COZYN/COZINE, VOLUME I by Mrs. E. T. Dorr.
In 1622, sixteen Dutch farmers living at the Bowery on Manhatten
Island began negotiations to buy a large tract of land between the
Hudson and Hackensack Rivers. One of these farmers was the pro-
genitor of this record, Gerritsen Cozyn, a wheelwright from Putten in
North Holland. This volume contains a well organized record of
Gerritsen's descendants. Little is known of Gerritsen's wife Vroutje

except that she was the mother of five children all born in New Amsterdam and baptised in The Dutch Reformed Church of New York. This volume, first in a set of two, charts the known descendants of Gerritsen for five generations through his children: Gerrit who married Belitje Jacobs Quick (the author's line); Margrietje who married first Herman Theuniszen, second Pieterse Haring and third Daniel de Clark; Hendrick (no records found); Geertje who married Andria Jureans; and Elsje (no records found).
Biographical narrations, photographs, copies and transcripts add interest and backing to this fine record. Illustrated, table of contents, indexed.
Paper— $20.00— 100pp-------------------------------------- Vendor #D1537

3536   - THE COYER CLAN AND THE CARRIER CONNECTION, 2d Ed., by John Edward Armstong. 1982.
This is a second edition of a condensed story of one branch of the Coyer family, and contains corrections and additions for the first eleven generations, restates the twelfth generation to include corrections and information not available earlier, and presents for the first time generation thirteen. The surname was originally French, Carrier.
Three hundred years of the Carrier/Coyer family is covered, starting with Jean Carrier and his wife Jeanne Dodier in Xaintes (Saintes) France early in the 17th Century. A lineal relationship is traced to Louis Jolliet, 1645-1700, the famed Mississippi River explorer. Other noteworthy ancestors include Gabriel Gosselin, Cardinal Begin, and Monseigneur Bourget. It focuses chiefly on ancestors and descendants of the three sons of Louis Coyer (1808-1886) and Margaret Deschene (1812-1892). They were: Louis, 1828-1911; Nelson, 1831-1915, and Edward, 1835-1914. It tells of the career of Private Joseph Coyer in the Civil War and his death in battle. The settlement trail of this family leads from St. Lawrence County, New York to Dodge County, Wisconsin to Minnesota.
A 30-page index is included, as well as some photos and several ancestor charts.
Paper—$18.00— 175pp----------------------------------- Vendor #D1538

3537   - GABRIEL PURDY, HIS ANCESTORS AND DESCENDANTS by Clayton C. Purdy. 1983.
Focused on the Purdy's of New England and Nova Scotia.
Paper—$22.50— 500pp----------------------------------- Vendor #D1539

3538   - THE STEVENS FAMILIES OF NOVA SCOTIA, REVISED EDITION by Robert Kim Stevens, Cj Stevens. 1983.
29 Stevens/Stephens/Stephen families who settled in Nova Scotia before Confederation. Fully indexed.
Paper—$25.00— 688+pp---------------------------------- Vendor #D1539

3539   - THE SALYER FAMILY—GENEALOGY AND RECORDS OF THEIR FIRST 250 YEARS IN AMERICA by Elisabeth L. W. Salyer. 1982.
Documented, illustrated, indexed.
Included are land surveys and grants, deeds, wills, inventories, marriage records, court records, maps, pictures and background history of the Salyers and allied families in North Carolina, Virginia and Kentucky.
Cloth—$52.00— 688pp----------------------------------- Vendor #D1542

3540   - THE COPENHAVER FAMILY OF SMYTH COUNTY, VIRGINIA compiled by Mildred (Manton) Copenhaver and Robert Madison Copenhaver, Jr. 1981.
A documented record of the descendants of Frederick and Eve Copenhaver, who came to Smyth County, Virginia, around 1800. Family line to 1728 emigrant. Thoroughly indexed.
Cloth—$33.90— 550pp----------------------------------- Vendor #D1543

3541   - THREADGILLS, BOOK II compiled by Janis Heidenreich Miller and Wordna Threadgill Wicker. 1983.
A more comprehensive genealogy than the first book with thousands of additions and changes to descendants of Deodatus Threadgill.

Extensive searching of court records has proven many more relationships. Completely indexed.
Cloth—$35.00—330pp-- Vendor #D1544

3542 - ROBERT CHAPMAN—DAVID THOMSON ALLIED FAMILY LINES by Dr. Dorothy Chapman Saunders. 1983.
93 allied lines from original emigrants, via descendants to author, from Robert Chapman, Saybrook, Connecticut 1635 and David Thomson, Portsmouth, New Hampshire 1623.
Related families: (Chapman) Baker, Bancroft, Bate, Berry, Bigge, Billiou, Bird, Bliss, Boyce, Buckland, Bushnell, Clarke, Collins, Crocheron, Curtice, Dayton, DuBois, Dutch, Freeman, French, Gould, Griggs, Harker, Hill, Hodgkins, Ingalls, Jessup, Jones, Key(es), Kirtland, Lacqueman, Lambe, Larzalere, Leeke, Loockermans, Look, Lord, Ludlam, Morse, Palmer, Pratt, Shaw, Sheather, Silsby, Southwick, Spencer, Steele, Stiles, Stowe, Stratton, Wellman, Wilkins, Withington.
(Thomson) Albee, Alley, Andrews, Bennett, Blower, Bor(d)eman, Bosworth, Brackett, Brownell, Burgess, Car(e)y, Darlin, Davis, Deighton, Francis, Gaunt, Gladding, Godfrey, Graves, Kin(g)sman, Lin(d)sey, Munro, Negus, Oxx, Pearce, Peckham, Pigge, Potter, Richmond, Rogers, Streete, Wagoner, Wardwell, Wight, Wilbore, Wood, Woodland, Wooley. Indexed.
Cloth—$25.00—349pp-------------------------------------- Vendor #D1545

3543 - HENRY RICE, THE PIONEER GRISTMILLER OF TENNESSEE, AND HIS TWELVE CHILDREN by Melvin Weaver Little. 1983.
Featuring also these surnames of sons-in-law and other descendants: Bailey, Brim, Miller, Morrow, Smith, Spence, Tuttle, Watson, Wilson. Fully indexed with maps and charts; also 96 District of South Carolina Land Records and East Tennessee.
Paper—$18.00—312pp------------------------------------- Vendor #D1546

3544 - JAMES AND ALVIN SANDERS, LIVESTOCK JOURNALISTS OF THE MIDWEST by Richard B. Helmer. 1984.
A history of Sanders/Saunders families. Descendants of Samuel Sanders (1766-1846) are traced from Rockbridge County, Virginia; Henry Sanders (1788-1862); James Sanders (1832-1899); Alvin Sanders (1860-1948). States: Virginia, Kentucky, Ohio, Iowa, Illinois. Related families: Reid, Rodgers, Ralston, Hildebrand. Full surname index and source appendix.
Cloth—$21.00—apx. 180pp-------------------------------- Vendor #D1547

3545 - OUR CRAWFORD COUNTY ILLINOIS HERITAGE compiled by Donna Gowin Johnston. 1983.
Some early pioneers of Crawford County, their nativity and known descendants. Many of these families were in this area before Illinois became a state.
Genealogies and biographical histories for Allen, Bailey, Enlow, Ford, Gowin, Hicks, Highsmith, Leeman, Littlejohn, Martin, Rash, Sanders, Thomas and Waggoner. Allied lines include: Higgins, Jones, Lindsay, Midgett, Montgomery, Paddick, Prier, Rich, Shipman, Taylor, Weger and many more. Numerous documents, over 200 pictures, completely referenced, and a complete index of 14,000 names. 8½"x11".
Cloth—$40.00—740pp------------------------------------ Vendor #D1548

3546 - A TALE OF SAMUEL GORTON INCLUDING ONE LINE OF DESCENT by Martha Stuart Helligso. 1980.
(1592-1677) of Rhode Island.
Paper—$6.00—31pp------------------------------------- Vendor #D1549

3547 - A TALE OF JOHN MASON INCLUDING ONE LINE OF DESCENT by Martha Stuart Helligso. 1982.
(1600-1672) of Connecticut.
Paper—$15.00—90pp----------------------------------- Vendor #D1549

3548 - CAPTAIN MICHAEL PIERCE INCLUDING ONE LINE OF DESCENT by Martha Stuart Helligso. 1981.
(1615-1676) of Massachusetts.
Paper—$15.00—85pp----------------------------------- Vendor #D1549

3549   - GEORGE MASON[1] INCLUDING ONE LINE OF DESCENT AND RELATED
LINES OF DEMOURVELL, FOWKE, FRENCH, LEE, NEALE, PRESLY,
RODHAM, SPENCE, STURMAN, TALBOTT, THOMPSON, THOROUGH-
GOOD AND YOUELL by Martha Stuart Helligso. 1983.
(1629-1686) of Virginia.
Paper—$15.00—125pp-- Vendor #D1549

3550   - THE ANCESTORS AND DESCENDANTS OF JAMES MONTANEY
(1799-1857) by Lois Stewart. 1983.
Fourteen generations of Americans, descended from Dr. Johannes
Mousnier de la Montagne (1595-1670) and his first wife Rachel
De Forest, are traced from France ca 1595, to Holland in 1619, Guiana
in 1624, Tobago in 1629, New Amsterdam in 1637, and Albany (Fort
Orange) in 1656. Thereafter, descendants of Dr. Montagne are
followed from Harlem to the Raritan Valley of New Jersey and the
Mohawk Valley of New York.
Descendants are named Montaney, Montanye, Montana. Allied families
include: Avery, Bowers, Buck, Clemons, Davis, Gallup, Gardiner,
Hayes, Kip, Lamphere, Mosher, Nellis, Porter, Quackenbush,
Randall, Reed, Robinson, Rockwell, Silvernail, Slingerland,
Sponable, Stahl, Stowell, Teeple, Timmerman, Van Gorder,
Van Huyse, Van Imbroch, Van Vleck, Veeder, Vermilye, Vosseller,
Walrath, Westfall, Williams, Wintersteen, Youker, Young.
Complete index, 50 pictures, maps, signatures.
Cloth—$25.00—448pp--- Vendor #D1550

3551   - DAVID BOAZ (1806-1876) AND HIS DESCENDANTS, 2 Volumes, by
T. D. Boaz, Jr. and Ann (Riley) Heath. 1982.
Kentucky (especially Paducah), Michigan, California, Florida.
Over 3,500 names, geographical location list, consanguinity chart.
Other families: Brown, Davidson, Downs, Edwards, Ellis, Gough,
Grimm, Hall, Harper, Johnson, Jones, McClure, Moore, Nance, Reed,
Riley, Rives, Schonover, Shaffer, Smith, Sullivan, Swartzell, Taylor,
Thompson, Turner, Whitis, Williams.
Paper—$22.50—734pp--- Vendor #D1553

3552   - JOSHUA BOAZ (1810-1890) AND HIS DESCENDANTS by Thurmond
DeWitte Boaz, Jr. 1981.
Surname list. Index over 1,800 names, geographical location list,
Texas (especially East Texas), Kentucky, California.
Other families: Brown, Cooper, Gough, Holland, McIntosh,
Puryear, Smith, Treadway, West, Williams.
Paper—$12.50—426pp--- Vendor #D1553

3553   - SAMUEL BOAZ (1809-1894) AND HIS DESCENDANTS by Thurmond
DeWitte Boaz, Jr. 1981.
Surname list. Index over 900 names, geographical location list,
Fort Worth, other Texas, Western Kentucky.
Other families: Davis, Elliston, Hovenkamp, Latta, Wright.
Paper—$10.00—205pp--- Vendor #D1553

3554   - GARRETT HENRY RENNEKER (1830-1877) AND HIS DESCENDANTS
by T. D. Boaz, Jr. 1981.
Photographs, surname list, index over 1,300 names, geographical
location list, Arkansas, California, Missouri, Oregon, Texas.
Other families: Bates, Butler, Dally, Pressley, Sawyers, Shryock,
Temple, Thompson, Young.
Paper—$10.00—258pp--- Vendor #D1553

3555   - THE FAMILY OF MRS. J. G. MEACHAM—A RECORD OF DESCENDANTS
OF SUSAN CAROLINE (BOAZ) MEACHAM/WARD (1828-1889) by T. D.
Boaz, Jr. 1974.
Western Kentucky, over 300 names.
Other families: Boaz, Callahan, Farabough, Roberts. Includes
Josephus Smith Boaz family.
Paper—$5.00—85pp--- Vendor #D1553

3556 - THE FAMILY OF MRS. J. B. SNOW—A RECORD OF THE DESCENDANTS OF NANCY ADELINE (BOAZ) SNOW (1833-1902) by T. D. Boaz, Jr. 1974.
Louisiana, Florida, Texas, Kentucky. Over 5000 names.
Other families: Boaz, Bushart, Dillard, Jack.
Paper—$5.00—108pp-- Vendor #D1553

3557 - FREDERICK WILLIAM WENNEKER, JR. (1822-1904) AND HIS DE-SCENDANTS by Thurmond DeWitte Boaz, Jr. and Elnora Mae (Wenneker) Smyser. 1983.
16 photographs, over 1,300 names, geographical location list, Missouri, Arkansas, Illinois, consanguinity chart.
Other families: Dally, Horton, Jenkins, Renneker, Roberts, Smyser, Temple.
Paper—$16.50—274pp--- Vendor #D1553

3558 - THE FAMILY OF MRS. J. S. MURCHISON—A RECORD OF DESCENDANTS OF ANN ELIZA (BOAZ) MURCHISON (1853-1935) by T. D. Boaz, Jr. 1974.
Western Kentucky, over 550 names. Also Alabama.
Other families: Boaz, Craig, Davis, Jonakin, Norman.
Paper—$5.00—92pp-- Vendor #D1553

3559 - FROM BOYT TO BOYETTE—THE DESCENDENTS OF THOMAS BOYET by Wendy L. Elliott, C. G. 1983.
Includes documentation on Boyett, Froneberger, Graves, Headden, Hill, Howell, Jones, King, Langston, Thompson, Whitley, and others in Virginia, North Carolina, Tennessee, Mississippi, Arkansas, Texas, and other southern states.
Cloth—$30.00—252+pp--- Vendor #D1556

3560 - SWINNERTON FAMILY HISTORY by Lt. Col. I. S. Swinnerton.
Quarterly Journal published March/June, September, December.
10 issues per Volume. Commenced 1974.
(Current issue—Volume 5, Number 7) ISSN 0508-6755.
Subscription—$8.00/Vol.—20pp--------------------------------- Vendor #D1558

3561 - SWYNNERTON AND THE SWYNNERTONS by Rev. B. T. Swinnerton.
A short history of a Staffordshire village and of the family of the same name.
Paper—$3.00—24pp--- Vendor #D1558

3562 - SWINNERTON FAMILY TREES (VOLUME I).
A reprint of trees from Volume VII of the *Collections For A History of Staffordshire.*
Paper—$4.00—10pp--- Vendor #D1558

3563 - AN INTRODUCTION TO THE HISTORY OF THE FAMILY OF SWYN-NERTON by The Rev. Charles Swynnerton, F.S.A. Repr.
An introduction written in 1888 to Part II of Volume VII of *Collections For A History of Staffordshire.*
Paper—$3.00—15pp--- Vendor #D1558

3564 - TWO ANCIENT PETITIONS FROM THE PUBLIC RECORD OFFICE CONCERNING SWYNNERTON by The Rev. Charles Swynnerton, F.S.A. Repr.
A reprint of the article from Number 7 of *The Ancestor* (1904).
Paper—$3.00—10pp--- Vendor #D1558

3565 - PULVERTAFT PAPERS: A NEWSLETTER ON THE PULVERTOFTS/PULVERTAFTS by Captain David M. Pulvertaft, R. N.
A family history newsletter printed twice each year in June and December describing research into the Pulvertoft family which lived in Lincolnshire, England, from the end of the 13th Century to the middle of the 19th Century (now extinct) and the Pulvertaft family whose origins were in Cork, Ireland, and are now thinly distributed round the world.
First issue December 1981—A5—free to family members; $1.00 per issue plus P&P to others.
Paper—$1.00/issue--Vendor #D1559

3566 - THE HISTORY AND LINEAGE OF THE PALGRAVES by Derek A.
Palgrave and Patrick Palgrave-Moore.
This book deals with the origin of the surname and discusses the
variants. There are chapters devoted to the principal branches at
North Barningham, Thuxton, Pulham, Ludham, Rollesby and Great
Yarmouth. Branches of the family outside Norfolk and Suffolk are
included and data up to and including 1978 are presented. There is
a comprehensive survey of Palgrave Heraldry and a chapter describing
the foundation of the Palgrave Society to publish the History of the
family and circulate a quarterly magazine.
Cloth—$25.00— 283pp------------------------------------- Vendor #D1560

3567 - THE WYCKOFF HOUSE AND ASSOCIATION, INCORPORATED.
Yearly membership dues: Individual $10.00; Family (husband and
wife) $15.00; Junior 18 and under $5.00. Inquire for five year and
Life Membership.
Write to Membership Chairperson: Mrs. Margaret Moore,
266 Contour Drive, Cheshire, CT 06410
--- Vendor #D1562

3568 - ANNUAL BULLETINS AND NEWSLETTERS—THE WYCKOFF HOUSE
AND ASSOCIATION, INCORPORATED.
1937 thru 1979—as available $2.50 each.
1980 thru 1983—$3.50 each.
Collection of all available 1937 thru 1983—$54.00.
--- Vendor #D1562

3569 - THE WYCKOFF FAMILY IN AMERICA, 2d Ed. 1978, repr. of 1950 ed.
Cloth—$17.00—Paper—$12.00— 650pp----------------------- Vendor #D1562

3570 - THE WYCKOFF FAMILY IN AMERICA, 3d Ed., VOLUME I—NICHOLAS
LINE ONLY. 1980.
Cloth—Members $27.00—Non-Members $37.00— 749pp---------- Vendor #D1562

3571 - THE WYCKOFF FAMILY IN AMERICA, 3d Ed., VOLUME II—TEN
LINES—EXCEPTING NICHOLAS. 1983.
Cloth—Members $32.00—Non-Members $42.00— 567pp---------- Vendor #D1562

3572 - THE OLD WORLD PROGENITORS OF THE WYCKOFF FAMILY.
Repr. of 1937 ed.
Paper—$9.00— 103pp------------------------------------- Vendor #D1562

3573 - MAT(T)HIAS MILESTONES: THE GENEALOGY OF DANIEL MATHIAS,
SENIOR (A SOLDIER OF THE REVOLTUION) OF WESTMORELAND
COUNTY, PENNSYLVANIA AND STARK COUNTY, OHIO by Dorothy
Weiser Seale. 1984.
Includes related Appendix, Life of Michael Zehner/Sanor (Eighth Penn-
sylvania Regiment). German immigrants Mathias and Sanor served in
Revolution in Westmoreland County, Pennsylvania so descendants elig-
ible for DAR and SAR. Son Daniel Jr. married daughter Julyan Sanor.
Mathias Sr. and Jr. families settled 1806 Stark County, Ohio;
Michael Sanor 1804 Columbiana County, Ohio.
Includes full Index, documentation, Historical Background, biogra-
phies and military records of descendants. 100+ family photos, early
Pennsylvania and Ohio land and probate records.
Related families: Albright, Beck, Brifogle, Christman, Cope, Crouch,
Deihl, Dennis, Eldredge, Eshelman, Etchberger, Gilbert, Harris, Hart,
Hickerson, McKean, Olinger, Roland, Seanor/Saner, Sechrist, Sheraw,
Shrader, Slusser, Kemp, Stambaugh, Sweeney, Trump, Walter,
Weiser, Yount.
Cloth—$39.50— 465pp----------------------------------- Vendor #D1563

3574 - JACOB STUTZMAN (?-1775) HIS CHILDREN AND GRANDCHILDREN
by John Hale Stutesman, Jr. 1982.
Related families include: Abbott (Virginia), Baughman (Pennsylvania),
Carter (North Carolina), Dodds (Kentucky and Indiana), Gerhardt
(Baltimore, Maryland), Hars (Orange County, New York, Ohio, Indiana),
Lear (Pennsylvania, Ohio, Indiana), McBain (Indiana), McCorkle
(Pennsylvania, North Carolina, Tennessee, Kentucky, Ohio, Indiana),
Nesbitt (Maryland), Oliver (North Carolina), Randolph (Virginia),

Rinehart (Pennsylvania, Kentucky), Shields (Indiana), Snoddy (North Carolina, Tennessee, Kentucky), Stoner (Pennsylvania, Ohio), Ulrich (Pennsylvania, Maryland), Watkins (Virginia), Whitmore (Pennsylvania, Maryland), Wilson (Kentucky, Indiana).
This book studies a Brethren (Dunker) pioneer of Pennsylvania and Maryland in mid-18th Century and his six children who moved westward across Pennsylvania into Montgomery County, Ohio during last quarter of 18th and first quarter of 19th Centuries. Their children continued west into Indiana, Illinois, Missouri and on to Pacific. Collateral families include Scotch-Irish of mid-18th Century and early Virginia and North Carolina settlers.
Cloth—$15.00—308pp--- Vendor #D1564

3575   - THE TRABUE FAMILY IN AMERICA, 1700-1983 by Charles C. Trabue, IV, M. D. and Julie Trabue Yates. 1983.
Sets forth, separately and according to the sequence of their ages, the children of Antoine Trabue, a Huguenot who arrived in Virginia in 1700. It lists over 7,000 direct descendants and their spouses. Includes pertinent dates and places of births, deaths, marriages and, when available, biographical sketches.
Some allied families are: Smith, Guerrant, Dupuy, Moseley, Bryant, Watkins, Haskins, Clay, Minter, Sublett, Wooldridge, Willson, and Major. Includes photographs and an index of over 12,000 names.
Cover is stamped in gold and imprinted with Trabue coat-of-arms.
Cloth—$32.00—536pp---------------------------------- Vendor #D1565

3576   - REILLY OF BALLINTLEA by Joseph F. Reilly. 1981.
A genealogical study of the Reillys of Ballintlea in Kilrossanty, County Waterford, Ireland with a complete listing of three generations of American descendants of Patrick Reilly and Anastasia O'Brien.
Paper—$3.50—80pp-- Vendor #D1566

3577   - BANTA PIONEERS by Elsa M. Banta.
The history and genealogy of one branch of the Banta family covering eight generations from Epke Jacobse to Hendrick (1), Hendrick (2), Hendrick (3), Hendrick (4), Henry (5), Henry (6), Henry (7) and descendants of Henry (7). Traces Banta family back to 16th Century Friesland [Epke Luuesz (1569-1630)] with family backgrounds of their wives.
Allied families include Westervelt, Hendrickse, Brower, Terhune, Demarest, Stryker, Shuck, Fulton, Hopkins, Stockdale, Altizer, Webber, Conley. Maps and photographs. 300 pages, indexed.
Available from Elsa M. Banta, P. O. Box 93, Soldiers Grove, WI 54655.
Cloth—$21.75—Paper—$16.75—300pp---------------------- Vendor #D1568

3578   - THE ALTIZER BRANCH by Elsa M. Banta. 1983.
The descendants of Emera Altizer, Sr. who emigrated from Bingen, Germany about 1720 to Montgomery County, Virginia. Traces his son, Elias, Sr. to Posey County, Indiana and Elias, Jr. to Grant County, Wisconsin in 1850. Genealogy charts of Emera, Elias, Sr., Elias, Jr. and the children of Elias, Jr.
Maps, illustrations and photos. Xeroxed, with binder.
Paper—$8.00—120pp------------------------------------- Vendor #D1568

3579   - MONMOUTH FAMILIES VOLUME I by Ann Pette Miles. 1980.
Cloth—$35.00—272pp--------------------------------------Vendor #D1570

3580   - A FREED FAMILY HISTORY—ANCESTORS AND DESCENDANTS OF WALTER AND DOROTHY FREED OF WILLIAMSPORT, PENNSYLVANIA by Joyce Wilcox Graff and June Freed Wilcox. 1981.
Includes Antes, Doebler, Youngman, Singer, Starr, Lebkicher, Ludwig, Worman, Wagle, Shoemaker, Paulin, DeWees, Hinkal, Gearhart.
Cloth—$25.00—252pp------------------------------------ Vendor #D1571

3581   - CHRISTOPHER GIST OF MARYLAND AND SOME OF HIS DESCENDANTS, 3d Ed., by Jean Muir and Maxwell J. Dorsey. Repr.
A treasure of documented genealogy, the Dorseys researched records as far back as 1679. Includes reproductions of old documents, wills and letters.
Cloth—$60.00—300+pp----------------------------------- Vendor #D1572

3582   - MARFLEET SOCIETY NEWSLETTER edited by John K. Marfleet.
The *Marfleet Society Newsletter* (first published 1976) is a quarterly
(A4 size) publication relevent to the Marfleet Family.
Available by subscription. ISSN 0308-6380.
Subscription—$2.50/p.a.--Vendor #D1573

3583   - MARFLEET HISTORY edited by John K. Marfleet.
Marfleet History is a half-yearly publication (A5 size) issued free
with alternate issues of the *Marfleet Society Newsletter*.
Available by subscription to the *Marfleet Society Newsletter*.
--- Vendor #D1573

3584   - HALEY AND RELATED FAMILIES by Edward Franklyn Haley. 1979.
The long awaited story of the Haley family, and many other related
families, is now off the press. The book is comprised of 796 pages of
interesting history and genealogy pertaining to the Haley, Gregory,
Stuart, Pigg, Keatts, Collins, Garrett, Scearce, Madison and other
families. The book is bound in durable hardcover bindings,
attractively jacketed, and extensively indexed, allowing each family
to easily trace their own lineage.
Cloth—$30.00—796pp-- Vendor #D1574

3585   - BALL COUSINS, DESCENDANTS OF JOHN AND SARAH BALL AND OF
WILLIAM AND ELIZABETH RICHARDS OF COLONIAL PHILADELPHIA
COUNTY, PENNSYLVANIA by Margaret B. Kinsey. 1981.
Documents estate of Joseph Ball (died 1821 Pennsylvania), its
955 beneficiaries, their ancestors and descendants. Some other
families: Campbell, Chilton, Cleaver, Compton, Custer, Daniels,
Dewees, Fisher, Frank, Green, Hafer, Holloway, Kemper, Kunzman,
McWilliams, Mountjoy, Munford, Pate, Porter, Reeder, Rhoads,
Sailer, Stewart, Supplee, Yocum. Indexed.
Cloth—$20.00—366pp-- Vendor #D1575

3586   - THE CAPERTON FAMILY by Bernard M. Caperton. 1973.
John Caperton, immigrant, and Polly Thompson of Augusta County,
Virginia and Monroe/Giles (Virginia, West Virginia). Children:
Captain Hugh and Rhoda Stodghill (West Virginia); Adam and
Elizabeth Miller.
Cloth—$17.50—239pp-- Vendor #D1576

3587   - EARLY ADVENTURERS ON THE WESTERN WATERS, THE NEW RIVER
OF VIRGINIA IN PIONEER DAYS, 1745-1800, VOLUME I by E. B. Kegley
and Mary B. Kegley. 1980.
Grants, surveys, military records, entries, deeds, tax lists, wills, be-
ginning of Augusta, Botetourt, Fincastle and Montgomery Counties as
they pertain to New River Settlement. Maps, illustrations, photos
and 72 family sketches, including families of Bane, Barger, Beard,
Billups, Bingamin, Black, Boles, Broce, Buchanan, Byrn, Chrisman,
Conrad, Craig, Crewey, Draper, Elswick, Gresham, Harless, Harman,
Haven, Hornbarger, Keister, Kinzer, Kipps, Linkous, Lorton, McCoy,
McDonald, McGee, McMullen, Martin, Peterson, Poppicover(Cofer)
Preston, Price, Ribble, Ritchie, Shell, Smelser, Sperry, Stephens,
Surface, Taylor, Trigg, Vickers, Wall, Westcoat, Wood, Bell, Carty,
Cassiday, Charlton, Christian, Cloyd, Gardner, Grills, Ingles, Penner,
McCorkle, Reilly, Rife, Sallust, Skaggs, Thompson, Whitt, Wiley;
many connecting lines.
Cloth—$27.25—456pp-- Vendor #D1578

3588   - EARLY ADVENTURERS, ON THE WESTERN WATERS, VOLUME II by
Mary B. Kegley. 1982.
Marriage records, land records, wills, lawsuits, petitions of New River
area. Continuation of Volume I. Maps, illustrations, photos and
64 family sketches of founding families of what is now Pulaski County.
Includes: Addair, Anderson, Birch, Bish, Brown, Caddall, Carper,
Cecil, Cloyd, Crouch, Crow, Currin, Eaton, Goldman, Guthrie, Hance,
Hevner, Hickman, Hoge, Howe, Hudson, Ingram, Mairs, Edward and
Nathaniel Morgan, Patton, Pepper, Pickens, Shufflebarger, Sifford,
Starn, Stobaugh, Swope, Taylor, Thompson, Trinkle, Trollinger,

Waggoner, Williamson, Wygal, Wysor, Alford, Allison, Boyd, Crockett, Drake, Draper, Edwards, Feely, Flora, Foster, Galbraith, Honaker, Montgomery, Morehead, Patrick, Runner, Russell, Sayers, Shepherd; many connecting lines.
Cloth—$34.78—515pp--- Vendor #D1578

3589 - MARTIN: A MARTIN FAMILY GENEALOGY—SCOTLAND, IRELAND, NORTH AMERICA by R. G. Nash, M. E. Martin, G. R. Martin, M. W. Martin, and J. A. Martin. 1983.
8½"x11", 130 illustrations, indexed.
Primarily a genealogy of descendants from three Scotch-Irish emigrant brothers from Ireland to Pennsylvania and Canada between 1830 and 1850; but contains considerable history of the Scot immigration to Ireland and the Scotch-Irish to the North America. Most descendants moved west and many have become leaders, teachers, and ministers. Some associated families are: Armstrong, Bailey, Bedford, Boal, Bond, Buck, Cabeen, Copeland, Davis, Delzell, Dodds, Finlay, Gillespie, Gish, Haslett, Hay, Henry, Johnston, Kerr, Kilpatrick, McClurkin, McConahy, McKee, McKnight, Morris, Morrow, Nash, Nelson, Rohrer, Ward, Whitten, Wilson, Wood, Wylie.
Paper—$16.50—539pp-- Vendor #D1581

3590 - NASH: A FAMILY GENEALOGY by Ralph G. Nash. 1983.
8½"x11", 69 illustrations, indexed.
Primarily a family history of descendants from a Revolutionary War soldier, Edward Nash, from Maryland; but contains Nash history and seven appendixes of early Nash statistics. Edward was of Irish descent. His descendants moved to Greene County, Ohio, Warren County, Illinois, and then to all parts West. They intermarried with the Scotch-Irish, primarily.
Other surnames associated with early Nashes were: Ward, Galbreath, McKinney, Gowdy, Martin, Henderson, Wright, Black, Brown, Sisco, Miller, Walker, Hamilton, French, Turnbull, Caldwell, McClaughlin, Graham, Jackson, Watt, Peterson, Harshfield, Thorton, Ballinger, Vogal, Booth, Pence.
Paper—$13.50—229pp--------------------------------------- Vendor #D1581

3591 - ANCESTORS AND DESCENDANTS OF ANNIE REBECCA BETTS, 1850-1916, WILTON, CONNECTICUT by Marjorie Dikeman Chamberlain. 1982.
History/Genealogy charting two lines of descent from Thomas Betts (1625-1688) of Guilford, Milford, and Norwalk, Connecticut, through sons Daniel and James. Collateral families of Mead, Taylor, Comstock, Platt, Hanford, Miles, Hubbard, Cable, Sherwood, Tibbals, Tomlinson, Marvin, Bouton. Pictures, charts, index.
Paper—$12.00—92pp-- Vendor #D1582

3592 - JOSIAH DIKEMAN OF HEMPSTEAD, NEW YORK, AND HIS DESCENDANTS by Marjorie Dikeman Chamberlain. 1984.
History/Genealogy of one line of descent from Josiah and Jane (Pettit) Dikeman through son Isaac and Freelove (Haviland). Pictures, charts, documents, signatures. Another section of genealogy and biographical material of descendants through Josiah's children: Ann, Isaac, Henry, Robert and John, b. between 1780 and 1795. Index.
Paper—$12.00—82pp-- Vendor #D1582

3593 - JOHANNES DYCKMAN OF FORT ORANGE (ALBANY, NEW YORK), AND HIS DESCENDANTS by Marjorie Dikeman Chamberlain. 1986.
Johannes Dyckman was First Clerk of the West India Company in Amsterdam, Holland, arriving in New Amsterdam in 1651, served as Vice-Director of Fort Orange. His descendants, through sons Cornelis and Johannes, had soon spread to New York City, up the Hudson River, to Long Island, to New Jersey and Connecticut, often changing the spelling of the name to Dikeman or Dykeman.
(In process)-- Vendor #D1582

3594 - THE BRICKEY HERITAGE by Raymond Luther Brickey. 1983.
Covering over ten years research of the Brickey family history and
genealogy beginning with the arrival of John Brickey (Jean Bricquet),
a French Huguenot, at Charles Town, South Carolina, in 1680, to the
present generation. 450 page cloth hard back—$39.95 PP.
Cloth—$39.95—450pp-- Vendor #D1584

3595 - A HISTORY OF THE OTSTOT(T) FAMILY IN AMERICA; ALSO BEING
A GUIDE TO THE DESCENDENTS OF JOST AND KATHERINE OTSTADT
by Charles Mathieson Otstot. 1973; Supplements 1974 & 1976.
Jost Otstadt immigrated Berks County, Pennsylvania 1775 from
Gerolsheim/Gross-Bockenheim, Rhine-Pfalz; seven children.
Family migrated Lancaster York Counties, thence Ohio, Indiana,
Illinois and on! +3500 persons recorded, only 550 Otstots.
650 other family names in direct line of descent—fully indexed—include:
Keller, Jung, Dellinger, Altman, Bunyan, Collins, Ellinger, Feaser,
Gram, Hay(e)s, Kauf(f)man, Markhart, Roush, Smith, Stephens,
Tuttle, Wertz, Wright, Wilson. Also 1,200 other family names not in
direct line of descent. Includes many photographs and maps.
A periodic supplements being issued. Soon to be issued: families of
three Otstot sisters married in early 1800's to three Hartman brothers.
Paper—$20.00—942pp-- Vendor #D1585

3596 - "UREN THERE—JOURNAL OF THE UREN FAMILY HISTORY SOCIETY"
edited by Chris. Barrett. 1982.
Quarterly Journal containing biographies, information, technical
articles and historical background to the study of the history of
families of the name and its variant spellings, worldwide.
Paper— £5/yr—8pp-- Vendor #D1587

3597 - JOHN PENDERGRASS OF BUTE COUNTY, NORTH CAROLINA, AND
LANCASTER COUNTY, SOUTH CAROLINA by Robert Allison Pender-
gast. 1980.
John Pendergrass moved to South Carolina 1779, fought on both sides
in Revolution, was murdered by Tories 1783. Widow, three sons, re-
moved to Georgia 1810. Descendants of sons, Nathaniel, John and
Minrod, are traced to present.
Cloth—$20.00—291+pp-- Vendor #D1588

3598 - KIMZEY AND KIMSEY: FAMILY RECORDS FROM 1750—1981 by
Herbert B. Kimzey. 1982.
Records begin with Benjamin Kimzey, who immigrated to Maryland and
Virginia after 1750. Descendants of Benjamin and his brother James
are given in outline form with brief biographical sketches. There is
an index of given names as well as an index of allied families.
Cloth—$15.00—229pp-- Vendor #D1590

3599 - THREADS OF ANCESTORS, TELFORD—RITCHIE—MIZE by Leila
Ritchie Mize and Jessie Julia Mize. 1978, repr. of 1956 ed.
Documented Bible records, wills, deeds, land grants. Many allied
families covered. Family lineage from early ancestors in America,
from Virginia into the Carolinas and Georgia, etc., in four parts.
Indexed. Not copyrighted.
Cloth—$11.50—304pp-- Vendor #D1591

3600 - MIZE GENEALOGY IN AMERICA by Joel Sanford Mize, Claudia Chit-
wood Weller and Jessie Julia Mize. 1984.
Family record begins 1694 in Surry County, Virginia. Migrations from
border counties in southern Virginia to North Carolina, Georgia,
Alabama, Texas, Kentucky, Tennessee, Kansas.
Contents: family groups, United States census records for Mice,
Mise, Mize and allied families. Relationships identified by reference
numbers. Photographs, maps, index. Copyrighted.
Cloth—$20.00—824pp-- Vendor #D1591

3601 - HATHAWAYS OF AMERICA by Elizabeth S. Versailles. 1970.
Descendants of Nicholas Hathway of Taunton, Arthur Hathaway of
Dartmouth, William Hathaway of Virginia and many partial lines.
Cloth—$21.55—1426pp-- Vendor #D1592

3602 - HATHAWAYS 1200—1980 by Elizabeth S. Versailles. 1980.
Supplements *Hathaways of America.*
Cloth—$21.09—621pp------------------------------------- Vendor #D1592

3603 - WILLIAM AND ELIZA (JOHNSON) WOODS OF COUNTY ANTRIM,
IRELAND—THEIR DESCENDENTS AND SOME ALLIED FAMILIES by
J. Robert Woods and Laurence C. Baxter. 1984.
A historical account of the families of forty of the authors ancestors—
the Woods family of Buffalo and Evans, New York; the Massachusetts
families of Bloomfield, Boyce, Buffington, Buffum, Burton, Clark,
Gaskill, Maber, Osborn, Pope, Singletary, Southwick, and Upton of
Essex County; the Baker, Chase, Eldridge, Nickerson, O'Kelly, and
Twining families of Yarmouth; the Cole and Collier families of Plymouth;
the Busby family of Watertown; the Burt and Hathaway families of
Taunton; and the Hinckley and Smith families of Barnstable; the
Sherman, Tripp, and Paine families of Portsmouth, Rhode Island;
the Jackson, Starr, Moore, Wildman, and Yates families of Chester,
Lancaster, and Bucks Counties, Pennsylvania; the Bloomfield, Burton,
Pound, Shotwell, Smith, and Singletary-Dunham families of Essex and
Middlesex Counties, New Jersey; and the Iddenden and Soule families
of County Kent, England. Included is a brief summary of Irish
history ca 1534 to 1660. Also, accounts of actions of the 44th and
116th New York Volunteers in the Civil War. Many wills and land
records are included or identified. All information is referenced.
Appendices A and B list several hundred Woods and Johns(t)one
names found in Irish records--baptisms, deaths, marriages, residence,
wills; also the source of the record is identified.
Indexed; photographs; Bibliography; 6"x9".
Cloth—$35.00—520pp-------------------------------------- Vendor #D1593

3604 - HISTORY AND GENEALOGY OF CAPTAIN JOHN LOCKE OF RYE,
NEW HAMPSHIRE by Arthur H. Locke. Repr. of 1917 ed.
44 illustrations, indexed. Begins with a biographical and historical
sketch of Captain John Locke who landed in Portsmouth, New Hamp-
shire ca 1640 and settled on Locke's Neck in present-day Rye, New
Hampshire and traces his family to the tenth generation. Includes
a small genealogy of the family of Nathaniel Locke of Portsmouth,
New Hampshire, possibly John's brother.
Also has an historical account of the Locke family in England. 6"x9".
Cloth—$32.00—752pp-------------------------------------- Vendor #D1595

3605 - LOCKE GENEALOGY SUPPLEMENT VOLUME I by Donald P. Hayes, Jr.
1979.
13 illustrations, indexed. Supplements the genealogy of Captain
John Locke of Rye, New Hampshire by adding previously unpublished
lines from the fifth to the thirteenth generations. Also has a limited
updating of the genealogy of William Locke of Woburn, Massachusetts.
A twenty-page history of the Locke Family Association traces the
development of the organization responsible for the genealogies. 6"x9".
Cloth—$12.50—360pp-------------------------------------- Vendor #D1595

3606 - LOCKE FAMILY ASSOCIATION NEWSLETTER.
A tri-annual newsletter informing descendants of Captain John Locke
of Rye, New Hampshire about association activities, reunion plans,
available information and new developments in research. The subscription fee includes membership in the association. Published tri-annually.
Subscription—$5.00—4pp------------------------------- Vendor #D1595

3607 - THE RISLEY RECORD by Risley Family Association; edited by Roy
Goold.
Descendants of Richard Risley, Sr. 1610-1648 of Hartford, Connecti-
cut and all Risley, Wrisley, Rizley, Riseley families in America.
Founded 1889. Annual reunions, quarterly newsletter for members
with genealogy, historical and biographical articles, in 7th edition;
updating family genealogy; other publications available.
Send SASE for information.
Paper—10pp/issue------------------------------------- Vendor #D1596

3608 - THE STROSNIDER FAMILY IN AMERICA 1751-1981 by Ruth C.
Strosnider. 1982.
Numbering system, indexed, illustrated and documented.
Paper—$13.00—183pp------------------------------------- Vendor #D1598

3609 - THE BERKEY BOOK by Rev. William A. Berkey and Ruth Berkey
Reichley. 1984.
Descendants of Swiss-Mennonite origin who came to America from
persecution and settled mainly in Pennsylvania, Illinois, Ohio and
Iowa. Eight major spellings: Barkey, Berkey, Berky, Birky, Burkey,
Perkey in forty lines. Related families: Clark, Byers, Eichelberger,
Fischer, Gibson, Gingerich, Good, Heiser, Hochstettler, Ioder, John-
son, Kauffman, Lehman, Litwiller, Martin, Mast, Miller, Oyer,
Reichley, Roth, Saylor, Schrock, Schultz, Springer, Stalter, Sutter,
Unzicker, Yoder, Zehr, Zimmerman and many more.
135 page index with over 14,500 entries.
Cloth—$21.00—560pp------------------------------------- Vendor #D1599

3610 - THOMAS MINOR: DESCENDANTS, 1608-1981 by John A. Miner. 1982.
The most extensive volume on this family currently available. Includes
many biographical sketches, providing insight into life and times of
thousands of descendants down through several key periods in history
of our country. The 75 page index contains extensive background
material on the family, both in America and England, not found elsewhere. Illustrated, reference and indexed; has a large bibliography
for further study.
Cloth—$35.00—1014pp--------------------------------- Vendor #D1600

3611 - THE MINOR DIARIES, 1653-1720 by John A. Miner.
The diary of Thomas Minor, one of only seventeen American diaries
known to exist from the seventeenth century, has been bound in one
volume together with the diary of his son, Manasseh. It provides a
valuable insight into the actual day-by-day lives and times of our
earliest American ancestors.
Cloth—$35.00—403pp---------------------------------- Vendor #D1600

3612 - FINKLEA, EXUM, PURCELL, HYMAN: THEIR ROOTS AND BRANCHES
by Mary K. O'Doherty, C.G. 1984.
A genealogical history of four interrelated families with documentation
and a report by Debrett Ancestry Research, Winchester, England.
History of the Finklea family dates from 1600 in England and from the
migration of Dr. Thomas Finckley to the Virginia Colony prior to 1680.
His great grandson Thomas died in South Carolina before December,
1787. This Thomas was progenitor of Finkleas who migrated to Alabama
in 1820's. Alabama families are well documented with many references
quoted in full.
Section on Exum family identifies seven children (with proof) of
Colonel Benjamin Exum of Revolutionary War. Documentation clarifies
long-standing questions on Exum line. Descendants of Elijah Exum,
son of William and Patience (Purcell), who settled on Pee Dee River
in South Carolina, are named through four generations.
Family history of Pearsall/Purcell establishes relationship with Exum
and allied families (Bardin, Brown, Cain, Culpepper, Davis, Dozier,
Flowers, Gibbs, Hinnant, Hutchinson, Hyman, Myers, Porter, Sweet).
Pedigree chart traces each generation to Rollo, Duke of Normandy,
died A.D. 928. This line has been accepted by authorities including
National Society Magna Charta.
Hugh Hyman first appeared in North Carolina in 1720. His chilren
are listed and lineages of two grandsons and descendants are treated
in detail. These grandsons, Laurence and Eaton, migrated to Big
Swamp, South Carolina, in early 1800's. Connection with Manning
and Rouse families is explained.
Notes and references number 232. Index, 1,268 names. Body text
16 point type for easy reading. pp. xii, 190. 1984. Acid free,
cloth. Price: $40.00; Postage and Handling: $2.00.
South Carolina residents add 4% sales tax.
Cloth—$42.00—190+pp--------------------------------- Vendor #D1601

3613 - THE LATTIMORES. A FAMILY HISTORY by Esther Lattimore Jenkins.
1982.
The only published genealogy of the Lattimore Family in America.
From 1690 to present. Documented. Approximately 7,100 names
and 330 places indexed.
Paper—$17.95—329pp------------------------------------ Vendor #D1608

3614 - DESCENDANTS OF NATHAN E. GROSVENOR AND LAURA FULLER
1794-1973 (WITH HIS ANCESTRY) by Jeannette Grosvenor. 1974.
Removed from Mansfield, Connecticut to Claridon, Ohio 1854/5.
Identifies 400+ descendants in Ohio, Michigan, and Colorado.
382 pictures. Full-page reproductions of a family record, deed,
marriage license. Every name index.
Cloth—$25.00—327pp----------------------------------- Vendor #D1609

3615 - PILGRIM: A BIOGRAPHY OF WILLIAM BREWSTER by Mary B.
Sherwood. 1982.
Cloth—$25.00—272pp----------------------------------- Vendor #D1610

3616 - THE LIVESAY BULLETIN edited by Mrs. Virginia Gress Smith.
Published quarterly: contains genealogical material on Livesay,
Lifsey, Livasey Family. Information on annual three day meetings.
Covers entire United States.
Paper—Donation $8.00 or more—10-14pp-------------------- Vendor #D1611

3617 - THE SMELTZERS OF KILCOOLY AND THEIR IRISH-PALATINE
KISSING COUSINS by Marjorie R. Smeltzer. 1981.
Many branches Canada, United States; maps, photos.
Cloth—$18.45—198pp----------------------------------- Vendor #D1612

3618 - RATLIFF—KELLER, BOOK II, LOUISVILLE, TENNESSEE AND MEMOR-
ABILIA by Carl M. Ratliff, Jr. 1982, partial repr.
Contains 56 page reprint, *History of Louisville, Blount County, Ten-
nessee*, by Love, French and Prather, added maps, etc.
The remainder of the book is memorabilia and family history of the
following families. Only Keller, Crozier and Smith are associated
with Blount or Knox Counties. Ratliff 1642-1982 notes and photos;
Keller, old letters and papers, two booklet reprints *Keller-Wallace
Family Trees and Memories 1306-1965* by Keller(s), and *Lest We Forget*
by Lillian Keller 1973; *Crozier Biography and Ancestory of John Hervey
Crozier 1769-1838* by Lizzie Crozier French; *Woollen Autobiography of
James A. Woollen* b. 1821, written 1900; *Mack, Story of the Family* by
George H. Mack 1874-1968, Mack genealogy to 1740, Pelton to 1720,
and Slocum to 1778; Hall, *Leaves From the Hall Family Tree* by Isadore
Hall Wilson 1924, Colonial Quakers to Indiana in early 1800's;
Charles H. Smith 1881-1953 Obituary.
25 illustrations; 8½"x11"; 505 surname index.
Cloth—$15.00—216pp----------------------------------- Vendor #D1613

3619 - HALLER—HOLLAR—HOLLER GENEALOGY by Amelia C. Gilreath. 1981.
Early Pennsylvania, Virginia and Ohio—300 years—10 generations.
12 years research—indexed—pictures.
Cloth—$30.00—314pp----------------------------------- Vendor #D1614

3620 - ELIZABETH JANE LANIER, HER ANCESTORS FROM CIRCA 1540, AND
DESCENDANTS TO 1982 by Margaret Drody Thompson. 1982.
Including the families of Harold Drody, Alexander McIver, John Lanier
McIver, William Johnson, Matthew Benjamin Floyd, and Sidney Lanier,
beloved Southern Poet.
Paper—$9.50--- Vendor #D1617

3621 - DRADY, DRAWDY, DRODY, DRODDY, DRUDE, AND VARIANTS edited
and published by Margaret Drody Thompson.
Bi-annual magazine of The Genealogical Association For Uncommon
Surnames (researching colonial Virginia surnames).
Paper--- Vendor #D1617

3622 - "THE PIPER" edited and published by Margaret Drody Thompson.
Annual publication for Scottish Heritage of Clan MacIvor Society In
America.
Subscription—$4.50/yr-------------------------------- Vendor #D1617

3623 - THE STEVENS TREE by Joe M. Clark, Jr. 1982.
The Stevens Tree contains a **Family History of Obediah Stevens** born
in Pennsylvania on October 9, 1787 and includes narratives of contributing family members, some of which were kept from the 19th Century
and continues through to the present generations, which amounts to
over 1,000 direct descendants being documented. These family
histories have helped trace the family migration through Ohio, Indiana,
Iowa, Missouri, Oregon, California, and Texas.
Also included are selected pages of Obediah Stevens probate records,
War of 1812 service records, copies of family letters, marriage licenses,
cattle brands, family pictures and over 400 work sheets.
Allied families: Arrowwood, Bassett, Benton, Bilbrey, Bishop, Black-
burn, Bohanan, Booth, Bowe, Bowen, Bruzwits, Burnett, Byars,
Calhoun, Calk, Carroll, Carter, Clark, Collins, Cowan, Crowson,
Daughters, Davis, Dickinson, Dixon, Doolan, Doolittle, Dowlearn,
Eaton, Fair, Foster, Fudge, Franks, Farris, Friberg, Glass, Green,
Hailey, Hammock, Hartley, Hedden, Hicks, Hill, Hoch, Hubler,
Hudgeons, Hunt, Johnston, Keele, Klingalman, Koehler, LaFour,
Lawrence, Lawson, Lightfoot, Ligon, Manness, Mayne, McAlfresh,
McCutchan, McKinney, McMurrey, Midgett, Mitchell, Monk, Moore,
Munson, North, O'Connor, Pace, Parker, Pedeen, Perry, Peters,
Railford, Ratley, Rhodes, Roell, Rouse, Schaeffer, Snead, Sparks,
Socogin, Stubbs, Sullivan, Sumerlin, Sutton, Thompson, Tidwell,
Vick, Webster, Westbrook, Westlake, Westmoreland, Waterman,
Williams, Wolfe, Woods, Weaver.
Cloth—$30.00 plus $3.00 postage.
Cloth—$33.00—550pp--------------------------------------- Vendor #D1618

3624 - THE DESCENDANTS OF PETER MAUCK 1708-1980 by William R.
Wolph. 1981.
Peter Mauck, born in Germany, immigrated to America in 1733,
settling in Frederick County, Virginia, in 1735. First and second
generation descendants lived in Shenandoah County, Virginia, and
later in Sullivan and Washington Counties, Tennessee; Columbiana
County, Ohio; Gibson and Harrison Counties, Indiana; Knox County,
Illinois; and Adair and Knox Counties, Missouri.
Some related families are: Broyles, Crabill, Funkhouser, Heiser,
Pittman, Rhodes, Snapp, Strickler, Zumwalt. 11"x8½".
Cloth—$22.00—256pp--------------------------------------- Vendor #D1619

3625 - "YOU SHOULD MEET THEM"—YOUR ANCESTORS AND DESCENDANTS
OF WARNER, SANDERSON, DICKINSON, LEWIS, MARTIN, PAYNE,
DANIEL, HOLLIDAY, BICKEL, MURDY, DAVIS, MASSIE, 1600-1983
AND HISTORICAL ACCOUNTS by Elizabeth Warner Holliday Davis. 1983.
Centered around Warner of "UpHome" (West Virginia) 1800's—1900's;
Warner (Massachusetts 1700's) md. 1861 Dickinson (Warner of Vir-
ginia 1600's); and sections on Holliday, Davis, and Massie. Luther
Warner of Springfield and Whately, Massachusetts, md. 1700's Stebbins.
Their son md. 1815 Sanderson and moved 1840's to Fayette County,
(West) Virginia, built 1858 pre-Civil War home, "UpHome," md. 1861
Dickinson (ancestors were Landcraft, Meriwether, and Warner of
Virginia 1600's). Their son md. 1899 Daniel (ancestors were Spencer,
Payne, Poindexter of Virginia). Their daughter md. 1924 Holliday of
Wood County and settled in Charleston, (ancestors were Bickel, Murdy,
Ganz; Hollidays were from Berkeley County and possibly Winchester,
Virginia, 1700's. A son md. 1830 Custer related to George Washington).
Their daughter md. 1948 Davis, Naval officer, (ancestors from Wales
and Buckingham Courthouse, Virginia, md. 1800's Sprouse. A son
md. Hoover. Their son md. Massie, daughter of Showalter. Massie
ancestors were from Falling Springs Valley of Virginia, Hot Springs
and Sinking Springs, whose ancestors were Ryals, Daggs related to
Caesar Rodney, and Bowler Cocke).
Massachusetts: Several page account of colonial Whately, Indian Wars,
Minutemen.
Virginia: George Washington connection, "Castle Hill" in Charlottes-
ville, "Little Castle Hill," "White Hall" near Lynchubrg. other.

West Virginia: Fayette, Kanawha, Summers, Wood Counties. Brief account of state's emigrants from Virginia/Pennsylvania and Indian conflicts. Civil War times, old letters, 1910 children's letters, 1930 grandchildren's adventures on Warner Farm "UpHome." In Charleston, Depression through World War II.
Washington, D. C.: Historical eyewitness accounts of President Roosevelt's funeral procession, President Kennedy's funeral procession, Nixon's Inaugural Parade, and President Reagan's Inaugural Parade (and hostage release day).
Three Journals at end by author's ancestors: Dr. Walker 1750 explored Virginia into Kentucky; Captain Massie 1808 East Coast trip Alexandria to New York; Hudson Meriwether Dickinson, Civil War (West) Virginia, New River Gorge, and travels in United States. Enjoyable. 25 charts throughout. 300 illustrations. Extensive index. 600+ pages, 8½"x11", library bound hardcover. LC 83-71329. ISBN: 0-9611384-0-8. Publisher may reprint.
Cloth—600+pp-- Vendor #D1621

3626   - THE SQUIRE, DANIEL AND JOHN BOONE FAMILIES IN DAVIE COUNTY, NORTH CAROLINA by James W. Wall, Flossie Martin and Howell Boone. 1983, repr. of 1982 ed.
A thoroughly researched study utilizing deed books, court minutes, church and cemetery records to document the presence in Davie County of Squire Boone (1696-1765) , his eleven children including Daniel Boone (1734-1820) and Squire's nephew John Boone (1727-1803) and their families.
Paper—$3.00—12pp-- Vendor #D1622

3627   - HULSEY RESEARCHER by Lou Pero.
Searching all lines.
Montly newsletter, back issues 1980-83. $5.00 for one year.
Paper—$5.00/yr--- Vendor #D1623

3628   - HARDY AND HARDIE, PAST AND PRESENT by Dr. H. Claude Hardy and Rev. Edwin Noah Hardy. Repr. of 1935 ed.
Hardy and Hardie, Past and Present, by Dr. H. Claude Hardy and Rev. Edwin Noah Hardy. Reprint of 1935 edition. 6,200 indexed Hardy names; 9,000 indexed non-Hardy names. Colored Coat-of-Arms. Chapter headings as follows:
Thomas Hardy of Bradford, Massachusetts (628 pages);
John Hardy of Isle of Wight County, Virginia (90 pages);
Major Jonas Hardy;
George W. Hardy of Bradford County, Pennsylvania;
Richard Hardy of Concord, Massachusetts and Stamford, Connecticut;
Josiah Hardy of Virginia and Masachusetts;
Samuel Hardy of Beverly, Massachusetts;
Hugh Hardy of Juaniata Valley, Pennsylvania;
John Hardy of Salem, Massachusetts;
Hardies of Scotland and America.
Cloth—$29.95 PP; 1300 pages; 8½"x5½".
Cloth—$29.95—1300pp-------------------------------------- Vendor #D1625

3629   - ROGERS AND RELATED FAMILIES OF ESTILL COUNTY, KENTUCKY by Ellen Rogers and Diane Rogers. 1981, repr.
52 related families; 25 pictures; Indexed.
Cloth—$25.00—375pp------------------------------------- Vendor #D1626

3630   - CAPTAIN MATTHEW ARBUCKLE by Joseph C. Jefferds, Jr. 1981.
A Documentary Biography of Captain Matthew Arbuckle, Indian fighter and hero of the Battle of Point Pleasant, with some data on antecedents and descendants! Illustrations, photographs.
Cloth—$15.00-- Vendor #D1627

3631   - BLEDSOE GENEALOGY by Banks McLaurin, Jr. 1984.
To be published semi-annually, 50 pages per issue, beginning Summer, 1984.
Paper—$12.00—50pp/issue---------------------------------Vendor #D1496

3632 - BAUCOM GENEALOGY by Banks McLaurin, Jr. 1983.
Published in one or more issues yearly to supplement the Baucom
book by B. E. Bawcom, and increase interest in Baucom, Bawcom,
Baughcom, Balcombe, Balkcom genealogy.
Paper—$10.00—100pp-------------------------------------- Vendor #D1496

3633 - TILTON TERRITORY: A HISTORICAL NARRATIVE—WARREN TOWN-
SHIP, JEFFERSON COUNTY, OHIO 1775-1838 by Robert H. Richardson.
The activities of John Tilton, his family, and his associates, who were
the early settlers in northwestern Virginia and eastern Ohio.
Cloth—$10.00—300pp-------------------------------------- Vendor #D1630

3634 - A TIME AND PLACE IN OHIO by Robert H. Richardson.
A chronological account of certain historical and genealogical miscellany
in eastern Ohio, and specifically in Warren Township, with over fifty
historic photographs. There are over 3,000 names in the index with
a capsule genealogy on many, including Tilton, West, Carpenter,
Liston, Stringer, and many others.
Cloth—$19.95—365pp-------------------------------------- Vendor #D1630

3635 - THE LINKOUS FAMILY HISTORY by Clovis E. Linkous. 1982.
A German soldier named Heinrich Linckost was in the Revolutionary
War and remained in America. He changed his name to a unique one,
Henry Linkous (1742-1822). He settled in Montgomery County, Vir-
ginia. The indexed, hardback book containing 367 pages is the story
of his trail and contains over 5,000 of his descendants through both
male and female lines in thirteen generations.
Cloth—$22.00—367pp-------------------------------------- Vendor #D1631

3636 - HAWBAKER DESCENDANTS FROM 1737-1978 by Eliphalet H. Hawbaker
and Goldie Hawbaker Clark. 1978.
Paper—$5.00—147pp-------------------------------------- Vendor #D1632

3637 - PEARCE, BARTLETT, MATTHEWS, SMART, AND ALLIED FAMILIES
by James Alonzo Matthews, Jr.; partially updated by Lucille Pearce.
1983. 11"x8½".
The Pearce line has been traced back to 10th Century England, Percy,
Pearce, Pierce, Peirce, Pearse, no matter the spelling, origins were
the same. Bartletts are presented from 11th Century England's Adam
Barttelot. Matthews family goes back to 9th Century, Ludolf, Duke of
Saxony. Also brief origins of Allison, Harnsberger, Oswald, Tschudi
(Judy), and Vincent; and brief synoptical records of Bogardus,
Brouwer, Bussing, DuBois, Jansen, Vermilyea and Waldron families of
New York.
Allied families also include: Allin, Andersen, Anger, Atkinson, Atte-
bery, Bailey, Ballard, Baker, Barker, Bartolini, Berry, Borden,
Boughner, Brewer, Britt, Brown, Buckles, Burger, Burleson, Calla-
way, Cason, Challis, Coles, Collins, Cooper, Cornelison, Cox, Creed,
Dalenberg, Daniels, Davis, Delashmutt, Dollarhide, Drury, East,
Edwards, Evans, File, Foster, Giger, Gonterman, Gore, Greenlee,
Griffith, Hagler, Harris, Hauskins, Herrin, Hill, Howard, Hoxsey,
Huffman, Hunt, Johnson, Jones, Keller, Keown, King, Kirkpatrick,
Long, Manning, Martin, McAdams, McCoy, McMichael, Miles, Miller,
Mitchell, Norwood, Olive, Perkins, Powers, Ramey, Randle, Roberts,
Robinson, Rogers, Shivers, Smith, Stallings, Stepp, Stinson, Sutton,
Tabor, Taylor, Teas, Thomas, Thompson, Tye, Warderman, Warren,
Whiteside, Williams, Willeford, Wilson, Wood, Wright, Young and
many more. Includes pioneer settlers in almost all states and Canada.
Indexed over 11,000 names. Limited Edition 300 copies.
Cloth—$38.20—392pp-------------------------------------- Vendor #D1633

3638 - BUTTON FAMILIES OF AMERICA by R. Glen Nye. 1971.
Fully indexed history of three major Button lines in America.
Cloth—$21.35—941pp--- Sold Out ------------------------ Vendor #D1634

3639 - MORRISON FAMILY: JOSIAH, WILLIAM, DANIEL IN MONTGOMERY
COUNTY, TENNESSEE BY 1800 edited by Clara (Hamlett) Robertson.
Goal to find colonial forebears of early Morrison families in Middle
Tennessee. New publication. Queries free.
Paper—$1.00/yr—4pp/qtly-------------------------------- Vendor #D1635

3640   - HAMLET(T)-HAMBLET-HAMLIT NEWSLETTER: VIRGINIA, NORTH
      CAROLINA, SOUTH CAROLINA, TENNESSEE, KENTUCKY, 1800 edited
      by Clara (Hamlett) Robertson.
      Goal to find colonial forebears of Hamletts in Montgomery County,
      Tennessee by 1800. Queries free. New publication.
      Paper—$1.00/yr—4pp/qtly - Vendor #D1635

3642   - ROBERTSON-ROBINSON-ROBERSON-NEWSLETTER: LOUISA-
      ALBEMARLE COUNTIES, VIRGINIA BY 1781 edited by Clara (Hamlett)
      Robertson.
      Goal to find forebears of Louisa-Albemarle County Robertson/Robinson/
      Roberson families. New publication. Queries free.
      Paper—$1.00/yr—4pp/qtly - Vendor #D1635

3643   - ROTHWELL-ROATHWELL-RAUTHWELL-ROUTHWELL NEWSLETTER:
      LOUISA-ALBEMARLE COUNTIES, VIRGINIA BY 1781 edited by Clara
      (Hamlett) Robertson.
      Goal to find forebears of Louisa-Albemarle County Rothwell families.
      New publication. Queries free.
      Paper—$1.00/yr—4pp/qtly - Vendor #D1635

3644   - SWAMP YANKEE FROM MYSTIC by James H. Allyn. 1980.
      An account of a "family, region, and its roots." Twelve and more
      generations of one family with the first settlers in Massachusetts,
      Rhode Island, and Connecticut, many with ancestors from Great
      Britain. Ten pages of genealogical tables. One hundred ten families,
      including: Allyn, Arnold, Avery, Babcock, Brewster, Chesebrough,
      Clark(e), Crandall, Denison, Fenner, Greenman, Hempsted, Latham,
      Maxson, Minor (Miner), Morgan, Packer, Palmer, Park(e), Potter,
      Stillman, Swan, Winthrop.
      Map of southeastern Connecticut and southern Rhode Island. Indexed.
      Paper—$10.95—194pp - Vendor #D1636

3645   - HOBBS AND RELATED FAMILIES by Ralph L. Hobbs. Repr.
      Fully indexed, hard bound, cloth cover. Contains genealogical infor-
      mation from thirteen early states relating to Hobbs and families they
      married into. Hobbs in Revolutionary War, Confederate service
      records. Many branches of the Hobbs family included. Originally
      published in 1976, republished 1983. Volume II will be published
      late 1984.
      Cloth—$25.00--413pp - Vendor #D1637

3646   - "McCLINTOCK ANCESTORS AND DESCENDANTS" by Maureen
      McClintock Rischard. 1979.
      This book is a compendium of McClintock genealogies. It presents the
      statistics and facts as listed in the original source which is named.
      The index contains 34,000 names; 12,225 are McClintocks; 843 different
      surnames. Surnames mentioned ten times or more are: Bennet,
      Borgeson, Brown, Byrd, Clark, Craig, Curtice, Handley, Jackson,
      Jones, Kerr, Mann, Martin, McCormick, Mehaffey, Miller, Moore,
      Peterson, Ross, Shields, Smith, Thompson, Waters, Williams, and
      Young.
      Paper—$15.00—125pp - Vendor #D1640

3647   - THE ABBOTTS OF WEST VIRGINIA by David A. Turner. 1981, repr.
      Paper—$10.00—89pp - Vendor #D1641

3648   - WEBB FAMILIES OF THE VIRGINIAS by Ronald R. Turner. 1983.
      Paper—$11.00—162pp - Vendor #D1641

3649   - GENEALOGY OF THE FLOYD COOK FAMILY by David A. Turner.
      1980, repr.
      Paper—$10.00—47pp - Vendor #D1641

3650   - DESCENDANTS OF JOHN AND ELIZABETH SANSOM by Van Edwin
      Turner. 1982.
      Paper—$8.00—72pp - Vendor #D1641

3651   - DESCENDANTS OF THOMAS AND ESTHER BAXTER by Ronald R.
      Turner. 1982.
      Paper—$8.00—60pp - Vendor #D1641

3652 - PORTRAIT OF NEW CANAAN, THE HISTORY OF A CONNECTICUT TOWN by Mary Louise King. 1981.
This book chronicles the important town events, blending with the lives of the movers and shakers who helped shape the town. Families included are: Ayres, Benedict, Comstock, Hoyt, Lockwood, Raymond, Richards, St. John, Silliman and Weed.
Cloth—$16.00—342pp------------------------------------- Vendor #D1642

3653 - THE THOMAS PHILLIPS FAMILY, FIRST EDITION by Mabel Phillips Baker. 1981.
A family history of Thomas Phillips, Revolutionary War Veteran, his ancestry and his descendants. His ancestor, Rev. George Phillips came to America from England with Governor Winthrop to establish churches in the Massachusetts Bay Colony. George Phillips born 1593 in Raynham, County of Norfolk, England, son of Christopher Phillips, was educated at Gonville and Caius College, School of Religion, Cambridge, England. He was indispensable in assisting with the establishment of the colonies.
The first part is devoted to his descendants; last part to his ancestry. Family lines researched were Phillips, Walker, Holland, Rowan, Harris, Scott, Collett, Hinkle, Poling in Virginia and Massachusetts.
The book has a blue hard cover; 5½"x8½"; illustrated; indexed.
Cloth—$32.00—219pp------------------------------------- Vendor #D1643

3654 - THE REV. JOHN ROWAN FAMILY, FIRST EDITION by Mabel Phillips Baker. 1980. 162pp.
John Rowan, b. 1749, Baltimore, Maryland served in the Revolutionary War. He returned to Maryland where he married Elizabeth Howard, daughter of Thomas Cornelius Howard. After her father died they moved to West Virginia in 1808. They made their home in Randolph County near Mabie, West Virginia. He purchased land which he lost in fraudulent land deals. He was a school teacher and a Methodist minister, performing many of the marriages in the area. They had nine children: John, Thomas Cornelius Howard, Joseph, William, Francis, Nancy, Elizabeth, Bathany, Labanna.
The first part of the book is about the descendants; last part traces the family back to Ireland, Scotland, England, France.
Family lines researched were Rowan, Phillips, Howard, Worthington, Ridgely, Greenberry, Dorsey, Duvall, Lovelace, Gorsuch, Aucher, Barnes, Cornwallis, Sandys, Wilsford, Wroth, Rich, Garrard.
This book is blue hard cover; 5½"x8½"; illustrated; indexed.
Cloth—$25.00—162pp------------------------------------- Vendor #D1643

3655 - GAUNT—GANTT FAMILY: SOME OF THE DESCENDANTS OF PETER GAUNT OF SANDWICH, MASSACHUSETTS by Mary Chalfant Ormsbee. 1984.
Contains biographies of 41 descendants in Massachusetts, New Jersey, Pennsylvania, Nebraska. Related families of Butler, Fulton, Lobaugh, Ridgeway, Shourds, Smith, and Thompson. Family letters.
Indexed; illustrated.
Cloth—$15.50—200pp------------------------------------- Vendor #D1644

3656 - THE MORIARTY CLAN NEWSLETTER by Dan Moriarty.
The Moriarty Clan is a worldwide family-name newsletter published quarterly, with subscribers in 48 states and 10 countries. See booklet "How to Publish a Worldwide Family-Name Newsletter."
Subscription—$5.00/yr—8pp---------------------------- Vendor #D1645

3657 - UNDERHILL GENEALOGY, VOLUMES 5-6 by Edwin R. Deats and Harry Macy, Jr. 1980.
This two-volume set covers all the Underhill families of North America; the 152-page index contains almost 40,000 names.
Cloth—$50.00/Set—1725pp---------------------------- Vendor #D1646

3658 - GENEALOGY OF THE DYMOND, WILLIAMS, AND RELATED FAMILIES by Robert H. Dymond. 1981.
Related families: Mosher, Booth, Whitlock. Carr. Cooke. Coolbaugh. Davol. Martin. Patton. Sickler. Snyder; recording Northeastern Pennsylvania settlers from New York, New Jersey, and Connecticut.
Indexed, and clothbound.
Cloth—$11.50—256pp------------------------------------- Vendor #D1648

3659   - WATHEN FAMILY ORGANIZATION NEWSLETTER edited by Carol
Collins. 1982.
Surname exchange on all Wathens but concentrating on descendants
of John, d. 1704/5 Maryland.
Subscription—Paper—$15.00/yr—100pp/yr------------------ Vendor #D1649

3660   - YOUR INHERITANCE, VOLUME II by Robbie Lee Gillis Ross. 1978.
Volume II includes the Campbells of Halifax County, North Carolina,
Clarke, Dallas and Wilcox Counties, Alabama, and Carroll County,
Mississippi; Jones of Clarke County, Alabama; Blacknall of Granville
County, North Carolina and Clarke County, Alabama; Gillis and
McLeod of Kershaw District, South Carolina and Barbour County,
Alabama; Miles of Maryland, Orange and Caswell Counties, North
Carolina, Hancock and Baldwin Counties, Georgia, and Lowndes
County, Alabama, and Mississippi; and Davis of Morgan County,
Georgia and Autauga County, Alabama.
Cloth—$35.00—328pp-------------------------------------- Vendor #D1651

3661   CURRIER FAMILY RECORDS OF U. S. A. AND CANADA, Three
Volumes, by Philip J. Currier. 1984.
Volume I—Descendants of Richard Currier of Salisbury and Amesbury,
Massachusetts. He was in Salisbury by 1640; many of his descendants
are carried out to the present. Includes family index.
Volume II—Descendants of Jeffrey Currier of the Isles of Shoals and
Portsmouth, New Hampshire; Samuel Currier of Haverhill, Massachu-
setts; Deacon David Currier of Chester, New Hampshire; Alexander
Currier [Corea] of Lexington, Massachusetts; Joseph Currier [Cayer]
of Newport, Vermont; John Currier [Currie?] of Vershire and Wolcott,
Vermont, and Edward Currier of Sherbroke, P. Q., Canada and
Northern Vermont. There are also more than 100 other shorter and
unclassified lines. Includes family index.
Volume III—Combined indexes for both Volume I and Volume II.
       1.   Married Male Currier Index, arranged alphabetically by given
           name, followed by his spouse's maiden name and his genealogi-
           cal number.
       2.   Spouses of Male Curriers Index, arranged alphabetically by
           the spouse's surname, followed by the given name of Currier
           and his genealogical number.
       3.   Single Male Currier Index, arranged alphabetically and chrono-
           logically by birth date, first those single male Curriers known
           not to have married, secondly the single males of whom it is
           unknown whether or not they married and had issue. This
           index also includes date and place of birth when known,
           parents' names and his genealogical number.
       4.   Married Female Currier Index, arranged alphabetically by
           her spouse's surname, followed by her given name and genea-
           logical number.
       5.   Single Female Currier Index, arranged in the same manner as
           the single male index.
       6.   *Place Index of All Male Curriers Who Reached Maturity,*
           arranged alphabetically by states in the United States and
           the Provinces of Canada. Under each state or province the
           towns are listed alphabetically followed by the given name
           of the male and his genealogical number. A name may be
           found in a number of places, depending on how often he
           moved and how much information I have on that person. This
           index is especially helpful in locating an ancestor if you cannot
           find his name in one of the other indexes.
These volumes are of top quality, typeset and printed on acid free
sixty pound paper. The bindings are of heavy duty Record Buckram
with imitation gold lettering on the spine and front cover.
Volumes Sold Separately;
Special Three Volume Price: $90.00 postpaid.
Cloth—Volume I—$45.00—685pp--------------------------- Vendor #D1652
Cloth—Volume II—$35.00— 419pp------------------------- Vendor #D1652
Cloth—Volume III—$20.00— 214pp------------------------ Vendor #D1652

3662 - THE BICKNELL GENEALOGY—1981 SUPPLEMENT TO THE 1913 BICK-
NELL GENEALOGY by Phyllis Bicknell Carroll. 1981.
Descendants of Zachary Bicknell (1635 to Weymouth, Massachusetts).
Adds several generations to New England branch. Also chapters on
other branches: New Jersey, Philadelphia, Denver, colonial Charles-
town, plus explanation of Southern branch.
Indexed. Heavy acid-free paper.
Cloth—$35.00—272pp-- Vendor #D1653

3663 - THREE VAIL BROTHERS AND THEIR DESCENDANTS, 1790-1900 by
Lida E. Logan. 1981.
A history of the sons of William Vail of South Carolina, and their de-
scendants who removed to Alabama, and later to other states.
Texas residents add 5% tax.
Order from Lida E. Logan, 480 E. Olmos Dr., #4, San Antonio, TX 78212
Paper—$16.00—107pp-- Vendor #D1654

3664 - THE LOGANS OF OLD NINE-SIX AND THEIR DESCENDANTS by
Lida E. Logan. 1984.
A history of the Logans who were among the early settlers in the upper
country of South Carolina, and their descendants who removed to
North Carolina, Alabama, Mississippi, and Texas. Included are
allied lines: Arnold, Baber, Bryan, Dickson, Hickman, Kornegay,
Lewis, Meriwether, Pruyn, Pullen, Ragland, and Turner. Surname Index.
Texas residents add 5% tax.
Order from Lida E. Logan, 480 E. Olmos Dr., #4, San Antonio, TX 78212
Paper—$20.00—177+pp------------------------------------- Vendor #D1654

3665 - GRANDMAS AND GRANDPAS OF YESTERYEAR, AN ANCESTORY
OF THE MEDDAUGH AND DEMING FAMILIES by Catherine Meddaugh
Deming. 1982.
Early New England, New York, New Jersey, and Pennsylvania settlers.
Stories and lineages from the immigrant to 185 male and female ancestors
of todays updated Deming, Edwards, Jackson, and Meddaugh families.
Each are presented alphabetically. Adams, Allen, Allyn, Alvord
Angell, Angelo, Argento, Annable, Arnold, Axtell, Ayer, Backus,
Bacon, Barentsen, Barstow, Bass, Bates, Bergen, Biggs, Bingham,
Blanchan, Blanchard, Bliss, Bogart, Boughton, Bower, Bridges,
Brigham, Browne, Burhan, Burseley, Bushnell, Campbell, Carpenter,
Champney, Chapin, Church, Clapp, Clark, Cogswell, Collier, Conte,
Cross, Cypher, Dane, Danforth, Davis, Delamater, Deming (immigrant
was Damon), Dennison, Diederich, Dimmock, DuBois, Dudley, Dunster,
Edwards, Eggleston, Farnum, Fish, Foulke, Ford, French, Fuller,
Gager, Gardner, Gilmore, Girton, Goodale, Goodnow, Graves, Gray,
Green, Gregory, Gutterson, Halliwell, Hatch, Hauenstein, Hawkins,
Hazen, Heard, Hearnden, Hendriks, Holcomb, Hoskins, Hosmer,
John Howe, Robbart Howe, Thomas Hunt, William Hunt. Hurd, Hutchins,
Inman, Jackson, Jansen, Jenks, Jessup, Kellogg, Kent, Kingsbury,
Lakin, Lane, Lay, Leffingwell, Legg, Littlefield, Lockwood, Loomis,
Lovejoy, Lowrey, Marbury, Marsh, Marvin, McMain, Meddaugh, Mooar,
Moore, Mowry, Neale, Newberry, Norman, Norton, Oosterhout, Osgood,
Page, Palen, Parkhurst, Parmenter, Pettibone, Pidge, Plumbe, Poor,
Poulter, Pratt, Pray, Preston, Rapalje, Reece, Reed, Reiland, Petges,
Rice, Rich, Richards, Richardson, David Roe, Hugh Roe, Root, Rudd,
Schutt, Scott, Sherman, Christopher Smith, John Smith the mason,
Southworth, Spellman, Sperry, Starbuck, Stone, Storm, Strong,
Stryker, Sweetser, Taylor, Thayer, Theale, Tidd, Timberlake, Trap-
hagen, Trico, Tuttle, Van Vliet, Van Ysselstyn, Voar, Waldo, Warren,
John White, William White, Whiteley, Willard, Nicholas Wood, Thomas
Wood, Woods, Woodman, Woodward, Wright. Over 6,000 other surnamed
persons indexed; Extensive sibling data; 46 photographs; sources.
Cloth—$33.50—608pp--------------------------------------- Vendor #D1656

3666 - MIDDAGH—MEDDAUGH GIVEN NAME INDEX by Catherine Meddaugh
Deming. pub. continually as requested.
Fourteen year collection of informative data with connections and source
on each Middag-Middaugh since immigrant Aert Theuniszen Middag
1652. Order by given name desired.
Paper—$2.00 ea. given name—varies/manuscript------------- Vendor #D1656

3667 - THE PRESTONS OF SMITHFIELD AND GREENFIELD IN VIRGINIA:
DESCENDANTS OF JOHN AND ELIZABETH (PATTON) PRESTON
THROUGH FIVE GENERATIONS by John Frederick Dorman. 1982.
Cloth--$28.75—441pp------------------------------------- Vendor #D1657

3668 - HOEFELBAUER AND ALLIED FAMILIES by Beth Heffelbower Seebach.
1974.
Hoefelbauer, Hefelbower, Heflebower, Heffelbower and Heflybower
descendants of Johann Jacob of Nordheim, Württemberg.
Paper—$9.00—170pp------------------------------------- Vendor #D1658

3669 - BUCHANAN, A GENEALOGICAL HISTORY by John A. Blakemore.
1978.
Family history of James Buchanan and wives, Martha Allison and Mary
Reside, Augusta County, Virginia, 1702-1972, with more than 4,750
direct descendants.
Paper—$25.00—627pp------------------------------------- Vendor #D1660

3670 - MARY TIBBETTS DENNISON 1877-1970—HER GENEALOGICAL LINES
by Bertie Holmes Boodry. 1982.
Mrs. Dennison traced her lines to the following twenty-two immigrant
ancestors: Abbott, Austin, Boston, Canny, Drew, Estes, Goodwin,
Haines, Hoar, Huckins, Kennard, Kimball, Martyn, Nason, Otis,
Peary, Porter, Robinson, Tibbetts, Towne, Tyler, and Varney.
Paper—$10.00—76pp------------------------------------- Vendor #D1661

3671 - A COLLECTION OF CUBA, NEW YORK NEWSPAPER CLIPPINGS—
1896-1915 by Bertie Holmes Boodry. 1980.
Birth announcements, weddings, obituaries, and news items were sent
to a relative in Texas. Prominent family names are Brown, Clapp,
Clements, Eldridge, Platte, Roberts. Much genealogical data.
Paper—$3.00—37pp------------------------------------- Vendor #D1661

3672 - GENEALOGICAL HISTORY OF JOHN FRANCIS HUBER AND HIS DE-
SCENDANTS by Gloria C. Hartzell. 1983.
John Francis Huber arrived 1751 in Pennsylvania. Early descendants
of his in Pennsylvania besides Huber/Hoover were: Harris, Hepler,
Brader, Edwards, Remaly, Rabert, Ebert. Hess, Hill, Brobst, Seybert,
Weiss, Readler, Harter, Martz, Hildebrand, Benson. Scott—Columbia
County; Kleckner, Shipe, Martz, Datesman—Northumberland and Union
Counties; Keyber, Flory, Unangst, Frankenfield, Christman, Illick,
Moyer, Ritter, Eilenberger, Laubach, maybe Hutchins—Northampton
County; Ritter, Laubach—Bucks County. Many of these went west—
to where?
Cloth—$39.00—512pp------------------------------------- Vendor #D1662

3673 - JOHAN HEINRICH LOEHR OF NORTHAMPTON COUNTY, PENNSYL-
VANIA AND HIS DESCENDANTS by Elizabeth A. Hagenbuch. Repr.
of 1899 ed.
Also Lehr of mid-west states, 600 descendants, 1753-1899.
Paper—$4.00—18pp------------------------------------- Vendor #D1662

3674 - GENEALOGY OF THE DANNER FAMILY OF NORTHAMPTON COUNTY,
PENNSYLVANIA by George J. Spengler. Repr. of 1940 ed.
Also Donners of Mercer County, Pennsylvania, 1,900 descendants,
1749-1940.
Paper—$6.60—42pp------------------------------------- Vendor #D1662

3675 - THE HEARD (HERD, HIRD, HURD) JOURNAL edited by Elsie L.
Zarnowitz, of Family Tree Helpers. 1984.
The Heard Journal aims to help Heard/Herd/Hird/Hurd descendants
(regardless of surname) complete their family lines. Each issue will
be indexed; an annual index will be sold separately. Editor will be
assisted by a panel of Heard researchers: John H. Burger, Charles A.
Clemson, Harold Heard, many others. Contributions of documented
material needed. *The Journal* covers the U. S. A. except for New
England, New York, New Jersey, and Delaware. Only Heard variety
lines believed to have originated in the British Isles (includes Ireland)
are covered. The first issue in April 1984, then June, September,
December/January. The twenty pages of text initially planned equals

about twenty-eight pages of normal typed letter-size as it will be typed by letter quality printer onto 11"x14" paper, then reduced to letter-size, with ample margins. Send SASE for more details. Send your FGS's, ancestor charts, showing at least one Heard variety (see above specifications) in the background, with family data. Price guaranteed for 1984 only, as many factors cannot be controlled.
Subscription—Paper—$10.00/yr—20pp/issue----------------- Vendor #D1663

3676   - THE HISTORIC JOHNSTON FAMILY OF THE SOO by C. H. Chapman. 1982, repr. of 1877 pub.
Reprinted from *Michigan Pioneer and Historical Collection.*
Cloth—$12.00—168pp-- Vendor #D1665

3677   - LENORA A. CROWELL LETTERS 1882-1885. 1976.
Cloth—$7.00—68pp-- Vendor #D1665

3678   - JOURNAL OF GEORGE FREDERICK SEIBERT 1879. 1976.
Journal of a walking trip in the Upper Peninsula by Iron Mountain's first druggist.
Cloth—$5.00—54pp-- Vendor #D1665

3679   - DIARY OF LEWIS YOUNG WHITEHEAD: FATHER OF THE MENOMINEE RANGE, 1833-1908. 1976.
Cloth—$5.00—62pp-- Vendor #D1665

3680   - KISS EACH OTHER FOR ME: CIVIL WAR LETTERS OF RUFUS ANDRES 1861-1963. 1979.
Collection of letters written by a Civil War soldier to his wife and children in Stiles, Oconto County, Wisconsin.
Cloth—$6.00—73pp-- Vendor #D1665

3681   - DIARY OF SOREN KRISTIANSEN, LAKE MICHIGAN SCHOONER CAPTAIN, 1891-1983. 1981.
Cloth—$8.00—97pp-- Vendor #D1665

3682   - GODFREY AND MARY CLINE AND THEIR DESCENDANTS by Charlotte Gonser Russell. 1984.
Cline/Klein/Kline: Hunterdon/Sussex Counties, New Jersey; 1730-1835; Northumberland/Columbia Counties, Pennsylvania, 1785-1860; Clinton/DeKalb Counties, Missouri, 1868-present.
Gebhard/Kephart: Hunterdon County, New Jersey, 1776-1797; North-umberland County, Pennsylvania, 1798-1816.
Seibel/Seiple: Philadelphia County, Pennsylvania, 1746-1784; Bucks County, Pennsylvania, 1760-1829; Northampton County, Pennsylvania, 1804-1820; Columbia County, Pennsylvania, 1840-1845; Noxubee County, Mississippi, 1860.
Vanbuskark/Van Buskirk: Morris/Hunterdon Counties, New Jersey, 1772-1792; Northumberland County, Pennsylvania, 1793-1807.
Name indexed.
Cloth—$35.00—220pp--------------------------------------- Vendor #D1667

3683   - GONSER AND BAUMANN FAMILIES FROM BADEN-WÜRTTEMBERG by Charlotte Gonser Russell. 1979.
Gonser: Onstmettingen/Dusslingen, Württemberg, West Germany 1550-1880; Clinton/DeKalb Counties, Missouri, 1880-1928; descendants to present.
Baumann: Sonderriet, Baden, West Germany, 1615-1880; Clinton/DeKalb Counties, Missouri, 1880-present; Champaign County, Illinois, 1870-present; Jackson County, Minnesota, 1900-present.
Lineage charts. Name indexed.
Cloth—$30.00—241pp--------------------------------------- Vendor #D1667

3684   - A GENEALOGICAL HISTORY OF THE BERRIEN FAMILY by E. Renée Heiss. 1982.
This limited edition volume begins with Cornelius Jansen Berrien who settled in Long Island around 1664. His descendants (including many female laines) are followed to New Jersey where his grandsons Peter and John settled on the Millstone River and to Georgia where John Macpherson Berrien became a State Senator and later Attorney General under Andrew Jackson.
The book is enhanced with thirty-two hand-drawn illustrations of the

Berriens and their homes. Also included are several explanatory maps.
The book is made even more valuable with the inclusion of a full color,
documented family coat-of-arms.
An appendix includes the Berrien lineage to Charlemagne and the full
text of an address delivered before the Georgia Bar Association in 1891
praising the merits of John Macpherson Berrien.
The book is divided in half with the front section listing lines of
descent while the second section chronicles related information on the
history of the people.
Related lines include Burroughs (Georgia), Fish (Long Island),
Jones (Georgia), Lawrence (Long Island), Leverich (Long Island),
Montgomery (New Jersey) and Riker (New Jersey).
Cloth—$28.00—194pp-- Vendor #D1670

3685 - BENNETT FAMILY NEWSLETTER by Nancy Miller.
Deals with others researching this surname, family charts, histories
and other data quarterly newsletter.
Contact Nancy Miller, P. O. Box 31, Napa, CA 94559-0031.
Subscription—$7.50/yr—40pp/yr-------------------------- Vendor #D1671

3686 - CRAWFORD FAMILY NEWSLETTER by Nancy Miller.
Quarterly newsletter with family charts of other researchers, census
reports, histories and other data concerning this surname.
Contact Nancy Miller, P. O. Box 31, Napa, CA 94559-0031.
Subscription—$7.50/yr—40pp/yr-------------------------- Vendor #D1671

3687 - MARS FAMILY NEWSLETTER by Nancy Miller.
Semi-annual newsletter with family charts and censuses, histories plus
other history about this surname. Deals with Mar-Marr-Marrs-Mars.
Is an exchange of materials found concerning this surname.
Contact Nancy Miller, P. O. Box 31, Napa, CA 94559-0031.
Paper—$5.00—20pp------------------------------------- Vendor #D1671

3688 - GENEALOGY OF THE HAND, AND RELATED FAMILIES by Dorothy
Hand Dymond. 1982.
Related families: Bancroft, Bassett, Brewer, Coddington, Crandelmire,
Dunn, Goble, Gransden, Houghton, Insley or Ilsley, Miller, Perrin,
Platt, Price, Roy, Scranton, Stark, Stevens, Stratton, Treslar or
Tressler, Vanderbilt, Webb. Indexed.
Cloth—$16.50—424pp----------------------------------- Vendor #D1672

3689 - THE WOOTEN QUARTERLIES, VOLUME I (1981) edited by Richard C.
Wooton. 1981.
Major articles: Wooten emigrants to Virginia to 1725, North Carolina
land grants to Wootens, Early Wootens in South Carolina and Georgia,
Index, many documents.
Paper—Stapled—$20.00—223pp--------------------------- Vendor #D1674

3690 - THE WOOTEN QUARTERLIES, VOLUME II (1982) edited by Richard C.
Wooton. 1982.
Major articles: Wooten Revolutionary Soldiers in National Archives/
DAR/ and North Carolina Accounts, Early Texas Wootens, Shadrach
Wooten as Revolutionary Ancestor, Surry/Yadkin North Carolina
Wootens. Index, many documents.
Paper—Stapled—$20.00—194pp--------------------------- Vendor #D1674

3691 - THE WOOTEN QUARTERLIES, VOLUME III (1983) edited by Richard
C. Wooton. 1983.
Major articles: Revolutionary Soldiers Joel, Turner, and Silas Wooton;
Wooten Deeds Edgecombe County, North Carolina; Almost Wootens?
Hootons, Wrotons, and Wooters. Woottons of Halifax and Mecklen-
burg Counties, Virginia; Tennessee and Kentucky land grants to
Wootens, Uncle Dick Wootton. Index, many documents.
Paper—Stapled—$20.00—190pp--------------------------- Vendor #D1674

3692 - THE WOOTTONS OF ISLE OF WIGHT COUNTY, VIRGINIA (WOOTEN
STUDY NUMBER I) by Richard C. Wooton. 1981.
Follows family from Northamptonshire, England to Isle of Wight, Vir-
ginia, to Edgecombe/Pitt, North Carolina. Exposes incorrect traditional
lineage claims, including Jamestown Surgeon Thomas Wotton
Index and many documents, over 200 notes/references.
Paper—Stapled—$15.00—91pp--------------------------- Vendor #D1674

3693   - THE WOOTONS OF SURRY COUNTY, NORTH CAROLINA 1735-1820 (WOOTEN STUDY NUMBER IV) by Richard C. Wooton. 1982.

Shows George Wooton and sons in Orange County, Virginia to 1752; Thomas Wooton and sons in Granville/Bute/Franklin, North Carolina 1752-1770's and in Surry, North Carolina 1770's-1820, ending with migration to Randolph County, Indiana. Thomas Puckett and sons given heavy coverage in Surry 1770's-1820.

Index, documents, over 300 notes and references.

Paper—Stapled—$25.00—226pp------------------------------ Vendor #D1674

3694   - THE WOOTTENS OF YORK COUNTY, VIRGINIA (WOOTEN STUDY NUMBER V) by Richard C. Wooton. 1984.

Shows emigrant ancestor in Warwick, Virginia, follows branches to Elizabeth City County, Virginia, halifax and Walke, North Carolina, Wilkes County, Georgia, Smith County, Tennessee.

Index, key documents, copious notes/references.

Paper—Stapled—$20.00—ca 120pp-------------------------- Vendor #D1674

3695   - CHARLES WOOTON OF KENTUCKY (WOOTEN STUDY NUMBER VIII) by E. C. and Jessamine V. Wooton. 1982.

Explores possible ancestry of Charles Wooton b. Virginia; traces his two families in Clay and Greenup Counties, Kentucky, on to Missouri, Kansas, etc.

Index, documents, sources cited in text, includes twenty-three page supplement.

Paper—Stapled—$15.00—122pp----------------------------- Vendor #D1674

3696   - JOHN WOOTEN, SR. OF PITT COUNTY, NORTH CAROLINA AND HIS SONS (WOOTEN STUDY NUMBER XI) by Richard C. Wooton. 1981.

Gives full account of John Wooten, Sr. of Pitt, traces his seven sons to their deaths: Shadrach d. Columbus, North Carolina; John (Jr.) d. Wayne/Lenoir, North Carolina; William d. Pitt, North Carolina; Richard d. Wayne, North Carolina; Josiah d. Pitt, North Carolina; Levi d. Beaufort, South Carolina; and Council d. Monroe, Georgia. Identifies children of each of seven sons.

Index, twenty-one pages documents, 396 notes/references.

Paper—Stapled—$20.00—127pp----------------------------- Vendor #D1674

3697   - THE LOY FAMILY IN AMERICA by Jennie E. Stewart, edited and indexed by William E. Lynch, Jr. 1984.

A genealogical account of the Ley/Loy German immigrants into Pennsylvania from 1732. The five 'brothers' are George Christopher, Matthias, John George to Maryland, John Henry to Virginia, Martin to North Carolina. Some allied families mentioned are: Reid, Tressler, Lamm, Stocker, Ginther, Troud, Kline, Kumpf, Lampert, Lyon, Millslagle, Walls.

Family group sheets, pedigree charts, wills, deeds and an every name index are included. 6"x9".

Cloth—$22.50—260pp------------------------------------- Vendor #D1677

3698   - CAPON VALLEY: ITS PIONEERS AND THEIR DESCENDANTS 1698-1940, 2 Volumes, by Maud Pugh. 1982, repr.

Capon Valley is located in Hampshire County, West Virginia.

Volume I concerns the Pugh settlers of Welch descent from 1698. Some allied families: Bennett, Dye, Edwards, Giffin, Kidwell, McNeill, Offutt, Reid, Ward.

Volume II includes other Capon Valley pioneers, whom some are: Ambler, Anderson, Baker, Billmyre, Brill, Cline, Emmett, Frye, Haines, Hayden, Hiett, Hockman, LaFollette, Milleson, Monroe, McKeever, McDonald, Orndorff, Pepper, Powell, Sine, Slane, Smith, Slonaker, Spaid.

Each volume has a separate every name index. 6"x9".

Cloth—$32.50—746pp------------------------------------- Vendor #D1677

3699   - THE McKINNEY MAZE edited by Patricia McKinney Kirkwood.

Quarterly publication for all McKinney/McKenney surname searchers.

Paper—$10.00—100pp------------------------------------- Vendor #D1678

3700 - GENEALOGY OF MACY FAMILY AND SPOUSES 1635 TO 1868 by
Silvanus J. Macy. 1975 repr. of 1868 orig. ed.
2,000 genealogical entries from early Nantucket and North Carolina.
Cloth—$20.00 postpaid—457pp------------------------------ Vendor #D1679

3701 - JONATHAN CONGER OF KNOX AND GIBSON COUNTIES, INDIANA
AND HIS DESCENDANTS, 2d Ed., compiled by Lesba Lewis Thompson.
1981.
Complete index; over 1,800 names.
Allied families include Catt, Davidson, Edwards, Evans, Frederick,
Minor, Small, Wilcox (spouses of the children of Jonathan Conger),
also Hill, Hyneman, Johnson, Lindy, McAtee, Nixon and Phillips.
Jonathan Conger is an established DAR and U. S. D. of 1812 ancestor.
Paper—$20.00—286pp--------------------------------------- Vendor #D1680

3702 - THE MAHLOCH FAMILY HISTORY by Elaine S. Larson. 1984.
Traces the descendants of Philipp Mahloch (Maloch), born 1817 in
Dienheim (Rhineland), Germany. Married (1) Sophie Best; (2) Cath-
erine Duerrwaechter. Emigrated to Wisconsin in 1843. 8½"x5½"; indexed.
Cloth—$39.00—596pp------------------------------------- Vendor #D1681

3703 - TWELVE FAMILIES: AN AMERICAN EXPERIENCE by William F. O'Dell.
1981.
A novel-like family history based on genealogical data, placing ances-
tors in their historical settings. "This book is the ultimate goal of a
genealogist..." wrote the Colorado Genealogical Society in its review.
Based on thirty years of research, covering each line back to its
European emigrant. 226 pictures and illustrations. 14 ancestral charts.
Appendices include 2,000 plus names, suggestions for further research
and a universal relationship chart.
Aikman, Baer/Barr, Gant/Ghent, Green, Horning/Hornung,
Michell/Mitchell, Odell/O'Dell/Odle, Peerenboom, Riley, Rooks,
Springer, Swing/Schwing.
Cloth; 533 pages; 9"x6"; fully indexed; $27.50.
Cloth—$27.50—533pp------------------------------------- Vendor #D1683

3704 - COOK'S CRIER edited by Carl A. Patin.
Clearinghouse and forum for Cook families. Sixteenth year of publication.
Published quarterly. Subscription rate $10.00—four issues.
Each issue indexed by name and locality. Free queries to subscribers.
Cook's Crier, P.O. Box 993, Casselberry, FL 32707
Subscription—Paper—$10.00—24pp------------------------- Vendor #D1684

3705 - MORRELL/MORRILL FAMILIES NEWSLETTER by Ann Lisa Pearson.
Quarterly, Annual Index.
Information on descendants of early Colonial settlers, especially
Abraham, John and Thomas lines. Also families from England, Ireland,
France, Germany, Sweden and Canadian settlers. Queries. 1"x8½".
1981—Paper—$6.00—67pp----------------------------------- Vendor #D1687
1982—Paper—$7.00—74pp----------------------------------- Vendor #D1687
1983—Paper—$8.00—80pp----------------------------------- Vendor #D1687
1984—Paper—$10.00—100pp--------------------------------- Vendor #D1687

3706 - THE WENGER BOOK—A FOUNDATION BOOK OF AMERICAN WENGERS
by Samuel S. Wenger, Editor-in-Chief. 1978.
Includes variant spellings (thirty) such as Winger, Wanger, Whanger,
Wengert, Wengerd, Wingert, and Wingard plus sixty Non-Wenger
families. The work is large and comprehensive with appropriate illus-
trations. Records begin with Christian Wenger, immigrant of 1727, and
Eve Graybill, his wife who settled in Lancaster County, Pennsylvania.
Add $2.00 for mailing charges and Pennsylvania buyers pay $2.37 sales
tax. Address all orders to:
Elizabeth Wenger, Route 3 - Pleasant Valley Road, Ephrata, PA 17522.
Cloth—$39.50—1248pp------------------------------------- Vendor #D1688

3707 - HENRY SHARP (C1737-1800) OF SUSSEX COUNTY, NEW JERSEY AND
FAYETTE COUNTY, PENNSYLVANIA AND HIS WIFE LYDIA MORGAN
AND SOME OF THEIR DESCENDANTS...by Elizabeth C. Eastwood and
Helen S. Wickliffe. 1975.
Sons-in-law Robert Chalfant, Pennsylvania to Perry County, Ohio;

Abraham Depuy, New Jersey to Vermillion County, Indiana; James
Silverthorn, New Jersey to Ontario, Canada; Thomas Wheatley,
Wales to Mason County, Kentucky. Would like information from and
about descendants.
First supplement, 1978, paper, $4.50, 58 pages, 11"x8½".
Second supplement, 1985.
Cloth—$25.00—263pp--- Vendor #D1689

3708 - THE DESCENDANTS OF ANDREW FORD OF WEYMOUTH, MASSACHU-
SETTS PART III by Elizabeth C. Eastwood. 1985-86.
Part III will contain eighth and all later known generations; also
additions and corrections to Parts I and II. Would like information
from and about descendants.
(In process)-- Vendor #D1689

3709 - THE DESCENDANTS OF THE MARRIAGE OF SOLOMON AND HANNAH
(WELLS) COBB OF CAMBRIDGE, WASHINGTON COUNTY, NEW YORK,
revised compilation of John L. Cobb, 1984, orig. pub. 1966.
Index. 11"x8½".
Paper—$5.00+postage—26pp-------------------------------- Vendor #D1690

3710 - SOME ANCESTORS AND DESCENDANTS OF EDWARD BILL[4] AND OF
OLIVER[5] BILL compiled by John L. Cobb. 1978.
Index; 8½"x5½".
Paper—$7.50+postage—73pp-------------------------------- Vendor #D1690

3711 - DeTAR AND ALLIED FAMILIES by Ruth G. Hall and Lucille O'Brien.
1982.
Richly illustrated and documented and represents twenty years of
travel and correspondence. 11"x8½".Indexed.
Family lines include DeTar, Altman, Watterson, Harrold, Kepple,
Robb, Gribbs, Huckleberry, Siegfried, Schneider, Baer, Koontz,
Lauffer, Uncapher, Rugh, and Earhart, with most of the story before
1900.
About 1750, Marianne Joghs Tetoit (DeTar), a French lady, supposedly
sold her gold lace petticoat to finance the emigration to Pennsylvania
for her husband David (Jacob?) and children Jacob and Catherine.
Widowed 1754, Marianne married Anthony Altman and had three more
children. The Altmans and DeTars removed to Westmoreland County,
Pennsylvania, 1769, where they suffered the hardships of the Indian
frontier.
Jacob DeTar married Mary Huckleberry, and all DeTars trace their
lineage to this marriage. Jacob's granddaughter Margaret married
Reuben Perkins, son of Jacob Perkins and Elizabeth Kammerer.
(See advertisement for Perkins-Kammerer supplement.)
The story is told against the background of French Huguenot,
Pennsylvania, and Kansas history.
Paper—$20.00—325pp------------------------------------- Vendor #D1691

3712 - PERKINS—KAMMER AND ALLIED FAMILIES by Ruth G. Hall and
Lucille O'Brien. 1982.
A supplement to *DeTar and Allied Familes*, 1982, of Pennsylvania and
Kansas. Lines include Rugh, Smith, Markle, Mechling. History
begins ca 1400 in Europe. Illustrated; indexed; 11"x8½".
Paper—$20.00—350pp------------------------------------- Vendor #D1691

3713 - THE DESCENDANTS OF JAMES SHERARD AND NANCY CORNELISON
by Gerald E. Sherard. 1984.
Sherard: lists seven generations of descendants from Dekalb County,
Missouri, and Butler County, Ohio.
Allied families include Ackley, Cornelison, Daniel, Delp, Ekhoff,
Flanders, Huffman, Johnson, Jones, Maret, Middleton, Moorman,
Moss, Murphy, Shelly, Smith, Teeter, Thomas, Thornburg, Williams.
Index to all Sherard surnames and heads of households of other
surnames. Contains history, births, deaths, and marriages.
Does not contain pictures. 6"x9".
Cloth—$21.00—200pp------------------------------------- Vendor #D1692

3714 - STYER, GAHEN AND POEHNELT FAMILIES OF WISCONSIN, HISTORY AND LINEAGE, 1785-1935 by Betty M. and Leo E. Styer. 1981.
Styer: Eischen, Luxembourg—1785; Adams County, Wisconsin—1859; Dunn County, Wisconsin—1863.
Gahen: Prince Edward Island, Canada—1800; Glouster County, New Brunswick, Canada—1836; Adams County, Wisconsin—1850; Dunn County, Wisconsin—1876.
Poehnelt: Gohren, Austria—Hungary (Kliny, Czechoslovakia)—1844; Taylor County, Wisconsin—1883.
Related families include Barron, Bird, Branshaw, Buehler, Burns, Carney, Decker, Doyle, Gauvin, Heller, Karlik, Lemon, Liddy, Marsh, Schwartz, Stratton. A genealogy of three families with historical background of where they came from and how they settled in Wisconsin. It tells of their relationship to each other and traces their lineage to a time period when their descendants, now living, can connect their families to one or more of these lines. A detailed history of two of the Styer brothers service in the Civil War is also included.
Cloth—$10.00—112pp--- Vendor #D1693

3715 - SOME BOONE DESCENDANTS AND KINDRED OF THE ST. CHARLES DISTRICT by Lilian Hays Oliver. 1984, repr. of 1964 ed.
Genealogical lines and history of Daniel Boone and his kindred. Related families include Bryan, Callaway, Castlio, Darst, Hays, Howell, Stewart. Over 1,300 surnames listed. Indexed.
Paper—$33.00—463pp--- Vendor #D1694

3716 - THE CHAPPELL GENEALOGY by Phil E. Chappell and Eloise M. Chappell. 1983, repr.
A history of Chappell emigration to Tidewater Area, Virginia in 1635, and movement throughout the East, South and West. Chapters on Dickie, Pate, Garlington and Adams families. Reprint of 1900 edition with Hix Chappell Chapter added.
Cloth—$57.50—398pp--- Vendor #D1696

3717 - "OUR MEADOR FAMILIES IN COLONIAL AMERICA" by Victor P. Meador and Bernal M. Meador. 1983.
History of the Meador families in Virginia from immigration in 1630's to the Revolution. From records in Isle of Wight, Lancaster, Richmond, Essex, (old) Rappahannock, and Caroline Counties. Much information on allied families, including Allen, Armstrong, Awbrey, Barton, Bourne, Bramham, Coombs, Gatewood, Gouldman, Gower, Gregory, Reeves, Rust, Underwood, Waggoner, and Williamson.
Four maps. Indexed.
Paper—$8.00—186pp--- Vendor #D1698

3718 - DESCENDANTS OF CORNELIS AERTSEN VAN SCHAICK by Melwood W. Van Scoyoc. 1982.
Twenty-nine photographs, fully indexed. Lineage records begin with Cornelis Aertsen who came to America from Westbroek, Holland in 1636. Direct male descendant surnames are Van Schaick, Van Schoick, Van Schoiack, Van Scoik, Van Scoy, Vanscoy, Van Scoyk, Van Scoyoc, Van Scyoc, Van Skaik, Van Skike, Van Sky, Van Skyhawk, Van Skyock, Van Syoc. Included is a reproduction of the red and silver Coat-of-Arms which has been authenticated by the Centraal Bureau of Genealogie of The Hague, Holland.
Cloth—$47.50-postpaid; 9"x6".
Cloth—$47.50—787pp--- Vendor #D1700

3719 - RATHBUN—RATHBONE—RATHBURN FAMILY HISTORIAN edited by Frank H. Rathbun.
Sixteen pages each quarterly issue; paper, membership dues $15.00 annually (1984).
Subscription—$15.00/yr—16pp/qtly---------------------- Vendor #D1702

3720 - "ONE WATERS FAMILY" by Jeanne Waters Strong. 1980.
Descendants of Richard Waters of Salem, Massachusetts.
Cloth—$25.00—167pp--- Vendor #D1705

3721 - THE DAY JOURNAL edited by Sharon Bryant Hinkle.
Quarterly Newsletter for surname <u>Day</u>. $7.50 annual subscription
Back issues available.
Subscription—$7.50/yr---Ven___ ___

3722 - SUPPLEMENT TO THE GETMAN FAMILY GENEALOGY by George A.
Getman, Jr. 1982.
Additions and corrections to *The Getman Genealogy 1710-1974*;
not recommended without a copy of *The Getman Genealogy, 1710-1974*
(See #4221).
Paper—$8.50—124pp-- Vendor #D1710

3723 - THE WERNECKE FAMILY: JOHANN ANDREAS ERNST WERNECKE
(1788-1867) AND FRIEDERIKE MARIA REGINA SACHSE (1792-1857),
THEIR ANCESTORS AND DESCENDANTS by Gretchen Ann Wernecke
Warda. 1984.
They emigrated from Saxony, Prussia to Town of Newton, in Manitowoc
County, Wisconsin in 1848 with four children. The book follows both
male and female lines. Major families in addition to <u>Wernecke</u> are:
<u>Eberhardt</u>, <u>Jochimsen</u>, <u>Reinhardt</u>, <u>Rodewald</u>, <u>Roepke</u>, <u>Roseman</u>,
<u>Schroeter</u>, <u>Stammerjohn</u>, <u>Truettner</u>, and <u>Zarling</u>.
While many descendants are still in Manitowoc County major branches
have settled in Brown, Fond du Lac, Marathon, Milwaukee, Outa-
gamie, Ozaukee, Shawano and Sheboygan Counties in Wisconsin,
Jefferson and Gage Counties in Nebraska and Washington County,
Kansas. Individual families are spread throughout the country with
large numbers in California, Illinois, Minnesota, Ohio and Texas.
Wisconsin residents add 5% sales tax - $2.05.
Cloth—$40.95—478pp--- Vendor #D1711

3724 - GENEALOGIES OF THE HOCKER—HAWKER FAMILIES OF THE UNITED
STATES by Viron E. Payne, Sr. 1984.
Over 4,000 <u>Hockers</u>, Hawkers and descendants in seven lines, pedigrees of several branches included back to <u>Charlemagne</u>, <u>El Cid</u>,
<u>Alfred the Great</u>, Charles Martel, etc. Rich, imitation leather,
D-ring binders for easy update. Has data from five earlier genealogies
plus thousands of new names. Source references. Five narative
chapters. The rest is a computer listing of names and data in family
order. A genealogist's genealogy. The standard work on <u>Hocker</u>.
Major descending lines include <u>Bass</u>, <u>Boarman</u>, <u>Byrn</u>, <u>Dunn</u>, <u>Farlee</u>,
<u>Hector</u>, <u>Helvey</u>, <u>McCormack</u>, <u>Paxton</u>, <u>Powers</u>, <u>Seals</u>, <u>Shoffner</u>,
<u>Shumate</u> and <u>Ward</u>. Includes qualifiers for DAR, SAR and Colonial
Dames. Many adoptions shown. Indexed; 8½"x11".
Hardback D-ring—$30.00—apx. 300pp---------------------- Vendor #D1713

3725 - GENEALOGY OF THE TANKERSLEY FAMILY IN THE UNITED STATES
by Charles W. Tankersley. 1893, repr.
Xerox copy of eighteen page original plus fifteen pages of added data.
Unbound.
Paper—Unbound—$10.00—33pp----------------------------- Vendor #D1713

3726 - THE FAMILY OF WILLIAM WEBSTER OF RHODE ISLAND by Leo H.
Garman. 1982.
Illustrated, indexed.
Principal collateral families: <u>Hart</u>, <u>Oller</u>, <u>Rutherford</u>.
Paper—$23.00—468pp------------------------------------ Vendor #D1714

3727 - DESCENDANTS OF REVEREND BENJAMIN DOGGETT OF VIRGINIA
by Blanche Doggett Heflin and Martha McDaniel Thompson. 1984.
Rev. Benjamin <u>Doggett</u> of Virginia, his English ancestry and his de-
scendants in nearly every state in United States.
Research material included.
Paper—$15.00—150pp------------------------------------ Vendor #D1716

3728 - ELIZABETH WOOLSEY SPRUCE, 1873-1969; THE STORY OF MY
FAMILY AND THOSE WHO POWERFULLY TOUCHED MY LIFE by
Elizabeth W. Spruce. 1981.
Autobiography of Texas Methodist pioneers from Georgia, settling in
Colorado and Wilson Counties.
Paper—$10.00—94pp------------------------------------ Vendor #D1717

3729 - SLAUGHTER OF THE PFOST—GREENE FAMILY by O. J. Morrison.
1982., repr.
Includes history of Pfost and Greene families.
Paper—$5.50—96pp-- Vendor #D1720

3730 - STERRY FAMILY OF AMERICA 1670-1970 by W. B. Smith. 1973.
Cloth—$20.00—345pp------------------------------------- Vendor #D1722

3731 - HISTORY AND GENEALOGY OF THE LEXINGTON, MASSACHUSETTS
MUNROES by R. S. Munroe. 1966.
Cloth—$10.00—468pp------------------------------------- Vendor #D1722

3732 - BURIED TREASURE FROM ACETO GENEALOGICAL FILES by Charles
D. and Edna Townsend, Editors.
Subscription—$10.00/yr—36pp--------------------------------Vendor #D1722

3733 - ROTA-GENE INTERNATIONAL GENEALOGY MAGAZINE edited by
Charles D. Townsend.
Subscription—$15.00/yr—36pp--------------------------------Vendor #D1722

3734 - SCHNURR BROTHERS IN AMERICA by James and Theresa Tapper.
1981.
Five brothers from Baden, Germany, settled in Iowa/Illinois 1853.
Photos, maps, documents, family history. Complete listing of de-
scendants. Special section on unrelated Schnurr groups found by
authors.
Allied families include Altman, Anderson, Arnhalt, Bald, Evans, Fort-
ney, Hause, Hubbard, Krieger, Lamp, Leuenhagen, Potter, Ryberg,
Schlotterback, Sheehy, Wonders, Zinger, Derga, more. Indexed.
Paper—$11.00—185pp---------------------------------- Vendor #D1724

3735 - A VIETS GENEALOGY—JOHN VIETS AND MARY ANN PHELPS:
THEIR ANCESTORS AND DESCENDANTS by Dorothy Viets Schell.
1982.
"I would most seriously recommend to every genealogical society to
buy a copy of this book, to have on hand to show its members how to
'Write it Right!'"—*Genealogy Today*.
Paper—$16.50—200pp---------------------------------- Vendor #D1725

3736 - GREAT LAKES' FIRST SUBMARINE—L. D. PHILLIPS' "FOOL
KILLER" by Patricia A. Gruse Harris. 1982.
Descendants of David Phillips, New Hampshire and life of submarine
inventor, Lodner Phillips.
Paper—$11.45—86pp---------------------------------- Vendor #D1727

3737 - ABIJAH BIGELOW REVOLUTIONARY SOLDIER AND A BRIEF SKETCH
OF MY MOTHER'S LIFE by Mrs. William H. Harris and Ellen D.
Williams Haddock. 1976.
"Mother" is Lucy Bigelow Williams. Bigelow, Williams, Haddock families.
Paper—$2.50—33pp---------------------------------- Vendor #D1727

3738 - RESEARCHER'S LIST FOR CLAN McCULLOUGH/MCCULLOCH
(1984 AND UPDATES) compiled by Betty K. Summers.
Family group sheets and brief lineages of members and non-members
of Clan McCullough/McCulloch. Finding aid of names and places.
Paper—$15.00—250pp---------------------------------- Vendor #D1728

3739 - CLAN McCULLOUGH/McCULLOCH NEWSLETTER (QUARTERLY)
compiled by Mrs. Betty K. Summers.
Approximately 200 pages per year; all states; all time periods;
all spellings of surname. Back issues available at $3.00 each.
Include pedigree sheet and family group sheet of oldest ancestor
with order. Queries welcome, free.
Subscription—Paper—$10.00/yr—apx. 200pp/yr------------- Vendor #D1728

3740 - THE SCUDAMORES OF UPTON SCUDAMORE: A KNIGHTLY FAMILY
IN MEDIEVAL WILTSHIRE by Warren Skidmore. 1982.
Cloth—$22.50—168pp---------------------------------- Vendor #D1729

3741 - THOMAS SKIDMORE (SCUDAMORE), 1605-1684, OF WESTERLEIGH,
GLOS., AND FAIRFIELD, CONNECTICUT by Warren Skidmore. 1980.
Cloth—$27.50—350pp--- Vendor #D1729

3742 - SKIDMORE: RICKMANSWORTH, ENGLAND, DELAWARE, NORTH
CAROLINA, AND WEST by Warren Skidmore and William F. Skidmore.
1983.
Cloth—$28.50—623pp--- Vendor #D1729

3743 - THOMAS STONESTREET OF BIRCHDEN, WITHYHAM, EAST SUSSEX,
AND CHARLES COUNTY, MARYLAND. 1983.
Cloth—$22.50—119pp--- Vendor #D1729

3744 - NEWSLETTER OF THE PARKE SOCIETY edited by David L. Parke.
Pub. since 1963.
Society serves as clearing-house for all Park/e/s immigrant lines from
the British Isles.
Subscription—$6.00 dues plus $5.00 application fee—48pp/yr- Vendor #D1730

3745 - OSWALD OUTLINES by Donna Potter Phillips. 1984.
Intended clearinghouse for Oswald/Oswalt pedigrees and all miscellaneous
information. Irregularly published booklets. Indexed.
Paper—$5.63—25+pp--- Vendor #D1731

3746 - POTTER PROFILES by Donna Potter Phillips. 1985.
Intended clearinghouse for Potter pedigrees and all miscellaneous
information. Irregularly published booklets. Indexed.
(In process)—Paper—$5.63—25+pp-------------------------- Vendor #D1731

3747 - A WHIPPLE FAMILY HISTORY: JOSEPH WHIPPLE, 1753-1843; MARKS
WHIPPLE, 1805-1880; JOHN WHIPPLE, 1855-1941 by Judith C. Whipple
and Darrel K. Whipple. 1981.
This family history deals with the descendants of Joseph Whipple, of
Sharon, Connecticut and the movement of the family to Ohio, Iowa,
Missouri, and California.
Paper—$15.00—130pp------------------------------------- Vendor #D1732

3748 - A COX FAMILY HISTORY: THE ANCESTORS AND DESCENDANTS
OF RICHARD ALBERTSON COX, 1820-1909 by Judith C. Whipple and
Darrel K. Whipple. 1985.
A family history covering the Quaker Cox family in Wayne County,
North Carolina, Bartholomew and Jackson Counties, Indiana, and
Douglas County, Kansas.
(In process)—Paper—$18.00—apx. 150pp—------------------ Vendor #D1732

3749 - SCHWARTZ FAMILY—HESSE KASSEL GERMANY TO WASHINGTON,
D.C. by Bernard A. Schwartz. 1985.
Includes relatives in Rooney, Jordan, and Marshall families. 11"x8½".
Paper—$3.00—15pp--------------------------------------- Vendor #D1734

3750 - BARNES FAMILY—NORTHUMBERLAND COUNTY, VIRGINIA by
Bernard A. Schwartz. 1985.
Includes relatives in Sumner, Ogle, Richardson, and Vanlandingham
families. 11"x8½".
Paper—$3.00—15pp-- Vendor #D1734

3751 - BLAKELEY FAMILY JOURNAL, VOLUME II by Nancy B. Ruff. 1982.
Includes all spellings and locations.
Paper—$12.00—118pp------------------------------------ Vendor #D1736

3752 - GRANDFATHER WAS ALWAYS A VERY OLD MAN by Byron Sistler.
1972.
Sitzlers, Sistlers, Sitchlers, Gibsons, Rexers, Holloways,
Trovillions, Monroe County, Tennessee and Pope County, Illinois.
Cloth--$11.50—239pp------------------------------------ Vendor #D1737

3753 - "OUR ANCESTORS" by Miss Jessie Mae Ashford and Mrs. Adelle B.
Ashford. 1977.
Contains 4,459 names and genealogy of twenty-three families from
Virginia, North Carolina, South Carolina, Alabama, Tennessee, Arkan-
sas, Georgia, and Illinois.
Includes Ashford, Baker, Barnes, Brown, Garrett, Grantham, Huffman,

Jackson, Judkins, Lane, Lawhon, Lucas, Merritt, Moring, Northcutt, Oates, O'Kelly, Register, Scarborough, Smith, Thornton, Thorp and Trout. A second edition is in process, with many additional names.
Cloth—$23.00—293pp--- Vendor #D1738

3754 - "THE McCARLEY MEMORIES" by Jane Berry McAfee. 1980.
Descendants of Moses and Ruth Ford? McCarley of Spartanburg County, South Carolina mentioned in Moses McCarley's will in 1784. Covers southern states. Indexed.
Paper—$15.50—168pp------------------------------------- Vendor #D1739

3755 - THE FIELD AND FRENCH—HENRY FAMILIES—A UNION OF NORTH AND SOUTH by Charles Kellogg Field, III. 1984.
A genealogical, narrative history of the General Martin Field family of New England includes anecdotes of him, Hon. Roswell Field and Eugene Field (Poet), his children and grandchildren. It traces this Field ancestry back to Hubertus del la Feld of the 11th Century. The text provides an early history of the French family of Virginia and Texas and discusses their origin as Huguenots from Roscommon County, Ireland; portrays the early Henry family of Virginia and their ancient ancestors dating back to Charlamagne. Several original letters and anecdotes are compiled in this volume by the author.
Illustrations include Field, French, Henry and Dial Coats-of-Arms and a history of their meaning.
Family lineage records furnish extensive information on the Field, French and Henry families and collateral families of William Bartlett of Oakland, California; Blacklaw-Melvin of Scotland; Governor William Bradford of England and Massachusetts, Signer of the Mayflower Compact and his heirs through the Webb family; Colonel Richard Calloway of Virginia and Kentucky; William Comstock of England and Connecticut; Descendants of James Dial of Glasgow, Scotland; Lieutenant Joseph Kellogg of Hadley, Massachusetts; Major Benjamin Netherland of Virginia; Henry Scarborough of England and Virginia and his descendants; Wiggins-Fergus of England and Scotland; Francis Eugene Yates of Corpus Christi, Texas.
27 illustrations; Indexed; 8½"x5½".
Cloth—$32.50—350pp--- Vendor #D1740

3756 - VANDERPOOL NEWSLETTER, VOLUME II edited by Frances R. Nelson. 1984.
Vanderpools anywhere, anytime. 36 page quarterly plus annual index issue.
Paper--$10.00/yr—144pp/yr. plus index-------------------- Vendor #D1741

3757 - RUSSELL REGISTER, VOLUME 6 edited by Frances R. Nelson, contributing editor, George Ely Russell. 1983-84.
Russells anytime, anywhere, before 1900. Lineages and queries free for subscribers. 36 page quarterly plus annual index; ongoing.
Subscription—$10.00/yr—144pp/yr. plus index------------- Vendor #D1741

3758 - MILLER MONITOR, VOLUME 5 edited by Frances R. Nelson. 1983-84.
Millers anywhere, any time (before 1900). Lineages and queries free for subscribers. 36 page quarterly plus annual index issue.
Subscription—$10.00/yr—144pp/yr. plus index--------------Vendor #D1741

3759 - CAMPBELL CONTACTS, VOLUME 5 edited by Frances R. Nelson.
Campbells anywhere, any time (before 1900). Lineages and queries free for subscribers. 36 page quarterly plus annual index issue.
Subscription—$10.00/yr—144pp/yr. plus index--------------Vendor #D1741

3760 - NELSON NOTES, VOLUME 2 edited by Frances R. Nelson. 1984-85.
Nelsons anywhere, anytime (before 1900). Lineages and queries free for subscribers. 36 page quarterly plus annual index issue.
Subscription—$10.00/yr—144pp/yr. plus index------------- Vendor #D1741

3761 - JONES JOURNEYS, VOLUME II edited by Frances R. Nelson. 1983-84.
Joneses anywhere, anytime (before 1900). Lineages and queries free for subscribers. 36 page quarterly plus annual index issue.
Subscription--$10.00/yr—144pp/yr. plus index-------------Vendor #D1741

3762 - FINKE AND THEIR CONNECTIONS 1793-1981 by Billie E. Embree. 1982.
This book covers seven generations. Some surnames included are: Alexander, Cook, Embree, Hulpieu, Lefort, Meier, Owens, Scheeter, Schutt and Zemler.
Paper—$20.00—104pp--- Vendor #D1742

3763 - HISTORY OF A GOOD FAMILY. DESCENDANTS OF JACOB AND MARY BOSLEY GOOD OF CAMBRIA COUNTY, PENNSYLVANIA 1779-1978 by Mary Ellen Sappington Good. 1978.
The first known Good ancestor in this history-genealogy is Jacob Good, who married Mary Bosley. On the 7th of October, 1779, in Washington County, Maryland they had a son whom they named Christian Good. The family eventually settled in Qumahoning Township, Somerset County, (now Johnstown, Cambria County) Pennsylvania. Christian married Susannah Singer in 1798. They were the parents of: Jacob, Mary, Samuel, John, Elizabeth, Christian, Abraham and Susannah. Each child and his/her known descendants have been included. From these progenitors the known Good descendants have been traced for five generations with liberal copies of documents, background material, and a wonderful collection of photographs. It has a complete full-name index.
Cloth—$41.50—653pp------------------------------------- Vendor #D1743

3764 - FOOTE HISTORY—GENEALOGY, VOLUME I by Abram Foote. 1984, repr. of 1907 ed.
Includes many pictures.
Cloth--$50.00—607pp----------------------------------- Vendor #D1745

3765 - FOOTE HISTORY—GENEALOGY, VOLUME II by Abram Foote. 1981, repr. of 1932 ed.
Includes many pictures. Binding on the two volumes match.
Cloth—$47.50—725pp----------------------------------- Vendor #D1745

3766 - THE COLLINS—CADWELL GENEALOGY: ANCESTORS AND DESCEN-DANTS OF HIRAM COLLINS AND HIS WIFE ANNAR CADWELL COLLINS OF MIDDLESEX, NEW YORK—WITH ALLIED LINES UNDERWOOD, CLARK AND VAN HOUTEN by Margaret U. Lofquist. 1983.
First section contains information on early Collins families of Guilford and Litchfield, Connecticut; and Cadwell families of East Hartford, Connecticut and Fabius, New York. Also data on Hiram and Annar Collins (married 1807) and over 900 of their descendants.
Localities include Yates and Allegany Counties, New York; Grass Lake, Michigan; Belvidere, Illinois; Ord, Nebraska; Eugene, Oregon; Shell Rock, Iowa; and Porter County, Indiana.
Second Section, which consists of charts and thirty ancestral lines, includes data on related families of Atwell, Buell, Burr, Case, Folger, Loomis, Leete, Spencer, Warner, Westover and twenty others.
7"x10"; indexed.
Cloth--$18.50—396pp------------------------------------- Vendor #D1746

3767 - THE TURN OF THE WHEEL—A BURNS—TINKER GENEALOGY by Louis F. Burns. 1980.
Traces the descendants of John Tinker, 1622 of Connecticut and William Burns, 1718 of Virginia and their related families: Miles, Van Meters, Roy, Lessert, Harness and Meek. Indexed.
Cloth--$30.00—400pp------------------------------------- Vendor #D1747

3768 - THE LAST FREE LAND—A BLAKE—KINCANNON GENEALOGY by Ruth Blake Burns. 1981.
Traces the westward migration of the descendants of Francis Kincannon, 1740 and Joseph Blake, 1800 and their related families: Walden, Maddox, Johnstons, Duncans, Banks. Indexed.
Cloth--$30.00—434pp------------------------------------- Vendor #D1747

3769 - MAHAN SURNAME BOOKLET NUMBER TWO by Linda Pollick Shorb. 1983.
Mahan, Mahon, Mayhon, etc., census and marriage records. Six different branches from Tennessee, Virginia, Kentucky, and Georgia. Mimeographed. Indexed.
Paper—$5.00—43pp------------------------------------- Vendor #D1748

3770 - WILLIAM GAYLORD (1585-1673) AND DESCENDANTS compiled by Barry C. Wood. 1980.
Compilation from various sources on the descendants of William Gaylord, with supplements. Loose leaf, no binder.
Paper—768pp--- Vendor #D1750

3771 - WISE RESEARCH REPORTER—A RESEARCH AID FOR WISE RESEARCH-ERS AND DESCENDANTS edited and published by Jack E. Wise.
Includes all variant spellings of Wise. Fourth year of publication.
Published Quarterly--$6.00 per calendar year. Queries free to subscribers. Back issues available--$5.00 per volume.
Subscription--$6.00/yr--Vendor #D1751

3772 - PAMUNKEY NEIGHBORS—ORANGE COUNTY, VIRGINIA, First Ed., compiled by Ruth and Sam Sparacio. 1984.
Transcription of original court records in Virginia, Kentucky, and Missouri from 1660-1900. Primary families: Lindsay, Mills, Stevens, Mountague. Related families: Brockman, Burrus, Daniel, Hill, Merry, Roach, Robinson, Thomas, Thompson, Ware. Also over 1,000 other surnames. Contains genealogical information and events affecting these families primarily during two generations in Orange County but includes related information from earlier generations in Middlesex, Essex, Caroline, Spotsylvania Counties and later generations Kentucky and Missouri.
Cloth—$30.00—600pp--- Vendor #D1754

3773 - CANFIELD FAMILY ASSOCIATION: CAMFIELD, CAMPFIELD, CANFIELD organized and edited by Genevieve (Canfield) Martinson.
Canfield Family Association. Genevieve (Canfield) Martinson, Organizer-Editor. Quarterly publication of genealogical information for all spellings of name, and allied lines. Indexed.
Queries for members.
Subscription—$6.00/yr—16/18pp-------------------------- Vendor #D1755

3774 - 92 YEARS OF RECOLLECTIONS AND RECIPES by Mary (Marie) B. Vaught Long. 1980.
From the alert mind of ninety-two-year-old Mrs. Marie Vaught Long has come this delightful collection of family history, personal remin-iscences, words of faith and wisdom, poetry, and favorite family recipes. Mrs. Long and her daughter, Maxine Long Atkins, spent nearly three years compiling the information for this book and se-curing the 800 photographs and illustrations which appear throughout. Charmingly related in Mrs. Long's own words, as recorded by her daughter, the autobiographical portion of the book tells of her early life on a Missouri farm, her marriage to Charles Long at age eighteen, and her long married life, most of it spent in the town of Hannibal, Missouri. Interwoven throughout the autobiography is evidence of Mrs. Long's deep religious faith, her special interest in music, her intense devotion to her family, and her strong compassion for other people.
Certainly a unique and priceless legacy to Mrs. Long's children and grandchildren, this book will appeal to other readers who are interested in the human spirit and/or are always eager to discover "tried and tested" good family recipes.
Cloth—$29.00—485pp--- Vendor #D1758

3775 - SIX GENERATIONS OF LA RUES AND ALLIED FAMILIES: CARMAN, HODGEN, HELM, BUZAN, RUST, McDONALD, CASTLEMAN, WALTERS, ALEXANDER, MEDLEY, McMAHON, VERTREES, KEITH, WINTERSMITH, CLAY, NEILL, GRANTHAM, VanMETER, AND ENLOW by Otis M. Mather. facs. repr. of 1921 ed.
Contains sketch of Isaac LaRue, Senior, who died in Frederick County, Virginia, in 1795, and some account of his American ancestors and three generations of his descendants and families who were connected by intermarriage. Copies of six old wills and other old documents; various incidents connected with the settlement of the Nolynn Valley in Kentucky; also, a chapter on the LaRue family and the child Abraham Lincoln. 14 illustrations; indexed.
Cloth—$17.00—198pp--------------------------------- Vendor #D1759

3776 - THE PIERCES AND THEIR POSTERITY—A FAMILY HISTORY compiled by Clara Pierce, Jas. P. McClurkin and Graham L. Pierce. 1981.
A record of the family with traces of its earliest history to the more complete development of family lines in the Southern States embracing Virginia, North and South Carolina, Georgia, Louisiana, Mississippi, Texas, Oklahoma, Arkansas, and New Mexico.
Illustrations and charts with Coat-of-Arms in color as the frontispiece.
Coat-of-Arms sold separate (suitable for framing)—$5.00.
Cloth—$20.00—320pp--- Vendor #D1760

3777 - THE ABER QUARTERLY 1971-1972 (8 issues) and THE ABER BULLETIN 1973-1982 (20 issues) by Hugh T. Law, et al. 1971-1982.
Genealogical and historical articles and photographs on the Aber Family and descendants. Several lines traced to Europe. Very attractive publication. Photocopies of out-of-print issues.
Paper—$2.50 ea—24+pp--Vendor #D1762

3778 - JOHNSON JOURNAL edited and published by Miz Johnson.
Pub. 3 times/yr.
Clearinghouse for data on all Johnson families and related lines.
Pedigree charts, family group sheets—records of all kinds.
Free queries.
Subscription—$10.00/yr--Vendor #D1764

3779 - ROBERTS REGISTER edited and published by Maxine Roberts.
Pub. 3 times/yr.
Clearinghouse for data on all Roberts families and related lines.
Pedigree charts, family group sheets—records of all kinds.
Free queries.
Subscription—$10.00/yr--Vendor #D1764

3780 - FROM THE DANUBE TO THE SUSQUEHANNA: 350 YEARS OF THE KITZMILLER FAMILY by John M. Kitzmiller, II and John M. Kitzmiller. 1983.
From Helfenberg, Austria to Lancaster County, Pennsylvania, descendants of Joachim Kitzmüller are traced. Book contains over 120 photos and maps; indexed. Appendix has transcribed wills, deeds, etc.; and book is footnoted.
Cloth—$40.00—500+pp--- Vendor #D1765

3781 - VIRGINIA HISTORY AND WHITFIELD BIOGRAPHIES by Vallie Jo Whitfield. 1976.
Colonial Historic Records on Whitfields, of Virginia.
Paper—$25.00—415pp--- Vendor #D1766

3782 - THE HOELSCHER FAMILY OF TEXAS compiled by Theresa Gros Gold and Donald T. Hoelscher. 1978.
Anton and Mary Katherine Hoelscher landed in Texas in 1846. This book traces the Hoelscher genealogy back 100 years in Germany and forward to the present, listing all 12,000 descendants of the couple, said to be the largest family in Texas. Includes biographies of the first three generations, photographs, maps, documents.
Complete name index.
Paper—$11.00—616pp--- Vendor #D1767

3783 - THE DeREVERE FAMILY OF PEEKSKILL, NEW YORK by Donn Devine. 1982.
Ancestry and descendants of John W. DeRevere (1839-1914) and his wife Martha Goetschius (1844-1921). Ancestral families include Underhill, Drake, Van Tassel, Wessels, Lent, Babcock.
Paper—$5.00—48pp--- Vendor #D1772

3784 - HOUSE OF FRANCISCUS by John Allen Franciscus, Melba Taylor Hargis, and Jan Simmons Johnson. 1986.
Descendants of Christophel Franciscus born 1680 in Germany. Follows family migration to Virginia, Tennessee, Kentucky, Missouri, Colorado, Montana. Includes many female and Francisco lines, McGuire, McMinn, Shiflett, Simmons, Allison, Harrison, Steele, etc. in Lancaster County, Pennsylvania; Tazewell, Russell, Scott, Augusta Counties, Virginia; Hawkins, Meigs, Bradley Counties, Tennessee; Washington County.

Arkansas; Saline County, Missouri. Will answer short queries for SASE.
We approximate $75.00 for 2 or 3-volume set.
(In process)—Cloth—apx $75.00/Set—apx 2000pp------------ Vendor #D1773

3785   - COUSINS by Jan Simmons Johnson. 1981.
Descendants of Christian Simmons of Rogersville, Tennessee (b. 1765).
Includes Anderson, Bellah, Bellamy, Brewer, Brooks, Creech, Crumley,
Davidson, Eidson, Emmert, Gillenwater(s), Gross, Henard, Horne,
Isenberg, Kensinger, Klepper, Looney, Marshall, Miller, Molsbee,
Pilant, Price, Shanks, Sizemore, Still, Taylor.
Paper—$30.00—800pp----------------------------------- Vendor #D1773

3786   - FROM VIKING GLORY: NOTES ON THE McCORKLE FAMILY IN
SCOTLAND AND AMERICA by Rev. Louis W. McCorkle. 1982.
Historical notes on the McCorkle family: origin in Scotland; early
McCorkles in Ireland; early McCorkles in America including Robert of
Waxhaw, James of the Brandywine, William of the Valley of Virginia,
and Samuel of Paxtang with biographical sketches of some descendants;
genealogy of some descendants. Index of 43 pages with 3,000 names;
die-stamped cover; hardbound.
Cloth—$50.00—423pp---------------------------------- Vendor #D1774

3787   - BUNTING BOOK compiled by Elizabeth Potts Koleda. 1981.
Anthony and Ellen (Barker) Bunting's four sons; William, Samuel, John
and Job with descendants as far as known. Settled in New Jersey and
Pennsylvania, migrated to Ohio and the West.
Hardbound, 6¼"x9¼'. Every name index.
Cloth—$26.50—350pp---------------------------------- Vendor #D1775

3788   - THE MONGERS A FAMILY OF OLD VIRGINIA by Billie Jo Monger.
1981.
A compendium of East Rockingham families. 107 Documents—164 pictures
(many family groups). Primary emphasis upon family of William Henry
Monger, the first of the surname into the Shenandoah Valley. Some
families represented are Anderson, Armentrout, Aughe, Baugher,
Boring (Bowing), Breeden, Davis, Dean, Deck (Teck, Tack), Hensley,
Dofflemyer (Tofflemyer), Eddins, Eppard (Ebert), Ferris, Good,
Gooden, Lam (Lamb), Leap (Leib), Long, Meadows, Miller, Monger
(Manger, Minger, Mounger, Munger), Rumball, Shifflett, Sycks
(Six), Sullivan, Weder, Wigle, Williams, Wyant (Wiant). 1255 to present.
Includes those people captured at Ruddles Station in Kentucky on
June 20, 1780 and carried to Canada.
8½"x11¼"; double column; indexed.
Cloth—$35.00—488pp------------------------------------ Vendor #D1776

3789   - SOME FAMILIES OF THE SHENANDOAH VALLEY, VOLUME I by
Billie Jo Monger. 1984.
Families of Dofflemyer (Dofflemier, Tofflemier), Frazier, Kyger (Geiger).
-- Vendor #D1776

3790   - SOME FAMILIES OF THE SHENANDOAH VALLEY, VOLUME II by
Billie Jo Monger. 1984.
Families of Lilly, Maiden, Warvel (Warble).
-- Vendor #D1776

3791   - THE DUNN—ANDERSON STORY by Virginia Dunn Kraut. 1980.
This attractive hard-cover book of 285 pages is of great interest to the
many descendants of the "Benjamin Dunn" and the "John Anderson" of
this story.
The Dunn line in this book starts with Benjamin Dunn, born ca 1785 in
South Carolina, died 1855 in Tennessee and traces his family through his
son, Jackson L., born 1809 in Tennessee, died 1884 in Kentucky; his
son, William Carroll, born 1828 in Kentucky, died 1906 in Kentucky,
his son, William Thomas, born 1866 in Kentucky, died 1950 in Indiana;
and his son, William Ferris, born 1891 in Kentucky, died 1964 in
Oklahoma. Information on all of the children of William Thomas who
married Florence Clementine Anderson in 1885 and on all of the children
of his oldest son, William Ferris, is included.
The Anderson line in this book starts with John Anderson, born 1732 in

Scotland, died 1781 in South Carolina (killed in the Revolutionary War) and traces his family through his son, Vincent, born ca 1768 in Virginia, died 1840 in Texas; his son, Crawford, born 1793 in South Carolina, died 1870 in Kentucky; his son, Holland Livingston, born 1823 in Kentucky, died 1877 in Kentucky; his daughter, Florence Clementine, born 1866 in Kentucky, died 1894 in Kentucky; her son, William Ferris Dunn, the last Dunn mentioned in the paragraph above. (The author is the fourth oldest child of William Ferris Dunn.)

The Dunn Story and the Anderson Story are each told separately and biographical sketches of each ancestor is given. Many photographs are included and an Excursus is presented for each wife or husband. These stories include the names Clay, Stoneham, Newton and Mansfield on the Dunn line, and Carney, Terry, Cunningham and Adams on the Anderson line. Many other families, allied to these are also presented.

Records are listed and ancestor charts and family sheets for each ancestor are included. An empty Addenda page has been added for each subject so that owners may add their own supplementary information. The first ·170 pages are given to the Dunn and Anderson Stories and to each ancestor's story. The rest of the book is devoted to the twelve Dunn-Anderson children and then specifically to a special Dunn-Anderson son, William Ferris Dunn and his children. The last twelve pages are exclusively the "Author's Own Department."

The Table of Contents is designed to simplify research on any members of this family and there is a complete index of all names. Color plates of the Dunn and Anderson Coats-of-Arms are included and complete stories on them as well as the names themselves.

The price of this book is $15.00 and may be ordered from Virginia Dunn Kraut, P. O. Box 51, Green Lake, Wisconsin 54941.

Cloth—$15.00—285pp--------------------------------- Vendor #D1780

3792   - INDIAN HOLLOW ROAD—A 19TH CENTURY AMERICAN FAMILY, THEIR LETTERS, THEIR STORY—VOLUME ONE by JoAnne Meade Webster. 1984.

Author's narrative links 263 complete letters and reminiscences describing experiences of an extended family (Connecticut origins) migrating to Ohio 1818-28, spreading into Illinois, Wisconsin, Louisiana, Michigan, Iowa, and beyond, before the Civil War. Maps and details about Indian Hollow Road, Carlisle Township, Lorain County, Ohio (home of William Webster, Jr. to whom most letters were addressed). Reminiscences cover difficulties in north-central Illinois 1838-45. Letters describe growth of ElkHorn, Wisconsin 1844-60, and hardships in western Iowa 1853-64. Civil War letters describe Union soldiers' experiences at Cumberland Gap, Tennessee; Martinsburg, West Virginia; western Kentucky; Mississippi River area, southern Louisiana.

Story spans three generations of the following families (residing Lorain County, Ohio unless otherwise noted): Webster, William Sr. (1778-1843) and Abigail Johnson (1783-1862): sons William, Jr., Bethuel Johnson, Michigan (later LaGrange, Ohio), and Henry DeLafayette (multi-locations); sons-in-law Abram VanDeBerg, Mayfield, Illinois, Josiah Weston, Augusta and Lamoille, Illinois, Levi Lee, ElkHorn, Wisconsin, Harris Sheldon, Calvin Brooks.

Phillips, Henry J. (1786-1864) and Abigail Finch (1784-1833): sons Jeremiah, Belvidere, Illinois, William, and Edward; sons-in-law Don Carols Wilmot and -?- Sweeley, Adel, Iowa, Augustus White, Freeport, Illinois (later Denison, Texas), and John Burrell.

Kelsey, Asahel Allis (1768-1893) and Anna Johnson (1772-1854): sons Henry and Frederick; sons-in-law Joseph Merrick (Connecticut), and William Stow.

Johnson, Phineas (1768-1840) and Hannah Miller (1768-1826): sons William, Kishwaukee, Illinois, Phineas, eastern Wisconsin, Isaac, Kishwaukee (later Oberlin, Ohio); sons-in-law Hezekiah Brooks, Samuel Brooks, Norris Stow, Niram Bruce, Horatio Nelson Gates. Additional family names (marriages, deaths, neighbors) in text. 6¼"x9¼"; Kentucky residents add tax.

Cloth—$18.95—554pp----------------------------------- Vendor #D1782

3793 - INDIAN HOLLOW ROAD—A 19TH CENTURY AMERICAN FAMILY, THEIR LETTERS, THEIR STORY—VOLUME TWO by JoAnne Meade Webster. 1985.
To be published 1985, illustrations, 2-volume index.
Covering period 1865-1890. Purchasers of Volume One will be notified upon publication. 6¼"x9¼".
(In process)—Cloth—apx $19.00—apx 550pp----------------- Vendor #D1782

3794 - DESCENDANTS OF DAVID McCONNAUGHHAY AND MARTHA JANE RANSON by Gerald M. Born. 1982.
Paper—$11.50—125pp------------------------------------ Vendor #D1784

3795 - GRAVES ASSOCIATION NEWSLETTER edited by Gerald M. Born.
Paper—$10.00—pub. 4 x annually—pp vary----------------- Vendor #D1784

3796 - ARCHIBALD CLAN NEWSLETTER edited by Gerald M. Born.
Paper—$5.00—pub. 4 x annually—pp vary------------------ Vendor #D1784

3797 - JARNAGIN COLLECTION AND ALLIED FAMILIES by Glenn S. Clark. 1977.
Descendants of Captain Thomas Jarnagin and Mary Witt.
Allied families: Carmichael, Carson, Clark, Donaldson, Galbraith, Gill, Inman, Lea, Scruggs, Shields, Stokely, etc. 8½"x11", offset.
Paper—$25.00—512pp------------------------------------ Vendor #D1785

3798 - ANCESTORS AND DESCENDANTS OF ELISHA MARTIN FREEMAN by Effie Darnell Volkland. 1984.
Includes Family Histories, Charts, Vital Records, 1583-1983.
Over 80 photographs. Includes descendants of: Arlie S. Freeman and Kate Gardner; John P. Freeman and Dora Booher; Will S. Freeman and Carrie Bales; James M. Darnell and Effie E. Freeman; Sam Hegarty and Hattie Freeman.
Includes allied families: Anderson, Burt, Childs, Clark, Collins, Corley, Cott, Coulson, Cramer, Cunningham, Darnell, Durbin, Enns, Farnum, Frazer, Goheen, Hegarty, Hoar, Hopper, Kee, Logue, Martin, Marvin, Milam, Million, Moore, Olmsted, Parker, Sterling, Thies, Urton, Volkland, Waltrip, Wiegel, Wilcoxen, Willis, and Winnop.
Indexed.
Cloth—$55.00—650+pp---------------------------------- Vendor #D1787

3799 - METZLER FAMILY 1700-1981 by Martha Mae Schmidt. 1981.
Came from Harpertshausen, Germany 1851, settled at Lenzburg, St. Clair County, Illinois and Shumway, Effingham County, Illinois.
Includes related families of Waeltz, Winter, Steinheimer, Mueller, Keim, Stroh, Heil, Erb, Buechler, Engel, Brummerstedt, Kunze, Miller, Struse, Prediger, Kiefer, Wirth, Hammel, Quast, Schafer, Hoese, Petzing and Herzberg. Indexed.
Cloth—$34.50—312pp----------------------------------- Vendor #D1791

3800 - HAMMEL—LAUFER FAMILIES 1675-1978 by Martha Mae Schmidt. 1978.
Came from Steinwenden, Germany 1840, settled at Millstedt, St. Clair County, Illinois, later also lived in Randolph and Perry Counties, Illinois. Includes related families of: Buecher, Stahlman, Ray, Heuman, Miller, Schwartz, Muskopf, Thompson, Rettinghouse, Berger, Reinhardt, Henrici, Jansen, Heinen, Pritz, Schmalriede, Jung, Saal, Kocher, Mines, Hein, and Kimmel. Indexed.
Cloth—$19.50—300pp----------------------------------- Vendor #D1791

3801 - BACON FAMILIES ASSOCIATION NEWSLETTER edited by John W. Hammersmith.
Information on ancestors and descendants, All Bacon lines (quarterly); queries.
Subscription—$8.00/yr dues—ave. 60pp/yr----------------- Vendor #D1792

3802 - McKNIGHT GENEALOGY 1754-1981 by Lilla M. Licht and William B. Moore. 1981.
Indexed; Documents all the descendants of James McKnight (1754-1835), Pennsylvania, known at time of publication. A second section gives the early history in Scotland, Ulster Province, North Ireland, and Early Scotch Irish Settlements in America. Queries with SASE welcomed.
Cloth—$23.50—Paper—$22.00—476pp---------------------- Vendor #D1796

3803   - McKNIGHT NEWSLETTER edited and published by Lilla McKnight Licht.
Quarterly publication; publishes: New information and corrections to the *McKnight Genealogy 1754-1981*; a communication media for descendants of James McKnight; Clearinghouse and exchange for all other McKnights seeking their McKnight "roots"; Free queries.
Back issues available.
Subscription—$6.00/yr—6pp/issue------------------------- Vendor #D1796

3804   - PHILBRICK/PHILBROOK FAMILY FILE by Joseph L. Philbrick, Ph.D.
Family organization newsletter, queries, and genealogical supplements to family history.
Pub. monthly--Vendor #D1798

3805   - PHILBRICK/PHILBROOK FAMILY HISTORY by Rev. J. Chapman and J. L. Philbrick, Ph.D. 1983.
Definitive genealogies from Thomas Philbrick 1600's through nine generations. Supplement in preparation.
Paper—$24.95—158pp------------------------------------ Vendor #D1798

3806   - OUR DAWSON KIN by Sallie M. Patin. 1981.
The History of William Dawson and Dinah McCormick descendants.
Indexed. Includes some biographies, family Bible records, family cemeteries, official documents and pedigree charts.
William Dawson born 1772 and Dinah McCormick born 1775 in Virginia. she was the daughter of Samuel McCormick. They married in Rockbridge County, Virginia on January 1, 1795 and later moved to Amite County, Mississippi then to West Feleciana, Louisiana.
This includes listings of 177 persons of Dawson name and 528 allied names. There are 1,741 persons of allied names including Kennedy, McCarstle, Morrison, Peairs, Perry, Reeks, McCormick, Rogillio, Wicker, and Woodside.
Cloth—$22.00—240pp----------------------------------- Vendor #D1799

3807   - WHITFIELD HISTORY AND GENEALOGY OF TENNESSEE by Vallie Jo Whitfield. 1979, repr. of 1964 ed.
Tennessee records on Whitfields of several counties.
Cloth—$15.00—320pp---------------------------------- Vendor #D1766

3808   - PAINTER FAMILIES by Harold N. Painter. 1982.
Charts of various families of Painters.
Paper—$11.00—61pp----------------------------------- Vendor #D1800

3809   - PAINTER RECORDS by Harold N. Painter. 1983.
Vital statistics of Painters all over.
Paper—$11.00—64pp----------------------------------- Vendor #D1800

3810   - THE PAINTER CLAN by James L. Douthat.
Newsletter of Descendants of Painters of Wythe County, Virginia.
Subscription—$7.50/yr-------------------------------Vendor #D1800

3811   - HISTORY AND GENEALOGY OF THE EARLY MORMON CHURCH IN ARKANSAS (1897-1975) by Emogene Tindall. 1983.
The first branch of the Mormon Church in Arkansas was established at the Barney Community in Northern Faulkner County. The second was the Baker Branch located about three miles away. In the beginning, the Mormons were persecuted by other members of the community. When this community was established Mormons from all over the state moved there so they could worship as they pleased.
Contains information of their hardships and the genelaogy of two of the most prominant families (the Bakers and Nooners). These two branches were later divided into Conway, Russellville, and Searcy Wards. It contains a list of members, their parents, and date and place of birth, emigration to Utah, and ten pages of pictures. Other names include: Barkhimer, Bell, Brown, Cox, Davis, Edgmon, Franklin, Goodman, Haggard, Holeman, Johnson, Keeling, Larson, Lawrence, Long, McDonald, McFadden, McGaha, Martin, Morgan, Parker, Sherwood, Smith, Spradlin, Taylor, Thomas, Williams, Wilson and Young. 150 pages indexed, Velo-bind, soft cover.
Over 5,000 names. $17.00 postpaid.
Soft cover—$17.00—150pp----------------------------- Vendor #D1801

3812 - SIGMON GENEALOGY—THE SIGMONS AND THEIR KIN by Edith
McGhee Sigmon. 1983.
Paper—$16.00—159pp------------------------------------- Vendor #D1802

3813 - THREE CENTURIES WITH THE ROSENBERGER—ROSENBERRY
FAMILY 1698-1983 by Myra Fields and Edward Rosenberry. 1983.
This book provides a definitive work on the extensive Rosenberger-
Rosenberry family of South-Central Pennsylvania and their related
families. It begins by tracing colonial family roots and probable
European origins. Detailed consideration centers 1.) upon the life
and descendants of Abraham and Juliana Lang Rosenberger of Letter-
kenny Township, Franklin County, Pennsylvania and their four
sons: Daniel (born 1752), Abraham (born 1754), Jacob (born 1756),
John Martin (born 1759); 2.) upon the descendants of Henry and
Rebecca Rosenberger of West Pennsborough Township, Cumberland
County, Pennsylvania through their son Oliver (born 1772).
Many source documents (wills, inventories, obituaries, letters, etc.)
add to the genealogical outline.
Family lineages, based on twenty-five years of personal correspon-
dence and research in civil and ecclesiastical archives, furnish de-
tailed data on the family and collateral lines of Bashore, Beltz,
Brown, Carbaugh, Coons, Diehl, Dixon, Fields, Fleagle, Forrester,
Guyer, Horn, Johnson, Keefer, Long, Mackey, Miller, Myers,
Neusbaum, Peebles, Reed, Rexroth, Rotz, Williams, Witherow,
Yohe, and hundreds more. The fifty page index contains over
20,000 entries. 8½"x11"; 835 illustrations.
Cloth—$55.00—990pp------------------------------------- Vendor #D1804

3814 - GUARDIANS OF THE NEW WORLD by Doris H. Wackerbarth. 1982.
Living history and drama—researched over twenty years in the United
States and Great Britain. Daily lives of our earliest pioneers and their
secret guests: Whalley, and Goffe, refugee judges of Charles I—at the
time of King Philip's War. Map. Bibliography.
Includes surnames: Atherton, Barnard, Beers, Bodwell, Bull,
Chamberlain, Clark(e), Cook(e), Cooper, Cowles, Crawford,
Dickinson, Eastman (Tilton), Gilbert, Goodman, Goodwin, Granis,
Hawkes, Hawley, Jennings, Kellogg, Lewis, Marsh, Mosely, Nash,
Newell, Plympton, Porter, Pynchon, Russell, Savage, Smith (Samuel),
Stockwell, Talcott, Terry, Treat, Wait, Webster, Wells, White.
A thoughtful gift for Ancestor Hunters.
...colorful tapestry...a warm and poignant story...*Northampton Daily
Hampshire Gazette*;...wonderfully instructive...provocative informa-
tion about...the years of development in the colonies...*Smith College
Alumnae Quarterly*; Well-documented...fascinating reading—*Greenfield
Recorder*; Mystery and suspense...a story for all ages...*Springfield
Daily News*.
Cloth—$12.95—Paper—$6.95—278pp------------------------ Vendor #D1807

3815 - MISSOURI ORDEAL, 1862-1864; DIARIES OF WILLARD HALL
MENDENHALL transcribed by Margaret Mendenhall Frazier,
annotations by Dr. James W. Goodrich. 1985.
W. H. Mendenhall mentioned daily each individual his family contacted.
Information on several generations of antecedents of Willard Hall
Mendenhall and his wife, Mary Margaret Kavanaugh are included. The
index includes 350 individual names. Approximately 240 pages,
publication expected early 1985.
(In process)—apx 240pp------------------------------ Vendor #D1810

3816 - BLACKWELL NEWSLETTER edited by John D. Blackwell. 1979 to
date.
An international semi-annual on Blackwell family history.
Subscription—$7.00/yr—40pp/yr------------------------- Vendor #D1811

3817 - ALEXANDER BEALL—1649-1744 OF MARYLAND, ONE LINE OF
DESCENT IN AMERICA by William Hunter McLean. 1977.
The Alexander Beall line is traced from St. Andrews Parish, Fife
County, Scotland 1649 to Maryland ca 1666 and on to Texas in mid
1800's.

Early Fort Worth history—Frances Cooke Van Zandt—Well researched
and documented.
Some names included are: Bell, Beal, Beale, Bale, and Behil—
Ballantyne, Butler, Covode, Dreiss, Gleason, Hardwick, Hunnam,
Johnson, Lewis, Long, Magruder, McCaleb, McLean, Neal, Offutt,
Ryan, Sanders, Smith, Stevens, Thompson, Van Zandt and Wilson.
6"x9"; typeset; indexed.
Cloth—$17.50—90pp-- Vendor #D1812

3818   - FROM AYR TO THURBER, THREE HUNTER BROTHERS AND THE
WINNING OF THE WEST by William Hunter McLean. 1978.
From William Hunter born 1728 in Ayr County, Scotland to the three
sons of Adam Hunter (Robert Dickie, William and David) of Macoupin
County, Illinois and Mercer County, Missouri and their exploits in the
West. Buffalo hunting with Bill Cody—Cattle from Texas to Kansas
and Missouri—Texas and Pacific Coal Company of Thurber, Texas—
Early Fort Worth—Apple orchards and H3 Niobrara Ranch in Nebraska—
Blizzard of 1887—Lincoln County, New Mexico War 1877-1878—
Murphy-Chism Fued—Family pictures.
7"x10"; typeset; indexed; thoroughly researched; well documented.
Some names included are: Beall, Blair, Chisum, Crosby, Dillon,
Goodman, Lothian, Marston, McClatchie, McCown, McLean, Phelan,
Reynolds, Thurber, Waggoner.
Cloth—$25.00—158pp-- Vendor #D1812

3819   - RHINEHART/RINEHART AND ERVIN/IRWIN FAMILIES OF INDIANA
by Kathryn Rhinehart Bassett. 1983.
Frederick Rinehart (b 1788 Pennsylvania) and Catherine Burl were
parents of Jacob (b 1815) and Catherine (b 1821). James Irwin
(b 1789 Ireland) and Nancy Ann Herral (b 1796 Kentucky) married
1815 in Butler County, Ohio and were parents of Alexander (b 1823)
and Julia Ann (b 1827). Jacob married Julia Ann in 1847 and Alexander married Catherine in 1843. Both marriages Butler County,
Ohio. The Rinehart and Irwin families moved to Indiana. I will
check index for $1.00 and SASE.
The collateral families include: Ash, Dunlap, Hasty, Kellin, Landis,
Moulden, Rohrig, Stech, Thompson, Tinder, Vance, Wamsley.
Book incluces photos and vital records. Rinehart/Irwin spelled
Rhinehart/Ervin by current generations. 8½"x11".
Paper—$25.00—325pp--- Vendor #D1813

3820   - THE SHEPARD FAMILIES OF NEW ENGLAND, VOLUME I, RALPH
SHEPARD OF DEDHAM compiled by Gerald Faulkner Shepard, edited
by Donald Lines Jacobus. 1971.
Cloth—$28.00—612pp--- Vendor #D1814

3821   - THE SHEPARD FAMILIES OF NEW ENGLAND, VOLUME II, EDWARD
SHEPARD OF CAMBRIDGE compiled by Gerald Faulkner Shepard,
edited by Donald Lines Jacobus. 1972.
Cloth—$28.00—520pp--- Vendor #D1814

3822   - THE SHEPARD FAMILIES OF NEW ENGLAND, VOLUME III, ADDITIONAL
FAMILY GROUPS compiled by Gerald Faulkner Shepard, edited by
Donald Lines Jacobus. 1973.
All Three Volumes—$60.00
Cloth—$28.00—567pp--- Vendor #D1814

3823   - PHOTOCOPY OF THE 1927 PARDEE GENEALOGY by Donald Lines
Jacobus. 1927.
Paper—$50.00—693pp--- Vendor #D1814

3824   - THE EARLY DAYTONS AND DESCENDANTS OF HENRY, JR. by
Donald Lines Jacobus and Arthur B. Dayton. 1959.
Cloth—$19.50—93pp-- Vendor #D1814

3825   - BLISS AND HOLMES DESCENDANTS by Elinor Bliss Dayton and
Arthur B. Dayton. 1961.
Cloth—$30.50—184pp--- Vendor #D1814

3826   - TOWNSHEND HERITAGE by Doris B. Townshend. 1971.
       Cloth—$19.50—380pp--- Vendor #D1814

3827   - GENEALOGIES OF THE MOORES AND HOPKINSES OF GUILFORD AND
       ROCKINGHAM COUNTIES, NORTH CAROLINA by Beatrice M. Caffey
       and Mary A. Browning. 1981.
       Separate genealogies of the Moore and Hopkins families, both moving
       to North Carolina from the Eastern Shore of Maryland. Eight gener-
       ations of Moores, seven of Hopkinses. Other surnames prominently
       mentioned: Bevil, Burton, Caffey, Connor, Dilworth, Doggett,
       Golding, Huffines, Johnson, Joyce, McNairy, Scott, Walker, Whitsett
       and Wright. Standard genealogical format; detailed index.
       Cloth—$16.00—144+pp------------------------------------- Vendor #D1815

3828   - GENEALOGIES OF THE CAFFEYS, IRELANDS AND ISELEYS OF
       ROCKINGHAM, GUILFORD AND ALAMANCE COUNTIES, NORTH
       CAROLINA by Beatrice M. Caffey and Mary A. Browning. 1981.
       Separate genealogies for Caffeys, Iseleys and Irelands, eight gener-
       ations of each. Caffeys and Irelands to North Carolina from Eastern
       Shore of Maryland; Iseleys from Pennsylvania. Other frequently-
       mentioned surnames: Bevil, Brown, Daniely, Davis, Doggett, Gentry,
       Kernodle, Melvin, Moore, Pinnix, Rudd, Scott, Simpson, Smith,
       Summers. Standard genealogical format; detailed index.
       Cloth—$16.00—141+pp------------------------------------- Vendor #D1815

3829   - HALEYS PLUS by Clella Haley Combs. 1984.
       Photographs, genealogy charts, obituaries. Published by The Printery,
       Albany, Missouri. Haleys history begins with Barnabas Haley, 1759,
       of Virginia and Kentucky. Includes William Haley, John Haley,
       Granville Dee Haley, and descendants to present time. Family also
       lived in Illinois, Iowa, Missouri, Oklahoma, Texas, and Oregon.
       PLUS is research on Haley spouses. Eliza Jane Cornelison Haley's
       ancestry back to Cornelis Van Niewkercke, 1600; Amos Maupin,
       1600; Nicolas Gentry, 1697. Information about the Lang(s)ford
       family of Mt. Vernon, Kentucky, includes Matilda and her parents,
       Mary Warren and Stephen Langford. Minimal information about
       Nancy Riddle Haley. Cloth bound, approximately 100 pages.
       Cost $30.00 includes shipping.
       Cloth—$30.00—100pp------------------------------------- Vendor #D1816

3830   - THE JOHNSON FAMILY PICTORIAL AND BIOGRAPHICAL by Family
       Publications.
       "Instills new hope for the discouraged researcher."—Editor, *The John-*
       son Journal. A spectacular Johnson family review! 8½"x11".
       Paper—$6.50--- Vendor #D1817

3831   - THE WILLIAMS/WILLIAMSON FAMILY PICTORIAL AND BIOGRAPHICAL
       by Family Publications.
       "Interesting articles...beautifully done."—Editor, *Williams Newsletter.*
       The Williams/Williamson story in articles, biographies, and illustrations.
       8½"x11".
       Paper—$6.50--- Vendor #D1817

3832   - THE CARTMEL-CARTMELL-CARTMILL FAMILY QUARTERLY pub-
       lished quarterly by William Cartmel. 8½"x11".
       Paper—$18.95/yr--------------------------------------- Vendor #D1817

3833   - THE BROWN FAMILY PICTORIAL AND BIOGRAPHICAL by Family
       Publications.
       A much-acclaimed publication highlighting the Brown surname in pic-
       tures, articles, and biographies. 8½"x11".
       Paper—$6.50--- Vendor #D1817

3834   - ALBEMARLE COUNTY IN VIRGINIA by Rev. Edgar Woods. 1978,
       repr. of 1901 ed.
       Giving some account of what it was by nature and what it was made
       by man, and some of the men who made it. The first five chapters
       unfold the early history of the county. The remaining chapters give

brief genealogical sketches of early families, including Anderson, Brown, Carr, Carter, Clark, Dawson, Durrett, Fretwell, Garland, Garrett, Gooch, Hamner, Harris, Jefferson, Lewis, Meriwether, Monroe, Randolph, Rives, Rodes, Terrell, Timberlake, Watson, Wingfield, Wood, Woods, and many others.
Appendices give rosters of frontier militia, Revolutionary soldiers, military organizations of the county, county officers, emigrants from Albemarle to other states and a Necrology from 1744 through 1890. Indexed.
Cloth—$20.00—412pp--- Vendor #D1203

3835 - THE SMITH FAMILY PICTORIAL AND BIOGRAPHICAL by Family Publications.
A much-acclaimed publication highlighting the Smith surname in pictures, articles, and biographies. 8½"x11".
Paper—$6.50-- Vendor #D1817

3836 - THE JONES FAMILY PICTORIAL AND BIOGRAPHICAL by Family Publications.
"This magazine belongs with any collection of Jones material and can serve as a good reminder of how many men of distinction have brought special honor to the Jones name."—Editor, Jones Journeys. 8½"x11".
Paper—$6.50-- Vendor #D1817

3837 - THE DAVIS/DAVISON/DAVIDSON FAMILY PICTORIAL AND BIO-GRAPHICAL by Family Publications.
The unique story of these families is told in pictures, articles, and biographies. 8½"x11".
Paper—$6.50-- Vendor #D1817

3838 - THE CARTMELL PIONEERS by William Cartmel.
Highlighting the Cartmel-Cartmell-Cartmill families of America.
Allied lines: Hite, Crist, Froman, Van Meter, Grier. 8½"x11".
Paper—$10.00—52pp--- Vendor #D1817

3839 - THE MILLER FAMILY PICTORIAL AND BIOGRAPHICAL by Family Publications.
A much-acclaimed publication highlighting the Miller surname in pictures, articles, and biographies. 8½"x11".
Paper—$6.50-- Vendor #D1817

3840 - THE MARTIN FAMILY PICTORIAL AND BIOGRAPHICAL by Family Publications.
A much-acclaimed publication highlighting the Martin surname in pictures, articles, and biographies. 8½"x11".
Paper—$6.50-- Vendor #D1817

3841 - THE CARTERS, FROM COLONIZATION by Harold B. Carter.
Highlights the early families from England who settled in Maryland, Massachusetts, Connecticut, Delaware, Virginia, Ohio, and Indiana. 5½"x8½".
Paper—$12.00—76pp--- Vendor #D1817

3842 - A WITTER-WIDDER WORLD by Harold B. Carter and William Cartmel.
Highlights the early families of Pennsylvania, Missouri, Kansas, Oklahoma, Ohio, and other western states. 8½"x11".
Paper—$12.00--- Vendor #D1817

3843 - MOMENTS IN TIME: A HISTORY OF THE TORNILLO COMMUNITY AND ITS PEOPLE by Frances Segulia. 1981.
Tornillo is a small town that flanks Texas Highway 20 and the Southern Pacific Railroad in the extreme southwest section of Texas. It takes its name from the tornillo tree, a variety of mesquite native to southwestern United States and northern Mexico.
The history relates a comprehensive and somewhat nostalgic account of the town's beginnings and the development of surrounding farmland in the most rural section of El Paso County, the last acreage in the county to be included in the Rio Grande Irrigation Project following the completion of the Elephant Butte Dam in 1916.
Carefully researched detail along with candid personal recollections tell a story of a multi-cultural setting along the mid-section of the

Rio Grande, the international boundary between the Lone Star State and the Republic of Mexico.
It records family histories, photographs, and brief biographies of wome of the following families: Alarcon, Allison, Bailey, Beachler, Bell, Bidwell, Bonilla, Bramwell, Brown, Burrus, Cano, Carpenter, Chavez, Chesser, Cochran, Coker, Cox, Dudley, Flores, Gaines, Gardea, Garza, Gonzalez, Green, Henderson, Holguin, Jordan, Keith, LaSalde, Mebus, Miller, Owen, Palmer, Parker, Partridge, Pruitt, Rivera, Rodriguez, Samples, Sanders, Segulia, Shafer, Smith, Stahmann, Stallings, Stephens, Stewart, Thomas, Tippit, Whitehead, Williams, Wilson, Yahn, Young.
It includes over 400 black and white photographs and snapshots.
Cloth—$28.42—223pp-- Vendor #D1818

3844 - REV. JOHN HAMPTON DAVIS OF HIGHLAND COUNTY, OHIO, HIS FAMILY, ANCESTORS, DESCENDANTS by Joanne Cherry Johnson. 1983.
Ancestors from Loudoun County, Virginia. Every name index.
Davis, Miller, Hampton, Hixon, Tribby, Sheeler, Watts, Brown.
Paper—$7.50—91pp-------------------------------------- Vendor #D1819

3845 - THE GRASTY FAMILIES OF AMERICA, VOLUME ONE by Dolores I. Merritt, M. A. 1983.
Documented history of descendants of Sharshall Grasty (1687-1745). Synopsis of ancestors from 1280, specific descent proven from Randle (died 1604), authentic Coat of Arms (claimed 1664), plus records of Gresty/Gristy relatives of Barbadoes and Maryland. Female lines included when known, including much on: Bettisworth, Birdsong, Brannock, Clark, Coleman, FitzPatrick, Goodrich, Haskins, Jones, Kelly, Kenner, Lightfoot, Lyles, Stone, Pannill, Wadlington, Wooding, Wright of South Carolina and Virginia. Bible records, documents, pre-Civil War family letters reproduced. Indexed.
Paper—$16.00—119pp----------------------------------- Vendor #D1821

3846 - THE DIARIES OF GEORGE RILEY HAZARD (1854-1867)—BROOME COUNTY, NEW YORK AND SUSQUEHANNAH COUNTY, PENNSYL-VANIA by Dolores I. Merritt, M. A. 1981.
These diaries provide genealogist and historians with vital statistics and history not found elsewhere. Births, deaths, marriages, Civil War records and specific emigration for 2,000 individuals of 450 surnames concerning neighbors in both counties. Detailed Hazard history plus much: Barton, Bound, Blatchley, Buchannan, Buckingham, Conklin, Dickenson, Dobson, Guernsey, Jones, Judd, Odell, Patrie, Phillips, Snedaker, Spoor, Stevens, Trowbridge, Wilsey and others. Indexed.
Paper—$11.00—127pp----------------------------------- Vendor #D1821

3847 - THE MCCASLIN FINDER by Dolores I. Merritt, M. A. 1984.
Hundreds of birth, marriage, death, census records, family group sheets with researchers' addresses, transcriptions of Revolutionary and Civil War pension applications, plus much McCaslin miscellany collected during fourteen years surname research. Emphasis on Pennsylvania, Kentucky, Illinois, Indiana, Missouri, Oklahoma and Tennessee. Excellent "finding" aid.
Paper—apx. $11.00—apx 125pp--------------------------- Vendor #D1821

3848 - THE ANCESTRY AND DESCENDANTS OF PETER WILSEY—TWELVE GENERATIONS by Dolores I. Merritt, M. A. 1982.
From the immigrant Hendrick, son of Marten of Copenhagen, from 1658 to 1982. Through Theunise Hendricksen Wiltsee (bp 10 Jan 1674) to Hendrick Theunise Wiltsie (bp 29 June 1703) to Teunis (bp 25 Feb 1726) to Henry T. Wilsey (born 15 Jan 1753) to Peter (bp 19 Apr 1778) with all known descendants of Peter and Margaret (Falkner) Wilsey. Transcribed Revolutionary War pension applications of Henry and wife Margaret (Miller), plus 34 significant family letters from Kansas, Minnesota, Wisconsin, Illinois, Ohio. Indexed. Full bibliography of Wilsey sources for additional research.
Paper—$8.00—59pp------------------------------------- Vendor #D1821

3849 - MOLZEN FAMILY IN AMERICA by Marsha Hoffman Rising. 1981.
Ancestors and descendants of the Molzen family from Schleswig-
Holstein to Kansas.
Paper—$10.50—100pp-- Vendor #D1822

3850 - KILPATRICK AND ALLIED FAMILIES by Edward Floyd Kilpatrick.
1984.
This book traces the descendants of Jesse Kilpatrick 1768-1853,
Benjamin Hearnden/Errington/Harrington 1618-1687, William Withrow
1717-1770, and John Montanye (Dr. Johannes de la Montagne) 1595-
1670. This is believed to be the first comprehensive record of the
descendants of Jesse Kilpatrick and William Withrow. About 2,700
persons have been identified.
Among the allied families that are included are Auld, Axtell, Bair,
Benton, Bequeath, Bovey, Brawner, Bricker, Brickhous, Brown,
Chantry, Cockerham, Copes, Cowan, Darling, Davison, Day, Duerr,
Dunkle, Dyson, Gillan, Hammaker, Hardman, Harrington, Hassel-
quist, Hixson, Hurlbutt, Johnson, Jones, Landers, Larson, Lewis,
Lininger, McClintick, McCreary, McCurdy, Miles, Miller, Montanye,
Nehren, Nelson, Noonan, Nusbaum, Olney, Palmer, Park, Patterson,
Patton, Perdue, Phillips, Pugh, Raymond, Rhynas, Robison, Rosen-
berry, Scharff, Schulze, Seymour, Shearer, Smith, Snyder, Stinson,
Stoner, Strickler, Summers, Swain, Thomson, Trowbridge, Wagner,
Warner, Webb, Wilhelm, Wilson, Wineman, Witherow, Withrow, Woodrow,
Wyatt, Zeigler, and Zeis.
The Kilpatricks originally settled in and around Monmouth County,
New Jersey; the Harringtons in Boston and Providence; the Withrows
in Chester County, Pennsylvania; and the Montanyes in New Amster-
dam. Their descendants spread to nearly every state in the United
States but especially to central Illinois, northern Indiana, and south-
ern Michigan; southwestern Iowa and eastern Nebraska; central Ohio;
and south central Pennsylvania.
Cloth—$13.25—146pp------------------------------------- Vendor #D1827

3851 - "DESCENDANTS OF WILLIAM AND MARGARET McGAUGHEY" by Polly
Rachel McGaughey Sutton. 1984.
Fully indexed by McGaughey family and related families.
William and Margaret McGaughey sailed from Glasgow, Scotland and
settled in York County, Pennsylvania ca 1740. Their children were
James, John, Isabella, William, Alexander. Their descendants immi-
grated to Illinois, Iowa, Tennessee, Albama, Mississippi, Arkansas,
Texas, Oklahoma, plus many more states. Early court records, cem-
etery, church and family research made in the 1930's and many have
been brought to the present time. Family lineage records furnished
by personal contact and correspondence. Research in the National
Archives, state and county courthouses.
Related families: Bigham, Blair, Boyd, Britton, Brooker, Brown,
Carnahan, Chilcote, Davis, Dobson, Gammill, Gordon, Hall, Henry,
Linn, Marshall, Moore, McCain, McClellan/d, McPherson, Reed, McKean,
Robinson, Schrecongest, Smith, Stephenson, Stewart/d, Torrence,
Walker...plus many more—over 4,000 names.
Cloth—$26.00 postage paid—270 pages—11½"x8½".
Cloth—$26.00—270pp--------------------------------------- Vendor #D1831

3852 - THE DORTCH FAMILY REFERENCE BOOK by James Perrin. 1981.
A general reference book on Dortch and Dorch families in the South.
Contains family genealogies, census, marriage, and land records.
Indexed.
Paper—$12.00—248pp------------------------------------- Vendor #D1832

3853 - CHAMBERLAIN FAMILIES, VOLUME I—OF RECORDS OF THE CHAMBER-
LAIN ASSOCIATION OF AMERICA FOUNDED IN 1897 edited by Alison
C. Ogilvie. 1984.
Includes female lines as well as male where known of five original
New England immigrants. Send SASE to Chamberlain Association
of America, 15 McKesson Hill Road, Chappaqua, NY 10514, for
publishing date and costs and order form.
(In process)--- Vendor #D1839

3854   - AMERICAN NYES OF GERMAN ORIGIN—VOLUME I by L. Bert Nye, Jr. 1984.
Descendants in United States and Canada of Johann Nicholas and Johann Adam Neu who emigrated from Kleinich, Germany to Philadelphia in 1749 and five generations of their ancestry in Germany. Descendants names spelled variously Nye, Ney, Nigh or Nie. Over 6,300 related individuals, completely indexed. Thirty-five illustrations including Coat of Arms and maps. Boxed in rigid slipcase.
Cloth—$37.00—654pp-- Vendor #D1841

3855   - AMERICAN NYES OF GERMAN ORIGIN—VOLUME II by L. Bert Nye, Jr. 1984.
Descendants of Andreas Ney, Fallendin Neu, Joseph Neu, H. George and Johannes Ney, Georg Ludwig Neu, Johan Nicholas Neu, Frederick and Francois Ney, Peter Neu and Freidrich Nye who came to America from the German Palatinate or Luxembourg between 1733 and 1860. Many descendants use the Nigh or Neigh spelling. Included genealogies of twenty-two other Pennsylvania-German "Nye" families as yet untraced to their immigrant ancestor. Over 5,000 related individuals, complete indexed. Twenty-two illustrations including Coat of Arms and maps. Boxed in rigid slipcase.
Cloth—$37.00—613pp-- Vendor #D1841

3856   - THE DESCENDANTS OF GEORGE FLINT OF HOLBEACH, LINCOLN-SHIRE; AND ALLIED FAMILIES by John Dobson.
The George Flint of the title flourished at the end of the 18th Century. This work will include, besides his descendants in Holbeach and in Wisbech, Cambridgeshire, those of his grandson George Flint (1823-1906) who came ca 1855 to Stouffville, York County, Ontario. Allied families include Teed and Madgham of Boston, Lincs., Teed of Wisbech, Barnes of Stouffville, Breuls of Markham Township, York County, Hatchard of Dorsetshire and Toronto, Bartholomew and Weidmann of Upper Mt. Methel Township, Northampton County, Pennsylvania, and Markham Township, and Yetter and Mills of Iowa. Information still sought and enquiries welcome.
(In process)-- Vendor #D1847

3857   - THE NUNNS OF XVIIITH CENTURY VIRGINIA, WITH ROSTER OF 1300 DESCENDANTS OF THE HENRY COUNTY CLAN by O. Norris Smith. 1984.
Paper—$6.00—50pp-------------------------------------- Vendor #D1848

3858   - DESCENDANTS OF PETER SIMMONS, BRUNSWICK COUNTY, VIR-GINIA: ALLIED LINES, HIATT, MILLS, PATTON, JAMES, HARLESS, McGRIFF by Gwen Boyer Bjorkman. 1973.
Paper—$8.00—180pp------------------------------------ Vendor #D1849

3859   - THE CHAMPION FAMILY—350 YEARS IN AMERICA by Ruth Crawley Champion.
Includes a brief history of the early settlers of Long Island, Hempstead Town; New Jersey pioneers of Old Gloucester and Great Egg Harbor; Hamilton and Clermont Counties in Ohio; and the westward exodus. Family names include the Champions, Ingersolls, Campbells, Steelmen, Sculls, and others. $16.00 postage paid.
Cloth—$16.00—154pp--------------------------------- Vendor #D1851

3860   - THE SWISS ON LOOKING GLASS PRAIRIE published by Friends of Lovejoy Library. 1983.
Includes information on families of Ammann, Bosshard, Brodtbeck, Buchmann, Feickert, Gysin, Hagnauer, Huegy, Koepfli, Kuenne, Leutwiler, Menz, Ryhiner, Schott, Seybt, Spindler, Suppiger.
--- Vendor #D1854

3861   - NEW SWITZERLAND IN ILLINOIS published by Friends of Lovejoy Library.
Includes information on families of Koepfli, Suppiger, and Eggen.
--- Vendor #D1854

3862 - "THE BRIN(C)KERHOFF'S OF AMERICA" by Rev. Theodore Brinck-
erhoff. 1984.
The genealogy of the more than 5,000 descendants of Joris Dircksen
Brinckerhoff (born 1604) compiled by Rev. Theodore Brinckerhoff.
Contains family history, biographies, genealogy, photos, maps,
first and last name index (over 2,000 surnames indexed).
Hard cover has family crest embossed in antique gold leaf. 11"x8½".
Cloth—$35.00—495pp--- Vendor #D1856

3863 - PETER SCHAUN by Anthony Jones. 1981.
Family History and Genealogy; 3,047 listings in the Index, 11 genea-
logical charts, 10 pages containing maps and pictures. Hardbound,
8½"x11", imitation leather, 70 pound stock.
Ohio County, Kentucky surnames: Barnett, Bennett, Benton, Shown,
Stevens, Talbott, Wallace, Webb.
Clay County, Illinois surnames: Davis, Eytchison, Hoard, Hord,
Jones, Ooton, Tolliver, Willis.
Maryland surnames: Dorsey, Higgins, Hobbs, Howard, Schaun,
Shown, Spurrier, Wheatcraft, Whitcraft.
Cloth—$27.50—300pp-- Vendor #D1858

3864 - THE WALLTONS OF BRUNSWICK COUNTY, VIRGINIA; DESCENDANTS
OF GEORGE AND ELIZABETH (ROWE) WALTON by Joe C. Tinney. 1984.
Named are members of 1,147 families and 4,339 descendants by line of
descent from the five children of George and Elizabeth, each with
Walton ancestry identified. Other topics: "Other Walton Families in
Colonial America;" "Waltons in England" (back to 13th Century);
wills; pictures and stories; migrations; index.
Cloth—$17.95—386pp-- Vendor #D1859

3865 - THOSE MISSISSIPPI UPCHURCH'S, 1817-1984 by Genevieve Tharp
Little. 1984.
Paper—$15.00—190pp-- Vendor #D1866

3866 - ELKINS FAMILY EXCHANGE NEWSLETTER.
Quarterly for all Elkins researchers. Published February, May, August,
November. Queries free to members. $1 to others. SASE to
Barbara Martin Thompson, 1679 Centurion Drive, Santa Rosa, CA 95401.
Subscription—$10.00/yr--- Vendor #D1868

3867 - BALL BEGINNINGS by Claudette Maerz. 3 issues/yr.
Paper—$12.00/yr—120-150pp/yr---------------------------------- Vendor #D1869

3868 - WRIGHT FAMILY WORKBOOK by Claudette Maerz. 3 issues/yr.
Paper—$12.00/yr—120-150pp/yr---------------------------------- Vendor #D1869

3869 - CHAMBERS HELPING CHAMBERS by Claudette Maerz. 3 issues/yr.
Paper—$14.00/yr—120-150pp/yr---------------------------------- Vendor #D1869

3870 - WOODSON WATCHER by Claudette Maerz. 3 issues/yr.
Paper—$14.00/yr—120-150pp/yr---------------------------------- Vendor #D1869

3871 - WEST SAXONY 452 AMERICA 1982, 3 Volumes by Richard Patterson.
1983.
Volume I—The Genealogical History of the Jarr(e)att Line from Ingil's
King of West Saxony thru Robert Devereaux b. 1591 d. 1646, Closing
with Memoranda of (Fair) Rosamond Clifford, Mistress of Henry II.
Surnames included are: Smith, Jarr(e)att, Ingils, De Bohun, Devereux,
Plantagenet, De Sarisburie, Benton, Brown, Coffee, Crockett, Haldeman,
Hollowell, Hoover, Jamison, Johnson, Lillard, Manson, Morris, Nelson,
Norvell, Patterson, Peacock, Purdy, Quarles, Smotherman, Sublett,
Taylor, Thompson, Washington, Clopton, Gilliam, Hardaway, Hastings,
Gooch, King, Lamar, May, Miller, Mims, Ransom, Sedberry, Wade,
White, Williamson, Woodson, Yeargan, Chilton, Kimbro (Kimbrough).
Also in Volume I are: Cynric, Ceawlin, Eahlmund, Egbert, Ethelwulf,
Ethelbald, Ethelbert, Ethelred I, Alfred (The Great), Edward,
Eadgifu, Athelstan, Edgar, Cnut.
Volume II—The Genealogical History of the Major Lawrence Smith
Family, Emigrant from Devonshire, England to Gloucester, Virginia
in 1652. Major Robert Smith of the Lawrence Smith family, married

Mary Jarratt in 1774, of Goochland County, Virginia. This volume carries the Smith Line through the year 1982.
Volume III—A continuation of Volume I of the emigrant Robert Jarratt, b. 1625, m. Mary _____ of Ireland, d. 1707. Both died in New Kent County, Virginia and carries the Smith Line through 1982.
The Index to Volume I is applicable only to that Volume.
The Index to Volume II is applicable to the Smith Line; the Index in Volume III is applicable to the Jarratt Line and there are many cross-references. The Family Tree of all three volumes appears only in Volume I.
Single Volumes—$60.00
Cloth—$180.00/Set of 3 vols.—575pp------------------------Vendor #D1870

3872   - THE BONNER FAMILY RECORD by Mrs. W. Gill Bonner.
Surry/Sussex Counties, Virginia, Southward-Westward.
Over twenty-five years researching Bonner and Allied families for this publication. Surname index.
Paper—$16.25--- Vendor #D1871

3873   - PRATER, PRATHER, PRAYTOR by Mrs. W. Gill Bonner.
Over fifty year collection of the late E. S. Lillard, and all the original researching done for the late Miss Eva H. Prather, plus over thirty years personal researching including the eight years I published the *Family Bulletin*, some years ago. For pedigree chart, and all known of oldest generation, I will check and send connection, not "all the files," for $50.00. This is not indexed, but grouped in family and state files, etc. It often takes several hours to find connections.
--- Vendor #D1871

3874   - JOURNAL OF THE JOHANNES SCHWALM HISTORICAL ASSOCIATION by the Johannes Schwalm Historical Association. 1980-84.
The Johannes Schwalm Historical Association is a non-profit organization dedicated to researching, collecting and disseminating data on the descendants of Hessian soldiers. They publish an annual Journal which has included family genealogies of the descendants of Caspar Goebbel, Andreas Thormann, Peter Sippel, Henry Burger, Johann Eickhoff, Johan Wedeking, Peter Sippel, and Heinrich Grote, as well as considerable material on the Johannes Schwalm descendants which include large family groups with surnames including Klinger, Messersmith, Moser, Hoffa, Herb, Suber, Bobb, and Romberger.
Significant articles of historical interest have included The Diary of Phillip Waldeck; The Hessians of Prince Edward Island; Johann Leibheit and the Convention Army; and various Revolutionary War prisoner lists.
One of the more important projects of the JSHA has been to maintain a computerized listing of all Hessians who settled in America. This listing was published in Volume 2, Number 3 of the *Journal* and will periodically be republished as new information warrants.
Also note that JSHA published in 1983 a book of twenty-two color sketches of the Hessians of York County, Pennsylvania, by Lewis Miller. These prints are suitable for framing and each includes a biography of the subject.
Paper (all 8½"x11"):
Volume 1, Number 4, 1980, 72 pages, $6.50;
Volume 2, Number 1, 1981, 90 pages, $8.00;
Number 2, 1982, 64 pages, $7.50;
Number 3, 1983, 78 pages, $8.00;
Number 4, 1984, 92 pages, $8.00;
The Hessians of Lewis Miller, 1983, 68 pages, $15.00.
--- Vendor #D1872

3875   - NETTLES FAMILIES OF THE SOUTH by William F. Medlin. 1984.
Paper—$10.00—100pp----------------------------------- Vendor #D1877

3876   - YOUNG, CAMPBELL AND RELATED FAMILIES OF SOUTH CAROLINA by William F. Medlin. 1985.
Cummings, Davis, Guerry, Jackson, Livingston, Kennedy, Micheau, Reese, Rembert, Saverance, Wynn, many more.
(In process)—Paper—$10.00—80pp----------------------Vendor #D1877

3877   - LOWRY AND RUSHING FAMILIES OF NORTH AND SOUTH CAROLINA
by William F. Medlin. 1985.
(In process)—Paper—$15.00—124pp------------------------- Vendor #D1877

3878   - THE O'DELL DIGGIN'S edited and published by Kay O'Dell.
Genealogical research aid and clearinghouse for O'Dell/Odell/Odle
families...
Published four times a year (February), (May), (August), and
(November). Every name indexed. Locality index.
Subscription: $8.00 annually—queries FREE to subscribers—
$3.00 for non-subscribers—75 word maximum.
Odell genealogical material welcomed.
Volume One—1982, indexed, Paper—$11.00—42pp.
Volume Two—1983, indexed, Paper—$13.00—86pp.
Subscription—$8.00/annually—min. 86pp-------------------- Vendor #D1880

3879   - LOVE LETTERS edited and published by Kay O'Dell.
Genealogical research aid and clearinghouse for Love families...
published four times a year (February), (May), (August), and
(November). Every name indexed. Locality index.
Subscription: $10.00 annually—queries FREE to subscribers—
$3.00 for non-subscribers—75 word maximum.
Love genealogical material welcomed.
Subscription—$10.00/annually—min. 86pp------------------- Vendor #D1880

3880   - DICK DOCUMENTS edited and published by Kay O'Dell.
For all Dick researchers. Published four times a year (February),
(May), (August), and (November). Every name indexed.
Locality index.
Subscription: $10.00 annually—queries FREE to subscribers—
$3.00 for non-subscribers—75 word maximum.
Dick genealogical material welcomed.
Subscription—$10.00/annually—min. 86pp------------------- Vendor #D1880

3881   - KIN FOULKES edited and published by Kay O'Dell.
For all Foulkes/Fowlkes/Folks (and variant spellings).
Published four times a year (February), (May), (August), and
(November). Every name indexed. Locality index.
Subscription: $10.00 annually—queries FREE to subscribers—
$3.00 for non-subscribers—75 word maximum.
Foulkes genealogical material welcomed.
Subscription—$10.00/annually—min. 86pp------------------- Vendor #D1880

3882   - NICHOLS NOSTALGIA edited and published by Kay O'Dell.
For all Nichols/Nicols/Nickels (and variant spellings).
Published four times a year (February), (May), (August), and
(November). Every name indexed. Locality index.
Subscription: $10.00 annually—queries FREE to subscribers—
$3.00 for non-subscribers—75 word maximum.
Nichols genealogical material welcomed.
Subscription—$10.00/annually—min. 86pp------------------- Vendor #D1880

3883   - THE HISTORY OF THE BURR PORTRAITS: THEIR ORIGIN, THEIR
DISPERSAL AND THEIR RESEMBLAGE by John E. Stillwell, M.D. 1928.
Cloth—$55.00—106pp------------------------------------- Vendor #D1883

3884   - CHRISTOPHERS GENEALOGY: JEFFREY AND CHRISTOPHER
CHRISTOPHERS OF NEW LONDON, CONNECTICUT AND THEIR
DESCENDANTS by John R. Totten. Repr. of 1921 ed. (April 1919-
July 1921).
Paper—$11.00—178pp----------------------------------- Vendor #D1883

3885   - THE HATFIELDS OF WESTCHESTER, DESCENDANTS OF THOMAS
HATFIELD by Abraham Hatfield. 1935.
Cloth—$11.00—222pp----------------------------------- Vendor #D1883

3886   - THE "KING" FAMILY HERALDRY by George Austin Morrison. Repr.
of 1910 ed. (October 1910 Record).
Paper—$6.00—35pp------------------------------------- Vendor #D1883

3887 - THE LIVINGSTON FAMILY IN AMERICA AND ITS SCOTTISH
ORIGINS compiled by Florence Van Rensselaer. 1949.
Cloth—$25.00—413pp------------------------------------- Vendor #D1883

3888 - STILLWELL GENEALOGY, VOLUME IV by John E. Stillwell, M. D.
1931.
(Volumes I, II, III out of print)
Cloth—$30.00—376pp------------------------------------- Vendor #D1883

3889 - DESCENDANTS OF EDWARD TRE(A)DWELL THROUGH HIS SON JOHN
by William A. Robbins. Repr. of 1911 ed. (Record—April 1911).
Paper—$4.50—119pp------------------------------------- Vendor #D1883

3890 - JOHN UNDERHILL, CAPTAIN OF NEW ENGLAND AND NEW
NETHERLAND by Henry C. Shelley. 1932.
Cloth—$11.00—473pp------------------------------------- Vendor #D1883

3891 - THE UNDERHILL BURYING GROUND compiled by David Harris
Underhill and Francis Jay Underhill, with diagram. 1924.
Cloth—$9.00—79pp------------------------------------- Vendor #D1883

3892 - THE VAN RENSSELAERS IN HOLLAND AND IN AMERICA by Florence
Van Rensselaer. 1956.
Cloth—$14.00—103pp------------------------------------- Vendor #D1883

3893 - GENEALOGICAL NOTES RELATING TO WARNAER WESSELS AND HIS
DESCENDANTS by Drs. J. G. B. Bulloch and Arthur Adams. Repr.
of 1913 ed. (Record—October 1913).
Paper—$2.00—15pp------------------------------------- Vendor #D1883

3894 - MERRILLS OF 1850, VOLUME I-VIII ALL STATES by Howard and
Jean Merrill. 1985.
Completely abstracted and indexed listing of all Merrills (various
spellings) from 1850 census. Parentage given where known.
Volumes individually available: I— Massachusettes, Connecticut,
Rhode Island; II— Maine; III— New Hampshire, Vermont;
IV— New York; V— Middle Atlantic; VI— Southeast; VII- Midwest;
VIII— West.
(In process)—Paper—$120.00/8 Vols.—ca 400pp------------- Vendor #D1885

3895 - HISTORY OF THE DESCENDANTS OF JOHN KOONTZ by Lowell L.
Koontz. 1979.
First edition, *History of the Descendants of John Koontz*, born 1739
and lived in the Shenandoah Valley of Virginia. More than five years
of research containing 669 pages, 37 illustrations, complete 86 page
index of 7,296 names bound in cloth hard cover. From 187 to no less
than 20 different members are listed for these major allied families:
Aleshire, Allen, Baker, Bowers, Brubaker, Brumback, Buracker,
Burner, Coffman, Dovel, Foltz, Graves, Grove, Harter, Hite,
Huffman, Isley, Johnson, Jones, Keyser, Kibler, Kiblinger, Kite,
Lionberger, Long, Louderback, Mauck, Miller, Moore, Nauman,
Price, Roudabush, Ruffner, Shirley, Shuler, Smith, Snyder,
Spitler, Steger, Strickler, Strole, Timmons, Wilson.
Price $26.00—Lowell Koontz, 6327 Phyllis Lane, Alexandria, VA 22312
Cloth—$26.00—669pp------------------------------------- Vendor #D1886

3896 - ANCESTORS AND DESCENDANTS OF FRANCIS W. AND LUCINDA
(SHEARER) CORNBOWER (KORNBAU) by Harry A. Diehl. 1982.
Families of Shearer, Sterner, Gerberick, Kroll-Croll of York County,
Pennsylvania and Baltimore and Caroll Counties, Maryland.
Paper—$8.60—59pp------------------------------------- Vendor #D1887

3897 - CROWNOVER FAMILIES IN USA by Helen Crownover; illustrated by
Joe Crownover. 1984.
In 1625 Wolfert Van Kouwenhoven came from Holland. His great-great
grandson John Covenhoven married Lydia Predmore 1752 New Jersey;
settled in Berkeley County, Virginia 1772. We trace five sons through
USA to 1984. Indexed. 11"x8½".
Cloth—$35.00—Paper—$30.00—321pp---------------------- Vendor #D1889

3898   - HUGH HUTCHINS OF OLD ENGLAND by Jack Randolph Hutchins and
Richard Jasper Hutchings. 1984.
A history of the Hutchins-Hutchings-Hutchens-Huchins families extending back to the year 1276 in Old England. Included are all known
families of these names living in colonial America, Newfoundland,
Canada, and the Caribbean Islands. Six different books in this one
volume give specific details on: The ancient Hutchins families of Old
England; The migration of the Hutchins families to the New World with
summary charts of all known early Hutchins families including the
families of New England, the Caribbean, Capt. John Hutchins of
New York, Nicholas Hutchins of Maryland, the many Hutchins families
of Virginia, the Carolinas, Georgia and the large Colonel Anthony
Hutchins family of Mississippi; An updating of the Hutchins in the
book *Thomas Hutchins of Salem* and the history of this line back to
Dorset about 1480; A genealogy of the large Elias Hutchins-Hutchings
family of Nauvoo and Utah; A genealogy of the family of Enoch
Hutchins-Hutchings of Kittery, Maine; and A genealogy of the
Keckhafer-Hameister families of Minnesota and their allied lines.
This is a history of the origins of all early families regardless of
the spelling of the name or their geographical location and provides
new information helpful to any person interested in any Hutchins-
Hutchings-Hutchens family.
Cloth—$35.00—904pp-------------------------------------- Vendor #D1890

3899   - THOMAS HUTCHINS OF SALEM AND HISTORY OF ALLIED FAMILIES
by Jack Randolph Hutchins. 1972, 1984.
A reprint of the genealogy of the Thomas Hutchins family starting
with his marriage in Salem, Massachusetts, in 1719. His grandchildren
moved into New Hampshire, Vermont, New York, Ontario, and on west.
Genealogies of allied families: Newman, Taylor, Tinney, Hepburn,
Penn, Momany, Morgan and many others are included.
Cloth—$35.00—801pp-------------------------------------- Vendor #D1890

3900   - JOHN HUTCHINS OF HAVERHILL compiled by Dr. Edwin Colby Byam,
edited by Jack Randolph Hutchins. 1974.
A genealogy with data on over 4,550 members of the oldest New England
Hutchins family. John arrived in Newbury in 1638 and later settled
in Haverhill, Massachusetts. This family moved into all the New
England states, Quebec, New York, Pennsylvania and Ohio.
Cloth—$25.00—563pp-------------------------------------- Vendor #D1890

3901   - JACOB HUTCHINS OF ATHOL, REVOLUTIONARY SOLDIER
(Bicentennial Book) by Jack Randolph Hutchins. 1976.
A history of the military activities of Jacob Hutchins of Athol, Massachusetts, and of the other 195 Hutchins-Hutchings-Hutchens who
served during the Revolutionary War including data from their
military records and pension applications. This book also includes
reprints of the 1885 genealogy of the David Hutchins family of
Attleboro, Massachusetts, and the 1935 publication of Mrs. Crider
summarizing the Strangeman Hutchins family of Virginia, North Carolina,
Ohio and Indiana.
Cloth—$20.00—384pp-------------------------------------- Vendor #D1890

3902   - "ALLEY HIGHLIGHTS, YESTERDAY FOR TOMORROW" by Virginia
Miller Carey and Garnet Alley Hampton. 1983.
Follows line of descent from Thomas A. Alley ca 1720 Henrico County,
Virginia, his son, James, Sr., and lists descendants of Paul Alley,
grandson of James, Sr.
Three Sections: Genealogical, Memoirs, and Reminiscences.
Maps and pictures. Limited number available.
Hardback, 8½"x11", Maroon-Gold Lettering.
Cloth—$30.00—373pp-------------------------------------- Vendor #D1893

3903   - THE ARCHER QUARTERLY edited by George W. Archer. 1983—.
Archer, Archie, Archey, Archar, Archard, Archad, etc.
Quarterly publication of The Archer Association.
Off-set, 50 pages each. Indexed annually.
Publishes primary and secondary source materials and compiled gen-
alogies on the surname Archer and variants in America and Canada

for period early 1600's to present.
Annual Association membership: $18. Membership includes *Quarterly*, *Newsletter*, computerized search service, free queries and clearing house service to help those doing Archer-related research.
Membership—$18.00/yr--Vendor #D1894

3904 - HOSTETTER FAMILY, DESCENDANTS OF JACOB AND ANNA, OSWALD AND MARIA HOSTETTER, LANCASTER COUNTY, PENNSYLVANIA by Richard L. Hostetter and David J. Bachman. 1984.
Cloth—$37.00—408pp-------------------------------------- Vendor #D1896

3905 - THE TINCHER TRIBE AND CAESAR'S TENCTERI TRIBE by Lois Tincher Dorsey. 1974.
All by the name of Tincher in America as of date of publication go back to one man in Virginia, Samuel Tincher/Tencher (born ca 1718-1791), Greenbrier County, West Virginia. A second volume is to be printed in 1985.
Cloth—$21.50—424pp-------------------------------------- Vendor #D1897

3906 - CORN STALKS AND PREACHERS by Lois Tincher Dorsey. 1981. 4th pr.
Story of John Peter Corn, Revolutionary Soldier and his fifteen children, of Henderson County, North Carolina.
Plastic cover—$27.50—396pp----------------------------Vendor #D1897

3907 - THE JUSTICE FAMILY by Lois Tincher Dorsey. 1981. 2d pr.
Story of the Justice family of Henderson County, North Carolina. Mainly the story of James Dyer Justice and his fourteen children.
Plastic cover—$14.50—99pp---------------------------- Vendor #D1897

3908 - THE HUGGINS FAMILY by Lois Tincher Dorsey. 1979.
Mainly the story of Edward Huggins, an early pioneer family who helped settle Henderson County, North Carolina, and his eight children.
Plastic cover—$16.50—103pp----------------------------Vendor #D1897

3909 - "CHARLES ROANE THE EMMIGRANT AND HIS WIFE FRANCES ROANE" by J. Sinclair Selden, Jr. 1982.
Descendants listed by generation. Family records of all known descendants, both male and female, where born and date, education, military service if known, occupation, marriage date and where buried. If living, the last known address was listed.
Cloth—$42.32—897pp------------------------------------- Vendor #D1899

3910 - "SAMUEL SELDEN THE EMMIGRANT AND HIS WIFE REBECCA YEO SELDEN" by J. Sinclair Selden, Jr. 1981.
Descendants listed by generation, family records of all known descendants, both male and female, where born and date, education, military service if known, occupation, marriage date and where buried. If living, the last known address was listed.
Cloth—$20.00—410pp------------------------------------- Vendor #D1899

3911 - "THE SINCLAIR FAMILY OF VIRGINIA" by J. Sinclair Selden, Jr. 1964.
Descendants listed by generation, family records of all known descendants, both male and female, where born and date, education, military service if known, occupation, marriage date and where buried. If living, the last known address was listed.
Cloth—$20.00—387pp------------------------------------- Vendor #D1899

3912 - PALATINE PROGENY: THE AREY FAMILY OF ROWAN COUNTY, NORTH CAROLINA AND RELATED FAMILIES, 1749-1983 by Harriet Arey Davidson. 1983.
Petter Ihrig, the progenitor, immigrated to America in 1749 and by 1757 was living in Rowan County, North Carolina. The change that the surname underwent in America from Ihrig to Earry, Eary, Airey, etc. evolving as Arey is documented by signatures reproduced from official records. The immigrant Peter Earry had at least four children; Abraham, John, Zachariah, and Mary Catharine m. Edelman. The direct line is through Abraham[2] who died in 1844, age 86, and

his son Peter[3] (1783-1841). Peter[3] and his wife Phebe Thomas had
two sons and six daughters. Amelia m. Samuel Rothrock, Mary Ellen
m. David Barringer, Milas m. 1st Sophia Barringer 2nd Nancy Ann
Smith, and Jane m. Littleton William Coleman. These couples resided in Rowan County. Elizabeth m. Charles Barringer, Benjamin
m. Maria Raynor, Phebe m. Tobias Brown, Charlotte m. John Clark(e) II
and lived in neighboring Iredell County. A separate chapter is devoted to each of these eight children and the families they headed
including genealogical listings and charts of their descendants through
1983. An appendix contains information on the immigrant Gottlib
Ihrich who was most likely the progenitor of the Arey families of
Rockingham and Augusta Counties, Virginia.
Surnames of progeny: Anderson, Archie, Arie, Airy, Area, Atwood,
Bailey, Bain, Baker, Barkley, Barnette, Barrier, Bass, Beard,
Beaver, Bell, Biddle, Blackwood, Blankenship, Boehmler, Boland,
Bradley, Brandt, Brawley, Bray, Buhl, Butler, Caldwell, Carter,
Christenbury, Clement, Cline, Copes, Cornelius, Cowan, Cuthrell,
Darr, Davidson, Deaton, Dunn, Eller, Elliott, Erwin, Eubanks,
Evans, Faust, Fisher, Foster, Frick, Gabriel, Garner, Barnett,
Goodman, Gouthier, Griffin, Gulledge, Guy, Haden, Hall, Hallman,
Hambley, Hanser, Hartman, Harvard, Hauser, Healy, Hill, Hine,
Hobson, Hodgson, Hoffner, Holder, Houston, Hunt, Johnson, Jones,
Kestler, Kimbrough, Landau, Lawhon, Lee, Lester, Littlejohn,
Lyerly, Martin, Metheny, Miller, Moore, Morgan, Moser, Mountcastle,
Mulligan, McCauley, McCrorey, Naile, Negoescu, Nussman, Ohle,
O'Neal, Oxendine, Parker, Peake, Pearch, Peeler, Philemon, Phillips,
Plyler, Poehlman, Pope, Pou, Pressly, Quantz, Rendleman, Ridenhour,
Ritchie, Roseman, Rufty, Schaeffer, Shemwell, Sherrill, Shore,
Simpson, Sloop, Stephenson, Stevenson, Stinson, Stoker, Summers,
Sumner, Sumrell, Taylor, Terry, Thorne, Toland, Trexler, Trout-
man, Walker, Waller, Waugh, Weeks, Wilson, White, Womble, Wood.
225 illustrations. Indexed. 7"x10¼".
Cloth—$37.50—334pp-- Vendor #D1901

3913 - "ANCESTRY FROM A TO Z, AMOS, ZOLL AND RELATED FAMILIES
by Eugene P. Amos. 1980.
Kansas pioneer families over 100 years, including: Amos, Beverly and
Bristol (Osage County), Zoll and Harrod (Leavenworth), Garrett,
Flint and Keller (Anderson and Coffey), Graham, Crane, Goodale
and Keeney (Pawnee), and Thomas (Smith).
Sixty-four surname chapters with the following Colonial families:
Tyler, Ballard, Sparks, Martindale, Bird, Montayne, Hills, Beeman,
Parke, Freeman, Geer, Tracy, Griswold, Holt, Ingalls, Clough,
Skidmore, Beers, Clark, Robinson, Peck, Tuttle, Sanford, Hotchkiss,
Hitchcock, Stebbings, Mallory, Sherman, Seeley, Olmsted and more.
8½"x11".
Cloth—$32.25—509pp-- Vendor #D1902

3914 - THE DUPY FAMILY GENEALOGY by Timothy Struthers Dupy. 1983.
Two Part Genealogy—Part One covers author's paternal lineage;
Part Two maternal lineage. Surnames include: Dupy, Vidal, Struthers,
Kite, Nelson, Robertson, Gray and Meredith. Areas covered are
Ohio, Iowa, Illinois, Oklahoma and Southern France.
Part One has a complete surname index and bibliography with total
of fifteen sections.
Paper—$55.00—705pp-- Vendor #D1903

3915 - THE FAMILY OF CLYDE MULFORD ELDRIDGE AND OTHER DESCEN-
DANTS OF WILLIAM ELDRED OF YARMOUTH by Luella Eldridge. 1983.
A family history including lineage charts for more than 900 descendants
of William Eldred and Ann Lumpkin married Yarmouth, Massachusetts
1647.
Cloth—$11.00—213pp-- Vendor #D1906

3916 - THE FUGATE FAMILY NEWSLETTER by Mary D. Fugate. Pub. since
1981.
This quarterly contains Fugate records for all spellings, all locations,
primarily pre-1880. Author also provides a free clearinghouse service
for all Fugate researchers.
Subscription—$10.00/yr—at least 85pp/yr-------------------Vendor #D1907

3917 - THE FEAST AND THE FAST by Chaim Lipschitz and Neil Rosenstein.
1984.
Biography of famed Rabbi Yomtov Heller (17th Century) with forty-one
genealogical charts and 1,400-name index.
Paper—$8.90--- Vendor #D1908

3918 - HOUSER HUNTERS by E. A. Houser, Jr. and Francis C. Knight.
Houser Hunters—International Association of persons interested in
Houser Family History—600 members—all spellings, Hauser, Haeuser,
Heyser, Houser, Howser, etc. Index of Houser Family researchers
listing 350 active researchers exchanging Houser Family information.
Semi-annual—free to all listed in it. Bibliography of published Houser
Family information. Thirty page quarterly Newsletter—$10. per year.
Subscription—$10.00/yr—30pp/qtly------------------------ Vendor #D1909

3919 - "PIONEERS AND PATRIOTS" by James R. Wilkins. 1980.
A historical and genealogical study of the Wilkins, Tuck, Hite, Wall,
Winn and other early Virginia families, (1618-1979).
8½"x11", hardbound, many photos, crests, maps, etc.
Cloth—$26.98—300pp------------------------------------- Vendor #D1911

3920 - A McFADDEN CHRONOLOGY, 1710-1900 by William T. Skinner,
C.G.R.S. 1983.
This is a thoroughly documented account of the events in the history
of the line of McFaddens out of Chester District, South Carolina.
Indexed. Some allied names are: Barham, Culp, Ferguson, Gill,
McKinney, Moses, Steele, Walker, Wylie.
Paper—$10.00—64pp------------------------------------- Vendor #D1920

3921 - RAINEY TIMES, VOLUME 4 edited by Rachel Rainey. 1984.
Surname Publication of all spellings of Rainey/Raney/Reyney, etc.
Quarterly—July, October, January, April.
Features census, court records, extracts, queries, family histories,
Bible records, etc.
Back Volumes 1, 2, and 3 available at $12.50 each postpaid.
Also available on Annual Basis—*Rainey Times Charts*—*Volumes 2A,
3A and 4A* at $12.50 each postpaid.
Subscription—Paper—$12.50/yr---------------------------Vendor #D1921

3922 - McCUTCHEN TRACE.
Historical and genealogical newsletter for any spelling of McCutcheon
or for anyone with McCutchen ancestors, including McCutcheon/
McCutchen/McCutchan/McCutchin/MacCutcheon. Two newsletters per
year plus more when you join the McCutchen Trace Association.
For more information contact Vendor #D1922.
Subscription—Paper—$7.50/yr---------------------------Vendor #D1922

3923 - HERNDONS OF THE AMERICAN REVOLUTION, PART I: DESCENDANTS
OF JOHN HERNDON OF CHARLOTTE COUNTY, VIRGINIA by John Good-
win Herndon. 1950.
Cloth—$12.50—67pp------------------------------------- Vendor #D1924

3924 - HERNDONS OF THE AMERICAN REVOLUTION, PART II: DESCEN-
DANTS OF EDWARD HERNDON OF SPOTSYLVANIA COUNTY, VIRGINIA
by John Goodwin Herndon. 1951.
Cloth—$12.50—91pp------------------------------------- Vendor #D1924

3925 - HERNDONS OF THE AMERICAN REVOLUTION, PART III: DESCEN-
DANTS OF WILLIAM HERNDON OF ORANGE COUNTY, VIRGINIA by
John Goodwin Herndon. 1952.
Cloth—$12.50—106pp------------------------------------- Vendor #D1924

3926 - GEORGE BOONE, SON OF EDWARD BOONE, KILLED BY THE INDIANS
IN 1780, AND NEPHEW OF DANIEL BOONE, THE FAMED EXPLORER by
Dorothy Spears Campbell and Shirley Spears Nowicki. 1982.
Contains Boone Family History; data about Edward Boone (brother of
pioneer Daniel Boone) and his issue, with information on thirteen
children of George Boone (1767-1841) and their descendants;
photographs (one of Edward Boone's daughter Sarah), wills, law-
suits, land records, Civil War records, petition with signatures of
Daniel, Israel, and Edward Boone.
Allied families: Anderson, Austerman, Baker, Josiah Boone,
Bourland, Boykin, Bryan, Burton, Cleveland, Fisher, Ford,
Gibson, Gragson, Hazelrigg, James, Horner, Hunter, Miller,
Morgan, Muir, Nunn, Perkins, Reedy, Sellers, Shain, Spears
(Von Spiern), Stevens, Wilson, Wood, Wright, Wynne, and numerous
others. [Indexed; 8½"x11"; over 100 illustrations.]
Cloth—$40.00—336pp------------------------------------- Vendor #D1926

3927 - FREED FAMILY FACTS NEWSLETTER edited by James M. Freed, Ph.D.
Semi-annual newsletter, indexed. Particpants contribute research
(European and American). For all Freed (Fried, Friedt, Freet,
Fread, etc.) serious genealogists.
Subscription—Paper—$6.00/yr—18-24pp/yr----------------- Vendor #D1927

3928 - JOHN LOGUE OF NORTH CAROLINA—FAMILIES OF DELAWARE,
MARYLAND, PENNSYLVANIA, TENNESSEE, AND VIRGINIA by Jane
Gray Buchanan. 1980; Addendum (13pp) pub. Aug., 1984.
Indexed. Begins with Ephraim Logue (d. 1751) of Chester, Pennsyl-
vania and New Castle, Delaware. Son John went to Orange County,
North Carolina. Collateral lines include Allen, Lindsay, Robertson
(Robison), Thompson, Tinnin.
Paper—$10.00/set—54+13pp--------------------------------Vendor #D1928

3929 - AN AIRGOOD, AIRGOD, EHRGOTT GENEALOGY, SOME OF THE
DESCENDANTS OF MICHAL AIRGOD OF INDIANA COUNTY, PENN-
SYLVANIA by James M. Airgood. 1979.
Michal and Margaret Ehrgott from Germany about 1835.
Fully indexed, 38 photos, 1,200 names, 400 surnames:
Airgood, Shields, Lewis, Stiver, Kanouff, Harris, Winters, etc.
Paper—$7.00—127pp------------------------------------- Vendor #D1929

3930 - "THE HEYDON—HAYDEN—HYDEN FAMILIES" (QUARTERLY),
Gene Hyden, Editor/Publisher; Bill Hyden, Co-Editor. 1978-84.
Indexed annually. Biographical sketches, reprints of articles/Journals
pre-1934, extensive query/feedback section.
Subscription—Paper—$12.00/yr—128pp/yr----------------- Vendor #D1931

3931 - HERE COME THE DOUTHITS—COAST TO COAST ACROSS TWO
CENTURIES by Ruth Long Douthit and Davis Douthit. 1983.
The story of John and Mary (Scott) Douthit and their thousands of
descendants in America, 1700's to present. Index of 6,000-plus
names. Discusses Douthit origins, early immigrants, life in Carolinas,
the Moravian influence. Data for John Douthit sons and descendants
occupy 234 pages. Family charts on twenty-two pages.
Paper—$15.00—396pp------------------------------------- Vendor #D1936

3932 - WHEELAND/WIELAND/WHELAND/WEYLAND AND ALLIED FAMILIES—
VOLUME ONE: FAMILY HISTORY by Alvin Anderson. 1984.
Volume One is the earliest history, starting with Martin Weyland,
born about 1610, Bavaria, tracing a century of history in Württemberg,
then the Michael Weyland family in Northumberland County, Pennsyl-
vania, with a listing of the first five generations of descendants of
Michael and Magdalena (Baker) Weyland.
Paper—$7.00—102pp------------------------------------- Vendor #D1930

3933 - WHEELAND/WIELAND/WHELAND/WEYLAND AND ALLIED FAMILIES—
VOLUME SIX: DESCENDANTS OF SAMUEL AND SUSAN ESTHER
(MERTZ) WHEELAND by Alvin Anderson. 1984.
Volume Six contains a biographical listing of over two thousand de-
scendants of Samuel and Susan Esther (Mertz) Wheeland, indexed.

Many of the family still live in Lycoming County, Pennsylvania, where
Samuel and Susan lived till about 1834.
Some major allied families include: Woolever, Chaapel, Strunk, Fagles,
Fritz, Thomas, Young, Narber, Elder, Hepburn, Beamer, Rager,
Lane, Winter, Ritter, Wise, Collins, Thompson, Long, Maxwell,
Anderson, Cox, Keagle, Kimble, Smith, Goldy, Hagerman, Knaul,
Keys, Schriner, Houtz, Ogden, Pricher, McCoy, Mansel, Belles,
Heim, Ort, Stark, Williamson. 11"x8½".
Paper—$14.00—300+pp------------------------------------ Vendor #D1930

3934 - GOODENOUGHS' GHOSTS—GOODENOUGH—GOODNOW—GOODENOW—
GOODNO—GOODNOUGH FAMILIES edited by Carol McWain Goodenough.
A thirty page newsletter printed quarterly, helping families find their
Goodenough lines.
Subscription—Paper—$8.00/yr—30pp----------------------Vendor #D1939

3935 - HOTT ANCESTORS by Richard and Kathryn Hott. 1984.
The ancestors of Mr. Hott have been compiled in this 250 page book.
Ancestors included are: Conrath Hatt, and Levi Hott in Berks County,
Pennsylvania to Wabash County, Indiana; the Downing Smith family
from Madison County, Virginia to Kokomo, Indiana; the Henry Funk
and the Showalter families through Rockingham County, Virginia; the
Lorentz Erbaugh family to Montgomery County, Ohio; the Jacob Miller,
Yost Swope, and Daniel Spraker families through Monroe County,
West Virginia; the Gaar families from Virginia to Indiana.
Complete indexed. 8½"x11".
Cloth—$25.00—250pp---------------------------------- Vendor #D1940

3936 - GOLDNER ANCESTORS by Kathryn and Richard Hott. 1983.
Many of the ancestors of Mrs. Hott have been traced from their native
Germany through Pennsylvania to Adams County, Indiana. Surnames
include: Guldner/Goldner from Germany to Northampton and Carbon
Counties, Pennsylvania through Trumbull County, Ohio to Indiana;
Broadsword from Pennsylvania to Ohio; and Weidler from Germany to
Ohio and Indiana. Completely indexed. 8½"x11".
Cloth—$22.00—200pp--------------------------------- Vendor #D1940

3937 - HIGGINS ANCESTORS by Richard and Kathryn Hott. 1984.
The ancestors of Mr. Hott's mother have been compiled in this 240 page
book which traces their migration to Wells County, Indiana.
Surnames inclue: Higgins from Ohio; Ditzler, Brickley, Haflich,
Saurbaugh, and Haverstock from Pennsylvania through Ohio;
Chalfant from England; Cobbum from West Virginia; Wolfcale from
Virginia; and Conard from Germantown, Pennsylvania.
Completely indexed. 8½"x11".
Cloth—$25.00—250pp---------------------------------- Vendor #D1940

3938 - FIVE GERMAN FAMILIES by James C. Bengelsdorf. 1983.
Emigration, intermarrying, descendants, of Bengelsdorf, Guggenbühler
Schänkin, Zeitlow, Ziegler; Toledo, Ohio, Petersburg, Michigan.
Paper—$16.50—105pp---------------------------------- Vendor #D1941

3939 - CRUMP FAMILY NEWSLETTER by Beth Johnsen.
The Crump Family Newsletter is a quarterly publication of eight pages
in each issue. It is compiled from reasearch of the Crump surname
contributed by descendants.
Paper—$5.00—8pp/issue-------------------------------Vendor #D1945

3940 - HISTORICAL SKETCHES OF SUMTER COUNTY, 2 Volumes, by Cassie
Nicholes.
Information on early life, families, etc.
Volume I: Woodward, Barnwell, Haynesworth, Mayes, Moise, Mood,
Muldrow, Reese, Mellette, Singleton, White, Purdy, Brogdon,
Witherspoon, Mason, Cousar, Furman, Wilson, Sumter, Anderson,
Baker, Brunson, Smith, Bethune, Andrews, etc.
Volume II: Aycock, Barwick, Birnie, Brunson, Creech, Heath, Levi,
McKnight, Manning, Moses, Nash, O'Donnell, Osteen, Reynolds,
Shore, Walker, Wilkinson, Williams, Birnie, Bland, Brown, Bryan,

Crosswell, Cuttino, DuBose, Dwight, Edmunds, Furman, Gibson,
Gorgas, Ivey, Levy, McLaughlin, McLaurin, Miller, Murray,
Plowden, Poinsett, Richardson, Shaw, Stubbs, Touchberry, Williams,
etc.
See listing under Sumter County, SOUTH CAROLINA.
Cloth—$22.00/Volume-- Vendor #D1948

3941 - NATHALIE DeLAGE SUMTER by Sister Ignatia. 1984.
Story of the French countess who married Thomas Sumter, Jr.;
Activities Stateburg Area; organized the first Catholic Church in
Sumter District.
Paper—$7.50-- Vendor #D1948

3942 - MORRIS AND HAMPTON FAMILIES by Mary M. Tate.
Butler County, Kentucky; Lewis County, Missouri; and North Central
Texas; 1798-1910.
(In process)--- Vendor #D1949

3943 - THOMAS FAULCONER AND HIS DESCENDENTS by James G.
Faulconer. 1984.
History of many lines of the Faulconer family dating back to 1622.
Cloth—$15.00-apx 200pp----------------------------------- Vendor #D1950

3944 - THE BEREND DE JONG FAMILY - 100 YEARS IN AMERICA 1882-1982
by Frank DeJong, Barbara Hook, Ken DeJong, and Bob Niekerk. 1982.
Berend and Fokeltje crossed the Atlantic during the winter with their
first child, ten more children and 100 years later descendants are
listed in Who's Who and recently one was written up in Fortune
Magazine.
Book includes five indexes; 750 pictures; letters; documents.
Cloth— $20.00-368pp--------------------------------------- Vendor #D1951

3945 - VOLUME I: THE COLLINS FAMILY IN GREAT BRITAIN, ANCESTORS
OF THE REV. WILLIAM COLLINS AND DESCENDANTS THROUGH HIS
ELDEST SON by Margaret Hill Collins. 1977.
The ancestry of Isaac Collins, New Jersey Quaker printer (1746-1817)
is disclosed for the first time. It is traced through his grandfather,
Rev. William Collins, Vicar of Swansea, to the 15th Century in Wales.
Descendants of the Vicar's eldest son remained in Great Britain.
His direct descendant, Elizabeth Collins Shorland, contributed, The
Collins Family of Chew Magna. Fluid narrative style, well documented;
illustrations, wills, deeds, public offices, maps, genealogical charts,
bibliography, Index.
Looseleaf Hardback—$21.95—157pp------------------------- Vendor #D1954

3946 - VOLUME II: THE COLLINS FAMILY IN AMERICA, DESCENDANTS
OF THE THIRD SON OF THE REV. WILLIAM COLLINS, VICAR OF
SWANSEA, GLAMORGANSHIRE, WALES by Margaret Hill Collins and
Ellinor Collins Aird. 1976.
Charles Collins, third son of Rev. William Collins, immigrated to
America ca 1734. His son was the well-known Quaker printer, Isaac
Collins. The direct line for six generations is described and three
distant connections: Stephen Grellet, Mary Anna Longstreth, Marion
Russell Taber.
Fluid narrative style, well documented; illustrations, public records,
maps, genealogical charts (Collins, Longstreth, Morris, Smith,
Reeve, Remington, Page, Maule, Caldwell, Hayes, Aird), bibliogra-
phy, Index, and Directory of many "Living Descendants of Isaac
and Rachel Budd Collins."
Looseleaf Hardback—$21.95—143pp------------------------- Vendor #D1954

3947 - VOLUME III: THE COLLINS FAMILY: ANCESTORS OF THE DISTAFF
SIDE OF THE FIRST FIVE GENERATIONS OF THE COLLINS FAMILY IN
AMERICA by Margaret Hill Collins and Ellinor Collins Aird. 1980.
The ancestor in each family described, from yeoman to gentry, nearly
all Quakers, immigrated in early Colonial days to West Jersey, Phila-
delphia, or Maryland: Hammond, Stacy, Budd, Lloyd, Hill, Morris,
Evans, Mauleverer, Abbott, Conrad. Fluid narrative style, well
documented; illustrations, maps, marriage certificates, wills, inven-
tories, genealogical charts, bibliography, Index.
Looseleaf Hardback—$23.95—270pp------------------------- Vendor #D1954

3948   - THE EBENEZER HANKS STORY by Kerry William Bate. 1982.
The Ebenezer Hanks Story by Kerry William Bate (1982), 200 illustra-
tions, 2 maps, Indexed. Biography, genealogy. Includes "the only
account in print of the ancestry of WILLIAM SARGENT of Malden,
Mass."—*New York Genealogical & Biographical Record*, carefully doc-
umenting pedigree through Gifford family to royal lines of England and
Scotland.
In addition, there are genealogical sketches of the following additional
families: Allen, Bean, Buckalew, Bushnell, Case, Casper, Delano,
Durbin, Hall, Hanks, Hatch, Hawkins, Hillier, Kennedy, Lewis,
Linnell, Litten, Mahieu, Makernes, Manter, Marvin, Mitchell,
Partridge, Quennell, Rowley, Rudd, Sargent, Scott, Shelley,
Tracy, Warren, White.
"The book is fascinating reading throughout"—*The American Genealogist*.
"Minutely documented...extensive citation of sources"—*New York
Genealogical and Biographical Record*.
$25.00 Cloth, xi+311+unpaged three-column index, 11"x8½", typeset.
Cloth—$25.00—311+pp-- Vendor #D1955

3949   - KINFOLK IN GERMANY, KINFOLK IN MARYLAND by Arta F.
Johnson. 1984.
The German origins and relationships of the Brunner, Götzendanner,
Sturm, and Thomas families.
Paper—$6.80—44pp--- Vendor #D1956

3950   - CARMICHAEL CLAN WESTBROOK AND ALLIED FAMILIES by Opal
Carmichael Phoenix. 1984, repr. of 1963 ed.
Hardbound, 455 pages, indexed, proposed republishing date—Fall 1984.
Chapter 1. Carmichaels from Scotland and Ireland to America and
public records.
Chapter 2. Public records, Descendants of Arthur Abram, William,
Mary Ann and Robert Carmichael of South Carolina.
Chapter 3. Descendants of Daniel Carmichael and Sallie McCall of
North Carolina.
Chapter 4. Descendants of William Carmichael and wives Sallie Smith
and Elizabeth B. Williams of Virginia and North Carolina.
Chapter 5. Descendants of Joseph Carmichael and Elizabeth Macklin
of South Carolina and Georgia.
Chapter 6. Cornelius and Isabell Carmichael of Pennsylvania.
Chapter 7. Descendants of Archibald, Daniel, Duncan, Christian
Carmichael and Dougald McIntyre of North Carolina and South
Carolina.
Chapter 8. Descendants of Dougald, John "Ban" and Gilbert
Carmichael and McDuffies of South Carolina.
Chapter 9. Odd list of Carmichaels of USA.
Chapter 10. Allied Families of Banks, Bell, Blair, Boyd, Brooke,
Brown, Caldwell, Calhoun, Campbell, Donaldson, Edwards, Phoenix,
Eva, Fair, Hunter, Fambrough, Cole, Martin, McDonald, Moore,
Russell, Thompson, Walker, Ward, White, and Young.
Chapter 11. Westbrook and Allied Families of Baker, Black, Gainey,
Sewell, Sandefur, Taylor, Trimble, Vaughn, Fort, Lee, Jones,
Ramsey, Foster, etc.
Chapter 12. Descendants of Drewry Arthur Carmichael and Cora
Westbrook of Georgia.
Price: $42.00 plus $1.75 postage and handling from:
CLAN CARMICHAEL (USA), 2750 Minton Rd., Melbourne, FL 32901
Cloth—$43.75—455pp-- Vendor #D1957

3951   - THE McCUES AND MINIERS OF OHIO AND MICHIGAN by Margaret C.
Klein, Ed.D., C.G. 1984.
Well documented and indexed history of two families including
collateral lines.
(In process)—Paper—$20.00------------------------------------ Vendor #D1960

3952   - THE ANTECEDENTS OF JON WARREN HAMILTON OF WAXAHACHIE,
        TEXAS by Margaret C. Klein, Ed.D., C.G. 1984.
        Traces the antecedents of Jon Warren Hamilton through eighteen
        direct and fourteen collateral lines. Documented and Indexed.
        Direct ancestors include: Buckles, Coppage, Cumming, Finley,
        Grimes, Hankins, Hobbs, Hood, Moss, Nation, Snoddy, West and
        Wood.
        Paper—$21.50--- Vendor #D1960

3953   - JOSEPH GRAVELY OF LEATHERWOOD, VIRGINIA by Margaret C.
        Klein, Ed.D., C.G. 1984.
        Traces the descendants of Joseph Gravely from 1744 through present.
        Includes: Austin, Barker, Childress, Cox, Davis, Dillard, Doyle,
        Dunnigan, Dyer, Eanes, Edwards, Eggle(s)ton, Flippen, Giles,
        Hairfield, Hairston, Hix, Holman, Hundley, Hurd, King, Lavinder,
        Law, Lawrence, Manning, Martin, McCabe, Millner, Minter, Moore,
        Morrison, Overton, Payne, Pedigo, Philpott, Ramsey, Rice, Richardson,
        Riddle, Stegall, Stults(z), Townes, Wade, Warren and Wingfield.
        Documented and Indexed.
        Paper—$21.50—120pp-------------------------------------- Vendor #D1960

3954   - CRAPO CREDENTIALS, A QUARTERLY ON PETER CRAPO (CA 1670-
        1756, FRANCE—MASSACH SETTS) AND HIS DESCENDANTS edited
        and published by Diane Miles.
        (Male and female lines.) Diane Miles, Editor and Publisher.
        Includes: Ashley, Barden, Barney, Borden, Braley, Brooks, Cobb,
        DeMaranville, Fowler, Fox, Haskell, Haskins, Hills, Howe, Howland,
        Hyde, Kilbourne, Kirby, Lake, Lewis, Lindsay, McNitt, Pierce,
        Quimby, Reynolds, Rice, Rounsevell, Sears, Sherman, Skiff, Soules,
        Spooner, Streeter, Thomas, Washburn, Westgate.
        Indexed annually.
        Subscription—$16.00/annually----------------------------- Vendor #D1958

3955   - ALLENS, QUAKERS OF SHENANDOAH, ANCESTORS AND DESCEN-
        DANTS 1636-1984 by Rudelle Mills Davis and Peggy Davidson Dick.
        1984.
        Reuben Allen I, to Shenandoah Valley 1730's, ancestors to 1636;
        descendants of five known children: Mary Allen-Moore, Margaret
        Allen-Bond, Reuben II, Jackson and Joseph Allen. Many migrated to
        Ohio and Indiana.
        Cloth—$32.50—637pp------------------------------------- Vendor #D1962

3956   - THE CHADWELL FAMILY: DESCENDANTS OF THOMAS CHADWELL
        WHO SETTLED AT LYNN, MASSACHUSETTS IN 1637 by Marcia Wilson
        Wiswall. 1984.
        Includes all male descendants for thirteen generations, all females for
        seven generations; related families; charts; photos; complete index.
        Cloth—$18.50—190pp------------------------------------- Vendor #D1964

3957   - THE HARBOURS IN AMERICA by Louis J. Williams. 1982.
        The Dallas Genealogical Society's *Quarterly* states: "This book by the
        late Mr. Williams was a labor of love for his wife, Hazel Harbour
        Williams 1889-1970. He has traced Harbours from every part of the
        United States. This is a monumental work, beginning with Thomas
        Harbour born ca 1675-1695 in Wales and his wife, Sarah Witt of Vir-
        ginia. It brings many family lines up to the present time and has
        much information on the Witt family as well. The numbering system
        is easy to follow and there is a full name index of about 97 pages.
        It is well documented. There are approximately 50 pages of illustra-
        tions. A must for Harbours and related family researchers."
        All spellings of Harbour/Harbor/Harber/Harbur are given. Allied
        families listed in some detail in special sections include: Arrowsmith,
        Dalton, Fuson, Hall, Houchins, Pedigo, Pilson, Reynolds, Ross,
        Spurlock, Turman, Thomas, as well as Witt/Whitt/Whit.
        Cloth—$48.50—Paper—$35.00—763pp----------------------- Vendor #D1965

3958   - THE HARBOUR—WITT FAMILY ASSOCIATION, INC. QUARTERLY
        edited by Mrs. Bettye Atkins Cartwright.
        This publication of 32 or more pages per issue has been put out four
        times a year since 1978. The current membership, including the
        Quarterly, is $12.00 annually. Back issues available while the supply
        lasts. Materials cover all spellings of Harbour/Harbor/Harber/Harbur
        and Witt/Whitt/Whit. In addition, special articles on inter-related
        families appear regularly as well as articles of general genealogical
        and historical interest.
        Subscription—Paper—$12.00/yr—32pp/issue----------------- Vendor #D1965

3959   - EAST TENNESSEE LETTERS, NINETEENTH CENTURY by Willie
        Reeves Hardin Bivins. 1984.
        Letters to and from East Tennessee families, 1853-1900. Illustrations,
        Index, Genealogical Notes.
        Patterson, Hardin, Ramsey, Reeves, Lenoir, Gaines, Easley, DeVault,
        Witten, Avery, Jennings, Browder, Baker, Taff, Caldwell, Allen,
        Boyd, Bishop, Bittle, Blunt, Boggess, Brown, Carr, Childress, Corry,
        Dickey, Faucette, Faust, Fowler, Gettys, Griffith, Hunt, Love, Lowe,
        Matthews, Martin, Miller, Reagan, Sharp, Robeson, Smith, Taylor,
        many others.
        Paper—$18.00—218pp------------------------------------- Vendor #D1969

3960   - DESCENDANTS OF EDWARD REEVES AND JANE MELVIN by Willie
        Reeves Hardin Bivins. 1984.
        Edward Reeves, born 1721. 1898 manuscript, revised and extended.
        Paper—$6.00—42pp------------------------------------- Vendor #D1969

3961   - LIFE IN OKLAHOMA TERRITORY by Willie Reeves Hardin Bivins.
        1981.
        Bivins, Whicker, Hardin and their relatives in Greer County.
        Index, illustrations.
        Paper—$4.00—18pp------------------------------------- Vendor #D1969

3962   - LIFE IN 1775 by Willie Reeves Hardin Bivins. 1976.
        Acuff, Gaines, Woodson, Easley, Miller, Moore, Fleming, Hamilton,
        Witten, Laird, Lenoir, Gash, Gudger, Patterson, Hardin, Reeves,
        Avery, Melvin, others. Index, charts.
        Paper—$5.00—31pp------------------------------------- Vendor #D1969

3963   - DESCENDANTS OF REYNOLDS RAMSEY (1736-1816) AND NAOMI
        ALEXANDER by Willie Reeves Hardin Bivins. 1984.
        Indexed.
        Paper—$4.00—18pp------------------------------------- Vendor #D1969

3964   - INDEX FOR ANCESTRAL SKETCHES by Leroy Reeves. 1984.
        Paper—$1.50—15pp------------------------------------- Vendor #D1969

3965   - THE PARSONS FAMILY: DESCENDANTS OF CORNET JOSEPH
        PARSONS (C. 1618-1683), SPRINGFIELD, MASSACHUSETTS, 1636;
        NORTHAMPTON, MASSACHUSETTS, 1654, THROUGH HIS GRANDSON
        JONATHAN PARSONS (1693-1782) OF NORTHAMPTON, MASSACHU-
        SETTS; SUFFIELD, CONNECTICUT; SANDISFIELD, MASSACHUSETTS;
        AND DORSET, VERMONT by Gerald James Parsons. 1984.
        Illustrations; indexed. The appendix contains a study of the first three
        generations of the Cornet Joseph Parsons family.
        New York State residents add sales tax.
        Cloth—$30.00—398+pp------------------------------------- Vendor #D1970

3966   - FOURTEEN GENERATIONS "THE TROSSBACH'S" 1470-1984, 5th Ed.,
        by J. E. Trossbach. 1984.
        Tracing, research family names, do it yourself style, methods, instruc-
        tions, using authors surname as illustrations.
        Cloth—$20.00—130pp------------------------------------- Vendor #D1972

3967   - WARFEL AND ALLIED FAMILIES. 1979.
        835 pages of families, 35 pages Census; 53 page Index.
        Approximately 13,000 names; over 2,500 surnames.
        Cloth—$28.95—900pp------------------------------------- Vendor #D1973

3968 - THE CELLE FAMILY BOOK by Mrs. Carolyn Cell Choppin.
A genealogy of the American Cell(e), Gsell(e), Seale(s), Sell(s),
Sill(s), Zell(e) families, primarily of Pennsylvania German origin.
Mostly mimeographed, some photocopies. Looseleaf notebook binding.
$26.00 plus postage.
Paper—$26.00+—475pp-------------------------------------- Vendor #D1975

3969 - CELLE NEWSLETTERS by Mrs. Carolyn Cell Choppin.
Published quarterly for the American Cell(e), Gsell(e), Seale(s),
Sell(s), Sill(s), Zell(e), etc. Clan. Subscriptions 35¢ per issue or
$2.75 for two years (8 issues). All 53 back issues (160 pages)
available for $9.00.
Subscription—Paper—$2.75 for 2/yrs---------------------- Vendor #D1975

3970 - CLARY GENEALOGY: FOUR EARLY AMERICAN LINES AND RELATED
FAMILIES by Ralph Shearer Rowland and Star Wilson Rowland. 1980.
Clary Lines of Maryland, Massachusetts, Virginia, Wisconsin.
Related families include Armstrong, Deveron, Green, Kuykendall,
Westfall. First prize 1980 Maryland Historical Society's Genealogical
Book Contest.
Paper—$17.00— 588+pp--------------------------------- Vendor #D1977

3971 - BOWERMAN/BOWMAN FAMILY NEWSLETTER edited by Glenn C. Lukos.
Pub. qtly. since 1983.
Dedicated to encouraging proper documentation of Bowerman and
Bowman data. Concentrates on Thomas Bowerman (Burman, Boreman,
Boardman) of Sandwich and Falmouth, Massachusetts and his de-
scendants, many of whom were first Quakers in New England. Early
collateral lines include Allen, Annable, Gifford, Harper, Hoxie, Swift,
Varney, Wing. Indexed.
Subscription—$10.00/yr—Large Print Edition—$18.00/yr------ Vendor #D1979

3972 - SAMUEL GORTON OF RHODE ISLAND AND HIS DESCENDANTS by
Thomas Gorton. 1985.
Volume I (revised) and Volume 2 (new) combined; over 1,000 pages.
Cloth. Publication date: early 1985.
(In process)—Cloth— 1000+pp----------------------------- Vendor #D1981

3973 - THE GUILFORD FAMILIES 900-1982, VOLUMES I AND II by Margaret
Guilford-Kardell. 1983.
73 illustrations, 38 pages of charts, Indexed by birth dates; index
includes spouses.
Records begin with the Norman Gulafres and Gulfer, son of Hugh
de Neufchatel and continue through English generations and American
generations of all spellings of Guilford, including Gilford, Gulliford,
etc. to 1983.
Cloth—$75.00— 1026pp-------------------------------- Vendor #D1984

3974 - JOHN AND MARGARET BINGHAM'S FAMILY 1803-1983 by Josef A.
Jackson. 1983.
A history of John Bingham and Margaret Hawthorn of County Antrim,
Northern Ireland and their descendants who came to America in 1840's.
422 surnames, indexed. 6"x9".
Cloth—$25.00— 191pp-------------------------------- Vendor #D1989

3975 - DEACON JOHN BURNHAM OF IPSWICH AND EBENEZER MARTIN OF
REHOBOTH, MASSACHUSETTS, WITH THEIR DESCENDANTS by
Elisabeth P. Martin. 1985.
A thorough study of the 1637 immigrant John Burnham, later Deacon of
Chebacco Parish. His line includes Ebenezer of Windham, Connecticut,
Revolutionary soldier Joseph from Ashford, Connecticut, Alba an
innkeeper in Batavia, New York.
Ebenezer Martin joined the Revolution from Berkshire County, Massa-
chusetts; son Jarvis was canal contractor in New York. Jarvis' chil-
dren settled in western New York and Ashtabula County, Ohio.
Martin family charts to present. Allied lines are Andrews, Varney,
Holt, Durkee, Byles, Snow, Mason, Waters, Montgomery, Bieder.
Indexed. Cloth.
(In process)—Cloth-------------------------------- Vendor #D1990

3976 - BIDWELL FAMILY HISTORY 1587-1982 VOLUME I by Joan J. Bidwell. 1983.
A genealogy of the descendants of John Bidwell, 1620-1687, pioneer of Hartford, Connecticut. This book contains copies of fifty-five original documents and 133 pictures and has a 70,000 every name index.
Cloth—$45.00—1097pp--- Vendor #D1994

3977 - AN EMMONS GENEALOGY by Corwin J. Emmons and Wilbur D. Emmons. 1983.
A study of the 1,824 descendants of John (Jan) Emmons who was granted title to land in Gravesend, Kings County, Long Island in 1645. Early descendants settled principally in New Jersey.
Paper—$16.50—335pp-------------------------------------- Vendor #D1998

3978 - LESSLEY FAMILY RECORDS: SAMUEL LESSLEY OF THE CAROLINA WAXHAWS AND DESCENDANTS by Samuel B. Lessley. 1983.
Part One is a brief history of the ancient Scottish history of this family beginning in 1066. The name is spelled in many ways; Leslie, Lesslie, Lessley, Lesley, Lesly, Lasley and others.
Part Two the author tells the story of Samuel Lessley who married Sarah Hutchinson about 1756 and in 1767 he purchased land on Waxhaw Creek in Mecklenburg County, North Carolina, near the South Carolina line. His brother John Lessley, who had married Mary Hutchinson, his wife's sister, purchased land a few miles south, but in Lancaster County, South Carolina. This Part also deals with Sarah Hutchinson's five sisters—one of whom married Andrew Jackson, Sr., and they were the parents of Andrew Jackson, Jr., President of the United States. From records found in county courthouses, archives, cemeteries and many other sources, the Author follows the descendants of Samuel and Sarah across the Carolinas, Missouri, Arkansas, Tennessee, Oklahoma and California and contains thousands of Lessley descendants now scattered from east to west. Family lineage records were furnished by hundreds of correspondents.
The source of all recorded information is given and printed in bold type; all documents are printed in italics as true copies.
Part Three deals with John Lessley of Lancaster County, South Carolina, George and James Lessley of York County, South Carolina. On the basis of available evidence these four Lessley men appeared in this area at about the same time, and may well have been brothers.
This book contains Records, History, Genealogy, Pictures, Family Charts and Illustrations on 400 pages.
Allied families: Hutchinson, Faulkner, Jackson, Lathen, McElwee, Allison, Spradling, Kinder, Strickland, Hunter and others.
Samuel B. Lessley, P. O. Box 573, Claremore, OK 74018.
Cloth—$32.50—400pp------------------------------------ Vendor #D2000

3979 - LAGESSE LINEAGE LINES edited by Laura LaGess. 1984.
Current news by and about descendants of Jean Dagesse and Marie Anne Drouillard.
Associated names: Barrie, Beauvois, Berthiaume, Bescharde, Collette, Dumas, Dye, Fortin, Greenwood, Houle, Lafond, Mannie, Nolin, Paradis, Robidoux, Regnier, Roy, Simoneau, Viau.
Three or four pages, issued two to four times annually, beginning 1984. No charge, donations accepted.
Donations Only—3/4pp/issue---------------------------- Vendor #D2002

3980 - THE DOCKSTADER FAMILY—DESCENDANTS OF GEORG DACHSTÄTTER PALATINE EMIGRANT OF 1709 WHO SETTLED IN THE MOHAWK VALLEY OF NEW YORK, VOLUME ONE, GENERATIONS ONE THROUGH SIX compiled by Doris Dockstader Rooney. 1983.
Georg Dachstätter, the pioneer, was one of the "Palatines" who immigrated in 1709 with his wife Anna Elisabeth and son from the Palatinate, Rheinland-Pfalz, through England to America and settled in 1710 at Manor Livingston on the Hudson River. They were among the ninety-two Palatines to whom lands were granted at German Flats in the Burnetsfield Patent in 1725. Traces the known descendants of Georg and Anna Elisabeth Dachstätter in the male and female lines to

the present time (twelve generations). Documentation is included in
the text with references to original sources as well as to secondary
works.
Some of the more significant allied families mentioned are:
Countryman, Diefendorf, Dillenback, Ecker, Fonda, Fox, Klock,
Lathers, Lipe, Loucks, Nellis, Saltsman, Shults, Snell, Snyder,
Van Wie, Veeder, Vroman, Wagner, Walrath, Wemple, and Yates.
This Volume is the first of a set of four Volumes.
Volume Two: Generations Seven and Eight.
Volume Three: Generations Nine Through Twelve.
Volume Four: Complete Index and Bibliography.
Illustrated with over 100 pictures and maps; published privately.
Order and Check: Doris Dockstader Rooney/1918 La Mesa Drive/
Dodge City/Kansas 67801
Cloth—$68.50—992pp-- Vendor #D2006

3981   - PATCHWORKS: LABAR—LABARRE GENEALOGY by Phyllis M.
Parmley. 1985.
After several others attempted research, I was given challenge to put
it altogether with mine. "Patchworks" because it has been pieced together with both documented and traditional sources. Covers
300 year period including immigration, settlements, migration, etc.
Photos and blank pages provided for your individual lineages or
photos.
(In process)—400pp-- Vendor #D2007

3982   - THRICE BLESSED—A HISTORY OF SOME WEST VIRGINIA FAMILIES
THEIR ANCESTORS AND STATES OF ORIGIN by Barbara Prince-Tharp.
1981.
Cobb, Cobbs, and Veith families of West Virginia.
Additional information on Ashley, Holcomb, Jones, Morris and Upton
families and related lines.
Includes Braxton, Jackson, Kanawha, Lewis, Roane and Upshur
Counties, West Virginia, birth, death and marriage records, and
medical and personal information from Union Soldiers' Civil War
Records. Photographs.
Cloth—$26.00—283pp-- Vendor #D2009

3983   - THE FEARNS OF VIRGINIA AND SOME ALLIED FAMILIES by Eliza-
beth Lee Fearn Cabell Ferneyhough and Elizabeth Lee Lusk.
Fearn and Allied Families: Keene, Lee, Therriott and Wortham.
Virginia Counties: Albemarle, Buckingham, Gloucester, Goochland,
Isle of Wight, Lancaster, Middlesex and Northumberland 1623-1802.
Kentucky County, Bourbon 1786-1800.
Paper—$8.50—90pp-- Vendor #D2010

3984   - DANICO (DENICO, DENNICO, DINNICO, DINICO, DANACO) FAMILY
HISTORY (DRAFT) by Francis H. Danico. 1982.
Danico Family Genealogy from Joseph Danico, Acadian, probably born
before 1735, died before 1790, in Kennebunkport, Maine.
Up to nine generations listed with sources listed.
Paper—$10.00—64pp-- Vendor #D2011

3985   - CROSSROADS IN KANSAS: A STEARNS—ROSS GENEALOGY WITH
ALLIED FAMILIES by Phyllis Ross Kostner. 1982.
Part One: One branch of Charles Sterne (1620-) family who migrated
from Massachusetts, Western New York, Wisconsin, to Kansas;
sixty-eight allied families include Jenckes, Hinckley, Cotton, Brad-
street, Dudley and many from Stonington, Connecticut Area: Palmer,
Denison, Geer, Allyn, Lovett, Blott.
Part Two: William Ross, Jr. and Nancy Chinn (1753-1833);
allied families: Chinn, Ball, Bonnifield, Minear.
Cloth—$37.50—290pp-- Vendor #D2012

3986   - "SOME OF THE MANY BRANCHES ON THE GREENWELL FAMILY TREE"
by Betty Greenwell Burgelin. 1984.
Nine branch Greenwell Family History—1066 A.D.—1984 world-wide.
War, birth, death, marriage records, biographies, pictures, indexed.
Paper—$27.50—315pp-- Vendor #D2014

3987   - HENDERSON HERITAGE edited by Mary K. Hubbard.
Quarterly publication to research all Hendersons; computerized;
queries from members.
Subscription—$12.00/yr—30pp------------------------------Vendor #D2015

3988   - HELFERICH FAMILY HISTORY; ANCESTORS AND DESCENDANTS OF
JOHANNES HELFERICH by B. P. Helferich. 1983.
Traces family lines from 1700's in Germany to Holland, England,
Canada, U.S.A. Lists known descendants and allied families,
with thumbnail sketches of many. Illustrated, indexed.
Cloth—$9.50—112pp-------------------------------------- Vendor #D2018

3989   - BYRDS AND SONNERS OF SHENANDOAH VALLEY VIRGINIA AND
THEIR MIGRATIONS TO WELLS COUNTY, INDIANA by Marilyn K.
Harton and Harold K. and Carol J. Byrd. 1983.
Beginning in the early 1700's, these families are traced from Pennsyl-
vania, Virginia, and Maryland, through Kentucky and Ohio, to Indiana.
Included are sketches of the following families: Ambrose, Byrd (Bird),
Cailey, Cartwright, Crum, Geeting, Jones, McCorkle, Ruddle, Sonner.
All names are indexed. Appendix includes maps and photographs.
Indexed.
Paper—$15.00—160pp------------------------------------ Vendor #D2020

3990   - ANCESTORS AND DESCENDANTS OF LEMUEL PRUITT/PREWETT
AND CATHERINE BRANTLEY by Caroline E. Hughes. 1983.
Documented from 1636, Virginia, Georgia, Tennessee, Mississippi,
Texas; anecdotal incidents; lineages to 1983 as submitted. Indexed.
145 pages; 8½"x11", typeset.
Limited number include an abridged Supplement: *Lateral Lines of
Kirk Prewett:* Royston; Harris and Royal Lines; Arnold.
50 pages, indexed.
Copies including the abridged Supplement of *Lateral Lines of Kirk
Prewett* are $25.00.
Paper—$18.00—145pp------------------------------------ Vendor #D2022

3991   - THE FRENCHLINE by Mara T. French.
Quarterly computerized research on the surname French, approximately
eight pages each quarter. Write for sample.
The Frenchline, 521 River View Dr., San Jose, CA 95111
Subscription—Paper—$10.00/yr—apx 8pp/qtly---------------Vendor #D2023

3992   - FRENCH AND RELATED FAMILY GENEALOGY by Mara T. French.
1982.
French Family of England (1490-1982), immigration to Massachusetts
in 1630. 500+ photographs; 100+ documents.
Paper—$53.50—720pp----------------------------------- Vendor #D2023

3993   - THE KOENIG FAMILY OF BASEL 1799-1979 by Mara T. French. 1980.
Paper—$2.00—7pp------------------------------------- Vendor #D2023

3994   - THE TREADWAY FAMILY 1604-1940 by Mara T. French. 1982.
Paper—$10.00—48pp----------------------------------- Vendor #D2023

3995   - THE CUMMINGS FAMILY 1000-1866 by Mara T. French. 1982.
Paper—$2.50—11pp------------------------------------ Vendor #D2023

3996   - THE BLAIR FAMILY 1680-1875 by Mara T. French. 1982.
Paper—$2.00—5pp------------------------------------- Vendor #D2023

3997   - THE HUTTON FAMILY 1730-1889 by Mara T. French. 1982.
Paper—$1.50—3pp------------------------------------- Vendor #D2023

3998   - THE BARKER FAMILY 1610-1895 by Mara T. French. 1982.
Paper—$2.00—7pp------------------------------------- Vendor #D2023

3999   - THE HAYNES FAMILY 1583-1665 by Mara T. French. 1982.
Paper—$2.00—5pp------------------------------------- Vendor #D2023

4000   - THE JONES FAMILY 1615-1852 by Mara T. French. 1982.
Paper—$1.75—4pp------------------------------------- Vendor #D2023

4001   - THE BARROW FAMILY 1609-1855 by Mara T. French. 1982.
Paper—$1.50—3pp------------------------------------- Vendor #D2023

4002 - THE WARD FAMILY 1603-1760 by Mara T. French. 1982.
Paper—$1.50—3pp--- Vendor #D2023

4003 - THE LOBDELL FAMILY 1645-1971 by Mara T. French. 1982.
Paper—$2.50—13pp-- Vendor #D2023

4004 - THE HOWLAND FAMILY OF THE MAYFLOWER 1554-1671 by Mara T.
French. 1982.
Paper—$3.00—21pp-- Vendor #D2023

4005 - THE BREWSTER FAMILY OF THE MAYFLOWER 1565-1753 by Mara T.
French. 1982.
Paper—$2.00—7pp--- Vendor #D2023

4006 - THE ANDERSON FAMILY OF DENMARK AND NEW JERSEY 1815-1978
by Mara T. French. 1980.
Paper—$20.00—80pp--- Vendor #D2023

4007 - THE NILL FAMILY OF NEHREN, GERMANY 1796-1975 by Mara T.
French. 1978.
Paper—$8.00—25pp-- Vendor #D2023

4008 - THE MAYERHOFER FAMILY OF VIENNA 1849-1953 by Mara T. French.
1972.
Paper—$8.00—38pp-- Vendor #D2023

4009 - RILEY QUARTERLY SURNAME NEWSLETTER edited by Ethel M.
Rudy and Josephine Anderson. 4 issues/yr.
Subscription—Paper—$12.00/yr------------------------------ Vendor #D2027

4010 - RUDY QUARTERLY SURNAME NEWSLETTER edited by Ethel M. Rudy
and Josephine Anderson. 4 issues/yr.
Subscription—Paper—$12.00/yr------------------------------ Vendor #D2027

4011 - BERGER/BURGER QUARTERLY SURNAME NEWSLETTER edited by
Ethel M. Rudy and Josephine Anderson. 4 issues/yr.
Subscription—Paper—$12.00/yr------------------------------ Vendor #D2027

4012 - THE MUNSON RECORD, VOLUMES I AND II by Myron A. Munson.
Repr. of 1895 ed.
Cloth—$58.50—1235pp--------------------------------------- Vendor #D2028

4013 - BRANCHES OF ONE RIDDLE FAMILY TREE, VOLUME I by Dorotha
Riddle Marsh. 1981.
Early Chatham County, North Carolina Riddle's and their descendants.
5½"x8½". Index.
Paper—$30.00—179pp--- Vendor #D2029

4014 - THE POSTERITY OF JOHN ADAM STAGER compiled by Clerice Z.
Fisher. 1983.
...who arrived Philadelphia 1732; settled Avon, Lebanon County,
Pennsylvania. Ten generations of descendants. Completely indexed.
Photos, maps. Allied lines, mainly Pennsylvania and Ohio: Bahner,
Bohner, Baker, Besecker, Deeter, Denlinger, Fourman, Lehman,
Miller, Oda, Sease, Shanaman, Staeger, Steger, Steager, Swinger,
Walters, Yingst, Zehrbach, others.
Cloth—$40.00—1196pp----------- --------------------------- Vendor #D2031

4015 - HALBERT—HOLBERT HISTORY, VOLUME I by Karen Halbert Moore.
1985.
Covers many lines of Halberts and Holberts who originated from Virginia
as early as 1650. Associated lines include Hill, Berry, Gresham, Acker,
Blackburn, Garrison. Includes Halberts and Holberts now residing in
Missouri, Kentucky, Tennessee, Alabama, Texas, Georgia, Illinois,
Indiana, New York, Massachusetts.
Cloth—$25.50—Paper—$18.95—628pp ---------------------- Vendor #D2034

4016 - JAMES HUGHES: 1843-1921, BIOGRAPHY OF A WESTERN PIONEER
by LaRoux K. Gillespie. 1983.
Follow this Massachusetts Irish lad to the Chicago Stockyards, Sherman's March to the sea, fighting Indians in Kansas, Homesteading in
Cowley County, Kansas, Soonering in the 1889 Oklahoma Land Rush

and fighting for gold in Alaska and Canada. Three hundred and
twenty-five of his and brother Pat's descendants are listed.
Two indices and fifteen photos are included.
Cloth—$40.00—Paper—$30.00— 245pp------------------------ Vendor #D2037

4017 - THE IRETONS OF KANSAS, AND OKLAHOMA: 1870-1920 by
LaRoux K. Gillespie. 1984.
The history of John Ireton of Ireland and his descendants are described from 1850 until the 1920's. Data on over 600 descendants is
presented, but the emphasis is on the story of their lives. Price to
be announced.
250pp-- Vendor #D2037

4018 - CHOTANKERS: A FAMILY HISTORY by A. Edward Foote. 1984.
Southern Foote family. Also Gargis.
Cloth—$29.95—336pp--------------------------------------- Vendor #D2043

4019 - A SWISS IMMIGRANT'S FAMILY—JACOB HUBER (1835-1914), HIS
ANCESTORS AND DESCENDANTS, VOLUME I by June Dorman. 1984.
From Switzerland to fifteen states in U.S.A. Traces 1805-1984, eight
generations, more than 500 people. Contains ancestral charts; name
and address directory; copies of pictures, maps, 19th Century docu-
ments; statistical extrapolations; cemetery listings.
First in two-volume series.
Paper—$13.50— 90pp------------------------------------- Vendor #D2045

4020 - HUGH McWHIRTER FAMILY HISTORY by Harry Walter Yoder.
Gilbert McWhirter came from Ballantrae, Scotland to New Richmond,
Quebec before 1825. His son, Hugh's family, spread through Michigan
and West in the United States. Scottish background, historical notes,
pedigrees, family sheets, diaries, letters, etc. Photocopied sheets.
Paper—$25.00—300pp-------------------------------------- Vendor #D2046

4021 - ROBERT LAITHE HOWE FAMILY HISTORY by Harry Walter Yoder.
Ancestors and descendants of Robert Laithe Howe of Westbrook,
Maine. Pedigrees, family sheets, diaries, letters, newspaper reports,
historical material. Photocopied sheets.
Paper—$20.00—200pp-------------------------------------- Vendor #D2046

4022 - JOHN P. YODER FAMILY HISTORY by Harry Walter Yoder.
Yoder Swiss background; Imm. Christian Jotter - Christian -
Jacob - Philip - John P. family, including maternal backgrounds.
Pedigrees, family sheets, diaries, photos, letters, historical
backgrounds, etc. Photocopied sheets.
Paper—$28.00—350pp-------------------------------------- Vendor #D2046

4023 - BENJAMIN FRANKLIN NICKEL FAMILY by Phyllis L. Ferrara.
Pennsylvania 1800, Ohio, Nebraska. Many pictures.
Cloth—$7.50—80pp-- Vendor #D2054

4024 - MORGAN MIGRATIONS edited and published by Priscilla (Dawson)
Kingston.
Published quarterly, January, April, July, October.
Seven year quarterly/clearinghouse on Morgan, Morgen, Morgin
families. Each issue contains birth, marriage, death, census records,
genealogy charts from subscribers, queries, articles, clippings, two
indexes, anything fit to print on name Morgan. SASE for more information. Editor Emeritus: Jeanne (Robey) Felldin (1977-1983).
For nominal fee, research will be done on all back issues for a Morgan
name and maidenname; otherwise, can not do outside research.
Subscribers may submit their own records for consideration of publication in future issues.
Subscription—Paper—$12.00/yr-------------------------- Vendor #D2055

4025 - DESCENDANTS OF WILLIAM AND CATHERINE (BECK) SANDY by
Dr. William A. Sandy, edited by John V. Beck. 1983.
Cloth—$16.08—220pp------------------------------------- Vendor #D2056

4026   - GENEALOGICAL RECORDS OF THE SEITZ/SITES FAMILY—VOLUME I
GEORGE SITES WHO DIED 1790 HARDY COUNTY, VIRGINIA (NOW
GRANT COUNTY, WEST VIRGINIA) AND HIS DESCENDANTS by John
V. Beck and Suzanne Sites Gibson. 1984.
Cloth—$21.00—350pp-- Vendor #D2056

4027   - BERRY/BERREY FAMILY, THE FAMILY OF ELIJAH BERRY, VIR-
GINIA, GEORGIA, ALABAMA AND TEXAS, 1700-1980 by Lynn Berry
Hamilton (Mrs. C. H. Hamilton, Jr.). 1980.
Records begin with subject's grandparents, John and Jemima Berry
of Culpeper County, Virginia, their eleven children, most of their
grandchildren. Remainder of book traces Elijah's descendants.
Copies and transcripts of early records such as John Berry's 1780
Estate Sale naming sixty purchasers, newspaper accounts, Civil War
letters, photographs are included. Indexed.
Price includes $1.38 for packaging/postage; Texas residents add
$1.12 tax.
Cloth—$23.88—300pp-- Vendor #D2058

4028   - THE HOFFMAN—SCHEMEL FAMILIES by Larry Hoehn. 1982.
132 photos; indexed; reviewed *Genealogical Helper*, Sept./Oct. 1983,
page 156. Surnames: Clifton, Dickinson, Hinkle, Hoehn, Hoffman,
Hotop, Pingel, Ruch, Rudisaile, Schemel, Schott, Schumer, Sides,
Unterreiner, Welker, Wills. SASE for brochure.
Cloth—$28.00—336pp-- Vendor #D2059

4029   - SKETCHES ABOUT LANGFORDS, BOOK II by George S. Langford.
1981.
This book provides historical and genealogical information in that it
names more than 2,300 Langford/Lankfords. Many of these were
pioneers who settled in America before, during and after the American Revolution. More than fifty (50) Langford/Lankford researchers
contributed information for the book and named some of their Langford
ancestry. Those researchers are named and their addresses are given
as of 1981.
Order from: George S. Langford, 4606 Hartwick Road, College Park,
Maryland 20740.
Cloth—$21.50—458pp-- Vendor #D2060

4030   - THE BREDING BOOK: THE FAMILY HISTORY OF BARDO OLSEN
BREDING by Kay Breding Netz. 1984.
Also includes the Buness, Garness, Sellie, Enget, Jermstad, and
many collateral families. This creatively designed book has unique
beauty and displayability. There is considerable background information on Norway and Norwegian immigration to Wisconsin, Minnesota,
and North Dakota. It contains many historical photographs, imagina-
tive graphics, original illustrations and maps. The book has been
acclaimed by archivists both in Norway and America for its professional research, clarity of organization, and artistic presentation.
A must-see model for genealogists and writers. Name index included.
Cloth—$40.00—300pp-- Vendor #D2061

4031   - IN SEARCH OF AN ANCESTRY - THE STONE—SHEARMIRE FAMILY
HISTORY by Pamela Stone Eagleson. 1984.
This book traces historical and genealogical backgrounds of the families
of Stone (Virginia, Ohio, Illinois, Missouri); Stover (Virginia);
Harper (Virginia and Missouri); Butts (with interrelated Culpeper
County, Virginia families of Broaddus, Gaines, Farguson, Brown,
Coleman); Terwilliger (with interrelated Ulster County, New York
families); Elliott (Ohio); Cosner (Pennsylvania and Illinois); Wiggins
(with emphasis on the Hambletons of Pennsylvania); and the Missouri
German families of Shearmire, Henze, Stoehr, Graue, and Fasse.
Cloth—$26.50—261pp-- Vendor #D2062

4032   - THE EPISTLE. 6 issues/yr.
Featuring all known United States branches of the Batchelder, Rice,
and Carpenter families; free queries; indexed.
Subscription—Paper—$15.00/yr-- Vendor #D2064

4033 - GROFF BOOK VOLUME ONE by Clyde L. Groff and Walter B. Groff.
1984.
Five generation history and genealogy of all Groff Families (all spellings), who settled in southeastern Pennsylvania in 17th and 18th Centuries; with European background.
Cloth—$30.00—300pp--Vendor #D2065

4034 - GROFF NEWSLETTER by Clyde L. Groff and Walter B. Groff. Pub. qtly.
History, genealogy and correspondence of Groffs across the United States.
Subscription—$5.00/yr— 6pp---------------------------------Vendor #D2065

4035 - BRANCHES OF THE PINGEL FAMILY OF PERRY COUNTY, MISSOURI by Carrol Geerling. 1982.
Paper—$7.50—120pp-------------------------------------- Vendor #D2066

4036 - THE CANFIELD FAMILY 1637-1978 by Hallie Canfield Kyle. 1978.
Follows the line from Matthew Canfield, England to Connecticut, New Jersey, and his descendants through New York to Randolph County, Virginia (now West Virginia). Two fifth generation brothers, Daniel and Josiah Canfield, settled in 1800 near Elkins, Randolph County; one son of each remained, and many descendants still live there. Relatives live in all parts of the United States. Includes marriages, births, deaths, places of burial, occupations, names of spouses' parents, when available. Information was drawn from deeds, wills, Bibles, military, church, newspapers, individual families, and census records. The descendants also include the daughters' families.
A partial list: Arbogast, Bartlett, Buckbee, Cain, Coberly, Collett, Crandall, Currence, Exline, Ferrier, Fox, Gainer, Godwin, Hamrick, Hart, Isner, Jacobs, Kibler, Long, McGinnis, Morningstar, Murphy, Myers, Nelson, Phillips, Schoonover, Scott, Skinner, Smith, Taylor, Triplett, Vanscoy, Wamsley, Webley, Wilmoth, Workman, Young. 70 pictures.
Cloth—$31.50—588+pp-------------------------------------- Vendor #D2067

4037 - A HISTORY OF THE STURGILL FAMILY by David A. and Mack H. Sturgill. 1983.
Published 1983, includes family records, sketches, maps, documents, photos. Sturgill—Sturgell, Sturgeon, Stargel, Stodghill, Stodgell data from 1650 to 1983. Orange County, Virginia, Ashe County, North Carolina, Southwest Virginia. Paper, 11"x8¼".
Paper—$25.00—650pp-------------------------------------- Vendor #D2071

4038 - CHILDRESS CHATTER RESEARCH QUARTERLY edited by Mrs. Molly Bateman Reigard.
$10.00 year. Free queries to subscribers. Childress/Childers, etc.
Subscription—$10.00/yr-------------------------------- Vendor #D2072

4039 - McGEHEE MESSENGER RESEARCH QUARTERLY.
$10.00 year. Free queries to subscribers.
Subscription—$10.00/yr---------------------------------Vendor #D2072

4040 - THE THREE BELLS RESEARCH QUARTERLY edited by Molly Bateman Reigard.
$10.00 year. Free queries to subscribers.
Subscription—$10.00/yr---------------------------------Vendor #D2072

4041 - ROGERS ROOTS RESEARCH QUARTERLY.
$10.00 year. Free queries to subscribers.
Subscription—$10.00/yr-------------------------- ------Vendor #D2072

4042 - THE ORIGINS OF THE BOWMANS OF CARROLL COUNTY, VIRGINIA: THE BOWMAN FAMILY HISTORY by Regina B. Manuel and Iva B. Manley. 1984.
Genealogical family history, from 1600's to present, including Branscombe, Marshall, Hancock, Hall, Jackson, Martin, McMillian, Quesenberry and many others.
Paper—$30.00—225pp------------------------- -----------Vendor #D2073

4043 - THE GILBERT FAMILY IN KANSAS by Larry D. Gilbert. 1982.
From Maryland (1600), Kentucky (1700) to Kansas (1850 to present).
Paper—$9.00—82pp--- Vendor #D2076

4044 - LEE LINEAGE, THE JONATHAN LEE FAMILY OF SOUTH CAROLINA
AND WESTWARD, 1810-1981, VOLUME I by Edna Earle Lee James. 1982.
From South Carolina to Alabama.
Allied families: Major, Teague, McComb, Cooper, Sims, Higginbotham,
Cowden, Self, Glenn. Maps, pictures, documents.
Cloth—$30.00—134pp--- Vendor #D2077

4045 - SELF HERITAGE by Larry Brown and Edna Earle James. 1984.
A Self collections including Isaac Self's (1750-1840) descendants,
from North Carolina, South Carolina, Tennessee, Georgia to Alabama,
and Westward.
Allied families: Johnson, Taylor, Hallmark, Love, Morton, Loggins,
Vann, Cooper, McComb, Ware, Lee. Maps, pictures, documents.
Cloth—$35.00—206pp--- Vendor #D2077

4046 - THE JOSEPH KITOWSKI FAMILY-1982 by Tim Siebert. 1982.
Listing of all descendants of the Joseph Kitowski family. Includes
main branches of Kitowski, Boyer and Mozuch. Lists as many people
as known with birth, death and marriage dates as known.
Paper—$2.50—32pp--- Vendor #D2080

4047 - TILSON GRIST MILL—MOUNTAIN FOLKLORE AND GENEALOGY by
Pat Alderman. 1981.
This 100-year-old mill was moved from Unicoi County to Nashville and
restored for use as an exciting centerpiece in the Pioneer Section of
the Tennessee State Museum. Includes interesting sketches of the life
and times of this pioneer family, which traces its American ancestors
bck to the Mayflower.
Paper—$5.00—48pp--- Vendor #D2081

4048 - WALKING WITH THE WALKERS by Edward R. Walker III. 1981.
This chronicle of the Walker family of Smythe and Wythe Counties in
southwest Virginia contains many old photos, copies of letters, etc.
Other family lines included are Bell, Bryant, Carter, Cleghorn, and
Gannaway. Surname and Walker first name index.
Paper—$15.00—128pp--- Vendor #D2081

4049 - LEONARD SHOUN AND WIFE BARBARA SLEMP OF JOHNSON COUNTY,
TENNESSEE AND THEIR DESCENDANTS by Carl B. Neal (1957);
indexed by Helen G. Price (1984), repr.
Leonard Shoun (1773-1845) and Barbara Slemp (1775-1851) have a
multiplicity of descendants through their eighteen children.
Associated Families: Barry, Butler, Cole, Donnelly, Dugger,
Garland, Harbin, Jenkins, Johnson, Lowe, Loyd, Mast, McEwen,
McQueen, Moore-Kiser, Murphey, Stout, Vaught, Wagner, Wills
and Wilson. Index includes approximately 8,700 names.
(In process)—Cloth—$25.00—Paper—$20.00—apx 250pp------- Vendor #D2081

4050 - RUGG-HOLT GENEALOGIES by Mary Rugg Dobbins.
Indexed; photographs; bibliography; illustrated.
Area: Connecticut, Massachusetts, Central New York, Southwest
Vermont. Includes Table of Important Historical Events, Churches
in Connecticut and Massachusetts including the Covenant of the
North Church in Salem, Massachusetts, 1629, which Covenant members
had to sign.
Some of the eighty-eight families (from early 1600's): Arms, Ball,
Blakeslee, Browne, Darbyshire, Frasier, Gleason, Graham, Grannis,
Holt, Ives, Mason, Moss, Palmer, Peck, Prescott, Priest, Rice, Rugg,
Snead, Stickney, Taylor, Todd, Tuttle, White, Wilder.
In the Prescott line are Royal Families in England, Italy, France and
Germany.
Revolutionary ancestors: Issac Gleason; Samuel Graham, Jr.;
Daniel Rugg, Jr.; Reuben Rugg; Lemuel Taylor, Sr.; Othniel Taylor, Sr.;
Hezekiah Todd, Sr.; Elphalet Stickney.
In the Appendix: Story of a Mountain Shepherd (Orie Rugg); Diary
of a Trip of Grandma Rugg.
Cloth—$22.00—Paper—$15.00—217pp----------------------- Vendor #D2082

4051 - HILBORN FAMILY JOURNAL edited by Robin Hilborn.
Founded 1978; 5 issues/year; $12. per year; 24 pages per issue;
circulation 140; ISSN 0707-3836.
Contact Robin Hilborn, 42 Sources Blvd., #1, Pointe Claire,
Quebec, H9S 2H9 Canada.
Subscription—$12.00/yr—24pp/issue------------------------Vendor #D2083

4052 - RICHARD BAILEY OF CHESTERFIELD AND TAZEWELL COUNTIES,
VIRGINIA AND HIS DESCENDANTS, VOLUME I by Mary Ellen Howe.
1984.
183 pictures, illustrations, maps, indexed, footnoted and documented,
20 Civil War letters. History of following areas included:
In Virginia—Chesterfield, Franklin, Tazewell Counties;
In West Virginia—Mercer, Wyoming, McDowell Counties, towns of
Princeton, Montcalm, and Bluefield;
In Kentucky—Franklin, Anderson Counties, towns of Bridgport and
Louisville.
Families included: Bailey, Belcher, Gates, Fuqua, Cheatham,
Jenkins, Stockton, Crockett, Rudd, Nunnally, Goode, Crump,
Davidson, Blankinship, Godfrey, Shrewsbury, McComas, Morgan,
Mitchem, Thompson, Wilson, Cook, Lambert, Walker, Lusk, Syres,
Hurst, Ferguson, Dillon, Harman, Davis, Stafford, King, Calfee,
Tuggle, Daniel, Tiller, Brown, Clay, Farley, Fraley, French,
Graham, Hill, Mills, Meadows, Porter, Roberts, Shrader, Taylor,
Straley, White, and many others. 6"x9".
Cloth—$35.00—622pp--------------------------------------Vendor #D2085

4053 - ANCESTORS AND DESCENDANTS OF LEWIS CONLEY BISHOP AND
ALLIED LINES compiled by Winnie Branen, Julia Dunn, and Gwen
Loveridge. 1980.
Earliest immigrant ancestors: John Bishop b. 1610 England, to Massa-
chusetts 1640; in Stamford, Connecticut as pastor 1644-1694.
William Tolman b. 1608 England, to Massachusetts 1630.
William Hewitt b. 1745 England, in 1781 married Sarah Krieg in
New Hampshire.
Lewis Conley Bishop b. 1818 Indiana; father of thirteen children;
step-father of five.
Allied lines: Whitehead, Tolman, Adams, Allen, Branen, Brown,
Buckner, Burnside, Cain, Camblin, Chappell, Coffin, Cunningham,
DeBusk, Dunn, Frey, Franklin, Gerloch, Glover, Griffin, Hayes,
Hazen, Howard, Kincaid, Kennedy, Koresky, Lambert, Lewis,
McKee, McGee, McNare, Petty, Peterson, Scott, Sharp, Smith,
Starr, Stone, Surber, Wallace, Woche, and others.
Records to 1978. Very early documented. Pictures, family stories.
8½"x11"; index; postage paid.
Cloth—$40.00—684pp------------------------------------Vendor #D2087

4054 - THE BOOK OF LIPPS AND RELATED FAMILIES OF CLINTON COUNTY,
INDIANA 1828-1983, VOLUMES I AND II by Francis L. Lipp. 1984.
Volume I has 756 pages of pictures, deeds, wills and information,
with forty-seven pages of index, given names of over 5,391, surnames
of 976, totalling over 8,000 individuals. Some ancestors go back to
15th, 16th, or 17th Century; ancestors from Europe, Virginia, Pennsylvania, Ohio, Indiana, Illinois, Kentucky, West Virginia, New
Jersey, and some up to date of the descendants. Most of the Lipp
names are in Volume I.
Also lists are collateral families: Pitman, Thornton, Fair, Fox,
Carter, Dunn, Baty or Beaty, Brandon, Thompson, Dallas, Askew,
Worth, Calvin and Samuel Pedigo, Copher, Denny, Walker, Kings-
lover, Hollcraft, Whitaker, Crawford, Boone, and many others.
Volume II has 681 pages of information, pictures, deeds, and wills,
45 pages of index, about 900+ surnames, over 8,000 individuals.
Going back to 15th, 16th, 17th Century from Europe and States:
Virginia, West Virginia, Pennsylvania, Ohio, New Jersey, Indiana,
Illinois, Kentucky.
List of collateral families: Offenbacker, Zerfas, Douglass, Pitman,
Phares, Smiley, Ross, Byers, McCray, Maxwell, Hunt, Sherard,
Cornelison, Zaring, Adams, Squire, Baxter, Bass, Alden, Paine,

Chambers, Williamson, Harpine, Baer, Miller, Browning, Desmarest,
Gibson, Brafford, Boothe, Dixon, Halberstadt, Trusler, Vanderventer,
Lipps, and many others.
This is also a record book, blanks are left for each family so they
can add as years go by. For information please feel free to write
me or call 317-659-2806.
Each book is numbered and name of person book is to be presented
to when ordering.
Cloth—Volume I and II—$37.50 each; Set of 2 Volumes—$75.00.
Cloth—$75.00/Set—apx 1500pp/Set------------------------- Vendor #D2088

4055 - THE BOOK OF ANTHONY HALBERSTADT AND HIS DESCENDANTS
FROM 1775-1974 by Francis Lipp. 1975.
History and genealogy of author's grandfather and his descendants up
to 1974. There are over 1,000 pages, which include pictures, maps,
charts, wills, deeds and births, birthplace, where buried and where
lived and a small biography of some persons.
Anthony Halberstadt was a Hession Soldier who came to America in
August, 1776, and took part in the Battle of Long Island, New
Rochelle, White Plains, Chatterton Hill and Trenton when he was
captured Christmas Eve of 1776, and chose to stay in America.
There are over 1,000 family names including: Adams, Allen, Bennett,
Brown, Butler, Carpenter, Cole, Copley, Davis, Dixon, Downey,
Fitzgerald, Halberstadt, Hall, Hazen, Henry, Herndon, Hilderbrand,
Kirkpatrick, Jackson, Lipp, Martin, Miller, Morris, Peterson,
Phenice, Pridmore, Reynolds, Romine, Smith, Snyder, Strawn,
Tellaeferro, Tyner, Warren, Waters, Weida, Williams, Woods, plus
over 7,000 persons named in this book. Each book is numbered.
Cloth—$25.00—1000+pp----------------------------------- Vendor #D2088

4056 - ZUG/ZUCK/ZOUCK/ZOOK GENEALOGY by Harry D. Zook. 1983.
Five generations of male lines from all Zaugg/Zug immigrants prior
to 1800. Early land warrantees and ninety percent of families in
1790 and 1850 censuses identified. Thousands of records reviewed.
Locations, migrations, legends, and European homelands described.
Illustrated. Comprehensive 4,000-name index includes 900 surnames.
Typeset.
Cloth—$15.00—428pp------------------------------------- Vendor #D2090

4057 - THE McCLUNG GENEALOGY by William McClung. 1983, repr. of
1904 ed.
A genealogical and biographical record of the McClung family and
their hundreds of allied families. It traces their emigration from
Scotland to Ulster, thence to Pennsylvania, the Valley of Virginia,
and throughout America from the years 1690 to 1904. Some 3,500
McClungs are mentioned. Indexed, illustrated.
Cloth—$25.00—336pp------------------------------------- Vendor #D2091

4058 - THE DOFFING FAMILY by Lucille Hammargren Doffing and Robert
J. Olson. 1982.
An intriguing genealogy of the Doffing family.
Cloth—$27.45—410pp------------------------------------- Vendor #D2092

4059 - A GENEALOGICAL RECORD OF THE DESCENDANTS OF BAZEAL
HAYES OF CHARLEY, LAWRENCE COUNTY, KENTUCKY by Thelma
C. Walter and Theodore B. Walter. 1981.
Bazeal Hayes born in Virginia 1806, came to Kentucky when a child
and settled at Charley, Lawrence County, Kentucky. He fathered
thirty-two children, by two wives. His children allied themselves,
by marriage, to the Packs, Bowlings, Carters, Murrays, Van Hooses,
Spencers, Thompsons, Travis, Jordans, Dixons, Moores, Prestons,
Cordle (Caudills), McKinsters, Daniels, Wellmans and Miller families
of the Big Sandy Valley of Eastern Kentucky. Bazeal Hayes' descendants have scattered across America. Indexed; over 350 pictures.
Cloth—$39.50—980pp------------------------------------- Vendor #D2096

4060 - A GENEALOGICAL RECORD OF THE DESCENDANTS OF ISREAL WALTER, VOLUME I by Theodore B. Walter. 1980.
Indexed, over 300 pictures of descendants, their spouses, Bible records, gravestones, churches, homes and other biographical data on the descendants of Isreal Walter, a well-known Baptist preacher in Russell County, Virginia, and the primogenitor of the Walter(s) family that settled in Floyd, now Lawrence County, Kentucky, about the year 1818. His descendants have scattered across America.
Cloth—$31.50—454pp--- Vendor #D2096

4061 - A GENEALOGICAL RECORD OF THE DESCENDANTS OF ISREAL WALTER, VOLUME II by Theodore B. Walter. 1983.
Volume II begins where Volume I ended. It includes over 650 pictures of the descendants, their homes, churches, gravestones, etc. The Walter family allied, by marriage, with the Grahams, Holbrooks, Deans, Wards, Swetnams, Woods, Sturgill, Gambill, Grubb, Burton, Ely, Patrick, Cooksey, Preston, Litteral and many other families of the Big Sandy Valley of Eastern Kentucky. Fully indexed.
Cloth—$39.00—853pp--- Vendor #D2096

4062 - MY McGEE AND JOYNER FAMILIES: PIONEERS, PATRIOTS, AND PREACHERS by Helen Bowling McKnight. 1983.
Descendants of John McGee (1716 Ireland-1773 Guilford County, North Carolina) and Revolutionary War heroine Martha McFarlane (1735-1820). Focusing on two sons: William, Presbyterian; John, Methodist—noted camp meeting evangelists early 1800's Kentucky, Tennessee, North Carolina. John's son-in-law Rev. Thomas Joyner (1802 Sumner County, Tennessee—1882 Marshall County, Mississippi). Northampton County, North Carolina and Virginia ancestors: Joyner, Burn, Daughtrey, Mandew.
Paper—$20.00—218pp--- Vendor #D2098

4063 - A FAMILY ODYSSEY: ANCESTORS AND DESCENDANTS OF JOSEPH H. AND ADA BELLE (MARSH) STAGER by Helen A. and Evelyn M. Stager. 1983.
Joseph Harrison Stager of Ohio and Nebraska and his wife Ada Belle Marsh of Wisconsin were chosen as the focus around which their grand-daughters organized sixty-eight chapters on ancestral lines marrying into the Stager and Marsh lines. Most ancestors go back to the early 1600's. Marshes originated in England and settled in Massachusetts and Maine. Stagers begin with Heinrich who immigrated to Pennsylvania in 1732. Some lines are carried back several generations in England. Photographs, historical background, and traditions are included. Each chapter has a list of good sources such as pension, probate, land, vital records, and local histories. Over 6,000 individual names appear.
Family lines are: Abbott, Albee, Barker, Carriel, Carver, Chadbourne, Chandler, Colburn, Conley, Cooke, Davenport, Davis, Dean, Downing, Eames, Eliot, Emery, Ford, Godfrey, Goldthwaite, Goodwin, Grant, Green, Hathorne, Heald, Hilton, Holbrook, Howland, Jenkins, King, Kingman, Lord, McFadden, Nason, Oldfield, Oldham, Pease, Phillips, Pierce, Richards, Robbins, Sampson, Shaw, Sillsbee, Simonds, Skelton, Smith, Spencer, Sprout, Stone, Story, Talmadge, Tozier, Thompson, Turner, Walker, Wetherill, Yiengst, Young, and more. 457 pages typeset.
Cloth—$37.00—Paper—$32.00—postpaid—457pp-------------- Vendor #D2099

4064 - WHITLOCK GLEANINGS by Thomas E. Roach. 1982.
A history of the Whitlock families of America.
Paper—$19.95—329pp--- Vendor #D2100

4065 - THE HONAKER FAMILY IN AMERICA by Joanne Coontz. 1985.
Descendants of Hans Jacob Honaker whose will dated in 1795 in Wythe County, Virginia, names his sons and daughters: Henry, Jacob, Nicholas, Joseph, Martin, Frederick, Peter, Benjamin, Isaac, Abraham, Elizabeth, Mary, Christiana, and Anna. Chapters are included on each of the sixteen children, who resided in Virginia, West Virginia, Kentucky, Georgia, etc., the Honaker's Revolutionary service and

their work as gunsmiths. Scheduled to be published in mid 1985.
Manuscript being compiled.
(In process)--- Vendor #D2101

4066 - YOUR PLACE IN THE LINE—A RYKER GENEALOGY by David E.
Ryker. 1984.
Genealogy of the Rycken, Riker, Ryker and allied families from 1635 to
present. Includes early history of New Netherlands, New York, New
Jersey from about 1635 to 1850; Biographies of Abraham Rycken,
Abraham, Jr., John, Gerardus, Gerardus, Jr., John Gerardus
Ryker and descendants; Family record sheets on more than 400 individ-
ual families who can trace ancestors back to 1635.
Family names follow: Alig, Anderson, Armond, Balif, Barber, Bryson,
Block, Burton, Callis, Collyear, Cook, Cope, Crafton, Cranford, Cull,
Cunliffe, Davis, Eckert, Elliott, Fein, Fewell, Fisher, France, Gray,
Green, Hall, Harris, Hampton, Hoge, Imel, Jackson, Jones, Judkins,
Keller, Kinney, Klein, Lane, Little, Lott, Lumsden, McAtee, McMannis,
Melton, Meredith, Mullins, Nichols, Palm, Palmer, Patton, Pech, Pender,
Richmond, Riker, Ryker, Ryhal, Salisbury, Salyers, Seegers, Sexton,
Short, Skidmore, Smith, Southard, Sparks, Stanley, Stiver, Taylor,
Utley, Walker, Waltz, Weaver, Werlie, Windenburg, Wilkins, Williamson,
Wilson, Woodfill. 8¼"x11". Indexed.
Cloth—$30.00—600pp--- Vendor #D2104

4067 - THE GUTHERY FAMILY OF CULLMAN COUNTY, ALABAMA by Ima Gene
Guthery Boyd. Revised 1979.
Covers eight generations from Henry Guthery (Gutry, Guthrie, Guttry,
etc.), born in Virginia (1770-80); his son, David Guthery and wife
Mary Ann Crone born 1811 South Carolina. They are in Alabama by
1840; they had eight children.
William Guthery married Martha Beatrice Speegle and they had sixteen
children.
Includes descendants of William and Martha Beatrice (Speegle) Guthery
to the current generation, over 1,000. Also has information on related
and allied families: Bradley, Cranford, Harris, Holloway, Jaggers,
Jones, Lett, McKoy, Persall, Sinyard, Still, Tucker, Vickery,
Williamson, Young. 29 pages of photographs.
Paper—$10.00—229pp--- Vendor #D2111

4068 - THE HAWK FAMILY OF NEW JERSEY AND ATHENS COUNTY, OHIO
IN THE NINETEENTH CENTURY by Nancy Aiken and Beverly
Schumacher. 1984.
Paper—$15.00—87pp+index--------------------------------------- Vendor #D2112

4069 - "IOWA COUSINS" compiled by Amelia (Wulf) Beck and Juanita
(Comegys) Gettman. 1983.
A genealogy and history of some of the families who came by wagon
train, leaving Kentucky ca 1845, remaining in Illinois fifteen months
and listed in Iowa in 1850 Federal Census: Bridges, Dawson, Linder,
Logsdon, Patterson, and Reynolds. In 1856 Iowa State Census:
Barstow, Millard, and Gardner from Washington County, Ohio.
Others: Beck, Campbell, Comegys, Strait, Fredregill, Gettman,
Grater, Eisenberg, Kerlin, Stauffer, Hunsicker, Sterling, Harley,
Cowan, Russell, Horning, Jones, Heath, Henderson, Wright, Stark
and many others, all related either by descent or marriage.
Also includes pictures, maps, and documents. Well indexed.
Privately published 1983, hardbound, over 570 pages, 8½"x11",
weighs six pounds. $47.50 postage paid.
Cloth—$47.50—570+pp--- Vendor #D2113

4070 - "OUR McFARLAND FAMILY IN EARLY KENTUCKY AND SINCE" by
R. M. McFarland, Jr. 1982.
Our McFarland Family in Early Kentucky and Since, the record of
descendants of Robert McFarland, ca 1731-1780, of Caswell County,
North Carolina, containing maps, old photographs, extracts of
wills and anecdotes. The result of five years of research. Full
alphabetical index. 8½"x11"; Perfect Binding.
Paper—$10.32—120pp--- Vendor #D2114

4071   - FARRINGTON AND KIRK FAMILY, 1600-1983. ANCESTORS AND
DESCENDANTS OF ABRAHAM FARRINGTON (1765-1840) OF NEW
JERSEY AND OHIO, AND HIS WIFE DEBORAH KIRK OF CHESTER
COUNTY, PENNSYLVANIA by Herschel B. Rochelle.
Most remote was Anthony Bunting (1600-1700) of Derbyshire, England,
fined for a religious meeting in his home (Quakers). Oldest Kirk was
Roger Kirk, a couper, of Lurgan, County Armagh, Ireland.
Bunting's granddaughter Phebe married Abraham Farrington (1690-1758)
of Burlington, New Jersey. His grandson, Abraham the Younger,
married Deborah Kirk, and their descendants are what the book is
about.
Irish church records are given, and accounts of Abraham the elder,
a noted Quaker preacher; and the journal of Abraham the younger,
including a mid-winter trip by sleigh from Ohio to New Jersey and
back, suffering from the cold, and his sleigh overturned on a rock,
requiring a blacksmith. He was a farmer, preacher, teacher, and
shoemaker. Also shown are photos, documents, maps, and Abraham's
handwriting. Other anecdotes of early days provide interest, and
care is taken to keep data orderly and easy to understand. The
index is in large, elite size type.
Allied names: Abel, Bowman, Dunlap, Dunn, Foreman, Fowler,
Heastand, Heard, Mosher, Moore, Reader, Watkins.
Illustrated; Index of 8,000 names. 8½"x11".
Cloth—$25.00—360pp-- Vendor #D2116

4072   - GENEALOGY OF THE BLISS FAMILY IN AMERICA, 3 Volumes, by
Aaron Tyler Bliss. 1982.
This work is monumental in size and scope, and is much more than a
listing of names and dates. It includes as many details as possible.
Biographical sketches, news articles, photographs and other materials
appear generously. Disconnected branches are included as well as
census records, and an index containing more than 86,000 persons.
More than 35,600 entries appear in the localities index. The family
history commences ca 1180 A.D. and is carried to the present and
contains the entire contents of the *Genealogy of the Bliss Family*,
by John Homer Bliss (1881), and selections from *The Bliss Book* by
Charles A. Hoppin (1913). Fourteen generations are shown in the
text along with the history of the family in England, full color coat-
of-arms, fragmentary information, extended female lines, survey
information are given in footnotes. Those interested in publishing
a family history should certainly consult this work, whether or not
their family surnames are included.
Cloth—$125.00—3059pp--------------------------------------- Vendor #D2117

4073   - A FAMILY NAMED CURTIS, THE DESCENDANTS OF THOMAS
CURTIS OF WETHERSFIELD, CONNECTICUT FROM 1598-1983
compiled by Rose Mary Goodwin. 1983, corrections and additions
included.
Contains more than 3,500 names from many lines of all Thomas
Curtis' children. Many of his descendants sent their records, as
well as mini-biographies, and/or incidents to include along with
pictures, etc. County, City and State History books from various
genealogical libraries were consulted. Family histories have contributed their bits.
Several other compilers of smaller works on this Thomas Curtis have
graciously given permission to incorporate their findings. Resources
are carefully accredited at the end of each family group.
These adventurous people gradually spread throughout New York,
Vermont and other of the New England States; then some went to
Canada as a result of the Revolutionary War and back into Michigan,
Wisconsin and on West.
Others joined the westward movement through Ohio and spread or
settled in almost all the states on the way to the West Coast, Iowa,
Nebraska, North and South Dakota, Kansas, Colorado, Wyoming,
Utah, Idaho, New Mexico, Nevada, California, Oregon, and
Washington.
Genealogical libraries and societies will want to add this volume to

their group of family genealogies for researchers of this family tree.
Experience in cataloging hundreds of family histories at the Heritage
Library in Glendale and the Southern California Genealogical Library
in Burbank enabled Mrs. Goodwin to choose a much used method of
arrangement of data, in an easy manner for researching the lines
included back to the immigrant, Thomas Curtis. Many of the
daughters' lines are included as well as the sons'.
8½"x11". Illustrated.
Cloth—$39.50—741pp--- Vendor #D2121

4074 - GEORG PETERSHEIM FAMILY by Petersheim Descendants. 1979.
The Georg and Christina (Nissley) Petersheim family emerges in the
Waldeck-Lippe regions of Germany. In 1810 they settled in Lancaster
County, Pennsylvania. The second generation springs from Lancaster
County, Somerset County, Pennsylvania and Ontario. The book has
over 5,000 entries interweaving 112 other Amish family names and
hundreds of others.
Included are: Bender, Blank, Brown, Byler, Erb, Esh, Fisher,
Gingrich, Glick, Hostetler, Jantzi, Kauffman, King, Martin, Mast,
Mayer, Miller, Schrock, Schwartz, Selders, Steinman, Stutzman,
Swartz, Umble, Weaver, Yoder, Zehr, and Zook.
Copies of many authentic European documents as passports, church
letters, and testimonials are included. An appendix contains brief
histories of associate families as Nissley, Schwartzentruber,
Gascho, Roth, Good, and Kropf. Accounts of Amish church commun-
ities of Wilmont, Canada, Aurora, West Virginia, Midland, Virginia,
and others are included.
Cloth—$11.50—615pp--- Vendor #D2123

4075 - TANGLEWOOD CHRONICLES by Debra Winfield Smithers. 1983.
Indexed, 69 photos, 36 chapters covering Allen, Bradley, Burchett,
Casteel, Davis, Gregg, Griffin, Hensley, Kelley, Laffoon, Lovan,
Lumpkin, McIntyre, Palmer, Pevehouse, Reardon, Rhodes, Richardson,
Schube, Sherard, Simms, Smethers, Stark, Trull, Wallace, Weaver,
Wild, Wilson, Winfield, White, Woodruff, Wooten.
Cloth—$25.00—512pp--- Vendor #D2124

4076 - BAKERS OF SISSINGHURST (CASTLE) AND OTHER RELATIVES by
Norma Baker McCullough. 1982.
Nineteen generations Bakers from 1490 in England to 1980 in America.
First American family 1698 Joseph Baker married Martha Woodward.
Children Mary (Yarnall), Richard, Anne (Sill), Sarah (Ottey),
Joseph, Rachel (Hampton), Nehemiah, John; 8,500 listings index.
SASE for information. Other lines included are McCullough, Taylor,
Tharp, Turner, Wilson, Zollars.
Cloth—$27.00—444pp--- Vendor #D2125

4077 - Le DESPENCER: JOURNAL OF SPENCER FAMILY ASSOCIATION
(ALL SPENCERS) INTERNATIONAL edited by Frances Spencer Powell.
Le Despencer is published quarterly and uses mostly primary type
records—wills, deeds, diaries, etc.—extracted and sent in by members
of The Spencer Family Association. Free queries to members.
Indexed in the October issue each year.
150pp/yr--- Vendor #D2126

4078 - THE FAMILY DIRECTORY WITH LISTINGS ON BAREFIELD/BARFIELD,
DALLAS, DAVIS, GILLEY, HOLLEY, NEWSOM, SPINKS, AND STARK
by Doris Barfield Sanders. 1980.
Cloth—$17.95—160pp--- Vendor #D2129

4079 - THE SHREINER FAMILY OF LANCASTER, PENNSYLVANIA by David
L. Shreiner. 1983.
Paper—Free—7pp--- Vendor #D2130

4080 - PEEBLES/ANTE 1600—1962 by Anne B. Peebles. 1962.
Peebles/Peeples/Peoples descendants of Captain David Peebles,
arrived Virginia 1649.
Cloth—$21.50—200pp--- Vendor #D2131

4081 - HART FAMILY HISTORY—SILAS HART, HIS ANCESTORS AND
DESCENDANTS by William Lincoln Hart. Repr. of 1942 ed.
Back to Mayflower and beyond. 1600's.
Hart, Sweet, Clark, Swift, Gilson, Truesdale, Janney, Ferguson, Smith,
Peckham, Gillingham, Schmid, McPherson, Rose, Milner, Day, Starr,
Shroyer, Hyde, Foster, Longabaugh, McNelly, Rigdon, Stitt, Pahner,
Crumley, DeVore, Pendleton, Mathews, King, Warren, many more.
Civil War Diary in back.
Paper—$10.00—218pp-- Vendor #D2132

4082 - SCALF FAMILY HISTORY by Elmer D. Scalf. 1982.
Traces the Scalf family back to 1719 where the North Carolina ancestors
lived in Colonial times. Also traces the descendants of John Scalf,
Revolutionary Soldier.
Paper—$20.00—233pp-- Vendor #D2133

4083 - SEALS FAMILY HISTORY by Elmer D. Scalf. 1984.
Traces the Seals (Seal) family line of William Seal of Halifax County,
Virginia. Emphasis on Seals families that settled in East Tennessee
and Southeast Kentucky.
Paper—$12.85—198pp-- Vendor #D2133

4084 - WELCH/WELSH/WALSH NEWSLETTER (THE FOUNTAIN) by Al and
Barbara Mahoney. 6 issues/yr.
Established bi-monthly newsletter. Queries free to subscribers.
Minimum twelve pages per issue.
Subscription—Paper—$6.00/yr—12pp/issue min.-------------- Vendor #D2135

4085 - THE GOLDEN THREADS, VOLUME I: WEGER, ANDERMANN, QUIT-
MEYER, LINDERWELL AND ALLIED LINES by William G. Weger. 1983.
Illustrated. Seventeen pedigree charts. Traces Weger family, 1650's,
near Ansbach, Bavaria; Andermann's, 1500's; Linderwell (Lindwedel),
1600's; Quitmeyer, 1700's; latter lines originate near Rodewald,
Hanover, Germany. Over 200 ancestors. Translated excerpts from
parish records, etc. 8½"x11".
Paper—$34.00—300+pp--- Vendor #D2136

4086 - THE GOLDEN THREADS, VOLUME II: HERZMANN, PEISCHAN,
REBASCHUS, ZICKLER AND LINDNER FAMILIES (INCLUDING BAUM-
GARTNER, RIEMATH AND ALL ALLIED LINES) by William G. Weger.
1984.
Illustrated. Pedigree charts. Traces Herzmann, Peischan, Rebaschus
families to 1700's, East Prussia; Zickler, Wattenbach, etc. to Unterellen-
Wartha, Germany, 1600's; Lindner's, 1600's, Bavaria.
Paper—$34.00—350+pp--- Vendor #D2136

4087 - THE SHOEN FOUNDATIONS by Cleo Shoen Van Lerberg. 1984.
William and Sally (Shepard) Shoen, New York State 1800's.
Shepard Shoen, wife Phylinda Wells, Samuel Shoen—Mary Duel—children.
Ten pages handwritten notes by eighty year old Dora Shoen.
150 photos.
Cloth—$20.00—153pp--- Vendor #D2137

4088 - THE SCHROEPFER CONNECTIONS by Cleo Shoen Van Lerberg. 1983.
Franz and Maria Schropfer, Bohemia. 1865—. Eckstein, Rathman,
Shoen—related families. New Ulm, Minnesota. 100 photos.
Cloth—$20.00—140pp--- Vendor #D2137

4089 - HASSINGER FAMILY, 1545—1983 by Bernice Shield Hassinger. 1984.
Beginning with Christmann Hassinger (1545-1589), Woerrstadt,
Germany, documented history and genealogy from unpublished
German archives, church and civil registers. All Hassingers found
German records listed. Johann Peter Hassinger (1796-1856) and
wife, Maria Sara Dörr, (1804-1885) with six children immigrated to
New Orleans, 1840, and traced to 1984. German records used until
immigration then Hassingers in published books noted. Hassingers
traced twelve generations and charted with thirty allied families on
Ancestral Chart with birth, death, and marriage dates and place.
Allied families: Doerr, Eulmus, Fürst, Gerhen (Gehrheim), Heintz,

Hoffman, Kaye (Kaegy, Kaye, Koechi), Kron, Marz, Metz, Rothenhauser, Rupp, Schneider, Schuber, Schumacher, Velten, Wendling, and Wickert. Chart included with each book.
41 illustrations. Indexed. Cloth $37.00; 155 pages; 11"x8".
Ancestral Chart (only) $10.00, 11"x25".
Cloth—$37.00—155pp------------------------------------- Vendor #D2140

4090 - REAGAN FAMILY JOURNAL. Pub. qtly.
Published by the Reagan Family Association, a non-profit organization dedicated to the assembling and preserving of genealogical and historical materials documenting the Regan/Ragan/Reagan family in North America. Variant spellings covered include, among others, Ragan, Ragen, Ragin, Ragon, Reagan, Reagin, Regan, Regin, Regans, Reigan, Rigan, Riggan, Riggin, Rigins, O'Ragan, and O'Reagan.
Subscription—Paper—$10.00/yr—64pp/yr------------------ Vendor #D2141

4091 - CORNELIUS McCLOW (McCLOE—MUCKLOW) AND HIS DESCENDANTS. THE McCLOW FAMILY HISTORY AND GENEALOGY by Arnold H. McClow, Editor, and Clarence S. McClow. 1983.
Traces family genealogy through nine generations from Cornelius and Elizabeth Brower McClow, and includes Brower family connection and other information before 1775.
Paper—$12.00—144pp-------------------------------------- Vendor #D2142

4092 - ANCESTORS AND DESCENDANTS OF HENRY SIMEON SAUNDERS by R. S. Sanders. 1983.
Sanders/Saunders; 8¼"x11"; 178 pages, documented; hard cover. Family indexed, $27.00.
William Saunders, born ca 1735, died 1790 in North Carolina, left five sons: John, George, Joseph, Jesse and James. Each major descendant is narrated, and over 3,000 descendants, including nearly 300 families of different surnames, are arranged in an easy-to-follow outline.
Son John served in the American Revolution then moved to South Carolina to rear his family.
Son George moved to Georgia where his descendants are written of and documented.
Simeon Saunders, son of George, is the great grandfather of the author.
Simeon deserted his family in Georgia and moved to Texas with a new wife in 1837 and died there in 1891. He was the father of twenty-one children.
Published by the Rio Valley Publishing Company, McAllen, Texas; Bound by H. V. Chapman and Sons, Abilene, Texas.
Order from the author: R. S. Sanders, Box 147, Weinert, TX 76388.
Cloth—$27.00—178pp----------------------------------- Vendor #D2143

4093 - THE GODDARD BOOK, VOLUMES I AND II by John W. Harms and Pearl Goddard Harms. 1984 (Vol. I), 1986 (Vol. II).
The Goddard Book - Volumes I and II...published by The Goddard Association of America; compiled and edited by John W. Harms and Pearl Goddard Harms. Volume I published in 1984 and Volume II, in 1986.
This will be the most comprehensive record of families with the name or ancestry of Goddard or Godard that has ever been published.
The two volumes, with indices in both, will contain about 1,200 pages. Volume I will contain about 9,000 to 10,000 surnames and place names. Both volumes in cloth binding: 6"x9"; printed on acid-free paper and will contain the Goddard Sheild in three colors with interpretation.
Also replicas of two ancient coats-of-arms (one Goddard and another, Godard) will be published in Volume II.
About 600 people in the United States and Canada have provided information. Two Goddard family historians living in England have assisted. Records covering about 900 years will be included.
The Goddard Book is sold only as a unit at the provisional price of $33.00 for the two volumes, which includes packaging and delivery.
A deposit of $20.00 is required for delivery of Volume I prior to

availability of Volume II.
Order from Secretary of The Goddard Assocation of America, Kathryn
Goddard Meyer, 118 South Volutsia, Wichita, KS 67211.
Telephone: 1-316/682-4942.
Cloth—$33.00/Set—apx 580pp-------------------------------Vendor #D2144

4094 - THE GODDARD NEWSLETTER edited by Mary L. Goddard.
The Goddard Newsletter...published three or four times annually by
The Goddard Assocation of America; Mary L. Goddard, Editor.
Contains general information of interest to those with the name or
ancestry of Goddard or Godard living in the United States, Canada,
and England. No charge for queries. The *Newsletter* is one of
services provided to members. For sample copy and information,
write to Secretary, Kathryn Goddard Meyer, 118 South Volutsia,
Wichita, KS 67211. Telephone: 1-316/682-4942.
Membership:
Individual: $10.00
Husband/Wife: $15.00
Family (includes husband/wife and dependent children as
Junior Members): $20.00
Subscription—Paper—8+pp-------------------------------- Vendor #D2144

4095 - REV. PETER PRUDDEN AND HIS DESCENDANTS IN AMERICA,
VOLUMES I AND II by Horton R. Prudden. 1983.
Genealogy of Rev. Peter Prudden (ca 1600-1656), first Pastor at
Milford, Connecticut, and his descendants. Rev. Prudden was born
in Kings Walden, Hertfordshire, England; came to New England in
1637 in the "Hector." Married ca 1637/38 Johanna Boyse.
Other blood-line surnames include: Abbott, Adams, Allen, Alling,
Andrew(s), Atwood, Bailey, Baldwin, Barnes, Beach, Beardsley,
Beeman, Beldings, Benedict, Bennett, Bidwell, Blanchard, Bliss,
Boardman, Booth, Bostwick, Bosworth, Bradley, Bristol, Brockaway,
Brown, Burns, Burr, Burrows, Callaghan, Camp, Campbell, Canfield,
Carpenter, Carraher, Case, Chase, Church, Clark(e), Clary, Cloyes,
Coe, Comstock, Cook(e), Cooley, Coxhead, Croff, Culver, Curtis(s),
Cushing, Davis, Dawson, Deming, Dewey, Dormer, Doty, Downs,
Dunn, Dunning, Eaton, Eddy, Ely, Evarts, Farmer, Ferguson, Field,
Finch, Fitch, Fogg, Foster, French, Fry, Fuller, Garvin, Gilbert,
Gillet(t)e, Goodrich, Graves, Hale, Hall, Hastings, Hawley, Heaton,
Henderson, Henry, Hine, Holley, Hoyt, Hubbell, Hulanski, Hull,
Hungerford, Hurd, Jacobs, James, Jocelyn, Johnson, Judson, King,
Kirtland, Kramer, Lane, Leonard, Maine, Marsh, McClenthen, McQueen,
Merrick, Miller, Minor, Moore, Morrison, Munson, Murray, Mygatt,
Newton, Nichols, Noble, Northrup, O'Dell, Parker, Parsons,
Patten(gill), Peck, Perry, Platt, Preston, Price, Raymond, Richardson,
Rorke, Ruggles, Runyan, Russell, Sanford, Scott, Searle, Seavey,
Seeber, Sexton, Shaw, Sherman, Sherwood, Smith, Spencer, Stevens,
Stilson, Stone, Strong, Stuart, Taylor, Thompson, Townsend, Tunis,
Tuttle, Upson, VanScoy, VanVliet, Wadham, Walston, Ward, Warriner,
Webster, Weed, Well(e)s, Wheaton, Whittlesey, Wilcox, Wild(er),
Willicut, Williams, Willis, Wilson, Wood, Woodruff, Wright, Wyncoop.
Maps; pictures.
Cloth—$350.00—1400pp------------------------------------ Vendor #D2147

4096 - THE COPPLE FAMILY TREE by Oscar A. Copple. 1983.
Over fifteen years of research provide this extensive compilation of
the Copple family lineage from the 1700's to the present. It has been
thoroughly researched and compiled from legal documents, census
records, family Bibles, manuscripts, etc. It includes proof for the
Daughters of the American Revolution that the early Copples were in
the War for Independence.
Paper—$15.00—113pp------------------------------------- Vendor #D2148

4097 - THE FAMILY OF JAMES DUFFIL SCOTT (1828-1913) AND ELLEN (MATHEWS) SCOTT (1827-1908) OF BUCKS COUNTY, PENNSYLVANIA by Robin Scott McDowell. 1983.
Biographies of James Scott (a county map publisher), his wife, and 121 descendants in five generations, including McDowell, Stilwell, Clemens, and Scott families. Ancestral table includes 105 Scott/ Mathews ancestors in nine generations. Detailed references and bibliography; illustrations; full index.
Paper—$6.00—67pp-- Vendor #D2152

4098 - "SIMPSON, A FAMILY OF THE AMERICAN FRONTIER".
Begins with the arrival of the founder of Fraser Clan in 1066 from Normandy and the establishment of Scottish Klan Fraser. The Simpson migration to Northern Ireland in 1625; migration in 1775 to South Carolina of John and Christian Simpson—six sons, William, David, Christopher, Samuel, Thomas and James with their descendants and their migrations.
Write to John W. Simpson, Box P-1, LeLand, MI 49654.
-- Vendor #D2155

4099 - JOHN ZIGLER AND ELIZABETH KLINE OF VIRGINIA by Floyd R. Mason. 1984.
Immigrant Philip Ziegler, the families in Pennsylvania, are given along with descendants who came to Virginia in 1811.
Paper—$3.45—20pp-- Vendor #D2157

4100 - JOHN MASON AND MARY ANN MILLER OF VIRGINIA by Floyd R. Mason. 1986.
Many of William Mason and Elizabeth Cline's children went west. The oldest, John, and his descendants are given.
(In process)—Cloth—apx $30.00—apx 350pp----------------- Vendor #D2157

4101 - MATHIAS MILLER AND SEVENTEEN CHILDREN by Floyd R. Mason. 1984.
Mathias moved to Rockingham County, VIRGINIA, 1794. I have working papers for you. You can help me.
Paper—$1.75—8pp-- Vendor #D2157

4102 - THE SEVEN SANDERS BROTHERS by Holden E. Sanders. 1984.
Softbound edition of the previous hardbound edition of *The Sanders Family: An American Odyssey*, LC 84-80397. Traces Sanderses from South Carolina at the time of the Revolution to Tennessee, their pioneering there and where the Brothers were born. Continues with their migration to southern Illinois and brings the family down to the present. Over two hundred photos and a Civil War section.
Paper—$27.50—312pp--------------------------------------- Vendor #D2158

4103 - WEISS FAMILY 1600-1983 FROM UHINGEN, WURTTEMBERG, GERMANY by Alta S. Waugh. 1983.
Cloth—$27.00—285pp-- Vendor #D2159

4104 - ELDRED GRIFFITH DAVIS, DISTINGUISHED CITIZEN OF WASHINGTON CITY by Mrs. Kearsley C. Stratton. 1982.
An account of family life in Washington, D. C. at the turn of the Century. Many photographs.
Paper—$8.50—110pp-- Vendor #D2160

4105 - DANIEL COBIA 1714 DESCENDANTS IN AMERICA by Minnie Lee Cobia Selleneit and Beth J. McCarty. 1979.
Daniel Cobia, born in 1714 in Charleston, South Carolina, had sons John Conrad, Francis Joseph, Daniel, Michael, Nicholas; daughters Mary (Worshing) and Ann (Patrick). Descendants spread across America. This culmination of thirty years of research includes 350 photos, 3,500 names, sources cited, indexed.
Paper—$25.00—618pp--------------------------------------- Vendor #D2161

4106 - McCLANAHAN FAMILIES FROM TENNESSEE TO MISSOURI, VOLUMES I AND II by Sibyl M. Baker.
Wright, Webster and Laclede Counties, Missouri.
Paper—$16.00/Volume—109pp, 152pp---------------------- Vendor #D2164

4107 - PEACOCK FEATHERS GENEALOGY OF ELLA FRENCH EDGERLY by
Luella Heether and Clara Peterson. 1983.
The History of England, Scotland from 475 A. D. to time of migration
to New England, it puts our ancestors where they were.
Allied families: Ball, Farbanks, Breck, Prescott, White, many more.
Source of English History.
Cloth—$20.00—178pp---Vendor #D2167

4108 - SONS OF FRONTIERSMEN, HISTORY AND GENEALOGY OF ROWLAND,
WHITMIRE AND ASSOCIATED FAMILIES by Billie Louise and Robert
James Owens. 1976.
Record of the Rolands or Rowlands and Whitmires that populated
eastern Missouri and their ancestors in South Carolina and Kentucky,
including Isbell, Parker, Crawford, Johnson, Hill, Ridgely, Isaac,
Pottinger, Beall, Westall, Hinson, and Hagood families.
Cloth—$9.00—137pp---Vendor #D2172

4109 - SIMS KIN, HISTORY AND GENEALOGY, THE DESCENDENTS
WILLIAM SYMES OF POUNDSFORD AND RELATED FAMILIES by
Billie Louise and Robert James Owens. 1982.
Contains a chapter of limited information on each of the early settler
families of Bridges, Everard, Isham, Duke, Byrd, Horsemanden,
Green, Hawkyns, Allison, Ogilvie, Harris, Moore, Thompson, Lewis,
and Fletcher.
Cloth—$15.00—323pp---Vendor #D2172

4110 - GENEALOGY OF JOHN W. AND MARY JONES OWENS OF POMEROY,
OHIO AND ASSOCIATES by Robert Percy Owens. 1977.
Includes information on Owens and Jones families coming from Wales in
1860 and the John H. Williams and Benjamin W. Price families of Wash-
ington County, Arkansas.
Paper—$6.00—133pp-- Vendor #D2172

4111 - POPE, MOORE, THORNTON AND ALLIED FAMILIES by Blanche L.
Pope and Kimmi Grulke. 1984.
Paper—$25.00—119pp--- Vendor #D2173

4112 - PARIS, PURCELL AND ALLIED FAMILIES by Blanche L. Pope and
Kemmi Grulke. 1984.
Paper—$22.00—98pp--- Vendor #D2173

4113 - PHILIP PAUL OF STOCKLINCH, SOMERSET, ENGLAND AND SOME
OF HIS DESCENDANTS IN OLD GLOUCESTER COUNTY, NEW JERSEY
AND ELSEWHERE by Gordon W. Paul. 1983.
Philip Paul, the progenitor of this line, was born in 1657 in the small
village of Stocklinch in the County of Somerset, England where his
family had lived for many years, and where his grandfather, John
Paul, was probably married in 1617. Philip was the second son of
James and Amy Lampre Paul. In 1685 Philip and his wife Susanna
immigrated to America, settling in Gloucester County, New Jersey.
This well-written record charts ten generations of the Philip Paul
line. The appendices include: the will of Jeremiah Paul; "The
Child's Assistant" printed for Jeremiah Paul, 1804; A collection of
the pantings of Jeremiah Paul, Jr.; Genealogical Charts of the
descendants of Nathan Paul. This family history includes over
forty photographs of churches, houses, historical sites and earlier
Paul family members, maps, historical text and genealogical charts.
A full-name index completes this excellent record.
Cloth—$27.50—228pp---Vendor #D2174

4114 - THE ARMSTRONG BORDERLAND by William A. Armstrong. 1985,
repr.
History of great Scottish Border family, from great strength of middle
ages, to dispersal in 18th-19th Centuries.
Cloth—$16.70—164pp---Vendor #D2175

4115 - DUNBAR'S 1000 YEARS by William Dunbar of Kilconzie. 1985, repr.
Story of Dunbar family in Scotland's southwest. New index;
excellent historical/genealogical study.
Paper—$10.50—120pp--- Vendor #D2175

4116   - ACCOUNT OF THE CONFEDERATION OF CLAN CHATTAN by Char
     Fraser Mackintosh of Drummond. 1985, repr.
     Unique reference work on non-Mackintosh families in Scotland's
     famous Clan Chattan alliance. MacGillivray, MacBean, MacPhail,
     MacQueen, Shaw, Clark, Gow, Davidson, MacLean, MacIntyre,
     MacAndrew, Farquharson. Full-page tartan swatches.
     Paper—$33.75—219pp- Vendor #D2175

4117   - THE HOUSE OF FORBES by Alistair and Henrietta Taylor. 1985, repr.
     Splendid historical and genealogical study of Scotland's House of Forbes;
     includes cadet branches.
     Cloth—$46.75—494pp- Vendor #D2175

4118   - THE STORY OF THE HAYS by Kenneth McLennan Hay. 1985, repr.
     History of Hay family in Scotland, plus prominent Hays and drawings
     of family homes.
     Paper—$11.70—131pp- Vendor #D2175

4119   - HISTORY OF THE HOUSE AND CLAN OF MACKAY by Robert
     Mackay. 1985, repr.
     Extensive history of Scotland's Mackays, 1200-1800.
     Collateral material on Sutherland, Irvine, Sinclair, Gordon,
     Mackintosh, Duffus, Forbes, Gunn, Innes, MacDonald, MacLeod,
     Murray.
     Cloth—$49.75—592pp- Vendor #D2175

4120   - THE MAXWELLS by James Taylor. 1984, repr.
     Introductory history of Maxwells, descended from Saxon nobles, and
     later one of Scotland's greatest noble houses. Tartan swatch.
     Paper—$6.70—54pp- Vendor #D2175

4121   - HISTORY OF THE CLAN GUNN by Mark Rugg Gunn. 1984, repr.
     History of main branches of important Scottish family, from Norse-
     Celtic beginnings through 19th Century Genealogical charts.
     Cloth—$26.75—280pp- Vendor #D2175

4122   - HISTORICAL AND GENEALOGICAL ESSAY UPON THE FAMILY OF
     BUCHANAN by William Buchanan of Auchmar. 1984, repr.
     Originally published 1723, remarkable family history of important
     Scottish clan whose lands border eastern shore of Loch Lomond.
     Tartan swatch.
     Paper—$11.25—99pp- Vendor #D2175

4123   - AN OFFICIAL SHORT HISTORY OF THE CLAN MacDOUGALL by
     Michael Starforth. 1983, repr.
     Excellent short history of one of Scotland's four oldest extant clans.
     Descended from Somerled, MacDougalls dominated Argyll, Mull,
     Jura, Lismore. Tartan swatch.
     Paper—$7.75—50pp- Vendor #D2175

4124   - THE CLAN AND NAME OF FERGUSON by James Ferguson, Younger
     of Kinmundy. 1984, repr.
     Introductory history of famous Scottish clan, including prominent
     branches and individuals. Tartan swatch.
     Paper—$6.25—32pp- Vendor #D2175

4125   - THE HOUSE OF ARGYLL AND COLLATERAL BRANCHES OF CLAN
     CAMPBELL. 1983, repr.
     Historical and genealogical study of primary branches of Scotland's
     famous Clan Campbell.
     Cloth—$31.75—239pp- Vendor #D2175

4126   - THE LAMONT CLAN 1235-1935: SEVEN CENTURIES OF CLAN
     HISTORY by Hector McKechnie. 1984, repr.
     Comprehensive history of Lamonts in Scotland. Cadet branches
     included, plus pedigrees, arms, extensive reference notes.
     Cloth—$41.75—602pp- Vendor #D2175

CLAN ROSS, WITH GENEALOGIES OF THE VARIOUS
lexander M. Ross. 1983, repr.
vey of Scottish family with biographical sketches of
dian, and United States descendants.
5–212pp-- Vendor #D2175

LS OF ROSS AND THEIR DESCENDANTS by Francis
d. 1985, repr.
extensive genealogical history of Scottish descendants of
Malco... Earl of Ross (1165-1214) into 19th Century. Much primary material.
Cloth–$18.70–142pp-- Vendor #D2175

4129 - THE CARMICHAEL CLAN, WESTBROOK AND ALLIED FAMILIES by Mrs. Opal Carmichael Phoenix. 1984, repr.
Detailed genealogical account of Carmichaels in America, plus thirty-five allied families: Baker, Bell, Calhoun, Donaldson, MacDonald, Martin, Thompson, Vaughn, Westbrook.
Cloth–$43.75–455pp-- Vendor #D2175

4130 - MEMOIRS OF CLAN FINGON by Donald D. Mackinnon. 1984, repr.
Traces Mackinnon family through 19th Century. Well researched history of Scottish family; biographies of prominent Mackinnons.
Paper–$17.75–249pp-- Vendor #D2175

4131 - CHIEFS OF CLAN DONNACHAIDH, 1275-1749, AND THE HIGHLANDERS AT BANNOCKBURN by James Robertson. 1983, repr.
History of Scotland's famous Robertson family, plus account of Bannockburn, Scotland's battle for independence.
Cloth–$13.75–80pp-- Vendor #D2175

4132 - CASTLE IN THE SEA by Robert Lister Macneil. 1984, repr.
Account of the revitalization of Kisimul Castle, on Scotland's Isle of Barra, and of the Clan Macneil, whose home it is.
Paper–$11.70–190pp-- Vendor #D2175

4133 - A HISTORY OF THE DENNIS FAMILY by William L. Dennis. 1984.
A collection of genealogical material primarily on the Southern Branch of the Dennis family. $8\frac{1}{2}$"x11", printed offset and saddle stitched.
Paper–$12.00–56pp-- Vendor #D2177

4134 - RACKLEY: A SOUTHERN COLONIAL FAMILY by Eloise Fretz Potter and Timothy Wiley Rackley. 1984.
Edward Rackley came to Virginia in 1639, and his descendants moved to North Carolina about 1740. Later they dispersed throughout the Sunbelt. Appendixes treat estates records, Civil War letters, American Rackleys not descended from Edward, and confusing collateral lines.
Approximately 3,000 related families include Adams, Alderman, Baines, Barnes, Bass, Blanchard, Bryant, Brown, Butler, Carpenter, Carter, Chapman, Chesnutt, Claxton, Cockrell, Collins, Cooper, Drew, Etheridge, Evans, Ezzell, Fowler, Hendricks, Hunt, Lindsey, Manning, Matthews, Morgan, Parker, Peterson, Pridgen, Reddell, Rivenbark, Robinson, Rose, Sanders, Tatum, Tidwell, Tucker, Vester, Vick, Wall, Ward, Warren, West, Whitley, Winstead, Wright.
Indexed; 53 illustrations; 11"x$8\frac{1}{2}$".
Cloth–$35.00–676pp-- Vendor #D2179

4135 - A COMBS FAMILY by Mae Frazier. 1982.
Descendants of Shadrack Combs born 1784, grandson of John Combs, the first Combs to settle in Eastern Kentucky.
Seven chapters, 20 photographs, Combs coat-of-arms, sample family tree and a cousins chart.
Allied families included are: Adams, Ison, Collins, Frazier, Caudill, Brown, Cornett, Smith, Banks, Morgan, Breeding, Whitaker, Hogg, Dixon, Blair, Back, Sexton, Hall, Jones, Stamper, Maggard, Holbrook, Fields, Halcomb, Amburgy, Adkins, Martin, Sumner, Bates, Baker, Brashear, Gibson, Day, Johnson, Mullins, Polly, Hampton, Stallard,

Wright, Campbell, Fugate, Franklin, Madden, Craft, Shepherd, Wooten,
Williams, Miller, Watts, Haynes, Boggs, and Webb.
Paper—$26.30—425pp--- Vendor #D2182

4136 - GENEALOGY OF THE HIGHLAND SCOT CLARK FAMILY FROM THE
ISLE OF JURA SCOTLAND by Col. Victor Clark. 1983.
Alexander Clark, emigrant, with sons Gilbert, John, Daniel and
Archibald came from the Isle of Jura to present day Harnett County,
North Carolina, in September 1739. We follow one Clark line to the
author's grandson—Cameron Clark.
Paper—$20.00—120pp--- Vendor #D2183

4137 - WOMMELSDORFF FAMILY HISTORY by Otto Wommelsdorff. 1983.
Wommelsdorff Family History by Otto Wommelsdorff contains original
German manuscript and English translation by Mildred Smith, checked
by Otto before he died. Sixty years of German research going back
to about 1400. Latter part discusses Womelsdorfs in Womelsdorf,
Pennsylvania. 240 pages, indexed, 8¼"x11", paper cover.
Paper—$33.00—240pp--- Vendor #D2184

4138 - ORIGINS AND DISTRIBUTION OF THE SURNAME O'BRIEN IN
IRELAND by Andrew J. Morris. 1984.
Distribution for all 325 Irish baronies ca 1850.
Paper—$5.00—20pp--- Vendor #D2185

4139 - ORIGINS AND DISTRIBUTION OF THE SURNAME SLATTERY IN
IRELAND by Andrew J. Morris. 1984.
Distribution for all 325 Irish baronies ca 1850.
Paper—$5.00—19pp--- Vendor #D2185

4140 - ORIGINS AND DISTRIBUTION OF THE SURNAME KENNEDY IN
IRELAND by Andrew J. Morris. 1984.
Distribution for all 325 Irish baronies ca 1850.
Paper—$5.00—20pp--- Vendor #D2185

4141 - ORIGINS AND DISTRIBUTION OF THE SURNAME MORRIS IN
IRELAND by Andrew J. Morris. 1984.
Distribution for all 325 Irish baronies ca 1850.
Paper—$5.00—20pp--- Vendor #D2185

4142 - BOOTHS IN HISTORY: THEIR ROOTS AND LIVES, ENCOUNTERS
AND ACHIEVEMENTS by Dr. John Nicholls Booth.
In twenty-six chapters, 240 pages (ph. neutral paper), with fifty-two
portraits, charts and illustrations, the rise, spread and careers of
innumerable Booths in history since 1225 A. D. are traced: tycoons,
Earls, Lords, inventors, actors, film pioneers, church leaders,
England's greatest forger, etc. Genealogy comes alive. Added know-
ledge of your roots or unsuspected ancestors may appear.
Connecting families to author: Scott, Hudson, Christie, Nicholls,
Kriger, Holbrook, Chapman
Very impressive book—National Genealogical Society.
Congratulations for a good job well done—American Antiquarian
Society. Beautifully published; ideal gift. Cloth: $28.95 postpaid.
Softcover: $16.95 postpaid.
Cloth—$28.95—Paper—$16.95—240pp---------------------- Vendor #D2186

4143 - JOHN NICHOLAS MAYER AND ALL KNOWN DESCENDANTS by
Sallyann Jean Seaman. 1981.
From Galena, Illinois to Stockton, California 1849.
Cloth—$18.00—140pp--- Vendor #D2189

4144 - YESTERDAY'S TOMORROW—A HISTORY OF STRAWN, KANSAS AND
SURROUNDING TERRITORY by Mary Lou DeLong Atherly. 1982.
310 page chronological history of Strawn, Kansas and Surrounding
Territory (California, Ottumwa and Pleasant Townships of Coffey
County, Kansas). 1806-1972. Hundreds of birth, death and marriage
records documented dating from the earliest settlers.
Strawn, DeLong, Baxter, Hoover, Hamman, Hutchinson, Meek,
Hughes, Jacobs, Houser, Pieratt, Applegate, Allen, Antrim, Evans,
Hamlin, Kennedy, Mark, Wingard, Taylor, Bowman, Farmer, Fry,
Newkirk, Smith, Williamson and many, many others.
Cloth—$18.60—Paper—$15.60—310pp---------------------- Vendor #D2191

4145 - MORRIS-WALDEN: FAMILY GROUP RECORDS OF THE ANCESTORS
AND DESCENDANTS OF HIRAM MORRIS AND SARAH WALDEN MORRIS
by Phillip Stephen Morris. 1980.
Family lineage records including collateral links to Flournoy, Trabue,
Dowdy, Andreuccetti, Cronshey, McAlexander, Eubanks, Franke,
Gowen, Hill, Henson, McNabb, Duscoe, Gish, Ozier, Ritter, and
Reinhardt.
Paper—$12.50—22pp------------------------------------- Vendor #D2193

4146 - OATES-CRITTENDEN: FAMILY GROUP RECORDS OF THE ANCES-
TORS AND DESCENDANTS OF STEPHEN KILBEY OATES AND CELIA
JANE CRITTENDEN by Phillip Stephen Morris. 1980.
Family lineage records including collateral links to Ivey, Oates, Crit-
tenden, Gwyn, Benson, Kotrla, Price, Rodgers, Cutbirth, Hooker,
Ballard, Hoskins, DeVore, Whitten, Morris, Doyle, Jordan, Gaither,
Atkeison, Stainback, Seagraves, Keltner, Gauthier, Brownhill, and
Newby.
Paper—$12.50—37pp------------------------------------- Vendor #D2193

4147 - THE EDWARDS JOURNAL (A FAMILY PERIODICAL) edited by Elaine
Nelson.
Here's the magazine for anyone interested in the Edwards surname.
Each issue is loaded with genealogical data from marriage, land,
death and Bible records, wills, veteran pension files and much
more. Try it and we'll guarantee you'll like it, or your money
refunded. Free queries to subscribers. Published quarterly.
Subscription—$12.00/yr-------------------------------------Vendor #D2196

4148 - ROBERT NEWMAN: HIS LIFE AND LETTERS 1752-1804 by Robert
Newman Sheets. 1975.
Revealing the life and times of the Sexton of Boston's Old North
Church, who April 18, 1775, held two lanterns aloft from its steeple
at the request of Paul Revere! Includes Newman Family Genealogy,
complete map of Boston 1775, many pictures and much information
never before published.
Cloth—$9.95—Paper—$4.25—60pp-------------------------- Vendor #D2199

4149 - BENSON MAGAZINE OF RESEARCH, VOLUMES I, II, III, IV
(continuing) by Christine Knox Wood, C.G.
General information for Benson family research such as Bible records;
court records; cemetery headstones. Includes variant spellings of
Benson. Two issues per volume. Full name index in November issue.
Paper—$16.25/yr—100+pp/vol---------------------------- Vendor #D2201

4150 - KNOX BOOK OF RESEARCH, VOLUME I (continuing) by Christine
Knox Wood, C.G. 1984.
Full name index. General information for Knox family research such
as Bible records; court records; cemetery headstones.
Paper—$16.25—100+pp--------------------------------- Vendor #D2201

4151 - KNOX MEMORIAL, VOLUMES I AND II by Christine Knox Wood, C.G.
1972.
Descendants of George Knox who migrated from Ireland to Wheeling,
West Virginia, to Howard County, Missouri by 1820. Family scattered
after the Civil War. Photographs; illustrations; full name index.
Paper—$16.25/Set—225pp------------------------------- Vendor #D2201

4152 - THOSE REEVES GIRLS, VOLUMES I AND II by Christine Knox Wood,
C.G. 1973.
Descendants of Thomas Reeves born ca 1789 in North Carolina and
Rosannah Reeves, born in Ireland. Son Robert S. Reeves, born
1810-1820 not located. Daughters: Elizabeth married James A. Thatch;
Frances married Thomas Carnes; Jane married William Henry Hales;
Sarah Matilda married Edmund Pace Jarvis; Harriet Neal married
John W. D. F. Thomas; Permelia Caroline married Thomas S. Patterson.
In Greene County, Alabama 1818; several daughters in Pontotoc
County, Mississippi by 1860. Photographs; maps; illustrations;
full name index.
Paper—$16.25/Set—254pp------------------------------- Vendor #D2201

4153 - KALEIDOSCOPIC FAMILY BASS, 1769-1971 by Christine Knox Wood, C.G. 1971.
The descendants of two brothers, Peter and Lawrence Bass, both born in Baltimore, Maryland. They finished out their lives in Boone County, Missouri. Full name index.
Paper—$16.25—182pp------------------------------------- Vendor #D2201

4154 - WOOD WORKS, VOLUMES I AND II by Christine Knox Wood, C.G. 1972.
This history records over 1,000 descendants of William Wood whose will was witnessed 22 January 1787 in Spartanburg District, South Carolina. Main line followed is through son Moses Wood, of Revolutionary War. Moses' widow took family to Jefferson County, Alabama, and then to Pontotoc County, Mississippi. A few members of the tenth generation are listed. Full name index.
Paper—$16.25/Set—220pp------------------------------- Vendor #D2201

4155 - WOOD WORKS, VOLUME III by Christine Knox Wood, C.G. 1978.
The numbering system for Volumes I and II was worked out so that it would be possible to present additional volumes with no disturbance of the original numbers. Volume III stands alone as a genealogical work, yet it contains updated and additional material to follow Volumes I and II. Full name index.
Paper—$16.25—205+pp--------------------------------- Vendor #D2201

4156 - THE TURKNETT FAMILY, DESCENDANTS OF JACOB, CA 1757-1816 compiled and edited by the late Frank D. Jenkins.
Photographs; maps; illustrations; Bible records. Full name index.
Paper—$11.25—107pp------------------------------------- Vendor #D2201

4157 - STRAYER'S WEST, THE BOOK OF SAMUEL VOLUME I by Frances Elizabeth Strayer Hanson. 1985-86.
A Kinolgy of Samuel Strayer, his wife Mary Rebecca Gruber from Bedford-Blair County, Pennsylvania to Newton County, Missouri. Genealogy of Samuel and Mary, their descendants. Families include Clapper, Long, Block, Douthitt, Humphrey. Maps, documents, newspaper account, personal notes, lots of pictures. Time period 1800-1984.
(In process)—Cloth—$40.00—apx 400pp------------------- Vendor #D2202

4158 - McCULLOUGH MEMOS—ALL SPELLINGS by W. R. Yarwood.
Any McCullough—anytime—anyplace.
Queries. Quarterly.
Subscription—Paper—$10.00/yr—56pp/issue---------------- Vendor #D2203

4159 - SOME DESCENDANTS OF WILLIAM WARD (AND PHEBE) OF MIDDLETOWN, CONNECTICUT by M. W. Molyneaux.
Five generations proved by town, church and probate records; indexed.
Paper—$8.95—42pp--- Vendor #D2204

4160 - THE ENGLISH ANCESTRY AND AMERICAN POSTERITY OF JOSEPH SOUTHWICK, 1703-1980 by Neal S. Southwick. 1981.
This book focuses on a Mormon emigrant from England who died within weeks of his 1849 arrival in America. His widow and small children crossed the plains with the Mormon pioneers and established themselves in Utah. Joseph Southwick's ancestry is shown back to 1703 and descendants charts show his posterity down to 1980. The book is more than a genealogy. It contains a written history of the people. Major surnames include: Creamer, Ellis, Hulse, Lauder, Marriott, Southwick, Summers, Walters, and many others. It also describes the origin of surnames in England and contains newly discovered information about Lawrence and Cassandra Southwick who came to Massachusetts in the early 1600's. Over 320 illustrations. Indexed.
Cloth—$21.40—416pp------------------------------------- Vendor #D2206

4161 - A GLIMPSE OF THE PAST—THE HARNESS FAMILY HISTORY by Harold Duncan Harness. 1983.
History, autobiography, and genealogy of the Michael Harness family of the South Branch of the Potomac near Moorefield, West Virginia (formerly Virginia). Covers the period 1649-1982.

Documented; indexed; hardbound; acid free paper; smythe sewn.
Contains over 540 descendants; documents; and pictures.
Maryland residents add $1.25.
Cloth—$27.50—213pp-- Vendor #D2208

4162 - BRADSHAW AND RELATED FAMILIES compiled by Evelyn M. Wright.
1984.
The early history of the ancient Bradshaw family in England and
Northern Ireland, is recorded in this book, from 1042 to 1700's. James
Bradshaw 1715-1776, emigrated to America 1727. He married Ruth
Lowther and they had twelve children. They were Quakers, residing
in Buckingham Township, Bucks County, Pennsylvania. Four sons
and five daughters stayed there, and three sons came to the Niagara
area of Ontario 1788-1800. Members of this family were involved in
the American Revolutionary War and in the War of 1812 in Canada.
Their descendants, through ten generations, are followed through-
out the U. S. A. and Canada.
Some early related families in Bucks County, Pennsylvania: Child,
Dyer, Preston, Shaw, Gilbert, Welding, Carver, Kinsey, Hill,
Michener, Meredith, Fell, Paiste, Lippincott.
In Niagara area, Ontario: Beckett, Darling, Willson, Goff, Wills,
Burdsall, Crane, Bowman, O'Reilly, Vanderlip, Kent, Crosthwaite,
Bostwick, Moore, Durand.
Hardbound, about 500 pages, fully indexed, many old photographs,
letters, documents and stories, with a blue cover, bearing the
Bradshaw arms in silver. Published 1984. Compiled after thirty
years resarch by Evelyn M. (Bradshaw) Wright, 500 Teeple Terrace,
London, Ontario N6J 1T3 Canada.
Price: $40.00 (U. S. Funds) postpaid.
In Canada $47.00 (Canadian Funds) postpaid.
Payment to Evelyn M. Wright.
Cloth—$40.00 (US)—$47.00 (Canadian)—apx 500pp-----------Vendor #D2209

4163 - A SHORT LINE ACROSS AMERICA: DESCENDANTS OF JOHN AND
MARY HANSFORD SHORT compiled by Pauline Williams Wright. 1984.
Traces Short family from Virginia across the United States.
Allied families: Jester, Wright, Payte, Whitten, Long, Grant,
Armstrong, Tidwell, Montgomery, Kile, Whisenhunt, Forga,
Hurst, Williams.
Cloth—$35.00—400pp--- Vendor #D0509

4164 - "THE CHESAPEAKERS", WALLERS AND ALLIED FAMILIES AS THEY
MIGRATE SOUTH-WEST AND NORTH FROM THE CHESAPEAKE BAY,
OLD SOMERSET COUNTY, OF THE EASTERN SHORE OF THE PRO-
VINCE OF MARYLAND by Charles S. Waller, Sr. March, 1985.
Second Edition to *Wallers in America*.
Emigrant John Waller from England; his ancestors back to 1066 as
a soldier of William the Conqueror. John 1st in 1654 settled on Vir-
ginia Peninsula, Accomac County, married in 1660 to Alice Major;
first two children born here. 1665 migrated up the Chesapeake Bay
to Old Somerset County, on the Eastern Shore of the Province of
Maryland, to Wallers Adventure Homestead.
Old Somerset County, Maryland: "The Chesapeakers". Allied
families: Fitzgerald, Reid, Patterson, Bozman, Dashiells, Baily,
Rhodes.
Sussex County, Delaware: 1715 Thomas Waller home was in Old
Somerset County, Maryland (1767 became part of Sussex County).
North Carolina: Zephaniah Waller born February, 1744 in Maryland;
Nathan Waller born in Maryland.
Georgia: 1795, three Waller brothers: John Sr., Joseph Sr.,
Nathaniel Sr. (sons of Captain Nathaniel of Maryland and Delaware);
James Waller (son of James Sr., Maryland and Delaware).
Richard Waller III migrated from Georgia to Kentucky, Illinois, Iowa,
Texas. Emily Waller (daughter of John K. C.) married Daniel Marion
Oliver, migrated to Lisbon Union County, Arkansas, 1883.
Margaret Peggie Waller (daughter of Joseph Sr. and Elizabeth Flint
Waller) married Alex Sample 1797, migrated to Alabama, then Texas.

Nathaniel Waller (son of Joseph Sr.) married Telitha Tool, 1802, Hancock County, migrated to Alabama in 1818. Thomas Flint Waller migrated to Texas; Nathaniel Waller, Jr. migrated to Selma, Alabama. Nathaniel Green Waller migrated to Montgomery, Alabama, 1833.
Allied Families: Tegg-Teague-Teauge: Edward Tegg, Chesapeake Bay Area, died 1697; the Joshua Teague Branch, North and South Carolina, Alabama, Texas. Thomason-Thomasson: Thomas Thomason came from Norfolk County, England, 1677, to Caroline County, Virginia; migrated to Georgia after the Revolutionary War; settled in Hancock County, then Troup County, Georgia, then to Alabama.
Related families: Fitzgerald, Reid, Patterson, Bozman, Dashiells, Baily, Rhodes, Phillips, Bradley, Hearn, Wilson, Cottman, Howard, Parrish, Marshall, Laws, Lyon, Umstead, Hedgepeth, Veasey, Dupree, Tillery, Flemming, Winston, Holbrook, Newsom, Humber, Flowers, Davis, Sample, Moore, Thomason, Hearn, Dismukes, Fleming, Harrison, Knight, Harris, Hughins, Slaughter, etc.
Cloth—$30.00—apx 550pp--------------------------------------Vendor #D2195

4165 - SPANISH-MEXICAN FAMILIES OF EARLY CALIFORNIA: 1769-1850, VOLUME II by Marie E. Northrop.
A new compilation covering the same time period as Volume I: includes twenty-seven of same surnames but different family groups. Has over 100 new families, giving names and information on spouses, most of their parents and all known children.
It is a genealogical dictionary of some 265 Early California families. They are the following:
Husbands: Abrego, Alanis, Alvarado, Alvarez, Arana, Arangure, Archuleta, Arellano, Avila, Ayala, Bandini, Beltran, Boronda, Botiller, Briones, Bustamante, Call, Calvo, Camero, Cano, Cantua, Carlon (Cortez), Carrillo, Castro, Cordero, Coronel, Cortes, Cota, Dominguez, Duarte, Estrada, Estudillo, Fernandez, Fitch, Gallardo, Garcia, Garibay, German, Gomez, Gonzales, Guerrero, Guevara, Guillen, Guzman, Hartnell, Hernandez, Higuera, Hill, Juarez, Lara, Larios, Leyba, Lobo (Villalobo), Lopez, Lorenzana, Lugo, Machado, Malarin, Mariner (Marine), Marquez, Martinez, Mejias, Mesa, Miramontes, Montiel, Morales, Moreno, Morillo (Murillo), Navarro, Nieto, Olivares, Olivas, Olvera, Ontiveros, de la Osa, Pacheco, Padilla, Palomares, Parra, Patino, Pico, Polanco, Pryor, Quijada, Quintero, Rendon, Reyes, Rice (Reis), Rico, Rios, Rodriguez, Romero, Rosas, Rubio, Ruiz, Salazar, Samaniego, Sanchez, Serrano, Silvas, Soberanes, Sotelo, Sunol, Talamantes, Tapis, Temple, de la Torre, Uribes, Urquidez, Valdez, Valencia, Valenzuela, del Valle, Vallejo, Vanegas, Vasquez, Velarde, Verdugo, Villalobo, Villavicencio, White, Wilhart, Wilson, Wolfskill, Ybarra, Zamorano, Zurita.
Wives: Acebedo, Aceves, Aguilar, Alanis, Alcala, Alcantara, Alili, Alvarez, Amador, Amesquita, Arguello, Armenta, Avila, Ayala, Beatriz, Beltran, Bernal, Berreras, Botiller, Briones, Camacho, Campos, Canedo, Cardenas, Carrasco, Carrillo, Castillo, Castro, Chicalia, Cordero, Cota, de la Cruz, Delgado, Dominguez, Duarte, Elisalde (Lisalde), Espinosa, Estrada, Estudiollo, Feliz, Flores, Garcia, Garibay, German, Gomez, Graciano, de la Guerra, Guillen, Gutierrez, Haro, Heredia, Hernandez, Higuera, Horcasitas, Jimenez, Landera, Landeros, Leon, Leyba, Limon, Linares, Lisalde, Lopez, Lorenzana, Lugo, Marquez, Marron, Martinez, Miranda, Mora, Moraga, Moreno, Morillo, Munoz, Nieto, Noriega, Ontiveros, Ortega, Ortiz (Ortel), Osuna, Pacheco, Padilla, Palomares, Parra, Pena, Peralta, Perez, Pico, Pinto, Pinuelas, Poyorena, Quijada, Quintero, Ramirez, Rayales, Renteria, Reyes, Rivera, Rochin, Rodriguez, Romero, Rosas, Rubio, Saez, Salazar, Sanchez, Sandoval, Sepulveda, Serrano, Silvas, Sinova, Sinusin, Sobreda (Sobrevia), Sotelo, Soto, Sotomayor, Talamantes, Uribes, Vales, Valencia, Valenzuela, Vallejo, Vanegas, Varelas, Vasquez, Vastida (Bastida), Vejar, Velasquez, Verdugo, Villalobo (Lobo), Villavicencio, Workman, Yorba, Zamora.
Volume II contains all eleven 1781 pobladores—settlers of El Pueblo de Los Angeles and forty-six of the soldiers accompanying them to San Gabriel from Mexico.
Complete index covers over 1,000 names of Early Californians.
Cloth—$32.00+ 6½%sales tax—apx 400pp--------------------Vendor #D2026

4166 - NEWSLETTER—PILGRIM EDWARD DOTY SOCIETY by Mary Lee
Merrill, Governor, Doty Soc.
There are three Newsletters per year; March, July and November for
the members of the Pilgrim Edward Doty Society. The length of the
Newsletter varies with the amount of information at the time
(five to six pages). We would like the price to be $1.00 per copy
for those subscribing.
Subscription—$1.00/copy--------------------------------- Vendor #D2163

4167 - RASK FAMILY: OLE SELMER CHRISTIANSON RASK: 1810-1875,
DESCENDANTS AND SPOUSES by Robert E. Erickson. 1983.
Contains names and dates of 1,315 descendants and spouses of this
man who left the Hallingdal District of Norway in 1857, and settled
in Houston County, Minnesota. 1,125 are living in twenty-nine states,
Canada, and Germany. The 400 family sketches vary from two para-
graphs to two pages.
The forty pages of geneaogical tables are made more readable by
varied type and many half and full page photos of family groups.
The line of descent is traced back to Old King Gorm, who died in
935, one of the Scandinavian kings who conducted the commerce and
government of England peacefully for more than 100 years, according
to *Encyclopedia Britannica*, 15th ed., 16:308.
The book itself is state of the art, with title and coat-of-arms in
gold on maroon cloth. The photos are crisp and beautiful. The paper
and binding are sturdy, as needed in an heirloom expected to last
for centuries.
Some of the more widely-known descendants or spouses are Robert
Anderson, Patrick Born, Howard Edwin Carver, Carlin Dahler,
Dale DeLaitsch, Allen Leroy Elvick, Ole P. Engen, Beth Marian
Erickson, Marjorie Gene Erickson, Rudolph Julius Erickson, Nils
Fauchald, Samuel Garness, Donald Marvin Johnson, Erik Karlsbraaten,
Steven Lee Knudson, Wesley Knutson, Odin Krageland, Walter H.
Larson, Rev. Wilhelm A. Larson, David Lee, Ulrich Heinrich Wilhem
Munkel, Michael Charles Murdock, John Harold Murray, Christian
Olson Rask, Howard C. Rask, Louis Gilbert Rask, Olaf Norris Rask,
Olaf Selmer Rask, Ole Peter Rask, Olaf Harold Rask, Peter Selmer
Rask, Petter Olesen Rask, Samuel Albert Rask, Theodore Luros Rask,
Dennis Wayne Ryan, James Michael Schaffhausen, Charles Clair Seaton,
Esther Priscilla Stewart, John Gilbert Stewart, and Charles Wolden.
260 photos (half in full-colour), three indexes.
Cloth—$38.00 U.S.—200pp--------------------------------- Vendor #D2211

4168 - WAHL ANCESTORS, DESCENDANTS AND RELATED FAMILIES OF
ALSACE AND BUTLER COUNTY, PENNSYLVANIA 1631-1982 by
Ardelle McMillen Reed. 1982.
Over 2,300 names, including spouses, maiden names, in-laws, and
others. Documented, maps, photographs, charts. Families include
Besnecker, Billin, Binder, Black, Boggs, Buhl, Burr, Burry,
Cashdollar, Childs, Covert, Dambach, Davidson, Dunbar, Ernig,
Fiser, Frame, Girbig, Graham, Green, Griffin, Hall, Haushalter,
Holbein, Jacox, Ketterer, Koerner, Kretzer, Kriess, Kuhn, Laderer,
Leighton, Lotz, Lutz, Maitland, Marburger, Markel, McBride,
McCandless, McMillen, Mickley, Nicklas, Nolsheim, Peters, Pfeifer,
Rahiser, Reiger, Rieger, Ripper, Ross, Rummel, Sloan, Spence,
Twentier, Voegtly, Voltz, Wahl, Walker, Wanger, Watson, Wehr,
Wilkins, Winger, Zeigler, Ziegler. Indexed; 8½"x11".
Legal Binding—$22.00—278pp---------------------------Vendor #D2216

4169 - LEAVES FROM McCRACKEN FAMILY TREES by Marilyn McCracken,
Mar Mac Genie-Aids. 1984.
McCracken family genealogy. Pedigree and family sheets welcomed
for inclusion in book.
(In process)—50pp------------------------------------- Vendor #D2219

4170 - LEAVES FROM ATCHISON FAMILY TREES by Marilyn McCracken,
Mar Mac Genie-Aids. 1985.
John <u>Atchison</u>'s descendants beginning in Scotland, to Pennsylvania,
Ohio, etc. Pedigree and family sheets welcomed for inclusion in book.
(In process)—60pp--- Vendor #D2219

4171 - LEAVES FROM SIMPSON FAMILY TREES by Marilyn McCracken,
Mar Mac Genie-Aids. 1985.
<u>Simpson</u> family descendants—England, Maryland, Ohio, etc.
Pedigree and family sheets welcomed for inclusion in book.
(In process)—60pp--- Vendor #D2219

4172 - LEAVES FROM KIRKPATRICK FAMILY TREES by Marilyn McCracken,
Mar Mac Genie-Aids. 1985.
<u>Kirkpatrick</u> descendants, beginning in Ireland/Scotland, New Jersey
and further west. Pedigree and family sheets welcomed for inclusion
in book.
(In process)—200pp-- Vendor #D2219

4173 - LEAVES FROM LING FAMILY TREES by Marilyn McCracken, Mar Mac
Genie-Aids. 1985.
Anthony <u>Ling</u> descendants, sons John, Peter, Philip, Christian,
and daughters Maria Elizabeth and Margaret, as well as other lines.
Germany, Pennsylvania, Ohio, Indiana, Illinois, Kansas, Iowa, etc.
Pedigree and family sheets welcomed for inclusion in book.
(In process)—apx 100pp----------------------------------- Vendor #D2219

4174 - NICHOLAS COUNTY, WEST VIRGINIA CEMETERIES. 1983.
Fully indexed. Includes research notes on <u>Smith</u>, <u>Jones</u>, <u>Williams</u>
and <u>Foster</u> families, So. West Virginia.
Paper—$13.00—322+pp------------------------------------- Vendor #D2210

4175 - THE KELLY CONNECTION, Second Edition, by Ernestine Hammond.
1985.
Names: <u>Jones</u>, <u>Francisco</u>, <u>Looney</u>, <u>Vineyard</u>, <u>Hammock</u>, <u>Conway</u>,
James, <u>Woodside</u>, <u>Willson</u>, <u>Doniphan</u>, (Virginia and West Virginia)
(1600's Virginia to present). Many family group sheets;
b. m. d. w. documents; author's notes.
(In process)—Paper------------------------------------- Vendor #D2220

4176 - THE EMMERSON CONNECTION by Ernestine Hammond. 1985.
(Scotland, England, United States)
Names: <u>Carmichael</u>, <u>McIntyre</u>, <u>Taylor</u>, <u>Morison</u>, <u>Douglas</u>, <u>Donnelly</u>,
<u>Robinson</u>, <u>Hammond</u>.
(In process)—Paper------------------------------------- Vendor #D2220

4177 - THE FRANCISCO CONNECTION by Ernestine Hammond. 1985.
Names: <u>Franciscus</u>, <u>Trout</u>, <u>Abbott</u>, <u>Brad</u>, <u>Fowler</u>.
Diary of <u>Lewis</u> 1860's (Virginia).
(In process)—Paper------------------------------------- Vendor #D2220

4178 - THE JONES CONNECTION by Ernestine Hammond. 1985.
Moses Wheeler <u>Joanes</u> (Maryland to West Virginia) and descendants.
Names include <u>Parsons</u>, <u>Canterbury</u>, <u>McMillian</u>, <u>Burgess</u>, <u>Witt</u>,
<u>Mullens</u> (Maryland, Virginia, West Virginia).
(In process)—Paper------------------------------------- Vendor #D2220

4179 - RENDERS AND THEIR RELATIVES. JOSHUA RENDER OF MARYLAND,
VIRGINIA by Pearl O. Smith. 1985.
Descendants in Georgia, Illinois, Kentucky, Texas, etc.
(In process)—Cloth------------------------------------- Vendor #D2221

4180 - THE HOUSE OF HILL by Kathryn Hill Arbogast. 1982.
The <u>Hill</u> family from Virginia, since 1695...photos, maps, wills...
allied families <u>Florence</u>, <u>Schleich</u>, <u>Hott</u>, <u>Robison</u>, <u>Sharp</u>, <u>Galbreath</u>,
<u>McKinley</u>, <u>Covington</u>, <u>Strother</u>, etc.
Cloth—$22.00—288pp------------------------------------- Vendor #D2222

4181 - THE CAPERTON FAMILY by Bernard M. Caperton. 1973.
John Caperton, immigrant, and Polly Thompson of Augusta County,
Virginia and Monroe/Giles (Virginia, West Virginia). Children:
Captain Hugh and Rhoda Stodghill (West Virginia); Adam and
Elizabeth Miller (Madison County, Kentucky); Sarah and James Gibson
(Tennessee); Mary and George Swope (Rutherford County, Tennessee);
Nancy and James Kelly (Cooper County, Missouri); Elizabeth and
Joshua Townsend (Tennessee and Alabama); William and Lucy Woods
(Kentucky, Tennessee, Mississippi); James and Sally Wells (Tennessee).
Descendants throughout the West.
Cloth—$17.50—239pp-- Vendor #D1576

4182 - BRANCHES OF ONE RIDDLE FAMILY TREE, VOLUME I by Dorotha
Riddle Marsh. 1981.
Early Chatham County, North Carolina Riddle's and their descendants.
5½"x8½". Index.
Paper—$30.00—179pp-------------------------------------- Vendor #D2029

4183 - BRANCHES OF ONE RIDDLE FAMILY TREE, VOLUME II, A SUPPLE-
MENT TO VOLUME I by Dorotha Riddle Marsh. 1983.
Early Chatham and Moore Counties, North Carolina Riddle and Minter
descendants. Index; 10"x11½".
Cloth—$40.50—290pp------------------------------------- Vendor #D2029

4184 - THE ANDREW PHILLIPS FAMILY, FIRST EDITION by Mabel Phillips
Baker. 1974.
Andrew Jackson Phillips b. January 21, 1830, Randolph County, West
Virginia, and Martha E. Rowan b. May 28, 1837, Barbour County,
West Virginia, were married May 5, 1854, Randolph County, West Vir-
ginia; moving later that year to Whiteside County, Illinois. They
moved to Upton, Iowa in 1865; later that year to Scotland County,
Missouri, where they lived the rest of their life. They had eleven
children: Elizabeth, Mary, Francis, William, Randolph, Benjamin,
Thomas, Edward, George, Emma who died when seven months old,
Lewis. The book covers the ancestry and descendants.
Blue soft cover, 5½"x8½"; Phillips family picture in front of book.
Paper—$7.50—70pp-- Vendor #D1643

4185 - THE WILLIAM WOOD AND RELATED FAMILIES OF ALBEMARLE
COUNTY, VIRGINIA AND BARREN COUNTY, KENTUCKY IN THE
1800'S by Henry C. Peden, Jr. 1984.
Paper—$8.00—45pp-- Vendor #D0099

4186 - THOMPSONS FORT, NEW RIVER, VIRGINIA by Patricia Givens
Johnson. 1985.
William Thompson descendants, Virginia, West Virginia, Alabama,
Mississippi, Georgia, Tennessee, Hickman, Farley, Cloyd, McManes,
Alexander, Anderson, Gardner, McCreary, Glover, Anderson,
Buchanan.
Paper—$12.00—140pp------------------------------------- Vendor #D0364

4187 - THE GOODRICH FAMILY IN AMERICA edited by L. W. Case for
Goodrich Family Memorial Association. 1984 repr. of 1889 ed.
A beautiful genealogy, published first in 1889, of the descendants of
John and William Goodrich, Wethersfield, Connecticut (1634), Richard
Goodrich, Guilford, Connecticut (1639), and William Goodridge,
Watertown, Massachusetts (1642).
Includes a history of the family in England, the origin of the name,
and a description of Goodrich Castle. Added is a code and section
to update the contents.
Cloth—$35.00—419pp------------------------------------- Vendor #D2226

4188 - THE SEARCH FOR HOLMES, ROBSON, HIND, STEELE, AND GRAHAM
FAMILIES OF CUMBERLAND AND NORTHUMBERLAND, ENGLAND by
Anne Hait Christian, M.A. 1984.
A unique book which provides historical settings, lifestyle, and
relationships that are universal to those who share a common bond
of Northern England ancestry.
Demonstrates use of parish and civil records with local history and

family memorabilia to reconstruct family life. Major families researched from 1650 to present. Cumberland Parishes searched are Bewcastle, Brampton, Lanercost, Nether Denton, and Walton. Northumberland Parishes searched are Allendale, Falstone, Haltwhistle, Knaresdale, Simonburn, and Wark. Can serve as inspiration to those who might wish to search in these specific areas of Cumberland and Northumberland, England. Additional lineages searched include Abram, Armstrong, Askey, Atkinson, Bell, Campbell, Charleton, Chipchase, Davidson, Dodd, Dodgson, Gardhouse, Harding, Hayton, Hetherington, Slater, Swan, Taylor, Tweddle, Wannop, Waugh, and Weir. Map of Cumberland area inside front cover; Map of Northumberland area inside back cover. Fully indexed by family names; complete bibliography; citations in text; 7"x10"; 45 photos; numerous documents, maps, and illustrations.
Cloth—$19.45—184pp--- Vendor #D2227

4189   - JOHN LOTHROPP (1584-1653): A PURITAN BIOGRAPHY AND GENEALOGY by Richard Woodruff Price. 1984.
In celebration of his 400th anniversary of birth this new book has been published and includes a biography, six-generation English and American pedigree and much more.
Paper—$14.40—38pp--- Vendor #D2228

4190   - "OUR KIN," BEDFORD COUNTY, VIRGINIA FAMILIES by Mary Denham Ackerly and Lula Eastman Jeter Parker. 1976, repr. of 1930 ed. Some of the early families who made history in the founding and development of Bedford County, Virginia. Families included are Ackerly, Bolling, Buford, Burks, Callaway, Davis, Douglas, Gwatkin, Hatcher, Jeter, Johnson, Joplin, Logwood, Moorman, Otey, Parker, Phillips, Poindexter, Robertson, Robinson, Slaughter, Sledd, Snead, Spencer, Talbot, Turpin, Wallace, White, Wright and many others. Added Addendum of Corrections. Illustrations; Index.
Cloth—$42.50—840pp--- Vendor #D1203

4191   - THE CABELLS AND THEIR KIN—A MEMORIAL VOLUME OF HISTORY, BIOGRAPHY AND GENEALOGY by Alexander Brown. 1978, repr. of 1939 ed.
Other families include Alexander, Anderson, Anthony, Blair, Bolling, Breckenridge, Brown, Bruce, Callaway, Campbell, Carrington, Carter, Clark, Coles, Crawford, Danniel, Davis, Garland, Gordon, Harris, Harrison, Henry, Henderson, Horsley, Jackson, Jefferson, Johnson, Jones, Jordan, Lewis, McCulloch, Meredith, Nelson, Payne, Preston, Randolph, Read, Reid, Rives, Rose, Scott, Smith, Taylor, Thompson, Venable, Walker, Winston, Woodson, and many others. Illustrations; Index.
Cloth—$42.50—708pp--- Vendor #D1203

4192   - VIRGINIA COUSINS by G. Brown Goode. 1981, repr. of 1887 ed.
A study of the ancestry and posterity of John Goode of Whitby, a Virginia Colonist of the Seventeenth Century, with notes on related families. A key to Southern Genealogy and a History of the English surname Gode, Goad, Goode and Good, from 1148 to 1887.
Appendices describe the family in England, some ancestral families with coats-of-arms. Illustrations; Index.
Cloth—$32.50—665pp--- Vendor #D1203

4193   - HISTORY OF THE DESCENDANTS OF JOHN HOTTEL. (IMMIGRANT FROM SWITZERLAND). AN AUTHENTIC GENEALOGICAL FAMILY REGISTER OF TEN GENERATIONS FROM THE FIRST OF THE NAME IN AMERICA 1732 TO THE PRESENT TIME, 1929, WITH NUMEROUS BRIEF BIOGRAPHICAL SKETCHES, COLLECTED AND COMPILED FROM MANY INDISPUTABLE SOURCES: COURT AND CHURCH RECORDS, OLD AND LATE FAMILY RECORDS AND TOMBSTONES OF THE MANY STATES IN THE UNION by Rev. W. D. Huddle and Lulu May Huddle. 1982, repr.
An impressive record of the John Hottel family. Progenitor of the

record, Johannes (John) Hottel, was born in Europe about 1700. John, his wife Margaret (?), and five children under the age of sixteen immigrated to America arriving at Port Philadelphia in September, 1732. The family located in the northern part of Bucks County, Pennsylvania where they lived for eighteen years. John, Margaret and three children Charles, George, and Barbara Ann, emigrated in 1750 to the Shenandoah Valley in Virginia, where their descendants are legion today. John and Margaret's sons John and Henry remained in Pennsylvania. The text of this major genealogical contribution consists of three branches, each headed by one of the three children of John and Margaret who emigrated to Virginia: Charles and wife Barbara(?) through their eleven children; George whose wife's name is unknown, however it is known that he is the father of nine children; Barbara Ann and husband George Keller through their nine children. The record is well documented, illustrated, and completely indexed.
6"x 9"; Illustrations; Index.
Cloth—$42.50—1183+pp--------------------------------------- Vendor #D1203

4194 - HISTORIC HOMES OF THE SOUTH-WEST MOUNTAINS, VIRGINIA by Edward D. Mead. 1978, repr. of 1899 ed.
The famous Colonial Homes of the Dickenson's, Everett's, Gordon's, Jefferson's, Page's, Lewis', Meriwether's, Randolph's, Rives', and others; includes biographical information and genealogical sketches of these famous Virginia families. (Albemarle and Orange Counties, Virginia.) Illustrations.
Cloth—$17.50—275pp--------------------------------------- Vendor #D1203

4195 - THE DESCENDANTS OF CAPT. THOMAS CARTER OF "BARFORD," LANCASTER COUNTY, VIRGINIA, 1652-1912 by J. Lyon Miller. 1982, repr. of 1912 ed.
Allied families include Allen, Ball, Bacon, Beale, Bronaugh, Campbell, Davis, Taylor, Taliaferro, White, Worth, and many others.
Illustrations; Index.
Cloth—$32.50—388pp--------------------------------------- Vendor #D1203

4196 - ANNALS OF BATH COUNTY, VIRGINIA by Oren F. Morton. 1978, repr. of 1917 ed.
Twenty-five chapters concerning the discovery and settlement, the Lewis Land Grant, mineral springs, early political history, life in the Pioneer days, ten years of Indian Wars, the Point Pleasant Campaign, the Revolution; War of 1861, Roster of Confederate Soldiers, surnames of Bath, list of early marriages, family sketches. Surnames included are: Abercrombie, Anglin, Armstrong, Baxter, Beard, Benson, Black, Blanton, Bollar, Bonner, Bourland, Bratton, Brown, Burns, Burnside, Byrd, Callison, Cameron, Carlile, Carpenter, Cartmill, Cleek, Clements, Clendennin, Coffey, Cowardin, Crawford, Crockett, Daugherty, Davis, Dean, Donally, Dunlap, Eddy, Feamster, Fudge, Frame, Fulton, Gay, Given, Graham, Gregory, Hall, Hamilton, Hicklin, Hodge, Insminger, Jameson, Kelso, Keyser, Kincaid, Knox, LaRue, Laverty, Lewis, Lockridge, Madison, Mallow, Mann, Massie, Mayse, McAvoy, McAllister, McCay, McClung, McCreery, McDannald, McFarland, McGuffin, Millroy, Mitchell, Moore, Morris, Muldrock, Mustoe, O'Hara, Persinger, Porter, Putnam, Rainey, Ramsey, Renick, Rhea, Scott, Sitlington, Sloan, Stuart, Swearingen, Thompson, Usher, Vance, Waddell, Wallace, Ward, Warwick, Watson, Williams, Wilson, Winthrow, Wright, etc.
Also includes a chapter on Alleghany County, Virginia. Map; Index.
Cloth—$17.50—208pp--------------------------------------- Vendor #D1203

4197 - GENEALOGY OF THE PAGE FAMILY IN VIRGINIA: ALSO A CONDENSED ACCOUNT OF THE NELSON, WALKER, PENDLETON AND RANDOLPH FAMILIES, WITH REFERENCES TO THE BLAND, BURWELL, BYRD, CARTER, CARY, DUKE, GILMER, HARRISON, RIVES, THORNTON, WELLFORD, WASHINGTON, AND OTHER DISTINGUISHED FAMILIES IN VIRGINIA, 2d ed., by Richard Channing Moore Page, M.D. 1983, repr. of 1893 ed.
Begins with John Page, son of Francis Page, of the Parish of Bedfont,

Middlesex County, England.
Part I: Page Family in Virginia.
Part II: Nelson Family (York County, Virginia).
Part III: Walker Family (Of Virginia, came from Staffordshire, England).
Part IV: Pendleton Family (of Norwich, England and New Kent County, and Caroline County, Virginia).
Part V: Randolph Family (of Turkey Island, Henrico County, Virginia). Illustrations; Index.
Cloth— $22.50— 288pp--- Vendor #D1203

4198 - ANNALS OF AUGUSTA COUNTY, VIRGINIA, 1726-1871, 2d ed., by Joseph A. Waddell. 1979, repr. of 1902 ed.
Contains a wealth of information on Augusta County, Virginia, which, at one time, included most of the land westward to the Mississippi and Northwest to the Great Lakes. The early settlement and foundation of the first County Court, the Indian Wars from 1753-1764, the Battle of Point Pleasant, the Revolutionary War, emigration from Augusta and some of the emigrants, periods from 1800-1865, Augusta County and the War of Secession, 1860-1862, during the War, 1862-1865, reconstruction after the war, 1865-1871, rosters of soldiers, excerpts from diaries, and sketches of some of the early families, including Jones, Brown, Hamilton, Cummings, Madison, Breckinridge, McDowell, Preston, Alexander, Wilson, Christian, Campbell, Smith, Harrison, Allen, Moffett, Trimble, Bowyer, Fleming, Crawford, Floyd, McKee, McNutt, Moore, McClanahan, Poage, Cunningham, Bell, Posey, Gamble, Mathews, Tate, Blackburn, Baxter, Doak, Waddell, Anderson, Warwick, Cameron, Nelson, Lyle, Stuart/Stewart, Baldwin, Banks. Map; Index.
Cloth— $35.00 - 545pp--- Vendor #D1203

4199 - SETTLERS BY THE LONG GREY TRAIL by J. Houston Harrison. 1975, repr. of 1935 ed.
Some pioneers of Old Augusta County, Virginia and their descendants of the family of Harrison and allied lines, including Bear, Bowman, Brown, Burkholder, Byrd, Campbell, Chrisman, Conrad, Craven, Creed, Davis, Davison, Decker, Ewing, Gaines, Gordon, Hanna, Henkel, Henton, Herring, Hamphill, Lincoln, Moore, Williams, Yancey, and others. Illustrations; Index. Color Coat-of-Arms (1935).
Cloth—$35.00—665pp--- Vendor #D1203

4200 - HOPKINS OF VIRGINIA AND RELATED FAMILIES by Walter Lee Hopkins. 1980, repr. of 1931 ed.
Dr. Arthur Hopkins of Goochland, William Hopkins of New Kent and James City Counties, Francis Hopkins of Bedford County, Virginia, John Hopkins, Hanover County, Virginia, John Hopkins, James City and Frederick County, Virginia, Joseph Hopkins of Chesterfield and Henrico Counties, Virginia, Rev. John A. Hopkins of Nelson and Albemarle Counties, Virginia, David Hopkins of Loudoun County, Virginia, Stephen Hopkins of Henrico County, Virginia, Gerard Hopkins of Maryland and Virginia, Stephen Hopkins of South Carolina. Other families include Cabell, Carter, Cocke, Cox, Davis, Hancock, Jefferson, Jones, Lee, Leftwich, Lewis, Martin, Miller, Muse, Mitchell, Otey, Price, Rives, Robertson, Scott, Smith, Swanson, Taylor, Thomas, Thompson, Turner, Walker, White, Williams, Wright. Illustrations; Index. LC31-10487.
Cloth— $32.50— 405pp--- Vendor #D1203

4201 - LEFTWICH—TURNER FAMILIES OF VIRGINIA AND THEIR CONNEC- TIONS by Walter Lee Hopkins. 1980, repr. of 1931 ed.
Augustine Leftwich, Sr., of Caroline and Bedford Counties, Virginia, and sons William, Thomas, Augustine, Jr., Uriah, John, Jabez, Littleberry, Joel, and daughter Mary; James Horsley Leftwich and Thomas Leftwich of King William County, Virginia.
Other families include Ayres, Brown, Davis, Early, Franklin, Fuqua, Goggin, Harris, Harrison, Johnson, Jones, Mitchell, Moorman, Otey, Saunders, Smith, Steptoe, Stone, Stratton, Walker, Ward, Williams, Wright, others. Illustrations; Index. LC 31-13352.
Cloth— $32.50- 351pp--- Vendor #D1203

4202 - THE PAYNES OF VIRGINIA, SECOND EDITION, WITH ALL NEW
PERSONAL NAME INDEX by Brooke Payne. 1977, repr. of 1937 ed.
Descendants of the several branches of the Payne Family of Eastern
Virginia. Allied families include Anderson, Ball, Barker, Berryman,
Blackwell, Brent, Brooke, Brown, Bruce, Carter, Clapham, Clarkson,
Cooke, Cox, Daingerfield, Davenport, Edmonds, Fairfax, Fant,
Farrow, Fitzhugh, Fleming, Glendenning, Grant, Green, Harlan,
Heale, Hilleary, Hooe, Hume, Hunton, Jennings, Jett, Johnson,
Jones, Keith, Kelly, Lawson, Lunsford, Meredith, Mitchell, Monroe,
Morris, Morson, Pace, Pannell, Quesenberry, Richards, Richardson,
Scott, Shipp, Smith, Stone, Sturman, Thacker, Towles, Turner,
Walker, Washington, West, Winston, Winter, Wirt, Woodville, and others.
Index.
Cloth—$42.50 – 728pp-------------------------------------Vendor #D1203

4203 - FORERUNNERS (STRICKLER GENEALOGY) by Harry M. Strickler.
1977, repr. of 1925 ed.
A history and genealogy of the Strickler families and other early
families of Shenandoah, Rockingham, Augusta, Frederick and Page
Counties in the Shenandoah Valley of Virginia.
Allied families include Brumback, Brubaker, Burner, Coffman,
Funkhouser, Grove, Hershberger, Hite, Huffman, Kagey, Keyser,
Koontz, Long, Martin, Mauck, Miller, Moore, Neff, Painter, Price,
Rhodes, Rothgeb, Ruffner, Shenk, Smith, Spitler, Stephens, Stover,
others. Illustrations; Index.
Cloth—$32.50—425pp-----------------------------------Vendor #D1203

4204 - THE FAMILY PICTORIAL AND BIOGRAPHICAL SERIES by Family
Publications.
esigned to instill family pride in young and old alike! Each edition
highlights a different surname in pictures, articles, and biographies.
Added features include profiles of historical, political, and celebrity
figures; surname history; cities and international landmarks bearing
the name; coats of arms; book reviews; family newsletters and associa-
tions; and unique pursuits of surname bearers, plus much more!
Issues Now Available: *Smith, Johnson, Williams/Williamson, Brown,
Jones, Miller, Davis/Davison/Davidson, and Martin.* What do the
professionals say? "Interesting articles...beautifully done."—Editor,
Williams Newsletter. "I have read and re-read the numerous articles
and find them more enjoyable each time."—Editor, *The Johnson
Journal.* "A new type of endeavor in the genealogy field...adding
color and interest to a family tree."—Editor, *The Kansas City
Genealogist.* 8½"x11".
Paper—$6.50/issue--------------------------------------- Vendor #D1817

4205 - ANNALS OF TAZEWELL COUNTY, VIRGINIA FROM 1800-1922 by
John Newton Harman, Sr. Repr. of 1922 ed.
Abstracts of all wills (1800-1924); marriages 1800-1868; soldiers of
Revolutionary, Civil and World War I. Besides transcriptions of
marriages, 1800-1853, Military Records Revolutionary War through
World War I, the following families treated very fully: Baldwin,
Bandy, Barnes, Bowen, Chapman, Copenhaven, Coulling, Crockett,
Deskins, Gillespie, Harrison, Johnston, Gose, Graham, Graybeal,
Greeves, Hankins, Harman, Higginbotham, Hopkins, Leece/Leech,
Linkous, Litz, Lockhart, McGuire, Maxwell, Martin, May, Mays,
Moore, Moss, Mustard, Peery, St. Clair, Stras, Sparks, Thompson,
Whitley, Williams, Witten, Wohlford, Yost, Young.
New every-name index of 100 pages.
Cloth—$35.00—1152pp----------------------------------Vendor #D1257

4206 - ARCHIVES OF THE PIONEERS OF TAZEWELL COUNTY, VIRGINIA by
Netti Schreiner-Yantis. 1973.
This work is an assemblage of a great many of the public records
created by the people living in this county before 1820. County,
state, and federal records are included. Approximately 30,000 references are contained in the index.
The greater portion of the book is a transcription or abstraction of
primary source materials. A section entitled "Descendants of the
Pioneers" includes lineages for as many as six or seven generations,

however, and there is a study of the immigration and emigration routes, illustrated by maps, and discussed in detail. The author—who has specialized in research in this area for a number of years—has added copious informative footnotes about many of the pioneers. To be found in this work: Abstract of Order Book #1, 1800-1810; Personal Property and Land Tax Lists; Legislative and Executive Petitions; Land Grants made in the County, 1800-1820; Wills, Appraisements, and Sale Bills, 1800-1832; Death Records; Pension Applications; The Davidson Cabin and Family—a Case Study; Immigrational and Emigrational Data.

Those names that have fifty or more references: Adkins/Atkins, Allen, Asberry/Asbury, Bailey, Bane, Barnes, Belcher, Belsha/Belshe, Blankenship, Boothe, Bowen, Bowling, Brewster, Bristow, Brooks, Brown(e), Campbell, Carter, Cartmill, Cecil/Sissel, Christian/Christen, Clark, Claypool, Compton, Cooke, Corder, Crockett, Dailey/Dayley, Daniel(s), Davidson, Davis/Davies, Day, Deskins, Dill(i)on, Elkins, Elswick, Evans, Farley, Ferguson, Fletcher, Gent, Ghent, George, Gibson, Gillespie, Godfrey, Goodwin, Gose, Green(e), Greenup, Griffiths, Grills, Hager, Hall, Hankins, Harman, Harper, Harrison, Hedrick, Heninger/Henager, Hicks, Higginbotham, Horton, Johns(t)on, Jones, Justice, Kendrick/Kindrich, Kidd, King, Laird, Lambert, Lesley/Leslie/Lestley, Lock(h)(e)art/Lockhard, Lusk, Mar(r)s/Marr/ Mare, Maxwell, McBroom(e), McComas, McGuire, McIntosh, Milam, Mitchell, Moore, Morgan, Mor(r)ison, Muncey, Murr(a)y/M(a)ury, Neal/Neil/Neel, On(e)y/Owney, Orr, Owens, Patton, Peery, Pickens, Powers, Prewett/Pruet(t)/Pruit, Rat(c)liff/Radcliff, Rif(f)e, Rineh(e)art, Rei(g)n(t)rart/Rynheart, Roark/Rowark/Rorux, Runyon/Run(n)ion, Sayres/Sawyers, Shannon, Skaggs/Scaggs/Skegs, Smith, Star(r), Steel(e), Stephe(n)son/Stevenson, Stewart/Stuart/Steward, Stob(a)ugh/Stobough, Stokes, Strutton/Stratton, Stump, Suiter/ Suitor/Suter/Sewter, Taylor, Thompson, Thorne, Tollett, Trent, Trigg, Vandike/Vandyke, Vincel(l)/Vincil(e), Wag(g)oner/Wagner, Walker, Wallace, Ward, Webb, White, Whitley, W(h)itt, Williams, Wilson, W(h)itten, Workman, Wynn(e)/Winn, Young. 8¼"x11".
Paper—$25.00—344pp------------------------------------- Vendor #D1257

4207   - A HISTORY OF THE MIDDLE NEW RIVER SETTLEMENTS AND CONTIGUOUS TERRITORY by David E. Johnston. 1906.
Sketches on the following families: Bailey, Bane, Belcher, Black, Barnes, Bowen, Burke, Calfee, Caperton, Chapman, Christian, Cecil, Clay, Cloyd, Davidson, Emmons, French, Gillespie, Hale, Hare, Hoge, Howe, Johnston, Kirk, Lybrook, M'Claugherty, M'Comas, Meadows, M'Donald, Napier, Pack, Peck, Pearis, Peters, Shannon, Smith, Snidow, Straley, Witten.
Area covered included present Giles, Bland, Tazewell, Pulaski Counties, Virginia; Mercer, Monroe and Summers Counties, West Virginia. New every-name index.
Cloth—$26.50—500+pp------------------------------------- Vendor #D1258

4208   - MAJOR GENERAL THOMAS MALEY HARRIS, INCLUDING ROSTER OF THE 10TH WEST VIRGINIA VOLUNTEER INFANTRY REGIMENT, 1861-1865 by H. E. Matheny. 1963.
This biography brings together for the first time the true facts of General Harris's life, Civil War campaigns and his work as a member of the Military Commission that tried Mrs. Mary Surratt and others for the assassination of President Abraham Lincoln—obscure facts that are a part of our American Heritage. Annotated; Illustrated; Indexed.
Cloth—$13.75--- Vendor #D0968

4209   - A BIOGRAPHICAL SKETCH OF THE LIFE OF THE LATE CAPTAIN MICHAEL CRESAP by John J. Jacob. 1971, repr. of 1866 ed.
Introduction by Dr. Otis K. Rice. Reprint of text retains original format and typography.
Cloth—$11.25--------------------------------------- Vendor #D0968

4210 - MEMOIR OF INDIAN WARS, AND OTHER OCCURRENCES by John Stuart. 1971, repr. of 1833 ed.
Col. John Stuart, born 1749 in Augusta County, Virginia, settled in what is now Greenbrier County, West Virginia in 1769. He served as a captain in the Battle of Point Pleasant. This is an interesting account of the settlement of this area and of the Battle. Reprint retains the original format and typeface of the memoirs and transmittal letter. Introduction by Dr. Otis K. Rice.
Cloth—$11.00--- Vendor #D0968

4211 - DRAKE—ARRINGTON, WHITE—TURNER, LINN—BROWN AND TWO DOZEN RELATED SOUTHERN LINES: TREADWELL, SLADE, LACEY, HARRISON, CATHEY, REDWINE, KRIDER, WOOD, McNAIR, PEDEN, SANDEFER, TOMPKINS, BENNETT, HODGES, GOODRICH, BECHINOE, WILLIAMS, BUSTIN, OUTLAW, FOX, SMITH, GEORGE, DOLL AND STAHLE by Jo White Linn, C. G. 1984.
Casebound, 490 pages, 7½"x10", charts, maps, illustrations, copies of original documents, letters, Bible records. $35.00 postpaid.
Order from Mrs. Stahle Linn, Jr., Box 1948, Salisbury, NC 28144.
Brochure and index search on receipt of SASE.
Cloth—$35.00—490pp-------------------------------------- Vendor #D0104

4212 - DULANY—FURLONG AND KINDRED FAMILIES by Roland Dulany Furlong. 1975.
Dennis Dulany, 1776 settler, ancestor of surname in Greene, Fayette, Washington, Monongalia, Wetzel, Ohio, Marion, counties in Pennsylvania and West Virginia. Intermarried with Fox, Haines, Headlee, John, Lemley, Pitcock, Shiver, and other families. John Furlong settled in Cambria County, Pennsylvania. About 7,500 names from authentic sources. Indexed.
Cloth—$26.50--- Vendor #D0968

4213 - HOLT—BENNETT FAMILY HISTORY by Margaret Holt Early. 1974.
This history of two prominent West Virginia families contains intimate stories, old letters, pictures of Confederate treasurer, United States Senator, governor, judges, bishops and educators.
Cloth—$11.25--- Vendor #D0968

4214 - CHRISTOPHER CALE'S FAMILY OF PRESTON COUNTY, WEST VIRGINIA, 1741-1973 by Janice Cale Sisler. 1973.
From the 1795 settlement of Christopher Cale in Preston County, 5,400 descendants have been traced all over the United States. Details from Civil War records; information from deeds dating from before the courthouse fire in Kingwood. 132 pictures. Indexed.
Cloth—$26.50—754pp------------------------------------- Vendor #D0968

4215 - THE MORGANS OF REDROCK GAP by Opal Morgan Wolfe. 1978.
This legend was handed down through the descendants of Abraham and Elizabeth Ealy Morgan (his wife), who came from Wales and settled near Beuna Vista, Virginia (Bedford County) before the Revolution. Their son, Thomas Morgan, became one of the first four white settlers of Wyoming County (1804). The story contains much of the musical quality and rhythm found in Hiawatha; and tells how the Morgans were influenced by the tales of "an ancient wrinkled Indian Chief."
Paper—$9.00--- Vendor #D0968

4216 - THE KINNAN MASSACRE, INCLUDING REPRINT OF THE ORIGINAL TRUE NARRATIVE OF THE SUFFERINGS OF MARY KINNAN by Boyd B. Stutler. 1969.
Gives background information not included in the original Kinnan narrative, printed in 1795 of which only two copies are known to exist. Reproduced with the original format.
Paper—$7.00--- Vendor #D0968

4217   - A BOY OF OLD SHENANDOAH by Robert Hugh Martin. 1977.
A newspaper editor recalls his experiences and observations of the
Civil War when a very young boy in Mount Jackson, Virginia, and
tells of his growing years in the country. Written about 1928.
Included are letters written by his father while serving in the
Stonewall Brigade.
Cloth—$11.00-- Vendor #D0968

4218   - GENERAL JAMES "PETE" LONGSTREET, LEE'S "OLD WAR HORSE",
SCAPEGOAT FOR GETTYSBURG by Wilbur D. Thomas. 1979.
Eight years after Gettysburg, and after he became a Republican,
two Confederate generals of questionable reputation falsely accused
General Longstreet of behaving badly during the battle, although
his performance there and elsewhere during the war was superior
to all others. This calumny, without the slightest foundation, is
fully exposed in this book.
Cloth—$22.50-- Vendor #D0968

4219   - YE HISTORIE OF YE TOWN OF GREENWICH, COUNTY OF FAIR-
FIELD AND STATE OF CONNECTICUT, WITH GENEALOGICAL NOTES
ON THE ADAMS, AVERY, BANKS, BETTS, BROWN, BRUNDAGE,
BRUSH, BUDD, BUSH, CLOSE, DAVIS, DAYTON, DENTON, FERRIS,
FINCH, GREEN, HENDRIE, HOBBY, HOLLY, HOLMES, HORTON,
HOWE, HUBBARD, HUSTED, INGERSOLL, KNAPP, LOCKWOOD, LYON,
MARSHALL, MEAD, MERRITT, MILLS, PALMER, PECK, PURDY,
REYNOLDS, RITCH, RUNDLE, SACKETT, SCOFIELD, SELLECK,
SEYMOUR, SHERWOOD, SLATER, SMITH, STUDWELL, SUTHERLAND,
SUTTON, TODD, WARING, WATERBURY, WEBB, WEED, WHITE,
WILCOX, WILSON, AND WORDEN FAMILIES; BEING A REVISION,
AMPLIFICATION, AND CONTINUATION OF THE HISTORY OF THE
TOWN OF GREENWICH, PUBLISHED IN 1857, BY DANIEL M. MEAD,
MAJOR 10TH REGIMENT, CONNECTICUT VOLUNTEER INFANTRY by
Spencer P. Mead, LL.B. 1979, repr. of 1911 ed.
This very rare town history, up to now commanding prices of $85 to
$100 on the out-of-print market, is now available at an affordable
price, printed on acid-free paper and sturdily bound. It includes
genealogies of fifty-seven Greenwich families. To genealogists,
Spencer Mead's work is a treasure trove of information. Its comprehensive lists of military personnel in past American wars, its alphabetical lists of landowners and, above all, its genealogies make it a
reference tool indispensable to anyone engaged in genealogical research. Profusely illustrated, maps. Index includes over 9,000 names.
Cloth—$37.50—768pp-- Vendor #D0948

4220   - WALWORTH GENEALOGY, 1878-1984, DESCENDANTS OF JOHN
WILSON WALWORTH AND LENORA BELLE BOODY OF EATON COUNTY,
MICHIGAN by Victor Harold Walworth. 1984.
Contains ancestry and life of pioneer couple and all descendants,
as well as spouses. Well illustrated with 157 photos, maps, and
sketches. Index to 430 names. 6"x9".
Cloth—$15.00—176pp-- Vendor #D2223

4221   - SECOND PRINTING OF THE GETMAN FAMILY GENEALOGY, 1710-
1974.
Over 5,000 names, at a pre-publication cost of $20.00 postpaid,
to be available in 1985.
[See also Family History #3722 - *Supplement.*]
(In process)—Paper—$20.00 pre-publication—563pp---------- Vendor #D1710

4222 - NATIONAL GENEALOGICAL SOCIETY BIBLE RECORDS COLLECTION.
The Society has a large collection of Bible records, and solicits others.
If you have any such records you will assure their being permanently
preserved by sending a photocopy of them to the Society. You will
also be making it possible for distant cousins to share the contents.
Please include all residences of the family known to you. Also include
date of publication of the Bible so it can be discerned if the inscriptions were made at the time of the event or copied from another
source.
The Bible records listed below are listed by the principal surname.
Dates, places of residence, if known, and other surnames appearing
in the record are included. The charge to obtain a photocopy of a
Bible record is 25¢ per page, or a minimum of $1.00 per order. The
number of pages contained in each collection is given. Please enclose
correct amount *and a large self-addressed stamped envelope* (SASE)
with your order [indicating records you desire by name *and* letter,
for example, ADAMS-a or WILLIAMS-fn] to------------------ Vendor #D2229

a. ADAMS: Smyrna Landing, Delaware, 1863-1930; Betts, Doyle,
Frost, Marshall, Salmon, Walls, Walters, Watson. 7pp.   --$1.75

b. ALBERTY: 1817-1855; Atwater, Buchanan, Clark, Gregory, Hoy,
Kinsley, Kinne, McLaren, Macy. Pennington, Perry, Rumery,
Shipman, Soper, Stacy, Trowbridge, VanValkenberk, Viers. 6pp. --$1.50

c. ALGYER: New York/Illinois, 1811-1886; Gowen, Mills, Ridlon,
Smelser. 7pp.   --$1.75

d. ALLEN: Mercer and Lawrence Counties, Pennsylvania; 1804-1882;
Blair, Fisher, Frazier. Hagen. Neely. Zediker. 4pp.   --$1.00

e. AMES: 1831-1912; Joynes. 2pp.   --$1.00

f. AMES: 1862-1891; Edwards, Givler, Mears, Nock, Roberts. 6pp. --$1.50

g. ANDREW: Huntington County, Indiana, 1868-1913; Crago,
Fooshee, Haneline, Kissinger, Newton, Weber. 2pp.   --$1.00

h. ANDREW: Canada, 1862-1945; Cretzler. Freeman, Hareson,
Miller. Towers. 6pp.   --$1.50

i. BACKUS: Connecticut/Minnesota/Wisconsin, 1809-1924; Berry,
Bunnell, Byholt, Frink. Lindermann, Morrill, Nilsson, Rew,
Ring, Soule, Svendsen. 4pp.   --$1.00

j. BAKER: Harrellsville, North Carolina, 1859-1929; Betts, Harrell,
Mitchell, Robertson, Watson. 2pp.   --$1.00

k. BAKER: Isle of Wight County, Virginia to Hertford County, North
Carolina, 1816-1898; Barker, Beasley, Betts, Browne, Cullens,
Dunning, Harrell, Hurchison, Mitchell, Outlaw, Perry, Rawles,
Robertson, Savage, Sheperd, Sowell, Tayloe, Watson, Willaford,
Winborne. 4pp.   --$1.00

l. BEESON: 1809-1869; Barrickman, Downer, Miller, Rogers,
Skiles, Tumbleston, Vail. 4pp.   --$1.00

m. MIDWELL: 1788-1898; Dudley, Foote, Grant, Holmes. 7pp.   --$1.75

n. BORK: Prussia/New York, 1750-1839; Chissom, Schermerhorn,
Wire. 2pp.   --$1.00

o. BORK: 1812-1872; Mosure. 2pp.   --$1.00

4222 (cont.)

p. BRADY: Michigan, 1804-1894; Biggs, McKee, Oberlin, Torrey. 5pp. --$1.25

q. BROWN: 1818-1935; Bleecker, Clinton, Stead. 12pp. --$3.00

r. BROWN: 1800-1886; Creekmore. 4pp. --$1.00

s. BRYAN: Atlanta, Georgia, 1802-1879; Daniels, Faulk, Johnson, McNabb. 5pp. --$1.25

t. CALDWELL: 1788-1847; Chitwood, Clarke, Daugherty, Farrar, Hall, Kinkead, Linthacum, McDonald, McDoniel. 7pp. --$1.75

u. CANTWELL: 1816-1947; Beach, Bell, Blount, Day, Eggleston, Finnell, Gill, Hanlon, Marshall, Parrish, Rundle, Watson. 2pp. --$1.00

v. CHAPEL: 1861-1944; Chase, Durgin, Morgan, Winegarden. 2pp. --$1.00

w. CHILDS: 1794-1935; Caldwell, Carson, Cochran, Dennison, Dodson, Hawks, Houston, Johnston, Motz. 5pp. --$1.25

x. CHILDS: New York, Massachusetts, 1784-1942; Chubb, Conn, Crouch, Dyer, Faulkner, Graham, Hoke, Long, Naramore, Nash, Peek, Purrington, Sheldon, Sherwood, Skinner, Smith, Tobey, Winslow, Wolf. 5pp. --$1.25

y. CLAYTON: Chesterfield County, Virginia, 1824-1892; Abbitt, Eminck, Ferguson, Jennings, Mack, Watkins. 8pp. --$2.00

z. COCKRELL: 1818-1884 (Contains Black slave birth records); Carpenter. 16pp. --$4.00

aa. COFFEY: Illinois, 1774-1894; Benbrook, Brower, Campbell, Conner, Daigh, Hutchinson, Porter, Tomlinson, Wills. 17pp. --$4.25

ab. COMPTON: 1814-1936; Auckeson, Boyd, Darling, Crawford, Karr, Love, McConnell, McFarland, Sullivan. 2pp. --$1.00

ac. DAMERON: Greene County, Missouri, 1872-1929; Akin. 5pp. --$1.25

ad. DARNALL: Charles County, Maryland, and Champaign County, Ohio, 1801-1851; Brown, Kelly. 5pp. --$1.25

ae. DAVIS: North Carolina, 1791-1890; Baker, Boon, Cook, Greene, Lancaster, Leonard, Portis, Robertson, Ruffin. 4pp. --$1.00

af. DELLINGER: 1810-1908; Clifford, Laney. 6pp. --$1.50

ag. DIEHL: 1836-1930; Bauer. 3pp. --$1.00

ah. DIETZ: 1798-1871; Borrows, Gose, Phinney. 2pp. --$1.00

ai. DINGMAN: 1803-1962; Bailey, Patterson. 6pp. --$1.50

aj. DOUGLASS: Pennsylvania/Minnesota, 1843-1888; Foster, Grove. 7pp. --$1.75

ak. DRESSLAER: 1835-1885; Barclay, Boring, Clark, Duket, Estes, Fumuliner, Gordon, Graves, Hamm, Hayes, Kabler, Lucas, McLean, Mattis, Neal, Mease, Noble, Parrigon, Penny, Ritchhart, Robinson, Rolan, Samth, Schueller, Stewart, Woolridge. 22pp. --$5.50

al. DUNLAP: Oakland, California, 1830-1944; Burgess, Durand, Knight, McCollum, Wood. 2pp. --$1.00

4222 (cont.)

am. EAGLE: 1762–1873; Barnard, Conine, deVere, Lawlor, Macfarlane, Tew. 3pp.   --$1.00

an. EDDY: Monroe County, Ohio, 1825–1922; Battin, Drume, Straight, Woods. 9pp.   --$2.25

ao. EDWARDS: 1850–1969; Ames, Crawford, Messerly, Strevey, Tolin. 5pp.   --$1.25

ap. EDWARDS: 1823–1856; Gilmore, Tyler. 3pp.   --$1.00

aq. ELLENBRAND: Strassburg, Germany, and St. Louis, Missouri, 1828–1928; Hausman. 5pp.   --$1.25

ar. ELLISON: 1857–1875; Andrews, Bowen, Gainer, Gibson, Hatton, Holliday, Johnston, Pope, Robertson. 2pp.   --$1.00

as. FARISH: Conway County, Arkansas, 1814–1857; Vincent, Whitehead. 5pp.   --$1.25

at. FERGUSON: Sangerfield, New York, 1783–1896; Button, Dix, Hewett, King, McCartney. 1pp.   --$1.00

au. FERRELL: 1853–1895; Dixon, Long. 1pp.   --$1.00

av. FIFE: Scotland/South Carolina, 1780–1963; Connelley, Jones, Miles, Reed, Showdecker, Swindell, Taber, Williams. 9pp.   --$2.25

aw. FINNELL: 1871–1971; Kyle, McConnell, Watson. 2pp.   --$1.00

ax. FINNELL: 1801–1845; Anderson, Burton, Case, Cleet, Hosman, Marshall, Roberts, Sleet. 2pp.   --$1.00

ay. FINNELL: Kentucky/Iowa, 1827–1910; Hisle, Oliver, Rielly, Sykes, Tuttle, White, William. 4pp.   --$1.00

az. FINNELL: Iowa, 1791–1890; Scanlon, Seely, Wolfe. 2pp.   --$1.00

ba. FITZSIMMONS: Illinois, 1867–1892; Burns, Cooke, Ettenberger, Humphrey, Jones, Nuss, Watts. 9pp.   --$2.25

bb. FORTNER: 1832–1933; Conley, Pittman, Stewart. 5pp.   --$1.25

bc. FOUTS: 1770–1858; Mason, Sink. 4pp.   --$1.00

bd. FOUTS: Montgomery County, Ohio, 1749–1794; Byrkett, Waymire. 3pp.   --$1.00

be. FRAZIER: Kanawha County, Virginia, 1847–1894; Baldwin, Bell, Lewis, Tams, Turpin, VonStomgel, Waters. 8pp.   --$2.00

bf. FRAZIER: Staunton, Virginia/Louisville, Kentucky, 1882–1927; Freeman, Lightner, Miller. 7pp.   --$1.75

bg. FREEMAN: Mechanicsburg, Pennsylvania, 1858–1924; Cretzler, Sheffield, Swartz, VanRaden. 2pp.   --$1.00

bh. FRENCH: Cincinnati, Ohio, 1765–1919; Chapman, Coss, Dicksey, Duton, Gilpin, Glover, Pope, Reid, Wate, Wilson. 2pp.   --$1.00

bi. FULTON: 1762–1890; Alexander, Hoffman, McClure. 11pp.   --$2.75

bj. GARRISS: Southampton County, Virginia/Northampton County, North Carolina, 1803–1870; Deloatch, Harrell, Jordan, Mitchell, Stephenson, Whitehead. 4pp.   --$1.00

4222 (cont.)

bk. GOODE: 1803-1913; Graham, Studdard. 3pp.   --$1.00

bl. GORDON: Missouri/Minnesota, 1798-1949; Brennan, Dresslear,
     Duncan, Embrey, Frederickson, Hindman, Howard, Ingram,
     Jones, Keys, Lentier, Mastin, Proctor, Ray, Sandres, Stout,
     Stutesman, Wilson. 14pp.   --$3.50

bm. GREER: 1797-1876; Finnell. 2pp.   --$1.00

bn. GROSECLOSE: 1869-1913; Farrier. 2pp.   --$1.00

bo. HACKER: Naavsey and Kendall, Illinois, 1818-1964; Apel,
     Atkinson, Jansen, Tiarkp, Williams. 1pp.   --$1.00

bp. HALL: Alabama/Mississippi, 1885-1970; Ashe, Burrow, Hughes,
     James, Potter, Smith. 14pp.   --$3.50

bq. HAMPSHIRE: Baltimore County, Maryland/Mercer County, Ohio,
     1813-1912; Dearduff, Huffman. 6pp.   --$1.50

br. HAMSCHER: Northampton County, Pennsylvania, 1753-1901;
     Marchsall. 4pp.   --$1.00

bs. HARDING: 1763-1869; Brach, Mix. 5pp.   --$1.25

bt. HASLETT: 1912-1945. 2pp.   --$1.00

bu. HATCH: 1806-1869; Field. 6pp.   --$1.50

bv. HELGENOLD: Arkansas/Tennessee, 1792-1920; Irvine, Kearby,
     Loy, Milligan. 4pp.   --$1.00

bw. HESS: Washington County, Indiana, 1825-1902; Alonzo, Chrisman,
     Coker, Haley, Hannah, Robinson, Williams. 4pp.   --$1.00

bx. HILL: Lane County, Oregon, 1813-1967; Bailey, Baker, Darneill,
     Drake, McClure, Merrell, Mood, Smith, Stickels, Wilson. 9pp.   --$2.25

by. HOMSHER: Lancaster County, Pennsylvania, 1826-1852;
     Gibson. 4pp.   --$1.00

bz. HOMSHER: Lancaster County, Pennsylvania, 1879-1903;
     Baughman. 3pp.   --$1.00

ca. HOMSHER: Lancaster County, Pennsylvania, 1799-1847;
     Huber. 6pp.   --$1.50

cb. HOMSHER: Lancaster County, Pennsylvania, 1827-1905; Groff,
     Huber. 4pp.   --$1.00

cc. HOMSHER: Lancaster County, Pennsylvania, 1784-1872; Boone,
     Coon, Coulter, James, Leech, Sperrin, Supplee, Townsend. 9pp.   --$2.25

cd. HOWARD: 1755-1922; Bennett, Biggerstaff, Black, Burgin,
     Deatherage, Grubb, Jones, Karr, Neale, Riley, Scruggs, Smith,
     Starnes, Tolson, Watts. 7pp.   --$1.75

ce. HOWELL: 1779-1853. 4pp.   --$1.00

cf. HOWLAND: Ireland/New Hampshire/Puerto Rico, 1823-1881;
     Sherry. 5pp.   --$1.25

cg. HOXIE: Massachusetts/Rhode Island, 1816-1871; Head. 1pp.   --$1.00

4222 (cont.)

ch. HUBIN: 1849-1940; Bachman, Brubacher, Muller, Rupp. 9pp. --$2.25

ci. JOHANSSON: 1855-1870; Gustafson. 1pp. --$1.00

cj. JOHNSON: Crawford County, Indiana, 1794-1948; Abel, Adney, Claycomb, Fancher, Goldman, Hoover, Jones, Key, Mazlott, Pankey, Weathers, Wuille. 3pp. --$1.00

ck. JONES: Taneytown, Maryland, 1772-180; Morris. 5pp. --$1.25

cl. JONES: Missouri, 1864-1974; Cary, Dale, Davidson, DeTour, Gordon. 6pp. --$1.50

cm. JORDON: Wayne County, Indiana, 1792-1904; Barnett, Burnell, Pollard. 7pp. --$1.75

cn. JORDON: Wayne County, Indiana, 1841-1924; Cain, Dennis, Davidson, Reynolds, Thornburgh, Ward. 4pp. --$1.00

co. JORDON: Indiana, 1792-1870; Atkinson, Barnett, Cecil, Davidson, Lumpkin, McClelland, McCluson, Pollard. 2pp. --$1.00

cp. JOYNES: 1812-1875; Dunton, Scott. 6pp. --$1.50

cq. KELLER: Lebanon County, Pennsylvania/Tuscarawas County, Ohio, 1758-1940; Armstrong, Campbell, Coventry, Elton, Embich, Goode, Graham, Green, Heacock, Hildt, Oliphant, Orth, Randall, Sebrell, Southworth, Strickle, Studdard, Stull, Wharton. 31pp. --$7.75

cr. LEONHARDT: Prussia, New York/Kansas, 1808-1968; Carpenter, Hobson, Hulbert, Johnston, Lewis, Martindale, Persinger, Rehfeld, Rudy, Sharpe, Swingle. 8pp. --$2.00

cs. LETTS: Orleans County, New York, 1786-1949; Allen, Benson, Gorman, Weatherwax. 10pp. --$2.50

ct. LEWIS: Vermont/Pennsylvania/New York/Wisconsin/Minnesota, 1818-1948; Christman, Shilleto, Williams. 2pp. --$1.00

cu. LINN: Michigan, 1837-1931; Craft, Swick. 2pp. --$1.00

cv. LIPPINCOTT: Morristown, New Jersey, 1746-1872; Dudley, Evans, Matlack, Roberts, Stiles. 4pp. --$1.00

cw. LIPPINCOTT: Morristown, New Jersey, 1776-1892; Andrews, Ballinger, Brian, Buzby, Conrow, Dudley, Eldridge, Evans, Haines, Hancock, Hilton, Jarrett, Matlack, Parry, Roberts, Shoemaker, Thorne, Walton, Zelly. 3pp. --$1.00

cx. LOVELAND: 1860-1936; Armstrong, Barrow, Partridge, Strong. 6pp. --$1.50

cy. LYLES: New York, 1778-1908; Corson, Crisfield, Gardiner, Garrison, Henry, Little, Lott, Neefris, Prince, Stothoff, Voorhes, Wells, Whitmore, Zabriskie. 9pp. --$2.25

cz. MABBETT: 1689-1733. 4pp. --$1.00

da. McCALEB: Virginia, 1879-1976; Cale, Campbell, Green, Groseclose, Harley, LeRoy, Mills, Oxenreider, Robertson, Walker. 8pp. --$2.00

4222 (cont.)

db. McCRACKEN: Bucks County, Pennsylvania, 1762-1932; Bodine,
Field, Garges, Grotz, Kensey, Malone, Matthews, Scott, Twining,
Walton, Woodruff, Egertsen, Lavers, McFaddin, Ryan. 4pp.   --$1.00

dd. McEWAN: 1870-1889; Lamont. 5pp.   --$1.25

de. McFARLAND: Buncombe County, North Carolina/Cooper County,
Missouri, 1823-1913; Alexander, Embree, George, Hunt, McMillon,
Mitchell, Pierce. 5pp.   --$1.25

df. MAIN: 1833-1899; Ferguson, Forsythe, Martin, Semple. 2pp.   --$1.00

dg. MAPP: Accomack County, Virginia, 1779-1906; Ames, Bull, Davis,
Edmunds, Harrison, Holt, Stott, Turlington. 5pp.   --$1.25

dh. MAPP: Accomack County, Virginia, 1733-1862; Ames, Davis,
Downing, Fletcher, Glen, Stott, Thomas, Willis. 4pp.   --$1.00

di. MARTIN: Missouri/Oklahoma, 1849-1916; Cooper, Fuller,
Young. 1pp.   --$1.00

dj. MASON: New York/Ohio, 1842-1920; Bell, Bunhisel, Crouch,
Dodds, Dwyer, Hilfinger, Kirby, Klinefellow, Marks,
Ospaugh. 2pp.   --$1.00

dk. MAXWELL: Delaware County, New York/Whiteside County, Illinois,
1776-1903; Austin, Coburn, Cole, Coyer, Guines, Hulse, Jeffers,
Meacham, Owen, Patrick, Pinney, Saxon, Schelf, Scott. 2pp.   --$1.00

dl. MEARS: 1857-1913; Ames, Battaile, Bell, Byrd, Custis, Hower,
Kahle, Tregor. 6pp.   --$1.50

dm. MENDUM: 1764-1894. 17pp.   --$4.25

dn. MERRICK: Ohio/Iowa, 1898-1859; Carlson, Harmon, Myers,
Nelson, Petterson. 1pp.   --$1.00

do. MILES: Baltimore, Maryland/Lawrence County, Pennsylvania,
1815-1847; Foster. 6pp.   --$1.50

dp. MILLER: Indiana County, Pennsylvania, 1783-1938; Hopkins,
Leasure, Lydick, McKelvey, Pollock, Renkin, Smeyers,
Streams. 6pp.   --$1.50

dq. MILLER: New York/Illinois/Iowa, 1826-1891; Albrook, Alden,
Black, DuBois, Flanigan. 3pp.   --$1.00

dr. MILLER: Knox County, Indiana, 1786-1860; Allen, Combs,
Healey, Howell, O'Donald, Richardson, Sims, Westfall. 9pp.   --$2.25

ds. MITCHELL: Surry County, Virginia/Limestone County, Alabama/
Homer, Louisiana, 1742-1879; Moody, Rives, Rose, Seward, Soloman,
Turner, Whitby. 18pp.   --$4.50

dt. MOE: 1781-1935; Mulholland, Ogden, Palmer, Sholl, Shull,
Welch. 3pp.   --$1.00

du. NEWTON: Ellis County, Texas, 1794-1909; Barnett, Beadford,
Hawkins, Hinkley, Neely, Stell, Stiles, Stockton, Vinson,
Wilson. 12pp.   --$3.00

dv. OBERLIN: Missouri/Michigan, 1839-1941; Boyles, Griffeth, Hubbs,
Iness, Lansker, Rood, Sonley, Trout, Wicks, Woolly. 6pp.   --$1.50

4222 (cont.)

dw. O'DONALD: Greene County, Indiana, 1813-1885; Crook, Gainey, Vest. 1pp. --$1.00

dx. OGDEN: Ross County, Ohio, 1799-1940; Bradley, Clawson, Garrett, Hull, Hurst, Roseboom, Smith. 2pp. --$1.00

dy. OLSON: Minnesota, 1857-1921; Belsheim, Carver, Hope, Josephson, Spencer. 5pp. --$1.25

dz. OSGOOD: 1819-1923; Hill, Partridge, Pauley, Payne, Wilcox. 6pp. --$1.50

ea. PATTON: Adams County, Ohio, 1850-1919; Allison, Heaton, Kirkpatrick, Morrison, Schneider. 6pp. --$1.50

eb. PAYNE: Shenandoah County, Virginia, 1797-1831; Chancellor, Cooper, Edwards, Frazer, Gaines, Gaw, Harrison, King, Miller, Pound, Rector, Sargent, Scullin, Wroe. 3pp. --$1.00

ec. PETERSON: 1843-1946; Emil, Moore, Myrti, Nilson, Theodoria, Willhelm, Wilgran. 1pp. --$1.00

ed. POTEET: Nebraska/Kansas, 1799-1942; Boles, Karr, LeHuquet, MacCorkle, Randolph, Titlow, Witman. 2pp. --$1.00

ee. PRUNER: 1807-1946; Gage, Philbin, Reno, Secon, Speece. 7pp. --$1.75

ef. REED: New York/Wisconsin, 1806-1916; Andrews. 10pp. --$2.50

eg. REEVES: Trumbull County, Ohio, 1808-1899; Adams, Ayres, Espy, Huston, Little, Malcolm, Paisley, Quimby, Tylee. 8pp. --$2.00

eh. RHEY: Indiana County, Pennsylvania, 1805-1929; Cochrane, McCunn, Ray. 2pp. --$1.00

ei. ROBERTS: 1814-1914; Neblett. 4pp. --$1.00

ej. ROACH: Kansas, 1842-1872; Berry, Brodie, Grant, Lemon, Monzell, Polson, Tressella. 3pp. --$1.00

ek. ROBASON: Martin County, North Carolina, 1742-1833; Coltrain, Cook, Danniel, Duggan, Goddard, Guffin, Hardison, Myzelle, Peel, Riddick, Rogerson, Stallings, Wollard. 5pp. --$1.25

el. ROBERTSON: Williamston, North Carolina, 1884-1952; Baker, Ellison, Faucette, Gardner, Harrell, Pottage, Waters. 2pp. --$1.00

em. ROBERTSON: Martin County, North Carolina, 1854-1948; Andrews, Bowen, Ellison, Hatton. 2pp. --$1.00

en. RODGERS: Accomack County, Virginia, 1776-1923; Ames, Bundick, Kendall, Miles, Parsons, Reade. 3pp. --$1.00

eo. ROOS: Sweden/Goodhue County, Minnesota, 1848-1896; Persson. 7pp. --$1.75

ep. ROSE: Lawrence County, Pennsylvania, 1815-1933; Davidson, Espy, Gardner, Geddes, Gibson, Hartzel, Huntley, Mayne, Rowe, Warnock. 4pp. --$1.00

eq. ROTSCHAFER: Germany/Drake, Missouri, 1818-1943; Grote, Pillmeyer, Proett, Ridder, Schopeskoetter, VanLob. 1pp. --$1.00

er. RUNIONS: 1746-1931; Fyke, Johnstone, Silsbee, Ward. 1pp. --$1.00

4222 (cont.)

es. SCHLABACH: 1857-1894; Hinemann, Jansen, Leidel, Seidel. 5pp. --$1.25

et. SCOTT: 1819-1824. 1pp. --$1.00

eu. SCULL: Hertford County, North Carolina. 1769-1835; Hayes, Norfleet, Outlaw, Sharp, Speight. 2pp. --$1.00

ev. SHOOK: Pennsylvania/Monroe County, Ohio, 1814-1890. 10pp. --$2.50

ew. SIMPSON: North Carolina/Indiana, 1792-1885; Collins, Dunn. 13pp. --$3.25

ex. SMITH: 1837-1921; Shaver, Williams. 4pp. --$1.00

ey. SPRAGG: 1829-1865; Knewstep, Salmons. 1pp. --$1.00

ez. STELLE: Washington, D.C., 1842-1933; Coles, Delare, Ducker, Gordon, Halladay, Hopkinson, McPherson, Whiting. 10pp. --$2.50

fa. STREITER: 1738-1860; Avis, Crawford, Drake, Dunkman, Eichelberger, Howard, Engle, Harris, Hendricks, Kennedy, Keyes, Knott, Link, Moler, O'Laughlin, Peters, Plummer, Roberts, Strider, Thompson, VanMeter, Whittman, Woodward, Young. 9pp. --$2.25

fb. STUBBS: England/Norway, 1802-1872; Bossom, Heljesen, Johannson, Solberg. 2pp. --$1.00

fc. SUTTON: Randolph County, Indiana, 1845-1963; Johnson, Noffsinger, Schneider, Smith. 11pp. --$2.75

fd. TAYLOR: Philadelphia, 1800-1866; Massey, Merrill, Reynolds, Soloman, Vickers. 13pp. --$3.25

fe. TITLO: Pennsylvania/Kansas, 1856-1893. 8pp. --$2.00

ff. TRACY: Vermont/Wisconsin, 1833-1960; Banker, Bingham, Bowdle, Brigham, Burns, Clarke, Cole, Copeland, Craig, Dean, Drew, Fitch, Frazier, Fuller, Gilluly, Harnagel, Hines, Hosmer, Luccock, Maddock, Melvin, Mitchell, Newton, Parker, Pendleton, Rogers, Sevcik, Stigler, Stillhorn, Stoddard, Terry, Todd, Welch, Westerhide, Willis. Also included: Bible of Edward Terry, 1813-1936; France, Sparhaw, Stevens, Stevenson, Stratton, Tannott, Thoms. 10pp. --$2.50

fg. TUBBS: Steuben County, Indiana, 1845-1967; Collins, Elliott, Harpster, Helme, Lahnum, Morse. 7pp. --$1.75

fh. TUCKER: Stockes, North Carolina, 1815-1880; Andrews, Barton, Hicks, Rose, Swain, Wiatt. 5pp. --$1.25

fi. VanVALKENBURGH: Greene County, New York, 1807-1932; Bloodgood, Britt, Holdridge, Johnson, Kipp, Rickmyer, Scoville, Shoemaker, Smith. 9pp. --$2.25

fj. WARD: Tuscaloosa County, Alabama, 1786-1898; Caonegay, Champin, Clemins, Deweeso, Hanly, Thomson. 4pp. --$1.00

fk. WEBB: 1890-1972; Alberty, Anderson, Bancroft, Borst, Fogle, Holloway, Kuhles, Laing, Lindahl, Pettry, Soper, Stuart, Tice, Toal. 10pp. --$2.50

fl. WEBB: Canadaigua, New York, 1811-1971; Alberty, Bancroft, Batchelor, Evans, Fletcher, Fogle, Huntington, Underwood. 8pp. --$2.00

4222 (cont.)

fm. WEST: 1873-1976; Barnett, Beall, Bibb, Boltwood, Bowman, Buczek, Busby, Coleman, Craft, Daniel, Ennis, Gardner, Harless, Hilwig, Lipp, Peircy, Petett, Rohr, Salisbury, Sandwich, Swick, Theimer, Viotette. 6pp. --$1.50

fn. WILLIAMS: Wayne County, Indiana, 1820-1892; Birkhmer, Fouts, Jacobs, Stomm. 3pp. --$1.00

fo. WILLIAMS: 1804-1917; Shaver, Wilson. 3pp. --$1.00

fp. WILSON: Highland and Pike Counties, Ohio, 1806-1839; Bowar, Core, Horn, Jolly, Perrill, Williams. 4pp. --$1.00

fq. WOODRUFF: 1815-1922; Cobb, Gaut, Springer, Young. 6pp. --$1.50

fr. ALLEN: Mercer and Lawrence Counties, Pennsylvania, 1824-1828; Rodgers. 3pp. --$1.00

fs. ALLSTON: New Castle County, Delaware/Kent County, Maryland, 1821-1853; Ashcroft, Vandegrift, Woods. 11pp. --$2.75

ft. ATKINSON: Madison County, Indiana, 1857-1945; Floyd, Hocker, Moore, Ostrander, Wilson. 1pp. --$1.00

fu. BEDOW: Kasota, Minnesoita, 1790-1866; Baker, Luce, Morris, Rich, Sharp. 8pp. --$2.00

fv. BEHRENBERG: 1874-1879. 4pp. --$1.00

fw. BERGMAN: Sweden/Oregon, 1874-1924; Anderson, Bergeson, Sandstrom, Seaquist. 11pp. --$2.75

fx. BINGHAM: Toronto, Canada/Trenton, New Jersey, 1842-1896; Cullen, Greenley, Johnston, McNulty, Pace. 8pp. --$2.00

fy. BRENIZER: Morrow County, Ohio, 1798-1971; Aldrige, Barry, Bond, Carpenter, Curren, Dailey, Denton, Doty, Elliott, Hartpence, Sheeler, Williams. 11pp. --$2.75

fz. BRIGHT: Greenbrier County, West Virginia, 1829-1903; Burter, Clarke, Conner, Henning, Legg, Plunger, Pollock, Ransbarger, Reynolds. 6pp. --$1.50

ga. CARMALT: Philadelphia, Pennsylvania, 1765-1843; Bryant, Christie, Gaskill, Hudson, Matlack, Newlings, Price. 12pp. --$3.00

gb. CONNER: Greenbrier County, West Virginia, 1842-1923; Bright, Foglesoug (Foglesong?), Leach, Mahood. 9pp. --$2.25

gc. deBOER: 1866-1940; Chambery, Hersken, Kooeman, Roltman, Ten Cate, Van Stilton. 1pp. --$1.00

gd. FINNELL: 1805-1866; Lang, Meneffee, Miller, Phelps. 8pp. --$2.00

ge. HATTON: Indiana/Ohio/Illinois, 1800-present; Alexander, Bearden, Blankenship, Bodkin, Coppock, Galloway, Griffin, Havel, Haven, Jones, Loring, Moody, Peacock, Pratt, Shoop, Swank, Winter. 25pp. --$6.25

gf. LEONARD: Middleboro, Massachusetts, 1775-1860; Bartlett, Childs, Clapp, Combs, Hill, Rice, Town, Warren, Weatherell. 7pp. --$1.75

gg. LUMLEY: Dallas County, Texas/California, 1846-1935; Bensett, Haught, Leach, Miller, Mathis, Parnell, Porter, Robertson, Summers. 12pp. --$3.00

4222 (cont.)

gh. McJUNKIN: South Carolina Upcountry, 1755-1859; Black, Bogan, O'Keefe, Thomas, Bankhead, Caldwell, Ogletree, Sayre. 8pp. --$2.00

gi. McJUNKIN: Northeast Georgia, 1828-1943; Bradley, Daniel, Forster, McHargue, Ogletree. 16pp. --$4.00

gj. MAHOOD: Fayette County, West Virginia, 1845-1882; Gauthrie, Huddleston, Lewis. 8pp. --$2.00

gk. MASON: Rappahannock and Giles Counties, Virginia, 17601-1873; Bush, Evans, Finch, Hoge, Peck, Porter, Williams. 4pp. --$1.00

gl. MITCHELL: Lanarkshire, Scotland/Trumbull County, Ohio, 1810-1915; Akins, Armstrong, Evans, Forrest, Hamilton, Hogg, Ptolemy, Watson. 7pp. --$1.75

gm. OSTERHOUT: 1826-1945; Beevers, Bush, Curtis, Davenport, Dibble, George, Hoagland, McCarbery, Newell, Peterson, Pocklington. 2pp. --$1.00

gn. Rock County, Minnesota; Abbott, Bartlett, Blackburn, Bross, Brown, Eberlein, Hawkins, Hettinges, Johnson, Jones, Kelley, Lathrop, Long, McBride, McDermo, McNeil, Newton, Price, Shoemaker, Sischo, Swenson, Wilder. 7pp. --$1.75

go. SIMMONS: Bertie County, North Carolina, 1855-1877; Holt. 4pp. --$1.00

gp. SMITH: Illinois/Nebraska/Iowa, 1781-1913; Booker, Crum, Harbour, Nunn, Packwood, Ross, Wilson. 7pp. --$1.75

gq. TEASDALE: 1855-1945; Gothie, Madison, Sertzinger, Vaughan. 3pp. --$1.00

gr. THOMAS: Elkton, Maryland, 1806-1923; Bevyley, Brown, Carter, Jones, Mooney, Pavard, Robb, Ritchie. 14pp. --$3.50

gs. TRAVER: New York/Iowa, 1831-1900; Clark, Clapp, DePew, Ferguson, Riddle, Schroeder, Spicer. 9pp. --$2.25

gt. WHITSON: Marshall County, Iowa, 1811-1920; Avery, Conner, Draper, Lamb, Pearison. 12pp. --$3.00

gu. ALLEMAN: 1860-1867; Hubbins, Kuhn. 4pp. --$1.00

gv. ATKINSON: Florida, 1810-1902; Brewer. 2pp. --$1.00

gw. BARNES: Montgomery and St. Louis Counties, Missouri, 1845-1942; Blakey, Chester, Dyer, Ellaby, Grigg, Hamlett, Hilde, Hildebrand, Kolling, Lewelling, McCrea, Percy, Veale. 5pp. --$1.25

gx. BEECHER: 1812-1868; Baldwin, Curtiss, Mise, Scott. 6pp. --$1.50

gy. BILBREY: Overton County, Tennessee, 1803-1862; Copeland, Gore. 1pp. --$1.00

gz. BOND: 1864-1913; McCarver. 3pp. --$1.00

ha. BUCHANAN: 1804-1892; Androm, Billings, Boner, Browning, Lacy, Lantz, McConnell, Porter, Ragan, Stephens, Walton. 16pp. --$4.00

hb. BUMGARDNER: Augusta County, Virginia, 1767-1881; Gabbert, Gibbons, Kunkle, McGilvray. 7pp. --$1.75

4222 (cont.)

hc. COOPER: Chesterville, Mississippi, 1872-1951; <u>Dandridge</u>,
<u>Keitt</u>, <u>McGilliand</u>, <u>Odell</u>, <u>Peevy</u>, <u>Phillips</u>. 6pp.   --$1.50

hd. CRAWFORD: Middletown, Pennsylvania, 1765-1892; <u>Plummer</u>,
<u>Sharp</u>. 1pp.   --$1.00

he. DUDLEY: Augusta County, Virginia, 1858-1939; <u>Dull</u>, <u>Pettit</u>,
<u>Snead</u>, <u>Vannerman</u>. 7pp.   --$1.75

hf. ENDERS: 1872-1900. 2pp.   --$1.00

hg. FISHER: 1785-1852; <u>Blake</u>, <u>Emmons</u>, <u>Evans</u>, <u>Hawkins</u>, <u>Lafayett</u>,
<u>Metcalf</u>, <u>North</u>, <u>Richardson</u>, <u>Simpson</u>, <u>Thompson</u>, <u>Warrin</u>,
<u>Wilmot</u>. 5pp.   --$1.25

hh. FORSYTH: 1803-1848; <u>Blaurock</u>, <u>Collins</u>, <u>Kitchin</u>. 1pp.   --$1.00

hi. FOWKE: Gunston Hall, Virginia, 1716-1969; <u>Campbell</u>, <u>Fossaker</u>,
<u>Harrison</u>, <u>Jenkins</u>, <u>Jackson</u>, <u>Marshall</u>, <u>Porterfield</u>, <u>Reed</u>. 3pp.   --$1.00

hj. GARRETT: Kentucky/Ohio, 1780-1905; <u>Cochran</u>, <u>Hornback</u>,
<u>Paris</u>, <u>Pursely</u>, <u>Reed</u>, <u>Rosenfelf</u>. 2pp.   --$1.00

hk. GATES: Wendell, Massachusetts, 1791-1866; <u>Johnson</u>. 1pp.   --$1.00

hl. GILLILAND: Alleghany County, Virginia/Charleston, West
Virginia, 1829-1880. 3pp.   --$1.00

hm. GLASCOCK: Hancock County, Indiana, 182-1928; <u>Plummer</u>. 1pp.   --$1.00

hn. HERRON: Yalobusha County, Mississippi, 1838-1891; <u>Shaw</u>. 10pp.   --$2.50

ho. HORNBARGER: Clifton Forge, Virginia, 1862-1914; <u>Dunn</u>, <u>Dudley</u>,
<u>Evan</u>, <u>Gilliland</u>, <u>Leffel</u>, <u>Mynes</u>. 7pp.   --$1.75

hp. JACKSON: 1739-1897; <u>Brickley</u>, <u>Cooper</u>, <u>Moore</u>. 15pp.   --$3.75

hq. JOHNSTON: Georgia, 1783-1846; <u>Clower</u>, <u>Hines</u>, <u>Martin</u>,
<u>Rucker</u>, <u>Underwood</u>, <u>Willis</u>. 1pp.   --$1.00

hr. KEELER: Erie, Pennsylvania, 1806-1908; <u>Adkins</u>, <u>Allen</u>, <u>Anderson</u>,
<u>Byrnes</u>, <u>Cole</u>, <u>Dyer</u>, <u>Flint</u>, <u>Godfrey</u>, <u>Hawson</u>, <u>Hills</u>, <u>Howe</u>,
<u>Hubbell</u>, <u>Hungerford</u>, <u>Lanfear</u>, <u>Lyon</u>, <u>McKee</u>, <u>Pierce</u>, <u>Russell</u>,
<u>Thrall</u>, <u>Tracy</u>, <u>Watts</u>, <u>Wickiser</u>, <u>Williams</u>, <u>Wilson</u>, <u>White</u>. 12pp.   --$3.00

hs. KELLEY: Greenbrier County, (West) Virginia, 1776-1896;
<u>Bright</u>, <u>Caraway</u>, <u>Conner</u>, <u>Handley</u>, <u>McCorkle</u>, <u>Vandall</u>. 11pp.   --$2.75

ht. KNOWLES: Frederick County, Mary;and/Ohio, 1750-1975;
<u>Alexander</u>, <u>Bliss</u>, <u>Bradley</u>, <u>Carpenter</u>, <u>Costerisan</u>, <u>Cusick</u>,
<u>Dahlin</u>, <u>Dearholt</u>, <u>Emerson</u>, <u>Fawcett</u>, <u>Flitcroft</u>, <u>Fraser</u>, <u>Grote</u>,
<u>Hanes</u>, <u>Hood</u>, <u>Jennings</u>, <u>Kearney</u>, <u>Kosta</u>, <u>Mackey</u>, <u>Main</u>, <u>Maxham</u>,
<u>McConnell</u>, <u>McQueen</u>, <u>McRoberts</u>, <u>Neitzel</u>, <u>Price</u>, <u>Richards</u>,
<u>Santos</u>, <u>Schultz</u>, <u>Sebring</u>, <u>Spitzley</u>, <u>Stewart</u>, <u>Stoughtenger</u>.
<u>Torpewski</u>, <u>Waldo</u>, <u>Weidman</u>, <u>Westenhaver</u>, <u>White</u>, <u>Young</u>. 15pp.   --$3.75

hu. ARMSTRONG: Adams County, Ohio, 1845-1925; <u>Fischer</u>,
<u>Hughes</u>, <u>McClure</u>, <u>Rhoads</u>, <u>Wallace</u>, <u>West</u>, <u>White</u>. 7pp.   --$1.75

hv. BAMBERGER: Dauphin County, Pennsylvania/Champaign County,
<u>Ohio</u>, 1806-1954; <u>Carey</u>, <u>Farris</u>, <u>Jones</u>, <u>Kennedy</u>, <u>Owen</u>, <u>Owens</u>,
<u>Parthemer</u>, <u>Saxbe</u>, <u>Sceva</u>, <u>Swisher</u>, <u>VanNess</u>, <u>Walbern</u>. 3pp.   --$1.00

hw. BORDEN: Shenandoah County, Virginia, 1850-1922; <u>Lee</u>. 9pp.   --$2.25

4222 (cont.)

hx. BOWIE: Hagerstown, Maryland, 1854-1942; Beatty. 8pp.   --$2.00

hy. DANIELL: Dallas County, Arkansas, 1857-1974; Brewer,
Watson. 5pp.   --$1.25

hz. DIBRELL: Wayne County, Kentucky, 1709-1861; Bailey, Bates,
Burton, Carter, Chamberlin, Conner, Eastland, Harbert, Herd,
Jenkins, Leftwich, Miller, Mooney, Pattison, Putney, Whitfield,
Sullivan. 20pp.   --$5.00

ia. FREY: Adams County, Pennsylvania, 1874-1879; Sell. 4pp.   --$1.00

ib. GATES: 1817-1930; Black, Fanning, Holderness, Langen, Scoggan,
Standish, Swan. 15pp.   --$3.75

ic. GOODBAR: Overton County, Tennessee, 1786-1940; Anderson,
Audirou, Bohamon, Cullom, Douglass, Draper, Marchbanks,
Masters, McCulley, Sayre. 11pp.   --$2.75

id. GRAHAM: 1821-1887. 5pp.   --$1.25

ie. GROSH: Mercersburg, Pennsylvania, 1843-1928; Basou, Gillin,
Myers. 9pp.   --$2.25

if. HALL: Iowa/New York, 1874-1902; Dinkel, Rappleye, Robb. 7pp.   --$1.75

ig. HENTHORN: Maryland, 1905-1963; Bullock, Henthorn, Hazwell,
Lowdenslage, Rawlings. 8pp.   --$2.00

ih. HOOVER: 1828-1928; Beaner, Denlinger. 5pp.   --$1.25

ii. JONES: 1774-1899; Buster, Hall. 3pp.   --$1.00

ij. KRAFFT: Erie County, New York, 1868-1960; Allen, Beers,
Bowley, Haney, Pichard, Stickles. (Filed Under HALL). 4pp.   --$1.00

ik. LARIMORE: 1776-1913; Bennett, Burbanks, Burkhart, Byram,
Dunton, Hoskins, McBride, McCormick, Newman, Oliver, Perkins,
Stevens. 8pp.   --$2.00

il. LATIMER: 1803-1877; Mecker, Moses, Pettibone, Phelphs,
Pierson, Wilcox. 16pp.   --$4.00

im. LEONARD: Bridgewater, Vermont, 1752-1843; Bartlett, Childs,
Clapp, Hill, Rin, Warren. 4pp.   --$1.00

in. McGAUGHY: 1825-1866; Horner, McAllen. 9pp.   --$2.25

io. MORAND: New York, 1851-1872; Caldwell, Cantrell, Child,
Converse, George, Lewis, Mellon, Peck, Wilbur. 8pp.   --$2.00

ip. PARK: 1779-1835; Cowden, Kincade, Nichols, Wier. 6pp.   --$1.50

iq. PATTY: Tennessee/Oregon, 1809-1870; Bewley, Brown, Easterly,
Gudger, Reynolds, Sunderland. 3pp.   --$1.00

ir. PEARRE: Frederick County, Maryland, 1835-1915; Clemson,
Dudderar, Lindsay. 6pp.   --$1.50

is. PEARRE: Columbia County, Georgia, 1825-1934; Bacon, Blackwood,
Hall, Hobbs, Lott, Tarver, Wall. 15pp.   --$3.75

4222 (cont.)

it. PEARRE: 1890-1973; <u>Newlin</u>, <u>Pitts</u>, <u>Sawyer</u>, <u>Skinner</u>, <u>Thornton</u>, <u>Waddon</u>, <u>Webb</u>. 1pp. --$1.00

iu. PEARRE: Missouri, 1859-1894; <u>Bitschy</u>, <u>Patterson</u>, <u>Stewart</u>, <u>Uhrin</u>. 8pp. --$2.00

iv. RECK: 1798-1869. 4pp. --$1.00

iw. SCHUFF: Thurmont, Maryland, 1877-1934; <u>Miller</u>, <u>Stitely</u>. 9pp. --$2.25

ix. STONE: Huron County, Ohio/Nemaha County, Kansas, 1782-1897; <u>Hoyt</u>. 7pp. --$1.75

ja. TILLEY: Queens County, New York, 1841—   ; <u>Whaley</u>. 12pp. --$3.00

jb. TRYON: 1850-1903; <u>Jackson</u>, <u>Luthan</u>, <u>McIntire</u>, <u>Sharpe</u>. 1pp. --$1.00

jc. TYUS: Memphis, Tennessee, 1872-1918; <u>Collins</u>, <u>Dobbins</u>, <u>Haley</u>, <u>Johnson</u>, <u>Matthews</u>, <u>McKinne</u>, <u>Morris</u>, <u>Pearre</u>, <u>Peters</u>, <u>Stevens</u>, <u>Tucker</u>. 15pp. --#.75

jd. TYUS: 1872-1972; <u>Haley</u>, <u>Johnson</u>, <u>Pearre</u>, <u>Peters</u>. 12pp. --$3.00

je. VAN GIESEN: 1787-1936; <u>Decker</u>, <u>Glass</u>, <u>Graham</u>, <u>Jacobus</u>, <u>Jenkins</u>, <u>Kiestead</u>. 7pp. --$1.75

jf. WATSON: 1827-1869; <u>Bundy</u>. 5pp. --$1.25

jg. WILSON: 1852-1871; <u>Lutz</u>. 11pp. --$2.75

jh. KUNKEL: Augusta County, Virginia, 1810-1937; <u>Dudley</u>, <u>Hill</u>, <u>Kunkle</u>, <u>Mahaney</u>, <u>McCutchen</u>. 2pp. --$1.00

ji. KUNKLE: 1781-1881. 2pp. --$1.00

jj. LIBBY: 1796-1901; <u>White</u>. 5pp. --$1.25

jk. LITTLE: 1855-1892; <u>Royer</u>. 3pp. --$1.00

jl. MANSON: New Hampton, New Hampshire, 1802-1866; <u>Bartlett</u>, <u>Bean</u>, <u>Bowles</u>, <u>Burnham</u>, <u>Carpenter</u>, <u>Dame</u>, <u>Day</u>, <u>Dickerson</u>, <u>Eaton</u>, <u>Joy</u>, <u>Lancaster</u>, <u>Lanpher</u>, <u>Leavy</u>, <u>Marston</u>, <u>Morse</u>, <u>Philbrick</u>, <u>Smith</u>, <u>Turner</u>, <u>Whittier</u>. 7pp. --$1.75

jm. McCUTCHAN: Augusta County, Virginia, 1750-1893; <u>Armstrong</u>, <u>Benson</u>, <u>Bibb</u>, <u>Brown</u>, <u>Dunlap</u>, <u>Durben</u>, <u>Firebaugh</u>, <u>Henderson</u>, <u>Higbee</u>, <u>Hodge</u>, <u>Jameson</u>, <u>Kunkle</u>, <u>McClung</u>, <u>McKnight</u>, <u>McNight</u>, <u>McRae</u>, <u>Nelson</u>, <u>Patrick</u>, <u>Wilson</u>, <u>Youel</u>. 11pp. --$2.75

jn. McJUNKIN: Green County, Georgia, 1876-1938; <u>Hall</u>, <u>Johnson</u>, <u>Stephens</u>, <u>Stall</u>. <u>Jones</u>. 9pp. --$2.25

jo. McWILLIAMS: Texas, 1824-1889; <u>Freeman</u>, <u>Lindsley</u>, <u>Porter</u>, <u>Pryor</u>, <u>Robertson</u>, <u>Stromber</u>. 5pp. --$1.25

jp. NICKESON: 1822-1880; <u>Host</u>, <u>Hughs</u>, <u>Kelley</u>. 8pp. --$2.00

jq. ODELL: Dawson, Texas, 1858-1953; <u>Bond</u>, <u>Boone</u>, <u>Hollingsworth</u>, <u>McCabe</u>, <u>Martin</u>, <u>Staaden</u>. 9pp. --$2.25

jr. OWSLEY: Kentucky/Missouri/Kansas, 1815-1961; <u>Bell</u>, <u>Black</u>, <u>Bowles</u>, <u>Catherman</u>, <u>Cherry</u>, <u>Childs</u>, <u>Cole</u>, <u>Constable</u>, <u>Davidson</u>, <u>Durg</u>, <u>Gilchrist</u>, <u>Johnson</u>, <u>Judd</u>, <u>Levine</u>, <u>Lewis</u>, <u>Lonegan</u>, <u>Lyne</u>, <u>McCallan</u>, <u>Parrott</u>, <u>Proctor</u>, <u>Reuter</u>, <u>Richards</u>, <u>Shepard</u>, <u>Stuart</u>, <u>Yates</u>. 11pp. --$2.75

4222 (cont.)

js. PARRISH: Williamson County, Tennessee/Yalobush County,
Mississippi, 1812-1844; Herron, Jones, North. 10pp. --$2.50

jt. PASLEY: Buckingham County, Virginia/Owen County, Kentucky,
1762-1844; Adcock, Blunt, Carter, Collin, Manary, McGinnis,
Scott, Tinder. 1pp. --$1.00

ju. PORTER: Wythe County, Virginia, 1826-1892; Barker, Davidson,
Dyer, Ewing, Flanagan, Huddle, Pearman, Sublett. 3pp. --$1.00

jv. PRICE: New Jersey/Pennsylvania/Mercer County, Illinois/Clark
County, Iowa, 1825-1913; Barton, Bates, Cardiff, Crowl, Dietrick,
Groff, Lutz, Mahaffey, Newman, Sipes, Steven, Thornton,
Winans. 9pp. --$2.25

jw. REPASS: Wythe County, Virginia, 1819-1865; Brown, Earheart,
Gerberin, Harkrader, Mollerin, Patterson, Sharitz, Spies,
Umburger. 18pp. --$4.50

jx. RIDEOUT: 1833-1864; Gloyd, Lloyd. 7pp. --$1.75

ka. SEARLE: 1773-1903; Alcott, Butler, Crocker, Dunn, Giles,
Hungerford, Scott, Thurston, Shuttuch. 5pp. --$1.25

kb. SPALDING: Plainfield, Connecticut, 1757-1854; Hewit,
VanWie. 1pp. --$1.00

kc. SPENCER: 1784-1960; Kirkland, MacDonald, Post, Sherman,
Windsor. 8pp. --$2.00

kd. SWARTLEY: North Wales/Montgomery County, Pennsylvania,
1849-1923; Heller, Kile, Kerper, Ruth. 7pp. --$1.75

ke. THORNTON: Pennsylvania/Long Beach, California, 1812-1929;
Biddle, Britt, Chowning, Garvin, Lee, Moore, Norbury, Partridge,
Vernon, Willets. 8pp. --$2.00

kf. TITLO: Pennsylvania, 1863-1944; Schoenly, Stockton,
Shuster. 1pp. --$1.00

kg. WASHINGTON: Hinman, Virginia, 1766-1858; Asbury, Johnson,
Kelley, Muse, Piles, Reed, Sutton, Williamson, Wilson. 4pp. --$1.00

kh. WATSON: Monroe County, Georgia, 1769-1930; Bradley, Cherry,
Gordon, Lassiter, Mobley, Shannon. 3pp. --$1.00

ki. WHITTEMORE: New York/Michigan, 1786-1844; McCrossin,
Peck, Richmond, Wheeler, White. 4pp. --$1.00

kj. WILKERSON: Logan County, Kentucky, 1830-1894; Appling,
Elliott, Hall, Harris, Herndon, Hollins, Neals, Peart, Price. 2pp. --$1.00

kk. WILSON: 1878-1920; Hall, Jefferson, McDaniel, Virginia. 4pp. --$1.00

kl. BIRDSALL: 1730-1849; Colant, Sutton. 4pp. --$1.00

km. BOYCE: 1810-1905; Archer, Exline, Mitchell. 4pp. --$1.00

kn. CARSON: Massachusetts/District of Columbia/Michigan/Wisconsin,
1920-1971; Ehlenfeldt, Jeffries. 7pp. --$1.75

ko. CHAMBERLIN: Summit County, Ohio, 1819-1904; Bush, Chidsey,
Clarkson, Cromack, Hull, Moore, Paxson, Paxton, Post, Ramsey,
Smith, Thompson, Wells. 6pp. --$1.50

4222 (cont.)
kp. CLARRIDGE: Palestine, Ohio, 1822-1884; McCafferty, Murphy, Southward. 2pp. --$1.00

kq. COSBEY: Ohio, 1816-1899; Agnew, Blair, Ferris, Heick, Kennedy, Magee, Mathis, Peckingpaugh. 6pp. --$1.50

kr. DAFF/DAFT/DAFFT: Ohio, 1798-1971. 1pp. --$1.00

ks. DAVIS: 1871-1950; Carson, Crider, Jecikinson, Phillips. 7pp. --$1.75

kt. FRY/FREY: Montgomery County, Maryland, 1768-1908; Fox. 11pp. --$2.75

ku. GARDETTE: Emigrated from Agen, France, 1783-1887; Badger, Brown, Carriere, DesMarain, DesMarias, Johnson, Maury, Pepper, Thompson. 5pp. --$1.25

kv. GOING: Ypsilanti and Pontiac, Michigan, 1822-1938; Beach, Becker, Hoffman, Parkins. 1pp. --$1.00

kw. HAMILTON: Illinois/Kansas, 1816-1935; Freeman, Leonard, Sheffield. 1pp. --$1.00

kx. JOHN: Whiteley Township, Greene County, Pennsylvania, 1781-1888; Fox, Hostutler/Hostetler, Robison, Wells. 3pp. --$1.00

la. JONES: 1808-1925; Cole, Goss, Livesay, Logan, Meadows, Testerman, Vines, Wallace, Willis. 10pp. --$2.50

lb. KANE: New Jersey/Ohio, 1774-1870; Drunhill, Miley, Smith, Wallace. 12pp. --$3.00

lc. LAWRENCE: Green County, Ohio/Leavenworth and Douglas Counties, Kansas; McConnell, McLawrence, McLellen. 2pp. --$1.00

ld. LUGENBEEL: Carroll County, Maryland, 1802-1933; Buckingham, Lindsay, Pearre, Shriner. 4pp. --$1.00

le. MARTIN: Talbot County, Georgia, 1818-1892; Baldwin, Carson, Collier, Leonard, Lewis, Oslin, Stephens. 2pp. --$1.00

lf. PEARRE: Carroll County, Maryland, 1857-1947; Buckingham, Lindsay, Lugenbeel, Shriner. 15pp. --$3.75

lg. SMITH: Pennsylvania/Iowa/Indiana, 1828-1947; Andrews, Berry, Culver, Hanes, Harrah, Read, Rex, Selby, Smith, Wildman, Whistler. 3pp. --$1.00

lh. SMITH: 1836-1931; Henry. 5pp. --$1.25

li. THOMAS: Ohio/Missouri/Oklahoma, 1803-1882; Ball, Boice, Burton, Clarridge, Halloway, Larey, McCafferty, Murphy, Southward, VanBuskirk. 7pp. --$1.75

lj. TIBBITS: 1794-1888; Davis, Simonton. 3pp. --$1.00

lk. TULLIS: Kansas?, 1812-1906; Ball, Blue, Burns, Calison, Meredith. 4pp. --$1.00

lm. WALLACE: Odd, West Virginia, 1808-1925; Cole, Goss, Jones, Livesay, Logan, Meadows, Testerman, Vines, Willis. 4pp. --$1.00

ln. WELKER: Pennsylvania/Maryland, 1760-1831; Korndorffein, Rule. 1pp. --$1.00

4222 (cont.)

lo. WILL: Lancaster County, Pennsylvania/Ohio/LaGrange County,
Indiana, 1796-1914; Clugston, Handley, Wade. 4pp.   --$1.00

lp. AMENT: Nashville, Tennessee/Palmyra, Missouri/Muscatine,
Iowa, 1823-1879; Davidson, Robbins, Ruff, Seymour. 5pp.   --$1.25

lq. BANDEL: Baltimore, Maryland, 1786-1871; Baxter, Clarke,
Johnson, Kerner, McJilton, Sagaser, Thomas. 17pp.   --$4.25

lr. BATEMAN: Hamilton County?, Ohio?, 1787-1870;
Westcoat/Westcott. 1pp.   --$1.00

ls. BONORDEN: Iowa/Missouri/Illinois/California, 1835-1917;
Doellinger/Dollinger. 3pp.   --$1.00

lt. BROWN: Nausy County, Georgia, 1857-1943; Duckett, Lindermann,
Molder, Orcutt, Skinner. 5pp.   --$1.25

lu. CRIST: Newport, Perry County, Pennsylvania, 1823-1870;
Diehl. 10pp.   --$2.50

lv. DAVIDSON: 1812-1922; Chenoweth, Cole, Cox, Meek, Roach,
Wilson. 5pp.   --$1.25

lw. DAVIDSON: Iowa, 1874-1962; Aichlee, Ament, Ashcraft, Bowen,
Brazell, Carey, Giesler, Gott, Greer, Gwathmey, Haber, Hodgkin,
Hunt, Kaselow, Martin, McCloud, Newman, Smith, Van Dyk,
Walker, Worthington, Zawiski. 11pp.   --$2.75

lx. DOAN: 1801-1965; Brady, Brown. 9pp.   --$2.25

ly. DUNN: Paisley, Scotland, Oneida and Cayuga Counties, New York/
Indiana, 1836-1848. 2pp.   --$1.00

lz. ERVIN: Williamsburgh, South Carolina, 1871-1928; Carsden,
Rose, Sullivan, Taylor, Wilson. 10pp.   --$2.50

ma. FELT: Connecticut, 1775-1904; Austin, Buel, Card, Davis,
Gunsaulus, Hayward, Henry, Spencer, Wheeler. 10pp.   --$2.50

mb. GORDON: Moundsville, West Virginia/Wayne County, Iowa/Fergus
County, Montana, 1827-1904; Ammons, Jefferson, Martin, Mitchell,
Phillips, Shepherd. 2pp.   --$1.00

mc. GORDON: Derrycughan, Armagh County, Northern Ireland, 1800-
1915; Barber, Boyden, DeGras/DeGress, Johnston. 1pp.   --$1.00

md. GRAY: Saranac Lake, New York, 1845-1934. Drake, Sratt, Tovar,
Washer. 7pp.   --$1.75

me. GRAY: Covington, Tioga County, Pennsylvania/Bloomington,
Illinois, 1821-1913; Chamerlain, Hamill, Roberts, Shays, Stewart,
Wetherbee. 5pp.   --$1.25

mf. GREGG: Ohio County, Virginia (Marshall County, West Virginia)/
Des Moines County, Iowa, 1805-1886; Boner, Delashmutt, Evans,
Gearhart, Gorrell, Hall, Lamon, Mills, Perry. 2pp.   --$1.00

mg. HATCHETT: King and Queen County, Virginia/New Orleans,
Louisiana/Wetumpka, Alabama, 1788-1940; Baylor, Chandler,
Gwathmey, Marbury, Starke, Thomas, White, Wyatt. 7pp.   --$1.75

mh. HICKLING: 1798-1956; Allison, Bradford, Bygrave, Cockrell,
Conway, Darling, Dorr, Edes, King, O'Reilly, Sever, Webber,
White. 11pp.   --$2.75

4222 (cont.)

mi. HOLE: White Grove, Clinton County, Ohio/Monrovia, Morgan
County, Indiana/Boulder, Colorado/Contra Costa, California,
1853-1954. 3pp.   --$1.00

mj. JEFFERSON: Marshall County, West Virginia, 1823-1899,
Mundell. 3pp.   --$1.00

mk. JEFFERSON: Wheeling, West Virginia, 1767-1878; Amick,
Strobel, Vanderveer, Wright. 2pp.   --$1.00

ml. JEFFERSON: Alexandria, Virginia/Moundsville, Ohio County,
West Virginia, 1793-1874; Freeland, Zimmerman. 2pp.   --$1.00

mm. LAMB: 1805-1920; Brink, Bundy, Carr, Chappell, Colwell,
Derby, Elliott, Fish, French, Guernsey, Hubbard, Jenks,
Lynch, Northrup, Secor, Starr, Studwell, Taylor, Williams,
Young. 10pp.   --$2.50

mn. LINCOLN: 1841-1949; Baker, Margoll, Turman. 6pp.   --$1.50

mo. McCUBBIN: 1843-1934; Berry, McPhail. 1pp.   --$1.00

mp. McCUTCHAN: Indiana/Ohio, 1768-1979; Bell, Craig, Crawford,
Edmondson, Gray, Guthrie, Holmes, Kennedy, Liggett, Lucas,
McClure, Meek, Neely, Nichols, Peterson, Segersman, Smith,
Taylor, Trotter, Ward, Young. 16pp.   --$3.75

mq. MILNER: Kentucky?, 1784-1961; Anderson, Benefiel,
Combs, Garrigus, Land, Melone, Parks, Sawyer, Shephard,
Shepherd. 2pp.   --$1.00

mr. MOREHEAD: Virginia/Audrain County, Missouri/California, 1805-
1909; Foley, Hocker, Lipp, Read, Thomas. 4pp.   --$1.00

ms. MUMPER: Carroll Township, York County, Pennsylvania, 17810
1910; Bailey, Beelman, Dorsheimer, Heiges. 1pp.   --$1.00

mt. MUNDEL: Greene County, Pennsylvania, 1758-1807; Barnhill. 6pp. --$1.50

mu. MUNDEL: Greene County, Pennsylvania, 1807-1928; Grove, Hill,
Mengus, Reeves, Waycoff. 2pp.   --$1.00

mv. MUNDELL: Greene County, Pennsylvania, 1802-1890; Barice,
Colbert, Dorman, Lindsay, Miller, Reeves, Thomas. 3pp.   --$1.00

mw. PETTUS: Virginia/Lincoln and Green Counties, Kentucky, 1761-
1814; Ament, Dawson, Dillard, Madison, Wilcox. 2pp.   --$1.00

mx. RING: Pennsylvania/Ohio/Indiana, 1806-1936; Blatchley, Carroll,
Cromb, Flanders, Ingle, Kew, Middleton, Pegdon, Stewart,
Turner. 7pp.   --$1.75

my. ROBERTS: Moundsville, Marshall County, West Virginia; 1819-
1905; Shepherd. 2pp.   --$1.00

mz. SEVER: Boston and Cambridge, Massachusetts, 1728-1974; Abbott,
Adams, Bygrave, Cockrell, Conway, Darling, DuClos, Hermanson,
Keith, King, Little, Morrill, O'Reilly, Russell, Warren, White,
Winslow. 8pp.   --$2.00

na. SHAW: 1786-1931; Cary, Colt, Esterbrook, McCubbin,
Rehbein. 6pp.   --$1.50

4222 (cont.)

nb. SHEPHERD: 1797-1877; Gregg, Hubbard, Patterson, Robertson, Simmons. 3pp. --$1.00

nc. STEPHEN: Highland County, Virginia?, 1767-1860; Blagg, Bradshaw, Keyser. 2pp. --$1.00

nd. TADLOCK: 1798-1890; Blair, Moyse. 4pp. --$1.00

ne. TEMPLE: Beaver County, Pennsylvania, 1836-1908; Diehl, Dougherty, Glasser, Harper, Johnston, Kerr, Long. 2pp. --$1.00

nf. TILLSON: Massachusetts/Illinois/Kansas/California, 1801-1965; Broussard, Bruce, Chernow, Dorenbos, Dunne(?), Hasser, Howell, Hunter, Laster, Lewis, McKay, Ricketts, Rogers, Simmons, Thompson, Trude, Tunnell, Walker. 6pp. --$1.50

ng. WELLNER: Cayuga County, New York/Indiana, 1886-1919; Baker, Dunn, Estes, Mitchell, Shoup. 10pp. --$2.50

nh. WILSON: Westmoreland County, Pennsylvania, 1836-1952; Heagy, McGuire, Mitcheltree, Ray, Woolslayer. 6pp. --$1.50

ni. YATES: 1806-1881; Jones, Tolson, Woods. 5pp. --$1.25

nj. BOWERS: Woodstock, Connecticut/Chepaket, Rhode Island/Brookbank, Connecticut, 1805-1937; Heredeen/Herendeen. 1pp. --$1.00

nk. MILLER: New Jersey/New York City, 1842-1950. Lamb, Bockeven, Browning, Hagedon, Miller, Williams. 4pp. --$1.00

nl. CHASE: New Hampshire/Maine, 1792-1885; Brewster, Chase, Grime, Hale, Higgins, Hill, Horton, Korgman, Lincoln, Lord, Pratt, Street, Woodman. 5pp. --$1.25

nm. HALE: Dover, New Hampshire, 1775-1887; Chase, Hill, Joy, Kimball, Lincoln, Pratt, Turner, Woodman. 4pp. --$1.00

nn. OLDHAM: Lexington, Kentucky, 1854-1922; Bayless, Bogie, Chenault, Clay, Dearing, Hainline, Jeter, Morse, Oldham, Woodford. 2pp. --$1.00

no. DAVIS: 1747-1836; Brandon, Hampton, Jeter, Lewis, Smith, Walton. 5pp. --$1.25

np. DENT: Annmore, Harrison County, Wisconsin, 1899-1939; Dent, Stuart. 4pp. --$1.00

nq. FRANZMEIER: Dakota County, Minnesota, 1834-1983; Burkhart, Cordes, Herbst, Koop, Langer, Moran, Prine, Salzman, Schindeldecker, Schmidt, Turpen. 13pp. --$3.25

nr. FRIER: Hazelhurst, Georgia, 1775-1954; Ashley, DeLoach, Dent, Durance/Durrance, Ellis, Frier, Girtmon, Harrell, Lott, McCall, McDuffie, Peacock, Pellicer, Smith, Wilcox, Williams. 12pp. --$3.00

ns. GOYER: 1838-1910; Burgess, Erwin, Goyer, Hamilton, Holmes, Keller, Wilburn, Woodley. 5pp. --$1.25

nt. GREENLIEF: Mound Prairie, Jasper County, Iowa/California, 1868-1932; and, CURE: Decatur County, Indiana, 1868-1932: Cure, Greenlief, Roney, Rumbaugh. 6pp. --$1.50

4222 (cont.)

nu. GRIFFEY: Gibson and Obion Counties, Tennessee, 1837-1887; Bowman, Griffey, Harrison, Hurt, Parnell, Tattermore, Wilkes, Woods. 2pp. --$1.00

nv. JEROLOMAN: 1819-1939; Derling, Jeroloman, Kingsland, Mesler, Norton, Vliet. 6pp. --$1.50

nw. JOYCE: 1778-1898; Hague, Joyce, Tison, Ward. 6pp. --$1.50

nx. KENT: Amherst County, Virginia, 1801-1925; Caldwell, Cash, Drindard, Foster, Hopkins, Kent, Luck, Lyons, Raine, Turner, Wright. 9pp. --$2.25

ny. KIZER: Illinois, 1815-1924; Bailey, Butts, Davis, Kizer, Wortham. 2pp. --$1.00

nz. KLEIN: Germany, 1682-1727; Kohl, Klein, Sickerling(?). 7pp. --$1.75

oa. McLAIN: Warren, Ohio/Nassau in the Bahamas, 1801-1949; Bower, Cramer, Cross, Doughton, Geinmill, Hess, Kearsley, Reynolds, Stratton, Thompson, McLain. 9pp. --$2.25

ob. McPHERSON: Greenbrier County, Virginia (West Virginia), 1830-1887; Austin, Harris, McClung, McPherson. 3pp. --$1.00

oc. MEHN/MAIN: Frederick County, Maryland, 1746-1878; Bruchey, Derr, Jautze, Mehn/Main, Weil. 9pp. --$2.25

od. MUMPER: Montrose, Illinois/Osceola, Iowa, 1812-1958; Beedle, Campbell, Collins, Cornett, Green, Gracey, Hargis, Merritt, Mumper, Oye, Reece, Schoonover. 5pp. --$1.25

oe. OSBORN: Long Bottom, Ohio, 1876-1939; Curtis, DeWolf, Holter, Osborn. 3pp. --$1.00

of. SMITH: 1761-1967; Bracey, Doares, Edmund, Lytch, McDirmid(?), Parish, Quine(?), Smith, Windham. 7pp. --$1.75

og. SWAYZE: Harrisonburg, Louisiana/Elgin and Taylor, Texas, 1858-1906; Graham, Swayze. 5pp. --$1.25

oh. SWAYZE: Wilkinson County, Mississippi/Catahoula Parish, Louisiana, 1820-1887; Tillingsley, Boles, Brundige, Davis, Graham, Miles, Pieper, Routon, Sanders, Swayze, Watkins, Wren. 3pp. --$1.00

oi. VANCE: DeSoto County, Mississippi/Shelby County, Tennessee/ Boone County, Arkansas, 1840-1873; McKnight, Vance. 3pp. --$1.00

oj. WHITEAKER: Putnam County, Tennessee, 1820-1950; Eller, Whiteaker. 1pp. --$1.00

ok. WILLSON: Independence (Warren), New Jersey, 1810-1919; Shotwell, Willson. 5pp. --$1.25

ol. EAKLE: New York, New York/Tompkinsville and Louisville, Kentucky/ Monroe County, Kentucky/Jackson County, Tennessee, 1797-1975; Eakle, Hammer(?), Steen(?), York. 2pp. --$1.00
Photocopies—25¢/pg.—minimum $1.00/order & SASE----------Vendor #D2229

4223 - POGUE/POLLOCK GENEALOGY AS MIRRORED IN HISTORY FROM
SCOTLAND TO NORTHERN IRELAND, OHIO, AND WESTWARD by
Lloyd Welch Pogue. 1985.
Lineage charts from mid-11th Century when William the Conqueror
granted the Pollock Lands in Renfrewshire, Scotland, to Progenitor
Fulbert. Descendant Sir Robert Pollock, Baronet (1703), was common
ancestor to Pollock, Pogue, and Polk families. James K. Polk, the
outstanding eleventh United States President, was a member of this
family. Little-known facts of history enlivens the genealogy through-
out. Sections include a Narrative, Vignettes of selected Members,
Family Charts, Illustrations and Maps, an Appendix with selected
support papers, and alphabetical list of ca 1,500 names of descendants
and spouses with lineage tracings of all line-descendants to John
Pogue/Pollock who reached America in 1789, and an Index. 6"x9".
Publication expected in Spring of 1985.
(In process)—Cloth—$35.00—apx 480pp--------------------- Vendor #D0030

4224 - THE CAUDLE FAMILY, THE DESCENDANTS OF WILLIAM CAUDLE by
Joyce B. Hensen. 1976.
Married Gracie Broadway in Granville County, North Carolina;
to Surry County, North Carolina; to Wright County, Missouri.
Paper—$6.00—50pp------------------------------------- Vendor #D2252

4225 - HISTORY OF A MISSOURI FARM FAMILY: THE O. V. SLAUGHTERS,
1700-1944 by S. Slaughter. 1978.
Extensive data on Havron, Davenport, Slaughter, Simpson and other
families. Homestead was a neighbor of President Truman in Independence. Twenty-eight pages of genealogies. Illustrations.
Cloth—$15.00—378pp----------------------------------- Vendor #D0948

4226 - VIRGINIA LINEAGES, LETTERS AND MEMORIES by Alice Jean
Nelson. 1984.
Families of Alexander, Ball, Carter, Catlett, Pope, Stuart,
Taliaferro, Thornton, Waring, Washington, Warner, etc.
Cloth—$21.50—302pp----------------------------------- Vendor #D2253

4227 - BIBLE RECORDS.
Rugh (Roof/Rook), Unger, Kerns, Bradley, Wise, Ensminger—
Cumberland County, Pennsylvania, 1700's to 1850; Cass County,
Indiana, 1850+.
Wise, Gregory—Stark County, Ohio, Warren County, Illinois, 1820-1900.
Six Wise brothers: Samuel, born 1813, died Canton, Ohio; Abraham,
born 1815, died St. Louis, Missouri; Jacob, born 1818, died Wells-
ville, Ohio; William born 1820, died Monmouth, Illinois; Henry, born
1828, died Kirkwood, Illinois; Levi, born 1830, died Kirkwood, Illinois.
Photocopies—$2.00 (free to proven relatives)—6pp---------- Vendor #D1257

4228 - ROOK (ROOF/RUGH) BIBLE RECORDS.
Old German testament dated 1803; data written in German. Cumber-
land County, Pennsylvania. Rook (Roof/Rugh)—Immanuel (born 1810),
Elizabeth (1812), John (1814), Peter (1817), Susanna? or Anna? (1823).
Unger, Catharina (married 1805?).
Photocopies—$2.00 (free to proven relatives)—2pp---------- Vendor #D1257

4229 - HANSARD—HANSFORD FAMILY HISTORY, VOLUMES I AND II by
Winnie Hansford Garrett. 1984.
Comprising the surnames of Hansforde, Handford, Hanford, Hansard,
Hanserd, Hansird, Hansford, and the variant forms from A.D. 15__ to
A.D. 1984.
Information contained in this work has been obtained from authentic
public and private records, documents, parish registers, town and
county files, church records, federal records, vital statistics, very
extensive correspondence, and personal knowledge.
Published in two volumes, with the complete Index in Volume II.
Traces the descendants of William Hansard/Hansford and his wife
Bathsheba Archer, who settled in the Colony of Virginia before 1740,
through their four known sons to the present time—through the
eighth and ninth generations in America. It also traces the ances-
trage of William back six generations to his English forebears and
their marriage in Middlesex County, England, in 1560.
Cloth—$52.30/set—1109+pp--------------------------------- Vendor #D2255

4230 - McDOWELL AND RELATED FAMILIES - A GENEALOGY by John A.
Crook, Jr., M.D. 1975.
McDowell: Antrim, Ireland—1787; Rockbridge County—1803; Botetourt
County, Virginia—1827; Greenville, Tennessee—1865.
McNair: Robeson, Scotland, and Richmond Counties, North Carolina—
1865; Barbour County, Alabama—1900.
McKay: Robeson, Scotland, and Richmond Counties, North Carolina—
1865; Barbour County, Alabama—1927.
Related families include Allen, Baker, Barnett, Boyes, Brown, Buie,
Burkhart, Compton, Chronister, Crook, Dean, Delaney, Dent, Ellixon,
Ely, Gage, Gillespie, Greer, Johnston, Lee, Levinski, Little, May,
Mays, Maxwell, McBride, McDonald, McFarland, McGill, McKay, McNair,
McRae, Moffett, Montalbano, Morgan, Patterson, Patton, Pritchard,
Randall, Ramsey, Robalis, Saunders, Singletary, Stewart, Stubbs,
Sylvester, Thrush, VanPatton, Walker, Wilkerson, Williams, Wood,
Woodley. These families are scattered over many of the fifty states.
Geographically the story involves the Shenandoah Valley of Virginia;
Greeneville, Tennessee; Alabama; Robeson, Scotland, and Richmond
Counties, North Carolina; and other places.
There's a great deal of early history of the Presbyterian Church
and much Civil War history. It includes over 35 pictures and repro-
ductions of daguerreotypes and tintypes of two Confederate soldiers
in their uniforms. Portion of Confederate soldier's Civil War diary
is included. The McDowells and most of the related families were
Scotch-Irish immigrants.
Cloth—$17.00—Paper—$20.00—117pp ----------------------- Vendor #D2481

4231 - EVEN STEVEN (STEPHENS-STEVENS-STEPHENSON-STEVENSON)
by A. Maxim Coppage. 1980.
The SECOND SERIES—January 1971-Spring 1977, a run of 176 pages,
has been indexed by name and location—thanks to Mrs. Jenna V. Owen-
by of Amarillo, Texas. This adds another 34 pages making a total of
210 pages.
Back-ordering the entire set with an index would be about $57.00 un-
bound. We are hoping to receive enough orders to be able to produce
a hardcover, bound book which can sell for $25.00 pre-publication cost.
Send a check in the amount of $25.00. It will be deposited in a special
account. If enough orders have not been received in six months, we
will refund your money. Libraries and organizations may order and ask
to be invoiced in the usual manner.
Cloth—$25.00—210pp -------------------------------------- Vendor #D3122

4232 - BURTON FAMILY QUARTERLY by A. Maxim Coppage.
Back issues available at $2.00 each.
Paper—$7.50/yr -- Vendor #D3122

Index to Family Genealogy Section

Audirou, 4222-ic
Auer, 3523a, 3523b
Aughe, 3788
Augur, 1217
Auld, 3850
Aulls, 3026, 3028
Austad, 3523k, 3523k
Austerman, 3926
Austin/Austen, 39, 819
  1218, 3046, 3061, 3076
  3398, 3520, 3523j, 3526
  3670, 3953, 4222-dk
  4222-ma, 4222-ob
Austinson, 3523j
Autry, 3523h
Auyer, 3377
Avent, 3418
Averett, 3467
Averill, 3077
Avery, 41, 1219, 1220
  1221, 1222, 3075, 3087
  3228, 3550, 3644, 3959
  3962, 4219, 4222-gt
Aves, 3438
Avila, 4165
Avis, 4222-fa
Awbrey, 3717
Axtell, 42, 1223, 3665
  3850
Ayala, 3460, 4165
Aycock, 3267, 3940
Aydelott, 3221
Ayer/Ayr, 3074, 3075
  3665, 3818
Aylsworth, 3371
Ayres, 1103, 1224, 1225
  3438, 3652, 4201
  4222-eg
Azbell, 3014

Baaldwin, 1243
Babbitt, 132, 3076
Babcock, 1226, 1227, 2126
  3028, 3074, 3228, 3530
  3644, 3783
Baber, 3664
Babington, 3523e
Bach, 3442
Bachilar, 1273
Bachman, 3217, 3258
  4222-ch
Back, 1228, 4135
Backus, 1229, 3665
  4222-i
Bacon, 1230, 1860, 3079
  3348, 3353, 3438, 3523e
  3665, 3801, 4195
  4222-is
Bacus, 3028
Badcock, 1231
Badger, 1232, 3523e
  4222-ku
Badg(e)ro(w), 3523g.
  3523k
Badie, 3028
Baer, 3217, 3703, 3711
  4054
Bahner, 4014
Bailey/Baillie/Baily, 45
  143, 213, 748, 1233
  1234, 3074, 3322, 3384
  3438, 3479, 3504, 3523g
  3543, 3545, 3589, 3637
  3843, 3912, 4052, 4095
  4164, 4206, 4207
  4222-ai, 4222-bx
  4222-hz, 4222-ms
  4222-ny
Baillie-See Bailey.
Baily-See Bailey.
Bain, 3912
Bainbridge, 3077

Baines, 4134
Bair, 3850
Baird, 168, 3221, 3401
Baisley, 3077
Baity, 3206
Baker, 46, 47, 749, 798
  1235, 1236, 1237, 1238
  2318, 3076, 3087, 3132
  3137, 3141, 3226, 3227
  3228, 3247, 3258, 3267
  3326, 3361, 3384, 3438
  3457, 3521, 3542, 3603
  3637, 3698, 3753, 3811
  3895, 3912, 3926, 3932
  3940, 3950, 3959, 4014
  4076, 4129, 4135
  4222-j, 4222-k, 4222-ae
  4222-bx, 4222-el
  4222-fu, 4222-mn
  4222-ng, 4230
Bakke, 3523i
Bakken, 3523a, 3523b
  3523c, 3523d, 3523e
  3523g
Balch, 1239, 1240
Balcom(be)/Balkcom, 1241
  3153, 3490, 3632
Bald, 3734
Baldwin, 49, 747, 1242
  1243, 1657, 2739, 3076
  3079, 3130, 3523e, 4095
  4198, 4205, 4222-be
  4222-gx, 4222-le
Bale/Bales, 3438, 3798
  3817
Balfour, 50
Balif, 4066
Balkcom-see Balcom(be)
Ball, 51, 52, 53, 395
  1244, 1245, 1246, 3073
  3079, 3136, 3399, 3457
  3518, 3585, 3867, 3985
  4050, 4107, 4195, 4202
  4222-li, 4222-lk, 4226
Ballantine/Ballantyne, 3360
  3817
Ballard, 1247, 2740, 3228
  3351, 3398, 3637, 3913
  4146
Balleine, 3385
Ballengee, 3449
Ballentine, 3345, 3363
Ballinger, 3132, 3438
  3590, 4222-cw
Ballou, 1248
Balthaser, 2076
Baltzer, 936
Bamberger, 4222-hv
Bamford, 3523e
Bancroft, 3542, 3688
  4222-fk, 4222-fl
Bandel, 4222-lq
Bandini, 4165
Bandy, 4205
Bane, 3587, 4206, 4207
Bangs, 1249, 3169
Banker/Bankor, 1250
  4222-ff
Bankhead, 4222-gh
Bankor-see Banker
Banks, 3077, 3153, 3463
  3464, 3768, 3950, 4135
  4198, 4219
Bankson, 3262
Banning, 1251
Banta, 55, 1252, 3577
Barbaree, 3087
Barber, 57, 658, 1253
  1254, 1255, 3110, 3228
  4066, 4222-mc
Barbour, 58, 568, 3073
Barclay, 1256, 4222-ak
Barclift, 3268, 3293
Barcroft, 1257

Bard, 3221
Barden/Bardin, 3612, 3954
Barefield, 4078
Barentsen, 3665
Barfield, 4078
Barger, 1258, 3587
Bargy, 3377
Barham, 3920
Barice, 4222-mv
Barker, 768, 2741, 2742
  2743, 3110, 3443, 3637
  3787, 3953, 3998, 4063
  4202, 4222-k, 4222-ju
Barkey, 3609
Barkhimer, 3811
Barkley, 3438, 3912
Barkman, 3531
Barksdale, 3467
Barlow, 476, 1259, 3028
  3333, 2828
Barnard, 3076, 3814
  4222-am
Barnes, 1260, 1261, 1613
  1694, 2786, 3074, 3087
  3206, 3654, 3750, 3753
  3856, 4095, 4134, 4205
  4206, 4207, 4222-gw
Barnett, 3863, 3912
  4222-cm, 4222-co
  4222-du, 4222-fm, 4230
Barnette, 3323, 3912
Barney, 2744, 3954
Barnhard, 3048
Barnhart, 3438
Barnhill, 4222-mt
Barnwell, 3940
Baron-see Barron,
Barr, 1262, 3703
Barraud, 3358
Barrett, 981, 1263, 3076
  3087, 3401
Barrickman, 4222-l
Barrie-see Barry/Barrie.
Barrier, 3912
Barringer, 3221, 3912
Barrington, 3132
Barron/Baron, 135, 3247
  3454, 3714
Barrow, 1264, 3384, 4001
  4222-cx
Barry/Barrie, 2745, 3401
  3523d, 3979, 4049
  4222-fy
Barstow, 3665, 4069
Bartee, 3088, 3351
Barten, 3438
Barthelme, 3379
Bartholomew, 63, 805
  1265, 3415, 3465, 3856
Bartlett, 68, 1266, 1267
  1268, 2651, 3075, 3637
  3755, 4036, 4222-gf
  4222-gn, 4222-im
  4222-jl
Bartolini, 3637
Barton, 1269, 3079, 3132
  3207, 3328, 3523e, 3717
  3846, 4222-fh, 4222-jv
Bartow, 69, 1270
Barttelot, 3637
Bartzen, 3523a, 3523b
  3523c, 3523d, 3523e
  3523g
Barwick, 3940
Bascom, 460, 1271
Basham, 3457
Bashore, 3170, 3813
Baskerville, 70, 72
Basou, 4222-ie
Bass, 73, 1272, 3200
  3368, 3401, 3665, 3724
  3912, 4054, 4134, 4153
Basset/Bassett, 1129
  3228, 3322, 3342, 3521

  3530, 3623, 3688
Bastida, 4165
Batchelder, 1273, 1274
  3260, 4032
Batcheller, 1273
Batchelor, 4222-fl
Bate/Bates, 74, 75, 1275
  1276, 1277, 1613, 3076
  3087, 3133, 3542, 3554
  3665, 3948, 4135
  4222-hz, 4222-jv
Bateman, 3112, 3151, 3152
  4222-lr
Bathurst, 567
Batt/Batts, 1278, 3362
Battaile, 4222-dl
Battelle, 1279
Battin, 3228, 4222-an
Baty, 4054
Baucom/Baucum/Bawcom,
  3153, 3490, 3632
Baucum-see Baucom.
Bauer, 3523j, 4222-ag
Baughan, 3258
Baughcom, 3153, 3490
  3632
Baugher, 3788
Baughman, 3526, 3574
  4222-bz
Baulstone, 3228
Bauman/Baumann, 998, 3683
Baumgardner, 3438
Baumgartner, 4086
Bauscher, 3247
Bausher, 3247
Bawcom-see Baucom.
Baxter, 537, 3064, 3073
  3651, 4054, 4144, 4196
  4198, 4222-lq
Bayle, 3109
Bayless, 4222-nn
Bayley, 3076, 3358
Baylor, 4222-mg
Beach, 1280, 3028, 3036
  4095, 4222-u, 4222-kv
Beachler, 3843
Beachy, 3216, 3219
Beadford, 4222-du
Beadle/Beadles, 3193
  3194, 3221
Beal/Beale/Beall, 1196
  1281, 1384, 3107, 3266
  3817, 3818, 4108, 4195
  4222-fm
Beals, 3076, 3114, 3118
Beaman/Beeman, 1144, 3488
  3523e, 3913, 4095
Beamer, 3933
Bean, 1282, 3948, 4222-jl
Beane, 1537
Beaner, 4222-ih
Bear, 1283, 3218, 3237
  4199
Beard, 168, 1284, 3075
  3401, 3587, 3912, 4196
Bearden, 4222-ge
Beardsley, 76, 513, 1285
  4095
Bears, 1277
Bearse, 1286
Bearss, 1286
Beasecker, 3132
Beasley, 4222-k
Beason, 3455
Beatrix, 4165
Beattie, 3087
Beatty, 77, 320, 851
  1287, 1569, 4222-hx
Beaty, 4054
Beau, 210
Beauforest, 3322
Beaumont, 3077
Beauvois, 3979
Beaver, 78, 3912

Carraher, 4095
Carrasco, 4165
Carraway, 3335
Carrell, 3138
Carrico, 3023
Carriel, 4063
Carrier, 3536
Carriere, 4222-ku
Carriger, 3159
Carrillo, 4165
Carrington, 4191
Carroll, 2642, 3087, 3107
3207, 3237, 3623
4222-mx
Carruth, 1437
Carsden, 4222-lz
Carson, 3075, 3523c, 3797
4222-w, 4222-kn
4222-ks, 4222-le
Carter, 567, 1129, 1438
1439, 3073, 3136, 3206
3250, 3262, 3348, 3364
3574, 3623, 3834, 3841
3912, 4048, 4054, 4059
4134, 4191, 4195, 4197
4200, 4202, 4206
4222-gr, 4222-hz
4222-jt, 4226
Cartmel/Cartmell, 3832
3838
Cartmill, 3832, 3838
4196, 4206
Cartwright, 3333, 3348
3384, 3401, 3989
Carty, 3587
Carver, 3155, 4063, 4162
4167, 4222-dy
Carvill, 3420
Cary-see Carey,
Casavant, 2767
Case, 1444, 1445, 3073
3525, 3766, 3948, 4095
4222-ax
Casey, 1446, 3322, 3469
Cash, 4222-nx
Cashdollar, 4168
Cashwell, 3065
Cason, 3119, 3348, 3637
Caspar, 936
Casper, 3948
Cassel, 3214
Cassiday, 3587
Cassidy, 3077, 3523c
Casteel, 4075
Castello, 3523h
Castetter, 3523g
Castillo, 4165
Castleman, 3775
Castlio, 3715
Castner, 1989
Castor, 1447
Castro, 4165
Caswell, 3438
Cate/Cates, 1448, 3257
Catesby, 567
Catherman, 4222-jr
Cathey/Cathy, 3440, 4211
Catlett, 860, 4226
Catlin, 3444
Catt, 3701
Caudill/Caudle, 4059
4135, 4224
Caughron, 3523e
Cavender, 3438
Cavendish, 1428
Caverly, 1449
Caverno, 1450
Cavins, 3092
Cawson, 3360
Cayer, 3661
Caywise, 3523e
Ceawlin, 3871
Cecil, 3588, 4206, 4207

4222-co
Cell/Celle, 3968, 3969
Cessna, 169, 170, 1451
Chaapel, 3933
Chadbourne, 4063
Chadwell, 3956
Chaffee, 3228
Chalfant, 3707, 3937
Chalker, 3073
Challis, 3637
Chamberlain, 1453, 3075
3079, 3523m, 3814, 3853
Chamberlin, 4222-hz
4222-ko, 3523m
Chambers, 3077, 3132
3154, 3517, 3869, 4054
Chambery, 4222-gc
Chamblin, 1454
Chamerlain, 4222-me
Champ, 3523b
Champes, 1129
Champin, 4222-fj
Champion, 1455, 3399
3530, 3859
Champney, 3665
Chancellor, 4222-eb
Chancey, 3210
Chandler, 171, 1456, 1457
1458, 1459, 1460, 2338
3074, 3228, 4063
4222-mg
Chantry, 3850
Chapel, 4222-v
Chapin, 1461, 1462, 1463
3665
Chapman, 1464, 1465, 1466
3073, 3087, 3089, 3438
3523g, 3542, 4134, 4142
4205, 4207, 4222-bh
Chappell, 174, 1467, 3075
3077, 3716, 4053
4222-mm
Charlamagne, 3755
Charlemagne, 3206, 3684
3724
Charles, 3320, 3523e
3523g
Charles I, 3814
Charleton/Charlton, 3587
4188
Charlick, 3401
Chase, 1289, 1452, 1468
1469, 1470, 1471, 1472
3073, 3087, 3228, 3256
3399, 3470, 3523e
3523h, 3603, 4095
4222-v, 4222-nl
4222-nm
Chatfield, 1473
Chattan, 4116
Chatten, 3523g
Chauncey, 1474, 3381
Chavez, 3843
Cheatham, 4052
Cheeseman, 3334, 3352
3361
Cheesman, 3352
Cheever, 1475, 1476, 1477
1478
Chelton, 3411
Chenault, 175, 4222-nn
Cheney, 1479
Chenoweth, 497, 1480
3132, 3370, 4222-lv
Chernow, 4222-nf
Cherry, 4222-jr, 4222-kh
Chesebrough, 3644
Cheshire, 3348
Chesman, 1481
Chesnutt, 4134
Chesser, 3843
Chessman, 1481
Chester, 1482, 1483, 1484

4222-gw
Chestnut/Chestnutt, 3076
Chevalier, 884, 1195
Chew, 3002
Cheyney, 3228
Chicalia, 4165
Chichester, 3351, 3523g
Chickering, 1485, 3228
Chidsey, 4222-ko
Chilcote, 3851
Child/Childe, 1486, 4162
4222-io
Childers, 4038
Childress, 3438, 3953
3959, 4038
Childrey, 3384
Childs, 1486, 3798, 4168
4222-w, 4222-x, 4222-gf
4222-im, 4222-jr
Chiles, 3517
Chilton, 3585, 3871
Chinn, 3985
Chipchase, 4188
Chipman, 981, 1487, 1488
1489, 2354
Chirbury, 3337
Chisman, 3361
Chisolm, 176, 1490
Chissom/Chis(u)m, 3818
4222-n
Chiswell, 763
Chittenden, 1491
Chitwood, 4222-t
Chiverton, 3087
Choate, 1492
Chouteau, 1493
Chown, 3523c
Chowning, 4222-ke
Chrisman, 3587, 4199
4222-bw
Christain, 3322
Christen, 4206
Christenbury, 3912
Christian, 152, 3066
3587, 4198, 4206, 4207
Christie, 4142, 4222-ga
Christman, 3573, 3672
4222-ct
Christmas, 3258
Christophers, 3884
Christopherson, 3523h
Chronister, 4230
Chubb, 4222-x
Chumbley, 3077
Church, 177, 1494, 1495, 3340
3360, 3443, 3665, 4095
Churchill, 178, 875, 1496
1497, 3398, 3523d
Churton, 3486
Chute, 179
Cilley, 1498
Cinnamon, 3075
Clagett, 3050
Claiborne, 180
Clapham, 3028, 4202
Clapp, 3131, 3132, 3523c
3665, 3671, 4222-gf
Clapper, 366, 3076, 4157
Clark, 46, 183, 677, 798
1144, 1499, 1500, 1503
1972, 2919, 3073, 3079
3087, 3210, 3213, 3262
3267, 3348, 3399, 3401
3419, 3485, 3523a
3523b, 3523e, 3603
3606, 3623, 3644, 3646
3665, 3797, 3798, 3814
3834, 3845, 3912, 3913
4081, 4095, 4116, 4136
4191, 4206, 4222-b
4222-ak, 4222-gs, 3766
Clarke, 184, 185, 186

570, 735, 1501, 1502
1503, 1504, 1841, 2908
3169, 3207, 3384, 3483
3523d, 3542, 4222-t
4222-ff, 4222-fz
4222-lq, 3644, 3814
3912, 4095
Clarkson, 4202, 4222-ko
Clarridge, 4222-kp
4222-li
Clary, 3970, 4095
Clason/Classon, 1505
Clatterbuck, 3505
Claty, 3442
Clauson/Clawson, 1505
3523h, 4222-dx
Claxton, 4134
Clay, 190, 191, 1506
1910, 3262, 3575, 3775
3791, 4052, 4207
4222-nn
Claycomb, 4222-cj
Clayland, 3036
Claypool/Claypoole, 416
4206
Clayton, 3112, 3379
4222-y
Cleaveland, 194, 2769
Cleaver, 3522, 3585
Cleckner, 3379
Cleek, 4196
Cleet, 4222-ax
Cleghorn, 4048
Cleiveland, 1511
Clemens, 1507, 1509, 3132
3377, 4097
Clement/Clements, 1508
1510, 3351, 3671, 3912
4196
Clementine, 3791
Clemins, 4222-fj
Clemons, 3550
Clemson, 3675, 4222-ir
Clendennin, 4196
Clendinen, 3150
Cleveland, 194, 1511
1716, 2769, 2770, 3087
3398, 3523e, 3926
Clevenger, 3052
Clifford, 3523c, 3871
4222-af
Clifton, 4028
Cline, 3682, 3698, 3912
4100
Clinton, 3438, 4222-q
Clock, 1126, 3132
Clopton, 3258, 3326, 3871
Close, 4219
Closson, 1505
Cloud, 3159
Clough, 3913
Cloughton, 3523b
Clouse, 3340, 3342
Clower, 4222-hq
Clowes, 3348
Cloyd, 3587, 3588, 4186
4207
Cloyes, 4095
Clugston, 4222-lo
Clute, 3087
Cnut, 3871
Coaldwell, 1424
Coan, 3487
Coates/Coats, 1512, 3073
3221
Cobb/Cobbs, 2771, 2937
3077, 3221, 3228, 3261
3709, 3954, 3982
4222-fq
Cobbum, 3937
Coberly, 4036
Cobia, 4105
Cobin, 2354

[Numerical reference is to the Surname Index Number - in left hand column of pages 1323 thru 1686.]

Godbout, 3523c
Gode, 4192
Godfrey, 3087, 3261, 3349
 3542, 4052, 4063, 4206
 4222-hr
Goding, 1874
Godwin, 3028, 4036
Goebbel, 3874
Goetschius, 3783
Goff/Goffe, 3160, 3814
 4162
Goforth, 3323
Goggin, 3517, 4201
Goheen, 3798
Gohn, 3058
Goin, 3159, 3455
Going, 3220, 4222-kv
Golden, 3119
Goldfinch, 3523a, 3523b
 3523c, 3523d, 3523e
 3523g
Golding, 3119, 3523c
 3523g, 3827
Goldman, 3588, 4222-cj
Goldner, 3936
Goldsack, 3523c, 3523d
 3523e, 3523g
Goldsberry, 3071, 3503
Goldsborough, 3527
Goldsmith, 3525
Goldthwaite, 1873, 4063
Goldy, 3933
Gomez, 4165
Gonser, 3683
Gonterman, 3637
Gonzales/Gonzalez, 3843
 4165
Gooch, 3834, 3871
Good/Goode, 3313, 3609
 3763, 3788, 4052, 4074
 4192, 4222-bk, 4222-cq
Goodale, 3665, 3913
Goodbar, 4222-ic
Goodell, 2809
Gooden/Goodin, 3443, 3788
Coodenough, 3934
Goodenow, 3934
Goodhue, 1872
Goodin-see Gooden,
Goodman, 3463, 3811, 3814
 3818, 3912
Goodno/Goodnough, 3934
Goodnow, 1871, 3665, 3934
Goodrich, 411, 1870, 3064
 3074, 3381, 3845, 4095
 4187, 4211
Goodridge, 412, 1868
 1869, 4187
Goodsell, 3077
Goodson, 3153
Goodwin, 1533, 1864, 1865
 1866, 1867, 2277, 2303
 2811, 3028, 3075, 3077
 3087, 3222, 3258, 3523m
 3670, 3814, 4063, 4073
 4206
Goodwind, 951
Goodyear, 1863, 3028
Gookin, 884, 1862, 3340
 3347, 3355
Gooll, 2421
Gootee, 3245
Gordon, 860, 3077, 3132
 3441, 3460, 3523c
 3523d, 3523e, 3523g
 3532, 3533, 3851, 4119
 4191, 4194, 4199
 4222-ak, 4222-bl
 4222-cl, 4222-ez
 4222-kh, 4222-mb
 4222-mc
Gordy, 3202
Gore, 1861, 3637, 4222-gy
Gorgas, 3214, 3940

Gorman, 4222-cs
Gornto, 3333
Gorrell, 4222-mf
Gorsuch, 413, 3654
Gorton, 3207, 3546, 3972
Gose/Goss, 183, 1859
 3322, 4205, 4206
 4222-ah, 4222-la
 4222-lm
Gosnell, 3523e
Gosnold, 1860
Gosselin, 3536
Gothie, 4222-gq
Gotskalksson, 3523h
Gott, 1858, 4222-lw
Gottshall, 1857
Gotzendanner, 3949
Gouch, 3322
Goucher, 3368
Gough, 3262, 3551, 3552
Goughenour, 3031
Gould, 693, 1851, 1856
 3079, 3523d, 3523g
 3542
Goulding, 711
Gouldman, 3717
Gouldner, 3936
Gouldsmith, 3420
Gourley, 1878
Gouthier, 3912
Gove, 1879
Gow, 4116
Gowdy, 3590
Gowen/Gowin, 3545, 4145
 4222-c
Gower, 3717
Goyer, 4222-ns
Graber, 3379
Gracey, 4222-od
Graciano, 4165
Gradeless, 3146
Grady, 414
Graff, 415
Grafton, 2354
Gragson, 3926
Graham/Grahams, 567, 918
 3076, 3106, 3132, 3159
 3247, 3441, 3460, 3590
 3913, 4050, 4052, 4061
 4168, 4188, 4196, 4205
 4222-x, 4222-bk
 4222-cq, 4222-id
 4222-je, 4222-og
 4222-oh
Gram, 3595
Gramling, 3207
Granber(r)y, 2810, 3332
 3335, 3341, 3343, 3348
 3349, 3351, 3354
Grandy, 3523a
Granger, 417, 1880
Granis/Grannis, 1881
 1882, 3814, 4050
Gransden, 3688
Grant, 649, 1883, 1884
 3252, 3399, 3523c
 3523g, 4063, 4163, 4202
 4222-m, 4222-ej
Grantham, 3753, 3775
Grass, 2496
Grasty, 3845
Grater, 4069
Graue, 4031
Gravely, 3953
Graves, 419, 540, 1885
 1886, 1887, 3028, 3074
 3110, 3222, 3542, 3559
 3665, 3795, 3895, 4095
 4222-ak
Gray, 1502, 1888, 2354
 3033, 3064, 3076, 3206
 3362, 3486, 3665, 3914
 4066, 4222-md, 4222-me
 4222-mp

Graybeal, 4205
Graybill, 514, 3215, 3706
Grayson, 860, 3089
Greeley, 3532
Green/Greene, 327, 422
 598, 1889, 1890, 1891
 2134, 2812, 2813, 2814
 3074, 3075, 3087, 3169
 3207, 3253, 3379, 3401
 3411, 3456, 3501, 3523c
 3523d, 3523e, 3529
 3585, 3623, 3665, 3703
 3729, 3843, 3970, 4063
 4066, 4109, 4168, 4202
 4206, 4219, 4222-ae
 4222-cq, 4222-da
 4222-od
Greenawalt, 3527
Greenberry, 3654
Greenleaf/Greenlief, 1892
 1893, 1894, 4222-nt
Greenlee/Greenley, 423
 3637, 4222-fx
Greenman, 3644
Greenough, 1895
Greenup, 4206
Greenwade, 3266
Greenway, 3401
Greenwell, 3986
Greenwood, 3076, 3979
Greer, 3112, 3159, 4222-bm
 4222-lw, 4230
Greeves, 4205
Gregg, 337, 3417, 4075
 4222-mf, 4222-nb, 3119
Gregory, 2815, 3087, 3418
 3584, 3665, 3717, 4196
 4222-b, 4227
Grellet, 3946
Gresham, 1896, 3119, 3348
 3438, 3587, 4015
Gresty, 3845
Grevie, 3523i
Gribbs, 3711
Grier, 3838
Griesemer, 3228
Griffen, 860
Griffeth, 4222-dv
Griffey, 4222-nu
Griffin, 425, 973, 1566
 3523e, 3912, 4053, 4075
 4168, 4222-ge
Griffing, 1897, 3364
Griffith(s), 815, 3052
 3523e, 3637, 3959, 4206
Grigg/Griggs, 1898, 1899
 3542, 4222-gw
Grigsby, 1900
Grills, 3587, 4206
Grim/Grimm, 3428, 3523e
 3551
Grime(s), 427, 918, 3438
 3462, 3952, 4222-nl
Grisham, 3119
Grissinger, 3237
Gristy, 3845
Griswold, 1901, 3028
 3077, 3530, 3913
Groff, 3215, 3217, 4033
 4034, 4222-cb, 4222-jv
Grommon, 3523e
Groo, 1904
Groome, 428
Groseclose, 4222-bn
 4222-da
Grosh, 4222-ie
Gross, 3785
Grosvenor, 3614
Grote, 3874, 4222-eq
 4222-ht
Grotz, 4222-db
Grout, 711, 1902
Grove(s), 429, 1903, 2930
 3028, 3110, 3895, 4203

 4222-aj, 4222-mu
Grover, 3077
Grow, 1904
Grubb, 3088, 3438, 4061
 4222-cd
Gruber, 4157
Grumling, 3207
Grymes, 3063
Gsell(e), 3968, 3969
Guay, 3206
Gudgane, 3064
Gudger, 3962, 4222-iq
Guerin, 3221
Guernsey, 3465, 3846
 4222-mm
Guerrant, 3221, 3575
Guerrero, 4165
Guerry, 3876
Guest, 2207
Guevara, 4165
Guffin, 4222-ek
Guggenbuhler, 3938
Guier, 3220
Guild, 1905, 1906
Guile, 1906
Guilford, 3973
Guillen, 4165
Guines, 4222-dk
Gulafres, 3973
Guldner, 3936
Gulledge, 3912
Gulliford, 3973
Gullikson, 3523j
Gump, 3253
Gunby, 3411
Gunderson, 3523j
Gundlach, 3523e
Gunn, 432, 3064, 4119
 4121
Gunnell, 3322
Gunning, 3438
Gunnison, 433, 1907
Gunsaulus, 4222-ma
Gunter, 3167, 3251, 3258
Gunterbergh, 3523m, 3523n
Gurgany, 3347
Gurgell, 4037
Gustafson, 4222-ci
Guthery, 4067
Guthrie, 10, 303, 1908
 2505, 2816, 3588, 4067
 4222-mp
Gutierrez, 4165
Gutry/Guttry, 4067
Gutterson, 3665
Guy, 1909, 3347, 3912
Guyer, 3813
Guyett, 3523e
Guzman, 4165
Gwathmey, 4222-lw
 4222-mg
Gwatkin, 4190
Gwinn/Gwyn, 578, 4146
Gwydir, 1155
Gyntersberg, 3523m
Gysin, 3860

Gaag, 3523d
Haak, 3335
Haar, 3523n
Haber, 4222-lw
Habersham, 144, 1910
Hack, 3355
Hacker, 4222-bo
Hackett, 3340, 3342
Haddix, 3073
Haddock, 3737
Haden, 875, 3912
Hadley, 1911, 1912, 3024
 3114, 3118, 3417
Haeffner, 488
Haen, 3348

3418, 3574, 4164
4222-ay, 4222-ik
Olivera, 3460
Oller, 3726
Olmstead/Olmsted, 741
　2307, 3087, 3384,
　3439, 3798, 3913
Olness, 3523b
Olney, 742, 2309, 3850
Olson, 3523h, 4222-dy
Olstad, 3523e
Oltman, 3523e
Olvera, 4165
O'Maley, 3245
O'Meagher, 2308
Onderdonk, 2310
O'Neal, 3245, 3912
Oney/Ony, 4206
Ontiveros, 4165
Oosterhout, 3665
Ooton, 3863
Opdycke/OpDyck/Opdyke,
　744
O'Ragan, 4090
Orcutt, 4222-lt
Ord, 3523b
Ordiway/Ordway, 3489
O'Reagan, 4090
O'Reilly, 4162, 4222-mh
　4222 mz
Orem, 3523g
Ormerod, 3523g
Ormsby, 2311, 2312
Orndorff, 3698
O'Rourke, 3028
Orr, 757, 4206
Orrison, 3247
Ort, 3933
Ortega, 4165
Ortel, 4165
Orth, 320, 4222-cq
Ortiz, 4165
Orton, 758, 2313, 2315
Orvis, 2314
Osbodby, 3438
Osborn/Osborne, 3028
　3075, 3082, 3088, 3118
　3132, 3165, 3418, 3523h
　3525, 3603, 4222-oe
Osgood, 2316, 3665
　4222-dz
Oslin, 4222-le
Osmundsdatter, 3523j
Osmundsdtr, 3523m
Osmundson, 3523j
Ospaugh, 4222-dj
Osteen, 3940
Osterhoudt, 1408
Osterhout, 4222-gm
Ostrander, 4222-ft
Osuna, 4165
Oswald, 3637, 3745
Oswalt, 3745
Otey, 4190, 4200, 4201
Otis, 760, 2317, 2318
　3670
Otstadt, 3595
Otstot(t), 3595
Otte, 3289
Ottey, 4076
Otto, 3523d
Ould, 739
Oulton, 3073
Oursler, 3107
Ousley, 3159, 3455
Oustad, 3523k
Outh, 1287
Outlaw, 4211, 4222-k
　4222-eu
Overholt, 3076
Overly, 3506
Overmyer, 761
Overstreet, 3517
Overton, 3258, 3523e

3525, 3953
Overzee, 3340
Owen/Owens, 61, 1196
　3153, 3159, 3228, 3467
　3530, 3762, 3843, 4110
　4206, 4222-dk, 4222-hv
Own, 3348
Owney, 4206
Owsley, 4222-jr
Oxendine, 3912
Oxenreider, 4222-da
Oxx, 3542
Oye, 4222-od
Oyer, 3377, 3609
Ozier, 4145
Ozment, 3401

Pabodie/Pabody, 2346
Pace, 3011, 3112, 3623
　4202, 4222-fx
Pacheco, 4165
Pack/Packs, 3207, 4059
　4207
Packard, 835, 2319, 3074
　3398, 3460
Packer, 3076, 3644
Packwood, 4222-gp
Pacy, 3399
Paddick, 3545
Paddock, 240
Paden, 3030
Padgett, 3245
Padilla, 4165
Pagan, 3259
Page, 764, 860, 1911
　2320, 2321, 2322, 2323
　3075, 3079, 3132, 3260
　3322, 3329, 3397, 3665
　3946, 4194, 4197
Pahner, 4081
Paine, 766, 2324, 2325
　2326, 2328, 3169, 3228
　3261, 3523e, 3523g
　3603, 4054
Painter/Paynter, 2338
　3073, 3348, 3808, 3809
　3810, 4203
Paisley, 4222-eg
Paiste, 4162
Palen, 3665
Palett, 3076
Palgrave, 2327, 3566
Pallet, 3348
Palm, 3529, 4066
Palmer, 765, 2329, 3087
　3197, 3213, 3260, 3397
　3439, 3523c, 3523d
　3542, 3644, 3843, 3850
　3985, 4050, 4066, 4075
　4219, 4222-dt
Palo, 3523a, 3523b
Palomares, 4165
Pamunkey, 3772
Pancoast, 538, 3005
Pankey, 4222-cj
Pannell, 4202
Pannill, 3845
Papen, 3214
Paradis, 3979
Parcel, 3073
Pardee, 3823
Paris, 4112, 4222-hj
Parish/Parrish, 2338
　3186, 4164, 4222-u
　4222-js, 4222-of
Park(e)/Park(e)(s), 183
　431, 1221, 1222, 1323
　2330, 2331, 3028, 3077
　3212, 3247, 3438, 3501
　3644, 3744, 3850, 3913
　4222-ip, 4222-mq
Parker, 2332, 2333, 2334

2335, 3074, 3079, 3087
3153, 3159, 3228, 3253
3267, 3333, 3335, 3348
3420, 3523e, 3623, 3798
3811, 3843, 3912, 4095
4108, 4134, 4190
4222-ff
Parkhill, 3501
Parkhurst, 2336, 3665
Parkins/Parkyns, 2364
　4222-kv
Parlin, 2337
Parmenter, 3665
Parnell, 4222-gg, 4222-nu
Parra, 4165
Parrigon, 4222-ak
Parrir, 2651
Parrish-see Parish,
Parrott, 3259, 4222-jr
Parry, 4222-cw
Parshall, 769, 2339, 3073
Parsley, 3107, 3463
Parsons, 770, 1716, 1978
　2340, 3965, 4095, 4178
　4222-en
Parthemer, 4222-hv
Parthemore, 771, 2341
Parther, 3873
Partrick, 3087
Partridge/Parttridge, 2342
　2343, 2344, 3075, 3530
　3843, 3948, 4222-cx
　4222-dz, 4222-ke
Pascoe, 3523e
Pasley, 3112, 4222-jt
Pasmore, 3064
Pasteur, 3351
Pastorius, 3214
Patchell, 3523d
Pate/Payte, 3112, 3438
　3585, 3716, 4163
Patentee, 2498
Paterson-see Patterson,
Patino, 4165
Paton-see Patton,
Patrick, 3087, 3362, 3438
　3588, 4061, 4105
　4222-dk, 4222-jm
Patrie, 3846
Patten, 701, 2345, 4095
Pattengill, 4095
Patterson/Paterson, 511
　3073, 3075, 3079, 3159
　3169, 3237, 3247, 3440
　3523c, 3523e, 3850
　3871, 3959, 3962, 4069
　4152, 4164, 4222-ai
　4222-iu, 4222-jw
　4222 nb, 4230
Pattison, 4222-hz
Patton/Paton, 3164, 3165
　3173, 3401, 3523e, 3588
　3658, 3667, 3850, 3858
　4066, 4206, 4222-ea, 4230
Patty, 4222-iq
Paul(s)/Paull, 2993, 3228
　3523e, 3523g, 4113
Pauley, 4222-dz
Paulin/Paullin, 3000
　3580
Paulson, 3206
Pavard, 4222-gr
Pawley, 3228
Paxson, 3420, 4222-ko
Paxton, 774, 3438, 3441
　3523e, 3724, 4222-ko
Paybody, 776, 2346
Payn, 2326
Payne/Paynes, 775, 2326
　3011, 3075, 3438, 3501
　3521, 3523c, 3523g
　3625, 3953, 4191, 4202
　4222-dz, 4222-eb
Paynter-see Painter,

Payson, 1402
Payte-see Pate,
Peabody, 776, 2346, 2347
　2348, 3228
Peacock, 3871, 4222-ge
　4222-nr
Peairs, 3806
Peak/Peake, 3113, 3912
Pearce/Pearse/Peirce, 781
　796, 2349, 2353, 2354
　2355, 3228, 3523d, 3542
　3637
Pearch, 3912
Pearis, 4207
Pearison, 4222-gt
Pearman, 4222-ju
Pearre, 4222-ir, 4222-is
　4222-it, 4222-iu
　4222-jc, 4222-jd
　4222-ld, 4222-lf
Pearsall, 3612
Pearse-see Pearce,
Pearson/Pierson, 798
　2381, 2382, 3079, 3299
　3399, 4222-il
Peart, 4222-kj
Peary, 3670
Pease, 777, 778, 779
　2350, 3076, 4063
Peaslee/Peasley, 2351
　3384
Pebworth, 3348
Pech, 4066
Pechacek, 3523i
Peck, 2320, 2333, 2352
　3073, 3237, 3530, 3913
　4050, 4095, 4207, 4219
　4222-gk, 4222-io
　4222-ki
Pecker, 2248
Peckham, 3074, 3542, 4081
Peckingpaugh, 4222-kq
Pedan, 3030
Pedeen, 3623
Peden, 3030, 4211
Pedigo, 3953, 3957, 4054
Peebles, 3033, 3464, 3813
　4080
Peek, 4222-x
Peel, 4222-ek
Peeler, 3323, 3912
Peeples, 4080
Peerenboom, 3703
Peery, 4205, 4206
Peevy, 4222-hc
Pef(f)ley/Peffly, 389
Pegdon, 4222-mx
Pegues, 3438
Peirce-see Pearce,
Peircy, 4222-fm
Peischan, 4086
Pejepscot, 1074
Pell, 1096
Pellicer, 4222-nr
Pelton, 3618
Pember, 2356, 3188
Pemberton, 2357
Pembroke, 3337
Pena, 4165
Pence, 2358, 3590
Pender, 4066
Pendergrass, 3597
Pendleton, 764, 3260
　4081, 4197, 4222-ff
Penhall, 3523e, 3523g
Penhallow, 2360
Penick, 3221, 3258, 3467
Penix, 3132, 3467
Penn, 200, 449, 2359
　3899
Penne-see Penney,
Pennell, 3228
Penner, 3587
Penney/Penne, 2361, 3523j

Youngblood, 3398
Youngman, 1159, 3523e
  3580
Yount, 3368, 3573
Yours, 340
Yows, 3401
Ysenring, 3220

Zabriskie, 4222-cy
Zachary, 3153
Zall, 3463

Zamora, 4165
Zamorano, 4165
Zaring, 4054
Zarling, 3723
Zaros, 3379
Zartman, 1161
Zaugg, 4056
Zawiski, 4222-lw
Zediker, 4222-d
Zehner, 3573
Zehr, 3609, 4074
Zehrbach, 4014
Zeigler, 3850, 4168

Zeis, 3850
Zeitlow, 3938
Zell(e), 3968, 3969
Zeller, 3438
Zelly, 4222-cw
Zemler, 3762
Zerfas, 4054
Zickler, 4086
Ziegler/Zigler, 3170
  3938, 4099, 4168
Zimmer, 3442
Zimmerman, 3215, 3438
  3523e, 3609, 4222-ml

Zinger, 3734
Zoll, 3913
Zollars, 4076
Zolman, 3379
Zook, 3013, 3216, 3219
  4056, 4074
Zouck, 4056
Zuber, 1162
Zuck, 4056
Zug, 3013, 4056
ZumBrunnen, 2984
Zumwalt, 3624
Zurita, 4165